VW

JETTA, RABBIT, GTI, GOLF
2006-11 REPAIR MANUAL

CHILTON'S

Covers U.S. and Canadian models of
New Jetta (2005), Jetta (2006 through 2011),
GLI (2006 through 2009), Rabbit (2006 through 2009),
GTI (2006 2.0L engine models), GTI (2007 through 2011),
Golf (2010 and 2011)

*Does not include 2005 Jetta (based on the A4 platform) or 2006 1.8L GTI models,
2011 2.0L 8-valve Sedan models (based on the A6 platform),
diesel engine or information specific to R32 models*

by Jeff Killingsworth

CHILTON *Automotive Books*

PUBLISHED BY **HAYNES NORTH AMERICA, Inc.**

Manufactured in USA
©2012 Haynes North America, Inc.
ISBN-13: 978-1-56392-950-2
ISBN-10: 1-56392-950-3
Library of Congress Control Number 2012937620

Haynes Publishing Group
Sparkford Nr Yeovil
Somerset BA22 7JJ England

Haynes North America, Inc
861 Lawrence Drive
Newbury Park
California 91320 USA

ABCDE
FGHIJ
KLMNO
PQRST

Contents

Mechanic and photographer with a 2007 VW Jetta

ACKNOWLEDGEMENTS

Wiring diagrams provided exclusively for Haynes North America, Inc. by Valley Forge Technical Information Services.

About this manual

ITS PURPOSE

The purpose of this manual is to help you get the best value from your vehicle. It can do so in several ways. It can help you decide what work must be done, even if you choose to have it done by a dealer service department or a repair shop; it provides information and procedures for routine maintenance and servicing; and it offers diagnostic and repair procedures to follow when trouble occurs.

We hope you use the manual to tackle the work yourself. For many simpler jobs, doing it yourself may be quicker than arranging an appointment to get the vehicle into a shop and making the trips to leave it and pick it up. More importantly, a lot of money can be saved by avoiding the expense the shop must pass on to you to cover its labor and overhead costs. An added benefit is the sense of satisfaction and accomplishment that you feel after doing the job yourself.

USING THE MANUAL

The manual is divided into Chapters. Each Chapter is divided into numbered Sections. Each Section consists of consecutively numbered paragraphs.

At the beginning of each numbered Section you will be referred to any illustrations which apply to the procedures in that Section. The reference numbers used in illustration captions pinpoint the pertinent Section and the Step within that Section. That is, illustration 3.2 means the illustration refers to Section 3 and Step (or paragraph) 2 within that Section.

Procedures, once described in the text, are not normally repeated. When it's necessary to refer to another Chapter, the reference will be given as Chapter and Section number. Cross references given without use of the word "Chapter" apply to Sections and/or paragraphs in the same Chapter. For example, "see Section 8" means in the same Chapter.

References to the left or right side of the vehicle assume you are sitting in the driver's seat, facing forward.

Even though we have prepared this manual with extreme care, neither the publisher nor the author can accept responsibility for any errors in, or omissions from, the information given.

➡ **NOTE**

A *Note* provides information necessary to properly complete a procedure or information which will make the procedure easier to understand.

❋❋ **CAUTION**

A *Caution* provides a special procedure or special steps which must be taken while completing the procedure where the Caution is found. Not heeding a Caution can result in damage to the assembly being worked on.

❋❋ **WARNING**

A *Warning* provides a special procedure or special steps which must be taken while completing the procedure where the Warning is found. Not heeding a Warning can result in personal injury.

Introduction

Volkswagen Jetta models are available in either a four-door sedan or 5-door sports wagon body style. The Rabbit, GTI and Golf are only available in a two-door hatchback model.

There are three different engines available depending on year and model: a 2.0L (FSI) turbocharged, 16-valve, DOHC four-cylinder engine, a 2.0L (TSI) turbocharged, DOHC four-cylinder engine, or a 2.5L, 20-valve, DOHC five-cylinder engine.

Automatic transaxle models come equipped with either a Tiptronic six-speed automatic transaxle or a 6-speed Direct Shift Gearbox (DSG) (which is a cross between an automatic transaxle and a manual transaxle). Manual transaxle models are equipped with either a five-speed or six-speed manual transaxle.

The front suspension on all models is independent, using McPherson struts and a stabilizer bar. The rear suspension on all models except the 2011 Jetta is a four-link design which consists of an upper transverse link (control arm), a lower control arm and tie-rod, a trailing arm, individual coil springs, shock absorbers and a stabilizer bar. 2011 Jetta models use a torsion beam axle supported by coil springs and shock aborbers.

The steering system consists of a rack-and-pinion steering gear and two adjustable tie-rods. Power steering is provided by an electro-mechanical motor and control module mounted directly to the steering gear.

The brakes are disc at the front and rear, with power assist standard. An Anti-lock Brake System (ABS) is standard equipment.

Vehicle identification numbers

Modifications are a continuing and unpublicized process in vehicle manufacturing. Since spare parts lists and manuals are compiled on a numerical basis, the individual vehicle numbers are necessary to correctly identify the component required.

VEHICLE IDENTIFICATION NUMBER (VIN)

This very important identification number is stamped on a plate attached to the dashboard inside the windshield on the driver's side of the vehicle (see illustration). The VIN also appears on the Vehicle Certificate of Title and Registration. It contains information such as where and when the vehicle was manufactured, the model year and the body style.

VIN ENGINE AND MODEL YEAR CODES

Two particularly important pieces of information found in the VIN are the engine code and the model year code. Counting from the left, the engine code letter designation is the 5th digit and the model year code letter designation is the 10th digit.

On the vehicles covered by this manual the model year codes are:

5	2005
6	2006
7	2007
8	2008
9	2009
A	2010
B	2011

On the vehicles covered by this manual the VIN engine codes are:

2.0L four-cylinder turbo (BPY) - timing belt models
  2006 through 2008 models............... A and K

2.0L four-cylinder turbo (CBFA, CCTA) - timing chain models
  2006 and 2007 models.....................J and V
  2008 and later models ....A, D, J and V

2.5L five-cylinder (BGP, BGQ, CBTA, CBUA)
  2006 and 2007 models.....................F, G, R and S
  2008 and later models ....A, M and Z

On the vehicles covered by this manual the transaxle codes are:

➡ Note: All transaxle codes are stamped onto the top and side of the transaxle.

0A4	5-speed manual transaxle
02Q	6-speed manual transaxle transaxle
09G/09GL	6-speed automatic transaxle
02E	6-speed direct shift gearbox (DSG) transaxle

VEHICLE CERTIFICATION LABEL

The Vehicle Certification Label is attached to the driver's side door post (see illustration). Information on this label includes the name of the manufacturer, the month and year of production and the Vehicle Identification Number.

ENGINE IDENTIFICATION NUMBER

Locations of the engine identification numbers:

2.0L four-cylinder engines: The engine code letters and serial number are stamped onto the left rear corner of the engine block, and the engine code letters are stamped onto the front left corner of the cylinder head.

2.5L five-cylinder engine: The engine code letters and serial number are stamped onto the back side of the engine block just above the oil pan, and the engine code letters are on a sticker attached to the top of the valve cover.

The VIN number is visible through the windshield on the driver's side

The Vehicle Certification Label is affixed to the driver's side door post

Recall information

Vehicle recalls are carried out by the manufacturer in the rare event of a possible safety-related defect. The vehicle's registered owner is contacted at the address on file at the Department of Motor Vehicles and given the details of the recall. Remedial work is carried out free of charge at a dealer service department.

If you are the new owner of a used vehicle which was subject to a recall and you want to be sure that the work has been carried out, it's best to contact a dealer service department and ask about your individual vehicle - you'll need to furnish them your Vehicle Identification Number (VIN).

The table below is based on information provided by the National Highway Traffic Safety Administration (NHTSA), the body which oversees vehicle recalls in the United States.

➡ **Note: This a partial list containing only the Volkswagen dealer recalls. There are additional aftermarket recalls available.**

The recall database is updated constantly. For the latest information on vehicle recalls, check the NHTSA website at www.nhtsa.gov, www.safercar.gov, or call the NHTSA hotline at 1-888-327-4236.

Recall date	Recall campaign number	Model(s) affected	Concern
June 28, 2005	05V0305000	2005 Jetta	On some models equipped with a five-cylinder gasoline engine, a fuel supply line clamp located in the engine compartment may not be positioned properly and could cause a fuel leak. Fuel leakage, in the presence of an ignition source, could result in a fire.
February 15, 2007	07V063000	2006 GTI	On some models, the brake light switch may malfunction if it was installed incorrectly. The brake lights could become inoperative, or remain on. Failure to provide the proper signal when braking could lead to a crash without warning.
June 21, 2007	07V284000	2006 Jetta	Some models with a five-cylinder gasoline engine may have a small plastic tab located on the windshield washer fluid reservoir that may chafe against the underhood fuel supply line. If this happens, the chafing has the potential to cause a fuel leak over time. Fuel leakage in the presence of an ignition source could result in a fire.
September 17, 2007	07V442000	2006, 2007, 2008 GTI and Rabbit 2006, 2007, 2008, 2009 Jetta	Certain models fail to comply with the requirements of Federal Motor Vehicle Safety Standard No. 108, "lamps, reflective devices, and associated equipment." Some vehicles may not have had a required cap installed which disables the headlight horizontal aim and some vehicles may contain a cap that disables the vertical aiming screw. Noncompliance can inhibit proper headlamp aim adjustment for roadway illumination; improperly aimed headlamps could cause reduced road visibility, increasing the risk of a crash.
May 13, 2009	09V164000	2006, 2007, 2008 Jetta	On some models with a four-cylinder engine, the fastening screw contact surfaces on the driveaxle cover plate may not have been manufactured to factory specifications. Some screws may not have been torqued properly during assembly and could loosen over time, causing a knocking sound when the vehicle is in motion. The driveaxle screws could loosen to the point where the driveaxle detaches from the gearbox. If the vehicle is moving when this happens, the detached driveaxle could cause damage the gearbox housing. A damaged gearbox housing could leak gearbox oil onto the street and create a risk of a vehicle crash for both the driver and other motorists.

Recall date	Recall campaign number	Model(s) affected	Concern
August 20, 2009	**09V333000**	2009, 2010 GTI and Jetta	On some models, the wiring harness of a temperature sensor in the direct shift gearbox (DSG) may have connector wires that were insufficiently crimped. With insufficiently crimped connector wires, a temperature sensor has the potential to falsely detect a high gearbox oil temperature, causing the transmission to abruptly shift to neutral. If this happens, the selector lever position indicator within the instrument panel will flash. In addition, the "depress brake pedal" indicator light will be illuminated, alerting the driver to apply the brakes. The abrupt shift to neutral could lead to a crash without warning.
December 14, 2010	**10V621000**	2006, 2007, 2008, 2009, 2010 Jetta 2007, 2008, 2009 Rabbit	On some models equipped with a five-cylinder engine, a small plastic tab located on the windshield washer fluid reservoir may chafe against an underhood fuel supply line. If chafing occurs, there is the potential for a fuel leak to develop. Fuel leakage, in the presence of an ignition source, could result in a fire.
March 25, 2011	**11V196000**	2011 Jetta	Some models may have an electrical wiring and fuse layout where the converter box is protected by the same fuse used by the signal horn and the anti-theft alarm system. Should that fuse be blown, the converter box will be disconnected from the power supply which, in turn, will shut off applications such as the engine management system, lighting system, and wipers. Should this happen while the vehicle is being driven, the engine could stall, or the headlights or wipers could turn off unexpectedly, potentially leading to a crash without warning.
September 07, 2011	**11E036000**	2011 Jetta	Volkswagen is recalling certain stainless steel exhaust tips, part number 1K0 071 910 U, sold as accessory equipment for use on model year 2011-2012 Jetta sedan vehicles manufactured from March 18, 2010, through August 22, 2011. These exhaust tips may extend beyond the original length of the factory-installed exhaust pipes. It is possible for inadvertent contact to occur with a person's leg. If the tailpipe extension is hot during inadvertent contact, a burn could occur.
September, 2011	**11V466000**	2011 Jetta	Some models had a stainless steel exhaust tip installed at the port during importation. These exhaust tips may extend beyond the original length of the factory-installed exhaust pipes. It is possible for inadvertent contact to occur with a person's leg. If the tailpipe extension is hot during inadvertent contact, a burn could occur.

Buying parts

Replacement parts are available from many sources, which generally fall into one of two categories - authorized dealer parts departments and independent retail auto parts stores. Our advice concerning these parts is as follows:

Retail auto parts stores: Good auto parts stores will stock frequently needed components which wear out relatively fast, such as clutch components, exhaust systems, brake parts, tune-up parts, etc. These stores often supply new or reconditioned parts on an exchange basis, which can save a considerable amount of money. Discount auto parts stores are often very good places to buy materials and parts needed for general vehicle maintenance such as oil, grease, filters, spark plugs, belts, touch-up paint, bulbs, etc. They also usually sell

tools and general accessories, have convenient hours, charge lower prices and can often be found not far from home.

Authorized dealer parts department: This is the best source for parts which are unique to the vehicle and not generally available elsewhere (such as major engine parts, transmission parts, trim pieces, etc.).

Warranty information: If the vehicle is still covered under warranty, be sure that any replacement parts purchased - regardless of the source - do not invalidate the warranty!

To be sure of obtaining the correct parts, have engine and chassis numbers available and, if possible, take the old parts along for positive identification.

Maintenance techniques, tools and working facilities

MAINTENANCE TECHNIQUES

There are a number of techniques involved in maintenance and repair that will be referred to throughout this manual. Application of these techniques will enable the home mechanic to be more efficient, better organized and capable of performing the various tasks properly, which will ensure that the repair job is thorough and complete.

Fasteners

Fasteners are nuts, bolts, studs and screws used to hold two or more parts together. There are a few things to keep in mind when working with fasteners. Almost all of them use a locking device of some type, either a lockwasher, locknut, locking tab or thread adhesive. All threaded fasteners should be clean and straight, with undamaged threads and undamaged corners on the hex head where the wrench fits. Develop the habit of replacing all damaged nuts and bolts with new ones. Special locknuts with nylon or fiber inserts can only be used once. If they are removed, they lose their locking ability and must be replaced with new ones.

Rusted nuts and bolts should be treated with a penetrating fluid to ease removal and prevent breakage. Some mechanics use turpentine in a spout-type oil can, which works quite well. After applying the rust penetrant, let it work for a few minutes before trying to loosen the nut or bolt. Badly rusted fasteners may have to be chiseled or sawed off or removed with a special nut breaker, available at tool stores.

If a bolt or stud breaks off in an assembly, it can be drilled and removed with a special tool commonly available for this purpose. Most automotive machine shops can perform this task, as well as other repair procedures, such as the repair of threaded holes that have been stripped out.

Flat washers and lockwashers, when removed from an assembly, should always be replaced exactly as removed. Replace any damaged washers with new ones. Never use a lockwasher on any soft metal surface (such as aluminum), thin sheet metal or plastic.

Fastener sizes

For a number of reasons, automobile manufacturers are making wider and wider use of metric fasteners. Therefore, it is important to be able to tell the difference between standard (sometimes called U.S. or SAE) and metric hardware, since they cannot be interchanged.

All bolts, whether standard or metric, are sized according to diameter, thread pitch and length. For example, a standard 1/2 - 13 x 1 bolt is 1/2 inch in diameter, has 13 threads per inch and is 1 inch long. An M12 - 1.75 x 25 metric bolt is 12 mm in diameter, has a thread pitch of 1.75 mm (the distance between threads) and is 25 mm long. The two bolts are nearly identical, and easily confused, but they are not interchangeable.

In addition to the differences in diameter, thread pitch and length, metric and standard bolts can also be distinguished by examining the bolt heads. To begin with, the distance across the flats on a standard bolt head is measured in inches, while the same dimension on a metric bolt is sized in millimeters (the same is true for nuts). As a result, a standard wrench should not be used on a metric bolt and a metric wrench should not be used on a standard bolt. Also, most standard bolts have slashes radiating out from the center of the head to denote the grade or strength of the bolt, which is an indication of the amount of torque that can be applied to it. The greater the number of slashes, the greater the strength of the bolt. Grades 0 through 5 are commonly used on automobiles. Metric bolts have a property class (grade) number, rather than a slash, molded into their heads to indicate bolt strength. In this case, the higher the number, the stronger the bolt. Property class numbers 8.8, 9.8 and 10.9 are commonly used on automobiles.

Strength markings can also be used to distinguish standard hex nuts from metric hex nuts. Many standard nuts have dots stamped into one side, while metric nuts are marked with a number. The greater the number of dots, or the higher the number, the greater the strength of the nut.

Metric studs are also marked on their ends according to property class (grade). Larger studs are numbered (the same as metric bolts), while smaller studs carry a geometric code to denote grade.

It should be noted that many fasteners, especially Grades 0 through 2, have no distinguishing marks on them. When such is the case, the only way to determine whether it is standard or metric is to measure the thread pitch or compare it to a known fastener of the same size.

Standard fasteners are often referred to as SAE, as opposed to metric. However, it should be noted that SAE technically refers to a non-metric fine thread fastener only. Coarse thread non-metric fasteners are referred to as USS sizes.

Since fasteners of the same size (both standard and metric) may have different strength ratings, be sure to reinstall any bolts, studs or nuts removed from your vehicle in their original locations. Also, when replacing a fastener with a new one, make sure that the new one has a strength rating equal to or greater than the original.

Tightening sequences and procedures

Most threaded fasteners should be tightened to a specific torque value (torque is the twisting force applied to a threaded component such as a nut or bolt). Overtightening the fastener can weaken it and cause it to break, while undertightening can cause it to eventually come loose. Bolts, screws and studs, depending on the material they are made of and their thread diameters, have specific torque values, many of which are noted in the Specifications at the end of each Chapter. Be sure to follow the torque recommendations closely. For fasteners not assigned a specific torque, a general torque value chart is presented here as a guide. These torque values are for dry (unlubricated) fasteners threaded into steel or cast iron (not aluminum). As was previously mentioned, the size and grade of a fastener determine the amount of torque that can safely be applied to it. The figures listed here are approximate for Grade 2 and Grade 3 fasteners. Higher grades can tolerate higher torque values.

Fasteners laid out in a pattern, such as cylinder head bolts, oil pan bolts, differential cover bolts, etc., must be loosened or tightened in sequence to avoid warping the component. This sequence will normally be shown in the appropriate Chapter. If a specific pattern is not given, the following procedures can be used to prevent warping.

Initially, the bolts or nuts should be assembled finger-tight only. Next, they should be tightened one full turn each, in a criss-cross or diagonal pattern. After each one has been tightened one full turn, return to the first one and tighten them all one-half turn, following the same

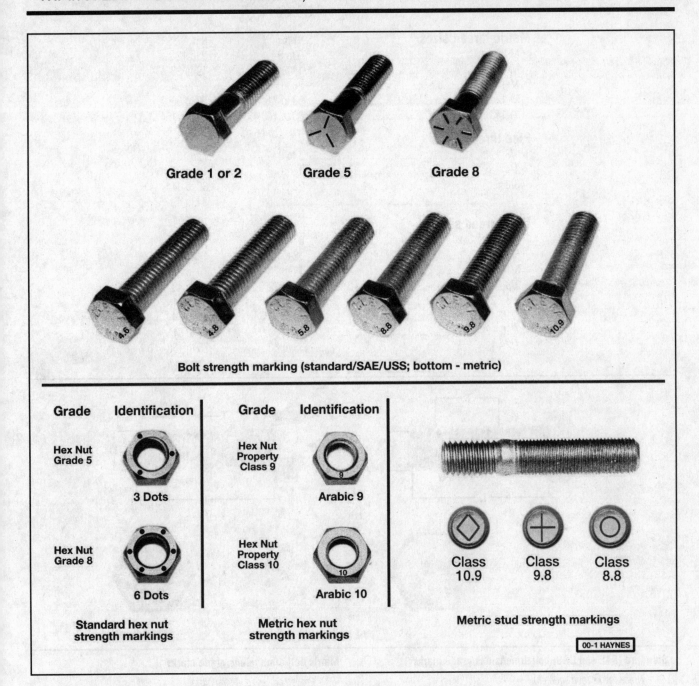

Bolt strength marking (standard/SAE/USS; bottom - metric)

Standard hex nut strength markings

Metric hex nut strength markings

Metric stud strength markings

00-1 HAYNES

pattern. Finally, tighten each of them one-quarter turn at a time until each fastener has been tightened to the proper torque. To loosen and remove the fasteners, the procedure would be reversed.

Component disassembly

Component disassembly should be done with care and purpose to help ensure that the parts go back together properly. Always keep track of the sequence in which parts are removed. Make note of special characteristics or marks on parts that can be installed more than one way, such as a grooved thrust washer on a shaft. It is a good idea to lay the disassembled parts out on a clean surface in the order that they were removed. It may also be helpful to make sketches or take instant photos of components before removal.

When removing fasteners from a component, keep track of their locations. Sometimes threading a bolt back in a part, or putting the washers and nut back on a stud, can prevent mix-ups later. If nuts and bolts cannot be returned to their original locations, they should be kept in a compartmented box or a series of small boxes. A cupcake or muffin tin is ideal for this purpose, since each cavity can hold the bolts and nuts from a particular area (i.e. oil pan bolts, valve cover bolts, engine

Metric thread sizes	Ft-lbs	Nm
M-6	6 to 9	9 to 12
M-8	14 to 21	19 to 28
M-10	28 to 40	38 to 54
M-12	50 to 71	68 to 96
M-14	80 to 140	109 to 154

Pipe thread sizes		
1/8	5 to 8	7 to 10
1/4	12 to 18	17 to 24
3/8	22 to 33	30 to 44
1/2	25 to 35	34 to 47

U.S. thread sizes		
1/4 - 20	6 to 9	9 to 12
5/16 - 18	12 to 18	17 to 24
5/16 - 24	14 to 20	19 to 27
3/8 - 16	22 to 32	30 to 43
3/8 - 24	27 to 38	37 to 51
7/16 - 14	40 to 55	55 to 74
7/16 - 20	40 to 60	55 to 81
1/2 - 13	55 to 80	75 to 108

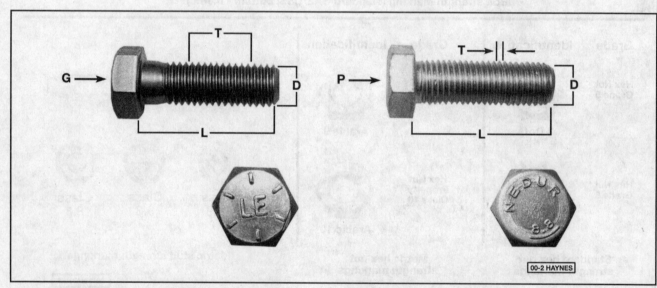

00-2 HAYNES

Standard (SAE and USS) bolt dimensions/grade marks

G   Grade marks (bolt strength)
L   Length (in inches)
T   Thread pitch (number of threads per inch)
D   Nominal diameter (in inches)

Metric bolt dimensions/grade marks

P   Property class (bolt strength)
L   Length (in millimeters)
T   Thread pitch (distance between threads in millimeters)
D   Diameter

mount bolts, etc.). A pan of this type is especially helpful when working on assemblies with very small parts, such as the carburetor, alternator, valve train or interior dash and trim pieces. The cavities can be marked with paint or tape to identify the contents.

Whenever wiring looms, harnesses or connectors are separated, it is a good idea to identify the two halves with numbered pieces of masking tape so they can be easily reconnected.

Gasket sealing surfaces

Throughout any vehicle, gaskets are used to seal the mating surfaces between two parts and keep lubricants, fluids, vacuum or pressure contained in an assembly.

Many times these gaskets are coated with a liquid or paste-type gasket sealing compound before assembly. Age, heat and pressure can sometimes cause the two parts to stick together so tightly that they are very difficult to separate. Often, the assembly can be loosened by striking it with a soft-face hammer near the mating surfaces. A regular hammer can be used if a block of wood is placed between the hammer and the part. Do not hammer on cast parts or parts that could be easily damaged. With any particularly stubborn part, always recheck to make sure that every fastener has been removed.

Avoid using a screwdriver or bar to pry apart an assembly, as they

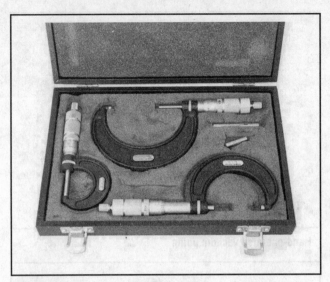

Micrometer set

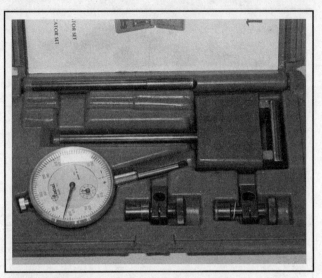

Dial indicator set

can easily mar the gasket sealing surfaces of the parts, which must remain smooth. If prying is absolutely necessary, use an old broom handle, but keep in mind that extra clean up will be necessary if the wood splinters.

After the parts are separated, the old gasket must be carefully scraped off and the gasket surfaces cleaned. Stubborn gasket material can be soaked with rust penetrant or treated with a special chemical to soften it so it can be easily scraped off.

✳✳ CAUTION:

Never use gasket removal solutions or caustic chemicals on plastic or other composite components.

A scraper can be fashioned from a piece of copper tubing by flattening and sharpening one end. Copper is recommended because it is usually softer than the surfaces to be scraped, which reduces the chance of gouging the part. Some gaskets can be removed with a wire brush, but regardless of the method used, the mating surfaces must be left clean and smooth. If for some reason the gasket surface is gouged, then a gasket sealer thick enough to fill scratches will have to be used during reassembly of the components. For most applications, a non-drying (or semi-drying) gasket sealer should be used.

Hose removal tips

✳✳ WARNING:

If the vehicle is equipped with air conditioning, do not disconnect any of the A/C hoses without first having the system depressurized by a dealer service department or a service station.

Hose removal precautions closely parallel gasket removal precautions. Avoid scratching or gouging the surface that the hose mates against or the connection may leak. This is especially true for radiator hoses. Because of various chemical reactions, the rubber in hoses can bond itself to the metal spigot that the hose fits over. To remove a hose, first loosen the hose clamps that secure it to the spigot. Then, with slip-joint pliers, grab the hose at the clamp and rotate it around the spigot. Work it back and forth until it is completely free, then pull it off. Silicone or other lubricants will ease removal if they can be applied between the hose and the outside of the spigot. Apply the same lubricant to the inside of the hose and the outside of the spigot to simplify installation.

As a last resort (and if the hose is to be replaced with a new one anyway), the rubber can be slit with a knife and the hose peeled from the spigot. If this must be done, be careful that the metal connection is not damaged.

If a hose clamp is broken or damaged, do not reuse it. Wire-type clamps usually weaken with age, so it is a good idea to replace them with screw-type clamps whenever a hose is removed.

TOOLS

A selection of good tools is a basic requirement for anyone who plans to maintain and repair his or her own vehicle. For the owner who has few tools, the initial investment might seem high, but when compared to the spiraling costs of professional auto maintenance and repair, it is a wise one.

To help the owner decide which tools are needed to perform the tasks detailed in this manual, the following tool lists are offered: *Maintenance and minor repair, Repair/overhaul* and *Special.*

The newcomer to practical mechanics should start off with the *maintenance and minor repair* tool kit, which is adequate for the simpler jobs performed on a vehicle. Then, as confidence and experience grow, the owner can tackle more difficult tasks, buying additional tools as they are needed. Eventually the basic kit will be expanded into the *repair and overhaul* tool set. Over a period of time, the experienced do-it-yourselfer will assemble a tool set complete enough for most repair and overhaul procedures and will add tools from the special category when it is felt that the expense is justified by the frequency of use.

Maintenance and minor repair tool kit

The tools in this list should be considered the minimum required for performance of routine maintenance, servicing and minor repair work. We recommend the purchase of combination wrenches (box-end and open-end combined in one wrench). While more expensive than open end wrenches, they offer the advantages of both types of wrench.

Combination wrench set (1/4-inch to 1 inch or 6 mm to 19 mm)
Adjustable wrench, 8 inch
Spark plug wrench with rubber insert

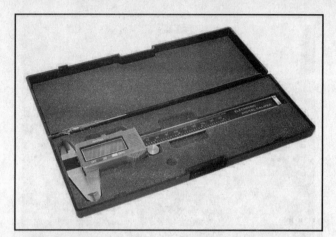

Dial caliper

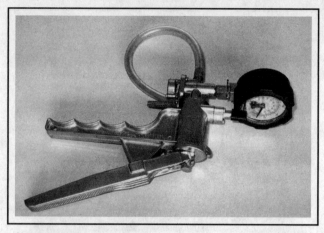

Hand-operated vacuum pump

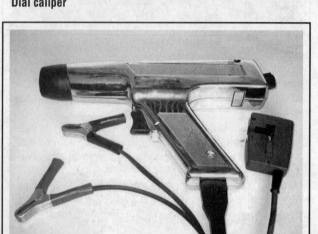

Timing light

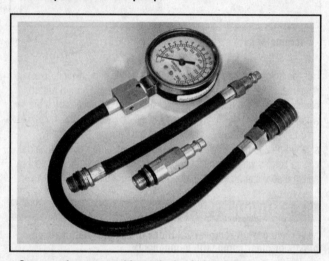

Compression gauge with spark plug hole adapter

Damper/steering wheel puller

General purpose puller

Hydraulic lifter removal tool

Spark plug gap adjusting tool
Feeler gauge set
Brake bleeder wrench
Standard screwdriver (5/16-inch x 6 inch)
Phillips screwdriver (No. 2 x 6 inch)
Combination pliers - 6 inch
Hacksaw and assortment of blades
Tire pressure gauge
Grease gun

Oil can
Fine emery cloth
Wire brush
Battery post and cable cleaning tool
Oil filter wrench
Funnel (medium size)
Safety goggles
Jackstands (2)
Drain pan

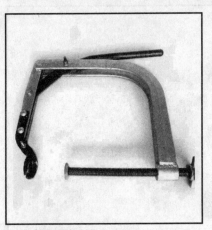

Valve spring compressor

Valve spring compressor

Ridge reamer

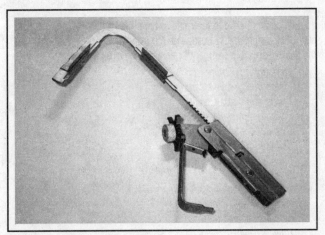

Piston ring groove cleaning tool

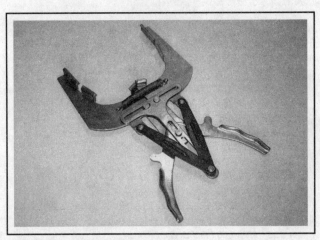

Ring removal/installation tool

Ring compressor

Cylinder hone

Brake hold-down spring tool

➥ **Note: If basic tune-ups are going to be part of routine maintenance, it will be necessary to purchase a good quality stroboscopic timing light and combination tachometer/dwell meter. Although they are included in the list of special tools, it is mentioned here because they are absolutely necessary for tuning most vehicles properly.**

Repair and overhaul tool set

These tools are essential for anyone who plans to perform major repairs and are in addition to those in the maintenance and minor repair tool kit. Included is a comprehensive set of sockets which, though expensive, are invaluable because of their versatility, especially when various extensions and drives are available. We recommend the 1/2-inch drive over the 3/8-inch drive. Although the larger drive is bulky and more expensive, it has the capacity of accepting a very wide range of large sockets. Ideally, however, the mechanic should have a 3/8-inch drive set and a 1/2-inch drive set.

Torque angle gauge

Clutch plate alignment tool

Socket set(s)
Reversible ratchet
Extension - 10 inch
Universal joint
Torque wrench (same size drive as sockets)
Ball peen hammer - 8 ounce
Soft-face hammer (plastic/rubber)
Standard screwdriver (1/4-inch x 6 inch)
Standard screwdriver (stubby - 5/16-inch)
Phillips screwdriver (No. 3 x 8 inch)
Phillips screwdriver (stubby - No. 2)
Pliers - vise grip
Pliers - lineman's
Pliers - needle nose
Pliers - snap-ring (internal and external)
Cold chisel - 1/2-inch
Scribe
Scraper (made from flattened copper tubing)
Centerpunch
Pin punches (1/16, 1/8, 3/16-inch)
Steel rule/straightedge - 12 inch
Allen wrench set (1/8 to 3/8-inch or 4 mm to 10 mm)
A selection of files
Wire brush (large)
Jackstands (second set)
Jack (scissor or hydraulic type)

➡ **Note: Another tool which is often useful is an electric drill with a chuck capacity of 3/8-inch and a set of good quality drill bits.**

Special tools

The tools in this list include those which are not used regularly, are expensive to buy, or which need to be used in accordance with their manufacturer's instructions. Unless these tools will be used frequently, it is not very economical to purchase many of them. A consideration would be to split the cost and use between yourself and a friend or friends. In addition, most of these tools can be obtained from a tool rental shop on a temporary basis.

This list primarily contains only those tools and instruments widely available to the public, and not those special tools produced by the vehicle manufacturer for distribution to dealer service departments. Occasionally, references to the manufacturer's special tools are included in the text of this manual. Generally, an alternative method of doing the job without the special tool is offered. However, sometimes there is no alternative to their use. Where this is the case, and the tool cannot be purchased or borrowed, the work should be turned over to the dealer service department or an automotive repair shop.

Valve spring compressor
Piston ring groove cleaning tool
Piston ring compressor
Piston ring installation tool
Cylinder compression gauge
Cylinder ridge reamer
Cylinder surfacing hone
Cylinder bore gauge
Micrometers and/or dial calipers
Hydraulic lifter removal tool
Balljoint separator
Universal-type puller
Impact screwdriver
Dial indicator set
Stroboscopic timing light (inductive pick-up)
Hand operated vacuum/pressure pump
Tachometer/dwell meter
Universal electrical multimeter
Cable hoist
Brake spring removal and installation tools
Floor jack

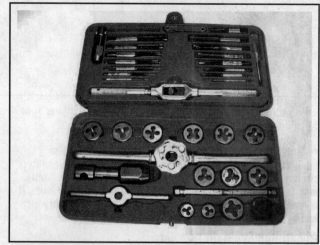

Tap and die set

Buying tools

For the do-it-yourselfer who is just starting to get involved in vehicle maintenance and repair, there are a number of options available when purchasing tools. If maintenance and minor repair is the extent of the work to be done, the purchase of individual tools is satisfactory. If, on the other hand, extensive work is planned, it would be a good idea to purchase a modest tool set from one of the large retail chain stores. A set can usually be bought at a substantial savings over the individual tool prices, and they often come with a tool box. As additional tools are needed, add-on sets, individual tools and a larger tool box can be purchased to expand the tool selection. Building a tool set gradually allows the cost of the tools to be spread over a longer period of time and gives the mechanic the freedom to choose only those tools that will actually be used.

Tool stores will often be the only source of some of the special tools that are needed, but regardless of where tools are bought, try to avoid cheap ones, especially when buying screwdrivers and sockets, because they won't last very long. The expense involved in replacing cheap tools will eventually be greater than the initial cost of quality tools.

Care and maintenance of tools

Good tools are expensive, so it makes sense to treat them with respect. Keep them clean and in usable condition and store them properly when not in use. Always wipe off any dirt, grease or metal chips before putting them away. Never leave tools lying around in the work area. Upon completion of a job, always check closely under the hood for tools that may have been left there so they won't get lost during a test drive.

Some tools, such as screwdrivers, pliers, wrenches and sockets, can be hung on a panel mounted on the garage or workshop wall, while others should be kept in a tool box or tray. Measuring instruments, gauges, meters, etc. must be carefully stored where they cannot be damaged by weather or impact from other tools.

When tools are used with care and stored properly, they will last a very long time. Even with the best of care, though, tools will wear out if used frequently. When a tool is damaged or worn out, replace it. Subsequent jobs will be safer and more enjoyable if you do.

HOW TO REPAIR DAMAGED THREADS

Sometimes, the internal threads of a nut or bolt hole can become stripped, usually from overtightening. Stripping threads is an all-too-common occurrence, especially when working with aluminum parts, because aluminum is so soft that it easily strips out.

Usually, external or internal threads are only partially stripped. After they've been cleaned up with a tap or die, they'll still work. Sometimes, however, threads are badly damaged. When this happens, you've got three choices:

1) Drill and tap the hole to the next suitable oversize and install a larger diameter bolt, screw or stud.

2) Drill and tap the hole to accept a threaded plug, then drill and tap the plug to the original screw size. You can also buy a plug already threaded to the original size. Then you simply drill a hole to the specified size, then run the threaded plug into the hole with a bolt and jam nut. Once the plug is fully seated, remove the jam nut and bolt.

3) The third method uses a patented thread repair kit like Heli-Coil or Slimsert. These easy-to-use kits are designed to repair damaged threads in straight-through holes and blind holes. Both are available as kits which can handle a variety of sizes and thread patterns. Drill the hole, then tap it with the special included tap. Install the Heli-Coil and the hole is back to its original diameter and thread pitch.

Regardless of which method you use, be sure to proceed calmly and carefully. A little impatience or carelessness during one of these relatively simple procedures can ruin your whole day's work and cost you a bundle if you wreck an expensive part.

WORKING FACILITIES

Not to be overlooked when discussing tools is the workshop. If anything more than routine maintenance is to be carried out, some sort of suitable work area is essential.

It is understood, and appreciated, that many home mechanics do not have a good workshop or garage available, and end up removing an engine or doing major repairs outside. It is recommended, however, that the overhaul or repair be completed under the cover of a roof.

A clean, flat workbench or table of comfortable working height is an absolute necessity. The workbench should be equipped with a vise that has a jaw opening of at least four inches.

As mentioned previously, some clean, dry storage space is also required for tools, as well as the lubricants, fluids, cleaning solvents, etc. which soon become necessary.

Sometimes waste oil and fluids, drained from the engine or cooling system during normal maintenance or repairs, present a disposal problem. To avoid pouring them on the ground or into a sewage system, pour the used fluids into large containers, seal them with caps and take them to an authorized disposal site or recycling center. Plastic jugs, such as old antifreeze containers, are ideal for this purpose.

Always keep a supply of old newspapers and clean rags available. Old towels are excellent for mopping up spills. Many mechanics use rolls of paper towels for most work because they are readily available and disposable. To help keep the area under the vehicle clean, a large cardboard box can be cut open and flattened to protect the garage or shop floor.

Whenever working over a painted surface, such as when leaning over a fender to service something under the hood, always cover it with an old blanket or bedspread to protect the finish. Vinyl covered pads, made especially for this purpose, are available at auto parts stores.

Jacking and towing

JACKING

⁂ WARNING:

The jack supplied with the vehicle should only be used for changing a tire or placing jackstands under the frame. Never work under the vehicle or start the engine while this jack is being used as the only means of support.

The vehicle should be on level ground. Place the shift lever in Park, and block the wheel diagonally opposite the wheel being changed. Set the parking brake.

Remove the spare tire and jack from stowage. Remove the wheel cover and trim ring (if so equipped) with the tapered end of the wheel bolt wrench by inserting and twisting the handle and then prying against the back of the wheel cover. Loosen the wheel bolts about 1/4- to-1/2 turn each. On models equipped with alloy wheels, using the hook from the tool bag, insert the hook into the wheel bolt cover and pull the covers off of the wheel bolts (see illustration).

Place the jack under the side of the vehicle and adjust the jack height until it engages the vertical rocker panel flange nearest the wheel to be changed. There is a front and rear jacking point on each side of the vehicle (see illustration).

Turn the jack handle clockwise until the tire clears the ground. Remove the wheel bolts and pull the wheel off, then install the spare.

Install the wheel bolts and tighten them snugly. Don't attempt to tighten them completely until the vehicle is lowered or it could slip off the jack. Turn the jack handle counterclockwise to lower the vehicle. Remove the jack and tighten the wheel bolts in a diagonal pattern.

Install the cover (and trim ring, if used) and be sure it's snapped into place all the way around.

Stow the tire, jack and wrench. Unblock the wheels.

TOWING

The manufacturer states that the only safe way to tow these vehicles is with a flatbed-type car carrier, a wheel-lift type tow truck with the front wheels raised. Other methods could cause damage to the drivetrain.

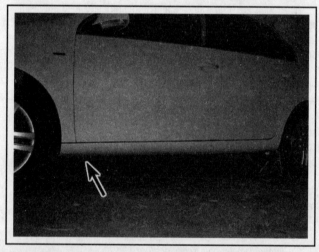

On alloy wheel models, use the hook from the tool bag to remove the wheel bolt covers

Place the jack so it engages the rocker panel nearest the wheel to be raised

Booster battery (jump) starting

Observe these precautions when using a booster battery to start a vehicle:

a) *Before connecting the booster battery, make sure the ignition switch is in the Off position.*

b) *Turn off the lights, heater and other electrical loads.*

c) *Your eyes should be shielded. Safety goggles are a good idea.*

d) *Make sure the booster battery is the same voltage as the dead one in the vehicle.*

e) *The two vehicles MUST NOT TOUCH each other!*

f) *Make sure the transaxle is in Neutral (manual) or Park (automatic).*

g) *If the booster battery is not a maintenance-free type, remove the vent caps and lay a cloth over the vent holes.*

Remove the battery cover, if equipped.

Connect the red-colored jumper cable to the positive (+) terminal of the booster battery and the other end to the positive (+) terminal of the dead battery. Then connect one end of the black jumper cable to the negative (-) terminal of the booster battery, and the other end of that cable to a good ground point on the engine of the disabled vehicle, preferably not too near the battery.

Start the engine using the booster battery and let the booster vehicle run at 2000 rpm for a few minutes to put some charge into the weak battery, then, with the engine running at idle speed, disconnect the jumper cables in the reverse order of connection.

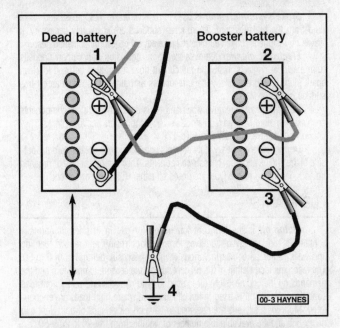

Make the booster battery cable connections in the numerical order shown (note that the negative cable of the booster battery is NOT attached to the negative terminal of the dead battery)

Automotive chemicals and lubricants

A number of automotive chemicals and lubricants are available for use during vehicle maintenance and repair. They include a wide variety of products ranging from cleaning solvents and degreasers to lubricants and protective sprays for rubber, plastic and vinyl.

CLEANERS

Carburetor cleaner and choke cleaner is a strong solvent for gum, varnish and carbon. Most carburetor cleaners leave a dry-type lubricant film which will not harden or gum up. Because of this film it is not recommended for use on electrical components.

Brake system cleaner is used to remove brake dust, grease and brake fluid from the brake system, where clean surfaces are absolutely necessary. It leaves no residue and often eliminates brake squeal caused by contaminants.

Electrical cleaner removes oxidation, corrosion and carbon deposits from electrical contacts, restoring full current flow. It can also be used to clean spark plugs, carburetor jets, voltage regulators and other parts where an oil-free surface is desired.

Demoisturants remove water and moisture from electrical components such as alternators, voltage regulators, electrical connectors and fuse blocks. They are non-conductive and non-corrosive.

Degreasers are heavy-duty solvents used to remove grease from the outside of the engine and from chassis components. They can be sprayed or brushed on and, depending on the type, are rinsed off either with water or solvent.

LUBRICANTS

Motor oil is the lubricant formulated for use in engines. It normally contains a wide variety of additives to prevent corrosion and reduce foaming and wear. Motor oil comes in various weights (viscosity ratings) from 0 to 50. The recommended weight of the oil depends on the season, temperature and the demands on the engine. Light oil is used in cold climates and under light load conditions. Heavy oil is used in hot climates and where high loads are encountered. Multi-viscosity oils are designed to have characteristics of both light and heavy oils and are available in a number of weights from 0W-20 to 20W-50.

Gear oil is designed to be used in differentials, manual transmissions and other areas where high-temperature lubrication is required.

Chassis and wheel bearing grease is a heavy grease used where increased loads and friction are encountered, such as for wheel bearings, ball-joints, tie-rod ends and universal joints.

High-temperature wheel bearing grease is designed to withstand the extreme temperatures encountered by wheel bearings in disc brake equipped vehicles. It usually contains molybdenum disulfide (moly), which is a dry-type lubricant.

White grease is a heavy grease for metal-to-metal applications where water is a problem. White grease stays soft under both low and high temperatures (usually from -100 to +190-degrees F), and will not wash off or dilute in the presence of water.

Assembly lube is a special extreme pressure lubricant, usually containing moly, used to lubricate high-load parts (such as main and rod bearings and cam lobes) for initial start-up of a new engine. The assembly lube lubricates the parts without being squeezed out or washed away until the engine oiling system begins to function.

Silicone lubricants are used to protect rubber, plastic, vinyl and nylon parts.

Graphite lubricants are used where oils cannot be used due to contamination problems, such as in locks. The dry graphite will lubricate metal parts while remaining uncontaminated by dirt, water, oil or acids. It is electrically conductive and will not foul electrical contacts in locks such as the ignition switch.

Moly penetrants loosen and lubricate frozen, rusted and corroded fasteners and prevent future rusting or freezing.

Heat-sink grease is a special electrically non-conductive grease that is used for mounting electronic ignition modules where it is essential that heat is transferred away from the module.

SEALANTS

RTV sealant is one of the most widely used gasket compounds. Made from silicone, RTV is air curing, it seals, bonds, waterproofs, fills surface irregularities, remains flexible, doesn't shrink, is relatively easy to remove, and is used as a supplementary sealer with almost all low and medium temperature gaskets.

Anaerobic sealant is much like RTV in that it can be used either to seal gaskets or to form gaskets by itself. It remains flexible, is solvent resistant and fills surface imperfections. The difference between an anaerobic sealant and an RTV-type sealant is in the curing. RTV cures when exposed to air, while an anaerobic sealant cures only in the absence of air. This means that an anaerobic sealant cures only after the assembly of parts, sealing them together.

Thread and pipe sealant is used for sealing hydraulic and pneumatic fittings and vacuum lines. It is usually made from a Teflon compound, and comes in a spray, a paint-on liquid and as a wrap-around tape.

CHEMICALS

Anti-seize compound prevents seizing, galling, cold welding, rust and corrosion in fasteners. High-temperature anti-seize, usually made with copper and graphite lubricants, is used for exhaust system and exhaust manifold bolts.

Anaerobic locking compounds are used to keep fasteners from vibrating or working loose and cure only after installation, in the absence of air. Medium strength locking compound is used for small nuts, bolts and screws that may be removed later. High-strength locking compound is for large nuts, bolts and studs which aren't removed on a regular basis.

Oil additives range from viscosity index improvers to chemical treatments that claim to reduce internal engine friction. It should be noted that most oil manufacturers caution against using additives with their oils.

Gas additives perform several functions, depending on their chemical makeup. They usually contain solvents that help dissolve gum and varnish that build up on carburetor, fuel injection and intake parts. They also serve to break down carbon deposits that form on the inside surfaces of the combustion chambers. Some additives contain upper cylinder lubricants for valves and piston rings, and others contain chemicals to remove condensation from the gas tank.

MISCELLANEOUS

Brake fluid is specially formulated hydraulic fluid that can withstand the heat and pressure encountered in brake systems. Care must be taken so this fluid does not come in contact with painted surfaces or plastics. An opened container should always be resealed to prevent contamination by water or dirt.

Weatherstrip adhesive is used to bond weatherstripping around doors, windows and trunk lids. It is sometimes used to attach trim pieces.

Undercoating is a petroleum-based, tar-like substance that is designed to protect metal surfaces on the underside of the vehicle from corrosion. It also acts as a sound-deadening agent by insulating the bottom of the vehicle.

Waxes and polishes are used to help protect painted and plated surfaces from the weather. Different types of paint may require the use of different types of wax and polish. Some polishes utilize a chemical or abrasive cleaner to help remove the top layer of oxidized (dull) paint on older vehicles. In recent years many non-wax polishes that contain a wide variety of chemicals such as polymers and silicones have been introduced. These non-wax polishes are usually easier to apply and last longer than conventional waxes and polishes.

CONVERSION FACTORS

LENGTH (distance)

Inches (in)	X	25.4	= Millimeters (mm)	X 0.0394	= Inches (in)
Feet (ft)	X	0.305	= Meters (m)	X 3.281	= Feet (ft)
Miles	X	1.609	= Kilometers (km)	X 0.621	= Miles

VOLUME (capacity)

Cubic inches (cu in; in^3)	X	16.387	= Cubic centimeters (cc; cm^3)	X 0.061	= Cubic inches (cu in; in^3)
Imperial pints (Imp pt)	X	0.568	= Liters (l)	X 1.76	= Imperial pints (Imp pt)
Imperial quarts (Imp qt)	X	1.137	= Liters (l)	X 0.88	= Imperial quarts (Imp qt)
Imperial quarts (Imp qt)	X	1.201	= US quarts (US qt)	X 0.833	= Imperial quarts (Imp qt)
US quarts (US qt)	X	0.946	= Liters (l)	X 1.057	= US quarts (US qt)
Imperial gallons (Imp gal)	X	4.546	= Liters (l)	X 0.22	= Imperial gallons (Imp gal)
Imperial gallons (Imp gal)	X	1.201	= US gallons (US gal)	X 0.833	= Imperial gallons (Imp gal)
US gallons (US gal)	X	3.785	= Liters (l)	X 0.264	= US gallons (US gal)

MASS (weight)

Ounces (oz)	X	28.35	= Grams (g)	X 0.035	= Ounces (oz)
Pounds (lb)	X	0.454	= Kilograms (kg)	X 2.205	= Pounds (lb)

FORCE

Ounces-force (ozf; oz)	X	0.278	= Newtons (N)	X 3.6	= Ounces-force (ozf; oz)
Pounds-force (lbf; lb)	X	4.448	= Newtons (N)	X 0.225	= Pounds-force (lbf; lb)
Newtons (N)	X	0.1	= Kilograms-force (kgf; kg)	X 9.81	= Newtons (N)

PRESSURE

Pounds-force per square inch (psi; lbf/in^2; lb/in^2)	X	0.070	= Kilograms-force per square centimeter (kgf/cm^2; kg/cm^2)	X 14.223	= Pounds-force per square inch (psi; lbf/in^2; lb/in^2)
Pounds-force per square inch (psi; lbf/in^2; lb/in^2)	X	0.068	= Atmospheres (atm)	X 14.696	= Pounds-force per square inch (psi; lbf/in^2; lb/in^2)
Pounds-force per square inch (psi; lbf/in^2; lb/in^2)	X	0.069	= Bars	X 14.5	= Pounds-force per square inch (psi; lbf/in^2; lb/in^2)
Pounds-force per square inch (psi; lbf/in^2; lb/in^2)	X	6.895	= Kilopascals (kPa)	X 0.145	= Pounds-force per square inch (psi; lbf/in^2; lb/in^2)
Kilopascals (kPa)	X	0.01	= Kilograms-force per square centimeter (kgf/cm^2; kg/cm^2)	X 98.1	= Kilopascals (kPa)

TORQUE (moment of force)

Pounds-force inches (lbf in; lb in)	X	1.152	= Kilograms-force centimeter (kgf cm; kg cm)	X 0.868	= Pounds-force inches (lbf in; lb in)
Pounds-force inches (lbf in; lb in)	X	0.113	= Newton meters (Nm)	X 8.85	= Pounds-force inches (lbf in; lb in)
Pounds-force inches (lbf in; lb in)	X	0.083	= Pounds-force feet (lbf ft; lb ft)	X 12	= Pounds-force inches (lbf in; lb in)
Pounds-force feet (lbf ft; lb ft)	X	0.138	= Kilograms-force meters (kgf m; kg m)	X 7.233	= Pounds-force feet (lbf ft; lb ft)
Pounds-force feet (lbf ft; lb ft)	X	1.356	= Newton meters (Nm)	X 0.738	= Pounds-force feet (lbf ft; lb ft)
Newton meters (Nm)	X	0.102	= Kilograms-force meters (kgf m; kg m)	X 9.804	= Newton meters (Nm)

VACUUM

Inches mercury (in. Hg)	X	3.377	= Kilopascals (kPa)	X 0.2961	= Inches mercury
Inches mercury (in. Hg)	X	25.4	= Millimeters mercury (mm Hg)	X 0.0394	= Inches mercury

POWER

Horsepower (hp)	X	745.7	= Watts (W)	X 0.0013	= Horsepower (hp)

VELOCITY (speed)

Miles per hour (miles/hr; mph)	X	1.609	= Kilometers per hour (km/hr; kph)	X 0.621	= Miles per hour (miles/hr; mph)

FUEL CONSUMPTION *

Miles per gallon, Imperial (mpg)	X	0.354	= Kilometers per liter (km/l)	X 2.825	= Miles per gallon, Imperial (mpg)
Miles per gallon, US (mpg)	X	0.425	= Kilometers per liter (km/l)	X 2.352	= Miles per gallon, US (mpg)

TEMPERATURE

Degrees Fahrenheit = (°C x 1.8) + 32   Degrees Celsius (Degrees Centigrade; °C) = (°F - 32) x 0.56

It is common practice to convert from miles per gallon (mpg) to liters/100 kilometers (l/100km), where mpg (Imperial) x l/100 km = 282 and mpg (US) x l/100 km = 235

FRACTION/DECIMAL/MILLIMETER EQUIVALENTS

DECIMALS TO MILLIMETERS

Decimal	mm	Decimal	mm
0.001	0.0254	0.500	12.7000
0.002	0.0508	0.510	12.9540
0.003	0.0762	0.520	13.2080
0.004	0.1016	0.530	13.4620
0.005	0.1270	0.540	13.7160
0.006	0.1524	0.550	13.9700
0.007	0.1778	0.560	14.2240
0.008	0.2032	0.570	14.4780
0.009	0.2286	0.580	14.7320
		0.590	14.9860
0.010	0.2540		
0.020	0.5080		
0.030	0.7620		
0.040	1.0160	0.600	15.2400
0.050	1.2700	0.610	15.4940
0.060	1.5240	0.620	15.7480
0.070	1.7780	0.630	16.0020
0.080	2.0320	0.640	16.2560
0.090	2.2860	0.650	16.5100
		0.660	16.7640
0.100	2.5400	0.670	17.0180
0.110	2.7940	0.680	17.2720
0.120	3.0480	0.690	17.5260
0.130	3.3020		
0.140	3.5560		
0.150	3.8100		
0.160	4.0640	0.700	17.7800
0.170	4.3180	0.710	18.0340
0.180	4.5720	0.720	18.2880
0.190	4.8260	0.730	18.5420
		0.740	18.7960
0.200	5.0800	0.750	19.0500
0.210	5.3340	0.760	19.3040
0.220	5.5880	0.770	19.5580
0.230	5.8420	0.780	19.8120
0.240	6.0960	0.790	20.0660
0.250	6.3500		
0.260	6.6040		
0.270	6.8580	0.800	20.3200
0.280	7.1120	0.810	20.5740
0.290	7.3660	0.820	21.8280
		0.830	21.0820
0.300	7.6200	0.840	21.3360
0.310	7.8740	0.850	21.5900
0.320	8.1280	0.860	21.8440
0.330	8.3820	0.870	22.0980
0.340	8.6360	0.880	22.3520
0.350	8.8900	0.890	22.6060
0.360	9.1440		
0.370	9.3980		
0.380	9.6520		
0.390	9.9060		
		0.900	22.8600
0.400	10.1600	0.910	23.1140
0.410	10.4140	0.920	23.3680
0.420	10.6680	0.930	23.6220
0.430	10.9220	0.940	23.8760
0.440	11.1760	0.950	24.1300
0.450	11.4300	0.960	24.3840
0.460	11.6840	0.970	24.6380
0.470	11.9380	0.980	24.8920
0.480	12.1920	0.990	25.1460
0.490	12.4460	1.000	25.4000

FRACTIONS TO DECIMALS TO MILLIMETERS

Fraction	Decimal	mm	Fraction	Decimal	mm
1/64	0.0156	0.3969	33/64	0.5156	13.0969
1/32	0.0312	0.7938	17/32	0.5312	13.4938
3/64	0.0469	1.1906	35/64	0.5469	13.8906
1/16	0.0625	1.5875	9/16	0.5625	14.2875
5/64	0.0781	1.9844	37/64	0.5781	14.6844
3/32	0.0938	2.3812	19/32	0.5938	15.0812
7/64	0.1094	2.7781	39/64	0.6094	15.4781
1/8	0.1250	3.1750	5/8	0.6250	15.8750
9/64	0.1406	3.5719	41/64	0.6406	16.2719
5/32	0.1562	3.9688	21/32	0.6562	16.6688
11/64	0.1719	4.3656	43/64	0.6719	17.0656
3/16	0.1875	4.7625	11/16	0.6875	17.4625
13/64	0.2031	5.1594	45/64	0.7031	17.8594
7/32	0.2188	5.5562	23/32	0.7188	18.2562
15/64	0.2344	5.9531	47/64	0.7344	18.6531
1/4	0.2500	6.3500	3/4	0.7500	19.0500
17/64	0.2656	6.7469	49/64	0.7656	19.4469
9/32	0.2812	7.1438	25/32	0.7812	19.8438
19/64	0.2969	7.5406	51/64	0.7969	20.2406
5/16	0.3125	7.9375	13/16	0.8125	20.6375
21/64	0.3281	8.3344	53/64	0.8281	21.0344
11/32	0.3438	8.7312	27/32	0.8438	21.4312
23/64	0.3594	9.1281	55/64	0.8594	21.8281
3/8	0.3750	9.5250	7/8	0.8750	22.2250
25/64	0.3906	9.9219	57/64	0.8906	22.6219
13/32	0.4062	10.3188	29/32	0.9062	23.0188
27/64	0.4219	10.7156	59/64	0.9219	23.4156
7/16	0.4375	11.1125	15/16	0.9375	23.8125
29/64	0.4531	11.5094	61/64	0.9531	24.2094
15/32	0.4688	11.9062	31/32	0.9688	24.6062
31/64	0.4844	12.3031	63/64	0.9844	25.0031
1/2	0.5000	12.7000	1	1.0000	25.4000

Safety first!

Regardless of how enthusiastic you may be about getting on with the job at hand, take the time to ensure that your safety is not jeopardized. A moment's lack of attention can result in an accident, as can failure to observe certain simple safety precautions. The possibility of an accident will always exist, and the following points should not be considered a comprehensive list of all dangers. Rather, they are intended to make you aware of the risks and to encourage a safety conscious approach to all work you carry out on your vehicle.

ESSENTIAL DOS AND DON'TS

DON'T rely on a jack when working under the vehicle. Always use approved jackstands to support the weight of the vehicle and place them under the recommended lift or support points.

DON'T attempt to loosen extremely tight fasteners (i.e. wheel lug nuts) while the vehicle is on a jack - it may fall.

DON'T start the engine without first making sure that the transmission is in Neutral (or Park where applicable) and the parking brake is set.

DON'T remove the radiator cap from a hot cooling system - let it cool or cover it with a cloth and release the pressure gradually.

DON'T attempt to drain the engine oil until you are sure it has cooled to the point that it will not burn you.

DON'T touch any part of the engine or exhaust system until it has cooled sufficiently to avoid burns.

DON'T siphon toxic liquids such as gasoline, antifreeze and brake fluid by mouth, or allow them to remain on your skin.

DON'T inhale brake lining dust - it is potentially hazardous (see Asbestos below).

DON'T allow spilled oil or grease to remain on the floor - wipe it up before someone slips on it.

DON'T use loose fitting wrenches or other tools which may slip and cause injury.

DON'T push on wrenches when loosening or tightening nuts or bolts. Always try to pull the wrench toward you. If the situation calls for pushing the wrench away, push with an open hand to avoid scraped knuckles if the wrench should slip.

DON'T attempt to lift a heavy component alone - get someone to help you.

DON'T rush or take unsafe shortcuts to finish a job.

DON'T allow children or animals in or around the vehicle while you are working on it.

DO wear eye protection when using power tools such as a drill, sander, bench grinder, etc. and when working under a vehicle.

DO keep loose clothing and long hair well out of the way of moving parts.

DO make sure that any hoist used has a safe working load rating adequate for the job.

DO get someone to check on you periodically when working alone on a vehicle.

DO carry out work in a logical sequence and make sure that everything is correctly assembled and tightened.

DO keep chemicals and fluids tightly capped and out of the reach of children and pets.

DO remember that your vehicle's safety affects that of yourself and others. If in doubt on any point, get professional advice.

STEERING, SUSPENSION AND BRAKES

These systems are essential to driving safety, so make sure you have a qualified shop or individual check your work. Also, compressed suspension springs can cause injury if released suddenly - be sure to use a spring compressor.

AIRBAGS

Airbags are explosive devices that can CAUSE injury if they deploy while you're working on the vehicle. Follow the manufacturer's instructions to disable the airbag whenever you're working in the vicinity of airbag components.

ASBESTOS

Certain friction, insulating, sealing, and other products - such as brake linings, brake bands, clutch linings, torque converters, gaskets, etc. - may contain asbestos or other hazardous friction material. Extreme care must be taken to avoid inhalation of dust from such products, since it is hazardous to health. If in doubt, assume that they do contain asbestos.

FIRE

Remember at all times that gasoline is highly flammable. Never smoke or have any kind of open flame around when working on a vehicle. But the risk does not end there. A spark caused by an electrical short circuit, by two metal surfaces contacting each other, or even by static electricity built up in your body under certain conditions, can ignite gasoline vapors, which in a confined space are highly explosive. Do not, under any circumstances, use gasoline for cleaning parts. Use an approved safety solvent.

Always disconnect the battery ground (-) cable at the battery before working on any part of the fuel system or electrical system. Never risk spilling fuel on a hot engine or exhaust component. It is strongly recommended that a fire extinguisher suitable for use on fuel and electrical fires be kept handy in the garage or workshop at all times. Never try to extinguish a fuel or electrical fire with water.

FUMES

Certain fumes are highly toxic and can quickly cause unconsciousness and even death if inhaled to any extent. Gasoline vapor falls into this category, as do the vapors from some cleaning solvents. Any draining or pouring of such volatile fluids should be done in a well ventilated area.

When using cleaning fluids and solvents, read the instructions on the container carefully. Never use materials from unmarked containers.

Never run the engine in an enclosed space, such as a garage. Exhaust fumes contain carbon monoxide, which is extremely poisonous. If you need to run the engine, always do so in the open air, or at least have the rear of the vehicle outside the work area.

THE BATTERY

Never create a spark or allow a bare light bulb near a battery. They normally give off a certain amount of hydrogen gas, which is highly explosive.

Always disconnect the battery ground (-) cable at the battery before working on the fuel or electrical systems.

If possible, loosen the filler caps or cover when charging the battery from an external source (this does not apply to sealed or maintenance-free batteries). Do not charge at an excessive rate or the battery may burst.

Take care when adding water to a non maintenance-free battery and when carrying a battery. The electrolyte, even when diluted, is very corrosive and should not be allowed to contact clothing or skin.

Always wear eye protection when cleaning the battery to prevent the caustic deposits from entering your eyes.

HOUSEHOLD CURRENT

When using an electric power tool, inspection light, etc., which operates on household current, always make sure that the tool is correctly connected to its plug and that, where necessary, it is properly grounded. Do not use such items in damp conditions and, again, do not create a spark or apply excessive heat in the vicinity of fuel or fuel vapor.

SECONDARY IGNITION SYSTEM VOLTAGE

A severe electric shock can result from touching certain parts of the ignition system (such as the spark plug wires) when the engine is running or being cranked, particularly if components are damp or the insulation is defective. In the case of an electronic ignition system, the secondary system voltage is much higher and could prove fatal.

HYDROFLUORIC ACID

This extremely corrosive acid is formed when certain types of synthetic rubber, found in some O-rings, oil seals, fuel hoses, etc. are exposed to temperatures above 750-degrees F (400-degrees C). The rubber changes into a charred or sticky substance containing the acid. *Once formed, the acid remains dangerous for years. If it gets onto the skin, it may be necessary to amputate the limb concerned.*

When dealing with a vehicle which has suffered a fire, or with components salvaged from such a vehicle, wear protective gloves and discard them after use.

Troubleshooting

CONTENTS

This section provides an easy reference guide to the more common problems which may occur during the operation of your vehicle. These problems and their possible causes are grouped under headings denoting various components or systems, such as Engine, Cooling system, etc. They also refer you to the chapter and/or section which deals with the problem.

Remember that successful troubleshooting is not a mysterious black art practiced only by professional mechanics. It is simply the result of the right knowledge combined with an intelligent, systematic approach to the problem. Always work by a process of elimination, starting with the simplest solution and working through to the most complex - and never overlook the obvious. Anyone can run the gas tank dry or leave the lights on overnight, so don't assume that you are exempt from such oversights.

Finally, always establish a clear idea of why a problem has occurred and take steps to ensure that it doesn't happen again. If the electrical system fails because of a poor connection, check the other connections in the system to make sure that they don't fail as well. If a particular fuse continues to blow, find out why - don't just replace one fuse after another. Remember, failure of a small component can often be indicative of potential failure or incorrect functioning of a more important component or system.

ENGINE

1 Engine will not rotate when attempting to start

1 Battery terminal connections loose or corroded (Chapter 1).
2 Battery discharged or faulty (Chapters 1 and 5).
3 Automatic transaxle not completely engaged in Park (Chapter 7B) or clutch pedal not completely depressed (Chapter 6).
4 Broken, loose or disconnected wiring in the starting circuit (Chapters 5 and 12).
5 Starter motor pinion jammed in flywheel ring gear (Chapter 5).
6 Starter solenoid faulty (Chapter 5).
7 Starter motor faulty (Chapter 5).
8 Ignition switch faulty (Chapter 12).
9 Starter pinion or flywheel teeth worn or broken (Chapter 5).

2 Engine rotates but will not start

1 Fuel tank empty.
2 Battery discharged (engine rotates slowly) (Chapter 5).
3 Battery terminal connections loose or corroded (Chapter 1).
4 Leaking fuel injector(s), faulty fuel pump, pressure regulator, etc. (Chapter 4).
5 Broken timing belt or chain (Chapter 2A or 2B).
6 Ignition components damp or damaged (Chapter 5).
7 Fouled spark plugs (Chapter 1).
8 Broken, loose or disconnected wiring in the starting circuit (Chapter 5).
9 Broken, loose or disconnected wires at the ignition coil or faulty coil (Chapter 5).
10 Defective crankshaft or camshaft sensor (Chapter 6).

3 Engine hard to start when cold

1 Battery discharged or low (Chapter 1).
2 Malfunctioning fuel system (Chapter 4).

3 Faulty coolant temperature sensor or intake air temperature sensor (Chapter 6).
4 Faulty ignition system (Chapter 5).

4 Engine hard to start when hot

1 Air filter clogged (Chapter 1).
2 Fuel not reaching the fuel injection system (Chapter 4).
3 Corroded battery connections (Chapter 1).
4 Faulty coolant temperature sensor or intake air temperature sensor (Chapter 6).

5 Starter motor noisy or excessively rough in engagement

1 Pinion or flywheel gear teeth worn or broken (Chapter 5).
2 Starter motor mounting bolts loose or missing (Chapter 5).

6 Engine starts but stops immediately

1 Insufficient fuel reaching the fuel injector(s) (Chapters 1 and 4).
2 Vacuum leak at the gasket between the intake manifold/plenum and throttle body (Chapter 4).

7 Oil puddle under engine

1 Oil pan gasket and/or oil pan drain bolt washer leaking (Chapter 2A or 2B).
2 Oil pressure sending unit leaking (Chapter 2C).
3 Valve cover leaking (Chapter 2A or 2B).
4 Engine oil seals leaking (Chapter 2A or 2B).
5 Oil pump housing leaking (Chapter 2A or 2B).

8 Engine lopes while idling or idles erratically

1 Vacuum leakage (Chapters 2 and 4).
2 Leaking EGR valve (Chapter 6).
3 Air filter clogged (Chapter 1).
4 Malfunction in the fuel injection or engine control system (Chapters 4 and 6).
5 Leaking head gasket (Chapter 2A or 2B).
6 Timing chain and/or sprockets worn (Chapter 2A or 2B).
7 Camshaft lobes worn (Chapter 2A or 2B).

9 Engine misses at idle speed

1 Spark plugs worn or not gapped properly (Chapter 1).
2 Faulty coil(s) (Chapter 1).
3 Vacuum leaks (Chapter 1).
4 Uneven or low compression (Chapter 2C).
5 Problem with the fuel injection system (Chapter 4).

10 Engine misses throughout driving speed range

1 Fuel filter clogged and/or impurities in the fuel system (Chapters 1 and 4).
2 Low fuel pressure (Chapter 4).
3 Faulty or incorrectly gapped spark plugs (Chapter 1).

4 Faulty emission system components (Chapter 6).
5 Low or uneven cylinder compression pressures (Chapter 2C).
6 Weak or faulty ignition system (Chapter 5).
7 Vacuum leak (Chapters 2C and 4).

11 Engine stumbles on acceleration

1 Spark plugs fouled (Chapter 1).
2 Problem with fuel injection or engine control system (Chapters 4 and 6).
3 Fuel filter clogged (Chapters 1 and 4).
4 Intake manifold air leak (Chapter 2A or 2B).
5 Problem with the emissions control system (Chapter 6).

12 Engine surges while holding accelerator steady

1 Intake air leak (Chapter 4).
2 Fuel pump or fuel pressure regulator faulty (Chapter 4).
3 Problem with the fuel injection system (Chapter 4).
4 Problem with the emissions control system (Chapter 6).

13 Engine stalls

1 Fuel filter clogged and/or water and impurities in the fuel system (Chapters 1 and 4).
2 Faulty emissions system components (Chapter 6).
3 Faulty or incorrectly-gapped spark plugs (Chapter 1).
4 Vacuum leak (Chapters 2C and 4).

14 Engine lacks power

1 Obstructed exhaust system (Chapter 4).
2 Faulty or incorrectly-gapped spark plugs (Chapter 1).
3 Problem with the fuel injection system (Chapter 4).
4 Dirty air filter (Chapter 1).
5 Brakes binding (Chapter 9).
6 Automatic transaxle fluid level incorrect (Chapter 1).
7 Clutch slipping (Chapter 8).
8 Fuel filter clogged and/or impurities in the fuel system (Chapters 1 and 4).
9 Emission control system not functioning properly (Chapter 6).
10 Low or uneven cylinder compression pressures (Chapter 2C).

15 Engine backfires

1 Emission control system not functioning properly (Chapter 6).
2 Problem with the fuel injection system (Chapter 4).
3 Vacuum leak at fuel injector(s), intake manifold or vacuum hoses (Chapters 2 and 4).
4 Exhaust manifold air leak.

16 Pinging or knocking engine sounds during acceleration or uphill

1 Incorrect grade of fuel.
2 Fuel injection system faulty (Chapter 4).
3 Improper or damaged spark plugs or wires (Chapter 1).
4 Knock sensor defective (Chapter 6).

5 EGR valve not functioning (Chapter 6).
6 Vacuum leak (Chapters 2C and 4).

17 Engine runs with oil pressure light on

1 Low oil level (Chapter 1).
2 Idle rpm below specification (Chapter 1).
3 Short in wiring circuit (Chapter 12).
4 Faulty oil pressure sender (Chapter 2C).
5 Worn engine bearings and/or oil pump (Chapter 2).

18 Engine continues to run after switching off

1 Defective ignition switch (Chapter 12).
2 Faulty Powertrain Control Module (Chapter 6).
3 Faulty Body Control Module.
4 Leaking fuel injector (Chapter 4).

ENGINE ELECTRICAL SYSTEMS

19 Battery will not hold a charge

1 Drivebelt or tensioner defective (Chapter 1).
2 Battery electrolyte level low (Chapter 1).
3 Battery terminals loose or corroded (Chapter 1).
4 Alternator not charging properly (Chapter 5).
5 Loose, broken or faulty wiring in the charging circuit (Chapter 5).
6 Short in vehicle wiring (Chapter 12).
7 Internally defective battery (Chapters 1 and 5).

20 Alternator light fails to go out

1 Faulty alternator or charging circuit (Chapter 5).
2 Drivebelt or tensioner defective (Chapter 1).

21 Alternator light fails to come on when key is turned on

1 Instrument cluster defective (Chapter 12).
2 Fault in the Powertrain Control Module or wiring harness.

FUEL SYSTEM

22 Excessive fuel consumption

1 Dirty air filter element (Chapter 1).
2 Emissions system not functioning properly (Chapter 6).
3 Fuel injection system not functioning properly (Chapter 4).
4 Low tire pressure or incorrect tire size (Chapter 1).

23 Fuel leakage and/or fuel odor

1 Leaking fuel line (Chapters 1 and 4).
2 Tank overfilled.
3 Evaporative emissions control system problem (Chapters 1 and 6).
4 Problem with the fuel injection system (Chapter 4).

COOLING SYSTEM

24 Overheating

1 Insufficient coolant in system (Chapter 1).
2 Water pump drivebelt defective or out of adjustment (Chapter 1).
3 Radiator core blocked or grille restricted (Chapter 3).
4 Thermostat faulty (Chapter 3).
5 Electric coolant fan inoperative or blades broken (Chapter 3).
6 Expansion tank cap not maintaining proper pressure (Chapter 3).

25 Overcooling

1 Faulty thermostat (Chapter 3).
2 Inaccurate temperature gauge sending unit (Chapter 3).

26 External coolant leakage

1 Deteriorated/damaged hoses; loose clamps (Chapters 1 and 3).
2 Water pump defective (Chapter 3).
3 Leakage from radiator core or coolant reservoir (Chapter 3).
4 Engine drain or water jacket core plugs leaking (Chapter 2).

27 Internal coolant leakage

1 Leaking cylinder head gasket (Chapter 2A or 2B).
2 Cracked cylinder bore or cylinder head (Chapter 2C).

28 Coolant loss

1 Too much coolant in reservoir (Chapter 1).
2 Coolant boiling away because of overheating (Chapter 3).
3 Internal or external leakage (Chapter 3).
4 Faulty radiator cap (Chapter 3).

29 Poor coolant circulation

1 Inoperative water pump (Chapter 3).
2 Restriction in cooling system (Chapters 1 and 3).
3 Drivebelt or tensioner defective (Chapter 1).
4 Thermostat sticking (Chapter 3).

CLUTCH

30 Pedal travels to floor - no pressure or very little resistance

1 Master or release cylinder faulty (Chapter 8).
2 Hose/pipe burst or leaking (Chapter 8).
3 Connections leaking (Chapter 8).
4 No fluid in reservoir (Chapter 8).
5 Master cylinder faulty (Chapter 8).
6 Broken release bearing or fork (Chapter 8).
7 Faulty pressure plate diaphragm spring (Chapter 8).

31 Fluid in area of master cylinder dust cover and on pedal

Rear seal failure in master cylinder (Chapter 8).

32 Fluid on release cylinder

Release cylinder plunger seal faulty (Chapter 8).

33 Pedal feels spongy when depressed

Air in system (Chapter 8).

34 Unable to select gears

1 Faulty transaxle (Chapter 7).
2 Faulty clutch disc or pressure plate (Chapter 8).
3 Faulty release lever or release bearing (Chapter 8).
4 Faulty shift lever assembly or control cables (Chapter 8).

35 Clutch slips (engine speed increases with no increase in vehicle speed)

1 Clutch plate worn (Chapter 8).
2 Clutch plate is oil soaked by leaking rear main seal (Chapters 2 and 8).
3 Clutch plate not seated (Chapter 8).
4 Warped pressure plate or flywheel (Chapter 8).
5 Weak diaphragm springs (Chapter 8).
6 Clutch plate overheated. Allow to cool.

36 Grabbing (chattering) as clutch is engaged

1 Oil on clutch plate lining, burned or glazed facings (Chapter 8).
2 Worn or loose engine or transaxle mounts (Chapter 2).
3 Worn splines on clutch plate hub (Chapter 8).
4 Warped pressure plate or flywheel (Chapter 8).
5 Burned or smeared resin on flywheel or pressure plate (Chapter 8).

37 Transaxle rattling (clicking)

1 Release lever loose (Chapter 8).
2 Clutch plate damper spring failure (Chapter 8).

38 Noise in clutch area

1 Fork shaft improperly installed (Chapter 8).
2 Faulty bearing (Chapter 8).

39 Clutch pedal stays on floor

1 Clutch master cylinder piston binding in bore (Chapter 8).
2 Broken release bearing or fork (Chapter 8).

40 High pedal effort

1 Piston binding in bore (Chapter 8).
2 Pressure plate faulty (Chapter 8).

MANUAL TRANSAXLE

41 Knocking noise at low speeds

1 Worn driveaxle constant velocity (CV) joints (Chapter 8).
2 Worn side gear shaft counterbore in differential case (Chapter 7A).*

42　Noise most pronounced when turning

Differential gear noise (Chapter 7A).*

43　Clunk on acceleration or deceleration

1　Loose engine or transaxle mounts (Chapter 2).
2　Worn differential pinion shaft in case.*
3　Worn side gear shaft counterbore in differential case (Chapter 7A).*
4　Worn or damaged driveaxle inboard CV joints (Chapter 8).

44　Clicking noise in turns

Worn or damaged outboard CV joint (Chapter 8).

45　Vibration

1　Rough wheel bearing (Chapter 10).
2　Damaged driveaxle (Chapter 8).
3　Out-of-round tires (Chapter 1).
4　Tire out of balance (Chapters 1 and 10).
5　Worn CV joint (Chapter 8).

46　Noisy in neutral with engine running

1　Damaged input gear bearing (Chapter 7A).*
2　Damaged clutch release bearing (Chapter 8).

47　Noisy in one particular gear

1　Damaged or worn constant mesh gears (Chapter 7A).*
2　Damaged or worn synchronizers (Chapter 7A).*
3　Bent reverse fork (Chapter 7A).*
4　Damaged fourth speed gear or output gear (Chapter 7A).*
5　Worn or damaged reverse idler gear or idler bushing (Chapter 7A).*

48　Noisy in all gears

1　Insufficient lubricant (Chapter 7A).
2　Damaged or worn bearings (Chapter 7A).*
3　Worn or damaged input gear shaft and/or output gear shaft (Chapter 7A).*

49　Slips out of gear

1　Worn or improperly adjusted cable (Chapter 7A).
2　Shift cable does not work freely, binds (Chapter 7A).
3　Input gear bearing retainer broken or loose (Chapter 7A).*
4　Worn or bent shift fork (Chapter 7A).*

50　Leaks lubricant

1　Side gear shaft seals worn (Chapter 7).
2　Loose or broken input gear shaft bearing retainer (Chapter 7A).*
3　Input gear bearing retainer O-ring and/or lip seal damaged (Chapter 7A).*

51　Locked in gear

Lock pin or interlock pin missing (Chapter 7A).*

Although the corrective action necessary to remedy the symptoms described is beyond the scope of this manual, the above information should be helpful in isolating the cause of the condition so that the owner can communicate clearly with a professional mechanic.

AUTOMATIC TRANSAXLE

➡ **Note: Due to the complexity of the automatic transaxle, it is difficult for the home mechanic to properly diagnose and service this component. For problems other than the following, the vehicle should be taken to a dealer or transmission shop.**

52　Fluid leakage

1　Automatic transaxle fluid is a deep red color. Fluid leaks should not be confused with engine oil, which can easily be blown onto the transaxle by air flow.
2　To pinpoint a leak, first remove all built-up dirt and grime from the transaxle housing with degreasing agents and/or steam cleaning. Then drive the vehicle at low speeds so air flow will not blow the leak far from its source. Raise the vehicle and determine where the leak is coming from. Common areas of leakage are:

a)　*Dipstick tube (Chapters 1 and 7).*
b)　*Transaxle oil lines (Chapter 7).*
c)　*Speed sensor (Chapter 6).*
d)　*Driveaxle oil seals (Chapter 7).*

53　Transaxle fluid brown or has a burned smell

Transaxle fluid overheated (Chapter 1).

54　General shift mechanism problems

1　Chapter 7, Part B, deals with checking and adjusting the shift cable on automatic transaxles. Common problems which may be attributed to poorly adjusted cable are:

a)　*Engine starting in gears other than Park or Neutral.*
b)　*Indicator on shifter pointing to a gear other than the one actually being used.*
c)　*Vehicle moves when in Park.*

2　Refer to Chapter 7, Part B for the shift cable adjustment procedure.

55　Transaxle slips, shifts roughly, is noisy or has no drive in forward or reverse gears

There are many probable causes for the above problems, but the home mechanic should be concerned with only one possibility - fluid level. Before taking the vehicle to a repair shop, check the level and condition of the fluid as described in Chapter 1. Correct the fluid level as necessary or change the fluid and filter if needed. If the problem persists, have a professional diagnose the cause.

DRIVEAXLES

56　Clicking noise in turns

Worn or damaged outboard CV joint (Chapter 8).

57 Shudder or vibration during acceleration

1 Excessive toe-in (Chapter 10).
2 Worn or damaged inboard or outboard CV joints (Chapter 8).
3 Sticking inboard CV joint assembly (Chapter 8).

58 Vibration at highway speeds

1 Out-of-balance front wheels and/or tires (Chapters 1 and 10).
2 Out-of-round front tires (Chapters 1 and 10).
3 Worn CV joint(s) (Chapter 8).

BRAKES

➡ **Note: Before assuming that a brake problem exists, make sure that:**

a) *The tires are in good condition and properly inflated (Chapter 1).*
b) *The front end alignment is correct.*
c) *The vehicle is not loaded with weight in an unequal manner.*

59 Vehicle pulls to one side during braking

1 Incorrect tire pressures (Chapter 1).
2 Front end out of alignment (have the front end aligned).
3 Front, or rear, tire sizes not matched to one another.
4 Restricted brake lines or hoses (Chapter 9).
5 Malfunctioning caliper assembly (Chapter 9).
6 Loose suspension parts (Chapter 10).
7 Excessive wear of pad material or disc on one side (Chapter 9).
8 Contamination (grease or brake fluid) of brake pad material or disc on one side (Chapter 9).

60 Noise (high-pitched squeal when the brakes are applied)

Brake pads worn out. Replace pads with new ones immediately (Chapter 9).

61 Brake roughness or chatter (pedal pulsates)

1 Excessive lateral runout (Chapter 9).
2 Uneven pad wear (Chapter 9).
3 Defective disc (Chapter 9).

62 Excessive brake pedal effort required to stop vehicle

1 Malfunctioning power brake booster (Chapter 9).
2 Partial system failure (Chapter 9).
3 Excessively worn pads (Chapter 9).
4 Piston in caliper stuck or sluggish (Chapter 9).
5 Brake pads contaminated with oil or grease (Chapter 9).
6 Brake disc grooved and/or glazed (Chapter 9).

63 Excessive brake pedal travel

1 Partial brake system failure (Chapter 9).
2 Insufficient fluid in master cylinder (Chapters 1 and 9).
3 Air trapped in system (Chapter 9).
4 Defective master cylinder (Chapter 9).

64 Dragging brakes

1 Incorrect adjustment of brake light switch (Chapter 9).
2 Master cylinder pistons not returning correctly (Chapter 9).
3 Caliper piston stuck (Chapter 9).
4 Restricted brakes lines or hoses (Chapter 9).
5 Incorrect parking brake adjustment (Chapter 9).

65 Grabbing or uneven braking action

1 Malfunction of proportioning valve (Chapter 9).
2 Binding brake pedal mechanism (Chapter 9).
3 Contaminated brake linings (Chapter 9).

66 Brake pedal feels spongy when depressed

1 Air in hydraulic lines (Chapter 9).
2 Master cylinder mounting bolts loose (Chapter 9).
3 Master cylinder defective (Chapter 9).

67 Brake pedal travels to the floor with little resistance

1 Little or no fluid in the master cylinder reservoir caused by leaking caliper piston(s) (Chapter 9).
2 Loose, damaged or disconnected brake lines (Chapter 9).
3 Defective master cylinder (Chapter 9).

68 Parking brake does not hold

Parking brake improperly adjusted (Chapter 9).

SUSPENSION AND STEERING SYSTEMS

➡ **Note: Before attempting to diagnose the suspension and steering systems, perform the following preliminary checks:**

a) *Tires for wrong pressure and uneven wear.*
b) *Steering universal joints from the column to the rack and pinion for loose connectors or wear.*
c) *Front and rear suspension and the rack-and-pinion assembly for loose or damaged parts.*
d) *Out-of-round or out-of-balance tires, bent rims and loose and/or rough wheel bearings.*

69 Vehicle pulls to one side

1 Mismatched or uneven tires (Chapter 10).
2 Broken or sagging springs (Chapter 10).
3 Wheel alignment incorrect. Have the wheels professionally aligned.
4 Front brake dragging (Chapter 9).

70 Abnormal or excessive tire wear

1 Wheel alignment out-of-specification. Have the wheels aligned.
2 Sagging or broken springs (Chapter 10).
3 Tire out-of-balance (Chapter 10).
4 Worn strut damper (Chapter 10).
5 Overloaded vehicle.
6 Tires not rotated regularly.

71 Wheel makes a thumping noise

1 Blister or bump on tire (Chapter 10).
2 Improper strut or shock absorber damper action (Chapter 10).

72 Shimmy, shake or vibration

1 Tire or wheel out-of-balance or out-of-round (Chapter 10).
2 Worn wheel bearings (Chapter 10).
3 Worn tie-rod ends (Chapter 10).
4 Worn balljoints (Chapters 1 and 10).
5 Excessive wheel runout (Chapter 10).
6 Blister or bump on tire (Chapter 10).

73 Hard steering

1 Lack of lubrication at balljoints and/or tie-rod ends (Chapter 10).
2 Wheel alignment out-of-specifications. Have the wheels professionally aligned.
3 Low tire pressure(s) (Chapter 1).
4 Worn steering gear (Chapter 10).

74 Poor returnability of steering to center

1 Worn balljoints or tie-rod ends (Chapter 10).
2 Worn steering gear assembly (Chapter 10).
3 Wheel alignment out-of-specifications. Have the wheels professionally aligned.

75 Abnormal noise at the front end

1 Worn balljoints or tie-rod ends (Chapter 10).
2 Damaged shock absorber mounting (Chapter 10).
3 Worn control arm bushings or tie-rod ends (Chapter 10).
4 Loose stabilizer bar (Chapter 10).
5 Loose wheel bolts (Chapter 1).
6 Loose suspension bolts (Chapter 10).

76 Wander or poor steering stability

1 Mismatched or uneven tires (Chapter 10).
2 Lack of lubrication at balljoints and tie-rod ends (Chapters 1 and 10).
3 Worn strut or shock absorber assemblies (Chapter 10).
4 Broken or sagging springs (Chapter 10).
5 Wheels out of alignment. Have the wheels professionally aligned.

77 Erratic steering when braking

1 Wheel bearings worn (Chapter 10).
2 Broken or sagging springs (Chapter 10).
3 Leaking wheel cylinder or caliper (Chapter 10).
4 Excessive brake disc runout (Chapter 9).

78 Excessive pitching and/or rolling around corners or during braking

1 Loose stabilizer bar (Chapter 10).
2 Worn strut dampers or mountings (Chapter 10).
3 Broken or sagging springs (Chapter 10).
4 Overloaded vehicle.

79 Suspension bottoms

1 Overloaded vehicle.
2 Sagging springs (Chapter 10).

80 Cupped tires

1 Front wheel or rear wheel alignment out-of-specifications. Have the wheels professionally aligned.
2 Worn shock absorbers (Chapter 10).
3 Wheel bearings worn (Chapter 10).
4 Excessive tire or wheel runout (Chapter 10).
5 Worn balljoints (Chapter 10).

81 Excessive tire wear on outside edge

1 Inflation pressures incorrect (Chapter 1).
2 Excessive speed in turns.
3 Wheel alignment incorrect (excessive toe-in). Have professionally aligned.
4 Suspension arm bent or twisted (Chapter 10).

82 Excessive tire wear on inside edge

1 Inflation pressures incorrect (Chapter 1).
2 Wheel alignment incorrect (toe-out). Have professionally aligned.
3 Loose or damaged steering components (Chapter 10).

83 Tire tread worn in one place

1 Tires out-of-balance.
2 Damaged wheel. Inspect and replace if necessary.
3 Defective tire (Chapter 1).

84 Excessive play or looseness in steering system

1 Wheel bearing(s) worn (Chapter 10).
2 Tie-rod end loose (Chapter 10).
3 Steering gear loose (Chapter 10).
4 Worn or loose steering intermediate shaft U-joint (Chapter 10).

85 Rattling or clicking noise in steering gear

1 Steering gear loose (Chapter 10).
2 Steering gear defective.

Section

1

TUNE-UP AND ROUTINE MAINTENANCE

1 Maintenance schedule

The maintenance intervals in this manual are provided with the assumption that you, not the dealer, will be doing the work. These are the minimum maintenance intervals recommended by the factory for vehicles that are driven daily. If you wish to keep your vehicle in peak condition at all times, you may wish to perform some of these procedures even more often. Because frequent maintenance enhances the efficiency, performance and resale value of your car, we encourage you to do so. If you drive in dusty areas, tow a trailer, idle or drive at low speeds for extended periods or drive for short distances (less than four miles) in below freezing temperatures, shorter intervals are also recommended.

When your vehicle is new, it should be serviced by a factory authorized dealer service department to protect the factory warranty. In many cases, the initial maintenance check is done at no cost to the owner.

EVERY 250 MILES (400 KM) OR WEEKLY, WHICHEVER COMES FIRST

Check the engine oil level (see Section 4)
Check the engine coolant level (see Section 4)
Check the brake and clutch fluid level (see Section 4)
Check the windshield washer fluid level (see Section 4)
Check the tires and tire pressures (see Section 5)
Check the operation of all lights
Check the horn operation

EVERY 5,000 MILES (8000 KM) OR 3 MONTHS, WHICHEVER COMES FIRST

All items listed above, plus:
Change the engine oil and filter (see Section 6)
Check and replace, if necessary, the air filter element (see Section 7)

EVERY 6,000 MILES (9600 KM) OR 6 MONTHS, WHICHEVER COMES FIRST

All items listed above, plus:
Check the wiper blade condition (see Section 8)
Check and clean the battery and terminals (see Section 9)

Rotate the tires (see Section 10)
Check the seat belts (see Section 11)
Inspect underhood hoses (see Section 12)
Check the cooling system hoses and connections for leaks and damage (see Section 13)
Check the exhaust system (see Section 14)

EVERY 15,000 MILES (24,000 KM) OR 12 MONTHS, WHICHEVER COMES FIRST

All items listed above, plus:
Replace the interior ventilation filter (see Section 15)
Check the brake system (see Section 16)
Check the suspension/steering components and driveaxle boots (see Section 17)
Check the fuel system hoses and connections for leaks and damage (see Section 18)
Check the drivebelts and replace if necessary (see Section 19)

EVERY 30,000 MILES (48,000 KM) OR 24 MONTHS, WHICHEVER COMES FIRST

All items listed above, plus:
Replace the air filter element (see Section 7)
Change the brake fluid (see Section 20)
Replace the spark plugs (see Section 21)
Check the ignition coil(s) (see Chapter 5)

EVERY 40,000 MILES (64,000 KM) OR 36 MONTHS, WHICHEVER COMES FIRST

All items listed above, plus:
Change the Direct Shift Gearbox (DSG) transaxle fluid and filter (see Section 23)

EVERY 75,000 MILES (120,000 KM)

Replace the timing belt (four-cylinder BPY engines; see Chapter 2A)

Engine compartment layout (five-cylinder model, others similar)

1	*Engine oil dipstick*	*4*	*Battery*	*7*	*Windshield washer fluid reservoir*
2	*Engine oil filler cap*	*5*	*Fuse and relay block*	*8*	*Coolant expansion tank*
3	*Brake fluid reservoir*	*6*	*Drivebelt*	*9*	*Ignition coil and spark plug*

Typical front underside components (five-cylinder model, others similar)

1	Engine oil drain plug	4	Automatic transaxle (09G) fluid level	7	Outer driveaxle boot
2	Oil filter housing		check/fill plug	8	Balljoint
3	Lower radiator hose	5	Inner driveaxle boot	9	Front disc brake caliper
		6	Exhaust pipe	10	Drivebelts

Typical rear underside components

1	Fuel filter	4	Exhaust pipe	7	EVAP canister (under cover)
2	Fuel tank	5	Rear disc brake caliper	8	Rear muffler
3	Center muffler	6	Stabilizer bar		

2 Introduction

This Chapter is designed to help the home mechanic maintain their Jetta, Rabbit, GTI or Golf with the goals of maximum performance, economy, safety and reliability in mind.

Included is a master maintenance schedule, followed by procedures dealing specifically with each item on the schedule. Visual checks, adjustments, component replacement and other helpful items are included. Refer to the accompanying illustrations of the engine compartment and the underside of the vehicle for the locations of various components.

Servicing your vehicle in accordance with the mileage/time maintenance schedule and the step-by-step procedures will result in a planned maintenance program that should produce a long and reliable service life. Keep in mind that it's a comprehensive plan, so maintaining some items but not others at the specified intervals will not produce the same results.

As you service your vehicle, you will discover that many of the procedures can - and should - be grouped together because of the nature of the particular procedure you're performing or because of the close proximity of two otherwise unrelated components to one another.

For example, if the vehicle is raised for chassis lubrication, you should inspect the exhaust, suspension, steering and fuel systems while you're under the vehicle. When you're rotating the tires, it makes good sense to check the brakes since the wheels are already removed. Finally, let's suppose you have to borrow or rent a torque wrench. Even if you only need it to tighten the spark plugs, you might as well check the torque of as many critical fasteners as time allows.

The first step in this maintenance program is to prepare yourself before the actual work begins. Read through all the procedures you're planning to do, then gather up all the parts and tools needed. If it looks like you might run into problems during a particular job, seek advice from a mechanic or an experienced do-it-yourselfer.

OWNER'S MANUAL AND VECI LABEL INFORMATION

Your vehicle owner's manual was written for your year and model and contains very specific information on component locations, specifications, fuse ratings, part numbers, etc. The Owner's Manual is an important resource for the do-it-yourselfer to have; if one was not supplied with your vehicle, it can generally be ordered from a dealer parts department.

Among other important information, the Vehicle Emissions Control Information (VECI) label contains specifications and procedures for applicable tune-up adjustments and, in some instances, spark plugs. The information on this label is the exact maintenance data recommended by the manufacturer. This data often varies by intended operating altitude, local emissions regulations, month of manufacture, etc.

This Chapter contains procedural details, safety information and more ambitious maintenance intervals than you might find in manufacturer's literature. However, you may also find procedures or specifications in your Owner's Manual or VECI label that differ with what's printed here. In these cases, the Owner's Manual or VECI label can be considered correct, since it is specific to your particular vehicle.

3 Tune-up general information

The term tune-up is used in this manual to represent a combination of individual operations rather than one specific procedure.

If, from the time the vehicle is new, the routine maintenance schedule is followed closely and frequent checks are made of fluid levels and high wear items, as suggested throughout this manual, the engine will be kept in relatively good running condition and the need for additional work will be minimized.

More likely than not, however, there will be times when the engine is running poorly due to lack of regular maintenance. This is even more likely if a used vehicle, which has not received regular and frequent maintenance checks, is purchased. In such cases, an engine tune-up will be needed outside of the regular routine maintenance intervals.

The first step in any tune-up or diagnostic procedure to help correct a poor running engine is a cylinder compression check. A compression check (see Chapter 2C) will help determine the condition of internal engine components and should be used as a guide for tune-up and repair procedures. If, for instance, a compression check indicates serious internal engine wear, a conventional tune-up will not improve the performance of the engine and would be a waste of time and money.

Because of its importance, the compression check should be done by someone with the right equipment and the knowledge to use it properly.

MINOR TUNE-UP

Check all engine-related fluids (Section 4)
Check the air filter (Section 7)
Clean, inspect and test the battery (Section 9)
Check all underhood hoses (Section 12)
Check the cooling system (Section 13)
Check the drivebelt (Section 19)
Check the charging system (Chapter 5)

MAJOR TUNE-UP

All items listed under Minor tune-up, plus . . .
Replace the air filter (Section 7)
Replace the spark plugs (Section 21)

4 Fluid level checks (every 250 miles [400 km] or weekly)

1 Fluids are an essential part of the lubrication, cooling, brake and windshield washer systems. Because the fluids gradually become depleted and/or contaminated during normal operation of the vehicle, they must be periodically replenished. See *Recommended lubricants*

and fluids in this Chapter's Specifications before adding fluid to any of the following components.

➡ **Note: The vehicle must be on level ground when fluid levels are checked.**

ENGINE OIL

▶ **Refer to illustrations 4.2, 4.4 and 4.6**

2   The oil level is checked with a dipstick, which is located on the side of the engine (see illustration). The dipstick extends through a metal tube down into the oil pan.

3   The oil level should be checked before the vehicle has been driven, or about 5 minutes after the engine has been shut off. If the oil is checked immediately after driving the vehicle, some of the oil will remain in the upper part of the engine, resulting in an inaccurate reading on the dipstick.

4   Pull the dipstick out of the tube and wipe all the oil from the end with a clean rag or paper towel. Insert the clean dipstick all the way back into the tube and pull it out again. Note the oil at the end of the dipstick; the level should be between the MIN and MAX marks (see illustration).

5   Do not allow the level to drop below the minimum mark, or oil starvation may cause engine damage. Conversely, overfilling the engine (adding oil above the MAX mark) may cause oil fouled spark plugs, oil leaks or oil seal failures. The oil could also be whipped by the crankshaft, causing it to foam, which could cause accelerated wear of the friction surfaces in the engine due to lack of proper lubrication.

✳ CAUTION:

Damage to the catalytic converter may result if the oil level is overfilled.

6   To add oil, remove the filler cap from the valve cover (see illustration). After adding oil, wait a few minutes to allow the level to stabilize, then pull out the dipstick and check the level again. Add more oil if required. Install the filler cap and tighten it by hand only.

7   Checking the oil level is an important preventive maintenance step. A consistently low oil level indicates oil leakage through damaged seals, defective gaskets or past worn rings or valve guides. If the oil looks milky in color or has water droplets in it, the cylinder head gasket(s) may be blown or the head(s) or block may be cracked. The engine should be checked immediately. The condition of the oil should also be checked. Whenever you check the oil level, slide your thumb and index finger up the dipstick before wiping off the oil. If you see

4.2 Engine oil dipstick - five-cylinder engine shown, others similar

small dirt or metal particles clinging to the dipstick, the oil should be changed (see Section 6).

ENGINE COOLANT

▶ **Refer to illustration 4.9**

✳ WARNING:

Do not allow antifreeze to come in contact with your skin or painted surfaces of the vehicle. Flush contaminated areas immediately with plenty of water. Don't store new coolant or leave old coolant lying around where it's accessible to children or pets - they're attracted by its sweet smell. Ingestion of even a small amount of coolant can be fatal! Wipe up garage floor and drip pan spills immediately. Keep antifreeze containers covered and repair cooling system leaks as soon as they're noticed.

8   All vehicles covered by this manual are equipped with a coolant expansion tank, located in the right side of the engine compartment,

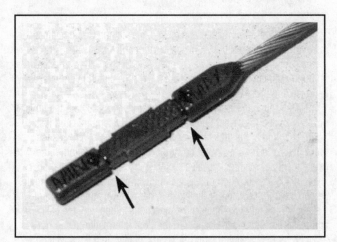

4.4 The oil level must be maintained between the MIN and MAX marks on the dipstick

4.6 Engine oil filler cap - five-cylinder engine shown, others similar

4.9 When the engine is cold, the coolant level should be between the MIN and MAX marks

4.15 Never let the brake fluid level drop below the MIN mark

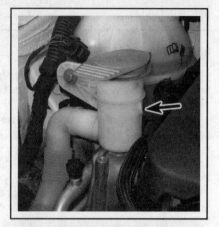

4.22 The windshield washer fluid reservoir is located in the passenger's side of the engine compartment

and connected by hoses to the cooling system.

9   The coolant level in the tank should be checked regularly.

☀ WARNING:

Never remove the pressure cap when the engine is warm!

The level in the tank varies with the temperature of the engine. When the engine is cold, the coolant level should be between the MIN and MAX marks on the tank (see illustration). If it isn't, remove the cap from the tank and add coolant to the tank.

☀ WARNING:

Remove the cap slowly. If you hear a hissing sound when unscrewing the cap, wait until it stops, then proceed.

10   Drive the vehicle and recheck the coolant level. If only a small amount of coolant is required to bring the system up to the proper level, water can be used. However, repeated additions of water will dilute the antifreeze and water solution. In order to maintain the proper ratio of antifreeze and water, always top up the coolant level with the correct mixture. Don't use rust inhibitors or additives. An empty plastic milk jug or bleach bottle makes an excellent container for mixing coolant.

11   If the coolant level drops consistently, there may be a leak in the system. Inspect the radiator, hoses, filler cap, drain plugs and water pump (see Section 13). If no leaks are noted, have the expansion tank cap pressure tested by a service station.

12   If you have to remove the pressure cap, wait until the engine has cooled completely, then wrap a thick cloth around the cap and turn it to the first stop. If coolant or steam escapes, or if you hear a hissing noise, let the engine cool down longer, then remove the cap.

13   Check the condition of the coolant as well. It should be relatively clear. If it's brown or rust colored, the system should be drained, flushed and refilled. Even if the coolant appears to be normal, the corrosion inhibitors wear out, so it must be replaced at the specified intervals.

BRAKE AND CLUTCH FLUID

▶ **Refer to illustration 4.15**

14   The brake master cylinder is located in the driver's side of the

engine compartment, under the cowl cover near the firewall. On vehicles with manual transaxles, the clutch master cylinder is connected by a hose to the brake master cylinder reservoir.

15   To check the fluid level, remove the access cover from the left cowl cover, then look at the MAX and MIN marks on the reservoir (see illustration). The level should be within the specified distance from the maximum fill line.

16   If the level is low, wipe the top of the reservoir cover with a clean rag to prevent contamination of the brake or clutch system before lifting the cover.

17   Add only the specified brake fluid to the brake reservoir (refer to *Recommended lubricants and fluids* in this Chapter's Specifications, or to your owner's manual). Mixing different types of brake fluid can damage the system. Fill the brake master cylinder reservoir only to the MAX line.

☀ WARNING:

Use caution when filling either reservoir - brake fluid can harm your eyes and damage painted surfaces. Do not use brake fluid that is more than one year old or has been left open. Brake fluid absorbs moisture from the air. Excess moisture can cause a dangerous loss of braking.

18   While the reservoir cap is removed, inspect the master cylinder reservoir for contamination. If deposits, dirt particles or water droplets are present, the fluid should be changed (see Section 20 for the brake fluid replacement procedure, or Chapter 8 for the clutch hydraulic system bleeding procedure).

19   After filling the reservoir to the proper level, make sure the lid is properly seated to prevent fluid leakage and/or system pressure loss.

20   The fluid in the brake master cylinder will drop slightly as the brake pads at each wheel wear down during normal operation. If the master cylinder requires repeated replenishing to keep it at the proper level, this is an indication of leakage in the brake system, which should be corrected immediately. If the brake system shows an indication of leakage, check all brake lines and connections, along with the calipers and master cylinder (see Section 16 for more information).

21   If, upon checking the brake master cylinder fluid level, you discover the reservoir empty or nearly empty, the brake and clutch systems should be thoroughly inspected (see Chapters 8 and 9).

WINDSHIELD WASHER FLUID

▶ **Refer to illustration 4.22**

22 Fluid for the windshield washer system is stored in a plastic reservoir located at the right rear of the engine compartment (see illustration).

23 In milder climates, plain water can be used in the reservoir, but it should be kept no more than 2/3 full to allow for expansion if the water freezes. In colder climates, use windshield washer system antifreeze, available at any auto parts store, to lower the freezing point of the fluid. Mix the antifreeze with water in accordance with the manufacturer's directions on the container.

> **✻✻ CAUTION:**
> Do not use cooling system antifreeze - it will damage the vehicle's paint.

5   Tire and tire pressure checks (every 250 miles [400 km] or weekly)

▶ **Refer to illustrations 5.2, 5.3, 5.4a, 5.4b and 5.8**

1 Periodic inspection of the tires may spare you the inconvenience of being stranded with a flat tire. It can also provide you with vital information regarding possible problems in the steering and suspension systems before major damage occurs.

2 The original tires on this vehicle are equipped with 1/2-inch wide bands that will appear when tread depth reaches 1/16-inch, at which point they can be considered worn out. Tread wear can be monitored with a simple, inexpensive device known as a tread depth indicator (see illustration).

3 Note any abnormal tread wear (see illustration). Tread pattern irregularities such as cupping, flat spots and more wear on one side than the other are indications of front end alignment and/or balance problems. If any of these conditions are noted, take the vehicle to a tire shop or service station to correct the problem.

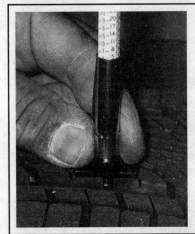

5.2 A tire tread depth indicator should be used to monitor tire wear - they are available at auto parts stores and service stations and cost very little

UNDERINFLATION

CUPPING

Cupping may be caused by:
- Underinflation and/or mechanical irregularities such as out-of-balance condition of wheel and/or tire, and bent or damaged wheel.
- Loose or worn steering tie-rod or steering idler arm.
- Loose, damaged or worn front suspension parts.

OVERINFLATION

INCORRECT TOE-IN OR EXTREME CAMBER

FEATHERING DUE TO MISALIGNMENT

5.3 This chart will help you determine the condition of your tires, the probable cause(s) of abnormal wear and the corrective action necessary

4   Look closely for cuts, punctures and embedded nails or tacks. Sometimes a tire will hold air pressure for a short time or leak down very slowly after a nail has embedded itself in the tread. If a slow leak persists, check the valve stem core to make sure it is tight (see illustration). Examine the tread for an object that may have embedded itself in the tire or for a plug that may have begun to leak (radial tire punctures are repaired with a plug that is installed in a puncture). If a puncture is suspected, it can be easily verified by spraying a solution of soapy water onto the puncture area (see illustration). The soapy solution will bubble if there is a leak. Unless the puncture is unusually large, a tire shop or service station can usually repair the tire.

5   Carefully inspect the inner sidewall of each tire for evidence of brake fluid leakage. If you see any, inspect the brakes immediately.

6   Correct air pressure adds miles to the life span of the tires, improves mileage and enhances overall ride quality. Tire pressure cannot be accurately estimated by looking at a tire, especially if it's a radial. A tire pressure gauge is essential. Keep an accurate gauge in the glove compartment. The pressure gauges attached to the nozzles of air hoses at gas stations are often inaccurate.

7   Always check tire pressure when the tires are cold. Cold, in this case, means the vehicle has not been driven over a mile in the three hours preceding a tire pressure check. A pressure rise of four to eight pounds is not uncommon once the tires are warm.

8   Unscrew the valve cap protruding from the wheel or hubcap and push the gauge firmly onto the valve stem (see illustration). Note the reading on the gauge and compare the figure to the recommended tire

5.4a If a tire loses air on a steady basis, check the valve core first to make sure it's snug (special inexpensive wrenches are commonly available at auto parts stores)

pressure shown on the tire placard on the driver's side door. Be sure to reinstall the valve cap to keep dirt and moisture out of the valve stem mechanism. Check all four tires and, if necessary, add enough air to bring them up to the recommended pressure.

9   Don't forget to keep the spare tire inflated to the specified pressure (refer to the pressure molded into the tire sidewall).

5.4b If the valve core is tight, raise the corner of the vehicle with the low tire and spray a soapy water solution onto the tread as the tire is turned slowly - slow leaks will cause small bubbles to appear

5.8 To extend the life of your tires, check the air pressure at least once a week with an accurate gauge (don't forget the spare!)

6 Engine oil and filter change (every 3000 miles [5000 km] or 3 months)

▶ **Refer to illustrations 6.2, 6.7, 6.8, 6.14, 6.15, 6.16, 6.17 and 6.18**

1 Frequent oil changes are the best preventive maintenance the home mechanic can give the engine, because aging oil becomes diluted and contaminated, which leads to premature engine wear.

2 Make sure you have all the necessary tools before you begin this procedure (see illustration).

3 You should also have plenty of rags or newspapers handy for mopping up any spills.

4 The engine and exhaust components will be warm during the actual work, so try to anticipate any potential problems before the engine and accessories are hot.

5 Park the vehicle on a level spot. Start the engine and allow it to reach its normal operating temperature. Warm oil and sludge will flow out more easily. Turn off the engine when it's warmed up. Remove the filler cap from the valve cover.

➡ **Note: Place rags around the filter housing to catch any oil that might spill out.**

6 Raise the vehicle and support it securely on jackstands.

✳ WARNING:

Never get beneath the vehicle when it is supported only by a jack. The jack provided with your vehicle is designed solely for raising the vehicle to remove and replace the wheels. Always use jackstands to support the vehicle when it becomes necessary to place your body underneath the vehicle.

7 Remove the under-vehicle splash shield (see illustration).

8 Being careful not to touch the hot exhaust components, place the drain pan under the drain plug in the bottom of the pan and remove the plug (see illustration). You may want to wear gloves while unscrewing the plug the final few turns if the engine is hot.

➡ **Note: The manufacturer states the drain plug must be replaced after it has been removed.**

9 Allow the old oil to drain into the pan. It may be necessary to move the pan farther under the engine as the oil flow slows to a trickle.

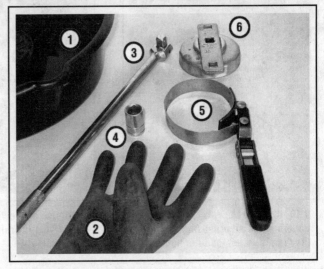

6.2 These tools are required when changing the engine oil and filter

1 *Drain pan* - It should be fairly shallow in depth, but wide in order to prevent spills
2 *Rubber gloves* - When removing the drain plug and filter, it is inevitable that you will get oil on your hands (the gloves will prevent burns)
3 *Breaker bar* - Sometimes the oil drain plug is pretty tight and a long breaker bar is needed to loosen it
4 *Socket* - To be used with the breaker bar or a ratchet (must be the correct size to fit the drain plug)
5 *Filter wrench* - This is a metal band-type wrench, which requires clearance around the filter to be effective
6 *Filter wrench* - This type fits on the bottom of the filter and can be turned with a ratchet or beaker bar (different size wrenches are available for different types of filters)

10 Inspect the old oil for the presence of metal shavings and chips.

11 After all the oil has drained, wipe off the drain plug with a clean rag. Even minute metal particles clinging to the plug would immediately

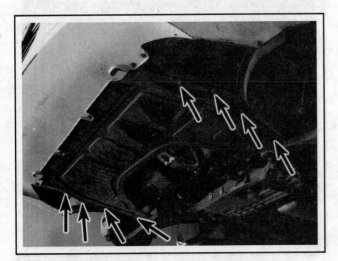

6.7 Splash shield fasteners

6.8 Use a proper size box-end wrench or socket to remove the oil drain plug and avoid rounding it off

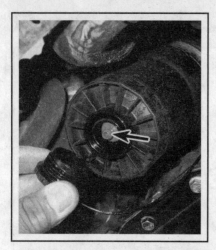

6.14 Unscrew the valve cap from the bottom of the filter housing and locate the drain valve in the filter housing

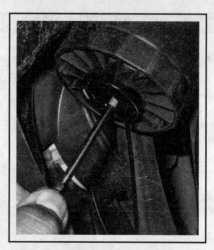

6.15 Use a screwdriver to depress the valve and drain the oil from the housing

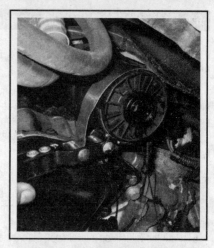

6.16 Use an oil filter wrench to remove the filter housing

contaminate the new oil.

12 Clean the area around the drain plug opening, install a new drain plug and tighten it to the torque listed in this Chapter's Specifications.

13 Locate the oil filter/housing and clean the area where the housing meets the engine.

14 Remove the valve dust cap from the bottom of the filter housing (see illustration).

15 Use a screwdriver to depress the valve at the bottom of the housing, allowing the oil in the filter housing to drain (see illustration).

16 Unscrew the oil filter housing (see illustration). The element is withdrawn with the oil filter housing, and can then be separated and discarded.

17 Wipe out the oil filter housing and cap using a clean rag, then install a new O-ring on the housing (see illustration).

18 Lubricate the O-ring(s) with clean engine oil, then install the filter element into the housing (see illustration).

19 Clean the surface where the filter housing meets the engine, then screw the filter housing onto the engine and tighten the housing securely.

20 Screw the valve dust cap into the bottom of the housing and tighten the cap securely.

21 Lower the vehicle and add new oil to the engine through the oil

filler cap in the valve cover. Use a funnel, if necessary, to prevent oil from spilling onto the top of the engine. Pour the specified type and amount of oil into the engine (refer to *Recommended lubricants and fluids* and *Capacities* in this Chapter's Specifications). Wait a few minutes to allow the oil to drain into the pan, then check the level (see Section 4). If the oil level is correct, install the filler cap hand tight, start the engine and allow the new oil to circulate.

✳✳ CAUTION:

Do not rev the engine.

22 Allow the engine to run for about a minute.

23 Wait a few minutes to allow the oil to flow back into the pan, then recheck the level on the dipstick and, if necessary, add enough oil to bring it to the correct level.

24 During the first few trips after an oil change, make it a point to check frequently for leaks and proper oil level.

25 The old oil drained from the engine cannot be reused in its present state and should be disposed of. Check with your local auto parts store, disposal facility or environmental agency to see if they will accept the oil

6.17 Pull the used element off of the filter housing stem and install a new O-ring in the housing

6.18 Install the new filter element

for recycling. After the oil has cooled, it can be drained into a container (capped plastic jugs, topped bottles, milk cartons, etc.) for transport to one of these disposal sites. Don't dispose of the oil by pouring it on the ground or down a drain!

SERVICE INDICATOR RESETTING

▶ Refer to illustration 6.26

➡ Note: After changing the engine oil, it's important to reset the service indicator so it can keep an accurate record of engine operating time/vehicle mileage.

26 Two buttons on the instrument cluster are used to reset the service indicator (see illustration).

➡ Note: On 09/2010 and later models, the windshield wiper lever switch or (if equipped) the steering wheel multi-function switch can also be used to reset the service indicator.

27 Turn the ignition key to the OFF position.

28 Press and hold the trip-odometer reset button (A), then turn the ignition key to the ON position, but do not start the engine. Release the button.

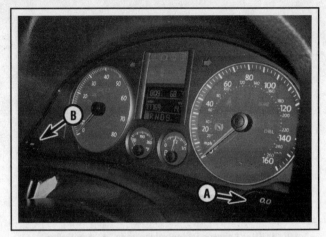

6.26 Buttons used for resetting the service indicator

A   *Trip-odometer reset button*   B   *Clock minute set button*

29 Press and release the clock minute set button (B) then turn the ignition key to the OFF position.

7   Air filter replacement (every 3000 miles [5000 km] or 3 months)

➡ Note: On four-cylinder BPY and five-cylinder engines, the air filter is incorporated in the engine cover.

FOUR-CYLINDER TIMING BELT ENGINE (BPY)

▶ Refer to illustration 7.1

1 Release the intake hose clamps at the rear of the engine cover and disconnect the intake hose from the Mass Air Flow (MAF) sensor (see illustration).

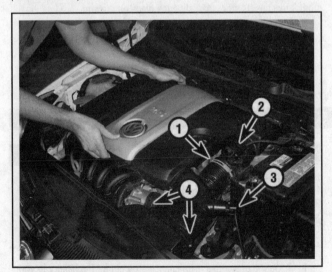

7.1 Engine cover details - five-cylinder engine shown, four-cylinder BPY models similar

1 Intake hose clamp	3 Smaller hose
2 Mass Air Flow (MAF) sensor electrical connector	4 Intake air duct screws

2 Disconnect the Mass Air Flow (MAF) sensor electrical connector.

3 Remove the fresh air intake air duct mounting screws at the front of the engine cover.

4 Lift the engine cover up from the right side of the ballstuds, then the left side, and remove the cover.

5 Place the cover upside down on a bench and remove the filter housing mounting screws (see illustration 7.19).

6 Rotate the housing up and unhook it from the engine cover, then remove the filter from the housing.

7 Clean the inside of the air filter housing with a damp cloth.

8 Installation is the reverse of removal.

FOUR-CYLINDER TIMING CHAIN ENGINES (CBFA AND CCTA)

➡ Note: To remove the engine cover, lift the cover up and off of the ballstuds.

9 Release the air guide top cover clips and remove the top cover.

10 Release the air guide lower clips and remove the guide.

11 Remove the fasteners that secure the cover of the filter housing. On models so equipped, also detach the smaller hose from the front of the filter housing.

12 Lift the cover up and remove the air filter element.

13 Clean the inside of the air filter housing with a damp cloth.

14 Installation is the reverse of removal.

FIVE-CYLINDER ENGINES

▶ Refer to illustrations 7.19 and 7.20

15 Release the intake hose clamp from the engine cover and disconnect the intake hose (see illustration 7.1).

7.19 Air filter housing fastener locations - five-cylinder engine shown, four-cylinder BPY models similar

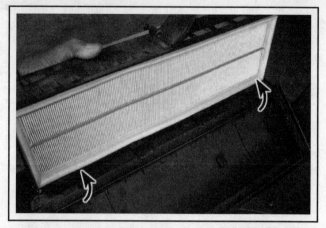

7.20 Rotate the housing up, then remove the filter element

16 Disconnect the Mass Air Flow (MAF) sensor electrical connector. On models so equipped, also detach the smaller hose from the front of the filter housing.

17 Remove the fresh air intake air duct mounting screws at the front of the engine cover.

18 Lift the cover up from the right side off of the ballstuds, then the left side, and remove the cover.

19 Place the cover upside down on a bench and remove the filter housing mounting fasteners (see illustration).

20 Rotate the housing up and unhook it from the engine cover, then remove the filter from the housing (see illustration).

21 Clean the inside of the air filter housing with a damp cloth.

22 Installation is the reverse of removal.

8 Windshield wiper blade inspection and replacement (every 6000 miles [9600 km] or 6 months)

1 The windshield wiper and blade assembly should be inspected periodically for damage, loose components and cracked or worn blade elements.

2 Road film can build up on the wiper blades and affect their efficiency, so they should be washed regularly with a mild detergent solution.

3 The action of the wiping mechanism can loosen bolts, nuts and fasteners, so they should be checked and tightened, as necessary, at the same time the wiper blades are checked.

4 If the wiper blade elements are cracked, worn or warped, or no longer clean adequately, they should be replaced with new ones.

5 Lift the arm assembly away from the glass, pivot the wiper blade until it reaches its stop, then slide the blade off the arm.

6 Installation is the reverse of removal.

9 Battery check, maintenance and charging (every 6000 miles [9600 km] or 6 months)

▶ Refer to illustrations 9.1, 9.6a, 9.6b, 9.7a, 9.7b and 9.8

※※ WARNING:

Certain precautions must be followed when checking and servicing the battery. Hydrogen gas, which is highly flammable, is always present in the battery cells, so keep lighted tobacco and all other open flames and sparks away from the battery. The electrolyte inside the battery is actually diluted sulfuric acid, which will cause injury if splashed on your skin or in your eyes. It will also ruin clothes and painted surfaces. When removing the battery cables, always detach the negative cable first and hook it up last!

※※ CAUTION:

If the battery is disconnected, several systems must be relearned before they will work properly (see Chapter 5, Section 3). Also, if the audio system is equipped with an anti-theft system, make sure you have the correct activation code before disconnecting the battery.

1 A routine preventive maintenance program for the battery in your vehicle is the only way to ensure quick and reliable starts. But before performing any battery maintenance, make sure that you have the proper equipment necessary to work safely around the battery (see illustration).

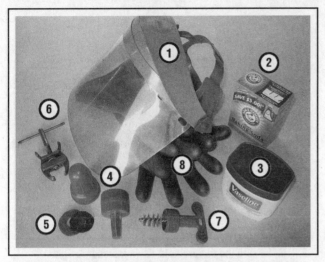

9.1 Tools and materials required for battery maintenance

1 *Face shield/safety goggles* - When removing corrosion with a brush, the acidic particles can easily fly up into your eyes

2 *Baking soda* - A solution of baking soda and water can be used to neutralize corrosion

3 *Petroleum jelly* - A layer of this on the battery posts will help prevent corrosion

4 *Battery post/cable cleaner* - This wire brush cleaning tool will remove all traces of corrosion from the battery posts and cable clamps

5 *Treated felt washers* - Placing one of these on each post, directly under the cable clamps, will help prevent corrosion

6 *Puller* - Sometimes the cable clamps are very difficult to pull off the posts, even after the nut/bolt has been completely loosened. This tool pulls the clamp straight up and off the post without damage

7 *Battery post/cable cleaner* - Here is another cleaning tool which is a slightly different version of number 4 above, but it does the same thing

8 *Rubber gloves* - Another safety item to consider when servicing the battery; remember that's acid inside the battery!

2   There are also several precautions that should be taken whenever battery maintenance is performed. Before servicing the battery, always turn the engine and all accessories off and disconnect the cable from the negative terminal of the battery (see Chapter 5).

3   The battery produces hydrogen gas, which is both flammable and explosive. Never create a spark, smoke or light a match around the battery. Always charge the battery in a ventilated area.

4   Electrolyte contains poisonous and corrosive sulfuric acid. Do not allow it to get in your eyes, on your skin or on your clothes. Never ingest it. Wear protective safety glasses when working near the battery. Keep children away from the battery.

5   Note the external condition of the battery. If the positive terminal and cable clamp on your vehicle's battery is equipped with a rubber protector, make sure that it's not torn or damaged. It should completely cover the terminal. Look for any corroded or loose connections, cracks in the case or cover or loose hold-down clamps. Also check the entire length of each cable for cracks and frayed conductors.

6   If corrosion, which looks like white, fluffy deposits (see illustration) is evident, particularly around the terminals, the battery should be removed for cleaning. Loosen the cable clamp bolts with a wrench, being careful to remove the ground cable first, and slide them off the terminals (see illustration). Then disconnect the hold-down clamp bolt and nut, remove the clamp and lift the battery from the engine compartment.

9.6a Battery terminal corrosion usually appears as light, fluffy powder

9.6b Removing a cable from the battery post with a wrench - sometimes a pair of special battery pliers are required for this procedure if corrosion has caused deterioration of the nut hex (always remove the negative cable first and hook it up last!)

7   Clean the cable clamps thoroughly with a battery brush or a terminal cleaner and a solution of warm water and baking soda (see illustration). Wash the terminals and the top of the battery case with the

9.7a When cleaning the cable clamps, all corrosion must be removed

9.7b Regardless of the type of tool used to clean the battery posts, a clean, shiny surface should be the result

9.8 Make sure the battery hold-down fastener is tight

same solution but make sure that the solution doesn't get into the battery. When cleaning the cables, terminals and battery top, wear safety goggles and rubber gloves to prevent any solution from coming in contact with your eyes or hands. Wear old clothes too - even diluted, sulfuric acid splashed onto clothes will burn holes in them. If the terminals have been extensively corroded, clean them up with a terminal cleaner (see illustration). Thoroughly wash all cleaned areas with plain water.

8   Make sure that the battery tray is in good condition and the hold-down clamp fasteners are tight (see illustration). If the battery is removed from the tray, make sure no parts remain in the bottom of the tray when the battery is reinstalled. When reinstalling the hold-down clamp bolts, do not overtighten them.

9   Information on removing and installing the battery can be found in Chapter 5. If you disconnected the cable(s) from the negative and/or positive battery terminals, see Chapter 5. Information on jump starting can be found at the front of this manual.

CLEANING

10 Corrosion on the hold-down components, battery case and surrounding areas can be removed with a solution of water and baking soda. Thoroughly rinse all cleaned areas with plain water.

11 Any metal parts of the vehicle damaged by corrosion should be covered with a zinc-based primer, then painted.

CHARGING

✳✳ WARNING:

When batteries are being charged, hydrogen gas, which is very explosive and flammable, is produced. Do not smoke or allow open flames near a charging or a recently charged battery. Wear eye protection when near the battery during charging. Also, make sure the charger is unplugged before connecting or disconnecting the battery from the charger.

12 Slow-rate charging is the best way to restore a battery that's discharged to the point where it will not start the engine. It's also a good way to maintain the battery charge in a vehicle that's only driven a few miles between starts. Maintaining the battery charge is particularly important in the winter when the battery must work harder to start the engine and electrical accessories that drain the battery are in greater use.

13 It's best to use a one or two-amp battery charger (sometimes called a "trickle" charger). They are the safest and put the least strain on the battery. They are also the least expensive. For a faster charge, you can use a higher amperage charger, but don't use one rated more than 1/10th the amp/hour rating of the battery. Rapid boost charges that claim to restore the power of the battery in one to two hours are hardest on the battery and can damage batteries not in good condition. This type of charging should only be used in emergency situations.

14 The average time necessary to charge a battery should be listed in the instructions that come with the charger. As a general rule, a trickle charger will charge a battery in 12 to 16 hours.

10 Tire rotation (every 6000 miles [9600 km] or 6 months)

▶ **Refer to illustration 10.2**

1 The tires should be rotated at the specified intervals and whenever uneven wear is noticed.

2 Refer to the accompanying illustration for the preferred tire rotation pattern.

3 Loosen the wheel bolts. Refer to the information in *Jacking and towing* at the front of this manual for the proper procedures to follow when raising the vehicle and changing a tire. If the brakes are to be checked, don't apply the parking brake as stated. Make sure the tires are blocked to prevent the vehicle from rolling as it's raised.

4 Preferably, the entire vehicle should be raised at the same time. This can be done on a hoist or by jacking up each corner, then lowering the vehicle onto jackstands placed under the frame rails. Always use four jackstands and make sure the vehicle is safely supported.

5 After rotation, check and adjust the tire pressures as necessary. Tighten the wheel bolts to the torque listed in this Chapter's Specifications.

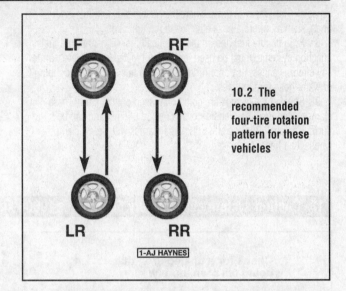

10.2 The recommended four-tire rotation pattern for these vehicles

11 Seat belt check (every 6000 miles [9600 km] or 6 months)

1 Check seat belts, buckles, latch plates and guide loops for obvious damage and signs of wear.

2 Where the seat belt receptacle bolts to the floor of the vehicle, check that the bolts are secure.

3 See if the seat belt reminder light comes on when the key is turned to the Run or Start position.

12 Underhood hose check and replacement (every 6000 miles [9600 km] or 6 months)

GENERAL

✳ CAUTION:

Replacement of air conditioning hoses must be left to a dealer service department or air conditioning shop that has the equipment to depressurize the system safely and recover the refrigerant. Never remove air conditioning components or hoses until the system has been depressurized.

1 High temperatures in the engine compartment can cause the deterioration of the rubber and plastic hoses used for engine, accessory and emission systems operation. Periodic inspection should be made for cracks, loose clamps, material hardening and leaks. Information specific to the cooling system hoses can be found in Section 13.

2 Some, but not all, hoses are secured to their fittings with clamps. Where clamps are used, check to be sure they haven't lost their tension, allowing the hose to leak. If clamps aren't used, make sure the hose has not expanded and/or hardened where it slips over the fitting, allowing it to leak.

VACUUM HOSES

3 It's quite common for vacuum hoses, especially those in the emissions system, to be color-coded or identified by colored stripes molded into them. Various systems require hoses with different wall thickness, collapse resistance and temperature resistance. When replacing hoses, be sure the new ones are made of the same material.

4 Often the only effective way to check a hose is to remove it completely from the vehicle. If more than one hose is removed, be sure to label the hoses and fittings to ensure correct installation.

5 When checking vacuum hoses, be sure to include any plastic T-fittings in the check. Inspect the fittings for cracks and the hose where it fits over the fitting for distortion, which could cause leakage.

6 A small piece of vacuum hose (1/4-inch inside diameter) can be used as a stethoscope to detect vacuum leaks. Hold one end of the hose to your ear and probe around vacuum hoses and fittings, listening for the hissing sound characteristic of a vacuum leak.

✳ WARNING:

When probing with the vacuum hose stethoscope, be very careful not to come into contact with moving engine components such as the drivebelt, cooling fan, etc.

FUEL HOSE

✳ WARNING:

There are certain precautions that must be taken when inspecting or servicing fuel system components. Work in a well-ventilated area and do not allow open flames (cigarettes, appliances, etc.) or bare light bulbs near the work area. Mop up any spills immediately and do not store fuel soaked rags where they could ignite. The fuel system is under high pressure, so if any fuel lines are to be disconnected, the pressure in the system must be relieved first (see Chapter 4 for more information).

7   Check all rubber fuel lines for deterioration and chafing. Check especially for cracks in areas where the hose bends and just before fittings, such as where a hose attaches to the fuel filter.

8   High quality fuel line, made specifically for high-pressure fuel injection systems, must be used for fuel line replacement. Never, under any circumstances, use unreinforced vacuum line, clear plastic tubing or water hose for fuel lines.

9   Spring-type clamps are commonly used on fuel lines. These clamps often lose their tension over a period of time, and can be sprung during removal. Replace all spring-type clamps with screw clamps whenever a hose is replaced.

METAL LINES

10 Sections of metal line are routed along the frame, between the fuel tank and the engine. Check carefully to be sure the line has not been bent or crimped and that cracks have not started in the line.

11 If a section of metal fuel line must be replaced, only seamless steel tubing should be used, since copper and aluminum tubing don't have the strength necessary to withstand normal engine vibration.

12 Check the metal brake lines where they enter the master cylinder and brake proportioning unit for cracks in the lines or loose fittings. Any sign of brake fluid leakage calls for an immediate and thorough inspection of the brake system.

13   Cooling system check (every 6000 miles [9600 km] or 6 months)

Check for a chafed area that could fail prematurely.

Check for a soft area indicating the hose has deteriorated inside.

Overtightening the clamp on a hardened hose will damage the hose and cause a leak.

Check each hose for swelling and oil-soaked ends. Cracks and breaks can be located by squeezing the hose.

13.4 Hoses, like drivebelts, have a habit of failing at the worst possible time - to prevent the inconvenience of a blown radiator or heater hose, inspect them carefully as shown here

▶ **Refer to illustration 13.4**

❊❊ WARNING:

Wait until the engine is completely cool before performing this procedure.

1   Many major engine failures can be attributed to a faulty cooling system. If the vehicle is equipped with an automatic transaxle, the cooling system also cools the transaxle fluid and thus plays an important role in prolonging transaxle life.

2   The cooling system should be checked with the engine cold. Do this before the vehicle is driven for the day or after it has been shut off for at least three hours.

3   Remove the cooling system pressure cap and thoroughly clean the cap, inside and out, with clean water. Also clean the opening in the expansion tank. All traces of corrosion should be removed. The coolant inside the expansion tank should be relatively transparent. If it is rust-colored, the system should be drained, flushed and refilled (see Section 26). If the coolant level is not up to the MIN mark, add additional anti-freeze/coolant mixture (see Section 4).

4   Carefully check the large upper and lower radiator hoses along with the smaller diameter heater hoses that run from the engine to the firewall. Inspect each hose along its entire length, replacing any hose that is cracked, swollen or shows signs of deterioration. Cracks may become more apparent if the hose is squeezed (see illustration).

5   Make sure all hose connections are tight. A leak in the cooling system will usually show up as white or rust-colored deposits on the areas adjoining the leak. If spring-type clamps are used at the ends of the hoses, it may be a good idea to replace them with more secure screw-type clamps.

6   Use compressed air or a soft brush to remove bugs, leaves, etc. from the front of the radiator or air conditioning condenser. Be careful not to damage the delicate cooling fins or cut yourself on them.

7   Every other inspection, or at the first indication of cooling system problems, have the cap and system pressure tested. If you don't have a pressure tester, most repair shops will do this for a minimal charge.

14 Exhaust system check (every 6000 miles [9600 km] or 6 months)

▶ **Refer to illustration 14.2**

1   With the engine cold (at least three hours after the vehicle has been driven), check the complete exhaust system from the manifold to the end of the tailpipe. Be careful around the catalytic converter, which may be hot even after three hours. The inspection should be done with the vehicle on a hoist to permit unrestricted access. If a hoist isn't available, raise the vehicle and support it securely on jackstands.

2   Check the exhaust pipes and connections for signs of leakage and/or corrosion indicating a potential failure. Make sure that all brackets and hangers are in good condition and tight (see illustration).

3   Inspect the underside of the body for holes, corrosion, open seams, etc. which may allow exhaust gasses to enter the passenger compartment. Seal all body openings with silicone sealant or body putty.

4   Rattles and other noises can often be traced to the exhaust system, especially the hangers, mounts and heat shields. Try to move the pipes, mufflers and catalytic converter. If the components can come in contact with the body or suspension parts, secure the exhaust system with new brackets and hangers.

14.2 Inspect the muffler (A) and all hangers (B) for signs of deterioration

15 Interior ventilation filter replacement (every 15,000 miles [24,000 km] or 12 months)

▶ **Refer to illustrations 15.2, 15.3a and 15.3b**

1   The interior ventilation filter is located inside a housing under the right (passenger's) side of the instrument panel.

2   Remove the trim panel fasteners and trim panel from under the glove box (see illustration).

3   To remove the ventilation filter, depress the tab and slide the cover to the right to release the clips that secure the cover, then lift the cover off and remove the ventilation filter element (see illustrations).

➡ **Note: On some models the cover is also secured with screws that must be removed before the cover will slide.**

4   Install the new filter with the arrows indicating air flow pointing down.

5   Installation is the reverse of the removal procedure.

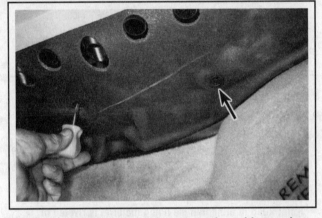

15.2 Remove the trim panel fasteners and panel from under the instrument panel

15.3a Depress the tab and slide the cover to release the clips

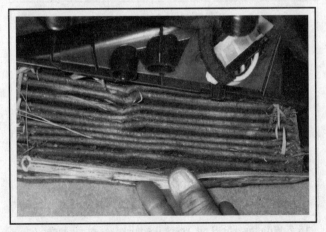

15.3b Remove the filter element

16 Brake system check (every 15,000 miles [24,000 km] or 12 months)

✳✳ WARNING:

The dust created by the brake system is harmful to your health. Never blow it out with compressed air and don't inhale any of it. An approved filtering mask should be worn when working on the brakes. Do not, under any circumstances, use petroleum-based solvents to clean brake parts. Use brake system cleaner only!

➡ **Note: For detailed photographs of the brake system, refer to Chapter 9.**

1 In addition to the specified intervals, the brakes should be inspected every time the wheels are removed or whenever a defect is suspected.

2 Any of the following symptoms could indicate a potential brake system defect: The vehicle pulls to one side when the brake pedal is depressed; the brakes make squealing or dragging noises when applied; brake pedal travel is excessive; the pedal pulsates; or brake fluid leaks, usually onto the inside of the tire or wheel. A brake pedal that sinks slowly to the floor, with no apparent external fluid leakage, indicates a faulty master cylinder.

➡ **Note: A faulty master cylinder can leak fluid into the power brake booster.**

3 Loosen the wheel bolts.
4 Raise the vehicle and place it securely on jackstands.
5 Remove the wheels.

DISC BRAKES

▶ **Refer to illustrations 16.7 and 16.9**

6 There are two pads (an outer and an inner) in each caliper. The pads are visible with the wheels removed.

7 Check the pad thickness by looking at each end of the caliper and through the inspection window in the caliper body (see illustration). If the lining material is less than the thickness listed in this Chapter's Specifications, replace the pads.

➡ **Note: Keep in mind that the lining material is riveted or bonded to a metal backing plate and the metal portion is not included in this measurement.**

16.7 With the wheel off, check the thickness of the inner brake pad through the inspection hole (front brake shown, rear brake similar)

8 If it is difficult to determine the exact thickness of the remaining pad material by the above method, or if you are at all concerned about the condition of the pads, remove the caliper(s), then remove the pads from the calipers for further inspection (see Chapter 9).

9 Once the pads are removed from the calipers, clean them with brake cleaner and re-measure them with a ruler or a vernier caliper (see illustration).

10 Measure the disc thickness with a micrometer to make sure that it still has service life remaining. If any disc is thinner than the specified minimum thickness, replace it (see Chapter 9). Even if the disc has service life remaining, check its condition. Look for scoring, gouging and burned spots. If these conditions exist, remove the disc and have it resurfaced (see Chapter 9).

11 Before installing the wheels, check all brake lines and hoses for damage, wear, deformation, cracks, corrosion, leakage, bends and twists, particularly in the vicinity of the rubber hoses at the calipers. Check the clamps for tightness and the connections for leakage. Make sure that all hoses and lines are clear of sharp edges, moving parts and the exhaust system. If any of the above conditions are noted, repair, reroute or replace the lines and/or fittings as necessary (see Chapter 9).

DRUM BRAKES

▶ **Refer to illustration 16.17**

12 Some 2011 models are equipped with rear drum brakes. Loosen the wheel bolts, raise the vehicle and support it securely on jackstands. Block the front tires to prevent the vehicle from rolling; however, don't apply the parking brake or it will lock the drums in place.

13 Remove the wheels, referring to *Jacking and towing* at the front of this manual if necessary.

14 Mark the hub so it can be reinstalled in the same position. Use a scribe, chalk, etc. on the drum, hub and backing plate.

15 Remove the brake drums. If the drum still won't come off, refer to Chapter 9

16 With the drums removed, carefully clean the brake assembly with brake system cleaner.

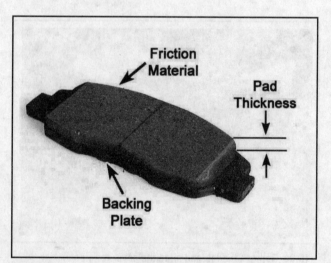

16.9 If a more precise measurement of pad thickness is necessary, remove the pads and measure the remaining friction material

✳✳ WARNING:

Don't blow the dust out with compressed air and don't inhale any of it (it is harmful to your health).

17 Note the thickness of the lining material on both front and rear brake shoes (see illustration). Compare the measurement with the limit given in this Chapter's Specifications; if any lining thickness is less than specified, then all of the brake shoes must be replaced (see Chapter 9). The shoes should also be replaced if they're cracked, glazed (shiny areas), or covered with brake fluid.

18 Make sure all the brake assembly springs are connected and in good condition.

19 Check the brake components for signs of fluid leakage. With your finger or a small screwdriver, carefully pry back the rubber cups on the wheel cylinder located at the top of the brake shoes. Any leakage here is an indication that the wheel cylinders should be replaced immediately (see Chapter 9). Also, check all hoses and connections for signs of leakage.

20 Wipe the inside of the drum with a clean rag and denatured alcohol or brake cleaner. Again, be careful not to breathe the dangerous brake dust.

21 Check the inside of the drum for cracks, score marks, deep scratches and hard spots which will appear as small discolored areas. If imperfections cannot be removed with fine emery cloth, the drum must be taken to an automotive machine shop for resurfacing.

22 Repeat the procedure for the remaining wheel. If the inspection reveals that all parts are in good condition, reinstall the brake drums, install the wheels and lower the vehicle to the ground.

BRAKE BOOSTER CHECK

23 Sit in the driver's seat and perform the following sequence of tests.

24 With the brake fully depressed, start the engine - the pedal should move down a little when the engine starts.

25 With the engine running, depress the brake pedal several times - the travel distance should not change.

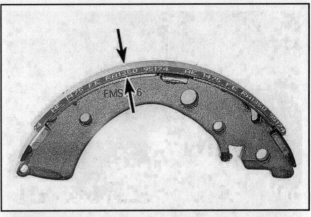

16.17 A more precise measurement of the brake shoe thickness can be made by measuring the shoes directly with the brake drum removed

26 Depress the brake, stop the engine and hold the pedal in for about 30 seconds - the pedal should neither sink nor rise.

27 Restart the engine, run it for about a minute and turn it off. Then firmly depress the brake several times - the pedal travel should decrease with each application.

28 If your brakes do not operate as described, the brake booster has failed. Refer to Chapter 9 for the replacement procedure.

PARKING BRAKE

➡ **Note: The rear brakes are self-adjusting, and do not require normal maintenance adjustments. Adjustment is only required after replacing brake discs, brake pads, brake calipers or parking brake cables.**

29 One method of checking the parking brake is to park the vehicle on a steep hill with the parking brake set and the shifter in Neutral (be sure to stay in the vehicle for this check!). If the parking brake cannot prevent the vehicle from rolling, it's in need of adjustment (see Chapter 9).

17 Suspension, steering and driveaxle boot check (every 15,000 miles [24,000 km] or 12 months)

➡ **Note: The steering linkage and suspension components should be checked periodically. Worn or damaged suspension and steering linkage components can result in excessive and abnormal tire wear, poor ride quality and vehicle handling and reduced fuel economy. For more information on the steering and suspension components, refer to Chapter 10.**

SHOCK ABSORBER CHECK

▶ **Refer to illustration 17.6**

1 Park the vehicle on level ground, turn the engine off and set the parking brake. Check the tire pressures.

2 Push down at one corner of the vehicle, then release it while noting the movement of the body. It should stop moving and come to rest in a level position within one or two bounces.

3 If the vehicle continues to move up-and-down or if it fails to return to its original position, a worn or weak shock absorber is probably the reason.

4 Repeat the above check at each of the three remaining corners of the vehicle.

5 Raise the vehicle and support it securely on jackstands.

6 Check the shock absorbers for evidence of fluid leakage (see

17.6 Check the shocks/struts for leakage at the indicated area

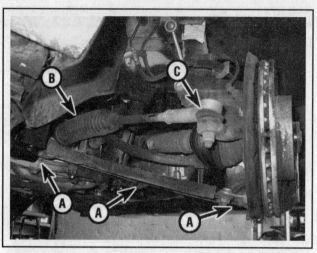

17.9 Examine the mounting points for the lower control arm (A), the steering gear boots (B), and the tie-rod ends (C)

illustration). A light film of fluid is no cause for concern. Make sure that any fluid noted is from the shocks and not from some other source. If leakage is noted, replace the shocks as a set.

7   Check the shocks to be sure that they are securely mounted and undamaged. Check the upper mounts for damage and wear. If damage or wear is noted, replace the shocks as a set (front or rear).

8   If the shocks must be replaced, refer to Chapter 10 for the procedure.

STEERING AND SUSPENSION CHECK

▶ **Refer to illustrations 17.9 and 17.11**

9   Visually inspect the steering and suspension components (front and rear) for damage and distortion. Look for damaged seals, boots and bushings and leaks of any kind. Examine the bushings where the control arms meet the chassis (see illustration).

10   Clean the lower end of the steering knuckle. Have an assistant grasp the lower edge of the tire and move the wheel in-and-out while

you look for movement at the steering knuckle-to-control arm balljoint. If there is any movement the suspension balljoint(s) must be replaced.

11   Grasp each front tire at the front and rear edges, push in at the front, pull out at the rear and feel for play in the steering system components (see illustration). If any freeplay is noted, check the steering gear mounts and the tie-rod ends for looseness.

12   Additional steering and suspension system information and illustrations can be found in Chapter 10.

DRIVEAXLE BOOT CHECK

▶ **Refer to illustration 17.14**

13   The driveaxle boots are very important because they prevent dirt, water and foreign material from entering and damaging the Constant Velocity (CV) joints. Because it constantly pivots back and forth following the steering action of the front hub, the outer CV boot wears out sooner and should be inspected regularly.

14   Inspect the boots for tears and cracks as well as loose clamps (see illustration). If there is any evidence of cracks or leaking lubricant, they must be replaced as described in Chapter 8.

17.11 With the steering wheel in the locked position and the vehicle raised, grasp the front tire as shown and try to move it back-and-forth - if any play is noted, check the steering gear mounts and tie-rod ends for looseness

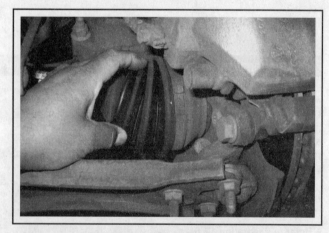

17.14 Inspect the inner and outer driveaxle boots for loose clamps, cracks or signs of leaking lubricant

18 Fuel system check (every 15,000 miles [24,000 km] or 12 months)

✳ WARNING:

Gasoline is flammable, so take extra precautions when you work on any part of the fuel system. Don't smoke or allow open flames or bare light bulbs near the work area, and don't work in a garage where a gas-type appliance (such as a water heater or clothes dryer) is present. Since fuel is carcinogenic, wear fuel-resistant gloves when there's a possibility of being exposed to fuel, and, if you spill any fuel on your skin, rinse it off immediately with soap and water. Mop up any spills immediately and do not store fuel-soaked rags where they could ignite. When you perform any kind of work on the fuel system, wear safety glasses and have a Class B type fire extinguisher on hand. The fuel system is under constant pressure, so, before any lines are disconnected, the fuel system pressure must be relieved (see Chapter 4).

1   If you smell fuel while driving or after the vehicle has been sitting in the sun, inspect the fuel system immediately.

2   Remove the fuel filler cap and inspect it for damage and corrosion. The gasket should have an unbroken sealing imprint. If the gasket is damaged, install a new cap.

3   Inspect the fuel feed line for cracks. Make sure that the connections in the fuel line are free of leaks.

✳ WARNING:

Your vehicle is fuel injected, so you must relieve the fuel system pressure before servicing fuel system components. The fuel system pressure relief procedure is outlined in Chapter 4.

4   Since some components of the fuel system - the fuel tank and feed lines, for example - are underneath the vehicle, they can be inspected more easily with the vehicle raised on a hoist. If that's not possible, raise the vehicle and support it on jackstands.

5   With the vehicle raised and safely supported, inspect the fuel tank and filler neck for punctures, cracks and other damage. The connection between the filler neck and the tank is particularly critical. Sometimes a rubber filler neck will leak because of loose clamps or deteriorated rubber. Inspect all fuel tank mounting brackets and straps to be sure that the tank is securely attached to the vehicle.

6   Carefully check all rubber hoses and metal lines leading away from the fuel tank. Check for loose connections, deteriorated hoses, crimped lines and other damage. Replace damaged sections as necessary (see Chapter 4).

19 Drivebelt check and replacement (every 15,000 miles [24,000 km] or 12 months)

1   The drivebelt(s) is/are located at the front of the engine and play(s) an important role in the overall operation of the vehicle and its components. Due to their function and material make-up, drivebelts are prone to failure after a period of time and should be inspected and adjusted periodically to prevent major engine damage.

2   Four-cylinder engines are equipped with a single self-adjusting serpentine drivebelt, which is used to drive all of the accessory components such as the alternator, power steering pump, water pump and air conditioning compressor. Five-cylinder engines use two serpentine drivebelts; the outer belt is used to drive the air conditioning compressor, and the inner belt (driven by the air conditioning compressor) is used to drive the alternator and water pump.

INSPECTION

▸ **Refer to illustration 19.4**

3   With the engine off, open the hood and locate the drivebelt at the front of the engine. Using your fingers (and a flashlight, if necessary), move along the belt checking for cracks and separation of the belt plies. Also check for fraying and glazing, which gives the belt a shiny appearance. Both sides of the belt should be inspected, which means you will have to twist the belt to check the underside.

4   Check the ribs on the underside of the belt. They should all be the same depth, with none of the surface uneven (see illustration).

5   The tension of the belt is automatically adjusted by the belt tensioner and does not require any adjustments.

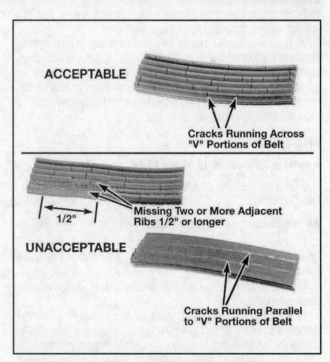

19.4 Here are some of the more common problems associated with drivebelts (check the belts very carefully to prevent an untimely breakdown)

19.6 Rotate the tensioner arm to relieve belt tension

19.10 Rotate the tensioner clockwise and lock the tensioner into place

REPLACEMENT

Four-cylinder engines

▶ **Refer to illustration 19.6**

6   On timing belt-equipped engines, rotate the tensioner clockwise using the cast square to relieve the tension on the belt (see illustration). On timing chain-equipped engines, use a box-end wrench to rotate the tensioner clockwise, and insert a drill bit into the cast hole to hold the tensioner in place.

7   Remove the belt from the auxiliary components and, on 2.0L timing belt engines, carefully release the tensioner.

8   Route the new belt over the various pulleys - again rotating the tensioner to allow the belt to be installed on timing belt engines - then release the belt tensioner. On timing chain models, rotate the tensioner enough to allow the drill bit to be removed, then slowly release the belt tensioner. Make sure the belt fits properly into the pulley grooves; it must be completely engaged.

Five-cylinder engines

▶ **Refer to illustrations 19.10 and 19.14**

9   Remove the front, driver's side section of the inner fender liner (see Chapter 11).

Air conditioning compressor (outer) belt

10   Use a box-end wrench and rotate the tensioner clockwise, then insert a drill bit or screwdriver into the cast hole to hold the tensioner in place (see illustration).

11   If the belt is to be re-used, mark the direction of rotation and remove the belt.

12   Route the new belt over the various pulleys, rotate the tensioner enough to allow the drill bit or screwdriver to be removed, then slowly release the belt tensioner. Make sure the belt fits properly into the pulley grooves - it must be completely engaged.

19.14 Rotate the tensioner clockwise, then insert a drill bit to lock the tensioner body

Alternator and water pump (inner) belt

13   Remove the air conditioning compressor outer belt (see Steps 10 and 11). Rotate the tensioner clockwise enough to remove the drill bit or screwdriver and slowly release the tensioner.

14   Using a box-end wrench or swivel wrench (see illustration), rotate the tensioner clockwise and insert a drill bit or screwdriver into the cast hole to hold the tensioner in place.

15   If the belt is to be re-used, mark the direction of rotation and remove the belt.

16   Route the new belt over the various pulleys, rotate the tensioner enough to allow the drill bit or screwdriver to be removed, then slowly release the belt tensioner. Make sure the belt fits properly into the pulley grooves - it must be completely engaged.

17   The remainder of installation is the reverse of removal.

TENSIONER REPLACEMENT

18 Remove the drivebelt (four-cylinder engines, see Steps 6 and 7; five cylinder engines, see Steps 9 through 15).

Four-cylinder timing belt engines

19 Remove the fasteners that secure the tensioner to the engine, then remove the tensioner.

20 Installation is the reverse of removal. Tighten the mounting bolt(s) to the torque listed in this Chapter's Specifications.

Four-cylinder timing chain engines

21 Apply the parking brake and block the rear wheels. Loosen the right front wheel lug bolts, then raise and support the vehicle on jackstands. Remove the under-vehicle splash shield (see illustration 6.7).

22 Remove the air guide top cover, the air guide and engine cover/air filter assembly (see Section 7).

23 Remove the right front wheel and front half of the inner fender liner (see Chapter 11).

24 On models with an auxiliary heater, remove the heater bracket mounting fasteners, then remove the heater muffler bracket clamp and bolt.

25 Using an engine support to support the engine as described in Chapter 2C, remove the front mount bolts (see Chapter 2A) and lower the engine a few inches.

26 Remove the tensioner mounting bolt from the back side of the tensioner and remove the tensioner from the front of the accessory bracket.

27 Installation is the reverse of removal. Tighten the mounting bolt(s) to the torque listed in this Chapter's Specifications.

Five-cylinder 2.5L engines

➡ **Note: On some models, the front engine mount may have to be removed to allow for removal of the tensioners (see Chapter 2B).**

28 Rotate the tensioner pulley mounting bolt and remove the 12-point tensioner mounting bolt and tensioner.

➡ **Note: The air conditioning belt tensioner must be removed first to gain access to the alternator and water pump tensioner.**

29 Installation is the reverse of removal. Tighten the mounting bolt(s) to the torque listed in this Chapter's Specifications.

---

20 Brake fluid change (every 30,000 miles [48,000 km] or 24 months)

❊❊ WARNING:

Brake fluid can harm your eyes and damage painted surfaces, so use extreme caution when handling or pouring it. Do not use brake fluid that has been standing open or is more than one year old. Brake fluid absorbs moisture from the air. Excess moisture can cause a dangerous loss of braking effectiveness.

➡ **Note: Used brake fluid is considered a hazardous waste and it must be disposed of in accordance with federal, state and local laws. DO NOT pour it down the sink, into septic tanks or storm drains, or on the ground.**

➡ **Note: On models equipped with a manual transaxle, the clutch master cylinder gets its fluid from the brake master cylinder reservoir. The clutch system fluid should be changed at the same time (see Chapter 8 for clutch bleeding).**

1 At the specified intervals, the brake fluid should be replaced. Since the brake fluid may drip or splash when pouring it, place plenty of rags around the master cylinder to protect any surrounding painted surfaces.

2 Before beginning work, purchase the specified brake fluid (see *Recommended lubricants and fluids* in this Chapter's Specifications).

3 Disconnect the fluid level sensor connector from the top of the master cylinder reservoir cap and unscrew the cap.

4 Using a hand-held suction pump or similar device, withdraw the fluid from the master cylinder reservoir.

5 Add new fluid to the master cylinder until the level of the fluid rises to the base of the filler neck. Install the cap.

6 Bleed the brake system as described in Chapter 9 at all four brakes until new and uncontaminated fluid is expelled from the bleeder screw. Be sure to maintain the fluid level in the master cylinder as you perform the bleeding process. If you allow the master cylinder to run dry, air will enter the system.

7 Refill the master cylinder with fluid, reconnect the fluid level sensor and check the operation of the brakes. The pedal should feel solid when depressed, with no sponginess.

❊❊ WARNING:

Do not operate the vehicle if you are in doubt about the effectiveness of the brake system.

21 Spark plug check and replacement (every 30,000 miles [48,000 km] or 24 months)

▶ **Refer to illustrations 21.2, 21.5, 21.9, 21.10, 21.11 and 21.12**

1   The spark plugs are located in the cylinder head.

2   In most cases, the tools necessary for spark plug replacement include a spark plug socket which fits onto a ratchet (this special socket is padded inside to protect the porcelain insulators on the new plugs and hold them in place), various extensions and a feeler gauge to check and adjust the spark plug gap (see illustration). Since these engines are equipped with an aluminum cylinder head, a torque wrench should be used when tightening the spark plugs.

3   The best approach when replacing the spark plugs is to purchase the new spark plugs beforehand, adjust them to the proper gap, then replace each plug one at a time. When buying the new spark plugs, be sure to obtain the correct plug for your specific engine. This information can be found in this Chapter's Specifications.

4   Allow the engine to cool completely before attempting to remove any of the plugs. During this cooling off time, each of the new spark plugs can be inspected for defects and the gaps can be checked.

5   The gap is checked by inserting the proper thickness gauge between the electrodes at the tip of the plug (see illustration). The gap between the electrodes should be as listed in this Chapter's Specifica-tions or in your owner's manual. Also check for cracks in the spark plug body (if any are found, the plug must not be used).

6   Cover the fender to prevent damage to the paint. Fender covers are available from auto parts stores but an old blanket will work just fine.

7   There is one centrally mounted spark plug per cylinder. The ignition coils are mounted directly over the plugs. Remove each ignition coil from the spark plug (see Chapter 5).

8   If compressed air is available, use it to blow any dirt or foreign material away from the spark plug area.

✷✷ WARNING:

Wear eye protection!

The idea here is to eliminate the possibility of material falling into the cylinder through the spark plug hole as the spark plug is removed.

9   Place the spark plug socket over the plug and remove it from the engine by turning it in a counterclockwise direction (see illustration).

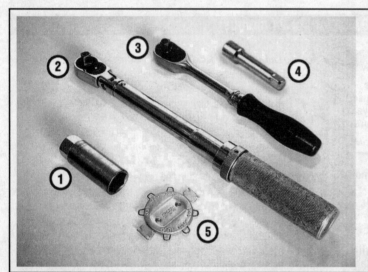

21.2 Tools required for changing spark plugs

1   *Spark plug socket* - This will have special padding inside to protect the spark plug porcelain insulator
2   *Torque wrench* - Although not mandatory, use of this tool is the best way to ensure that the plugs are tightened properly
3   *Ratchet* - Standard hand tool to fit the plug socket
4   *Extension* - Depending on model and accessories, you may need special extensions and universal joints to reach one or more of the plugs
5   *Spark plug gap gauge* - This gauge for checking the gap comes in a variety of styles. Make sure the gap for your engine is included

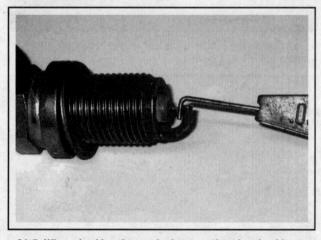

21.5 When checking the spark plug gap, the wire should slide between the electrodes with a slight drag

21.9 Use a socket and extension to unscrew the spark plugs

A normally worn spark plug should have light tan or gray deposits on the firing tip.

A carbon fouled plug, identified by soft, sooty, black deposits, may indicate an improperly tuned vehicle. Check the air cleaner, ignition components and engine control system.

An oil fouled spark plug indicates an engine with worn piston rings and/or bad valve seals allowing excessive oil to enter the chamber.

This spark plug has been left in the engine too long, as evidenced by the extreme gap- Plugs with such an extreme gap can cause misfiring and stumbling accompanied by a noticeable lack of power.

A physically damaged spark plug may be evidence of severe detonation in that cylinder. Watch that cylinder carefully between services, as a continued detonation will not only damage the plug, but could also damage the engine.

A bridged or almost bridged spark plug, identified by a build-up between the electrodes caused by excessive carbon or oil build-up on the plug.

21.10 Inspect the spark plug to determine engine running conditions

10 Compare the spark plug with the chart (see illustration) to get an indication of the overall running condition of the engine.

11 It's a good idea to lightly coat the threads of the spark plugs with an anti-seize compound (see illustration) to insure that the spark plugs do not seize in the aluminum cylinder head.

12 It's often difficult to insert spark plugs into their holes without cross-threading them. To avoid this possibility, fit a piece of rubber hose over the end of the spark plug (see illustration). The flexible hose acts as a universal joint to help align the plug with the plug hole. Should the plug begin to cross-thread, the hose will slip on the spark plug, preventing thread damage. Install the spark plug and tighten it to the torque listed in this Chapter's Specifications.

13 Repeat the procedure for the remaining spark plugs.

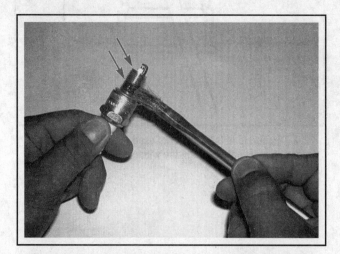

21.11 Apply a thin film of anti-seize compound to the spark plug threads to prevent damage to the cylinder head

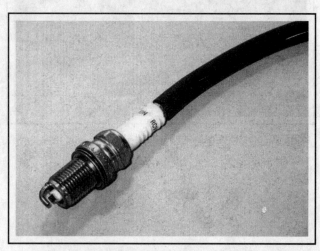

21.12 A length of snug-fitting rubber hose will save time and prevent damaged threads when installing the spark plugs

22 Automatic transaxle fluid change (every 30,000 miles [48,000 km] or 24 months)

◆ Refer to illustrations 22.5 and 22.7

❋ WARNING:

This procedure is potentially dangerous and is best left to a professional shop. The vehicle must be kept level while being safely raised high enough for access to the plugs on the transaxle.

➡ **Note: When the vehicle is serviced by a dealer or other qualified repair shop, a scan tool is used to read the transaxle fluid temperature. To perform the job at home, you will have to estimate the temperature of the fluid.**

➡ **Note: The engine must be running when checking the fluid level and when adding fluid.**

1   At the specified intervals, the transaxle fluid should be drained and replaced. Since the fluid will remain hot long after driving, perform this procedure only after everything has cooled down completely.

2   Before beginning work, purchase the specified transaxle fluid (see *Recommended lubricants and fluids* in this Chapter's Specifications).

3   Other tools necessary for this job include jackstands to support the vehicle in a raised position, a drain pan capable of holding several quarts, newspapers and clean rags.

4   Raise and support the vehicle on jackstands. Remove the under-vehicle splash shield (see illustration 6.7).

5   Place the drain pan underneath the transaxle. Remove the check/fill plug (see illustration), then unscrew the overflow tube through the check/fill plug opening and allow the fluid to drain.

6   Reinsert the overflow tube and tighten it to the torque listed in this Chapter's Specifications. Measure the amount of fluid drained (the same amount will be added to the transaxle later).

7   On these transaxles, the fluid is added through the check/fill plug hole. A special tool is available for this purpose, but a suction gun equipped with an angled nozzle can be used to pump the fluid up into the transaxle. The nozzle must pass through the opening in the overflow tube. Remove the check/fill plug (see illustration 22.5) and slowly add fluid through the check/fill hole until it runs out (see illustration). Temporarily reinstall the check/fill plug.

8   With the shifter in Park and the parking brake set, run the engine at a fast idle.

9   Move the gear selector through each range, pausing for about two seconds in each range, then back to Park. Let the engine idle for a few minutes, then remove the check/fill plug. If fluid runs out of the hole, allow it to run out until it just drips. If no fluid runs out, add fluid through the hole until it does run out, allowing it to flow out until it just drips.

➡ **Note: The ideal temperature of the fluid when adjusting the level should be 95 to 113-degrees F.**

10 Install a new seal on the check/fill plug, then reinsert the plug and tighten it to the torque listed in this Chapter's Specifications.

11 Reinstall the under-vehicle splash shield.

22.5 Automatic transaxle fluid level check/fill plug location

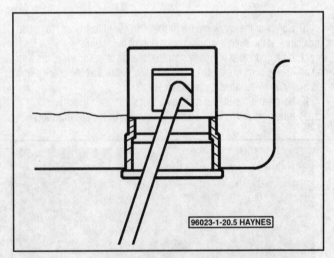

96023-1-20.5 HAYNES

22.7 The nozzle of the tool being used to add fluid to the transaxle must pass through the window in the overflow tube

23 Direct Shift Gearbox (DSG) fluid and filter change (every 40,000 miles [64,000 km] or 36 months)

※ WARNING:

This procedure is potentially dangerous and is best left to a professional shop. The vehicle must be kept level while being safely raised high enough for access to the plugs on the transaxle.

※ CAUTION:

If the battery is disconnected, several systems must be relearned before they will work properly (see Chapter 5, Section 3).

➡ Note: When the vehicle is serviced by a dealer or other qualified repair shop, a scan tool is used to read the transaxle fluid temperature. To perform the job at home, you will have to estimate the temperature of the fluid.

➡ Note: A minimum of 5.5 qts of DSG fluid must be added prior to starting the engine, and the engine must be running when checking the fluid level or when adding any more fluid.

1 At the specified intervals, the transaxle fluid should be drained and replaced. Since the fluid will remain hot long after driving, perform this procedure only after everything has cooled down completely.

2 Before beginning work, purchase the specified transaxle fluid (see *Recommended lubricants and fluids* in this Chapter's Specifications).

3 Other tools necessary for this job include jackstands to support the vehicle in a raised position, a drain pan capable of holding several quarts, newspapers and clean rags.

4 Raise the vehicle and support it securely on jackstands.

➡ Note: The vehicle must be level when checking or filling the transaxle, so the rear of the vehicle must be raised and supported as well.

5 Remove the splash shield under the engine (see illustration 6.7).

6 Remove the engine cover/air filter housing (see Section 7).

7 Disconnect and remove the battery and battery tray (see Chapter 5).

8 Move a drain pan, rags under the transaxle.

9 Using an open end wrench loosen the filter housing from the top of the transaxle but do not remove the filter housing. Once the filter housing is loosened allow it to sit for a few minutes, this will allow the oil in the housing to drain back into the transaxle and prevent excess fluid from spilling.

10 Remove the filter housing, pull the filter element out from the housing and take off the O-ring.

11 Clean out the filter housing and install a new O-ring to the housing.

12 Coat the end of the new filter element with DSG oil and install the filter, with the locating arrow pointing down into the transaxle.

13 Coat the O-ring on the filter housing with DSG oil, install the filter housing over the filter element and on to the transaxle. Tighten the filter housing to the torque listed in this Chapter's Specifications.

14 Working under the vehicle, remove the transaxle shield mounting bolts and shield, if equipped.

15 Move the drain pan under the transaxle check/drain plug and remove the plug. Once the plug is removed, use an Allen-wrench to unscrew and remove the overflow tube, allowing the fluid to drain out of the transaxle.

➡ Note: On early models, two check/drain plugs were installed; only remove the check/drain plug closest to the pendulum support mount.

16 After the lubricant has drained completely, reinstall the overflow tube and tighten the tube to the torque listed in this Chapter's Specifications. Measure the amount of fluid drained (the same amount will be added later).

17 On these transaxles, the fluid is added through the check/fill plug hole. A special tool is available for this purpose, but a suction gun equipped with an angled nozzle can be used to pump the fluid up into the transaxle. The nozzle must pass through the opening in the overflow tube. Slowly add fluid through the check/fill hole until it runs out (see illustration 22.7). Temporarily reinstall the check/drain plug.

➡ Note: Add at least 5.5 qts of DSG oil before starting the engine.

18 With the transaxle in Park and the parking brake set, start the engine.

19 Move the gear selector through each range, pausing for about three seconds in each range, then back to Park. Let the engine idle for a few minutes, then remove the check/drain plug. If fluid runs out of the hole, allow it to run out until it just drips. If no fluid runs out, add fluid through the hole until it does run out, allowing it to flow out until it just drips.

➡ Note: Every few seconds a small amount of oil will surge out due to the clutch operations, this does not mean there is too much oil in the transaxle and need to be factored in to determine the proper level. Also, the ideal temperature of the fluid when adjusting the level should be 95 to 113-degrees F.

20 Install a new seal on the check/drain plug, then reinsert the plug and tighten it to the torque listed in this Chapter's Specifications.

21 Reinstall the under-vehicle splash shield.

22 Lower the vehicle. The remainder of installation is the reverse of removal.

23 Drive the vehicle for a short distance, then check the check/drain plug and filter housing for leakage.

24 Manual transaxle lubricant change (every 60,000 miles [96,000 km] or 48 months)

5-SPEED MODELS

▶ Refer to illustrations 24.5 and 24.7

✳✳ CAUTION:

If the battery is disconnected, several systems must be relearned before they will work properly (see Chapter 5, Section 3).

➡ **Note: The fill plug located on the side of the transaxle is used to fill the transaxle only while it is out of the vehicle. Due to the angle of the engine, once the transaxle is installed, the fluid level is above the fill plug.**

1 Raise the vehicle and support it securely on jackstands.
2 Remove the splash shield under the engine (see illustration 6.7).
3 Remove the engine cover/air filter housing (see Section 7).
4 Disconnect and remove the battery and battery tray (see Chapter 5).
5 Push down on the selector shaft. While holding the shaft down, rotate the locking lever clockwise. The selector shaft is now locked and should not be able to be moved (see illustration).
6 Move a drain pan, rags, newspapers and wrenches under the transaxle.
7 Remove the drain plug, selector shaft journal fastener and journal from the bottom of the transaxle case (see illustration), and allow the lubricant to drain into the pan.
8 After the lubricant has drained completely, reinstall the drain plug and selector shaft journal and tighten them securely.

➡ **Note: Replace the O-ring on the selector shaft journal with a new one.**

9 Rotate the locking lever counterclockwise to unlock the selector shaft (see illustration 24.5).
10 Disconnect and remove the back-up light switch at the top of the transaxle. Using a hand pump, syringe or squeeze bottle, fill the transaxle with the specified amount of lubricant listed in this Chapter's Specifications. Reinstall the back-up light switch and tighten it securely.
11 Lower the vehicle.

12 Drive the vehicle for a short distance, then check the drain plug and selector shaft journal for leakage.

6-SPEED MODELS

✳✳ WARNING:

This procedure is potentially dangerous and is best left to a professional shop. The vehicle must be kept level while being safely raised high enough for access to the plugs on the transaxle.

13 This procedure should be performed after the vehicle has been driven so the lubricant will be warm and therefore will flow out of the transaxle more easily.
14 Raise the vehicle and support it securely on jackstands.

➡ **Note: The vehicle must be level when checking or filling the transaxle, so the rear of the vehicle must be raised and supported as well.**

15 Remove the splash shield under the engine (see illustration 6.7).
16 Move a drain pan, rags, newspapers and wrenches under the transaxle.
17 Remove the fill plug from the side of the transaxle case, then remove the transaxle drain plug at the bottom of the transaxle and allow the lubricant to drain into the pan.

➡ **Note: Two types of drain and fill plugs are used, a six point (hex) plug or a twelve point (triple square) plug. Both have different tightening specifications.**

18 After the lubricant has drained completely, reinstall the drain plug and tighten it securely.
19 Using a hand pump, syringe or squeeze bottle, fill the transaxle with the specified lubricant until it just reaches the bottom edge of the hole. Reinstall the fill plug and tighten it securely.
20 Lower the vehicle.
21 Drive the vehicle for a short distance, then check the drain and fill plugs for leakage.

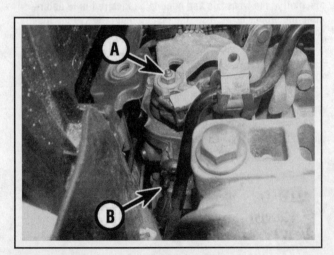

24.5 Five-speed selector shaft lock details

A Selector shaft　　　　　*B Locking pin*

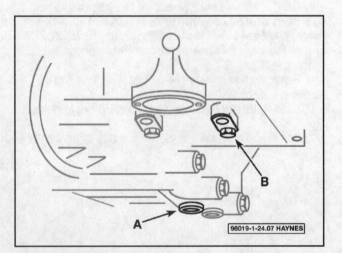

24.7 Five-speed drain plug (A) and selector shaft journal (B) locations

25 Fuel filter replacement (every 60,000 miles [96,000 km] or 48 months)

◆ **Refer to illustration 25.1**

✳✳ WARNING:

Gasoline is extremely flammable, so take extra precautions when you work on any part of the fuel system. Don't smoke or allow open flames or bare light bulbs near the work area, and don't work in a garage where a gas-type appliance (such as a water heater or clothes dryer) is present. Since gasoline is carcinogenic, wear fuel-resistant gloves when there's a possibility of being exposed to fuel, and, if you spill any fuel on your skin, rinse it off immediately with soap and water. Mop up any spills immediately and do not store fuel-soaked rags where they could ignite. When you perform any kind of work on the fuel system, wear safety glasses and have a Class B type fire extinguisher on hand. The fuel system is under pressure, so if any lines must be disconnected, the pressure in the system must be relieved first (see Chapter 4 for more information).

✳✳ CAUTION:

If the battery is disconnected, several systems must be relearned before they will work properly (see Chapter 5, Section 3).

✳✳ CAUTION:

On five-cylinder engines, the fuel system must be bled once the lines have been opened (see Chapter 4). Damage to the catalytic converter may result if the system is not bled.

1   The fuel filter is located under the rear of the vehicle, ahead of the right-rear wheel, adjacent to the fuel tank (see illustration).

2   The manufacturer does not give a replacement interval, but our suggested interval is based on experience with many other vehicles; replacing it is like inexpensive insurance and may prevent an untimely breakdown.

3   Depressurize the fuel system (see Chapter 4), then disconnect the cable from the negative terminal of the battery. Raise the vehicle and support it securely on jackstands.

4   Use compressed air or brake system cleaner to clean any dirt surrounding the fuel inlet and outlet line fittings.

➡ **Note: On some models, it is necessary to remove a plastic splash shield for access.**

5   Disconnect the fuel lines from the filter; refer to Chapter 4 for information on how to disconnect quick-connect fittings.

➡ **Note: Have rags ready to catch or wipe up gasoline that will spill from the filter.**

6   Remove the clamp screw and detach the filter.

7   Remove the retaining clip and remove the pressure regulator from the filter body.

8   Replace the gasket and O-ring to the pressure regulator, install the regulator to the filter body and insert the retaining clip.

9   Installation is the reverse of removal. Make sure the arrow on the side of the new filter is pointing toward the engine side of the fuel system, and check for leaks after running the vehicle.

25.1 Fuel filter details

A   *Clamp screw*   B   *Fuel line fittings*

26 Cooling system servicing (draining, flushing and refilling)

✳✳ WARNING:

Do not allow antifreeze to come in contact with your skin or painted surfaces of the vehicle. Rinse off spills immediately with plenty of water. Antifreeze is highly toxic if ingested. Never leave antifreeze lying around in an open container or in puddles on the floor; children and pets are attracted by it's sweet smell and may drink it. Check with local authorities about disposing of used antifreeze. Many communities have collection centers which will see that antifreeze is disposed of safely.

✳✳ WARNING:

Wait until the engine is completely cool before beginning this procedure.

1   Periodically, the cooling system should be drained, flushed and refilled to replenish the antifreeze mixture and prevent formation of rust and corrosion, which can impair the performance of the cooling system and cause engine damage. When the cooling system is serviced, all

hoses and the expansion tank cap should be checked and replaced if necessary.

DRAINING

▶ **Refer to illustration 26.7**

2 Apply the parking brake and block the wheels. If the vehicle has just been driven, wait several hours to allow the engine to cool down before beginning this procedure.

3 Raise and support the vehicle on jackstands. Remove the under-vehicle splash shield (see illustration 6.7).

4 Once the engine is completely cool, remove the expansion tank cap.

5 Move a large container under the radiator hose to catch the coolant.

6 **Four-cylinder engines:** Remove the clip for the coupler at the lower radiator hose or the radiator, then remove the hose, allowing the coolant to drain.

7 **Five-cylinder engines:** Loosen and remove the hose clamp from the lower radiator hose and allow the coolant to drain (see illustration).

8 While the coolant is draining, check the condition of the radiator hoses, heater hoses and clamps (refer to Section 9 if necessary). Replace any damaged clamps or hoses.

FLUSHING

9 Reconnect the lower radiator hose. Fill the cooling system with clean water, following the *Refilling* procedure (see Steps 15 through 21).

10 Start the engine and allow it to reach normal operating temperature, then rev up the engine a few times.

11 Turn the engine off and allow it to cool completely, then drain the system as described earlier.

12 Repeat Steps 9 through 11 until the water being drained is free of contaminants.

13 In severe cases of contamination or clogging of the radiator, remove the radiator (see Chapter 3) and have a radiator repair facility clean and repair it if necessary.

14 Many deposits can be removed by the chemical action of a cleaner available at auto parts stores. Follow the procedure outlined in the manufacturer's instructions.

➡ **Note: When the coolant is regularly drained and the system refilled with the correct antifreeze/water mixture, there should be no need to use chemical cleaners or descalers.**

REFILLING

➡ **Note: Always refill the cooling system with a 50/50 percent coolant and water mixture.**

15 Place the heater temperature control in the maximum heat position.

16 Add coolant to the expansion tank until the level is between the MIN and MAX marks on the expansion tank. Wait five minutes and recheck the coolant level, adding if necessary.

17 Install the expansion tank cap and run the engine in a well-ventilated area at 2000 rpm for three minutes.

18 Allow the engine to idle until both radiator hoses are warm (indicating that the thermostat has opened).

19 Raise the engine speed to 2000 rpm for one minute.

20 Turn the engine off and let it cool. Check the coolant level; add more coolant mixture, if necessary, to bring it up to the MAX mark on the expansion tank. Install the expansion tank cap.

21 Start the engine, allow it to reach normal operating temperature and check for leaks. Also, set the heater and blower controls to the maximum setting and check to see that the heater output from the air ducts is warm. This is a good indication that all air has been purged from the cooling system.

26.7 Loosen the lower radiator hose clamp, detach the hose and allow the coolant to drain

Specifications

Recommended lubricants and fluids

➡ **Note: Listed here are manufacturer recommendations at the time this manual was written. Manufacturers occasionally upgrade their fluid and lubricant specifications, so check with your local auto parts store for current recommendations.**

Engine oil	API - SM/SL; ACEA A2/A3 synthetic
Viscosity	5W-40 (see accompanying chart)
Fuel	
Four-cylinder engine	Unleaded gasoline, 91 octane minimum
Five-cylinder engine	Regular unleaded gasoline
Automatic transaxle fluid	VW part No. G 055 025
Manual transaxle lubricant	
5-speed	See authorized VW dealer
6-speed	VW part No. G 052 911 A1
6-speed (DSG)	VW part No. G 052 182 A2
Brake and clutch fluid	DOT 4 Super or DOT 4+ brake fluid
Engine coolant	Phosphate-free coolant 50/50 mixture of G12 (purple) antifreeze and distilled water
Hood and trunk hinge lubricant	Lubriplate, lubricant aerosol spray
Door hinge and check spring grease	NLGI no. 2 multi-purpose grease
Key lock cylinder lubricant	Graphite spray
Hood latch assembly lubricant	NLGI no. 2 multi-purpose grease
Door latch lubricant	NLGI no. 2 multi-purpose grease or equivalent

Capacities*

Engine oil (including filter)	
Four-cylinder engines	4.9 quarts (4.6 liters)
Five-cylinder engines	
2007 and earlier models	6.3 quarts (6.0 liters)
2008 and later models	5.8 quarts (5.5 liters)
Manual transaxle	
5-speed (0A4)	2.0 quarts (1.9 liters)
6-speed (02Q)	2.4 quarts (2.3 liters)
Automatic transaxle	
6-speed	
Drain and refill	Not specified. The best way to determine the amount to add is to measure the amount drained
From dry	7.4 quarts (7.0 liters)
6-speed (DSG)	
Drain and refill	5.5 quarts (5.2 liters)
From dry	7.6 quarts (7.2 liters)
Cooling system	
Four-cylinder engines	
2006 and 2007 (Rabbit and GTI models)	8.0 quarts (7.6 liters)
All others	8.5 quarts (8.0 liters)
Five-cylinder engines	10 quarts (9.5 liters)

*All capacities approximate. Add as necessary to bring to appropriate level.

Specifications

Brakes

Disc brake pad wear limit (lining only)   0.079 inch (2.0 mm)
Drum brake shoe wear limit (lining only)   0.098 inch (2.5 mm)

Ignition system

Spark plug type
    Four-cylinder engines   Bosch F6KPP332S
    Five-cylinder engines   NGK PZFR5J-11
Spark plug gap
    Four-cylinder engines
        Jetta models
            2005   0.035 to 0.043 inch (0.9 to 1.1 mm)
            2006 and later
                Engine code BPY   0.028 to 0.031 inch (0.7 to 0.8 mm)
                Engine codes CCTA and CBFA   0.039 to 0.043 inch (1.0 to 1.1 mm)
        Rabbit/GTI/Golf models
            Engine code BPY   0.028 to 0.031 inch (0.7 to 0.8 mm)
            Engine code CCTA and CBFA   0.039 to 0.043 inch (1.0 to 1.1 mm)
    Five-cylinder engine   0.039 to 0.043 inch (1.0 to 1.1 mm)
Firing order
    Four-cylinder engines   1-3-4-2
    Five-cylinder engines   1-2-4-5-3

Cylinder locations - four-cylinder engine

Cylinder locations - five-cylinder engine

Torque specifications   Ft-lbs (unless otherwise indicated)   Nm

➡ **Note: One foot-pound (ft-lb) of torque is equivalent to 12 inch-pounds (in-lbs) of torque. Torque values below approximately 15 foot-pounds are expressed in inch-pounds, because most foot-pound torque wrenches are not accurate at these smaller values.**

	Ft-lbs	Nm
Engine oil drain plug*	18	25
Oil filter housing-to-engine	18	25
Automatic transaxle check/fill plug	135 in-lbs	15
Automatic transaxle overflow tube-to-transaxle	27 in-lbs	3
DSG transaxle check/drain plug	33	45
DSG transaxle overflow tube-to-transaxle	27 in-lbs	3
DSG transaxle filter housing-to-transaxle	15	20

*Replace the drain plug after each use.

Torque specifications   Ft-lbs (unless otherwise indicated)   Nm

➡ **Note:** One foot-pound (ft-lb) of torque is equivalent to 12 inch-pounds (in-lbs) of torque. Torque values below approximately 15 foot-pounds are expressed in inch-pounds, because most foot-pound torque wrenches are not accurate at these smaller values.

	Ft-lbs	Nm
Manual transaxle		
6-speed models		
Check/fill plug		
Six point (hex) plug	22	30
Twelve point (triple square) plug	33	45
Drain plug		
Six point (hex) plug	22	30
Twelve point (triple square) plug	33	45
Spark plugs	18	25
Drivebelt tensioner mounting bolt(s)		
Four-cylinder timing belt engine	17	23
Four-cylinder timing chain engine	88 in-lbs	10
Five-cylinder engine	26	35
Wheel bolts	90	120

Notes

Section

Reference to other Chapters

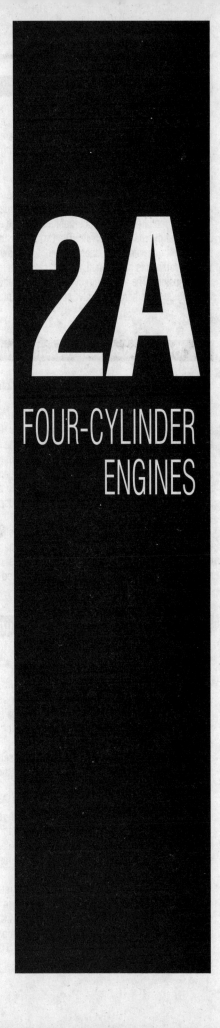

2A
FOUR-CYLINDER ENGINES

1 General information

This Part of Chapter 2 is devoted to in-vehicle repair procedures for the 2.0L four-cylinder gasoline engines. There are two engines offered: the timing belt (BPY) engine, which uses a timing belt and an oil pump/balance shaft drive that is externally mounted to the crankshaft, and the timing chain (CCTA, CBFA) engine, which uses a timing chain with two balance shafts mounted in the engine block. These engines utilize an aluminum engine block with an aluminum cylinder head. Both engines have a turbocharger that is incorporated with the exhaust manifold and utilize dual overhead camshafts. The two camshafts are driven by a timing belt or chain, each operating eight valves via roller rocker arms. Valve clearance is maintained automatically at zero lash by hydraulic lash adjusters. The aluminum cylinder head is equipped with pressed-in valve guides and hardened valve seats. The oil pump is mounted below the front of the engine and is chain driven from the crankshaft. The engine identification is stamped on a machined flat spot at the top of the cylinder block where the engine and transaxle meet. On some models, an additional engine identification sticker is attached to the upper half of the timing cover.

Information concerning intake and exhaust manifold removal and installation can be found in Chapter 4, Sections 14 or 15. Information concerning engine removal and installation and engine overhaul can be found in Part C of this Chapter.

The following repair procedures are based on the assumption that the engine is installed in the vehicle. If the engine has been removed from the vehicle and mounted on a stand, many of the steps outlined in this Part of Chapter 2 will not apply.

2 Repair operations possible with the engine in the vehicle

Many major repair operations can be accomplished without removing the engine from the vehicle.

Clean the engine compartment and the exterior of the engine with some type of degreaser before any work is done. It will make the job easier and help keep dirt out of the internal areas of the engine.

Depending on the components involved, it may be helpful to remove the hood to improve access to the engine as repairs are performed (refer to Chapter 11 if necessary). Cover the fenders to prevent damage to the paint. Special pads are available, but an old bedspread or blanket will also work.

If vacuum, exhaust, oil or coolant leaks develop, indicating a need for gasket or seal replacement, the repairs can generally be made with the engine in the vehicle. The intake and exhaust manifold gaskets, oil pan gasket, crankshaft oil seals and cylinder head gasket are all accessible with the engine in place.

Exterior engine components, such as the intake and exhaust manifolds, the oil pan, the oil pump, the water pump, the starter motor, the alternator and the fuel system components can be removed for repair with the engine in place.

Since the cylinder head can be removed without pulling the engine, camshaft and valve component servicing can also be accomplished with the engine in the vehicle. Replacement of the timing belt and pulleys is also possible with the engine in the vehicle.

In extreme cases caused by a lack of necessary equipment, repair or replacement of piston rings, pistons, connecting rods and rod bearings is possible with the engine in the vehicle. However, this practice is not recommended because of the cleaning and preparation work that must be done to the components involved.

3 Top Dead Center (TDC) for number one piston - locating

▶ **Refer to illustrations 3.6a and 3.6b**

1   Top Dead Center (TDC) is the highest point in the cylinder that each piston reaches as it travels up the cylinder bore. Each piston reaches TDC on the compression stroke and again on the exhaust stroke, but TDC generally refers to piston position on the compression stroke.

2   Positioning the piston(s) at TDC is an essential part of many procedures such as valve adjustment, camshaft, timing belt or timing chain/sprocket removal.

3   Before beginning this procedure, be sure to place the transaxle in Neutral and apply the parking brake or block the rear wheels.

4   Remove the spark plugs (see Chapter 1) and install a compression gauge in the number one spark plug hole (see Chapter 2C). It should be a gauge with a screw-in fitting and a hose at least six inches long.

5   Rotate the crankshaft using a socket and ratchet attached to the bolt threaded into the front of the crankshaft. Turn the bolt in a clockwise direction only. The moment the gauge shows pressure indicates that the number one cylinder has begun the compression stroke.

6   Once the compression stroke has begun, TDC for the compression stroke is reached by bringing the piston to the top of the cylinder.

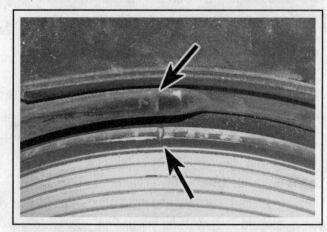

3.6a Align the notch on the crankshaft drivebelt pulley with the arrow on the timing belt cover - 2.0L timing belt (BPY) engines

Continue turning the crankshaft until the notch in the crankshaft damper is aligned with the "TDC" or the "0" mark on the timing chain cover (see illustrations). At this point, the number one cylinder is at TDC on the compression stroke. If the marks are aligned but there was no compression, the piston was on the exhaust stroke; continue rotating the crankshaft 360-degrees (1-turn).

➡ **Note: If a compression gauge is not available, you can simply place a blunt object over the spark plug hole and listen for compression as the engine is rotated. Once compression at the No.1 spark plug hole is noted the remainder of the Step is the same.**

7   After the number one piston has been positioned at TDC on the compression stroke, TDC for any of the remaining cylinders can be located by turning the crankshaft 180-degrees and following the firing order (refer to the Specifications). Rotating the engine 180 degrees past TDC #1 will put the engine at TDC compression for cylinder #3.

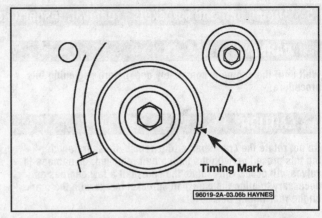

3.6b Align the notch on the crankshaft pulley with the mark on the timing belt cover - 2.0L timing chain (CCTA, CBFA) engines

4   Valve cover - removal and installation

➡ **Note: This procedure applies to the timing belt (BPY) engine only.**

REMOVAL

1   Remove the engine cover (see Chapter 1, Section 7).

2   Remove the timing belt upper cover retaining fasteners (see Section 5).

3   Remove the ignition coils (see Chapter 5).

4   Remove the PCV valve fasteners and pull the PCV housing away from the cover.

5   Remove the crankcase hose heat shield retaining fasteners from the turbocharger, and remove the shield.

6   Disconnect the electrical connectors and harness clipped to the valve cover.

7   Remove the retaining fasteners in the reverse order of installation (see illustration 4.11) and detach the valve cover from the cylinder head.

8   If the cover is stuck to the head, bump the end with a block of wood and a hammer to jar it loose. If that doesn't work, try to slip a flexible putty knife between the head and cover to break the seal.

✳ CAUTION:

Don't pry at the cover-to-head joint or damage to the sealing surfaces may occur, leading to oil leaks after the cover is reinstalled.

INSTALLATION

▶ **Refer to illustrations 4.10 and 4.11**

9   The mating surfaces of the cylinder head and cover must be clean when the cover is installed. Remove all traces of sealant and old gasket material including the spark plug tube seal gaskets, then clean the mating surfaces with brake system cleaner. If there's residue or oil on the mating surfaces when the cover is installed, oil leaks may develop. Also inspect the rubber end plug at the rear of the cylinder head for cracks and damage. Now would be a good time to replace it, if damage has occurred.

10 The rubber gasket can be reused if not damaged (see illustration).

11 Install the valve cover and any brackets removed, then tighten fasteners in sequence (see illustration) to the torque listed in this Chapter's Specifications.

12 Reinstall the remaining parts, run the engine and check for oil leaks.

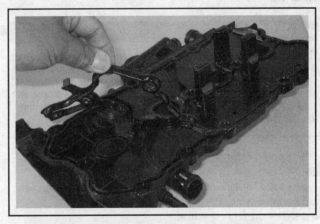

4.10 The gasket is reusable - clean it and press it into the groove in the valve cover

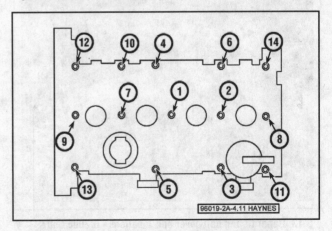

4.11 Valve cover bolt tightening sequence (loosening sequence is the reverse of tightening)

5 Timing belt and sprockets - removal, inspection and installation

✳✳ WARNING:

Wait until the engine is completely cool before beginning this procedure.

✳✳ CAUTION:

Do not rotate the crankshaft or the camshaft separately during this procedure with the timing belt removed, as damage to valves will occur. Only rotate the camshaft a few degrees as necessary to align the camshaft sprocket marks with the marks on the rear timing belt cover.

✳✳ CAUTION:

If the battery is disconnected, several systems must be relearned before they will work properly (see Chapter 5, Section 3).

➡ **Note:** This procedure applies to the BPY engine only.

REMOVAL

▸ **Refer to illustrations 5.13, 5.14, 5.16, 5.18, 5.26, 5.28a, 5.28b and 5.29**

✳✳ CAUTION:

The timing system is complex. Severe engine damage will occur if you make any mistakes. Do not attempt this procedure unless you are highly experienced with this type of repair. If you are at all unsure of your abilities, consult an expert. Double-check all your work and be sure everything is correct before you attempt to start the engine.

1   Disconnect the cable from the negative terminal of the battery (see Chapter 5).

2   Loosen the right front wheel bolts, raise the front of the vehicle and support it securely on jackstands. Block the wheels at the opposite end and remove the right front wheel.

3   Working under the vehicle, remove the lower splash shield below the engine (see Chapter 1, Section 6).

4   Disconnect the electrical connector from the fuel pump (see Chapter 4).

5   Working from above in the engine compartment, remove the engine cover (see Chapter 1, Section 7).

6   Mark and disconnect the fuel lines around the timing belt cover (see Chapter 4).

7   Drain some of the coolant from the cooling system (see Chapter 1), then disconnect the coolant pipe in front of the timing belt cover.

8   Remove coolant reservoir (see Chapter 3).

9   Remove the driver's side inner fender liner (see Chapter 11).

10   Remove the charge air cooler lower connector pipe retaining fasteners and lower connector pipe.

11   Mark the rotation direction of the drive belt, then remove the drive belt (see Chapter 1) and spark plugs.

➡ **Note:** After the belt is removed, remove the locking pin from the tensioner and slowly release the tensioner.

12   On 5/2006 and earlier production models, remove the timing belt inspection cover from the upper timing belt cover.

13   On 6/2006 and later production models, remove the timing belt upper cover fasteners (see illustration) and cover.

14   Rotate the engine in the normal direction of rotation (clockwise) until the No. 1 cylinder is located at TDC (see Section 3). Verify that the camshaft sprocket mark is aligned with the mark on the rear timing belt cover (see illustration).

15   Use an offset box wrench on the crankshaft center bolt to keep the crankshaft from rotating while removing the pulley retaining bolts. Loosen the crankshaft drive sprocket retaining bolt (only if the sprocket is to be removed) and the crankshaft pulley bolts, then remove the pulley (see Section 10). After the bolts are loosened, verify that the crankshaft has not moved from TDC.

➡ **Note:** Loosening the drive sprocket bolt is only required if the crankshaft drive sprocket is expected to be removed. It is not typically necessary to remove the drive sprocket when you're simply replacing a timing belt, but it will have to be removed if you are replacing the crankshaft front oil seal or housing. If you do remove the drive sprocket, obtain a new bolt (the manufacturer doesn't recommend re-using it).

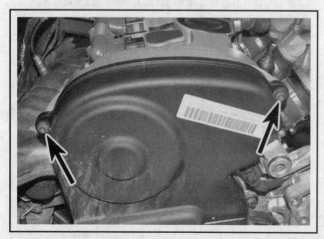

5.13 Upper timing belt cover bolt locations - 6/2006 and later production model engines

5.14 When the engine is positioned at TDC for the No. 1 cylinder on the compression stroke, the camshaft sprocket mark will be aligned with the mark on the rear timing belt cover

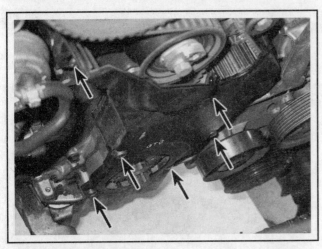

5.17 Lower timing belt cover fastener locations - 6/2006 and later production model engines

5.18 Typical engine support details

16 On 5/2006 and earlier production models, remove the lower timing belt cover retaining fasteners and lower cover.

17 On 6/2006 and later production models, remove the timing belt cover retaining fasteners that are visible (see illustration).

➡ **Note: There are two more retaining fasteners that can only be accessed once the engine mount has been removed.**

18 Support the engine from above with an engine support fixture (see illustration).

19 Remove the air conditioning line bracket clamps.

❋❋ **CAUTION:**

Do not disconnect the air conditioning lines.

20 Remove the front exhaust pipe/catalytic converter (see Chapter 4).

21 Disconnect the driveaxles from the transaxle (see Chapter 8).

22 Remove the pendulum mount (see Section 18) from under the vehicle.

23 Remove the front engine mount, engine mounting bracket bolts and bracket (see Section 18).

➡ **Note: The engine will have to be raised and lowered to remove the front engine retaining fasteners.**

24 Remove the remaining timing belt cover retaining fasteners and cover.

25 Loosen the tensioner pulley nut, then insert a hex tool into the tensioner pulley and turn the tensioner counterclockwise until the timing belt can be removed from the sprockets.

26 If you plan to re-use the timing belt, apply match marks on the sprocket and belt, and make an arrow indicating direction of travel on the belt (see illustration).

27 Remove the timing belt from the engine, taking care to avoid twisting or kinking it excessively.

➡ **Note: If you're removing the upper part of the belt only, for camshaft seal replacement or cylinder head removal, it isn't necessary to detach the belt from the crankshaft sprocket.**

28 If the crankshaft sprocket is worn or damaged, or if you have to replace the crankshaft front oil seal, remove the drive sprocket retaining bolt which was loosened in Step 15 and detach the crankshaft sprocket from the crankshaft (see illustrations).

➡ **Note: There is a diamond disc or washer located between the crankshaft sprocket and end of the crankshaft.**

5.26 If you intend to re-use the timing belt, apply directional marks on the belt

5.28a With the crankshaft drive sprocket retaining bolt removed . . .

5.28b . . . the crankshaft sprocket is easily detached from the engine. Note how the lug on the sprocket engages with the notch in the crankshaft

29 If the camshaft sprocket is damaged or needs to be removed for other procedures such as cylinder head removal, use a pin spanner wrench or similar tool to hold the sprocket in place as the sprocket retaining bolt is loosened (see illustration), then, use a two-jaw puller to remove the camshaft sprocket.

INSPECTION

▶ **Refer to illustration 5.31**

❋ CAUTION:

Do not bend, twist or turn the timing belt inside out. Do not allow it to come in contact with oil, coolant or fuel. Do not turn the crankshaft or camshaft more than a few degrees (if necessary for tooth alignment) while the timing belt is removed.

30 Spin the timing belt tensioner pulley (which is the large pulley bolted to the engine block) and the idler wheel (which is the small roller mounted on the tensioner body) and check the bearings for smooth operation and excessive play. Also inspect the remaining timing belt sprockets for any obvious damage. Replace all worn parts as necessary.
31 Examine the belt for evidence of contamination by coolant or lubricant. If this is the case, find the source of the contamination before progressing any further. Check the belt for signs of wear or damage, particularly around the leading edges of the belt teeth (see illustration).

❋ CAUTION:

If the belt appears to be in good condition and can be re-used, it is essential that it is reinstalled the same way around, otherwise accelerated wear will result, leading to premature failure.

32 Replace the belt if its condition is in doubt; the cost of belt replacement is negligible compared with potential cost of the engine repairs, should the belt fail in service. Similarly, if the belt is known to have covered more than 60,000 miles, it is a good idea to replace it regardless of condition, as a precautionary measure.

5.29 If necessary, the camshaft sprocket bolt can be loosened while holding the sprocket in place with a pin spanner wrench

INSTALLATION

▶ **Refer to illustration 5.37**

❋ CAUTION:

Before starting the engine, carefully rotate the crankshaft by hand through at least two full revolutions (use a socket and breaker bar on the crankshaft pulley center bolt). If you feel any resistance, STOP! There is something wrong - most likely, valves are contacting the pistons. You must find the problem before proceeding. Check your work and see if any updated repair information is available.

33 Ensure that the crankshaft is still set to TDC on No. 1 cylinder, as described in Section 3. If any of the timing sprockets or the tensioner pulley were removed for inspection or needed replacement, install them back onto the engine now. If the timing belt tensioner was removed, reinstall it now and tighten the bolts to the torque listed in this Chapter's Specifications, then install the tensioner pulley adjustment bolt loosely.
34 Make sure the camshaft sprocket mark is still in alignment with

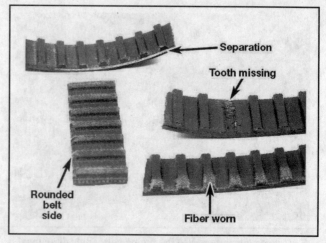

5.31 Check the timing belt for cracked and missing teeth - wear on one side of the belt indicates sprocket misalignment problems

the mark on the rear timing belt cover (see illustration 5.14).

35 Loop the timing belt loosely under the crankshaft sprocket.

✳ CAUTION:

Observe the direction of rotation markings on the belt.

36 Route the belt clockwise in this order: around the lower guide pulley, the tensioning roller, the camshaft sprocket, water pump sprocket, then the relay pulley (the small roller). Ensure the belt teeth seat correctly on the sprockets.

➡ **Note: Slight adjustments to the position of the camshaft sprocket may be necessary to achieve this.**

37 Using a hex wrench, rotate the tensioner clockwise until the notch is positioned above the tab (see illustration); this applies tension to the belt. Loosen the tensioner again, rotate the tensioner until the notch is aligned with the tab, then tighten the nut to the torque listed in this Chapter's Specifications.

38 Install the lower timing belt cover and the crankshaft pulley.

39 Rotate the crankshaft two complete revolutions, bringing it back to TDC on the compression stroke. Check the alignment marks again.

5.37 Timing belt tensioner details

A   Tab   B   Notch

Also re-check that the tensioner tab is positioned by the middle of the notch (see illustration 5.37).

40 The remainder of installation is the reverse of removal.

6   Timing chain cover, timing chains and tensioners - removal and installation

✳ WARNING:

Wait until the engine is completely cool before beginning this procedure.

✳ CAUTION:

Do not rotate the crankshaft or the camshafts separately during this procedure with the timing chain removed, as damage to valves may occur.

✳ CAUTION:

If the battery is disconnected, several systems must be relearned before they will work properly (see Chapter 5, Section 3).

➡ **Note: This procedure applies to the CCTA and CBFA engines only.**

TIMING CHAIN COVERS

Upper cover

Removal

1   Remove the engine cover (see Chapter 1, Section 7), then remove the oil dipstick tube retaining fasteners and the dipstick housing.

➡ **Note: Be sure to replace the O-ring at the base of the dipstick tube.**

2   On models equipped with a noise generator, open the locking ring on the charge air pipe, pull the fuel lines from the retaining clip, then remove the EVAP canister retaining bolts and canister (see Chapter 6). Move the charge air pipe to the side.

3   Push the coolant hoses away from the cover and tie them out of the way.

4   Disconnect the electrical connector to the camshaft adjustment

valve 1, then remove the adjustment valve retaining fasteners, the valve and seal.

➡ **Note: Always replace the adjustment valve seal and O-ring.**

5   Remove the upper timing chain cover retaining fasteners in a star pattern and remove the cover.

6   Discard the gasket; it must be replaced whenever it is removed. Check that the sealing faces are undamaged.

Installation

▶ **Refer to illustration 6.9**

7   Clean the cover and the cylinder head faces carefully, then install a new gasket onto the upper cover.

8   Install the cover to the cylinder head, ensuring as the cover is tightened that the gasket remains seated.

9   Working in sequence (see illustration), first tighten the cover bolts by hand only. Once all the bolts are hand-tight, go around once more in sequence, and tighten the retaining fasteners to the torque

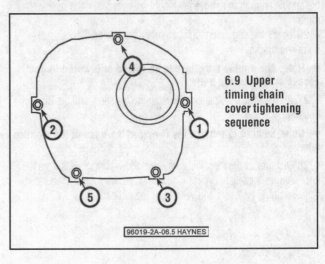

6.9 Upper timing chain cover tightening sequence

96019-2A-06.5 HAYNES

listed in this Chapter Specifications.

10 The remainder of installation is the reverse of removal. Run the engine and check for leaks.

Lower cover

Removal

11 Disconnect the cable from the negative terminal of the battery (see Chapter 5).

12 Loosen the right front wheel bolts, raise the front of the vehicle and support it securely on jackstands. Block the wheels at the opposite end and remove the right front wheel.

13 Working under the vehicle, remove the lower splash shield below the engine (see Chapter 1, Section 6).

14 Working from above in the engine compartment, remove the engine cover (see Chapter 1, Section 7).

15 Remove the right front inner fender liner (see Chapter 11).

16 Drain the engine oil (see Chapter 1).

17 Remove the air charge pipe retaining fasteners, the clamps at each end and the air charge pipe.

18 Loosen both hose clamps on the lower air charge hose and remove the hose.

19 Remove the drivebelt and tensioner (see Chapter 1).

20 Use an offset box wrench on the crankshaft center bolt and rotate the engine in the normal direction of rotation (clockwise) until the No. 1 cylinder is located at TDC (see Section 3). Verify that the notch on the crankshaft pulley is aligned with the mark on the lower timing chain cover.

21 Remove the crankshaft pulley (see Section 10) and reinstall the crankshaft pulley bolt.

❊❊ CAUTION:

To prevent damaging the splines on the end of the crankshaft install VW special tool #T10355 spacer or equivalent.

---

22 On models equipped with a noise generator, open the locking ring on the charge air pipe, then move the charge air pipe to the side.

23 Remove the alternator (see Chapter 5).

24 Support the engine from above with an engine support fixture (see illustration 5.18).

➡ **Note: On some 2009 and later models, the battery and battery tray must be removed for access to the lifting points.**

25 Remove the front engine mount-to-mount bracket bolts, raise the engine enough to remove the mount-to-body bolts and remove the mount.

26 Lower the engine enough to remove the engine mount bracket bolts and bracket.

➡ **Note: The engine may have to be raised or lowered to gain access or remove the bolts.**

27 Remove the oil dipstick tube retaining fasteners and the dipstick housing.

➡ **Note: Be sure to replace the O-ring at the base of the dipstick tube.**

28 Disconnect the electrical connector and vacuum hoses from the turbocharger wastegate bypass regulator valve. Remove the regulator valve retaining fasteners and valve from the turbocharger.

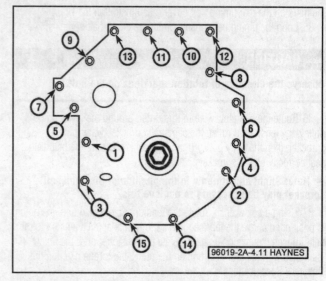

6.36 Lower timing chain cover tightening sequence

29 Remove the turbocharger support bracket retaining fasteners and bracket.

30 Remove the lower cover retaining fasteners in the reverse of the tightening sequence (see illustration 6.36) and carefully pry the cover from the engine block.

Installation

▶ **Refer to illustration 6.36**

31 Use a scraper to remove all traces of old sealant from the block and timing cover. Clean the mating surfaces with brake system cleaner.

32 Make sure the threaded bolt holes in the block are clean.

33 Check the timing chain cover flange for distortion, particularly around the bolt holes. Remove any nicks or burrs as necessary.

34 Apply a 3/16-inch wide bead of RTV sealant to the mating surface of the timing cover.

➡ **Note: Be sure to follow the sealant manufacturers recommendations for assembly and sealant curing times.**

35 Carefully position the timing cover on the engine block and install the timing cover retaining fasteners loosely.

36 Working in sequence (see illustration), first tighten the cover bolts by hand only. Once all the bolts are hand-tight, tighten the retaining fasteners in sequence to the torque listed in this Chapter Specifications.

37 The remainder of installation is the reverse of removal. Run the engine and check for leaks.

TIMING CHAIN AND TENSIONERS

❊❊ CAUTION:

The timing system is complex, and severe engine damage will occur if you make any mistakes. Do not attempt this procedure unless you are highly experienced with this type of repair. If you are at all unsure of your abilities, be sure to consult an expert. Double-check all your work and be sure everything is correct before you attempt to start the engine.

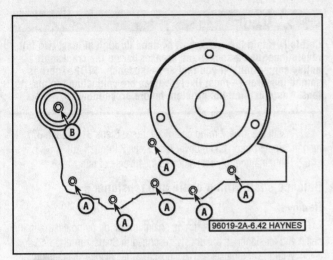

6.42 Remove the bearing retaining fasteners (A), then the bracket-to-exhaust camshaft bolt (B)

Removal

▶ **Refer to illustration 6.42**

38 Remove the upper timing chain cover (see Steps 1 through 6).
39 Use an offset box wrench on the crankshaft center bolt and rotate the engine in the normal direction of rotation (clockwise) until the No. 1 cylinder is located at TDC (see Section 3). Verify that the notch on the crankshaft pulley is aligned with the mark on the lower timing chain cover and the marks on the camshafts are pointing upwards (see illustration 3.6b).
40 Remove the lower timing chain cover (see Steps 11 through 30).
41 Insert VW special tool #10352 or equivalent into the two holes on the control valve, then rotate the valve clockwise and pull the valve out from the end of the camshaft.

➡ **Note: The control valve has left hand threads.**

42 Remove the bearing bracket retaining fasteners, bearing bracket-to-exhaust camshaft bolt and bearing bracket (see illustration).

Oil pump timing chain

43 Press the oil pump chain tensioner away from the chain and place a pin (a drill bit or paper clip will work) into the hole of the tensioner to hold it in the compressed position.
44 Remove the chain guide retaining pin and chain guide, then remove the chain.

Camshaft timing chain and tensioner

▶ **Refer to illustration 6.45**

45 Using a small screwdriver or pick, hold the chain tensioner ratchet arm away (UP) from the ratchet stem, then slowly compress the timing chain tensioner piston and place a pin (a drill bit or paper clip will work) into the hole to hold it in the compressed position (see illustration).
46 Remove the chain guide retaining pins and the chain guide from each side of the chain.
47 Remove the timing chain tensioner retaining fasteners and tensioner.

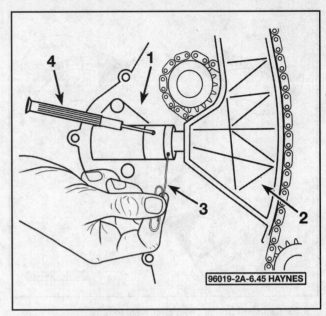

6.45 Timing chain tensioner details

1	Timing chain tensioner	3	Drill bit or paper clip
2	Timing chain guide	4	Small screwdriver

✳✳ CAUTION:

Do not remove the pin holding the tensioner piston in the compressed position once it's removed.

48 Remove the timing chain.

Installation

Camshaft timing chain and tensioner

▶ **Refer to illustration 6.53**

✳✳ CAUTION:

Before starting the engine, carefully rotate the crankshaft by hand through at least two full revolutions (use a socket and breaker bar on the crankshaft pulley center bolt). If you feel any resistance, STOP! There is something wrong - most likely, valves are contacting the pistons. You must find the problem before proceeding. Check your work and see if any updated repair information is available.

49 Remove all traces of old sealant from the timing chain covers and the mating surfaces of the engine block and cylinder head.
50 Make sure the crankshaft is at TDC and the balance shaft chain marks are aligned (see illustration 6.67).
51 Loop the timing chain around the crankshaft sprocket and align the No.1 colored link with the mark on the crankshaft sprocket. Place the timing chain over the exhaust camshaft and align the colored link with the mark on the exhaust camshaft sprocket.

➡ **Note: There are three bright or colored links on the timing chain. The No.1 colored link is the link farthest away from the two colored links that are closest together.**

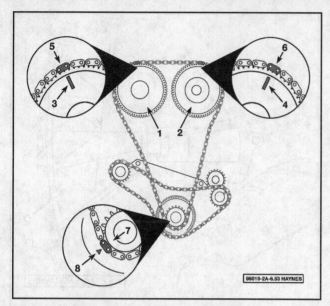

6.53 Camshaft timing chain alignment details

1	Exhaust camshaft	5	Colored link
2	Intake camshaft	6	Colored link
3	Exhaust camshaft timing mark	7	Crankshaft sprocket timing mark
4	Intake camshaft timing mark	8	Colored link

52 Using a wrench on the flat area of the intake camshaft, slightly rotate the intake camshaft counterclockwise to align the mark on the camshaft sprocket and the chain.

53 Once the camshaft sprocket and colored link are aligned (see illustration), install the chain on to the teeth of the camshaft sprocket.

✳✳ CAUTION:

Do not let go of the wrench holding the intake camshaft in place until the tensioner is installed.

54 Using your free hand, install the chain guides and retaining pins, then tighten the fasteners to the torque listed in this Chapter's Specifications.

55 Install the timing chain tensioner and tighten the retaining fasteners to the torque listed in this Chapter's Specifications.

56 Install the bearing bracket and tighten the retaining fasteners hand tight.

57 Remove the pin from the tensioner to release the tensioner piston to engage the chain guide, then slowly release the wrench holding the intake camshaft.

Oil pump timing chain

58 Loop the chain over the oil pump drive gear and the crankshaft gear.

59 Install the oil pump chain tensioner guide against the chain and retaining pin, then tighten the retaining pin to the torque listed in this Chapter's Specifications. Remove the pin from the tensioner to release the tensioner piston to engage the chain guide.

60 Tighten the bearing bracket retaining fasteners to the torque listed in this Chapter's Specifications.

✳✳ CAUTION:

Carefully rotate the crankshaft by hand through at least two full revolutions (use a socket and breaker bar on the crankshaft pulley center bolt). If you feel any resistance, STOP! There is something wrong - most likely, valves are contacting the pistons. You must find the problem before proceeding.

61 Install the lower timing chain cover (see Steps 31 through 37), then the upper timing chain cover (see Steps 7 through 10).

62 The remainder of installation is the reverse of removal.

Balance shaft timing chain and tensioner

Removal

63 Remove the camshaft timing chain covers, oil pump chain, timing chain and tensioner as previously described in Steps 1 through 48.

64 With the engine set at TDC, unscrew the balance shaft tensioner from the side of the cylinder block.

65 Remove the chain guide retaining pins, the chain guides from each side of the chain and the balance shaft chain.

Installation

▶ **Refer to illustrations 6.66 and 6.67**

✳✳ CAUTION:

Before starting the engine, carefully rotate the crankshaft by hand through at least two full revolutions (use a socket and breaker bar on the crankshaft pulley center bolt). If you feel any resistance, STOP! There is something wrong - most likely, valves are contacting the pistons. You must find the problem before proceeding. Check your work and see if any updated repair information is available.

66 Rotate the intermediate shaft sprocket and intake side balance shaft and align the timing marks on the gears (see illustration).

➡ **Note: The timing marks will only align every seven rotations.**

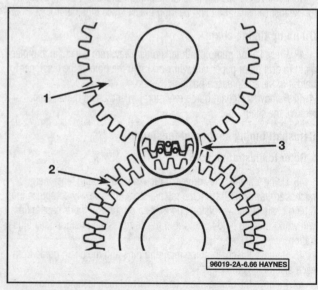

6.66 Intermediate shaft sprocket alignment details

1	Intake side balance shaft	3	Timing marks
2	Intermediate shaft sprocket		

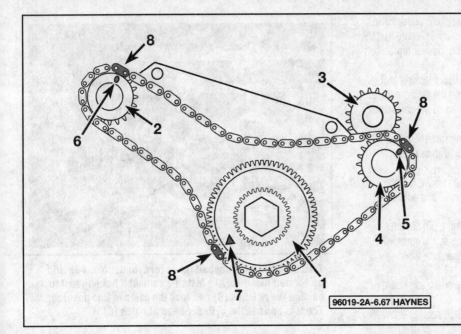

6.67 Balance shaft timing chain alignment details

1   Crankshaft sprocket
2   Exhaust side balance shaft
3   Intake side balance shaft
4   Intermediate sprocket
5   Intermediate sprocket timing mark
6   Exhaust side balance shaft timing mark
7   Crankshaft sprocket timing mark
8   Colored links

96019-2A-6.67 HAYNES

67 Loop the timing chain around the intermediate shaft sprocket and align one of the colored links of the chain with the mark on the intermediate shaft sprocket. Place the timing chain over the exhaust side balance shaft and crankshaft, then align the colored link with the mark on the exhaust side balance shaft sprocket and crankshaft (see illustration).

→ **Note: There are three bright or colored links equally spaced on the timing chain.**

68 Install the tensioner side chain guide, then the lower tensioner guide and upper chain guide and pins. Tighten the retaining pins to the torque listed in this Chapter's Specifications.

69 Apply thread locking sealer to the tensioner, then install the tensioner and tighten it to the torque listed in this Chapter's Specifications.

70 Check that all three balance shaft timing chain marks are correctly aligned.

71 The remainder of installation is the reverse of removal.

---

7   Camshafts, roller rocker arms and lash adjusters - removal, inspection and installation

✷✷ WARNING:

Wait until the engine is completely cool before beginning this procedure.

✷✷ CAUTION:

If the battery is disconnected, several systems must be relearned before they will work properly (see Chapter 5, Section 3).

✷✷ CAUTION:

Severe engine damage will occur if you make any mistakes. Do not attempt this procedure unless you are highly experienced with this type of repair. If you are at all unsure of your abilities, be sure to consult an expert. Double-check all your work and be sure everything is correct before you attempt to start the engine.

→ **Note: The camshafts and lifters should always be thoroughly inspected before installation and camshaft endplay should always be checked prior to camshaft removal. Although the hydraulic lifters are self adjusting and require no periodic service, there is an in-vehicle procedure for checking excessively noisy hydraulic lifters.**

REMOVAL

Timing belt (BPY) engine

♦ **Refer to illustration 7.10**

1 Disconnect the cable from the negative terminal of the battery (see Chapter 5).

2 Working from above in the engine compartment, remove the engine cover (see Chapter 1, Section 7) then remove the high pressure fuel pump (see Chapter 4).

3 Remove the valve cover (see Section 4).

4 Clamp the coolant hoses off at the end of the cylinder head, then disconnect and plug the coolant hoses from the coolant tube. Remove the coolant tube retaining fastener from the heat shield and remove the tube.

5 Disconnect the electrical connector from the camshaft adjustment valve and the vacuum hose from the vacuum pump.

6 Remove the electrical harness retaining fasteners and pull the harness away from the end of the cylinder head.

7 Remove the battery and battery tray (see Chapter 5).

8 Remove the camshaft adjuster housing retaining fasteners and the housing from the cylinder head.

9   Rotate the engine in the normal direction of rotation (clockwise) until the No. 1 cylinder is located at TDC (see Section 3). Verify that the camshaft sprocket mark is aligned with the mark on the rear timing belt cover (see illustration 5.14).

10 With the camshafts and crankshaft at TDC, use a locking tool (VW # T10252 or similar homemade tool) to fit into the facing notches on both camshafts; bolt the tool to the cylinder head so the camshafts cannot rotate (see illustration).

11 Press down on the top of the chain and compress the camshaft drive chain tensioner, then insert a drill bit or thick wire to retain the tensioner in the retracted position.

12 Hold the camshaft adjuster from turning and remove the bolt securing the camshaft adjuster, then remove the chain and adjuster together.

13 Remove the exhaust camshaft sprocket, using a pin spanner wrench or similar tool to hold the sprocket in place as the sprocket retaining bolt is loosened (see illustration 5.29), then use a two-jaw puller to remove the camshaft sprocket.

14 Remove the upper rear timing belt guard fasteners and guard from the cylinder head.

15 This engine does not have individual camshaft bearing caps. All of the caps are part of one assembly called a guide frame. Remove the camshaft guide frame bolts in the reverse of the tightening sequence (see illustration 7.53).

➡ **Note: Be sure to use NEW guide bolts, as the old bolts are stretch-type fasteners that will not provide the correct torque readings if reused.**

16 Remove the guide frame, then remove the camshafts and set them aside in a clean space. Remove all traces of gasket sealing material from the guide frame and cylinder head mating surfaces.

17 Do not reinstall camshaft and valve train components unless a thorough inspection proves they are in perfect condition.

Timing chain (CCTA, CBFA) engines

18 Disconnect the cable from the negative terminal of the battery (see Chapter 5).

19 Loosen the right front wheel bolts, raise the front of the vehicle and support it securely on jackstands. Block the wheels at the opposite end and remove the right front wheel.

20 Working under the vehicle, remove the lower splash shield below the engine (see Chapter 1, Section 6).

21 Working from above in the engine compartment, remove the engine cover (see Chapter 1, Section 7).

22 Remove the right front inner fender liner (see Chapter 11).

23 Remove the ignition coils (see Chapter 5) and the spark plugs (see Chapter 1).

24 Rotate the engine in the normal direction of rotation (clockwise) until the No. 1 cylinder is located at TDC (see Section 3).

25 Remove the air charge pipe retaining fasteners, the clamps at each end and the air charge pipe.

26 Loosen the hose clamps on the lower air charge hose and remove the hose.

27 Remove the drivebelt and tensioner (see Chapter 1).

28 Remove the high pressure fuel pump (see Chapter 4).

29 Remove the ground wire fastener below the vacuum pump and the bracket retaining fastener to the left of the ground wire.

30 Disconnect the vacuum hose from the pump, plug the hose and cap the port on the vacuum pump.

7.10 At TDC, the camshaft lobes for cylinder No. 4 should be pointed like this (A) - install a camshaft holding tool to engage the notches (B) and lock the cams in this position. The tool bolts to the cylinder head at holes (C)

31 Remove the vacuum pump fasteners at the 1 o'clock, 4 o'clock and 7 o'clock positions.

➡ **Note: Do not remove the fastener at the 11 o'clock position or disassemble the vacuum pump.**

32 Remove the upper timing chain cover (see Section 6).

33 Remove the control valve and bearing bracket (see Section 6, Steps 41 and 42).

34 Make alignment marks from the camshaft timing chain to the camshaft sprockets using a permanent marker.

➡ **Note: The marks will be used for reinstallation. If the marks are removed, the lower cover, camshaft timing chain and balance shaft timing chain will have to be removed, reset and reinstalled (see Section 6).**

35 Remove the tensioner access hole plug on the left side of the lower timing cover. Working through the access hole, use a small screwdriver or pick to hold the chain tensioner ratchet arm away (UP) from the ratchet stem, then slowly compress the timing chain tensioner piston by rotating the crankshaft pulley counterclockwise until the pin (a drill bit or paper clip will work) can be inserted into the hole to hold it in the compressed position (see illustration 6.45).

36 Remove the tensioner-side guide retaining pin from the camshaft timing chain.

37 Using a small screwdriver, release the locking clip and slide the timing chain upper guide rail out and off.

➡ **Note: With the lower timing chain cover in place, the loose timing chain cannot fall off.**

38 Remove the timing chain from the camshaft sprockets.

※※ **CAUTION:**

Do not rotate the engine once the timing chain has been removed or damage to the valves (and possibly pistons) may occur.

39 Remove the crankcase ventilation (see Chapter 6).

7.44 Measure the outside diameter of each camshaft journal and the inside diameter of each bearing surface on the cylinder head to determine the oil clearance measurement

7.46 Checking camshaft endplay with a dial indicator

40 Disconnect the charge air tube from the turbocharger (see Chapter 4).

41 Disconnect the electrical connector from the camshaft position sensor.

42 Remove the cylinder head cover bolts in the reverse of the installation sequence (see illustration 7.64), then remove the camshafts and set them aside in a clean space. Remove all traces of gasket sealing material from the cylinder head cover and cylinder head mating surfaces.

➡ **Note: Be sure to use NEW cover bolts, as the old bolts are stretch-type fasteners that will not provide the correct torque readings if reused.**

INSPECTION

▶ **Refer to illustrations 7.44, 7.46, 7.47 and 7.48**

43 Check the camshaft bearing surfaces for pitting, score marks, galling and abnormal wear. If the bearing surfaces are damaged, the cylinder head and guide frame will have to be replaced.

➡ **Note: If there is scoring on either the guide frame or the camshaft saddles in the cylinder head, both the cylinder head and the guide frame must be replaced.**

44 Measure the outside diameter of each camshaft bearing journal and record your measurements (see illustration). Then measure the inside diameter of each corresponding camshaft bearing and record the measurements. Subtract each cam journal outside diameter from its respective cam bearing bore inside diameter to determine the oil clearance for each bearing. Compare the results to the specified journal-to-bearing clearance. If any of the measurements fall outside the standard specified wear limits in this Chapter, either the camshaft or the cylinder head, or both, must be replaced.

45 Check camshaft runout by placing the camshaft back into the cylinder head and set up a dial indicator on the center journal. Zero the dial indicator. Turn the camshaft slowly and note the dial indicator readings. Record your readings and compare them with the specified runout in this Chapter. If the measured runout exceeds the runout specified in

this Chapter, replace the camshaft.

46 Place the camshafts back into the cylinder head and temporarily install the cylinder head cover or guide frame. Check the camshaft endplay by placing a dial indicator with the stem in line with the camshaft and touching the snout (see illustration). Push the camshaft all the way to the rear and zero the dial indicator. Next, pry the camshaft to the front as far as possible and check the reading on the dial indicator. The distance it moves is the endplay. If it's greater than the value listed in this Chapter's Specifications, check the bearing caps/guide frame for wear. If the bearing caps or guide frame are worn, the cylinder head must be replaced.

47 Compare the camshaft lobe height by measuring each lobe with a micrometer (see illustration). Measure each of the intake lobes and record the measurements and relative positions. Then measure each of the exhaust lobes and record the measurements and relative positions also. This will let you compare all of the intake lobes to one another and all of the exhaust lobes to one another. If the difference between the lobes exceeds 0.005 inch, the camshaft should be replaced. Do not compare intake lobe heights to exhaust lobe heights as lobe lift may be different. Only compare intake lobes-to-intake lobes and exhaust lobes-to exhaust lobes for this comparison.

7.47 Measuring the camshaft lobe height with a micrometer - make sure you move the micrometer to get the highest reading (top of cam lobe)

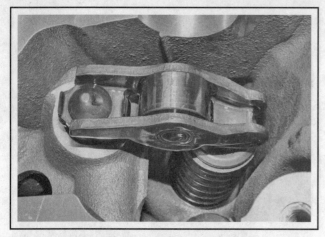

7.48 Roller rocker and lash adjuster installed in the cylinder head

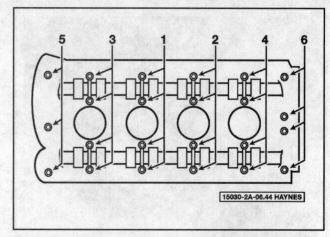

7.53 Timing belt engine (BPY) camshaft bearing guide frame bolt TIGHTENING sequence

48 Inspect the contact and sliding surfaces of each rocker arm roller for wear and scratches (see illustration).

➡ **Note: If the rocker roller is worn, it's a good idea to check the corresponding camshaft. Do not lay the lifters on their side or upside down, or air can become trapped inside and the lifter will have to be bled. The lifters can be laid on their side only if they are submerged in a pan of clean engine oil until reassembly.**

49 Check the contact surfaces of each lash adjuster.

INSTALLATION

Timing belt (BPY) engine

▶ **Refer to illustration 7.53**

50 Clean and lubricate the camshafts and the guide frame bearing surfaces with clean engine oil.

51 Install the camshafts in their original locations.

52 Before installing the guide frame, reinstall the exhaust camshaft seal, if necessary, then the exhaust camshaft timing belt sprocket.

53 Apply an even amount of sealer to the guide frame, then install the guide frame and tighten the new bolts to this Chapter's Specifications, in the order shown (see illustration).

54 Position the camshafts as shown in illustration 7.10, then install

the camshaft holding tool.

55 Reinstall the camshaft adjuster and the chain at the rear of the cylinder head, aligning the notch in the adjuster with the tab on the exhaust camshaft. Tighten the fasteners to the torque listed in this Chapter's Specifications.

➡ **Note: When engaging the chain with the intake camshaft, place it over the top of the sprocket first.**

56 Remove the locking pin from the chain tensioner.

57 Install the camshaft adjuster housing, using a new gasket, and tighten the bolts to the torque listed in this Chapter's Specifications.

58 Install the timing belt (see Section 5).

59 The remainder of installation is the reverse of removal.

> ❊❊ **CAUTION:**
>
> **Don't turn the crankshaft for 30 minutes. After 30 minutes, carefully rotate the crankshaft by hand through at least two full revolutions (use a socket and breaker bar on the crankshaft pulley center bolt). If you feel any resistance, STOP! There is something wrong - most likely valves are contacting the pistons. You must find the problem before proceeding. After two revolutions, ensure that both TDC marks still align.**

Timing chain (CCTA, CBFA) engines

▶ **Refer to illustration 7.64**

60 Clean and lubricate the camshafts and the cylinder head cover bearing surfaces with clean engine oil.

61 Make sure the roller rocker arms make proper contact with the valve stems (see illustration 7.48).

62 Rotate the crankshaft enough to make sure none of the pistons are at TDC.

63 Install the camshafts in their original location, with the recesses facing each other.

64 Apply a 1/8-inch (3 mm) bead of RTV sealant to the cylinder head cover mating surfaces, then install the cover and tighten the new bolts to this Chapter's Specifications, in the order shown (see illustration).

➡ **Note: Once the sealant is applied to the cylinder head cover, the cover must be installed within five minutes.**

65 Install the seal plug for the intake camshaft into the cylinder head and cylinder head cover.

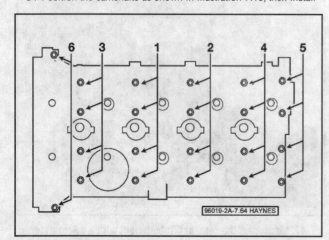

7.64 Timing chain engine (CCTA, CBFA) cylinder head cover bolt TIGHTENING sequence

➡ **Note:** The seal plug should not be recessed more than 0.12-inch (2 mm).

66 Rotate the crankshaft back to TDC, aligning the crankshaft pulley with the mark on the timing chain cover (see illustration 3.6b), place the timing chain over the camshaft sprockets and align the chain with the marks made in Step 34.

✳✳ **CAUTION:**

The marks on the chain and sprocket must align or damage will occur. If the marks do not align, see Section 6 and follow the procedure for camshaft timing chain removal and installation.

67 Install the camshaft upper guide, then remove pin holding the tensioner in the compressed position.

✳✳ **CAUTION:**

Don't rotate the crankshaft for 30 minutes. After 30 minutes, carefully rotate the crankshaft by hand through at least two full revolutions (use a socket and breaker bar on the crankshaft pulley center bolt). If you feel any resistance, STOP! There is something wrong - most likely, valves are contacting the pistons. You must find the problem before proceeding.

68 The remainder of installation is the reverse of removal.

8 Valve springs, retainers and seals - replacement

▸ **Refer to illustrations 8.4, 8.8, 8.10, 8.15a, 8.15b, 8.15c, 8.16 and 8.17**

➡ **Note:** Broken valve springs and defective valve stem seals can be replaced without removing the cylinder heads. Two special tools and a compressed air source are normally required to perform this operation, so read through this Section carefully and rent or buy the tools before beginning the job.

1   Remove the camshafts and roller rockers (see Section 7).

2   Remove the spark plug from the cylinder which has the defective component. If all of the valve stem seals are being replaced, all of the spark plugs should be removed.

3   Turn the crankshaft until the piston in the affected cylinder is at Top Dead Center (TDC) on the compression stroke (see Section 3). If you're replacing all of the valve stem seals, begin with cylinder number one and work on the valves for one cylinder at a time. Move from cylinder-to-cylinder following the firing order sequence (see this Chapter's Specifications).

4   Thread an adapter into the spark plug hole (see illustration) and connect an air hose from a compressed air source to it. Most auto parts stores can supply the air hose adapter.

➡ **Note:** Many cylinder compression gauges utilize a screw-in fitting that may work with your air hose quick-disconnect fitting.

5   Apply compressed air to the cylinder. The valves should be held in place by the air pressure.

✳✳ **WARNING:**

If the cylinder isn't exactly at TDC, air pressure may force the piston down, causing the engine to quickly rotate. DO NOT leave a wrench on the crankshaft drive sprocket bolt or you may be injured by the tool.

6   Stuff shop rags into the cylinder head holes around the valves to prevent parts and tools from falling into the engine.

7   Using a socket and a hammer, gently tap on the top of each valve spring retainer several times. This will break the bond between the valve keeper and the spring retainer and allow the keeper to separate from the valve spring retainer as the valve spring is compressed.

8   Use a valve spring compressor to compress the spring. Remove the keepers with small needle-nose pliers or a magnet (see illustration).

➡ **Note:** Several different types of tools are available for compressing the valve springs with the head in place. Be sure to purchase or rent the Import type that bolts to the top of the cylinder head. This type uses a support bar across the cylinder head for leverage as the valve spring is compressed. The lack of clearance surrounding the valve springs on these engines prohibits other types of valve spring compressors from being used.

9   Remove the valve spring and retainer.

8.4 You'll need an air hose adapter to reach down into the spark plug wells on the cylinder head - they're commonly available at auto parts stores

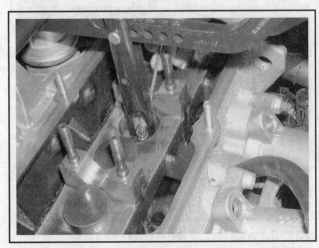

8.8 While the valve spring tool is compressing the spring, remove the keepers with a small magnet or pliers

8.10 The old valve stem seals can be removed with a pair of needle-nose pliers

8.15a Install the protective plastic sleeve over the valve end face to avoid damage to the valve seal as the seal is installed

➡ Note: If air pressure fails to retain the valve in the closed position during this operation, the valve face or seat may be damaged. If so, the cylinder head will have to be removed for repair.

8.15b Push a new valve stem seal over the valve and down to the top of the guide, then remove the plastic installation tool

10 Remove the old valve stem seals, noting differences between the intake and exhaust seals (see illustration).

11 Wrap a rubber band or tape around the top of the valve stem so the valve won't fall into the combustion chamber, then release the air pressure.

12 Inspect the valve stem for damage. Rotate the valve in the guide and check the end for eccentric movement, which would indicate that the valve is bent.

13 Move the valve up-and-down in the guide and make sure it doesn't bind. If the valve stem binds, either the valve is bent or the guide is damaged. In either case, the head will have to be removed for repair.

14 Reapply air pressure to the cylinder to retain the valve in the closed position, then remove the tape or rubber band from the valve stem.

15 Lubricate the valve stem with engine oil and install a new seal on the valve guide (see illustrations).

16 Install the valve spring and the spring retainer in position over the valve (see illustration).

8.15c Gently tap the new seal in place on the guide with a socket

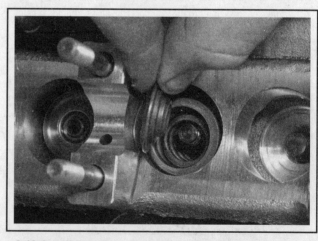

8.16 Install the valve spring and the retainer over the valve

17 Compress the valve spring and carefully position the keepers in the groove. Apply a small dab of grease to the inside of each keeper to hold it in place (see illustration).

18 Remove the pressure from the spring tool and make sure the keepers are seated.

19 Disconnect the air hose and remove the adapter from the spark plug hole.

20 Install the camshaft, lifters, timing belt and the valve cover by referring to the appropriate Sections.

21 Install the spark plug(s) and ignition coil(s).

22 Start and run the engine, then check for oil leaks and unusual sounds coming from the valve cover area.

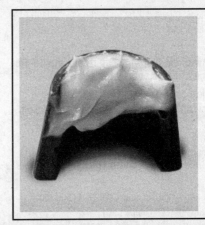

8.17 Apply a small dab of grease to each keeper as shown here before installation - it'll hold them in place on the valve stem as the spring is released

9 Cylinder head - removal and installation

⁜⁜ **WARNING:**

Wait until the engine is completely cool before beginning this procedure.

⁜⁜ **CAUTION:**

If the battery is disconnected, several systems must be relearned before they will work properly (see Chapter 5, Section 3).

⁜⁜ **CAUTION:**

Performing this procedure may cause a trouble code to be set, and require a scan tool to clear the trouble code (see Chapter 6).

REMOVAL

1 Relieve the fuel pressure (see Chapter 4), then disconnect the cable from the negative terminal of the battery (see Chapter 5).

2 Loosen the right front wheel bolts, raise the front of the vehicle and support it securely on jackstands. Block the wheels at the opposite end and remove the right front wheel.

3 Working under the vehicle, remove the lower splash shield below the engine (see Chapter 1, Section 6).

4 Working from above in the engine compartment, remove the engine cover (see Chapter 1, Section 7).

5 Remove the right front inner fender liner (see Chapter 11).

6 Drain the engine coolant (see Chapter 1). Set the engine to TDC (see Section 3).

Timing belt (BPY) engine

7 Remove the intake manifold (see Chapter 4, Section 12).

8 Remove the timing belt (see Section 5). Also remove the rear timing belt cover.

9 Remove the exhaust manifold/turbocharger assembly (see Chapter 4, Section 13).

10 Remove the valve cover (see Section 4).

11 On GTI models, remove the cowl panels (see Chapter 11).

12 Remove the front exhaust pipe/catalytic converter (see Chapter 6).

13 Remove the intercooler lower connector pipe retaining fasteners and the lower connector pipe.

14 Disconnect all electrical connectors from the turbocharger.

15 Remove the oil supply and coolant supply banjo bolts and plug the lines.

16 Remove the oil return line retaining fasteners and disconnect the return line from the turbocharger.

17 Remove the turbocharger support bracket retaining fasteners and support bracket.

18 Remove the battery and battery tray (see Chapter 5).

19 Remove coolant reservoir (see Chapter 3).

20 Clamp the coolant hoses off at the end of the cylinder head, then disconnect and plug the coolant hoses from the coolant tube.

21 Remove the coolant tube retaining fastener from the heat shield and remove the tube.

22 Disconnect the electrical connector from the camshaft adjustment valve and the vacuum hose from the vacuum pump.

23 Remove the electrical harness retaining fasteners and pull the harness away from the end of the cylinder head.

24 Disconnect the engine coolant temperature sensor (ECT) electrical connector, then remove the coolant housing retaining fasteners from the end of the cylinder head.

➡ **Note: Always replace the O-ring on the coolant housing.**

25 Working in the reverse of the sequence shown in illustration 9.72a, progressively loosen the cylinder head bolts, by half a turn at a time, until all bolts can be unscrewed by hand. Discard the bolts - new ones must be installed on reassembly.

26 Check that nothing remains connected to the cylinder head, then lift the head away from the cylinder block; seek assistance if possible, as it is heavy. If resistance is felt, carefully pry the cylinder head upward, beyond the gasket surface, at a casting protrusion.

27 Remove the gasket from the top of the block. Do not discard the gasket - it will be needed for identification purposes.

28 Before the cylinder head is reinstalled, an engine machine shop should inspect the cylinder head, valves, valve guides and other critical dimensions with precision measuring tools.

Timing chain (CCTA, CBFA) engines

▶ **Refer to illustration 9.59**

29 Remove the upper timing chain cover (see Section 6).

30 Remove the air charge pipe retaining fasteners, the clamps at each end and the air charge pipe.

31 Loosen the both hose clamps on the lower air charge hose and remove the hose.

32 Remove the front exhaust pipe/catalytic converter (see Chapter 6).

33 Remove the intercooler lower connector pipe retaining fasteners and lower connector pipe.

➡ **Note: Place a shop towel into the intercooler openings to prevent anything from getting in to the cooler.**

34 Disconnect all electrical connectors from the turbocharger.

35 Remove the oil supply and coolant supply banjo bolts and plug the lines.

36 Remove the oil return line retaining fasteners and disconnect the return line from the turbocharger.

37 Remove the turbocharger support bracket retaining fasteners and support bracket.

38 Remove the drivebelt and tensioner (see Chapter 1) and the power steering pump, if equipped (see Chapter 10).

39 Remove the high pressure fuel pump (see Chapter 4).

40 Remove the ground wire fastener below the vacuum pump and the bracket retaining fastener to the left of the ground wire.

41 Disconnect the vacuum hose from the pump, plug the hose and cap the port on the vacuum pump.

42 Remove the crankcase ventilation hose (see Chapter 6).

43 Remove the exhaust manifold heat shield retaining fasteners and shield.

44 On engine code CBFA models, disconnect the secondary air injection electrical connectors to access the coolant pipe retaining fasteners and remove the fasteners from the cylinder.

45 Disconnect the electrical connector to the intake manifold and EVAP canister.

46 Disconnect the coolant hose to the intake manifold, then remove the coolant tube-to-intake manifold retaining fasteners and tube.

47 Remove the intake manifold support bracket retaining fasteners and bracket from under the manifold.

48 Disconnect the heater hoses from the firewall.

49 Insert VW special tool #10352 or equivalent into the two holes on the control valve, then rotate the valve clockwise and pull the valve out from the end of the camshaft.

➡ **Note: The control valve has left hand threads.**

50 Remove the bearing bracket retaining fasteners, bearing bracket-to-exhaust camshaft bolt and bearing bracket (see illustration 6.42).

51 Rotate the engine in the normal direction of rotation (clockwise) until the No. 1 cylinder is located at TDC (see Section 3). Verify that the notch on the crankshaft pulley is aligned with the mark on the lower timing chain cover (see illustration 3.8b) and the marks on the camshafts are pointing upwards.

52 Make alignment marks from the camshaft timing chain to the camshaft sprockets and upper chain guide to timing chain using a permanent marker.

➡ **Note: The marks will be used for reinstallation. If the marks are removed, the lower cover, camshaft timing chain and balance shaft timing chain will have to be removed, reset and reinstalled (see Section 6).**

53 Remove the tensioner access hole plug on the left side of the lower timing cover. Working through the access hole, use a small screwdriver or pick to hold the chain tensioner ratchet arm away (UP) from the ratchet stem then slowly compress the timing chain tensioner piston by rotating the crankshaft pulley counterclockwise until the pin (a drill bit or paper clip will work) can be inserted into the hole to hold it in the compressed position (see illustration 6.45).

54 Remove the tensioner side, guide retaining pin from the camshaft timing chain.

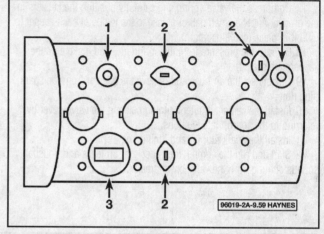

9.59 Cylinder head bolt cover details

1	Ballstud	3	Oil filler cap
2	Cylinder head bolt cover		

55 Using a small screwdriver, release the locking clip and slide the timing chain upper guide rail out and off.

➡ **Note: With the lower timing cover in place the loose timing chain cannot fall off.**

56 Remove the timing chain from the camshaft sprockets.

✳✳ CAUTION:

Do not rotate the engine once the timing chain has been removed or damage to the valves or pistons may occur.

57 Remove the ignition coils (see Chapter 5).

58 Disconnect the electrical connector from the camshaft position sensor.

59 Some of the cylinder head bolts are covered. To access the head bolts, remove the oil filler cap and unscrew the ballstuds from the cylinder head cover. Rotate the cylinder head bolt covers counterclockwise 90-degrees and remove the bolt covers (see illustration).

60 Remove the four smaller bolts at the front of the cylinder head first, then remove the cylinder head bolts in reverse order of the installation sequence (see illustration 9.72b).

61 The cylinder head assembly is heavy; you will have to attach a lifting sling or chain to the cylinder head. Position an engine hoist and connect the sling to it. Fasten the chains or slings to open bolt hole locations on the side of the cylinder head - ones that are strong enough to take the weight, but in locations that will provide good balance. Take up the slack until there is slight tension on the sling or chain. Position the chain on the hoist so it balances the cylinder head as it is lifted.

62 Carefully lift the cylinder head assembly out, making sure the timing chain guides rails are not damaged.

63 Lower the cylinder assembly down onto two blocks of wood, then remove the intake manifold and exhaust manifold/turbocharger.

✳✳ CAUTION:

The valves protrude past the bottom of the cylinder head and are easily damaged if the head is placed down on the valves.

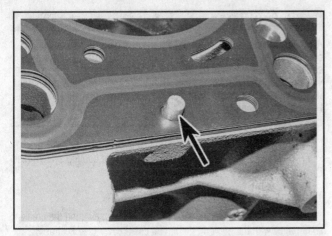

9.69a Center the gasket using the cylinder head dowel pins

9.69b Be sure the "TOP" mark faces upward

INSTALLATION

All models

▶ **Refer to illustrations 9.69a, 9.69b, 9.72a, 9.72b and 9.72c**

64 The mating faces of the cylinder head and cylinder block must be perfectly clean before installing the head. Use a hard plastic or wood scraper to remove all traces of gasket and carbon; also clean the piston crowns. Take particular care during the cleaning operations, as aluminum alloy is easily damaged. Also, make sure that the carbon is not allowed to enter the oil and water passages - this is particularly important for the lubrication system, as carbon could block the oil supply to the engine's components. Using adhesive tape and paper, seal the water, oil and bolt holes in the cylinder block.

65 Check the mating surfaces of the cylinder block and the cylinder head for nicks, deep scratches and other damage. If slight, they may be removed carefully with abrasive paper.

66 If warpage of the cylinder head gasket surface is suspected, use a straight-edge to check it for distortion. At no point should a 0.004-inch feeler gauge fit between the straightedge and the head's gasket surface.

67 Clean out the cylinder head bolt holes using a suitable tap. They must be clean and dry before installation of the head bolts.

68 It is possible for the piston crowns to strike and damage the valve heads if the camshaft is rotated with the timing belt or chain removed and the crankshaft set to TDC. For this reason, the crankshaft must be set to a position other than TDC on No. 1 cylinder before the cylinder head is reinstalled. Use a wrench and socket on the crankshaft pulley center bolt to turn the crankshaft in the opposite direction of rotation (counterclockwise), until all four pistons are positioned slightly down their bores - approximately 20-degrees before TDC.

69 Position the new head gasket on the cylinder block, engaging it with the dowel pins. Ensure that the manufacturer's "TOP" or part number markings are facing up (see illustrations).

70 With the help of an assistant, place the cylinder head centrally on the cylinder block, ensuring that the dowel pins engage with the recesses in the cylinder head. Check that the head gasket is correctly seated before allowing the full weight of the cylinder head to rest upon it.

➡ **Note: If the cylinder head had been disassembled for repair, be sure the camshafts are reinstalled on the cylinder head with recesses in the camshafts facing each other.**

71 Install the cylinder head bolts and screw them in hand tight. Use NEW cylinder head bolts, as the old bolts are stretch-type fasteners that will not provide the correct torque readings if reused.

72 Working in the sequence shown (see illustrations), tighten the

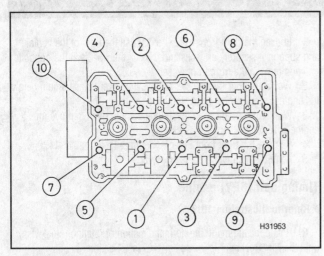

9.72a Cylinder head bolt TIGHTENING sequence - 2.0L timing belt (BPY) engines

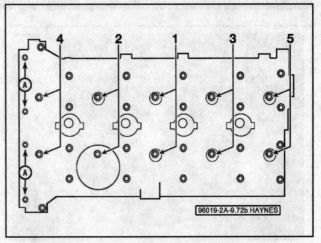

9.72b Tighten cylinder head bolts 1 through 5 (in sequence), then tighten the front bolts (A) - 2.0L timing chain (CCTA, CBFA) engines

9.72c Using an angle measurement gauge during the final stages of tightening

cylinder head bolts in stages to the torque and angle of rotation listed in this Chapter's Specifications.

➡ **Note:** It is recommended that an angle-measuring gauge be used during the final stages of the tightening, to ensure accuracy (see illustration). If a gauge is not available, use white paint to make alignment marks between the bolt head and cylinder head prior to tightening; the marks can then be used to check that the bolt has been rotated through the correct angle during tightening.

Timing belt (BPY) engine

73 Rotate the crankshaft clockwise to set the engine back at TDC. Be sure the alignment mark on the crankshaft pulley aligns with the mark on the front cover. Refer to Section 3, if necessary.

74 Install the timing belt tensioner and the camshaft sprocket on the engine if removed.

75 Install and adjust the timing belt as described in Section 5.

※ CAUTION:

After the timing belt has been installed, carefully rotate the crankshaft by hand through at least two full revolutions (use a socket and breaker bar on the crankshaft pulley center bolt). If you feel any resistance, STOP! There is something wrong - most likely, valves are contacting the pistons. You must find the problem before proceeding.

---

76 The remainder of the installation is the reverse of removal.

77 Change the engine oil and filter, and refill the cooling system (see Chapter 1). Run the engine and check for leaks.

Timing chain (CCTA, CBFA) engines

78 Rotate the crankshaft clockwise back to TDC, aligning the crankshaft pulley with the mark on the timing chain cover (see Section 3). Place the timing chain over the camshaft sprocket and align the chain with the marks made in Step 52.

※ CAUTION:

The marks on the chain and sprocket must align or damage will occur. If the marks do not align, see Section 6 and follow the procedure for camshaft timing chain removal and installation.

---

79 Install the camshaft upper guide and remove the pin holding the tensioner in the compressed position.

※ CAUTION:

Carefully rotate the crankshaft by hand through at least two full revolutions (use a socket and breaker bar on the crankshaft pulley center bolt). If you feel any resistance, STOP! There is something wrong - most likely, valves are contacting the pistons. You must find the problem before proceeding.

---

80 The remainder of installation is the reverse of removal.

81 Change the engine oil and filter, and refill the cooling system (see Chapter 1). Run the engine and check for leaks.

---

10 Crankshaft pulley - removal and installation

10.7 Crankshaft pulley retaining bolts - timing belt (BPY) engine

1 Loosen the right front wheel bolts, raise the front of the vehicle and support it securely on jackstands. Block the wheels at the opposite end and remove the right front wheel.

2 Working under the vehicle, remove the lower splash shield below the engine (see Chapter 1, Section 6).

3 Working from above in the engine compartment, remove the engine cover (see Chapter 1, Section 7).

4 Remove the right front inner fender liner (see Chapter 11).

5 Remove the drivebelts (see Chapter 1).

Timing belt (BPY) engine

▶ **Refer to illustration 10.7**

6 Rotate the engine in the normal direction of rotation (clockwise) until the No. 1 cylinder is located at TDC (see Section 3).

7 Hold the crankshaft stationary with a wrench on the center bolt, then unscrew the pulley bolts and remove the pulley from the crankshaft sprocket (see illustration).

Severe engine damage may occur or valve timing may change if the crankshaft is moved out of the TDC position when the crankshaft pulley is removed.

➡ **Note: If you remove the center bolt, obtain a new one (the manufacturer doesn't recommend re-using it).**

8   If it was removed, be sure to tighten the new crankshaft drive sprocket bolt to the torque and angle of rotation listed in this Chapter's Specifications.

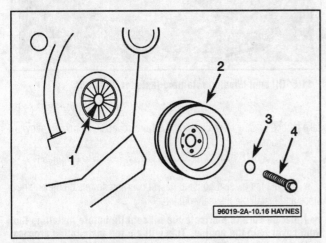

96019-2A-10.16 HAYNES

10.16 Crankshaft pulley details - timing chain (CCTA, CBFA) engines

1	Crankshaft tooth flat index	3	Crankshaft bolt O-ring
2	Crankshaft pulley	4	Crankshaft pulley bolt

9   Position the crankshaft pulley on the crankshaft drive sprocket and align the mounting holes. Note that the pulley can only go on one way.

10   Install the pulley retaining fasteners and tighten them to the torque listed in this Chapter's Specifications.

11   The remainder of installation is the reverse of removal.

Timing chain (CCTA, CBFA) engines

▶ **Refer to illustration 10.16**

12   Remove the air charge pipe retaining fasteners, the clamps at each end and the air charge pipe.

13   Loosen the both hose clamps on the lower air charge hose and remove the hose.

14   Rotate the engine in the normal direction of rotation (clockwise) until the No. 1 cylinder is located at TDC (see Section 3).

15   Prevent the crankshaft pulley from turning using VW special tool #T10355 (or equivalent) and remove the crankshaft pulley bolt.

Severe engine damage may occur or valve timing may change if the crankshaft is moved out of the TDC position when the crankshaft pulley is removed.

16   Install the crankshaft pulley to the crankshaft, making sure that both flats on the tooth contours align with the tooth contours on the end of the crankshaft (see illustration).

17   Install a new pulley retaining bolt and O-ring and tighten the bolt to the torque listed in this Chapter's Specifications.

18   The remainder of installation is the reverse of removal.

---

11 Crankshaft front oil seal and housing - replacement

TIMING BELT (BPY) ENGINE

▶ **Refer to illustrations 11.2, 11.4 and 11.5**

1   Remove the timing belt and crankshaft sprocket (see Section 5).

2   Note how far the seal is recessed in the bore, then carefully pry it out with a screwdriver or seal removal tool. Don't scratch the housing bore or damage the crankshaft in the process (if the crankshaft is damaged, the new seal will end up leaking).

➡ **Note: If a seal removal tool is unavailable, you can thread two self-tapping screws (180-degrees apart from one another) into the front seal to pry the seal out (see illustration).**

3   Clean the bore in the housing and coat the outer edge of the new seal with engine oil or multi-purpose grease. Apply multi-purpose grease to the seal lip.

11.2 If a seal removal tool is unavailable, the front seal can also be removed with self-tapping screws to pry out the seal

11.4 Lubricate the seal lip and drive the new crankshaft seal into place with a seal driver or a large socket and a hammer

11.5 Oil seal housing retaining fastener locations

4   Using a seal driver or a socket with an outside diameter slightly smaller than the outside diameter of the seal, carefully drive the new seal into place with a hammer (see illustration). Make sure it's installed squarely and driven in to the same depth as the original. If a socket isn't available, a short section of large diameter pipe will also work. Check the seal after installation to make sure the spring didn't pop out of place.

5   If the front oil seal housing needs to be removed for access to other components, remove the housing retaining fasteners and remove the housing from the engine while noting the installed position of the fasteners (see illustration). In some instances the front oil seal removal and installation is easier with the front housing removed, since the seal can be placed on a workbench and driven straight in and out of the bore with no special tools or adapters.

6   If the front of the oil pan gasket was damaged while removing the housing, use a razor blade or utility knife to cut the pan gasket off flush with front edge of the cylinder block. This part of the oil pan gasket will be replaced with RTV sealant upon installation of the cover.

7   Before installing the front cover, make sure the mating surfaces of the cover, the cylinder block and the oil pan rail are perfectly clean. Use a hard plastic or wood scraper to remove all traces of gasket material.

Take particular care when cleaning the front cover, as aluminum alloy is easily damaged.

8   Apply a 3/16-inch (5 mm) bead of RTV sealant to the oil pan flange.

9   Locate the oil seal housing gasket over the dowels on the engine block and install the oil seal housing.

➡ **Note: Be sure to lubricate the oil seal lip before installing the front cover onto the engine. This will aid the installation process and prevent dry start ups, which may damage the seal and lead to future oil leaks.**

10 Tighten the front oil seal housing bolts a little at a time to the torque listed in this Chapter's Specifications.

11 Reinstall the crankshaft sprocket and timing belt (see Section 5).

12 Run the engine and check for oil leaks at the front seal.

TIMING CHAIN (CCTA, CBFA) ENGINES

13 Remove the crankshaft pulley (see Section 10).

14 Refer to Steps 2, 3 and 4 to replace the seal.

15 Install the crankshaft pulley (see Section 10).

12 Oil pan(s) - removal and installation

REMOVAL

1   Set the parking brake and block the rear wheels.

2   Raise the front of the vehicle and support it securely on jackstands.

3   Working under the vehicle, remove the lower splash shield below the engine (see Chapter 1, Section 6).

4   Drain the engine oil (see Chapter 1).

Timing belt (BPY) engine

5   Remove the intercooler lower connector pipe retaining fasteners and lower connector pipe.

6   Remove the bolts that attach the bracket and EVAP hose to the side of the oil pan.

7   Remove the turbocharger oil return line retaining fasteners and return pipe from the side of the oil pan.

➡ **Note: Always replace the oil return pipe gasket.**

8   Remove the transaxle-to-oil pan bolts, then unscrew and remove the oil pan bolts in the reverse of the installation sequence (see illustration 12.24).

9   Remove the oil pan and the gasket if equipped. If it is stuck, tap it gently with a mallet to free it.

Timing chain (CCTA, CBFA) engines

Lower oil pan

10 Remove the lower oil pan retaining fasteners in the reverse of the installation sequence (see illustration 12.29).

11 Remove the oil pan and the gasket if equipped. If it is stuck, tap it gently with a mallet to free it.

Upper oil pan

12 Remove the air charge pipe retaining fasteners, the clamps at

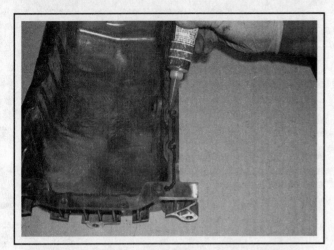

12.23 Apply a 1/8-inch (3 mm) bead of RTV sealant to the oil pan flange

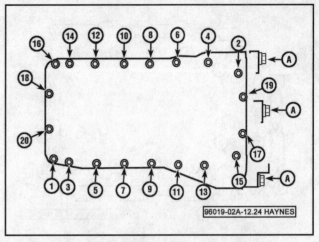

12.24 Oil pan bolt TIGHTENING sequence - (A) are the transaxle-to-oil pan bolts (timing belt [BPY] engine)

each end and the air charge pipe.

13 Loosen both hose clamps on the lower air charge hose and remove the hose.

14 Remove the lower oil pan (see Steps 10 and 11).

15 Remove the transaxle (see Chapter 7A or 7B.)

16 Remove the oil pump (see Section 13).

17 Remove the lower timing chain cover-to-oil pan bolts.

18 Using VW special tool #T10118 or equivalent, pull the oil pump drive chain tensioner spring clockwise and insert VW special tool #136 or an Allen wrench or drill bit into the guide rail hole to lock the tensioner.

19 Remove the oil pan bolts in the reverse of the installation sequence (see illustration 12.26). Remove the oil pan and the gasket if equipped. If it is stuck, tap it gently with a mallet to free it.

INSTALLATION

20 Use a scraper to remove all traces of old sealant from the block and oil pan. Clean the mating surfaces with brake system cleaner.

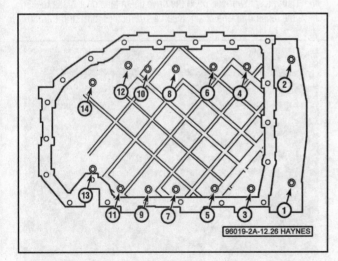

12.26 Upper oil pan bolt TIGHTENING sequence - timing chain (CCTA, CBFA) engines

21 Make sure the threaded bolt holes in the block are clean.

22 Check the oil pan flange for distortion, particularly around the bolt holes. Remove any nicks or burs as necessary.

Timing belt (BPY) engine

▶ Refer to illustrations 12.23 and 12.24

23 Apply a 1/8-inch (3 mm) bead of RTV sealant to the oil pan flange (see illustration).

➡ **Note: The oil pan must be installed within 5 minutes once the sealant has been applied.**

24 Carefully position the oil pan on the engine block. Install the oil pan-to-engine block bolts and tighten them by hand. Install the transaxle-to-oil pan bolts (see illustration). Tighten all bolts in steps, to the torque listed in this Chapter's Specifications.

Timing chain (CCTA, CBFA) engines

▶ Refer to illustrations 12.26 and 12.29

Upper oil pan

25 Apply a 1/8-inch (3 mm) bead of RTV sealant to the oil pan flange.

➡ **Note: The upper oil pan must be installed within 5 minutes once the sealant has been applied.**

26 Carefully position the oil pan on the engine block. Install the oil pan-to-engine block bolts and tighten them by hand (see illustration). Tighten all bolts in steps, to the torque listed in this Chapter's Specifications.

27 Remove the tool from the oil pump chain tensioner.

Lower oil pan

28 Apply a 1/8-inch (3 mm) bead of RTV sealant to the oil pan flange.

➡ **Note: The upper oil pan must be installed within 5 minutes once the sealant has been applied.**

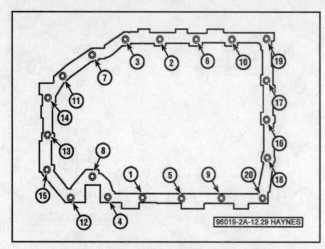

12.29 Lower oil pan bolt TIGHTENING sequence - timing chain (CCTA, CBFA) engines

29 Carefully position the oil pan on the upper pan. Install the lower oil pan-to-upper oil pan bolts and tighten them by hand (see illustration). Tighten all bolts in stages to the torque listed in this Chapter's Specifications.

All models

30 The remainder of installation is the reverse of removal.

➡ **Note: Be sure to follow the sealant manufacturer's recommendations on curing times and allow the sealant to properly cure before adding oil.**

31 Run the engine and check for oil pressure and leaks.

13 Oil pump - removal, inspection and installation

REMOVAL

Timing belt (BPY) engine

♦ **Refer to illustrations 13.3a, 13.3b, 13.4, 13.5, 13.8 and 13.9**

➡ **Note: If wear is found on the oil pump cover or oil pump rotors the oil pump and balance shaft drive must be replaced as an assembly.**

1   Set the engine to TDC on No 1 cylinder as described in Section 3.
2   Remove the oil pan as described in Section 12.
3   Using a small screwdriver, depress the tabs to release the retaining clips, and remove the chain/sprocket cover horizontally (see illustrations).
4   Use a Torx bit to loosen the oil pump drive sprocket retaining bolt approximately 1 turn (see illustration).
5   Using a screwdriver, push the drive chain tensioner blade to relieve the tension on the chain. Insert a 1/8 inch (3 mm) drill bit into

13.3a Depress the tabs . . .

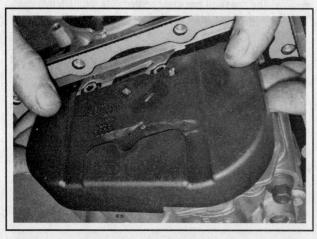

13.3b . . . and remove the chain/sprocket cover

13.4 Loosen the oil pump drive sprocket retaining bolt one turn

13.5 Locking the drive chain tensioner with a drill bit

13.8 Unbolt the drive chain tensioner fasteners

the hole in the tensioner assembly to lock the blade in this position (see illustration).

6   Remove the Torx bolt and pull the sprocket from the oil pump shaft. Disengage the sprockets from the chain.

7   Working from the outside-in, gradually and evenly loosen and remove the bolts securing the balance shaft housing and intermediate plate. Note the installed positions of the bolts - some are longer than others. Remove the balancer shaft housing and plate from the engine block, noting that the housing locates on dowels. Discard the retaining bolts; new ones must be installed. The manufacturer states that the intermediate plate must be replaced.

➡ **Note: Some models are equipped with an anti-foaming cover mounted to the balance shaft housing.**

8   Remove the retaining bolts and remove the drive chain tensioner from the balance shaft housing (see illustration).

9   If required, remove the oil pump cover retaining fasteners and cover (see illustration). Pull the inner and outer rotors from the pump.

Timing chain (CCTA, CBFA) engines

➡ **Note: Two people are required to remove the oil pump.**

10   Remove the lower oil pan (see Section 12).

11   Remove the oil baffle retaining fasteners and oil baffle.

12   This step requires the help of an assistant; remove the oil pump mounting bolts while an assistant pulls back on the oil pump chain

tensioner using VW special tool #T10118 or equivalent. Remove the oil pump from the chain.

13   Remove the oil pick-up tube retaining fastener and pick-up tube from the pump.

➡ **Note: Always replace the O-ring on the pick-up tube.**

INSPECTION

▶ **Refer to illustrations 13.17a and 13.17b**

➡ **Note: The oil pump on timing chain (CCTA, CBFA) engines is not serviceable and must be replaced as a unit if a problem is suspected. This procedure applies to timing belt (BPY) engines only.**

14   Remove the timing belt (see Section 5), then unbolt the crankshaft oil seal housing from the cylinder block (see Section 11) and remove the drive chain from the sprockets. Examine the drive chain for wear and damage.

15   It is not advisable to disassemble the balancer shafts and housing. No separate parts are available. If faulty, the complete assembly must be replaced.

16   If the oil pump has been disassembled, clean the components and check them for wear and damage. Examine the inner and outer rotors for scoring or any signs of wear/damage. If evident, replace the oil pump.

17   If the oil pump components are re-usable, install the outer and

13.9 Remove the cover from the oil pump

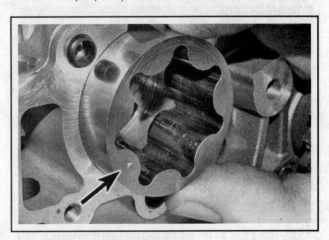

13.17a Outer rotor alignment mark

13.17b Install the inner rotor into the pump housing

inner rotors to the pump body, with the marks on the ends of the inner rotor facing inwards and the one on the outer rotor facing outwards (see illustrations). Install the pump cover and tighten all bolts to the torque listed in this Chapter's Specifications.

INSTALLATION

Timing belt (BPY) engine

▶ **Refer to illustrations 13.19, 13.22 and 13.23**

18 Install the chain tensioner assembly to the balancer shaft housing, and tighten the retaining bolts to the specified torque. Ensure the tensioner blade is in the locked position, as described in Step 5.

19 Apply a bead of sealant, approximately 5/64-inch (2.0 mm) thick, to the cylinder block side of the intermediate plate (see illustration). Take great care not to apply the sealant too thickly, as any excess may find its way into the oil galleries.

20 Position the intermediate plate over the locating dowels on the cylinder block sealing surface. On early versions, feed the drive chain through the intermediate plate.

21 Position the balancer shaft housing on the base of the cylinder block/intermediate plate, then insert the new bolts (make sure the new O-ring is installed to the appropriate bolt). Working from the inside,

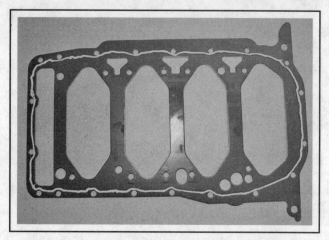

13.19 Apply sealant to the intermediate plate as shown

tighten the new bolts in stages to the torque listed in this Chapter's Specifications. Make sure the correct length bolt is installed to the correct positions.

22 Ensure the crankshaft pulley is still in the TDC position, then rotate the balancer shaft sprocket until the mark on the sprocket face is aligned with the locating hole, then insert a 13/64-inch (5.0 mm) drill bit into the hole to lock the sprocket in this position (see illustration).

23 Engage the drive chain with the balancer shaft sprocket, then install the oil pump sprocket into the chain. Install the sprocket on to the oil pump shaft, noting that the sprocket will only fit in one position - if necessary, rotate the oil pump shaft to enable the alignment of the sprocket (see illustration). Install the new sprocket retaining bolt and tighten it to the torque listed in this Chapter's Specifications.

24 Remove the balancer shaft sprocket locking tool (drill bit), and the Allen key locking the tensioner blade.

25 Install the cover over the drive sprockets, and secure it with the retaining clips.

Timing chain (CCTA, CBFA) engines

26 Install a new O-ring on the oil pick-up tube, then install the tube to the oil pump and tighten the retaining fastener to the torque listed in this Chapter's Specifications.

27 Have an assistant pull back on the oil pump chain tensioner using VW special tool #T10118 or equivalent, and install the oil pump

13.22 Use a drill bit to lock the balancer shaft sprocket in the TDC position

13.23 Oil pump sprocket locating flat

to the chain.

28 Install the oil pump retaining fasteners and tighten them to the torque listed in this Chapter's Specifications.

29 Install a new oil baffle and tighten the retaining fasteners to the torque listed in this Chapter's Specifications.

All models

30 Install the oil pan (see Section 12).

31 Add oil, start the engine and check for oil pressure and leaks.

32 Recheck the engine oil level.

---

14 Flywheel/driveplate - removal and installation

✷✷ CAUTION:

The manufacturer recommends replacing the flywheel bolts with new ones whenever they are removed.

REMOVAL

1 On manual transaxle models, remove the transaxle (see Chapter 7A) and clutch (see Chapter 8). Now is a good time to check/replace the clutch components.

2 On automatic transaxle models, remove the automatic transaxle as described in Chapter 7B.

Standard flywheel/driveplate

▶ **Refer to illustrations 14.3 and 14.5**

3 Use a center punch or paint to make alignment marks on the flywheel/driveplate and crankshaft to ensure correct alignment during reinstallation (see illustration).

4 Remove the bolts that secure the flywheel/driveplate to the crankshaft. If the crankshaft turns, wedge a screwdriver in the ring gear teeth to prevent it from turning.

5 Remove the flywheel/driveplate from the crankshaft. Since the flywheel is fairly heavy, be sure to support it while removing the last bolt. Automatic transaxle equipped vehicles have spacers on both sides of the driveplate (see illustration); keep them with the driveplate.

14.3 Mark the flywheel/driveplate and the crankshaft so they can be reassembled in the same relative positions

Dual-mass flywheel

▶ **Refer to illustrations 14.7 and 14.8**

6 On engines with the dual-mass flywheel, begin by making alignment marks between the flywheel and the crankshaft.

7 Rotate the outside of the dual-mass flywheel so that the bolts align with the holes (see illustration).

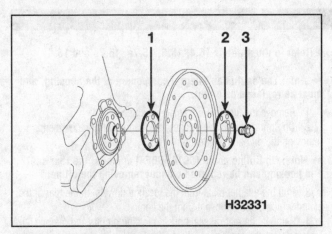

14.5 On vehicles with an automatic transaxle, there is a spacer plate on each side of the driveplate - mark each plate as it is removed so it can be installed back in the same position

1 *Backing plate*   2 *Shim*   3 *Bolt*

14.7 Align the holes with the bolts, then remove the bolts

14.8 Use a locking tool to hold the flywheel from turning

8   Use a locking tool to hold the flywheel (see illustration), then remove the bolts and the flywheel. Discard the bolts; new ones must be installed.

⁂ CAUTION:

In order not to damage the flywheel, do not use an air tool or impact driver to remove the bolts - only use hand tools.

9   The dual-mass flywheel has a needle-bearing insert that can be removed with a puller and installed with a bearing driver.

INSTALLATION

▶ **Refer to illustration 14.14**

10   Use brake system cleaner on the flywheel to remove any dust, grease and oil. Inspect the surface for cracks, rivet grooves, burned areas and score marks. Light scoring can be removed with emery cloth.

15   Rear main oil seal - replacement

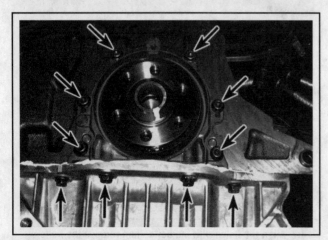

15.4   Crankshaft rear seal housing mounting bolt locations - timing belt (BPY) engine shown timing chain (CCTA, CBFA) engines similar

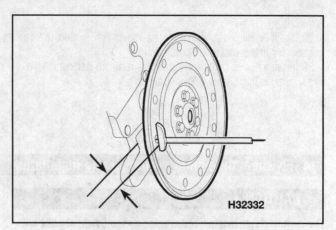

14.14 The driveplate installed height can be measured with a machinist's ruler or depth gauge, from the surface of the driveplate, through one of the holes to the engine block

Check for cracked and broken ring gear teeth. Lay the flywheel on a flat surface and use a straightedge to check for warpage.

11   Clean and inspect the mating surfaces of the flywheel/driveplate and the crankshaft. If the crankshaft rear seal is leaking, replace it before reinstalling the flywheel/driveplate.

12   Position the flywheel/driveplate and spacer (if used) against the crankshaft. Be sure to align the marks made during removal. Note that some engines have an alignment dowel or staggered bolt holes to ensure correct installation. Before installing the bolts, apply thread locking compound to the threads.

13   Use a locking tool to hold the flywheel (see illustration 14.8) from turning and tighten the bolts to the torque listed in this Chapter's Specifications. Follow a criss-cross pattern and work up to the final torque in three or four steps.

14   On vehicles equipped with an automatic transaxle, measure the installed height at three equal places around the driveplate and compare the average measurement to this Chapter's Specifications (see illustration). If the measurement is incorrect, the driveplate must be removed and shimmed to the proper height.

15   The remainder of installation is the reverse of removal.

▶ **Refer to illustrations 15.4, 15.6, 15.7a, 15.7b and 15.9**

➡ **Note: The seal is an integral component of the housing, and must be replaced as a unit.**

1   Remove the flywheel/driveplate (see Section 14).
2   On timing belt (BPY) engines, the manufacturer recommends removing the oil pan (see Section 12).

➡ **Note: On timing chain (CCTA, CBFA) engines, the rear seal and housing can be replaced without removing the oil pan.**

3   Pull the adapter plate from the locating dowels on the rear of the cylinder block, and remove it from the engine.
4   Remove the rear oil seal housing retaining bolts and remove the housing from the engine (see illustration), including the relevant oil pan bolts.
5   Before installing a new rear seal and housing, make sure the mating surfaces of the cover, the intermediate plate, the cylinder block and the oil pan rail are perfectly clean. Use a hard plastic or wood scraper to remove all traces of gasket material. Take particular care when cleaning

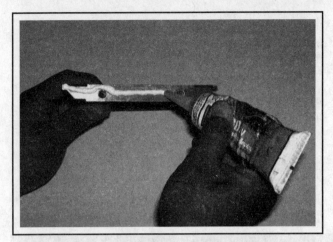

15.6 Apply a 1/8-inch (3 mm) bead of RTV sealant to the oil pan sealing surface on the rear oil seal housing

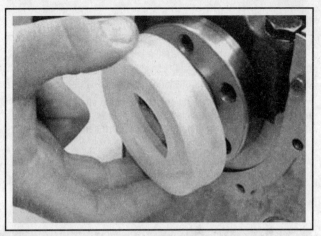

15.7a Install the seal installation tool over the end of the crankshaft . . .

the rear housing, as aluminum alloy is easily damaged.

6   Apply a 1/8-inch (3 mm) bead of RTV sealant to the new rear oil seal housing flange (see illustration).

7   The new seal is supplied with a guide sleeve installed to the center of the seal. Position the housing and seal over the end of the crankshaft and gently, evenly, push it into position (see illustrations).

➡ **Note: On timing chain (CCTA, CBFA) engines, do not apply sealant to the oil pan, as this will cause the sealant to be pushed inward into the oil pan as the rear oil seal housing is positioned on the block.**

8   Tighten the rear oil seal housing bolts evenly, in several steps to the torque listed in this Chapter's Specifications then remove the tool. Be sure to follow the sealant manufacturer's recommendations on curing times and allow the sealant to properly cure before adding oil.

9   Install the adapter plate, locating it over the oil seal housing, and onto the dowels at the back of the cylinder head (see illustration).

10 The remaining steps are the reverse of removal.

15.7b . . . and slide the oil seal and housing over the tool

15.9 Install the adapter plate, locating it as shown

16 Balance shafts - removal and installation

➡ **Note: This procedure applies to timing chain (CCTA, CBFA) engines only.**

REMOVAL

➡ **Note: The manufacturer requires the balance shaft(s) and intermediate shaft sprocket to be replaced with a new one, once it is removed from the cylinder block.**

1   Remove the oil pump chain, camshaft and balance shaft timing chains (see Section 6).

2   On the intake balance shaft, remove the water pump toothed belt drive sprocket (see Chapter 3, Section 7), then remove the intermediate sprocket retaining fastener and sprocket.

3   Remove the balance shaft(s) retaining bolt and slide the balance shaft(s) out of the cylinder block.

➡ **Note: If the balance shaft(s) will not come out by hand, use VW special puller #T10394 or equivalent.**

INSTALLATION

4   Place the new balance shaft in a freezer for approximately 30 minutes, then remove and coat the shaft with engine oil. As quickly as possible, install the balance shaft into the cylinder block.

➡ **Note: The clearance between the balance shaft and cylinder block is very tight. If the shaft will not side in, do not force it; remove the shaft and cool it again until it can be easily installed.**

5   Install the balance shaft retaining fastener and tighten it to the torque listed in this Chapter's Specifications.

6   If removed, replace the O-ring on the intermediate shaft and install the shaft to the cylinder block, aligning the pin on the sprocket shaft with the hole in the cylinder block. Install the intermediate shaft retaining fastener and tighten it to the torque listed in this Chapter's Specifications.

7   Align the timing marks of the intermediate sprocket with the mark on the intake balance shaft. Install the sprocket to the intermediate shaft, making sure the timing marks are aligned (see illustration 6.66).

8   Install the intermediate sprocket retaining fastener and tighten the fastener to the torque listed in this Chapter's Specifications.

9   Install the balance shaft, timing and oil pump chains (see Section 6).

10 The remaining steps are the reverse of removal.

17 Oil separator - removal and installation

➡ **Note: This procedure applies to timing chain (CCTA, CBFA) engines only.**

REMOVAL

1   Raise the front of the vehicle and support it securely on jackstands.

2   Working under the vehicle, remove the lower splash shield below the engine (see Chapter 1, Section 6).

3   Remove the oil separator cover retaining fasteners in the reverse of the removal sequence (see illustration 17.6).

4   Remove the separator cover and seal from the cylinder block.

INSTALLATION

▸ **Refer to illustrations 17.6**

5   Clean the mating surfaces of the cylinder block and cover, then install a new seal on to the separator cover.

6   Install the cover to the cylinder block and tighten the fasteners, in

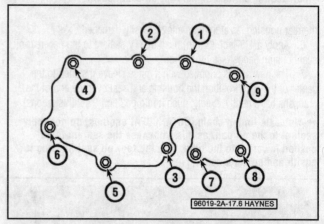

17.6 Oil separator tightening sequence - timing chain (CCTA, CBFA) engines

sequence (see illustration), to the torque listed in this Chapter's Specifications.

7   The remaining steps are the reverse of removal.

18 Engine mounts - check and replacement

1   Engine mounts seldom require attention, but broken or deteriorated mounts should be replaced immediately or the added strain placed on the driveline components may cause damage or wear.

CHECK

2   During the check, the engine must be raised slightly to remove the weight from the mounts.

3   Raise the vehicle and support it securely on jackstands, then position a jack under the engine oil pan. Place a large block of wood between the jack head and the oil pan, then carefully raise the engine just enough to take the weight off the mounts. Do not position the wood block under the drain plug.

✳✳ WARNING:

DO NOT place any part of your body under the engine when it's supported only by a jack!

4   Remove the splash shield under the engine, if equipped. Check the mounts to see if the rubber is cracked, hardened or separated from the metal plates. Sometimes the rubber will split right down the center.

5   Check for relative movement between the mount plates and the engine or frame (use a large screwdriver or pry bar to attempt to move the mounts). If movement is noted, lower the engine and tighten the mount fasteners.

REPLACEMENT

✳✳ WARNING:

The weight of the entire engine will be supported by the mounts not being removed during this procedure. Never place any part of your body directly under the engine when performing this procedure. Do not disconnect more than one mount at a time, except during engine removal.

6   Raise the vehicle and support it securely on jackstands (if not

already done). Support the engine as described in Step 3.

7 Remove the under-vehicle splash shield (see Chapter 1, Section 6).

Pendulum support mount

8 Remove the pendulum mount-to-subframe bolt, then the pendulum-to-transaxle bolts.

9 Pull the pendulum mount from the subframe.

10 Slide the pendulum mount into the subframe and install the transaxle-to-pendulum bolts first, then the pendulum-to-subframe bolt and tighten the bolts to the torque listed in this Chapter's Specifications.

11 Install the splash shield.

Driver and passenger side mounts

12 Disconnect the cable from the negative terminal of the battery and remove the battery and battery tray (see Chapter 5).

13 Raise the front of the vehicle and support it securely on jackstands. Block the wheels at the opposite end.

14 Working under the vehicle, remove the lower splash shield below the engine (see Chapter 1, Section 6).

✳ CAUTION:

Remove the heat shield over the inboard joint of the right drive-axle before raising the engine.

15 Working from above in the engine compartment, remove the engine cover (see Chapter 1, Section 7).

16 On models equipped with a noise generator, open the locking ring on the charge air pipe, pull the fuel lines from the retaining clip, then move the charge air pipe to the side.

17 Support the engine from above with an engine support fixture (see illustration 5.18), but do not lift the engine.

Passenger side (engine) mount

18 Remove the coolant reservoir (see Chapter 3).

➡ **Note: Depending on the model, it may be necessary to remove the windshield washer reservoir (see Chapter 12).**

19 Remove the support bracket retaining fasteners and bracket from the top of the engine mount.

20 With the engine and transaxle supported with a support fixture, slowly remove the engine mount-to-body fasteners.

21 Remove the engine mount-to-engine mount bracket fasteners and remove the engine mount.

22 Install the mount and the retaining fasteners, tighten the fasteners hand tight, then tighten all the fasteners to the torque listed in this Chapter's Specifications.

23 Installation is the reverse of the removal procedure.

Driver side (transaxle) mount

24 Slowly remove the transaxle mount-to-body bracket fasteners.

25 Remove the transaxle mount-to-transaxle mount bracket fasteners and remove the engine mount.

26 Install the mount and the retaining fasteners, tighten the fasteners hand tight, then tighten all the fasteners to the torque listed in this Chapter's Specifications.

27 Installation is the reverse of the removal procedure.

Specifications

General

Four-cylinder timing belt engine designation	BPY	
Four-cylinder timing chain engine designations	CCTA, CBFA	
Firing order	1-3-4-2	

FRONT OF VEHICLE

Cylinder numbering

Driveplate

Driveplate installed height	
Without intermediate plate	0.76 to 0.83 inch (19.5 to 21.1 mm)
With intermediate plate	0.74 to 0.80 inch (18.8 to 20.4 mm)

Camshafts

Endplay (maximum)	
Timing belt (BPY) engine	0.008 inch (0.20 mm)
Timing chain (CCTA, CBFA) engines	0.0067 inch (0.17 mm)

Torque specifications   Ft-lbs (unless otherwise indicated)   Nm

➡ **Note:** One foot-pound (ft-lb) of torque is equivalent to 12 inch-pounds (in-lbs) of torque. Torque values below approximately 15 foot-pounds are expressed in inch-pounds, because most foot-pound torque wrenches are not accurate at these smaller values.

Timing belt (BPY) engine

	Ft-lbs	Nm
Camshaft bearing guide bolts (in sequence - see illustration 7.53)		
Step 1	71 in-lbs	8
Step 2	Tighten an additional 90 degrees	
Cam adjuster sprocket bolt*		
Step 1	15	20
Step 2	Tighten an additional 45 degrees	
Camshaft adjuster housing bolts	88 in-lbs	10
Camshaft adjuster chain tensioner bolts	88 in-lbs	10
Camshaft sprocket bolt*		
Step 1	37	50
Step 2	Tighten an additional 180 degrees	
Crankshaft pulley bolt*		
Step 1	15	20
Step 2	Tighten an additional 90 degrees	
Crankshaft sprocket bolt*		
Step 1	66	90
Step 2	Tighten an additional 90 degrees	
Crankshaft seal retainer flange bolts		
Front	132 in-lbs	15
Rear	132 in-lbs	15
Cylinder head bolts (in sequence - see illustration 9.72a)		
Step 1	29.5	40
Step 2	Tighten an additional 90 degrees	
Step 3	Tighten an additional 90 degrees	
Exhaust manifold/turbocharger nuts	15	20
Flywheel/driveplate bolts		
Step 1	44	60
Step 2	Tighten an additional 90 degrees	

Torque specifications	Ft-lbs (unless otherwise indicated)	Nm

➡ **Note:** One foot-pound (ft-lb) of torque is equivalent to 12 inch-pounds (in-lbs) of torque. Torque values below approximately 15 foot-pounds are expressed in inch-pounds, because most foot-pound torque wrenches are not accurate at these smaller values.

Timing belt (BPY) engine (continued)

Engine mount		
Bracket bolts*		
Step 1	15	20
Step 2	Tighten an additional 90 degrees	
Mount-to-engine bracket bolts* (passenger side)		
Step 1	29.5	40
Step 2	Tighten an additional 90 degrees	
Mount-to-body bracket bolts* (passenger side)		
Step 1	44	60
Step 2	Tighten an additional 90 degrees	
Transaxle mount		
Mount-to-transaxle bracket bolts* (driver side)		
Step 1	29.5	40
Step 2	Tighten an additional 90 degrees	
Mount-to-body bracket bolts* (driver side)		
Step 1	44	60
Step 2	Tighten an additional 90 degrees	
Pendulum mount		
Mount-to-transaxle bolts*		
Step 1	29.5	40
Step 2	Tighten an additional 90 degrees	
Mount-to-subframe bolt*		
Step 1	74	100
Step 2	Tighten an additional 90 degrees	
Oil pan bolts*, in sequence (see illustration 12.24)		
Step 1, pan-to-engine block bolts	Hand tight	
Step 2, transaxle-to-pan bolts	Hand tight	
Step 3, pan-to-engine block bolts	Hand tighten again	
Step 4, transaxle-to-pan bolts	29.5	40
Step 5, pan-to-engine block bolts	132 in-lbs	15
Oil anti-foaming cover		
Cover bolt-to-balance shaft assembly (smaller)	71 in-lbs	8
Cover bolt-to-balance shaft assembly (larger)	29.5	40
Oil pump cover bolts	71 in-lbs	8
Oil pump/balance shaft assembly-to-block bolts		
Step 1	Hand tight	
Step 2	132 in-lbs	15
Step 3	Tighten an additional 90 degrees	
Oil pump sprocket bolt*		
Step 1	15	20
Step 2	Tighten an additional 90 degrees	
Oil pump chain tensioner bolt	132 in-lbs	15
Engine oil cooler fastener	18.5	25

*Replace with new bolt(s)

Torque specifications	Ft-lbs (unless otherwise indicated)	Nm

➡ **Note:** One foot-pound (ft-lb) of torque is equivalent to 12 inch-pounds (in-lbs) of torque. Torque values below approximately 15 foot-pounds are expressed in inch-pounds, because most foot-pound torque wrenches are not accurate at these smaller values.

Timing belt (BPY) engine (continued)

Engine oil filter bracket housing fastener		
Step 1	133 in-lbs	15
Step 2	Tighten an additional 90 degrees	
Timing belt cover bolts (upper and lower)	88 in-lbs	10
Timing belt tensioner nut	18.5	25
Turbocharger oil return line bolts	80 in-lbs	9
Lower idler roller bolt	26	35
Upper idler roller bolt	18.5	25
Valve cover bolts	88 in-lbs	10

Timing chain (CBFA, CCTA) engines

Accessory bracket bolts		
Step 1	15	20
Step 2	Tighten an additional 90 degrees	
Balance shaft mounting bolt	80 in-lbs	9
Balance shaft chain tensioner bolt	48	65
Bearing bracket-to-cylinder head bolts	80 in-lbs	9
Bearing bracket-to-exhaust camshaft bolt		
M6 size bolt		
Step 1	71 in-lbs	8
Step 2	Tighten an additional 90 degrees	
M8 size bolt		
Step 1	15	20
Step 2	Tighten an additional 90 degrees	
Camshaft adjustment valve bolt	80 in-lbs	9
Camshaft chain tensioner bolts	80 in-lbs	9
Crankshaft damper/pulley bolt*		
Step 1	110	150
Step 2	Tighten an additional 90 degrees	
Crankshaft rear seal retainer flange bolts		
Step 1	Hand tight	
Step 2	80 in-lbs	9
Cylinder head bolts* (in sequence - see illustration 9.72b)		
Bolt groups 1 through 5		
Step 1	29.5	40
Step 2	Tighten an additional 90 degrees	
Step 3	Tighten an additional 90 degrees	
A bolts (see illustration 9.72b)		
Step 1	71 in-lbs	8
Step 2	Tighten an additional 90 degrees	
Cylinder head cover bolts* (in sequence - see illustration 7.64)		
Step 1	Hand tight	
Step 2	71 in-lbs	8
Step 3	Tighten an additional 90 degrees	

*Replace with new bolt(s)

Torque specifications	Ft-lbs (unless otherwise indicated)	Nm

➡ **Note:** One foot-pound (ft-lb) of torque is equivalent to 12 inch-pounds (in-lbs) of torque. Torque values below approximately 15 foot-pounds are expressed in inch-pounds, because most foot-pound torque wrenches are not accurate at these smaller values.

Timing chain (CBFA, CCTA) engines (continued)

Drivebelt tensioner nut	88 in-lbs	10
Dual mass flywheel bolts		
Step 1	44	60
Step 2	Tighten an additional 90 degrees	
Driveplate bolts		
Step 1	44	60
Step 2	Tighten an additional 90 degrees	
Engine mount		
Bracket bolts*		
Step 1	15	20
Step 2	Tighten an additional 90 degrees	
Mount-to-engine bracket bolts* (passenger side)		
Step 1	29.5	40
Step 2	Tighten an additional 90 degrees	
Mount-to-body bracket bolts* (passenger side)		
Step 1	44	60
Step 2	Tighten an additional 90 degrees	
Transaxle mount*		
Mount-to-transaxle bracket bolts (driver side)		
Step 1	29.5	40
Step 2	Tighten an additional 90 degrees	
Mount-to-body bracket bolts (driver side)		
Step 1	44	60
Step 2	Tighten an additional 90 degrees	
Pendulum mount*		
Mount-to-transaxle bolts		
Step 1	29.5	40
Step 2	Tighten an additional 90 degrees	
Mount-to-subframe bolt		
Step 1	74	100
Step 2	Tighten an additional 90 degrees	
Intake camshaft control valve bolt (left-hand thread)	26	35
Lower oil pan bolts* (in sequence - see illustration 12.29)		
Step 1	Hand tight	
Step 2	71 in-lbs	8
Step 3	Tighten an additional 45 degrees	
Upper oil pan bolts* (in sequence - see illustration 12.26)		
Step 1	132 in-lbs	15
Step 2	Tighten an additional 90 degrees	
Oil baffle bolts	80 in-lbs	9
Oil dipstick bolts	80 in-lbs	9
Oil filter element	16.5	22

*Replace with new bolt(s)

Torque specifications	Ft-lbs (unless otherwise indicated)	Nm

➡ **Note:** One foot-pound (ft-lb) of torque is equivalent to 12 inch-pounds (in-lbs) of torque. Torque values below approximately 15 foot-pounds are expressed in inch-pounds, because most foot-pound torque wrenches are not accurate at these smaller values.

Timing chain (CBFA, CCTA) engines (continued)

Oil pump-to-upper oil pan bolts		
M6 size bolt	80 in-lbs	9
M8 size bolt	15	20
Oil pump chain tensioner bolt	15	20
Oil pump chain tensioner guide pin-to-cylinder		
block bolt	80 in-lbs	9
Oil separator fasteners	80 in-lbs	9
Timing chain cover bolts		
Upper cover	80 in-lbs	9
Lower cover		
Step 1	71 in-lbs	8
Step 2	Tighten an additional 45 degrees	
Timing chain guide pins	15	20
Timing chain tensioner bolts	80 in-lbs	9
Intermediate shaft sprocket bolts		
Step 1	88 in-lbs	10
Step 2	Rotate the sprocket	
	➡ **Note: No play must be felt when rotating**	
Step 3	22	30
Step 4	Tighten an additional 90 degrees	
Vacuum pump mounting bolts	80 in-lbs	9

Section

Reference to other Chapters

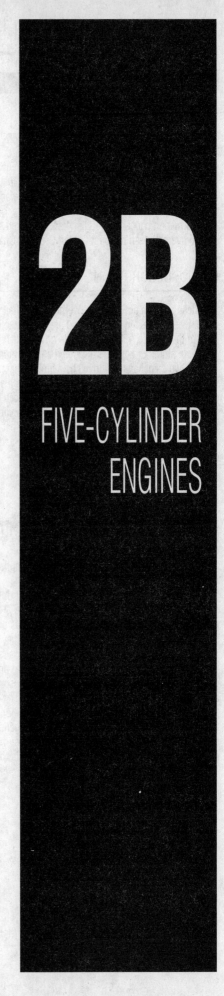

2B

FIVE-CYLINDER ENGINES

1 General information

HOW TO USE THIS CHAPTER

This Part of Chapter 2 is devoted to repair procedures possible while the engine is still installed in the vehicle. Since these procedures are based on the assumption that the engine is installed in the vehicle, if the engine has been removed from the vehicle and mounted on a stand, some of the preliminary dismantling steps outlined will not apply.

Information concerning engine/transaxle removal, replacement and engine overhaul, can be found in Part C of this Chapter.

ENGINE DESCRIPTION

These engines are a double overhead camshaft (DOHC), twenty-valve, five-cylinder, in-line type and are transversely mounted at the front of the vehicle, with the transaxle on the left-hand end. They incorporate an aluminum cylinder head and an aluminum cylinder block.

The two camshafts are driven by a timing chain, each operating ten valves via roller rocker arms. Valve clearance is maintained automatically at zero lash by hydraulic lash adjusters. Each camshaft rotates in five bearings that are line-bored directly in the cylinder head and the (bolted-on) camshaft guide frame. This means that the guide frame is not available separately from the cylinder head, and must not be interchanged with a guide frame from another engine.

These engines incorporate an aluminum camshaft chain cover, upper and lower oil pans, crankshaft front oil seal housing, rear oil seal housing and six crankshaft main caps. When working on these engines, note that Torx-type (both male and female heads) and hexagon socket (Allen head) fasteners are widely used. A good selection of sockets, with the necessary adapters, will be required, so that these can be unscrewed without damage and, on reassembly, tightened to the torque wrench settings specified.

LUBRICATION SYSTEM

The oil pump is driven via a chain from the front of the crankshaft, using the same sprocket that drives the timing chain. The pump forces oil through an externally mounted full-flow cartridge-type filter. From the filter, the oil is pumped into a main gallery in the cylinder block/crankcase, from where it is distributed to the crankshaft (main bearings) and cylinder head.

The connecting rod bearings are supplied with oil via internal drillings in the crankshaft. Each piston crown and connecting rod is cooled by a spray of oil.

The cylinder head is provided with two oil galleries, one on the intake side and one on the exhaust, to ensure constant oil supply to the camshaft bearings and lifters.

2 Repair operations possible with the engine in the vehicle

Many major repair operations can be accomplished without removing the engine from the vehicle.

Clean the engine compartment and the exterior of the engine with some type of degreaser before any work is done. It will make the job easier and help keep dirt out of the internal areas of the engine.

Depending on the components involved, it may be helpful to remove the hood to improve access to the engine as repairs are performed (refer to Chapter 11 if necessary). Cover the fenders to prevent damage to the paint. Special pads are available, but an old bedspread or blanket will also work.

If vacuum, exhaust, oil or coolant leaks develop, indicating a need for gasket or seal replacement, the repairs can generally be made with the engine in the vehicle. The intake and exhaust manifold gaskets, oil pan gaskets, front crankshaft oil seal and cylinder head gasket are all accessible with the engine in place.

Exterior engine components, such as the intake and exhaust manifolds, the lower oil pan, the water pump, the starter motor, the alternator and the fuel system components can be removed for repair with the engine in place.

Since the camshaft(s) and cylinder head can be removed without pulling the engine, valve component servicing can also be accomplished with the engine in the vehicle. Replacement of the timing chain and sprockets is also possible with the engine in the vehicle.

In extreme cases caused by a lack of necessary equipment, repair or replacement of piston rings, pistons, connecting rods and rod bearings is possible with the engine in the vehicle. However, this practice is not recommended because of the cleaning and preparation work that must be done to the components involved.

3 Top Dead Center (TDC) for number 5 piston - locating and locking

▶ Refer to illustrations 3.6 and 3.7

❄❄ **WARNING:**

Wait until the engine is completely cool before beginning this procedure.

❄❄ **CAUTION:**

If the battery is disconnected, several systems must be relearned before they will work properly (see Chapter 5, Section 3).

➡ **Note:** All timing and adjustments are set off of the number 5 cylinder.

➡ **Note:** You will need a crankshaft locking pin (VW special tool #T40069) to perform this procedure.

1 Disconnect the cable from the negative terminal of the battery (see Chapter 5).

2 Loosen the right front wheel bolts, raise the front of the vehicle and support it securely on jackstands. Block the wheels at the opposite end and remove the right front wheel.

3 Remove the under-vehicle splash shield (see Chapter 1, Section 6).

4 Working from above in the engine compartment, remove the engine cover (see Chapter 1, Section 7).

5 Remove the right front inner fender liner (see Chapter 11).

6 Using a wrench or socket on the crankshaft pulley bolt, rotate the crankshaft clockwise until the mark on the crankshaft pulley is aligned with the mark on the crankshaft front seal flange (see illustration).

➡ **Note:** This can be very difficult to see; if the marks can't be seen, you will need the crankshaft adapter tool (VW #T03003, or equivalent). Mount this tool to the crankshaft pulley and rotate the engine until the line on the tool is pointing straight down.

7 A locking pin hole is located near the lower right front corner of the engine block (on the firewall side) to provide a means of securing the engine on the no. 5 cylinder at TDC. When you locate this hole, remove the locking bolt (see illustration).

8 Using a mirror, look into the bolt hole and make sure the machined hole in the crankshaft is aligned with the threads of the locking bolt hole, then screw in the locking pin.

❄❄ **CAUTION:**

We don't recommend trying to fabricate a timing pin with a bolt because while you would be able to determine the correct bolt diameter and thread pitch, it is very difficult to determine what the length of the bolt should be. There is no way to determine the correct pin length without comparing it to a factory or aftermarket tool designed to be used with this engine. Using a bolt of the wrong length could damage the engine.

➡ **Note:** It may be necessary to rotate the crankshaft a little up or down to align the two holes.

9 Once the locking tool is correctly installed and the engine cannot be rotated, the engine is now locked at TDC for the no. 5 cylinder.

10 Before rotating the crankshaft again, make sure that the tool(s) are removed. Do not forget to install the locking bolt and tighten it securely.

11 Once no. 5 cylinder has been positioned at TDC on the compression stroke, TDC for any of the other cylinders can then be located by rotating the crankshaft clockwise 144-degrees at a time and following the firing order (see this Chapter's Specifications).

3.6 With the engine at TDC for no. 5 cylinder, the mark on the crankshaft pulley should be aligned with the mark on the crankshaft front seal flange

3.7 The TDC locking hole (A), is located behind the engine support bracket (B)

4 Valve cover - removal and installation

✳✳ WARNING:

Wait until the engine is completely cool before beginning this procedure.

✳✳ CAUTION:

If the battery is disconnected, several systems must be relearned before they will work properly (see Chapter 5, Section 3).

REMOVAL

1 Disconnect the cable from the negative battery terminal (see Chapter 5).

2 Working from above in the engine compartment, remove the engine cover (see Chapter 1, Section 7).

3 Remove the individual ignition coil assemblies from the spark plugs (see Chapter 5).

4 Remove the secondary air injection pipe and disconnect the crankcase housing ventilation hose from the corner of the cover.

5 Working progressively, unscrew the valve cover retaining fasteners in reverse order of the tightening sequence (see illustration 4.9), noting the (captive) spacer sleeve and rubber seal. Remove the cover.

6 Discard the cover gasket. This must be replaced if it is leaking or damaged.

INSTALLATION

▶ **Refer to illustration 4.9**

7 Clean the cover and cylinder head gasket faces carefully, then install a new gasket onto the valve cover, ensuring that it is located correctly by the rubber seals and spacer sleeves.

8 Install the cover to the cylinder head, ensuring as the cover is tightened that the gasket remains seated.

9 Working in sequence (see illustration), first tighten the cover bolts by hand only. Once all the bolts are hand-tight, go around once more in sequence, and tighten the bolts to the torque listed in this Chapter Specifications.

10 The remainder of installation is the reverse of removal. Run the engine and check for oil leaks.

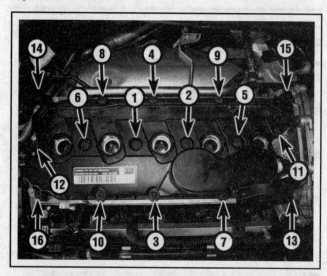

4.9 Valve cover fastener locations and tightening sequence

5 Valve timing - check and adjustment

✳✳ CAUTION:

The timing system is complex, and severe engine damage will occur if you make any mistakes. Do not attempt this procedure unless you are highly experienced with this type of repair. If you are at all unsure of your abilities, be sure to consult an expert. Double-check all your work and be sure everything is correct before you attempt to start the engine.

✳✳ CAUTION:

If the battery is disconnected, several systems must be relearned before they will work properly (see Chapter 5, Section 3).

➡ **Note: The valve timing must be adjusted any time the camshaft sprockets are loosened or removed.**

CHECK

▶ **Refer to illustration 5.10**

➡ **Note: You will need a crankshaft locking pin (VW special tool #T40069) and a camshaft holding tool (#T40070).**

1 Disconnect the cable from the negative terminal of the battery (see Chapter 5).

2 Loosen the right front wheel bolts, raise the front of the vehicle and support it securely on jackstands. Block the wheels at the opposite end and remove the right front wheel.

3 Remove the under-vehicle splash shield (see Chapter 1, Section 6).

4 Working from above in the engine compartment, remove the engine cover (see Chapter 1, Section 7).

5 Remove the right front inner fender liner (see Chapter 11).

6   Remove the valve cover (see Section 4).

7   Remove the locking bolt from the side of the engine (see illustration 3.7).

8   Using a wrench or socket on the crankshaft pulley bolt, rotate the crankshaft clockwise only.

✳✳ CAUTION:

Do not rotate the engine counterclockwise even a little.

9   Continue rotating the engine to the point that the machined hole in the crankshaft is 90-percent visible through the locking bolt hole. Use a mirror to make sure the hole has not gone past the opening.

10   Working from the top of the engine, look through the bolt holes of the camshaft guide frame and verify that the threaded holes in the camshafts align with holes of the guide frame (see illustration).

➡ **Note: If the holes in the camshafts and guide frame do not line up, rotate the crankshaft one full turn (360-degrees) and check again.**

11   Confirm that the threaded holes in the camshafts line up with the holes in the guide frame, then insert the locking pin #T40069 in the cylinder block and tighten the pin. The timing will be correct when the locking pin is installed and the threaded holes of the camshaft and camshaft guide frame are aligned.

12   If the camshafts are close but both do not fully align, install the camshaft holding tool #T40070 on to the end of the camshaft guide frame and screw the holding tool fasteners into the guide frame holes. Tighten the holding tool fasteners until the tool is flush with the flats on the camshafts. If the bolts cannot be easily tightened, use a wrench on the recess of the exhaust camshaft and rotate the exhaust camshaft slightly clockwise, taking up any slack or wear in the timing chain to align the holes. If the camshaft holding tool can now be easily installed, the timing is correct.

➡ **Note: The engine is not locked correctly in this position for any disassembly.**

13   If the camshaft holding tool cannot be easily installed, the timing is not correct and must be adjusted (see Steps 14 through 25).

ADJUSTMENT

14   Remove the upper timing chain cover (see Section 9).

15   With the engine in the timing check position (see Steps 1 through 11), remove the crankshaft locking pin and slightly rotate the crankshaft a few degrees clockwise to the no. 5 cylinder TDC position.

16   Install the camshaft holding tool #T40070 (see Step 12).

➡ **Note: It may be necessary to rotate the crankshaft slightly to help install the camshaft holding tool.**

17   Slightly rotate the crankshaft (if necessary) to the TDC position for the no. 5 cylinder and lock the crankshaft (see Section 3).

✳✳ CAUTION:

If the crankshaft is rotated more than a few degrees or is not locked in the TDC position for the no. 5 cylinder, the valves can be damaged.

18   With a screwdriver placed between the chain guide and the tensioner piston, slowly compress the timing chain tensioner piston and place a pin (a drill bit or paper clip will work) into the hole on the

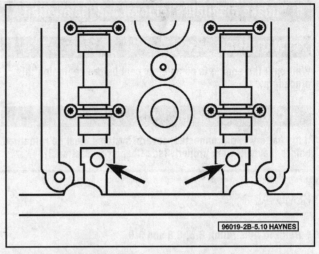

96019-2B-5.10 HAYNES

5.10 When the engine is positioned at TDC for cylinder no. 5, the threaded holes in the camshaft should align with the holes in the guide frame

tensioner body to hold it in the fully compressed position (see Section 9).

19   Remove the exhaust camshaft sprocket and intake camshaft adjuster sprocket center retaining fasteners and pull the sprockets off the ends of the camshaft until both sprockets can easily rotate on the ends of the camshafts.

20   Reinstall the sprockets and hand-tighten the new center retaining fasteners (see Section 9, if necessary); the sprockets must still be able to rotate by hand.

➡ **Note: Make sure the timing chain is properly seated against the chain guide.**

21   Remove the pin from the tensioner to release the tensioner piston and allow the piston to engage the chain guide.

22   Install a pin spanner wrench or similar tool to hold the exhaust sprocket in place (see Chapter 2A, illustration 5.29).

23   With the help of an assistant, use a spanner wrench to carefully rotate (clockwise) and hold pressure on the exhaust sprocket to keep the timing chain preloaded.

24   While the assistant holds the pressure against the chain, tighten the intake camshaft adjuster sprocket fastener to step one of the torque listed in this Chapter's Specifications, then tighten the exhaust camshaft sprocket fastener to step one of the torque listed in this Chapter's Specifications.

25   Tighten both the intake and exhaust sprocket fasteners to step two of the torque listed in this Chapter's Specifications.

26   Remove the camshaft holding tool and the crankshaft locking pin.

27   Rotate the engine by hand two full revolutions and check the timing (see Steps 1 through 11). If the timing is incorrect, repeat Steps 14 through 25 until it is correctly adjusted.

✳✳ CAUTION:

Before starting the engine, carefully rotate the crankshaft by hand through at least two full revolutions (use a socket and breaker bar on the crankshaft pulley center bolt). If you feel any resistance, STOP! There is something wrong - most likely, valves are contacting the pistons. You must find the problem before proceeding. Check your work and see if any updated repair information is available.

28   The remainder of installation is the reverse of removal.

6 Intake manifold - removal and installation

※ WARNING:

Wait until the engine is completely cool before beginning this procedure.

※ CAUTION:

If the battery is disconnected, several systems must be relearned before they will work properly (see Chapter 5, Section 3).

REMOVAL

▶ Refer to illustration 6.5, 6.8 and 6.9

1 Relieve the fuel system pressure (see Chapter 4)

2 Disconnect the cable from the negative battery terminal (see Chapter 5).

3 Working from above in the engine compartment, remove the engine cover (see Chapter 1, Section 7).

4 To disconnect the fuel supply lines (see Chapter 4) and vacuum line (if equipped), press the circlip in at the outer end of the connectors, then lift up on the connector to remove it.

5 Disconnect the electrical connectors to the fuel injectors, Camshaft Position (CMP) sensor and the EVAP canister purge valve (see illustration).

6 Unclip the wiring harness and EVAP hose clamp from the intake manifold, then open the locking ring and remove the EVAP canister purge valve.

7 Remove the throttle body (see Chapter 4) and power steering pump (see Chapter 10), if equipped.

8 Disconnect the Manifold Absolute Pressure (MAP) sensor electrical connector and remove the harness from the manifold (see illustration).

9 Remove the intake manifold support bracket fasteners (see illustration), then push the oil dipstick tube/grommet out from the molded bracket on the manifold.

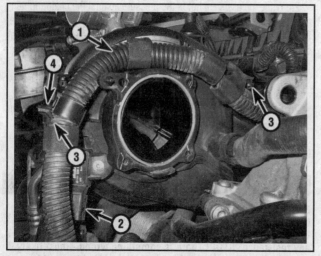

6.8 MAP sensor harness details

1	MAP sensor harness	3	Harness clips
2	MAP sensor electrical connector	4	Oil dipstick grommet/ molded bracket location

10 Remove the oil dipstick tube-to-engine block retaining fastener and rotate the tube out of the way.

11 The intake manifold is secured with nine bolts, four below and five along the top.

➡ **Note: The bolts should remain with the manifold during removal.**

Remove the bolts and pull the intake manifold away from the engine at a slight angle for clearance.

INSTALLATION

12 There are individual gaskets for each of the five ports of the intake manifold. Using new manifold gaskets, install the intake manifold. Tighten the bolts and nuts in several stages, working from the center out, to the torque listed in this Chapter's Specifications.

13 Installation is otherwise the reverse of removal.

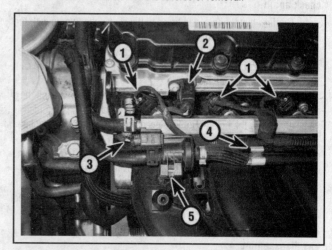

6.5 Disconnect the electrical connectors and clamp around the manifold

1	Fuel injector electrical connectors (3 of 5 shown)	3	EVAP canister purge electrical connector
2	CMP sensor electrical connector	4	Harness/hose clamp
		5	EVAP canister purge locking ring

6.9 Remove the intake manifold support bracket retaining fasteners

7 Exhaust manifold - removal, inspection and installation

⁂ WARNING:

Allow the engine to cool completely before beginning this procedure.

REMOVAL

1   Raise the vehicle and place it securely on jackstands.

2   When the engine has cooled, it will be helpful to soak the manifold heat shield retaining nuts with penetrating oil to loosen any rust. Remove the heat shield. Also apply penetrating oil to the exhaust manifold mounting fasteners.

3   Disconnect the exhaust pipe from the exhaust manifold (see Chapter 4). Remove and discard the old flange gasket.

4   Unplug the electrical connector for the oxygen sensor and remove the oxygen sensor from the exhaust manifold (see Chapter 6).

5   Remove the exhaust manifold mounting nuts, then remove the exhaust manifold and the old manifold gasket.

➡ **Note: On some models it may be necessary to remove the secondary air injection pipe to allow the manifold to be removed.**

6   Use a stud removal tool or two nuts tightened against each other to remove the old studs from the cylinder head.

INSPECTION

7   Inspect the exhaust manifold for cracks and any other obvious damage. If the manifold is cracked or damaged in any way, replace it.

8   Using a scraper, remove all traces of gasket material from the mating surfaces and inspect them for wear and cracks.

⁂ CAUTION:

When removing gasket material from any surface, especially aluminum, be very careful not to scratch or gouge the gasket surface. Any damage to the surface may cause an exhaust leak. Gasket removal solvents are available from auto parts stores and may prove helpful.

9   Using a straightedge and feeler gauge, inspect the exhaust manifold mating surface for warpage. Also check the exhaust manifold surface on the cylinder head. If the warpage on any surface exceeds the limits listed in this Chapter's Specifications, the exhaust manifold and/or cylinder head must be replaced or resurfaced at an automotive machine shop.

INSTALLATION

10 Install new exhaust studs in the cylinder head and install the manifold with a new gasket and new self-locking nuts.

➡ **Note: Coat the threads of the exhaust manifold studs with an anti-seize compound.**

Tighten the nuts in several stages, working from the center out, to the torque listed in this Chapter's Specifications.

11 The remainder of installation is the reverse of removal. Run the engine and check for exhaust leaks.

8 Crankshaft pulley - removal and installation

REMOVAL

▶ **Refer to illustration 8.4**

1   Remove the drivebelt (see Chapter 1).

8.4 Install the crankshaft pulley holding tool

2   Set the engine to TDC using the crankshaft locking tools (see Section 3).

3   The crankshaft must be held to prevent its rotation while the pulley bolts are unscrewed. A two-pin type spanner can be used to engage the hub and hold the crankshaft pulley.

⁂ CAUTION:

Use of a pry bar or similar tool can damage the crankshaft pulley.

4   Insert the holding tool into the spaces in the front face of the pulley (see illustration) to hold it in place while removing the crankshaft pulley retaining fasteners.

⁂ CAUTION:

Failure to hold the crankshaft pulley securely while removing the pulley bolts could result in engine damage. Severe engine damage may occur or valve timing may change if the crankshaft is moved out of the TDC position when the crankshaft pulley is removed.

5   Unscrew all the pulley bolts, then remove the holding tool and pulley.

INSTALLATION

6 Lightly coat the crankshaft front seal with clean engine oil, then install the crankshaft pulley.

→ **Note: If the seal shows signs of leakage, you may want to replace it before installing the crankshaft pulley (see Section 10).**

Install new crankshaft pulley bolts and hand tighten only.

7 Insert the holding tool into the pulley and tighten the crankshaft pulley bolts to the torque listed in this Chapter's Specifications.

8 Remove the crankshaft pulley holding tool and the threaded crankshaft alignment bolt from the pulley and front engine cover.

9 Remove the locking pin from the cylinder block.

10 The remainder of installation is the reverse of removal.

---

9   Upper timing chain cover, cover seal, camshaft timing chain and tensioner - removal and installation

---

✳✳ WARNING:

Wait until the engine is completely cool before beginning this procedure.

✳✳ CAUTION:

If the battery is disconnected, several systems must be relearned before they will work properly (see Chapter 5, Section 3).

UPPER TIMING CHAIN COVER

Removal

1 Remove the engine cover (see Chapter 1, Section 7).

2 Remove the battery and battery tray (see Chapter 5).

3 Loosen the right front wheel bolts, raise the front of the vehicle and support it securely on jackstands. Block the wheels at the opposite end and remove the right front wheel.

4 Remove the under-vehicle splash shield (see Chapter 1, Section 6).

5 Drain the coolant from the cooling system (see Chapter 1).

6 Remove coolant reservoir (see Chapter 3).

7 Remove the intake manifold (see Section 6).

8 Disconnect the vacuum hose from the vacuum pump.

9 Disconnect the coolant hoses from the thermostat housing (see Chapter 3).

10 Remove the coolant pipe from the thermostat housing by pulling the retaining clip up from the housing, then pull the pipe out of the housing.

11 Disconnect the engine coolant temperature switch, then remove the thermostat housing retaining fasteners. Remove the thermostat housing (see Chapter 3).

12 Working in a diagonal pattern, remove the upper timing chain cover retaining fasteners and carefully pry the cover from the cylinder head.

Installation

13 Installation is the reverse of removal, noting the following:

a) *Clean the mating surfaces of all sealant.*

→ **Note: Be careful not to gouge or use any abrasives on the mating surfaces.**

b) *Install the engine cover within four minutes of applying a 1/8-inch (3 mm) bead of RTV sealant.*

c) *Tighten the bolts a little at a time, in a diagonal pattern, to the torque listed in this Chapter's Specifications.*

d) *Install a new cover oil seal.*

e) *Check and, if necessary, adjust the valve timing as described in Section 5.*

CAMSHAFT CHAIN COVER SEAL

Removal

14 Remove the timing chain cover (see Steps 1 through 12).

→ **Note: The seal can only be removed from the back side of the camshaft chain cover.**

15 Using a socket or tube, drive the seal out of the camshaft cover from the back side.

16 Using a socket or tube, press the seal in to the cover until it is seated.

✳✳ CAUTION:

Support the cover on a flat surface when driving the cover seal in, or the housing may be damaged.

17 Installation is the reverse of removal.

CAMSHAFT TIMING CHAIN AND TENSIONER

✳✳ CAUTION:

The timing system is complex, and severe engine damage will occur if you make any mistakes. Do not attempt this procedure unless you are highly experienced with this type of repair. If you are at all unsure of your abilities, be sure to consult an expert. Double-check all your work and be sure everything is correct before you attempt to start the engine.

→ **Note: You will need VW special tools #T40069 (crankshaft locking pin) and #T40070 (camshaft holding tool) for this procedure.**

Removal

18 Remove the upper timing chain cover (see Steps 1 through 12).

19 Remove the valve cover (see Section 4).

20 Lock the crankshaft at the TDC for cylinder no. 5 (see Section 3).

21 Install the camshaft holding tool #T40070 (see Section 5).

22 With a screwdriver placed between the chain guide and the tensioner piston, slowly compress the timing chain tensioner piston and place a pin (a drill bit or paper clip will work) into the hole on the tensioner body to hold it in the fully compressed position.

23 Remove the exhaust camshaft sprocket and intake camshaft adjuster sprocket fasteners and pull the sprockets off the ends of the camshafts.

✳✳ CAUTION:

Remove the center mounting fastener on the camshaft sprockets; do not disassemble the camshaft adjuster sprocket.

24 Remove the tensioner mounting fastener, then slide the tensioner assembly, chain guide and tensioner guide off of the cylinder head dowels.

✳✳ CAUTION:

Do not remove the pin holding the tensioner piston in the compressed position.

25 Remove and discard the tensioner gasket and the strainer from the cylinder head.

26 Remove the timing chain from the housing.

➡ **Note: Mark the original direction of rotation on the chain if it is to be reused.**

Installation

27 Loop the camshaft timing chain around the double sprocket and secure the chain from falling off the sprocket.

28 Install the chain guide (left) and the tensioner guide (right) on to the cylinder head dowels.

29 Insert the tensioner strainer into the cylinder head.

30 Install the tensioner gasket and tensioner assembly on to the cylinder head dowels, then the tensioner fastener. Tighten the fastener to the torque listed in this Chapter's Specifications.

31 Install the intake camshaft adjuster sprocket to the intake camshaft, hand tightening the sprocket mounting fastener.

32 Loop the timing chain over the sprocket, then the exhaust camshaft sprocket. Install the exhaust sprocket and chain to the exhaust camshaft, hand tightening the sprocket mounting fastener.

33 Remove the pin from the tensioner and release the piston to engage the chain guide.

34 Adjust the valve timing (see Section 5).

35 The remainder of installation is the reverse of removal.

10 Crankshaft front oil seal flange - replacement

▶ **Refer to illustration 10.4**

➡ **Note: The front seal is integrated into the front sealing flange and cannot be replaced separately; if the front oil seal is leaking, the sealing flange must be replaced.**

1 Remove the drivebelt and tensioner (see Chapter 1).

2 Set the engine to TDC using the crankshaft locking tools (see Section 3).

3 Remove the crankshaft pulley (see Section 8).

4 Remove the sealing flange retaining fasteners (see illustration).

5 Starting at the alignment holes, work around the entire flange, then carefully pry the sealing flange from the cylinder block.

✳✳ CAUTION:

If the sealing flange is bent or distorted it must be replaced.

6 Remove the sealing flange from the engine.

7 Before installing the new sealing flange, make sure the mating surfaces of the cylinder block are perfectly clean. Use a hard plastic or wood scraper to remove all traces of gasket material. Take particular care when cleaning as aluminum alloy is easily damaged.

8 Slide VW special tool #T40069 into the crankshaft seal and allow the tool to remain in the seal during installation.

9 Apply a 1/8-inch (3 mm) bead of RTV sealant into the groove of the sealing flange.

10 Align special tool #T40069 over the end of the crankshaft, the carefully position the sealing flange on the engine block and install the

10.4 Sealing flange retaining fasteners

timing cover retaining fasteners loosely.

11 Working in a diagonal sequence, first tighten the flange retainers by hand only. Once all the fasteners are hand-tight, tighten the retaining fasteners in a diagonal sequence to the torque listed in this Chapter Specifications.

12 Rotate special tool #T40069 while pulling it off of the crankshaft, making sure the oil seal is not damaged.

13 The remainder of installation is the reverse of removal. Run the engine and check for leaks.

11 Camshafts, roller rocker arms and lash adjusters - removal, inspection and installation

※ WARNING:

Wait until the engine is completely cool before beginning this procedure.

※ CAUTION:

If the battery is disconnected, several systems must be re-learned before they will work properly (see Chapter 5, Section 3).

※ CAUTION:

Severe engine damage will occur if you make any mistakes. Do not attempt this procedure unless you are highly experienced with this type of repair. If you are at all unsure of your abilities, be sure to consult an expert. Double-check all your work and be sure everything is correct before you attempt to start the engine.

➡ Note: The camshafts and lifters should always be thoroughly inspected before installation and camshaft endplay should always be checked prior to camshaft removal. Although the hydraulic lifters are self-adjusting and require no periodic service, there is an in-vehicle procedure for checking excessively noisy hydraulic lifters.

REMOVAL

1   Lock the camshafts in the timing adjustment position as described in Section 5.

2   Remove the camshaft sprocket and the timing chain as described in Section 9.

➡ Note: When installing the camshafts, the lobes and the slots in the ends of the camshafts must be in the same positions.

3   This engine does not have individual camshaft bearing caps. All of the caps are part of one assembly called a camshaft guide frame. Working in the reverse of the tightening sequence (see illustration 11.17) loosen the camshaft guide frame bolts progressively by half a turn at a time. Work only as described, to gradually release pressure of the valve springs evenly on the guide frame.

➡ Note: Use NEW guide bolts, as the old bolts are stretch-type fasteners that will not provide the correct torque readings if reused.

4   Remove the guide frame, then remove the camshafts and set them aside in a clean space. Remove all traces of gasket sealing material from the guide frame and cylinder head mating surfaces.

5   Do not reinstall camshaft and valve train components unless a thorough inspection proves they are in perfect condition.

INSPECTION

▸ Refer to illustrations 11.9 and 11.10

6   Visually check the camshaft bearing surfaces for pitting, score marks, galling and abnormal wear. If the bearing surfaces are damaged, the cylinder head and guide frame will have to be replaced.

➡ Note: If there is scoring on either the guide frame or the camshaft saddles in the cylinder head, both the cylinder head and the guide frame must be replaced.

7   Measure the outside diameter of each camshaft bearing journal and record your measurements. Measure the inside diameter of each corresponding camshaft bearing and record the measurements. No manufacturer's specifications were available at the time of writing; if the camshafts, camshaft bearing surfaces, lifters or the cylinder head bores are excessively worn, new camshafts, new lifters and/or new camshaft guide frame and cylinder head may be required.

8   To check camshaft runout, place the camshaft back into the cylinder head and set up a dial indicator on the center journal. Zero the dial indicator. Turn the camshaft slowly and note the dial indicator readings. Record your readings and compare them with the specified runout in this Chapter. If the measured runout exceeds the runout specified in this Chapter, replace the camshaft.

9   Place the camshafts back into the cylinder head and temporarily install the cylinder head cover or guide frame. Check the camshaft endplay by placing a dial indicator with the stem in line with the camshaft and touching the snout (see illustration). Push the camshaft all the way to the rear and zero the dial indicator. Next, pry the camshaft to the front as far as possible and check the reading on the dial indicator. The distance it moves is the endplay. If it's greater than the value listed in this

11.9 Checking camshaft endplay with a dial indicator

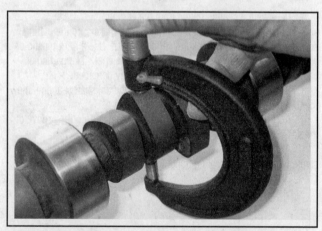

11.10 Measuring the camshaft lobe height with a micrometer - make sure you move the micrometer to get the highest reading (top of cam lobe)

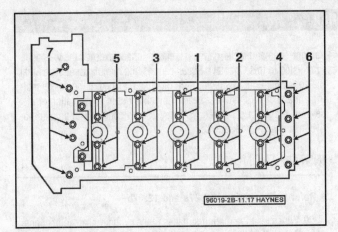

11.17 Camshaft guide frame tightening sequence

11.18 The tapered edge of the sealing plug should be flush with the cylinder head and camshaft guide frame

Chapter's Specifications, check the guide frame for wear. If the guide frame is worn, the cylinder head must be replaced.

10 Compare the camshaft lobe height by measuring each lobe with a micrometer (see illustration). Measure each of the intake lobes and record the measurements and relative positions. Measure each of the exhaust lobes and record the measurements and relative positions. This will let you compare all of the intake lobes to one another and all of the exhaust lobes to one another. If the difference between the lobes exceeds 0.005 inch, the camshaft should be replaced. Do not compare intake lobe heights to exhaust lobe heights as lobe lift may be different. Only compare intake lobes-to-intake lobes and exhaust lobes-to exhaust lobes for this comparison.

11 Inspect the contact and sliding surfaces of each lash adjuster and rocker arm roller for wear and scratches.

➡ **Note: If the rocker roller is worn, it's a good idea to check the corresponding camshaft. Do not lay the lash adjusters on their side or upside down, or air can become trapped inside and the lash adjuster will have to be bled. The adjusters can be laid on their side only if they are submerged in a pan of clean engine oil until reassembly.**

12 Check that each lash adjuster moves up and down freely in its bore on the cylinder head. If it doesn't, the valve may stick open and cause internal engine damage.

INSTALLATION

▶ **Refer to illustrations 11.17 and 11.18**

13 Lubricate the lash adjusters and roller rocker arms and install them in their original locations in the cylinder head.

14 Place the guide frame upside down on a flat surface, then clean and lubricate the guide frame bearing surfaces with clean engine oil. Clean and lubricate the camshafts with clean engine oil, then place the camshafts into the guide frame with the recesses of the camshaft facing each other. The intake camshaft sensor wheel should be pointing towards the camshaft sensor and the bearing journals of the camshafts should be seated squarely in the guide frame journals.

✳✳ **CAUTION:**

There are two sealing rings on the end of the intake camshaft; the open end of the rings must face up or down. If the rings face side to side, oil will leak past the rings.

15 With the help of an assistant, turn the guide frame over while keeping the camshafts from falling out. Rotate the camshafts until the threaded holes in the camshafts are aligned with the threaded holes in the camshaft guide frame (see illustration 5.10). Install camshaft holding tool #T40070 and tighten the holding tool to 15 ft-lbs (20 Nm).

16 Turn the guide frame back over and apply a 1/8-inch (3 mm) bead of RTV sealant around the spark plug holes and the outside edges of the guide frame, then immediately install the guide frame assembly to the cylinder head.

17 Install the new guide frame bolts and tighten them in the proper sequence (see illustration) to this Chapter's Specifications, wiping off any extra sealant.

➡ **Note: Follow the sealant manufacturer's recommendations on curing times and allow the sealant to properly cure before adding oil.**

18 Using a socket or pipe, carefully press the sealing plugs in to the end of the cylinder head and camshaft guide frame until the tapered edge of the plug is flush with the cylinder head and camshaft guide (see illustration).

19 Allow the engine to sit for 30 minutes before proceeding.

✳✳ **CAUTION:**

Do not turn the crankshaft during this time.

20 Adjust the valve timing (see Section 5), then remove the camshaft holding tool and the crankshaft locking pin.

✳✳ **CAUTION:**

Before starting the engine, carefully rotate the crankshaft by hand through at least two full revolutions (use a socket and breaker bar on the crankshaft pulley center bolt). If you feel any resistance, STOP! There is something wrong - most likely, valves are contacting the pistons. You must find the problem before proceeding. Check your work and see if any updated repair information is available.

21 Refill the cooling system (see Chapter 1).
22 The remainder of installation is the reverse of removal.

➡ **Note: Rotate the engine through two complete revolutions and ensure that both TDC marks still align.**

12 Cylinder head - removal, inspection and installation

☆☆ WARNING:

Wait until the engine is completely cool before beginning this procedure.

☆☆ CAUTION:

If the battery is disconnected, several systems must be relearned before they will work properly (see Chapter 5, Section 3).

REMOVAL

1 Relieve the fuel system pressure (see Chapter 4).

2 Remove the battery and battery tray (see Chapter 5).

3 Raise the front of the vehicle and support it securely on jackstands. Block the wheels at the opposite end.

4 Remove the under-vehicle splash shield (see Chapter 1, Section 6).

5 Remove the engine cover (see Chapter 1, Section 7).

6 Remove the alternator and ignition coils (see Chapter 5). Remove the power steering pump (see Chapter 10), if equipped.

7 Drain the cooling system (see Chapter 1).

8 Remove the coolant expansion tank (see Chapter 3).

9 Remove the valve cover (see Section 4).

10 Remove the intake manifold (see Section 6) and reinstall the support strap to aid in removing and installing the cylinder head.

11 Remove the camshaft chain cover (see Section 9).

12 Lock the camshafts (see Section 5), then remove the camshaft sprockets from the camshafts (see Section 11) and allow the camshaft timing chain to lie to the side.

13 Disconnect the exhaust pipe from the exhaust manifold.

14 Disconnect the oxygen sensor electrical connectors and move any harness retainers.

15 Remove the cylinder head bolts in the reverse order of installation (see illustration 12.27a).

➡ **Note: If the cylinder head bolt closest to the camshaft holding tool was not able to be removed, loosen the camshaft holding tool one turn and slide the tool away from the bolt. Remove the bolt and retighten the holding tool.**

INSPECTION

16 The mating faces of the cylinder head and cylinder block must be perfectly clean before replacing the head. Use spray-on gasket remover and a hard plastic or wood scraper to remove all traces of gasket and carbon.

17 Take particular care during the cleaning operations, as aluminum alloy is easily damaged. Also, make sure that the carbon is not allowed to enter the oil and water passages - this is particularly important for the lubrication system, as carbon could block the oil supply to the engine's components.

18 To prevent carbon entering the gap between the pistons and bores, smear a little grease in the gap. After cleaning each piston, use a small brush to remove all traces of grease and carbon from the gap, then wipe away the remainder with a clean rag.

19 Check the mating surfaces of the cylinder block and the cylinder head for nicks, deep scratches and other damage. Also check the cylinder head and cylinder block mating surfaces with a precision straight-edge and feeler gauges. If either surface exceeds the warpage limit listed in this Chapter's Specifications, the manufacturer states that the component out of specification must be replaced. If the gasket mating surface of your cylinder head or block is out of specification or is severely nicked or scratched, you may want to consult with an automotive machine shop for advice.

INSTALLATION

➡ **Refer to illustrations 12.27a and 12.27b**

20 Wipe clean the mating surfaces of the cylinder head and cylinder block. Install the alignment dowels into their original locations.

21 The cylinder head bolt holes must be free from oil or water. This is most important, because a hydraulic lock in a cylinder head bolt hole can cause a fracture of the block casting when the bolt is tightened. Note the location of the cylinder head alignment dowels in the block.

22 Apply a 1/8-inch (3 mm) bead of RTV sealant to the clean, sides of the timing chain area of the cylinder block.

➡ **Note: Follow the sealant manufacturer's recommendations on curing times and allow the sealant to properly cure before adding oil.**

23 The cylinder head gasket is easily damaged - only remove it from its packaging just before you're ready to install the gasket. Position a new gasket on the cylinder block surface over the alignment dowels, with the "TOP" mark is facing up.

24 Apply a 1/8-inch (3 mm) bead of RTV sealant to the top of the head gasket, at the rear side of the timing chain area (viewed from the driver's side fender looking at the gasket, on the right side, approximately two inches long). Once the sealant is applied to the cylinder head gasket, the cylinder head must be installed within five minutes.

25 As the cylinder head is such a heavy and awkward assembly to install, an assistant should be used. Install the cylinder head, guiding the camshaft chain through the opening at the end of the cylinder head.

26 Coat the new cylinder bolt threads with engine oil - do not apply more than a light film of oil. Install the new cylinder head bolts and screw them in hand-tight.

➡ **Note: New cylinder head bolts must be used.**

27 Working progressively and in the sequence shown (see illustration), tighten all the bolts to the Step 1 torque setting listed in this Chapter's Specifications. There are three tightening stages, the final two

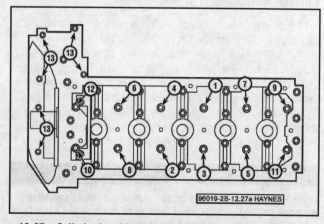

12.27a Cylinder head bolt tightening sequence

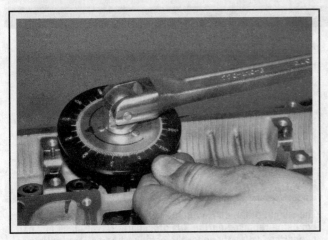

12.27b You can use a torque angle gauge, or you can carefully note the starting and stopping points of the wrench handle

using the angle torque method (see illustration).

28 Allow the engine to sit for 30 minutes.

※※ CAUTION:

Do not turn the crankshaft during this time.

29 Adjust the valve timing (see Section 5) and remove the camshaft holding tool and the crankshaft locking pin.

※※ CAUTION:

Before starting the engine, carefully rotate the crankshaft by hand through at least two full revolutions (use a socket and breaker bar on the crankshaft pulley center bolt). If you feel any resistance, STOP! There is something wrong - most likely, valves are contacting the pistons. You must find the problem before proceeding. Check your work and see if any updated repair information is available.

30 Replacement of the other components removed is a reversal of removal.

31 Change the engine oil and filter and refill the cooling system (see Chapter 1).

13 Oil pan - removal and installation

➡ **Note: This engine is equipped with a two-piece oil pan. The upper pan can only be removed with the engine out of the vehicle. Therefore the following procedure pertains only to removal and installation of the lower oil pan in the vehicle. Refer to Chapter 2C for removal and installation of the upper oil pan.**

REMOVAL

1 Set the parking brake and block the rear wheels.

2 Raise the front of the vehicle and support it securely on jackstands.

3 Remove the under-vehicle splash shield (see Chapter 1, Section 6).

4 Drain the engine oil (see Chapter 1).

5 Remove the lower oil pan retaining fasteners in a diagonal sequence.

6 Remove the oil pan, and the gasket if equipped. If it is stuck, tap it gently with a mallet to free it.

INSTALLATION

7 Use a scraper to remove all traces of old sealant from the upper oil pan and lower oil pan. Clean the mating surfaces with brake system cleaner.

➡ **Note: Use RTV sealant to seal the oil pan-to-cylinder block mating surface.**

8 Make sure the threaded bolt holes in the block are clean.

9 Check the oil pan flange for distortion, particularly around the bolt holes. Remove any nicks or burrs as necessary.

10 Apply a 1/8-inch (3 mm) bead of RTV sealant to the oil pan flange.

➡ **Note: The oil pan must be installed within 5 minutes once the sealant has been applied.**

11 Carefully position the lower oil pan on the upper pan. Install the lower oil pan-to-upper oil pan bolts and tighten them by hand. Tighten all bolts in a diagonal sequence, to the torque listed in this Chapter's Specifications.

12 The remainder of installation is the reverse of removal.

➡ **Note: Follow the sealant manufacturer's recommendations on curing times and allow the sealant to properly cure before adding oil.**

13 Run the engine and check for oil pressure and leaks.

14 Rear main oil seal - replacement

1 Remove the transaxle (see Chapter 7A or 7B).

2 Remove the flywheel/driveplate (see Section 15).

3 Pry the oil seal from the rear of the control housing. Be careful not to nick or scratch the crankshaft or the housing. Note how far it's recessed into the bore before removal, so the new seal can be installed to the same depth. Thoroughly clean the seal bore in the block with a shop towel. Remove all traces of oil and dirt.

4 Lubricate the outside diameter of the seal and install the seal over the end of the crankshaft. Make sure the lip of the seal points toward the engine. Preferably, a seal installation tool (available at some auto parts store) is needed to press the new seal back into place. If the proper seal installation tool is unavailable, use a large socket, section of pipe or a blunt tool and carefully drive the new seal squarely into the seal bore and flush with the edge of the engine block.

5 Install the flywheel/driveplate (see Chapter 2A).

6 Install the transaxle (see Chapter 7A or 7B).

15 Engine mounts - check and replacement

1 Engine mounts seldom require attention, but broken or deteriorated mounts should be replaced immediately or the added strain placed on the driveline components may cause damage or wear.

CHECK

2 During the check, the engine must be raised slightly to remove the weight from the mounts.

3 Raise the vehicle and support it securely on jackstands, then position a jack under the engine oil pan. Place a large wood block between the jack head and the oil pan to prevent oil pan damage, then carefully raise the engine just enough to take the weight off the mounts.

✳✳ WARNING:

DO NOT place any part of your body under the engine when it's supported only by a jack!

4 Check the mounts to see if the rubber is cracked, hardened or separated from the bushing in the center of the mount.

5 Check for relative movement between the mount and the engine or chassis. Use a large screwdriver or prybar to attempt to move the mounts. If movement is noted, lower the engine and tighten the mount fasteners.

REPLACEMENT

✳✳ CAUTION:

If the battery is disconnected, several systems must be relearned before they will work properly (see Chapter 5, Section 3).

➡ Note: Refer to Chapter 7B for information on the transaxle mounts.

6 Raise the vehicle and support it securely on jackstands (if not already done). Support the engine as described in Step 3.

7 Remove the under-vehicle splash shield (see Chapter 1, Section 6).

Pendulum support mount

▶ Refer to illustration 15.8

8 Remove the pendulum mount-to-subframe bolt, then the pendulum-to-transaxle bolts and bracket (see illustration).

9 Pull the pendulum mount from the subframe and remove the pendulum support.

10 Slide the pendulum mount into the subframe and install the bracket and transaxle-to-pendulum bolts. Install the pendulum-to-subframe bolt and tighten the bolts to the torque listed in this Chapter's Specifications.

11 Install the splash shield.

Passenger side (engine) mount

▶ Refer to illustration 15.15

✳✳ WARNING:

The weight of the entire engine will be supported by the mounts not being removed during this procedure. Never place any part of your body directly under the engine when performing this procedure. Do not disconnect more than one mount at a time, except during engine removal.

✳✳ CAUTION:

Remove the heat shield over the inboard joint of the right drive-axle before raising the engine.

12 Working from above in the engine compartment, remove the engine cover (see Chapter 1, Section 7).

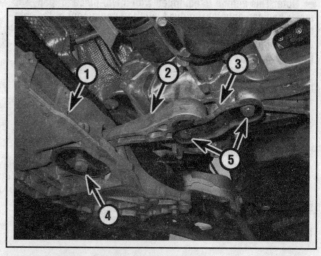

15.8 Pendulum support mount details

1 *Subframe*
2 *Pendulum support mount*
3 *Pendulum bracket*
4 *Pendulum mount-to-subframe retaining fastener*
5 *Pendulum bracket-to-transaxle retaining fasteners*

13 Remove the coolant reservoir (see Chapter 3).

➡ **Note: Depending on the model it may be necessary to remove the windshield washer reservoir (see Chapter 12).**

14 Place a floor jack under the engine with a wood block between the jack head and oil pan and raise the engine slightly to relieve the weight from the mounts.

15 Remove the fasteners and detach the support bracket and mount from the body and engine (see illustration).

16 Installation is the reverse of removal. Use thread-locking compound on the mount bolts and tighten them securely.

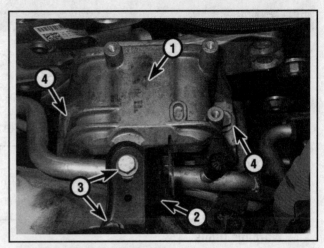

15.15 Engine mount details

1   Engine mount
2   Support bracket
3   Support retaining fasteners
4   Engine mount-to-bracket retaining fasteners

Specifications

General

Engine type	Five-cylinder, in-line, DOHC
Firing order	1-2-4-5-3
Compression pressure	See Chapter 2C
Oil pressure	See Chapter 2C

FRONT OF VEHICLE

Cylinder locations

Camshafts

Runout (maximum)	0.0014 inch (0.035 mm)
Endplay (maximum)	0.0067 inch (0.17 mm)

Warpage limits

Cylinder head gasket surfaces (head, manifolds and block)	0.002 inch (0.05 mm)

Torque specifications

	Ft-lbs (unless otherwise indicated)	Nm

➡ **Note:** One foot-pound (ft-lb) of torque is equivalent to 12 inch-pounds (in-lbs) of torque. Torque values below approximately 15 foot-pounds are expressed in inch-pounds, because most foot-pound torque wrenches are not accurate at these smaller values.

	Ft-lbs (unless otherwise indicated)	Nm
Camshaft chain cover fasteners	89 in-lbs	10
Camshaft guide frame (in sequence - see illustration 11.17)		
Step 1	Hand tighten all bolts	
Step 2	71 in-lbs	8
Step 3	Tighten an additional 90 degrees	
Exhaust camshaft sprocket bolt		
Step 1	44	60
Step 2	Tighten an additional 90 degrees	
Intake camshaft adjuster bolt		
Step 1	44	60
Step 2	Tighten an additional 90 degrees	
Crankshaft pulley bolts*		
Step 1	37	50
Step 2	Tighten an additional 90 degrees	
Cylinder head bolts (in sequence - see illustration 12.27a)		
Step 1	30	40
Step 2	Tighten an additional 90 degrees	
Step 3	Tighten an additional 90 degrees	
Valve cover bolts	89 in-lbs	10
Exhaust manifold nuts*	17	23
Engine mount*		
Bracket bolts		
Step 1	15	20
Step 2	Tighten an additional 90 degrees	
Mount-to-engine bracket bolts (passenger side)		
Step 1	30	40
Step 2	Tighten an additional 90 degrees	

*Replace with new fasterer(s)

Torque specifications	Ft-lbs (unless otherwise indicated)	Nm

→ **Note:** One foot-pound (ft-lb) of torque is equivalent to 12 inch-pounds (in-lbs) of torque. Torque values below approximately 15 foot-pounds are expressed in inch-pounds, because most foot-pound torque wrenches are not accurate at these smaller values.

Engine mount* (continued)		
Mount-to-body bracket bolts (passenger side)		
Step 1	44	60
Step 2	Tighten an additional 90 degrees	
Transaxle mount*		
Mount-to-transaxle bracket bolts (driver side)		
Step 1	30	40
Step 2	Tighten an additional 90 degrees	
Mount-to-body bracket bolts (driver side)		
Step 1	44	60
Step 2	Tighten an additional 90 degrees	
Pendulum mount*		
Mount-to-transaxle bolts		
Step 1		
8.8 stamped bolts	30	40
10.9 stamped bolts	37	50
Step 2	Tighten an additional 90 degrees	
Mount-to-subframe bolt		
Step 1	74	100
Step 2	Tighten an additional 90 degrees	
Flywheel/driveplate bolts		
Step 1	44	60
Step 2	Tighten an additional 90 degrees	
Intake manifold-to-cylinder head fasteners	80 in-lbs	9
Intake manifold-to-support bracket fasteners		
BGP and BGQ engines	15	20
CBTA and CBUA engines	144 in-lbs	16
Intake manifold support-to-cylinder block fasteners	18	25
Oil dipstick tube-to-cylinder block fastener	18	25
Lower oil pan-to-upper oil pan bolts	89 in-lbs	10
Timing chain tensioner fastener	89 in-lbs	10

*Replace with new fastener(s)

Notes

Section

Reference to other Chapters

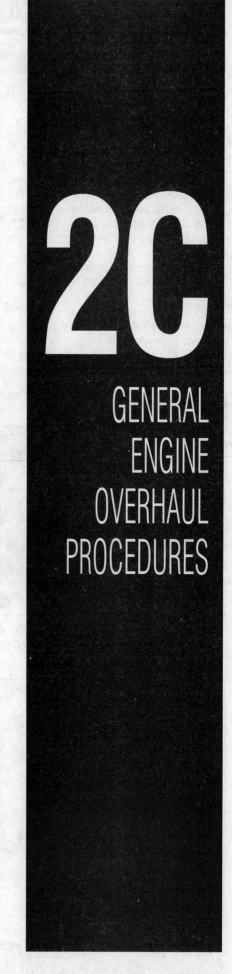

2C

GENERAL ENGINE OVERHAUL PROCEDURES

1 General information - engine overhaul

◆ **Refer to illustrations 1.1, 1.2, 1.3, 1.4, 1.5 and 1.6**

Included in this portion of Chapter 2 are general information and diagnostic testing procedures for determining the overall mechanical condition of your engine.

The information ranges from advice concerning preparation for an overhaul and the purchase of replacement parts and/or components to detailed, step-by-step procedures covering removal and installation.

The following Sections have been written to help you determine whether your engine needs to be overhauled and how to remove and install it once you've determined it needs to be rebuilt. For information concerning in-vehicle engine repair, see Chapter 2A or 2B.

It's not always easy to determine when, or if, an engine should be completely overhauled, because a number of factors must be considered.

High mileage is not necessarily an indication that an overhaul is needed, while low mileage doesn't preclude the need for an overhaul. Frequency of servicing is probably the most important consideration. An engine that's had regular and frequent oil and filter changes, as well as other required maintenance, will most likely give many thousands of miles of reliable service. Conversely, a neglected engine may require an overhaul very early in its service life.

Excessive oil consumption is an indication that piston rings, valve seals and/or valve guides are in need of attention. Make sure that oil leaks aren't responsible before deciding that the rings and/or guides are bad. Perform a cylinder compression check to determine the extent of the work required (see Section 3). Also check the vacuum readings under various conditions (see Section 4).

Check the oil pressure with a gauge installed in place of the oil pressure sending unit and compare it to this Chapter's Specifications (see Section 2). If it's extremely low, the bearings and/or oil pump are probably worn out.

Loss of power, rough running, knocking or metallic engine noises, excessive valve train noise and high fuel consumption rates may also point to the need for an overhaul, especially if they're all present at the same time. If a complete tune-up doesn't remedy the situation, major mechanical work is the only solution.

An engine overhaul involves restoring the internal parts to the specifications of a new engine. During an overhaul, the piston rings are replaced and the cylinder walls are reconditioned (rebored and/or honed) (see illustrations 1.1 and 1.2). If a rebore is done by an automotive machine shop, new oversize pistons will also be installed. The main bearings and connecting rod bearings are generally replaced with new ones and, if necessary, the crankshaft may be reground to restore the journals (see illustration 1.3). Generally, the valves are serviced as well, since they're usually in less-than-perfect condition at this point. While the engine is being overhauled, other components, such as the starter and alternator, can be rebuilt as well. The end result should be a like-new engine that will give many trouble-free miles.

➡ **Note: Critical cooling system components such as the hoses, drivebelts, thermostat and water pump should be replaced with new parts when an engine is overhauled. The radiator should be checked carefully to ensure that it isn't clogged or leaking (see Chapter 3). If you purchase a rebuilt engine or short block, some rebuilders will not warranty their engines unless the radiator has been professionally flushed. Also, we don't recommend overhauling the oil pump - always install a new one when an engine is rebuilt.**

1.1 An engine block being bored. An engine rebuilder will use special machinery to recondition the cylinder bores

1.2 If the cylinders are bored, the machine shop will normally hone the engine on a machine like this

1.3 A crankshaft having a main bearing journal ground

1.4 A machinist checks for a bent connecting rod, using specialized equipment

1.5 A bore gauge being used to check the main bearing bore

1.6 Uneven piston wear like this indicates a bent connecting rod

Overhauling the internal components on today's engines is a difficult and time-consuming task that requires a significant amount of specialty tools and is best left to a professional engine rebuilder (see illustrations 1.4, 1.5 and 1.6). A competent engine rebuilder will handle the inspection of your old parts and offer advice concerning the reconditioning or replacement of the original engine. Never purchase parts or have machine work done on other components until the block has been thoroughly inspected by a professional machine shop. As a general rule, time is the primary cost of an overhaul, especially since the vehicle may be tied up for a minimum of two weeks or more. Be aware that some engine builders only have the capability to rebuild the engine you bring them while other rebuilders have a large inventory of rebuilt exchange engines in stock. Also be aware that many machine shops could take as much as two weeks time to completely rebuild your engine depending on shop workload. Sometimes it makes more sense to simply exchange your engine for another engine that's already rebuilt to save time.

2 Oil pressure check

▶ **Refer to illustration 2.2**

1   Low engine oil pressure can be a sign of an engine in need of rebuilding. A "low oil pressure" indicator (often called an "idiot light") is not a test of the oiling system. Such indicators only come on when the oil pressure is dangerously low. Even a factory oil pressure gauge in the instrument panel is only a relative indication, although much better for driver information than a warning light. A better test is with a mechanical (not electrical) oil pressure gauge.

2   Locate the oil pressure indicator sending unit on the engine block. The oil pressure sending unit is located on the oil pump housing next to the VTEC solenoid (see illustration).

3   Unscrew and remove the oil pressure sending unit and then screw in the hose for your oil pressure gauge (see illustration). If necessary, install an adapter fitting. Use Teflon tape or thread sealant on the threads of the adapter and/or the fitting on the end of your gauge's hose.

4   Connect an accurate tachometer to the engine, according to the tachometer manufacturer's instructions.

5   Check the oil pressure with the engine running (normal operating temperature) at the specified engine speed, and compare it to this Chapter's Specifications. If it's extremely low, the bearings and/or oil pump are probably worn out.

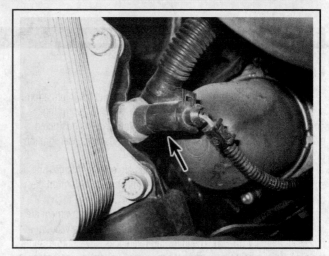

2.2 The oil pressure sending unit is located on top of the oil pump, near the VTEC solenoid

3 Cylinder compression check

▸ **Refer to illustration 3.6**

1   A compression check will tell you what mechanical condition the upper end of your engine (pistons, rings, valves, head gaskets) is in. Specifically, it can tell you if the compression is down due to leakage caused by worn piston rings, defective valves and seats or a blown head gasket.

➡ **Note: The engine must be at normal operating temperature and the battery must be fully charged for this check.**

2   Begin by cleaning the area around the spark plugs before you remove them (compressed air should be used, if available). The idea is to prevent dirt from getting into the cylinders as the compression check is being done.

3   Remove all of the spark plugs from the engine (see Chapter 1).

4   Block the throttle wide open.

5   Disable the ignition and fuel systems by unplugging the wiing harness connectors from the ignition coils (see Chapter 5) and by removing the fuel pump relay (see Chapter 4).

6   Install a compression gauge in the spark plug hole (see illustration).

7   Crank the engine over at least seven compression strokes and watch the gauge. The compression should build up quickly in a healthy engine. Low compression on the first stroke, followed by gradually increasing pressure on successive strokes, indicates worn piston rings. A low compression reading on the first stroke, which doesn't build up during successive strokes, indicates leaking valves or a blown head gasket (a cracked head could also be the cause). Deposits on the undersides of the valve heads can also cause low compression. Record the highest gauge reading obtained.

8   Repeat the procedure for the remaining cylinders and compare the results to this Chapter's Specifications.

9   Add some engine oil (about three squirts from a plunger-type oil can) to each cylinder, through the spark plug hole, and repeat the test.

10 If the compression increases after the oil is added, the piston rings are definitely worn. If the compression doesn't increase significantly, the leakage is occurring at the valves or head gasket. Leakage

3.6 Use a compression gauge with a threaded fitting for the spark plug hole, not the type that requires hand pressure to maintain the seal

past the valves may be caused by burned valve seats and/or faces or warped, cracked or bent valves.

11 If two adjacent cylinders have equally low compression, there's a strong possibility that the head gasket between them is blown. The appearance of coolant in the combustion chambers or the crankcase would verify this condition.

12 If one cylinder is slightly lower than the others, and the engine has a slightly rough idle, a worn lobe on the camshaft could be the cause.

13 If the compression is unusually high, the combustion chambers are probably coated with carbon deposits. If that's the case, the cylinder head(s) should be removed and decarbonized.

14 If compression is way down or varies greatly between cylinders, it would be a good idea to have a leak-down test performed by an automotive repair shop. This test will pinpoint exactly where the leakage is occurring and how severe it is.

15 After performing the test, don't forget to unblock the throttle plate.

4 Vacuum gauge diagnostic checks

▸ **Refer to illustrations 4.4 and 4.6**

1   A vacuum gauge provides inexpensive but valuable information about what is going on in the engine. You can check for worn rings or cylinder walls, leaking head or intake manifold gaskets, restricted exhaust, stuck or burned valves, weak valve springs, improper ignition or valve timing and ignition problems.

2   Unfortunately, vacuum gauge readings are easy to misinterpret, so they should be used in conjunction with other tests to confirm the diagnosis.

3   Both the absolute readings and the rate of needle movement are important for accurate interpretation. Most gauges measure vacuum in inches of mercury (in-Hg). The following references to vacuum assume the diagnosis is being performed at sea level. As elevation increases (or atmospheric pressure decreases), the reading will decrease. For every 1,000-foot increase in elevation above approximately 2000 feet, the gauge readings will decrease about one inch of mercury.

4   Connect the vacuum gauge directly to the intake manifold vac-

4.4 A simple vacuum gauge can be handy in diagnosing engine condition and performance

uum, not to ported (throttle body) vacuum (see illustration). Be sure no hoses are left disconnected during the test or false readings will result.

5   Before you begin the test, allow the engine to warm up completely. Block the wheels and set the parking brake. With the transaxle in Park, start the engine and allow it to run at normal idle speed.

❄❄ WARNING:

Keep your hands and the vacuum gauge clear of the fans and drivebelts.

6   Read the vacuum gauge; an average, healthy engine should normally produce about 17 to 22 in-Hg with a fairly steady needle (see illustration). Refer to the following vacuum gauge readings and what they indicate about the engine's condition:

7   A low steady reading usually indicates a leaking gasket between the intake manifold and cylinder head(s) or throttle body, a leaky vacuum hose, late ignition timing or incorrect camshaft timing. Check ignition timing with a timing light and eliminate all other possible causes, utilizing the tests provided in this Chapter before you remove the timing belt cover to check the timing marks.

8   If the reading is three to eight inches below normal and it fluctuates at that low reading, suspect an intake manifold gasket leak at an intake port or a faulty fuel injector.

9   If the needle has regular drops of about two-to-four inches at a steady rate, the valves are probably leaking. Perform a compression check or leak-down test to confirm this.

10   An irregular drop or down-flick of the needle can be caused by a sticking valve or an ignition misfire. Perform a compression check or leak-down test and read the spark plugs.

11   A rapid vibration of about four in-Hg variation at idle combined with exhaust smoke indicates worn valve guides. Perform a leak-down test to confirm this. If the rapid vibration occurs with an increase in engine speed, check for a leaking intake manifold gasket or head gasket, weak valve springs, burned valves or ignition misfire.

12   A slight fluctuation, say one inch up and down, may mean ignition problems. Check all the usual tune-up items and, if necessary, run the engine on an ignition analyzer.

13   If there is a large fluctuation, perform a compression or leak-down test to look for a weak or dead cylinder or a blown head gasket.

14   If the needle moves slowly through a wide range, check for a clogged PCV system, incorrect idle fuel mixture, throttle body or intake manifold gasket leaks.

15   Check for a slow return after revving the engine by quickly snapping the throttle open until the engine reaches about 2,500 rpm and let it shut. Normally the reading should drop to near zero, rise above normal idle reading (about 5 in-Hg over) and then return to the previous idle reading. If the vacuum returns slowly and doesn't peak when the throttle is snapped shut, the rings may be worn. If there is a long delay, look for a restricted exhaust system (often the muffler or catalytic converter). An easy way to check this is to temporarily disconnect the exhaust ahead of the suspected part and redo the test.

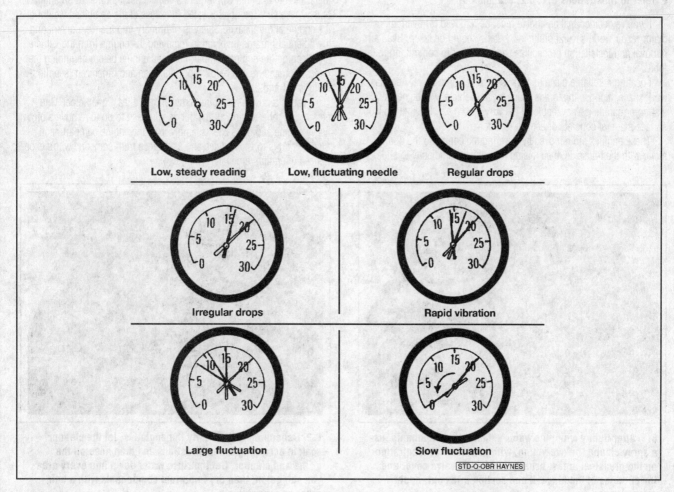

Low, steady reading   Low, fluctuating needle   Regular drops

Irregular drops   Rapid vibration

Large fluctuation   Slow fluctuation

STD-O-OBR HAYNES

4.6 Typical vacuum gauge readings

5 Engine rebuilding alternatives

The do-it-yourselfer is faced with a number of options when purchasing a rebuilt engine. The major considerations are cost, warranty, parts availability and the time required for the rebuilder to complete the project. The decision to replace the engine block, piston/connecting rod assemblies and crankshaft depends on the final inspection results of your engine. Only then can you make a cost effective decision whether to have your engine overhauled or simply purchase an exchange engine for your vehicle.

Some of the rebuilding alternatives include:

Individual parts - If the inspection procedures reveal that the engine block and most engine components are in reusable condition, purchasing individual parts and having a rebuilder rebuild your engine may be the most economical alternative. The block, crankshaft and piston/connecting rod assemblies should all be inspected carefully by a machine shop first.

Short block - A short block consists of an engine block with a crankshaft and piston/connecting rod assemblies already installed. All new bearings are incorporated and all clearances will be correct. The

existing camshafts, valve train components, cylinder head and external parts can be bolted to the short block with little or no machine shop work necessary.

Long block - A long block consists of a short block plus an oil pump, oil pan, cylinder head, valve cover, camshaft and valve train components, timing sprockets and belt or gears and timing cover. All components are installed with new bearings, seals and gaskets incorporated throughout. The installation of manifolds and external parts is all that's necessary.

Low mileage used engines - Some companies now offer low mileage used engines that are a very cost effective way to get your vehicle up and running again. These engines often come from vehicles that have been in totaled in accidents or come from other countries that have a higher vehicle turn over rate. A low mileage used engine also usually has a similar warranty like the newly remanufactured engines.

Give careful thought to which alternative is best for you and discuss the situation with local automotive machine shops, auto parts dealers and experienced rebuilders before ordering or purchasing replacement parts.

6 Engine removal - methods and precautions

▶ **Refer to illustrations 6.1, 6.2, 6.3 and 6.4**

If you've decided that an engine must be removed for overhaul or major repair work, several preliminary steps should be taken. Read all removal and installation procedures carefully prior to committing to this job.

Locating a suitable place to work is extremely important. Adequate work space, along with storage space for the vehicle, will be needed. If a shop or garage isn't available, at the very least a flat, level, clean work surface made of concrete or asphalt is required.

These engines are removed by lowering the engine to the floor, along with the transaxle, then raising the vehicle sufficiently to slide

the assembly out; this will require a vehicle hoist as well as an engine hoist. Make sure the hoist is rated in excess of the combined weight of the engine and transaxle. Safety is of primary importance, considering the potential hazards involved in removing the engine from the vehicle.

Cleaning the engine compartment and engine before beginning the removal procedure will help keep tools clean and organized (see illustrations 6.1 and 6.2).

If you're a novice at engine removal, get at least one helper. One person cannot easily do all the things you need to do to remove a big heavy engine and transaxle assembly from the engine compartment. Also helpful is to seek advice and assistance from someone who's experienced in engine removal.

6.1 After tightly wrapping water-vulnerable components, use a spray cleaner on everything, with particular concentration on the greasiest areas, usually around the valve cover and lower edges of the block. If one section dries out, apply more cleaner

6.2 Depending on how dirty the engine is, let the cleaner soak in according to the directions and then hose off the grime and cleaner. Get the rinse water down into every area you can get at; then dry important components with a hair dryer or paper towels

6.3 Get an engine stand sturdy enough to firmly support the engine while you're working on it. Stay away from three-wheeled models: they have a tendency to tip over more easily, so get a four-wheeled unit

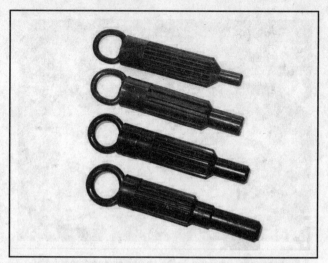

6.4 A clutch alignment tool is necessary if you plan to install a rebuilt engine mated to a manual transaxle

Plan the operation ahead of time. Arrange for or obtain all of the tools and equipment you'll need prior to beginning the job (see illustrations 6.3 and 6.4). Some of the equipment necessary to perform engine removal and installation safely and with relative ease are (in addition to a vehicle hoist and an engine hoist) a heavy duty floor jack (preferably fitted with a transmission jack head adapter), complete sets of wrenches and sockets as described in the front of this manual, wooden blocks, plenty of rags and cleaning solvent for mopping up spilled oil, coolant and gasoline.

Plan for the vehicle to be out of use for quite a while. A machine shop can do the work that is beyond the scope of the home mechanic. Machine shops often have a busy schedule, so before removing the engine, consult the shop for an estimate of how long it will take to rebuild or repair the components that may need work.

7 Engine - removal and installation

※※ WARNING:

The models covered by this manual are equipped with Supplemental Restraint systems (SRS), more commonly known as airbags. Always disable the airbag system before working in the vicinity of airbag system components to avoid the possibility of accidental deployment of the airbag, which could cause personal injury (see Chapter 12).

※※ WARNING:

Gasoline is extremely flammable, so take extra precautions when you work on any part of the fuel system. Don't smoke or allow open flames or bare light bulbs near the work area, and don't work in a garage where a gas-type appliance (such as a water heater or clothes dryer) is present. Since gasoline is carcinogenic, wear fuel-resistant gloves when there's a possibility of being exposed to fuel, and, if you spill any fuel on your skin, rinse it off immediately with soap and water. Mop up any spills immediately and do not store fuel-soaked rags where they could ignite. The fuel system is under constant pressure, so, if any fuel lines are to be disconnected, the fuel pressure in the system must be relieved first (see Chapter 4 for more information). When you perform any kind of work on the fuel system, wear safety glasses and have a Class B type fire extinguisher on hand.

※※ WARNING:

The engine must be completely cool before beginning this procedure.

※※ CAUTION:

If the battery is disconnected, several systems must be relearned before they will work properly (see Chapter 5, Section 3).

➡ Note: Engine removal on these models is a difficult job, especially for the do-it-yourself mechanic working at home. Because of the vehicle's design, the manufacturer states that the engine and transaxle have to be removed as a unit from the bottom of the vehicle, not the top. With a floor jack and jackstands the vehicle can't be raised high enough and supported safely enough for the engine/transaxle assembly to slide out from underneath. The manufacturer recommends that removal of the engine/transaxle assembly only be performed on a vehicle hoist.

REMOVAL

▶ **Refer to illustrations 7.5, 7.12a and 7.12b**

1 On four-cylinder timing belt (BPY) engines, have the air conditioning system discharged by an automotive air conditioning technician.

➡ Note: On all other models, only have the air conditioning system discharged if the condenser assembly is being removed or the air conditioning compressor is being replaced.

2 Park the vehicle on a frame-contact type vehicle hoist. The pads of the hoist arms must contact the body welt along each side of the vehicle.

7.5 Disconnect the wires to the engine compartment fuse/relay panel

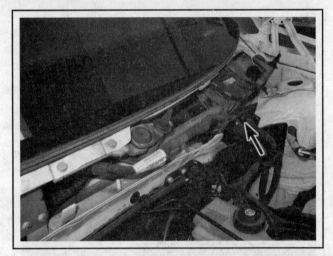

7.12a Release the wiring harness from the body by pressing the tab and pulling the plastic insert upwards

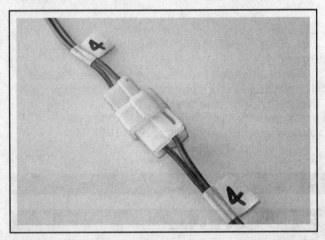

7.12b Label both ends of each wire or vacuum connection before disconnecting them

3 Remove the engine cover (see Chapter 1, Section 7).

4 Relieve the fuel system pressure (see Chapter 4). Remove the battery cover and disconnect the cable from the negative battery terminal (see Chapter 5).

5 Detach the wires from the engine compartment fuse and relay panel (see illustration).

6 Place protective covers on the fenders and cowl and remove the hood (see Chapter 11).

7 Remove the battery and battery tray (see Chapter 5).

8 Loosen the front wheel bolts and the driveaxle/hub bolts, then raise the vehicle on the hoist. Remove the under-vehicle splash shield (see Chapter 1, Section 6).

9 Drain the cooling system, engine oil, power steering fluid and transaxle fluid (see Chapter 1).

10 Remove the air conditioning compressor drivebelt (see Chapter 1), then unbolt the compressor and secure it out of the way using wire (see Chapter 3).

➡ **Note: On four-cylinder timing belt (BPY) engines, disconnect and remove the line from the air conditioning compressor to the condenser (see Chapter 3).**

11 Remove the windshield wiper motor (see Chapter 12) and cowl assembly (see Chapter 11).

12 Clearly label, then disconnect all vacuum lines, coolant and emissions hoses, wiring harness connectors (see illustration), ground straps and fuel lines. Masking tape and/or a touch up paint applicator work well for marking items (see illustration). Take instant photos or sketch the locations of components and brackets.

13 On models equipped with a noise generator, open the locking ring on the charge air pipe, pull the fuel lines from the retaining clip, then remove the EVAP canister retaining bolts and canister (see Chapter 6).

14 Remove the cover and disconnect the electrical connectors to the Engine Control Module (ECM) (see Chapter 6).

15 Remove the alternator and the starter (see Chapter 5).

16 Remove the power steering pump, if equipped (see Chapter 10).

17 Remove the coolant reservoir tank and set it aside (see Chapter 3).

18 On four-cylinder engines, remove the engine cooling fan (see Chapter 3).

➡ **Note: If the radiator is not taken out, it will still be necessary to detach the transaxle oil cooler lines from the bottom of the radiator on automatic transaxle equipped vehicles.**

19 Disconnect the shift cable(s) from the transaxle (see Chapter 7A or 7B). Also disconnect any wiring harness connectors from the transaxle.

20 Disconnect the radiator hoses, heater hoses and coolant recirculation pump, if equipped (see Chapter 3).

➡ **Note: On models equipped with a coolant recirculation pump, it may be necessary to remove the pump fasteners and pump after the hoses have been disconnected.**

21 If equipped with a manual transaxle, disconnect the clutch release cylinder from the transaxle (see Chapter 8).

22 Detach the exhaust pipe(s) from the exhaust manifold(s) (see Chapter 4).

23 Detach all remaining wiring harnesses and hoses from between the engine/transaxle and the chassis. Be sure to mark all connectors to facilitate reassembly.

24 Remove the driveaxle heat shield and driveaxles (see Chapter 8).

25 Remove the pendulum mount (see Chapter 2A, Section 17 or Chapter 2B, Section 15) and, on models so equipped, disconnect the power steering lines from the mounting clips.

26 Attach a lifting sling or chain to the engine. Position an engine hoist and connect the sling to it. If no lifting hooks or brackets are pres-

ent, you'll have to fasten the chains or slings to some substantial part of the engine - ones that are strong enough to take the weight, but in locations that will provide good balance. Take up the slack until there is slight tension on the sling or chain. Position the chain on the hoist so it balances the engine and the transaxle level with the vehicle.

27 Remove the front subframe (see Chapter 10).

28 Remove the transaxle mount and the engine mount.

29 Recheck to be sure nothing except the mounts are still connecting the engine to the vehicle or to the transaxle. Disconnect and label anything still remaining.

30 Slowly lower the engine/transaxle from the vehicle.

➡ **Note: Placing a sheet of hardboard or paneling between the engine and the floor makes moving the powertrain easier.**

31 Once the powertrain is on the floor, disconnect the engine lifting hoist and raise the vehicle hoist until the vehicle clears the powertrain.

32 Reconnect the chain or sling and raise the engine/transaxle with the hoist. Support the transaxle with a jack (preferably one with a transmission jack head adapter). Separate the engine from the transaxle (see Chapter 7).

33 Remove the flywheel/driveplate and mount the engine on a stand.

INSTALLATION

➡ **Note: The manufacturer recommends replacing all subframe and suspension fasteners with new ones whenever they are loosened or removed.**

34 Installation is the reverse of removal, noting the following points:

a) *Check the engine/transaxle mounts. If they're worn or damaged, replace them.*

b) *Attach the transaxle to the engine following the procedure described in Chapter 7.*

c) *Add coolant, oil, power steering and transaxle fluids as needed (see Chapter 1).*

d) *Align the subframe reference marks before tightening the bolts.*

e) *Tighten the subframe, suspension and steering fasteners to the torque listed in the Chapter 10 Specifications.*

f) *Reconnect the negative battery cable (see Chapter 5).*

g) *Run the engine and check for proper operation and leaks. Shut off the engine and recheck fluid levels.*

h) *Have the air conditioning system re-charged and leak tested by the shop that discharged it.*

8 Engine overhaul - disassembly sequence

1 It's much easier to remove the external components if it's mounted on a portable engine stand. A stand can often be rented quite cheaply from an equipment rental yard. Before the engine is mounted on a stand, the flywheel/driveplate should be removed from the engine.

2 If a stand isn't available, it's possible to remove the external engine components with it blocked up on the floor. Be extra careful not to tip or drop the engine when working without a stand.

3 If you're going to obtain a rebuilt engine, all external components must come off first, to be transferred to the replacement engine. These components include:

Clutch and flywheel (models with manual transaxle)
Driveplate (models with automatic transaxle)
Control housing cover
Emissions-related components
Engine mounts and mount brackets
Fuel injection components

Intake/exhaust manifolds
Oil filter
Ignition coils and spark plugs
Thermostat and housing assembly
Water pump

➡ **Note: When removing the external components from the engine, pay close attention to details that may be helpful or important during installation. Note the installed position of gaskets, seals, spacers, pins, brackets, washers, bolts and other small items.**

4 If you're going to obtain a short block (assembled engine block, crankshaft, pistons and connecting rods), remove the timing belt, cylinder head, oil pan, oil pump pick-up tube, oil pump and water pump from your engine so that you can turn in your old short block to the rebuilder as a core. See *Engine rebuilding alternatives* for additional information regarding the different possibilities to be considered.

9 Pistons and connecting rods - removal and installation

REMOVAL

▸ **Refer to illustrations 9.1, 9.3 and 9.4**

➡ **Note: Prior to removing the piston/connecting rod assemblies, remove the cylinder head and oil pans.**

1 Use your fingernail to feel if a ridge has formed at the upper limit of ring travel (about 1/4-inch down from the top of each cylinder). If carbon deposits or cylinder wear have produced ridges, they must be completely removed with a special tool (see illustration). Follow the manufacturer's instructions provided with the tool. Failure to remove the ridges before attempting to remove the piston/connecting rod assemblies may result in piston breakage.

9.1 Before you try to remove the pistons, use a ridge reamer to remove the raised material (ridge) from the top of the cylinders

9.3 Checking the connecting rod endplay (side clearance)

9.4 If the connecting rods and caps are not marked, use permanent ink or paint to mark the caps to the rods by cylinder number (for example, this would be the No. 4 connecting rod)

2   After the cylinder ridges have been removed, turn the engine so the crankshaft is facing up. Remove the balance shaft assembly (see Section 13).

3   Before the main bearing cap assembly and connecting rods are removed, check the connecting rod endplay with feeler gauges. Slide them between the first connecting rod and the crankshaft throw until the play is removed (see illustration). Repeat this procedure for each connecting rod. The endplay is equal to the thickness of the feeler gauge(s). Check with an automotive machine shop for the endplay service limit (a typical end play limit should measure between 0.005 to 0.015 inch [0.127 to 0.396 mm]). If the play exceeds the service limit, new connecting rods will be required. If new rods (or a new crankshaft) are installed, the endplay may fall under the minimum allowable. If it does, the rods will have to be machined to restore it. If necessary, consult an automotive machine shop for advice.

4   Check the connecting rods and caps for identification marks. The marks on the face of the rods and caps should always point towards the drivebelt end of the engine and the marks on the ends of the rods and caps are for cylinder designation. If they aren't plainly marked, use paint or marker to clearly identify each rod and cap (1, 2, 3, etc., depending on the cylinder they're associated with) (see illustration).

5   Loosen each of the connecting rod cap bolts 1/2-turn at a time until they can be removed by hand.

➡ **Note: New connecting rod cap bolts must be used when reassembling the engine, but save the old bolts for use when checking the connecting rod bearing oil clearance.**

6   Remove the number one connecting rod cap and bearing insert. Don't drop the bearing insert out of the cap.

7   Remove the bearing insert and push the connecting rod/piston assembly out through the top of the engine. Use a wooden or plastic hammer handle to push on the upper bearing surface in the connecting rod. If resistance is felt, double-check to make sure that all of the ridge was removed from the cylinder.

8   Repeat the procedure for the remaining cylinders.

9   After removal, reassemble the connecting rod caps and bearing inserts in their respective connecting rods and install the cap bolts finger tight. Leaving the old bearing inserts in place until reassembly will help prevent the connecting rod bearing surfaces from being accidentally nicked or gouged.

10   The pistons and connecting rods are now ready for inspection and overhaul at an automotive machine shop.

PISTON RING INSTALLATION

▶ **Refer to illustrations 9.13, 9.14, 9.15, 9.19a, 9.19b and 9.22**

11   Before installing the new piston rings, the ring end gaps must be checked. It's assumed that the piston ring side clearance has been checked and verified correct.

12   Lay out the piston/connecting rod assemblies and the new ring sets so the ring sets will be matched with the same piston and cylinder during the end gap measurement and engine assembly.

13   Insert the top (number one) ring into the first cylinder and square it up with the cylinder walls by pushing it in with the top of the piston (see illustration). The ring should be near the bottom of the cylinder, at the lower limit of ring travel.

14   To measure the end gap, slip feeler gauges between the ends of the ring until a gauge equal to the gap width is found (see illustration). The feeler gauge should slide between the ring ends with a slight amount of drag. A typical ring gap should fall between 0.010 and 0.020

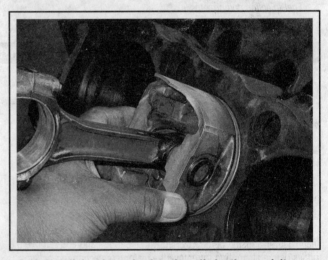

9.13 Install the piston ring into the cylinder then push it down into position using a piston so the ring will be square in the cylinder

9.14 With the ring square in the cylinder, measure the ring end gap with a feeler gauge

9.15 If the ring end gap is too small, clamp a file in a vise as shown and file the piston ring ends - be sure to remove all raised material

inch (0.25 to 0.50 mm) for compression rings and up to 0.030 inch (0.76 mm) for the oil ring steel rails. If the gap is larger or smaller than specified, double-check to make sure you have the correct rings before proceeding.

15 If the gap is too small, it must be enlarged or the ring ends may come in contact with each other during engine operation, which can cause serious damage to the engine. If necessary, increase the end gaps by filing the ring ends very carefully with a fine file. Mount the file in a vise equipped with soft jaws, slip the ring over the file with the ends contacting the file face and slowly move the ring to remove material from the ends. When performing this operation, file only by pushing the ring from the outside end of the file towards the vise (see illustration).

16 Excess end gap isn't critical unless it's greater than 0.0315 inch (0.8 mm). Again, double-check to make sure you have the correct ring type.

17 Repeat the procedure for each ring that will be installed in the first cylinder and for each ring in the remaining cylinders. Remember to keep rings, pistons and cylinders matched up.

18 Once the ring end gaps have been checked/corrected, the rings can be installed on the pistons.

19 The oil control ring (lowest one on the piston) is usually installed first. It's composed of three separate components. Slip the spacer/expander into the groove (see illustration). If an anti-rotation tang is used, make sure it's inserted into the drilled hole in the ring groove. Next, install the upper side rail in the same manner (see illustration). Don't use a piston ring installation tool on the oil ring side rails, as they may be damaged. Instead, place one end of the side rail into the groove between the spacer/expander and the ring land, hold it firmly in place and slide a finger around the piston while pushing the rail into the groove. Finally, install the lower side rail.

20 After the three oil ring components have been installed, check to make sure that both the upper and lower side rails can be rotated smoothly inside the ring grooves.

21 The number two (middle) ring is installed next. It's usually stamped with a mark which must face up, toward the top of the piston. Do not mix up the top and middle rings, as they have different cross-sections.

➡ **Note: Always follow the instructions printed on the ring package or box - different manufacturers may require different approaches.**

9.19a Installing the spacer/expander in the oil ring groove

9.19b DO NOT use a piston ring installation tool when installing the oil control side rails

ENGINE BEARING ANALYSIS

Debris

Babbitt bearing embedded with debris from machinings

Microscopic detail of debris

Microscopic detail of gouges

Overplated copper alloy bearing gouged by cast iron debris

Aluminum bearing embedded with glass beads

Microscopic detail of glass beads

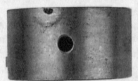

Damaged lining caused by dirt left on the bearing back

Misassembly

Result of a lower half assembled as an upper - blocking the oil flow

Excessive oil clearance is indicated by a short contact arc

Polished and oil-stained backs are a result of a poor fit in the housing bore

Result of a wrong, reversed, or shifted cap

Overloading

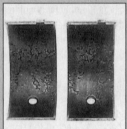

Damage from excessive idling which resulted in an oil film unable to support the load imposed

Damaged upper connecting rod bearings caused by engine lugging; the lower main bearings (not shown) were similarly affected

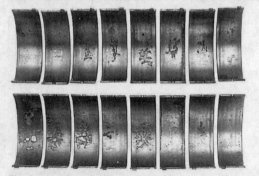

The damage shown in these upper and lower connecting rod bearings was caused by engine operation at a higher-than-rated speed under load

Misalignment

A warped crankshaft caused this pattern of severe wear in the center, diminishing toward the ends

A poorly finished crankshaft caused the equally spaced scoring shown

A tapered housing bore caused the damage along one edge of this pair

A bent connecting rod led to the damage in the "V" pattern

Lubrication

Result of dry start: The bearings on the left, farthest from the oil pump, show more damage

Result of a low oil supply or oil starvation

Severe wear as a result of inadequate oil clearance

Corrosion

Microscopic detail of corrosion

Corrosion is an acid attack on the bearing lining generally caused by inadequate maintenance, extremely hot or cold operation, or inferior oils or fuels

Microscopic detail of cavitation

Example of cavitation - a surface erosion caused by pressure changes in the oil film

Damage from excessive thrust or insufficient axial clearance

Bearing affected by oil dilution caused by excessive blow-by or a rich mixture

9.22 Use a piston ring installation tool to install the number 2 and the number 1 (top) rings - be sure the directional mark on the piston ring(s) is facing toward the top of the piston

22 Use a piston ring installation tool and make sure the identification mark is facing the top of the piston, then slip the ring into the middle groove on the piston (see illustration). Don't expand the ring any more than necessary to slide it over the piston.

23 Install the number one (top) ring in the same manner. Make sure the mark is facing up. Be careful not to confuse the number one and number two rings.

24 Repeat the procedure for the remaining pistons and rings.

INSTALLATION

25 Before installing the piston/connecting rod assemblies, the cylinder walls must be perfectly clean, the top edge of each cylinder bore must be chamfered, and the crankshaft must be in place.

26 Remove the cap from the end of the number one connecting rod (refer to the marks made during removal). Remove the original bearing inserts and wipe the bearing surfaces of the connecting rod and cap with a clean, lint-free cloth. They must be kept spotlessly clean.

Connecting rod bearing oil clearance check

▶ **Refer to illustrations 9.30, 9.35, 9.37 and 9.41**

27 Clean the back side of the new upper bearing insert, then lay it in place in the connecting rod.

28 Make sure the tab on the bearing fits into the recess in the rod. Don't hammer the bearing insert into place and be very careful not to nick or gouge the bearing face. Don't lubricate the bearing at this time.

29 Clean the back side of the other bearing insert and install it in the rod cap. Again, make sure the tab on the bearing fits into the recess in the cap, and don't apply any lubricant. It's critically important that the mating surfaces of the bearing and connecting rod are perfectly clean and oil free when they're assembled.

30 Position the piston ring gaps at 90-degree intervals around the piston as shown (see illustration).

31 Lubricate the piston and rings with clean engine oil and attach a piston ring compressor to the piston. Leave the skirt protruding about 1/4-inch to guide the piston into the cylinder. The rings must be compressed until they're flush with the piston.

32 Rotate the crankshaft until the number one connecting rod journal is at BDC (bottom dead center) and apply a liberal coat of engine oil to

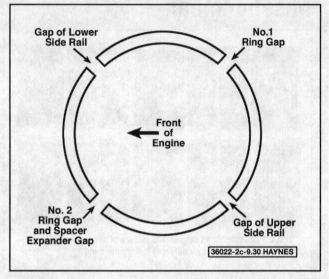

9.30 Position the piston ring end gaps as shown

the cylinder walls.

33 With the mark on top of the piston facing the front (timing belt or chain end) of the engine, gently insert the piston/connecting rod assembly into the number one cylinder bore and rest the bottom edge of the ring compressor on the engine block.

34 Tap the top edge of the ring compressor to make sure it's contacting the block around its entire circumference.

35 Gently tap on the top of the piston with the end of a wooden or plastic hammer handle (see illustration) while guiding the end of the connecting rod into place on the crankshaft journal. The piston rings may try to pop out of the ring compressor just before entering the cylinder bore, so keep some downward pressure on the ring compressor. Work slowly, and if any resistance is felt as the piston enters the cylinder, stop immediately. Find out what's hanging up and fix it before proceeding. Do not, for any reason, force the piston into the cylinder - you might break a ring and/or the piston.

36 Once the piston/connecting rod assembly is installed, the connecting rod bearing oil clearance must be checked before the rod cap is permanently installed.

9.35 Use a plastic or wooden hammer handle to push the piston into the cylinder

9.37 Place Plastigage on each connecting rod bearing journal parallel to the crankshaft centerline

9.41 Use the scale on the Plastigage package to determine the bearing oil clearance - be sure to measure the widest part of the Plastigage and use the correct scale; it comes with both standard and metric scales

37 Cut a piece of the appropriate size Plastigage slightly shorter than the width of the connecting rod bearing and lay it in place on the number one connecting rod journal, parallel with the journal axis (see illustration).

38 Clean the connecting rod cap bearing face and install the rod cap. Make sure the mating mark on the cap is on the same side as the mark on the connecting rod (see illustration 9.4).

39 Install the old rod bolts, at this time, and tighten them to the torque listed in this Chapter's Specifications.

➡ **Note: Use a thin-wall socket to avoid erroneous torque readings that can result if the socket is wedged between the rod cap and the bolt head. If the socket tends to wedge itself between the fastener and the cap, lift up on it slightly until it no longer contacts the cap. DO NOT rotate the crankshaft at any time during this operation.**

40 Remove the fasteners and detach the rod cap, being very careful not to disturb the Plastigage.

41 Compare the width of the crushed Plastigage to the scale printed on the Plastigage envelope to obtain the oil clearance (see illustration). The connecting rod oil clearance is usually about 0.001 to 0.002 inch (0.025 to 0.05 mm). Consult an automotive machine shop for the clearance specified for the rod bearings on your engine. One the covered vehicles, code numbers on the block and crankshaft are used to select the proper bearings, using a chart at a dealership service/parts department.

42 If the clearance is not as specified, the bearing inserts may be the wrong size (which means different ones will be required). Before deciding that different inserts are needed, make sure that no dirt or oil was between the bearing inserts and the connecting rod or cap when the clearance was measured. Also, recheck the journal diameter. If the Plastigage was wider at one end than the other, the journal may be tapered. If the clearance still exceeds the limit specified, the bearing will have to be replaced with an undersize bearing.

⁘ **CAUTION:**

When installing a new crankshaft always use a standard size bearing.

Final installation

43 Carefully scrape all traces of the Plastigage material off the rod journal and/or bearing face. Be very careful not to scratch the bearing -

use your fingernail or the edge of a plastic card.

44 Make sure the bearing faces are perfectly clean, then apply a uniform layer of clean moly-base grease or engine assembly lube to both of them. You'll have to push the piston into the cylinder to expose the face of the bearing insert in the connecting rod.

➡ **Note: If there was a large amount metal shavings or debris, replace the oil piston nozzle fastener and nozzle.**

45 Slide the connecting rod back into place on the journal, install the rod cap, install the new bolts and tighten them to the torque listed in this Chapter's Specifications.

⁘ **CAUTION:**

Install new connecting rod cap bolts. Do NOT reuse old bolts - they have stretched and cannot be reused. Again, work up to the torque in three steps.

46 Repeat the entire procedure for the remaining pistons/connecting rods.

47 The important points to remember are:

a) *Keep the back sides of the bearing inserts and the insides of the connecting rods and caps perfectly clean when assembling them.*

b) *Make sure you have the correct piston/rod assembly for each cylinder.*

c) *The mark on the piston must face the front (timing chain end) of the engine.*

d) *Lubricate the cylinder walls liberally with clean oil.*

e) *Lubricate the bearing faces when installing the rod caps after the oil clearance has been checked.*

f) *Make sure the piston oil spray nozzles were not bent or damaged.*

48 After all the piston/connecting rod assemblies have been correctly installed, rotate the crankshaft a number of times by hand to check for any obvious binding.

49 As a final step, check the connecting rod endplay, as described in Step 3. If it was correct before disassembly and the original crankshaft and rods were reinstalled, it should still be correct. If new rods or a new crankshaft were installed, the endplay may be inadequate. If so, the rods will have to be removed and taken to an automotive machine shop for resizing.

10 Crankshaft - removal and installation

REMOVAL

▶ **Refer to illustrations 10.1 and 10.3**

➡ **Note: The crankshaft can be removed only after the engine has been removed from the vehicle. It's assumed that the flywheel or driveplate, crankshaft pulley, crankshaft front oil seal flange, timing belt or timing chains, oil pans, oil pump body, control housing cover (five-cylinder engine), oil filter and piston/connecting rod assemblies have already been removed. On four-cylinder engines, the rear main oil seal retainer must be unbolted and separated from the block before proceeding with crankshaft removal.**

1   Before the crankshaft is removed, measure the endplay. Mount a dial indicator with the indicator in line with the crankshaft and just touching the end of the crankshaft as shown (see illustration).

2   Pry the crankshaft all the way to the rear and zero the dial indicator. Next, pry the crankshaft to the front as far as possible and check the reading on the dial indicator. The distance traveled is the endplay. A crankshaft endplay will fall between 0.003 to 0.009 inch (0.07 to 0.23 mm) for four-cylinder engines and 0.003 to 0.008 inch (0.07 to 0.21 mm) on five-cylinder engines. If it is greater than that, check the crankshaft thrust surfaces for wear after it's removed. If no wear is evident, new main bearings should correct the endplay.

3   If a dial indicator isn't available, feeler gauges can be used. Gently pry the crankshaft all the way to the front of the engine. Slip feeler gauges between the crankshaft and the front face of the thrust bearing or washer to determine the clearance (see illustration).

4   Loosen the main bearing cap bolts 1/4-turn at a time each, until they can be removed by hand. Loosen the bolts in the reverse of the tightening sequence (see illustration 10.19a, 10.19b or 10.19c). On four-cylinder timing chain (CCTA, CBFA) engines, remove the jack bolts (side bolts) before removing the bearing cap bolts.

5   Remove the main bearing caps, gently tap the caps with a soft-face hammer around its perimeter and pull the cap straight up and off the cylinder block.

6   Carefully lift the crankshaft out of the engine. It may be a good

idea to have an assistant available, since the crankshaft is quite heavy and awkward to handle. With the bearing inserts in place inside the engine block and main bearing caps, reinstall the main bearing caps onto the engine block and tighten the bolts finger tight.

INSTALLATION

7   Crankshaft installation is the first step in engine reassembly. It's assumed at this point that the engine block and crankshaft have been cleaned, inspected and repaired or reconditioned.

8   Position the engine block with the bottom facing up.

9   Remove the bolts and lift off the main bearing caps.

10 If they're still in place, remove the original bearing inserts. Wipe the bearing surfaces of the block and main bearing cap assembly with a clean, lint-free cloth. They must be kept spotlessly clean. This is critical for determining the correct bearing oil clearance.

Main bearing oil clearance check

▶ **Refer to illustrations 10.17, 10.19a, 10.19b, 10.19c and 10.21**

11 Without mixing them up, clean the back sides of the new upper main bearing inserts (with grooves and oil holes) and lay one in each main bearing saddle in the engine block. Each upper bearing (engine block) has an oil groove and oil hole in it.

✳✳ CAUTION:

The oil holes in the block must line up with the oil holes in the upper bearing inserts.

➡ **Note: The thrust bearing is located on the engine block number 3 (center) journal.**

Clean the back sides of the lower main bearing inserts and lay them in the corresponding location in the main bearing caps or the lower cylinder block. Make sure the tab on the bearing insert fits into its corresponding recess.

10.1 Checking crankshaft endplay with a dial indicator

10.3 Checking the crankshaft endplay with feeler gauges at the thrust bearing journal

10.17 Place the Plastigage onto the crankshaft bearing journal as shown

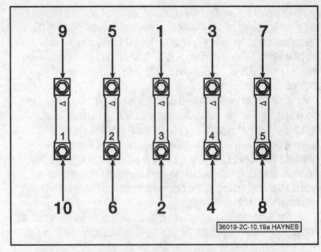

10.19a Main bearing cap beam bolt tightening sequence - four-cylinder timing belt (BPY) engines

❊❊ CAUTION:

Do not hammer the bearing insert into place and don't nick or gouge the bearing faces. DO NOT apply any lubrication at this time.

12 Clean the faces of the bearing inserts in the block and the crankshaft main bearing journals with a clean, lint-free cloth.

13 Check or clean the oil holes in the crankshaft, as any dirt here can go only one way - straight through the new bearings.

14 Once you're certain the crankshaft is clean, carefully lay it in position in the cylinder block. Lube and insert the thrust washer on either side of journal no. 3 for all engines.

➡ **Note: Install the thrust washers with the groove in the thrust washer facing the crankshaft and the smooth sides facing the main bearing saddle.**

15 Before the crankshaft can be permanently installed, the main bearing oil clearance must be checked.

16 Cut several strips of the appropriate size of Plastigage. They must be slightly shorter than the width of the main bearing journal.

17 Place one piece on each crankshaft main bearing journal, parallel with the journal axis as shown (see illustration).

18 Clean the faces of the bearing inserts in the main bearing caps or the lower cylinder block. Hold the bearing inserts in place and install the caps or the lower cylinder block onto the crankshaft and cylinder block. DO NOT disturb the Plastigage.

19 Apply clean engine oil to all bolt threads prior to installation, then install all bolts finger-tight. Tighten the bolts in the sequence shown (see illustrations) progressing in steps, to the torque listed in this Chapter's Specifications. DO NOT rotate the crankshaft at any time during this operation.

➡ **Note: Use the old bolts at this time not the new ones.**

20 Remove the bolts in the reverse order of the tightening sequence and carefully lift the caps straight up and off the block. Do not disturb the Plastigage or rotate the crankshaft.

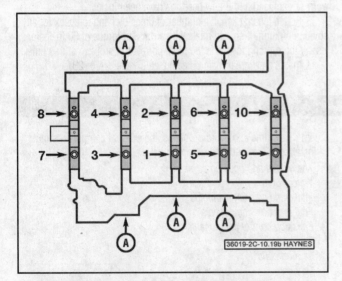

10.19b Main bearing cap beam bolt tightening sequence - four-cylinder timing chain (CCTA, CBFA) engines. (A) are the jack (side) bolts

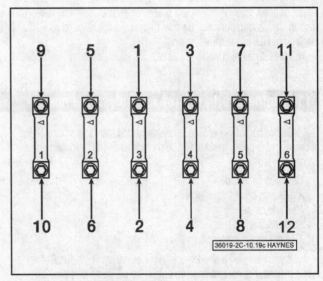

10.19c Main bearing cap beam bolt tightening sequence - five-cylinder engines

21 Compare the width of the crushed Plastigage on each journal to the scale printed on the Plastigage envelope to determine the main bearing oil clearance (see illustration). Main bearing oil clearance will fall between 0.007 to 0.0145 inch (0.17 to 0.37 mm) for four-cylinder engines and 0.009 to 0.017 inch (0.23 to 0.43 mm) on five-cylinder engines.

22 If the clearance is not as specified, the bearing inserts may be the wrong size (which means different ones will be required). Before deciding if different inserts are needed, make sure that no dirt or oil was between the bearing inserts and the cap assembly or block when the clearance was measured. If the Plastigage was wider at one end than the other, the crankshaft journal may be tapered. If the clearance still exceeds the limit specified, the bearing insert(s) will have to be replaced with an undersize bearing insert(s).

23 The upper bearing inserts are installed with different thicknesses. Colored dots serve to identify the bearing thicknesses; S-black, R-red, G-yellow, B-blue and W-white. On four-cylinder timing belt (BPY) engines, these letters are marked on the lower sealing surface of the cylinder block where the oil pan is mounted. The first letter, starting from the belt side of the engine, and reading right to the left is for bearing cap no. 1, the second letter is for bearing cap no. 2, through all five caps to identify which bearing thickness must be installed in which location. On four-cylinder timing chain (CCTA, CBFA) engines, these letters are marked on the end of the crankshaft. The first letter, starting from the left and reading to the right is for bearing cap no.1, the second letter is for bearing cap no. 2, through all five caps. On five-cylinder engines, these letters are marked on the lower sealing surface of the cylinder block where the oil pan is mounted. The first letter, starting from the belt side of the engine, and reading left to right is for bearing cap no. 1, the second letter if for bearing cap no. 2, through all six. The lower bearing inserts are always installed with Y-yellow dotted inserts, for all engines.

➡ **Note: If the colored dots cannot be properly identified, always replace the inserts with blue dotted inserts.**

24 Carefully scrape all traces of the Plastigage material off the main bearing journals and/or the bearing insert faces. Be sure to remove all residue from the oil holes. Use your fingernail or the edge of a plastic card - don't nick or scratch the bearing faces.

25 Carefully lift the crankshaft out of the cylinder block.

26 Clean the bearing insert faces in the cylinder block, then apply a thin, uniform layer of moly-base grease or engine assembly lube to each of the bearing surfaces. Be sure to coat the thrust faces as well as the journal face of the thrust bearing.

27 Make sure the crankshaft journals are clean, then lay the crank-

10.21 Use the scale on the Plastigage package to determine the bearing oil clearance - be sure to measure the widest part of the Plastigage and use the correct scale; it comes with both standard and metric scales

shaft back in place in the cylinder block.

28 Clean the bearing insert faces and apply the same lubricant to them. Clean the engine block and the bearing caps/lower cylinder block thoroughly. The surfaces must be free of oil residue.

29 Install the main bearing caps with the arrows on the caps facing the front of the engine.

30 Prior to installation, apply clean engine oil to all bolt threads wiping off any excess, then install all bolts finger-tight.

➡ **Note: The manufacturer requires using NEW bolts for the main caps and jack bolts (side bolts) on four-cylinder timing chain (CCTA, CBFA) engines.**

31 Tighten the new main bearing cap bolts, following the correct torque sequence (see illustrations 10.19a, 10.19b and 10.19c). Torque the bolts to the Specifications listed in this Chapter. On four-cylinder timing chain (CCTA, CBFA) engines, tighten the jack bolts (side bolts) at the same time as the bearing cap bolts.

32 Recheck the crankshaft endplay with a feeler gauge or a dial indicator. The endplay should be correct if the crankshaft thrust faces aren't worn or damaged and if new bearings have been installed.

33 Rotate the crankshaft a number of times by hand to check for any obvious binding. It should rotate with a running torque of 50 in-lbs or less. If the running torque is too high, correct the problem at this time.

34 Install a new rear main oil seal (see Chapter 2A or 2B).

11 Engine overhaul - reassembly sequence

1 Before beginning engine reassembly, make sure you have all the necessary new parts, gaskets and seals as well as the following items on hand:

Common hand tools
A 1/2-inch drive torque wrench
New engine oil
Gasket sealant
Thread locking compound

2 If you obtained a short block it will be necessary to install the cylinder head, the control housing cover, the oil pump and pick-up tube, upper and lower the oil pans, the water pump, the timing belt/chain and timing cover, and the valve cover (see Chapter 2A or 2B). In order to save time and avoid problems, the external components must be installed in the following general order:

Thermostat and housing cover
Water pump
Intake and exhaust manifolds
Fuel injection components
Emission control components
Spark plugs
Ignition coils
Oil filter
Engine mounts and mount brackets
Clutch and flywheel (manual transaxle)
Driveplate (automatic transaxle)

12 Control housing cover (five-cylinder engine) - removal and installation

REMOVAL

▶ **Refer to illustration 12.7**

1   Remove the engine (see Section 7) and separate the transaxle from the engine (see Chapter 7).
2   Remove the camshaft chain cover (see Chapter 2B).
3   Remove the flywheel/driveplate (see Chapter 2A)
4   Remove the cylinder head (see Chapter 2B).
5   Remove the brake booster vacuum pump mounting fasteners and remove the vacuum pump (see Chapter 9).
6   Unclip the speed sensor harness and remove the speed sensor (see Chapter 6).
7   Remove the control housing cover retaining fasteners (see illustration), then carefully pry the housing from the cylinder block and upper oil pan, starting at the dowels, on each side of the cover.

INSTALLATION

8   Use a scraper to remove all traces of old sealant from the block and upper oil pan. Clean the mating surfaces with brake system cleaner.

➡ **Note: Before removing all the traces of the old sealant from the control housing cover, follow the outline of the sealant and copy it, to apply the new sealant along the same line.**

9   Make sure the threaded bolt holes in the block are clean.
10 Check the cover housing for distortion, particularly around the bolt holes. Remove any nicks or burrs as necessary.
11 Apply a 1/16-inch (2 mm) bead of RTV sealant to the control housing flange.
12 Carefully position the housing cover on to the alignment dowels,

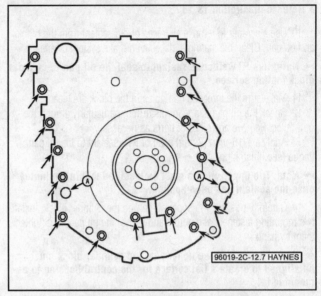

12.7 Remove the control housing cover retaining bolts, then pry the cover off, starting at the dowel (A) locations

install the retaining fasteners and tighten them by hand.
13 Tighten all control housing retaining fasteners to the torque listed in this Chapter's Specifications.
14 Install the brake booster vacuum pump (see Chapter 9).
15 The remainder of installation is the reverse of removal.

➡ **Note: Be sure to follow the sealant manufacturer's recommendations on curing times and allow the sealant to properly cure before adding oil.**

13 Upper oil pan (five-cylinder engine) - removal and installation

REMOVAL

▶ **Refer to illustration 13.9**

1   Remove the engine (see Section 7) and separate the transaxle from the engine (see Chapter 7).
2   Remove the lower oil pan (see Chapter 2B).
3   Remove the crankshaft front oil seal flange (see Chapter 2B).
4   Loosen the camshaft sprockets (see Chapter 2A, Section 5).
5   Remove the control housing (see Section 12).
6   Remove the oil pump chain tensioner and guide (see Section 14).
7   Remove the pick-up tube retaining fasteners and pick-up tube.
8   Remove the pick-up tube-to-oil pump seal.
9   Remove the upper oil pan mounting fasteners (see illustration) and carefully pry the oil pan off.

➡ **Note: Pry the oil pan at the number 6 and number 1 crankshaft bearing caps using a flat blade screwdriver or equivalent tool.**

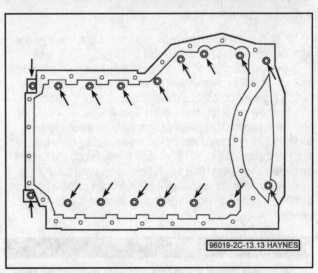

13.9 Upper oil pan mounting fastener locations

INSTALLATION

▶ **Refer to illustration 13.13**

10 Use a scraper to remove all traces of old sealant from the block and oil pan. Clean the mating surfaces with brake system cleaner.

➡ **Note: Use RTV silicone sealant to seal the oil pan-to-cylinder block mating surface.**

11 Make sure the threaded bolt holes in the block are clean.

12 Check the oil pan flange for distortion, particularly around the bolt holes. Remove any nicks or burrs as necessary.

13 Apply a 1/16-inch (2 mm) bead of RTV sealant to the oil pan flange (see illustration).

➡ **Note: The upper oil pan must be installed within 5 minutes once the sealant has been applied.**

14 Carefully position the upper oil pan on the cylinder block, install two mounting fasteners at the front and rear of the oil pan, and tighten them by hand.

➡ **Note: The ends of the upper pan and cylinder block must be aligned to create a flat surface for the control housing to be mounted to.**

15 Install VW special tool #2036/1, or equivalent to each side of the engine block.

➡ **Note: This tool has two flat metal bars that are bolted to the cylinder block to keep the oil pan aligned with the cylinder block when the pan is installed.**

16 Align the oil pan with the special tool, check that the edge of the block and the edge of the oil pan are flush, then install the remaining

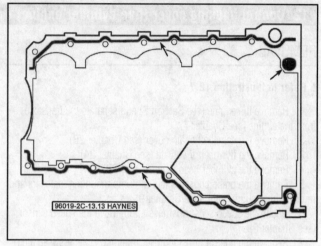

13.13 Apply a 1/16-inch (2.0 mm) thick bead of sealant to the upper pan at these points

oil pan bolts (see illustration 13.9). Tighten all mounting fasteners in a diagonal sequence, to the torque listed in this Chapter's Specifications.

17 Install the oil pick-up tube to the pump with a new seal, then install the pick-up tube mounting fasteners to the oil pan, tightening all mounting fasteners to the torque listed in this Chapter's Specifications.

18 Install the oil pump timing chain and tensioner (see Section 14).

19 The remainder of installation is the reverse of removal.

➡ **Note: Be sure to follow the sealant manufacturer's recommendations on curing times and allow the sealant to properly cure before adding oil.**

14 Oil pump, timing chain and tensioner (five-cylinder engine) - removal and installation

➡ **Note: The oil pump is not serviceable; if there is a problem, the oil pump it must be replaced.**

REMOVAL

▶ **Refer to illustration 14.8**

1 Remove the engine (see Section 7), then separate the transaxle from the engine (see Chapter 7A or 7B).

2 Remove the upper oil pan and oil pick-up tube (see Section 13).

3 Remove the crankshaft front oil seal flange (see Chapter 2B).

4 Loosen the camshaft sprockets (see Chapter 2A, Section 5).

5 Remove the control housing (see Section 12).

6 With a screwdriver placed between the chain guide and the tensioner piston, slowly compress the oil pump timing chain tensioner piston and place a pin (a drill bit or paper clip will work) into the hole on the tensioner body to hold it in the fully compressed position.

7 Remove the tensioner mounting fastener then slide the tensioner assembly, chain guide and tensioner guide off of the cylinder block dowels.

✳ CAUTION:

Do not remove the pin holding the tensioner piston in the compressed position.

14.8 Use a holding tool on the oil pump drive sprocket to remove the retaining bolt

8 While holding the oil pump drive sprocket with a suitable tool, remove the sprocket retaining bolt from the oil pump, then remove the sprocket and chain (see illustration).

9 Remove oil pump retaining fasteners, then the oil pump and O-ring.

➡ **Note: Always replace the O-ring with a new one.**

INSTALLATION

10 Lock the crankshaft in the TDC position (see Chapter 2B, Section 3).

11 Install a new O-ring onto the pump, then install the oil pump and hand tighten the retaining fasteners.

12 Place the oil pump sprocket onto the pump, with the lettering on the sprocket facing outwards. Install the sprocket retaining bolt and tighten it to the torque listed in this Chapter's Specifications.

13 Loosen the oil pump bolts so that the oil pump can slide, then use VW special alignment tool #T03005 to align the oil pump sprocket with the crankshaft sprocket.

➡ **Note: On 2011 models, special shim #T03005/1 must be installed between the alignment tool and crankshaft.**

14 Mount the tool to the end of the crankshaft and tighten the tool mounting bolts to 22 ft-lbs (30 Nm).

15 Slide the oil pump sprocket towards the tool, which has magnets attached, and allow the sprocket to contact to the magnets.

➡ **Note: The magnets and sprocket must be clean and free from any metal shavings.**

16 Remove the crankshaft locking pin.

17 Press the crankshaft towards the front (drivebelt side) and hold it in place using a shim or screwdriver between the last main bearing cap and the crankshaft counter weight.

18 Press the oil pump body lightly towards the oil pump chain side. Tighten the two oil pump retaining bolts at the back of the pump, then the bolt at the front of the pump, to the torque listed in this Chapter's Specifications.

19 Lock the crankshaft in the TDC position again (see Chapter 2B, Section 3), and remove the special alignment tool.

20 If a new pump is being installed, fill the oil pump through the pick-up tube opening with oil, while rotating the oil pump sprocket several times.

21 Place the oil pump chain onto the sprockets and check to make sure the chain runs in a straight line between three sprockets.

22 Install the upper oil pan (see Section 13).

23 Install the chain guide, the tensioner guide and the tensioner assembly onto the cylinder block dowels, then install the tensioner fastener and tighten it to the torque listed in this Chapter's Specifications.

24 Remove the pin from the tensioner and release the piston to engage the chain guide.

25 The remainder of installation is the reverse of removal.

15 Initial start-up and break-in after overhaul

❈❈ WARNING:

Have a fire extinguisher handy when starting the engine for the first time.

1 Once the engine has been installed in the vehicle, double-check the engine oil and coolant levels.

2 With the spark plugs out of the engine and the fuel pump disabled (see Chapter 4, Section 3), crank the engine until oil pressure registers on the gauge or the light goes out.

3 Install the spark plugs, hook up the plug wires and restore the ignition system and fuel pump functions.

4 Start the engine. It may take a few moments for the fuel system to build up pressure, but the engine should start without a great deal of effort.

5 After the engine starts, it should be allowed to warm up to normal operating temperature. While the engine is warming up, make a thorough check for fuel, oil and coolant leaks.

6 Shut the engine off and recheck the engine oil and coolant levels.

7 Drive the vehicle to an area with minimum traffic, accelerate from 30 to 50 mph, then allow the vehicle to slow to 30 mph with the throttle closed. Repeat the procedure 10 or 12 times. This will load the piston rings and cause them to seat properly against the cylinder walls. Check again for oil and coolant leaks.

8 Drive the vehicle gently for the first 500 miles (no sustained high speeds) and keep a constant check on the oil level. It is not unusual for an engine to use oil during the break-in period.

9 At approximately 500 to 600 miles, change the oil and filter.

10 For the next few hundred miles, drive the vehicle normally. Do not pamper it or abuse it.

11 After 2,000 miles, change the oil and filter again and consider the engine broken in.Specifications

GLOSSARY

B

Backlash - The amount of play between two parts. Usually refers to how much one gear can be moved back and forth without moving the gear with which it's meshed.

Bearing Caps - The caps held in place by nuts or bolts which, in turn, hold the bearing surface. This space is for lubricating oil to enter.

Bearing clearance - The amount of space left between shaft and bearing surface. This space is for lubricating oil to enter.

Bearing crush - The additional height which is purposely manufactured into each bearing half to ensure complete contact of the bearing back with the housing bore when the engine is assembled.

Bearing knock - The noise created by movement of a part in a loose or worn bearing.

Blueprinting - Dismantling an engine and reassembling it to EXACT specifications.

Bore - An engine cylinder, or any cylindrical hole; also used to describe the process of enlarging or accurately refinishing a hole with a cutting tool, as to bore an engine cylinder. The bore size is the diameter of the hole.

Boring - Renewing the cylinders by cutting them out to a specified size. A boring bar is used to make the cut.

Bottom end - A term which refers collectively to the engine block, crankshaft, main bearings and the big ends of the connecting rods.

Break-in - The period of operation between installation of new or rebuilt parts and time in which parts are worn to the correct fit. Driving at reduced and varying speed for a specified mileage to permit parts to wear to the correct fit.

Bushing - A one-piece sleeve placed in a bore to serve as a bearing surface for shaft, piston pin, etc. Usually replaceable.

C

Camshaft - The shaft in the engine, on which a series of lobes are located for operating the valve mechanisms. The camshaft is driven by gears or sprockets and a timing chain. Usually referred to simply as the cam.

Carbon - Hard, or soft, black deposits found in combustion chamber, on plugs, under rings, on and under valve heads.

Cast iron - An alloy of iron and more than two percent carbon, used for engine blocks and heads because it's relatively inexpensive and easy to mold into complex shapes.

Chamfer - To bevel across (or a bevel on) the sharp edge of an object.

Chase - To repair damaged threads with a tap or die.

Combustion chamber - The space between the piston and the cylinder head, with the piston at top dead center, in which air-fuel mixture is burned.

Compression ratio - The relationship between cylinder volume (clearance volume) when the piston is at top dead center and cylinder volume when the piston is at bottom dead center.

Connecting rod - The rod that connects the crank on the crankshaft with the piston. Sometimes called a con rod.

Connecting rod cap - The part of the connecting rod assembly that attaches the rod to the crankpin.

Core plug - Soft metal plug used to plug the casting holes for the coolant passages in the block.

Crankcase - The lower part of the engine in which the crankshaft rotates; includes the lower section of the cylinder block and the oil pan.

Crank kit - A reground or reconditioned crankshaft and new main and connecting rod bearings.

Crankpin - The part of a crankshaft to which a connecting rod is attached.

Crankshaft - The main rotating member, or shaft, running the length of the crankcase, with offset throws to which the connecting rods are attached; changes the reciprocating motion of the pistons into rotating motion.

Cylinder sleeve - A replaceable sleeve, or liner, pressed into the cylinder block to form the cylinder bore.

D

Deburring - Removing the burrs (rough edges or areas) from a bearing.

Deglazer - A tool, rotated by an electric motor, used to remove glaze from cylinder walls so a new set of rings will seat.

E

Endplay - The amount of lengthwise movement between two parts. As applied to a crankshaft, the distance that the crankshaft can move forward and back in the cylinder block.

F

Face - A machinist's term that refers to removing metal from the end of a shaft or the face of a larger part, such as a flywheel.

Fatigue - A breakdown of material through a large number of loading and unloading cycles. The first signs are cracks followed shortly by breaks.

Feeler gauge - A thin strip of hardened steel, ground to an exact thickness, used to check clearances between parts.

Free height - The unloaded length or height of a spring.

Freeplay - The looseness in a linkage, or an assembly of parts, between the initial application of force and actual movement. Usually perceived as slop or slight delay.

Freeze plug - See Core plug.

G

Gallery - A large passage in the block that forms a reservoir for engine oil pressure.

Glaze - The very smooth, glassy finish that develops on cylinder walls while an engine is in service.

H

Heli-Coil - A rethreading device used when threads are worn or damaged. The device is installed in a retapped hole to reduce the thread size to the original size.

I

Installed height - The spring's measured length or height, as installed on the cylinder head. Installed height is measured from the spring seat to the underside of the spring retainer.

J

Journal - The surface of a rotating shaft which turns in a bearing.

K

Keeper - The split lock that holds the valve spring retainer in position on the valve stem.

Key - A small piece of metal inserted into matching grooves machined into two parts fitted together - such as a gear pressed onto a shaft - which prevents slippage between the two parts.

Knock - The heavy metallic engine sound, produced in the combustion chamber as a result of abnormal combustion - usually detonation. Knock is usually caused by a loose or worn bearing. Also referred to as detonation, pinging and spark knock. Connecting rod or main bearing knocks are created by too much oil clearance or insufficient lubrication.

L

Lands - The portions of metal between the piston ring grooves.

Lapping the valves - Grinding a valve face and its seat together with lapping compound.

Lash - The amount of free motion in a gear train, between gears, or in a mechanical assembly, that occurs before movement can begin. Usually refers to the lash in a valve train.

Lifter - The part that rides against the cam to transfer motion to the rest of the valve train.

M

Machining - The process of using a machine to remove metal from a metal part.

Main bearings - The plain, or babbitt, bearings that support the crankshaft.

Main bearing caps - The cast iron caps, bolted to the bottom of the block, that support the main bearings.

O

O.D. - Outside diameter.

Oil gallery - A pipe or drilled passageway in the engine used to carry engine oil from one area to another.

Oil ring - The lower ring, or rings, of a piston; designed to prevent excessive amounts of oil from working up the cylinder walls and into the combustion chamber. Also called an oil-control ring.

Oil seal - A seal which keeps oil from leaking out of a compartment. Usually refers to a dynamic seal around a rotating shaft or other moving part.

O-ring - A type of sealing ring made of a special rubberlike material; in use, the O-ring is compressed into a groove to provide the sealing action.

Overhaul - To completely disassemble a unit, clean and inspect all parts, reassemble it with the original or new parts and make all adjustments necessary for proper operation.

P

Pilot bearing - A small bearing installed in the center of the flywheel (or the rear end of the crankshaft) to support the front end of the input shaft of the transmission.

Pip mark - A little dot or indentation which indicates the top side of a compression ring.

Piston - The cylindrical part, attached to the connecting rod, that moves up and down in the cylinder as the crankshaft rotates. When the fuel charge is fired, the piston transfers the force of the explosion to the connecting rod, then to the crankshaft.

Piston pin (or wrist pin) - The cylindrical and usually hollow steel pin that passes through the piston. The piston pin fastens the piston to the upper end of the connecting rod.

Piston ring - The split ring fitted to the groove in a piston. The ring contacts the sides of the ring groove and also rubs against the cylinder wall, thus sealing space between piston and wall. There are two types of rings: Compression rings seal the compression pressure in the combustion chamber; oil rings scrape excessive oil off the cylinder wall.

Piston ring groove - The slots or grooves cut in piston heads to hold piston rings in position.

Piston skirt - The portion of the piston below the rings and the piston pin hole.

Plastigage - A thin strip of plastic thread, available in different sizes, used for measuring clearances. For example, a strip of plastigage is laid across a bearing journal and mashed as parts are assembled. Then parts are disassembled and the width of the strip is measured to determine clearance between journal and bearing. Commonly used to measure crankshaft main-bearing and connecting rod bearing clearances.

Press-fit - A tight fit between two parts that requires pressure to force the parts together. Also referred to as drive, or force, fit.

Prussian blue - A blue pigment; in solution, useful in determining the area of contact between two surfaces. Prussian blue is commonly used to determine the width and location of the contact area between the valve face and the valve seat.

R

Race (bearing) - The inner or outer ring that provides a contact surface for balls or rollers in bearing.

Ream - To size, enlarge or smooth a hole by using a round cutting tool with fluted edges.

Ring job - The process of reconditioning the cylinders and installing new rings.

Runout - Wobble. The amount a shaft rotates out-of-true.

S

Saddle - The upper main bearing seat.

Scored - Scratched or grooved, as a cylinder wall may be scored by abrasive particles moved up and down by the piston rings.

Scuffing - A type of wear in which there's a transfer of material between parts moving against each other; shows up as pits or grooves in the mating surfaces.

Seat - The surface upon which another part rests or seats. For example, the valve seat is the matched surface upon which the valve face rests. Also used to refer to wearing into a good fit; for example, piston rings seat after a few miles of driving.

Short block - An engine block complete with crankshaft and piston and, usually, camshaft assemblies.

Static balance - The balance of an object while it's stationary.

Step - The wear on the lower portion of a ring land caused by excessive side and back-clearance. The height of the step indicates the ring's extra side clearance and the length of the step projecting from the back wall of the groove represents the ring's back clearance.

Stroke - The distance the piston moves when traveling from top dead center to bottom dead center, or from bottom dead center to top dead center.

Stud - A metal rod with threads on both ends.

T

Tang - A lip on the end of a plain bearing used to align the bearing during assembly.

Tap - To cut threads in a hole. Also refers to the fluted tool used to cut threads.

Taper - A gradual reduction in the width of a shaft or hole; in an engine cylinder, taper usually takes the form of uneven wear, more pronounced at the top than at the bottom.

Throws - The offset portions of the crankshaft to which the connecting rods are affixed.

Thrust bearing - The main bearing that has thrust faces to prevent excessive endplay, or forward and backward movement of the crankshaft.

Thrust washer - A bronze or hardened steel washer placed between two moving parts. The washer prevents longitudinal movement and provides a bearing surface for thrust surfaces of parts.

Tolerance - The amount of variation permitted from an exact size of measurement. Actual amount from smallest acceptable dimension to largest acceptable dimension.

U

Umbrella - An oil deflector placed near the valve tip to throw oil from the valve stem area.

Undercut - A machined groove below the normal surface.

Undersize bearings - Smaller diameter bearings used with re-ground crankshaft journals.

V

Valve grinding - Refacing a valve in a valve-refacing machine.

Valve train - The valve-operating mechanism of an engine; includes all components from the camshaft to the valve.

Vibration damper - A cylindrical weight attached to the front of the crankshaft to minimize torsional vibration (the twist-untwist actions of the crankshaft caused by the cylinder firing impulses). Also called a harmonic balancer.

W

Water jacket - The spaces around the cylinders, between the inner and outer shells of the cylinder block or head, through which coolant circulates.

Web - A supporting structure across a cavity.

Woodruff key - A key with a radiused backside (viewed from the side).

Specifications

General

Engine designations	
Four-cylinder timing belt engine	BPY
Four-cylinder timing chain engines	CCTA, CBFA
Five-cylinder engine	BGP, BGQ, CBTA, CBUA
Displacement	
Four-cylinder engines	121 cubic inches (2.0 liters)
Five-cylinder engine	151 cubic inches (2.5 liters)
Bore and stroke	
Four-cylinder engines	3.25 x 3.65 inches (82.5 x 92.8)
Five-cylinder engine	3.25 x 3.65 inches (82.5 x 92.8)
Compression ratio	
Four-cylinder timing belt engine	10.5:1
Four-cylinder timing chain engines	9.6:1
Five-cylinder engine	9.5:1
Cylinder compression	
Four-cylinder engines	
Minimum/maximum	160 to 203 psi (1,110 to 1,400 kPa)
Variation between cylinders	44 psi (303 kPa)
Five-cylinder engines	
Minimum/maximum	130 to 188 psi (896 to 1,296 kPa)
Variation between cylinders	43 psi (296 kPa)
Oil pressure	
2000 rpm @ 176-degrees F	39 to 65 psi (269 to 448 kPa)
Maximum pressure	102 psi (703 kPa)

Torque specifications	Ft-lbs (unless otherwise indicated)	Nm

➡ **Note: One foot-pound (ft-lb) of torque is equivalent to 12 inch-pounds (in-lbs) of torque. Torque values below approximately 15 foot-pounds are expressed in inch-pounds, because most foot-pound torque wrenches are not accurate at these smaller values.**

Connecting rod bolts (new)		
Four-cylinder timing belt (BPY) engines		
Step 1	22	30
Step 2	Tighten an additional 90 degrees	
Four-cylinder timing chain (CCTA, CBFA) engines		
Step 1	33	45
Step 2	Tighten an additional 90 degrees	
Five-cylinder (BGP, BGQ, CBTA, CBUA) engines		
Step 1	22	30
Step 2	Tighten an additional 90 degrees	
Control housing cover fasteners		
Step 1	89 in-lbs	10
Step 2	18.5	25
Main bearing bolts (new) (tighten in sequence, see illustrations 10.19a, 10.19b, 10.19c)		
Four-cylinder timing belt (BPY) engines		
Step 1	48	65
Step 2	Tighten an additional 90 degrees	

Torque specifications	Ft-lbs (unless otherwise indicated)	Nm

➡ **Note:** One foot-pound (ft-lb) of torque is equivalent to 12 inch-pounds (in-lbs) of torque. Torque values below approximately 15 foot-pounds are expressed in inch-pounds, because most foot-pound torque wrenches are not accurate at these smaller values.

	Ft-lbs (unless otherwise indicated)	Nm
Main bearing bolts (new) (tighten in sequence, see illustrations 10.19a, 10.19b, 10.19c)		
Four-cylinder timing chain (CCTA, CBFA) engines		
Step 1	Tighten all bolts by hand	
Step 2 cap bolts	48	65
Step 3 cap bolts	Tighten an additional 90 degrees	
Step 4 jack bolts (side bolts)	15	20
Step 5 jack bolts (side bolts)	Tighten an additional 90 degrees	
Five-cylinder (BGP, BGQ, CBTA, CBUA) engines		
Step 1	30	40
Step 2	Tighten an additional 90 degrees	
Oil pump fasteners	18.5	25
Oil pump pick-up tube fasteners	89 in-lbs	10
Oil pump sprocket retaining bolt (new)		
Step 1	15	20
Step 2	Tighten an additional 90 degrees	
Oil pump tensioner fastener	89 in-lbs	10
Piston oil spray nozzle fastener	20	27
Upper oil pan mounting fasteners	18.5	25

Notes

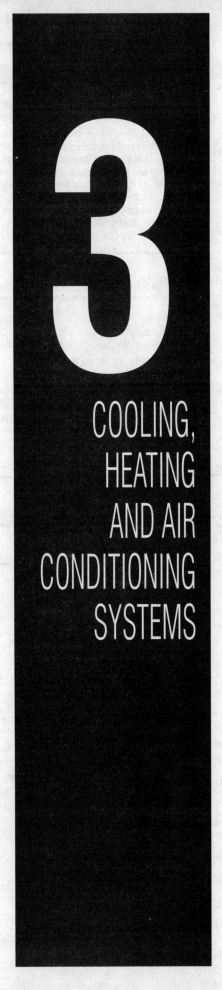

3

COOLING, HEATING AND AIR CONDITIONING SYSTEMS

Section

Reference to other Chapters

1 General information

※※ WARNING:

Do not allow antifreeze to come in contact with your skin or painted surfaces of the vehicle. Rinse off spills immediately with plenty of water. Antifreeze is highly toxic if ingested. Never leave antifreeze lying around in an open container or in puddles on the floor; children and pets are attracted by its sweet smell and may drink it. Check with local authorities about disposing of used antifreeze. Many communities have collection centers which will see that antifreeze is disposed of safely. Never dump used antifreeze on the ground or pour it into drains.

ENGINE COOLING SYSTEM

All modern vehicles employ a pressurized engine cooling system with thermostatically controlled coolant circulation. The cooling system consists of a radiator, an expansion tank or coolant reservoir, a pressure cap (located on the expansion tank or radiator), a thermostat, a cooling fan, and a water pump.

The water pump circulates coolant through the engine. The coolant flows around each cylinder and around the intake and exhaust ports, near the spark plug areas and in close proximity to the exhaust valve guides.

A thermostat controls engine coolant temperature. During warm up, the closed thermostat prevents coolant from circulating through the radiator. As the engine nears normal operating temperature, the thermo-

stat opens and allows hot coolant to travel through the radiator, where it's cooled before returning to the engine.

HEATING SYSTEM

The heating system consists of a blower fan and heater core located in a housing under the dash, the hoses connecting the heater core to the engine cooling system and the heater/air conditioning control head on the dashboard. Hot engine coolant is circulated through the heater core. When the heater mode is activated, a flap door in the housing opens to expose the heater core to the passenger compartment through air ducts. A fan switch on the control head activates the blower motor, which forces air through the core, heating the air.

AIR CONDITIONING SYSTEM

The air conditioning system consists of a condenser mounted in front of the radiator, an evaporator mounted adjacent to the heater core, a compressor mounted on the engine, a receiver-drier or accumulator and the plumbing connecting all of the above components.

A blower fan forces the warmer air of the passenger compartment through the evaporator core (sort of a radiator-in-reverse), transferring the heat from the air to the refrigerant. The liquid refrigerant boils off into low pressure vapor, taking the heat with it when it leaves the evaporator.

2 Troubleshooting

COOLANT LEAKS

▶ **Refer to illustration 2.2**

1   A coolant leak can develop anywhere in the cooling system, but the most common causes are:

   a) A loose or weak hose clamp
   b) A defective hose
   c) A faulty pressure cap
   d) A damaged radiator
   e) A bad heater core
   f) A faulty water pump
   g) A leaking gasket at any joint that carries coolant

2   Coolant leaks aren't always easy to find. Sometimes they can only be detected when the cooling system is under pressure. Here's where a cooling system pressure tester comes in handy. After the engine has cooled completely, the tester is attached in place of the pressure cap, then pumped up to the pressure value equal to that of the pressure cap rating (see illustration). Now, leaks that only exist when the engine is fully warmed up will become apparent. The tester can be left connected to locate a nagging slow leak.

COOLANT LEVEL DROPS, BUT NO EXTERNAL LEAKS

▶ **Refer to illustrations 2.5a and 2.5b**

3   If you find it necessary to keep adding coolant, but there are no external leaks, the probable causes include:

2.2 The cooling system pressure tester is connected in place of the pressure cap, then pumped up to pressurize the system

   a) A blown head gasket
   b) A leaking intake manifold gasket (only on engines that have coolant passages in the manifold)
   c) A cracked cylinder head or cylinder block

4   Any of the above problems will also usually result in contamination of the engine oil, which will cause it to take on a milkshake-like appearance. A bad head gasket or cracked head or block can also result in engine oil contaminating the cooling system.

5   Combustion leak detectors (also known as block testers) are available at most auto parts stores. These work by detecting exhaust

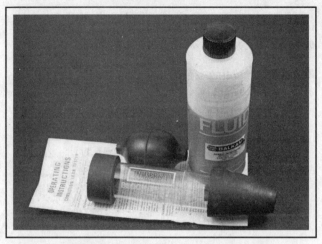

2.5a The combustion leak detector consists of a bulb, syringe and test fluid

2.5b Place the tester over the cooling system filler neck and use the bulb to draw a sample into the tester

gases in the cooling system, which indicates a compression leak from a cylinder into the coolant. The tester consists of a large bulb-type syringe and bottle of test fluid (see illustration). A measured amount of the fluid is added to the syringe. The syringe is placed over the cooling system filler neck and, with the engine running, the bulb is squeezed and a sample of the gases present in the cooling system are drawn up through the test fluid (see illustration). If any combustion gases are present in the sample taken, the test fluid will change color.

6   If the test indicates combustion gas is present in the cooling system, you can be sure that the engine has a blown head gasket or a crack in the cylinder head or block, and will require disassembly to repair.

PRESSURE CAP

▶ Refer to illustration 2.8

⁂ WARNING:

Wait until the engine is completely cool before beginning this check.

7   The cooling system is sealed by a spring-loaded cap, which raises the boiling point of the coolant. If the cap's seal or spring are worn out, the coolant can boil and escape past the cap. With the engine completely cool, remove the cap and check the seal; if it's cracked,

2.8 Check the cooling system pressure cap with a cooling system pressure tester

hardened or deteriorated in any way, replace it with a new one.

8   Even if the seal is good, the spring might not be; this can be checked with a cooling system pressure tester (see illustration). If the cap can't hold a pressure within approximately 1-1/2 lbs of its rated pressure (which is marked on the cap), replace it with a new one.

9   The cap is also equipped with a vacuum relief spring. When the engine cools off, a vacuum is created in the cooling system. The vacuum relief spring allows air back into the system, which will equalize the pressure and prevent damage to the radiator (the radiator tanks could collapse if the vacuum is great enough). If, after turning the engine off and allowing it to cool down you notice any of the cooling system hoses collapsing, replace the pressure cap with a new one.

THERMOSTAT

▶ Refer to illustration 2.10

10 Before assuming the thermostat (see illustration) is responsible for a cooling system problem, check the coolant level (see Chapter 1), drive-

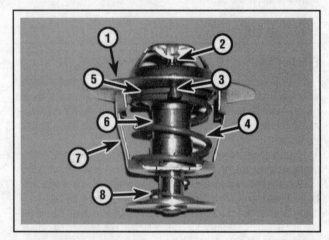

2.10 Typical thermostat:

1	Flange	5	Valve seat
2	Piston	6	Valve
3	Jiggle valve	7	Frame
4	Main coil spring	8	Secondary coil spring

2.28 The water pump weep hole is generally located on the underside of the pump

belt tension (see Chapter 1) and temperature gauge (or light) operation.

11 If the engine takes a long time to warm up (as indicated by the temperature gauge or heater operation), the thermostat is probably stuck open. Replace the thermostat with a new one.

12 If the engine runs hot or overheats, a thorough test of the thermostat should be performed.

13 Definitive testing of the thermostat can only be made when it is removed from the vehicle. If the thermostat is stuck in the open position at room temperature, it is faulty and must be replaced.

❊ CAUTION:

Do not drive the vehicle without a thermostat. The computer may stay in open loop and emissions and fuel economy will suffer.

14 To test a thermostat, suspend the (closed) thermostat on a length of string or wire in a pot of cold water.

15 Heat the water on a stove while observing thermostat. The thermostat should fully open before the water boils.

16 If the thermostat doesn't open and close as specified, or sticks in any position, replace it.

COOLING FAN

Electric cooling fan

17 If the engine is overheating and the cooling fan is not coming on when the engine temperature rises to an excessive level, unplug the fan motor electrical connector(s) and connect the motor directly to the battery with fused jumper wires. If the fan motor doesn't come on, replace the motor.

18 If the radiator fan motor is okay, but it isn't coming on when the engine gets hot, the fan relay might be defective. A relay is used to control a circuit by turning it on and off in response to a control decision by the Powertrain Control Module (PCM). These control circuits are fairly complex, and checking them should be left to a qualified automotive technician. Sometimes, the control system can be fixed by simply identifying and replacing a bad relay.

19 Locate the fan relays in the engine compartment fuse/relay box.

20 Test the relay (see Chapter 12).

21 If the relay is okay, check all wiring and connections to the fan motor. Refer to the wiring diagrams at the end of Chapter 12. If no obvious problems are found, the problem could be the Engine Coolant

Temperature (ECT) sensor or the Powertrain Control Module (PCM). Have the cooling fan system and circuit diagnosed by a dealer service department or repair shop with the proper diagnostic equipment.

Belt-driven cooling fan

22 Disconnect the cable from the negative terminal of the battery and rock the fan back and forth by hand to check for excessive bearing play.

23 With the engine cold (and not running), turn the fan blades by hand. The fan should turn freely.

24 Visually inspect for substantial fluid leakage from the clutch assembly. If problems are noted, replace the clutch assembly.

25 With the engine completely warmed up, turn off the ignition switch and disconnect the negative battery cable from the battery. Turn the fan by hand. Some drag should be evident. If the fan turns easily, replace the fan clutch.

WATER PUMP

26 A failure in the water pump can cause serious engine damage due to overheating.

Drivebelt-driven water pump

▶ **Refer to illustration 2.28**

27 There are two ways to check the operation of the water pump while it's installed on the engine. If the pump is found to be defective, it should be replaced with a new or rebuilt unit.

28 Water pumps are equipped with weep (or vent) holes (see illustration). If a failure occurs in the pump seal, coolant will leak from the hole.

29 If the water pump shaft bearings fail, there may be a howling sound at the pump while it's running. Shaft wear can be felt with the drivebelt removed if the water pump pulley is rocked up and down (with the engine off). Don't mistake drivebelt slippage, which causes a squealing sound, for water pump bearing failure.

Timing chain or timing belt-driven water pump

30 Water pumps driven by the timing chain or timing belt are located underneath the timing chain or timing belt cover.

31 Checking the water pump is limited because of where it is located. However, some basic checks can be made before deciding to remove the water pump. If the pump is found to be defective, it should be replaced with a new or rebuilt unit.

32 One sign that the water pump may be failing is that the heater (climate control) may not work well. Warm the engine to normal operating temperature, confirm that the coolant level is correct, then run the heater and check for hot air coming from the ducts.

33 Check for noises coming from the water pump area. If the water pump impeller shaft or bearings are failing, there may be a howling sound at the pump while the engine is running.

➡ **Note: Be careful not to mistake drivebelt noise (squealing) for water pump bearing or shaft failure.**

34 It you suspect water pump failure due to noise, wear can be confirmed by feeling for play at the pump shaft. This can be done by rocking the drive sprocket on the pump shaft up and down. To do this you will need to remove the tension on the timing chain or belt as well as access the water pump.

All water pumps

35 In rare cases or on high-mileage vehicles, another sign of water

pump failure may be the presence of coolant in the engine oil. This condition will adversely affect the engine in varying degrees.

➡ **Note: Finding coolant in the engine oil could indicate other serious issues besides a failed water pump, such as a blown head gasket or a cracked cylinder head or block.**

36 Even a pump that exhibits no outward signs of a problem, such as noise or leakage, can still be due for replacement. Removal for close examination is the only sure way to tell. Sometimes the fins on the back of the impeller can corrode to the point that cooling efficiency is diminished significantly.

HEATER SYSTEM

37 Little can go wrong with a heater. If the fan motor will run at all speeds, the electrical part of the system is okay. The three basic heater problems fall into the following general categories:

   a) *Not enough heat*
   b) *Heat all the time*
   c) *No heat*

38 If there's not enough heat, the control valve or door is stuck in a partially open position, the coolant coming from the engine isn't hot enough, or the heater core is restricted. If the coolant isn't hot enough, the thermostat in the engine cooling system is stuck open, allowing coolant to pass through the engine so rapidly that it doesn't heat up quickly enough. If the vehicle is equipped with a temperature gauge instead of a warning light, watch to see if the engine temperature rises to the normal operating range after driving for a reasonable distance.

39 If there's heat all the time, the control valve or the door is stuck wide open.

40 If there's no heat, coolant is probably not reaching the heater core, or the heater core is plugged. The likely cause is a collapsed or plugged hose, core, or a frozen heater control valve. If the heater is the type that flows coolant all the time, the cause is a stuck door or a broken or kinked control cable.

AIR CONDITIONING SYSTEM

41 If the cool air output is inadequate:

   a) *Inspect the condenser coils and fins to make sure they're clear*
   b) *Check the compressor clutch for slippage.*
   c) *Check the blower motor for proper operation.*
   d) *Inspect the blower discharge passage for obstructions.*
   e) *Check the system air intake filter for clogging.*

42 If the system provides intermittent cooling air:

   a) *Check the circuit breaker, blower switch and blower motor for a malfunction.*
   b) *Make sure the compressor clutch isn't slipping.*
   c) *Inspect the plenum door to make sure it's operating properly.*
   d) *Inspect the evaporator to make sure it isn't clogged.*
   e) *If the unit is icing up, it may be caused by excessive moisture in the system, incorrect super heat switch adjustment or low thermostat adjustment.*

43 If the system provides no cooling air:

   a) *Inspect the compressor drivebelt. Make sure it's not loose or broken.*
   b) *Make sure the compressor clutch engages. If it doesn't, check for a blown fuse.*
   c) *Inspect the wire harness for broken or disconnected wires.*
   d) *If the compressor clutch doesn't engage, bridge the terminals of the A/C pressure switch(es) with a jumper wire; if the clutch now engages, and the system is properly charged, the pressure switch is bad.*
   e) *Make sure the blower motor is not disconnected or burned out.*
   f) *Make sure the compressor isn't partially or completely seized.*
   g) *Inspect the refrigerant lines for leaks.*
   h) *Check the components for leaks.*
   i) *Inspect the receiver-drier/accumulator or expansion valve/tube for clogged screens.*

44 If the system is noisy:

   a) *Look for loose panels in the passenger compartment.*
   b) *Inspect the compressor drivebelt. It may be loose or worn.*
   c) *Check the compressor mounting bolts. They should be tight.*
   d) *Listen carefully to the compressor. It may be worn out.*
   e) *Listen to the idler pulley and bearing and the clutch. Either may be defective.*
   f) *The winding in the compressor clutch coil or solenoid may be defective.*
   g) *The compressor oil level may be low.*
   h) *The blower motor fan bushing or the motor itself may be worn out.*
   i) *If there is an excessive charge in the system, you'll hear a rumbling noise in the high pressure line, a thumping noise in the compressor, or see bubbles or cloudiness in the sight glass.*
   j) *If there's a low charge in the system, you might hear hissing in the evaporator case at the expansion valve, or see bubbles or cloudiness in the sight glass.*

3   Air conditioning and heating system - check and maintenance

AIR CONDITIONING SYSTEM

▶ **Refer to illustration 3.1**

※ WARNING:

The air conditioning system is under high pressure. Do not loosen any hose fittings or remove any components until after the system has been discharged. Air conditioning refrigerant should be properly discharged into an EPA-approved recovery/ recycling unit at a dealer service department or an automotive air conditioning repair facility. Always wear eye protection when disconnecting air conditioning system fittings.

※ CAUTION 1:

All models covered by this manual use environmentally friendly R-134a. This refrigerant (and its appropriate refrigerant oils) are not compatible with R-12 refrigerant system components and must never be mixed or the components will be damaged.

3.1 Evaporator drain hose

3.9 Insert a thermometer in the center vent, turn on the air conditioning system and wait for it to cool down; depending on the humidity, the output air should be 30 to 40 degrees cooler than the ambient air temperature

❄❄ CAUTION 2:

When replacing entire components, additional refrigerant oil should be added equal to the amount that is removed with the component being replaced. Be sure to read the can before adding any oil to the system, to make sure it is compatible with the R-134a system.

1   The following maintenance checks should be performed on a regular basis to ensure that the air conditioning continues to operate at peak efficiency.

   a) *Inspect the condition of the compressor drivebelt. If it is worn or deteriorated, replace it (see Chapter 1).*
   b) *Check the drivebelt tension (see Chapter 1).*
   c) *Inspect the system hoses. Look for cracks, bubbles, hardening and deterioration. Inspect the hoses and all fittings for oil bubbles or seepage. If there is any evidence of wear, damage or leakage, replace the hose(s).*
   d) *Inspect the condenser fins for leaves, bugs and any other foreign material that may have embedded itself in the fins. Use a fin comb or compressed air to remove debris from the condenser.*
   e) *Make sure the system has the correct refrigerant charge.*
   f) *If you hear water sloshing around in the dash area or have water dripping on the carpet, check the evaporator housing drain tube (see illustration) and insert a piece of wire into the opening to check for blockage.*

2   It's a good idea to operate the system for about ten minutes at least once a month. This is particularly important during the winter months because long term non-use can cause hardening, and subsequent failure, of the seals. Note that using the Defrost function operates the compressor.

3   If the air conditioning system is not working properly, proceed to Step 6 and perform the general checks outlined below.

4   Because of the complexity of the air conditioning system and the special equipment necessary to service it, in-depth troubleshooting and repairs beyond checking the refrigerant charge and the compressor clutch operation are not included in this manual. However, simple checks and component replacement procedures are provided in this Chapter.

5   The most common cause of poor cooling is simply a low system refrigerant charge. If a noticeable drop in system cooling ability occurs, one of the following quick checks will help you determine if the refrigerant level is low.

Checking the refrigerant charge

▶ **Refer to illustration 3.9**

6   Warm the engine up to normal operating temperature.

7   Place the air conditioning temperature selector at the coldest setting and put the blower at the highest setting.

8   After the system reaches operating temperature, feel the larger pipe exiting the evaporator at the firewall. The outlet pipe should be cold (the tubing that leads back to the compressor). If the evaporator outlet pipe is warm, the system probably needs a charge.

9   Insert a thermometer in the center air distribution duct (see illustration) while operating the air conditioning system at its maximum setting - the temperature of the output air should be 30 to 40 degrees F below the ambient air temperature (down to approximately 40 degrees F). If the ambient (outside) air temperature is very high, say 110 degrees F, the duct air temperature may be as high as 60 degrees F, but generally the air conditioning is 30 to 40 degrees F cooler than the ambient air.

10   Further inspection or testing of the system requires special tools and techniques and is beyond the scope of the home mechanic.

Adding refrigerant

▶ **Refer to illustrations 3.11 and 3.13**

❄❄ CAUTION:

Make sure any refrigerant, refrigerant oil or replacement component you purchase is designated as compatible with R-134a systems.

11   Purchase an R-134a automotive charging kit at an auto parts store (see illustration). A charging kit includes a can of refrigerant, a tap valve and a short section of hose that can be attached between the tap valve and the system low side service valve.

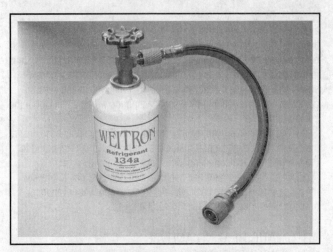

3.11 R-134a automotive air conditioning charging kit

3.13 Location of the low-side charging port

❋❋ CAUTION:

Never add more than one can of refrigerant to the system. If more refrigerant than that is required, the system should be evacuated and leak tested.

12 Back off the valve handle on the charging kit and screw the kit onto the refrigerant can, making sure first that the O-ring or rubber seal inside the threaded portion of the kit is in place.

❋❋ WARNING:

Wear protective eyewear when dealing with pressurized refrigerant cans.

13 Remove the dust cap from the low-side charging port and attach the hose's quick-connect fitting to the port (see illustration).

❋❋ WARNING:

DO NOT hook the charging kit hose to the system high side!

The fittings on the charging kit are designed to fit only on the low side of the system.

14 Warm up the engine and turn On the air conditioning. Keep the charging kit hose away from the fan and other moving parts.

➡ **Note: The charging process requires the compressor to be running. If the clutch cycles off, you can put the air conditioning switch on High and leave the car doors open to keep the clutch on and compressor working. The compressor can be kept on during the charging by removing the connector from the pressure switch and bridging it with a paper clip or jumper wire during the procedure.**

15 Turn the valve handle on the kit until the stem pierces the can, then back the handle out to release the refrigerant. You should be able to hear the rush of gas. Keep the can upright at all times, but shake it occasionally. Allow stabilization time between each addition.

➡ **Note: The charging process will go faster if you wrap the can with a hot-water-soaked rag to keep the can from freezing up.**

16 If you have an accurate thermometer, you can place it in the center air conditioning duct inside the vehicle and keep track of the output

air temperature. A charged system that is working properly should cool down to approximately 40 degrees F. If the ambient (outside) air temperature is very high, say 110 degrees F, the duct air temperature may be as high as 60 degrees F, but generally the air conditioning is 30 to 40 degrees F cooler than the ambient air.

17 When the can is empty, turn the valve handle to the closed position and release the connection from the low-side port. Reinstall the dust cap.

18 Remove the charging kit from the can and store the kit for future use with the piercing valve in the UP position, to prevent inadvertently piercing the can on the next use.

HEATING SYSTEMS

19 If the carpet under the heater core is damp, or if antifreeze vapor or steam is coming through the vents, the heater core is leaking. Remove it (see Section 11) and install a new unit (most radiator shops will not repair a leaking heater core).

20 If the air coming out of the heater vents isn't hot, the problem could stem from any of the following causes:

   a) *The thermostat is stuck open, preventing the engine coolant from warming up enough to carry heat to the heater core. Replace the thermostat (see Section 4).*
   b) *There is a blockage in the system, preventing the flow of coolant through the heater core. Feel both heater hoses at the firewall. They should be hot. If one of them is cold, there is an obstruction in one of the hoses or in the heater core, or the heater control valve is shut. Detach the hoses and back flush the heater core with a water hose. If the heater core is clear but circulation is impeded, remove the two hoses and flush them out with a water hose.*
   c) *If flushing fails to remove the blockage from the heater core, the core must be replaced (see Section 11).*

ELIMINATING AIR CONDITIONING ODORS

▶ **Refer to illustration 3.24**

21 Unpleasant odors that often develop in air conditioning systems are caused by the growth of a fungus, usually on the surface of the evaporator core. The warm, humid environment there is a perfect breeding ground for mildew to develop.

22 The evaporator core on most vehicles is difficult to access, and

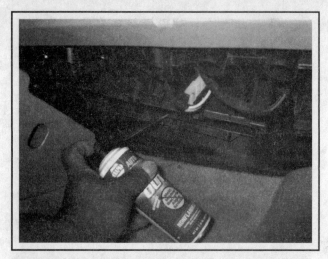

3.24 Remove the interior ventilation filter and spray the disinfectant into the blower housing with the blower on high (be sure to wear safety goggles)

factory dealerships have a lengthy, expensive process for eliminating the fungus by opening up the evaporator case and using a powerful disinfectant and rinse on the core until the fungus is gone. You can service your own system at home, but it takes something much stronger than basic household germ-killers or deodorizers.

23 Aerosol disinfectants for automotive air conditioning systems are available in most auto parts stores, but remember when shopping for them that the most effective treatments are also the most expensive. The basic procedure for using these sprays is to start by running the system in the RECIRC mode for ten minutes with the blower on its highest speed. Use the highest heat mode to dry out the system and keep the compressor from engaging by disconnecting the wiring connector at the compressor.

24 The disinfectant can usually comes with a long spray hose. Insert the nozzle into an intake port inside the cabin, and spray according to the manufacturer's recommendations (see illustration).

25 Once the evaporator has been cleaned, the best way to prevent the mildew from coming back again is to make sure your evaporator housing drain tube is clear (see illustration 3.1).

AUTOMATIC HEATING AND AIR CONDITIONING SYSTEMS

26 Some vehicles are equipped with an optional automatic climate control system. This system has its own computer that receives inputs from various sensors in the heating and air conditioning system. This computer, like the PCM, has self-diagnostic capabilities to help pinpoint problems or faults within the system. Vehicles equipped with automatic heating and air conditioning systems are very complex and considered beyond the scope of the home mechanic. Vehicles equipped with automatic heating and air conditioning systems should be taken to dealer service department or other qualified facility for repair.

4 Thermostat - replacement

⁂ WARNING:

The engine must be completely cool when this procedure is performed.

⁂ CAUTION:

Don't drive the vehicle without a thermostat! The computer may stay in open loop mode and emissions and fuel economy will suffer.

⁂ CAUTION:

If the battery is disconnected, several systems must be relearned before they will work properly (see Chapter 5, Section 3).

➡ **Note: Some modes are equipped with a by-pass thermostat located in the top line of the by-pass hose.**

1 Remove the engine cover (see Chapter 1, Section 7).
2 Disconnect the cable from the negative terminal of the battery (see Chapter 5).
3 Raise the front of the vehicle and support it securely on jackstands.
4 Remove the under-vehicle splash shield (see Chapter 1, Section 6).
5 Drain the coolant from the radiator (see Chapter 1). If the coolant

is new, save it and reuse it. If it is to be replaced, see Section 1 for cautions about proper handling of used antifreeze.

FOUR-CYLINDER BPY ENGINE

▶ **Refer to illustration 4.10**

6 Remove the drivebelt (see Chapter 1).
7 Remove the alternator (see Chapter 5).
8 Disconnect the radiator hose clamp and remove the radiator hose from the thermostat housing.
9 Remove the upper coolant hose clamps, hose and the coolant tube fastener, then pull the tube and O-ring from the housing.
10 Remove the coolant distribution housing fasteners, then detach the housing (see illustration). Be prepared for some coolant to spill as the gasket seal is broken.

➡ **Note: The thermostat and housing are one piece and must be replaced as a unit.**

Clean the mating surfaces of the engine block and the thermostat.

11 Install a new O-ring and reattach the thermostat housing to the engine block. Tighten the bolts to the torque listed in this Chapter's Specifications.
12 The remainder of installation is the reverse of the removal procedure.

4.10 Remove the thermostat (coolant distribution) housing fasteners and remove the housing - 2.0L BPY engine

➡ **Note: Coat the accessory bracket fasteners with thread locking compound before installation.**

13 Refer to Chapter 1 and refill and bleed the system, then run the engine and check carefully for leaks.

FOUR-CYLINDER CCTA, CBFA ENGINES

14 On models equipped with a noise generator, open the locking ring on the charge air pipe, disconnect the electrical connector to the charge air pipe, then remove the mounting fastener and the charge air pipe.

15 Remove the wiring harness retaining strap fastener and strap from under the radiator hose.

16 Remove the after-run coolant pump bracket fastener.

17 Remove the radiator hoses located behind the air conditioning compressor (see Chapter 1).

18 Loosen the intake manifold support bracket fasteners and move the bracket to the right.

19 Remove the oil separator (see Chapter 2A).

20 Remove the thermostat cover retaining fasteners and cover.

➡ **Note: A centering pin is mounted in the thermostat cover; if the cover is turned over, the pin may fall out of the cover.**

Be prepared for some coolant to spill as the cover is removed.

21 Note how the thermostat is installed (spring end inside the water pump housing), then remove the thermostat from the water pump housing.

22 Clean the mating surfaces of the water pump housing and the thermostat cover.

23 Install the thermostat and make sure the correct end faces out; the spring end is installed into the water pump housing.

24 Install a new O-ring to the thermostat cover and reattach the cover to the pump housing. Tighten the retaining fasteners to the torque listed in this Chapter's Specifications.

25 The remainder of installation is the reverse of the removal procedure.

26 Refer to Chapter 1 and refill and bleed the system, then run the engine and check carefully for leaks.

FIVE-CYLINDER ENGINES

27 Remove the intake manifold (see Chapter 2B).

➡ **Note: Reinstall the oil dipstick tube to prevent coolant from running into the oil pan.**

28 Remove the thermostat cover retaining fasteners and cover.

29 Note how the thermostat is installed (jiggle valve on top, and the spring end inside the thermostat housing), then remove the thermostat from the housing.

30 Remove the seal from the thermostat housing and clean the mating surfaces of the thermostat housing and the thermostat cover.

31 Install the thermostat seal to the housing. Install the thermostat, making sure the correct end faces out - with the jiggle valve up and the spring end installed into the housing.

32 Install a new O-ring to the thermostat cover and reattach the cover to the thermostat housing. Tighten the retaining fasteners to the torque listed in this Chapter's Specifications.

33 The remainder of installation is the reverse of the removal procedure.

34 Refer to Chapter 1 and refill and bleed the system, then run the engine and check carefully for leaks.

5 Engine cooling fans - removal and installation

▶ **Refer to illustrations 5.7, 5.8 and 5.9**

✳✳ WARNING:

Keep hands, tools and clothing away from the fan. To avoid injury or damage, DO NOT operate the engine with a damaged fan. Do not attempt to repair fan blades - always replace a damaged fan with a new one.

✳✳ CAUTION:

If the battery is disconnected, several systems must be relearned before they will work properly (see Chapter 5, Section 3).

1 Remove the engine cover (see Chapter 1, Section 7). Disconnect the cable from the negative terminal of the battery (see Chapter 5).

2 Raise the front of the vehicle and support it securely on jackstands.

3 Remove the under-vehicle splash shield (see Chapter 1, Section 6).

4 On four-cylinder BPY engines, remove the air conditioning line support bracket fasteners at the right side of the frame and move the lines away from the fan shroud.

5 On four-cylinder CCTA and CBFA engines equipped with a noise generator, open the locking ring on the charge air pipe, disconnect the electrical connector to the charge air pipe, then remove the mounting fastener and the charge air pipe (see Chapter 4).

5.7 Disconnect the engine harness connector to the cooling fan connector

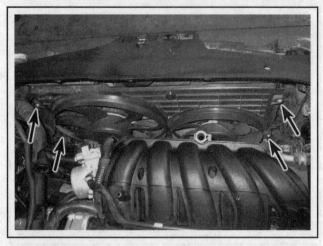

5.8 Remove the fan shroud retaining fasteners

6   On five-cylinder engines, unclip the lower radiator hose from the fan shroud and disconnect the Engine Coolant Temperature (ECT) sensor electrical connector (see Chapter 6).

7   Disconnect the electrical connector(s) from the cooling fan(s) harness (see illustration).

8   Remove the cooling fan shroud fasteners (see illustration) and remove the assembly from the bottom of the vehicle.

9   Disconnect, then separate the electrical connector for the cooling fans, remove the cooling fan motor fasteners and fans from the shroud (see illustration).

10   If the fan blades or the fan motor are damaged, they can be replaced by removing the fan blade from the fan motor.

11   The remainder of installation is the reverse of the removal procedure.

5.9 Fan shroud and cooling fan details

1   Fan shroud
2   Cooling fan motor connection
3   Cooling fan retaining fasteners

6   Radiator and expansion tank - removal and installation

✳✳ WARNING:

The engine must be completely cool when this procedure is performed.

✳✳ CAUTION:

If the battery is disconnected, several systems must be relearned before they will work properly (see Chapter 5, Section 3).

RADIATOR

▸ Refer to illustrations 6.10a and 6.10b

1   Raise the front of the vehicle and support it securely on jackstands. Disconnect the cable from the negative terminal of the battery (see Chapter 5).

2   Remove the under-vehicle splash shield (see Chapter 1, Section 6) and drain the cooling system as described in Chapter 1. Refer to the coolant **Warning** in Section 1.

3   Remove the engine cover (see Chapter 1, Section 7).

4   On four-cylinder BPY engines, remove the lower hoses to the intercooler (see Chapter 4).

5   On four-cylinder BPY engines and five-cylinder engines, remove the front bumper and place the radiator support panel in the service position (see Chapter 11).

5   On four-cylinder CCTA and CBFA engines equipped with a noise generator, open the locking ring on the charge air pipe, disconnect the electrical connector to the charge air pipe, then remove the mounting fastener and the charge air pipe (see Chapter 4).

6   Remove the hoses from the radiator (see Chapter 1).

7   Remove the fan shroud (see Section 5).

8   Remove the air duct fasteners from each side of the radiator and remove the ducts, if equipped.

6.10a Radiator mount retaining fastener location (right side shown, left side similar) - five-cylinder engines

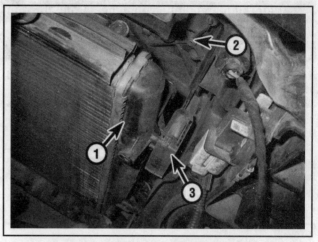

6.10b Radiator mount details - five-cylinder engines

1 *Radiator*
2 *Radiator support (in the service position)*
3 *Radiator mount*

9   On five-cylinder engines, remove the condenser-to-radiator mounting fasteners.

10 Remove the radiator mounting fasteners and lower the radiator from the vehicle.

➡ **Note: On five-cylinder engines, remove the radiator mount fasteners, slide the radiator out (away from the radiator support panel) and remove the radiator mounts and radiator from above (see illustrations).**

11 Prior to installation of the radiator, replace any damaged hose clamps and/or radiator hoses.

12 Installation is the reverse of removal.

13 Refill and bleed the system, then run the engine and check carefully for leaks (see Chapter 1).

EXPANSION TANK

6.15 Expansion tank details

1 *Expansion tank*	4 *Coolant hose (lower hose*
2 *Coolant level sensor*	*connection not visible)*
3 *Mounting screw*	

▶ **Refer to illustration 6.15**

14 Drain the cooling system as described in Chapter 1 until the expansion tank is empty. Refer to the coolant **Warning** in Section 1.

15 Detach the upper coolant hose from the expansion tank (see illustration).

16 Disconnect the coolant level sensor connector. Remove the expansion tank mounting screw, then lift the expansion tank up and disconnect the lower hose.

17 Remove the expansion tank from the engine compartment.

18 Prior to installation, make sure the reservoir is clean and free of debris which could be drawn into the radiator (wash it with soapy water and a brush if necessary, then rinse thoroughly).

19 Installation is the reverse of removal.

7   Water pump and after-run coolant pump - replacement

※ CAUTION:

If the battery is disconnected, several systems must be relearned before they will work properly (see Chapter 5, Section 3).

WATER PUMP

※ WARNING:

Wait until the engine is completely cool before starting this procedure.

1   Remove the engine cover (see Chapter 1, Section 7).

2   Disconnect the cable from the negative terminal of the battery (see Chapter 5).

3   Raise the front of the vehicle and support it securely on jackstands.

4   Remove the lower splash shield below the engine (see Chapter 1, Section 6).

5   Drain the cooling system (see Chapter 1). If the coolant is new save it and reuse it. If it is to be replaced, see Section 1 for cautions about proper handling of used antifreeze.

Four-cylinder BPY engine

6   Remove the timing belt (see Chapter 2A).

7   Remove the water pump mounting fasteners and remove the pump.

8   Remove the O-ring located between the housing and block and discard it; a new one should be used on installation.

9   Installation is the reverse of removal. Be sure to install a new O-ring between the water pump housing and the engine block, and tighten the fasteners to the torque listed in this Chapter's Specifications. Refer to Chapter 2A and install the timing belt.

10 Refill and bleed the cooling system (see Chapter 1). Start the engine and check for the proper coolant level and the water pump and hoses for leaks.

Four-cylinder CCTA and CBFA engines

▶ Refer to illustration 7.29

11 On models equipped with a noise generator, open the locking ring on the charge air pipe, disconnect the electrical connector to the charge air pipe, then remove the mounting fastener and the charge air pipe.

12 Disconnect the electrical connectors above the small coolant pipe and pull the harness back enough to access the pipe.

13 Remove the small coolant pipe-to-cylinder block mounting fasteners. Disconnect the heater hose clamp from the top end of the coolant pipe and the clamp from the connection at the bottom of the pipe (where it meets the turbocharger coolant pipe).

14 Remove the coolant pipe from the hoses and from the water pump housing.

→ **Note: Always replace the small coolant pipe-to-water pump housing O-ring.**

15 Remove the throttle body assembly (see Chapter 4).

16 Remove the wiring harness retaining strap fastener and strap from under the radiator hose.

17 Remove the after run coolant pump bracket fastener.

18 Remove the radiator hoses located behind the air conditioning compressor (see Chapter 1).

19 Remove the intake manifold runner control valve (see Chapter 4) and move it to the side.

20 Remove the water pump (toothed) belt cover fasteners and cover.

21 Use a wrench or socket to hold the crankshaft pulley from turning, then remove the bolt that holds the water pump (toothed) belt and drive gear to the end of the balance shaft. Remove the belt.

※ CAUTION:

The water pump belt drive gear mounting bolt is left hand thread.

22 Remove the intake manifold support bracket fasteners and bracket.

23 Remove the engine coolant temperature sensor (see Chapter 6).

24 Remove the water pump mounting fasteners in the reverse order of the tightening sequence (see illustration 7.29), then lift the water pump off of the center pins.

→ **Note: The centering pins can stick in the water pump when the pump is removed. Remove the pins from the pump and install them back in the cylinder block.**

25 As the water pump is removed, the connector between the oil cooler and water pump should remain in the oil cooler.

26 Remove the connector from the oil cooler and replace both O-rings on the connector, then install the connector back into the oil cooler.

27 Clean the surface of the cylinder block and new water pump, then install the seal to the water pump housing.

28 Slide the water pump onto the connector piece in the oil cooler then onto the centering pins.

→ **Note: Make sure the water pump housing is seated on the centering pins, use a small mirror if necessary.**

29 Install the mounting fasteners and tighten, in sequence (see illustration) to the torque listed in this Chapter's Specifications. The

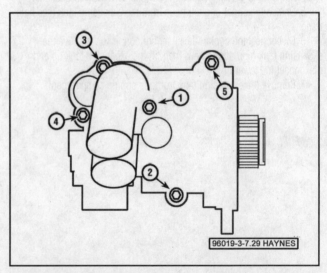

7.29 Water pump mounting fastener tightening sequence - four-cylinder CCTA and CBFA engines

manufacturer recommends replacing the drive gear seal whenever the drive gear is removed, as follows:

  a) *Note how the seal is installed - the new one must be installed to the same depth and facing the same way. Carefully pry the oil seal out of the cylinder block with a seal puller or a small screwdriver. Be very careful not to scratch the balance shaft! Wrap electrician's tape around the tip of the screwdriver to avoid damage to the balance shaft.*

  b) *Apply clean engine oil or multi-purpose grease to the outer edge of the new seal and balance shaft, then install it over the balance shaft and in the cylinder block with the lip (spring side) facing IN. Drive the seal into place with a seal driver or a large socket and a hammer. Make sure the seal enters the bore squarely and stop when the front face is at the proper depth.*

30 Place the water pump (toothed) belt over the water pump pulley, then place the drive gear at the bottom of the belt and install a new drive gear bolt, tightening it to the torque listed in this Chapter's Specifications.

31 Install the water pump (toothed) belt cover and fasteners, then tighten the fasteners to the torque listed in this Chapter's Specifications.

32 Installation is the reverse of removal.

33 Refill and bleed the cooling system (see Chapter 1). Start the engine and check for the proper coolant level and the water pump and hoses for leaks.

Five-cylinder engines

▸ **Refer to illustration 7.42**

34 Remove the battery and battery tray (see Chapter 5).

35 Remove the drivebelt (see Chapter 1).

36 Remove the exhaust pipe-to-exhaust manifold fasteners and secure the exhaust pie to the side.

37 Remove the pendulum support (see Chapter 2B, Section 15).

38 On manual transaxles, remove the shift levers (see Chapter 7A).

39 On automatic transaxles, disconnect the selector lever cable (see Chapter 7B).

40 Remove the cowl cower and grille (see Chapter 11).

41 Remove the transport strap fasteners and remove the strap from the cylinder head.

42 Install an engine support fixture (see illustration) and slightly raise the engine.

43 Remove the windshield wiper reservoir and coolant expansion tank fasteners, then move both tanks to the side.

44 Remove the engine mount (see Chapter 2B).

45 Loosen the transaxle mount bolts and slide the engine as far back as possible.

46 Remove the water pump mounting bolts and carefully maneuver the pump out of the vehicle (at an angle).

47 Install the water pump into the engine block with the sealed plug facing downwards.

48 Install the water pump bolts and tighten them to the torque listed in this Chapter's Specifications.

49 The remainder of the installation procedure is the reverse of removal. Refill and bleed the cooling system (see Chapter 1).

50 Start the engine and check for the proper coolant level, and check the water pump and hoses for leaks.

AFTER-RUN COOLANT PUMP

⁑ WARNING:

Wait until the engine is completely cool before starting this procedure.

➡ **Note: Not all models are equipped with this pump; it's available only on models in countries with high-temperature climates. On 2.0L (BPY) engines, the after-run pump is called a coolant recirculation pump.**

51 Raise the vehicle and support it securely on jackstands.

52 Drain the coolant (see Chapter 1).

53 On four-cylinder CCTA and CBFA engines equipped with a noise generator, open the locking ring on the charge air pipe, disconnect the electrical connector from the charge air pipe, then remove the mounting fastener and the charge air pipe.

54 Remove the inlet and outlet hoses from the after-run coolant pump.

55 Disconnect the electrical connector from the pump, then remove the retaining bracket bolt and detach the after-run coolant pump from the engine.

56 Installation is the reverse of removal. Refill and bleed the cooling system (see Chapter 1).

7.42 Support the engine using an appropriate engine support fixture

8 Coolant temperature gauge sending unit - check and replacement

CHECK

> ※※ **WARNING:**
>
> **Wait until the engine is completely cool before beginning this procedure.**

1 The coolant temperature indicator system consists of the temperature gauge, a sensor mounted on the engine or lower radiator hose and the vehicle's main computer. The Engine Coolant Temperature (ECT) sensor provides a signal to the Powertrain Control Module (PCM) (see Chapter 6). The PCM uses this signal to control the temperature gauge.

2 If the temperature gauge goes above normal and begins to read hot, check the coolant level in the system (see Chapter 1). Also, refer to the *Troubleshooting* Section before assuming that the temperature indicator is faulty.

3 Start the engine and monitor it while it warms up for 10 minutes. If the gauge has not moved from the cold position, check the wiring harness connections going to the instrument cluster and the sensor.

4 If there is a problem with the ECT sensor, it is likely that the CHECK ENGINE light will come on and the sensor will have to be replaced or the circuit will have to be repaired (see Chapter 6).

REPLACEMENT

5 Refer to Chapter 6 for the engine coolant temperature sensor replacement procedure.

9 Blower motor - removal and installation

▶ **Refer to illustrations 9.2 and 9.3**

> ※※ **WARNING:**
>
> **These models have airbags. Always disable the airbag system before working in the vicinity of any airbag system component to avoid the possibility of accidental deployment of the airbag(s), which could cause personal injury (see Chapter 12).**

➡ **Note: The blower control module is an integral part of the blower motor and can't be replaced separately.**

1 Remove the trim panel fasteners and trim panel from under the glove box (see Chapter 1, Section 15).

2 Disconnect the electrical connector from the blower motor (see illustration).

3 Pull the locking tab on the blower motor downwards, rotate the blower motor assembly counterclockwise and withdraw the blower motor (see illustration).

➡ **Note: Some models may have a retaining screw that will need to be removed before the housing will rotate.**

4 Installation is the reverse of removal; rotate the blower housing until it contacts the stop.

9.2 Disconnect the blower motor electrical connector from the motor

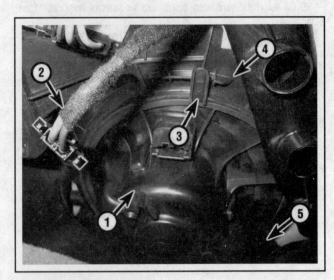

9.3 Blower motor details

1	Blower motor	4	Locking tab stop
2	Blower motor electrical connector	5	Retaining screw (if equipped)
3	Locking tab		

10 Heater and air conditioning control assembly - removal and installation

▶ Refer to illustrations 10.3a, 10.3b, 10.4 and 10.5

※ WARNING:

These models have airbags. Always disable the airbag system before working in the vicinity of any airbag system component to avoid the possibility of accidental deployment of the airbag(s), which could cause personal injury (see Chapter 12).

※ CAUTION:

If the battery is disconnected, several systems must be relearned before they will work properly (see Chapter 5, Section 3).

1   Disconnect the negative battery cable (see Chapter 5).
2   Remove the center vent assembly (see Chapter 11).

➡ Note: On some models, it will be necessary to remove the radio to access the trim screws for the control assembly (see Chapter 12).

3   Remove the trim panel retaining screws and carefully pry out the panel (see illustrations).
4   Remove the control head fasteners and lift out the control head (see illustration).
5   Disconnect the electrical connectors from the rear of the control head (see illustration).
6   Installation is the reverse of removal.

10.3a Remove the retaining fasteners at the top of the center trim panel . . .

10.3b . . . then carefully pry out the trim panel

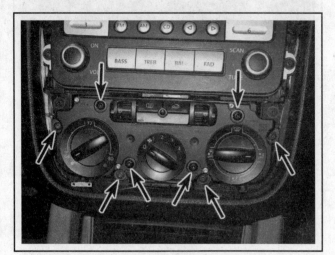

10.4 Control head fastener locations

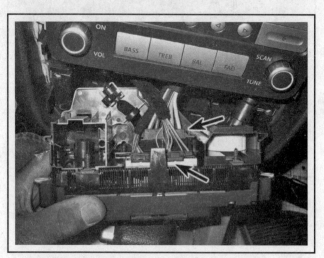

10.5 Unplug all the electrical connectors from the control assembly

11 Heater core - removal and installation

▶ Refer to illustrations 11.5 and 11.9

※ WARNING:

Wait until the engine is completely cool before beginning this procedure.

※ WARNING:

These models have airbags. Always disable the airbag system before working in the vicinity of any airbag system component to avoid the possibility of accidental deployment of the airbag(s), which could cause personal injury (see Chapter 12).

※ CAUTION:

If the battery is disconnected, several systems must be relearned before they will work properly (see Chapter 5, Section 3).

1 Remove the engine cover (see Chapter 1, Section 7).
2 Disconnect the cable from the negative terminal of the battery (see Chapter 5).
3 Drain the cooling system (see Chapter 1). If the coolant is new, save it and reuse it. If it is to be replaced, see Section 1 for cautions about proper handling of used antifreeze.
4 Remove the battery and battery tray (see Chapter 5).

5 Mark the heater hoses, then remove the locking clips and disconnect the hoses at the heater core inlet and outlet on the engine side of the firewall (see illustration).
6 Once the heater hoses are removed, loosen the small bolt in between the coolant pipes.
7 Using a suction gun, remove as much of the coolant as possible from the heater core tubes and plug the open tubes.
8 Remove the center console lower side trim (see Chapter 11).
9 Remove the heater core cover fasteners and the cover (see illustration).

➡ Note: The temperature door lever may be in the way of the top retaining fastener. If the lever is in the way, rotate the hot and fresh air controls until the lever is moved out of the way.

10 Loosen the heater core tube clamp fasteners.

➡ Note: Cover the carpet with plastic sheeting to prevent coolant from getting on the carpet.

Place a rag or a small drain pan under the tubes and carefully separate the tubes from the core. Once the remaining coolant has drained, pull the heater core from the housing.

11 Installation is the reverse of removal.

➡ Note: When reinstalling the heater core, make sure any original insulating/sealing materials are in place around the heater core pipes and around the core.

12 Refill and bleed the cooling system (see Chapter 1).
13 Start the engine and check for proper operation.

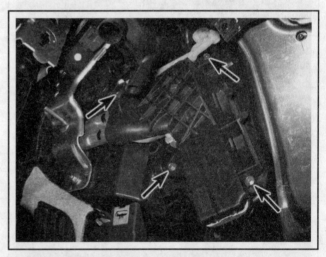

11.5 Remove the heater hose locking clips

11.9 Remove the heater core cover fasteners

12 Heater and air conditioning housing - removal and installation

✳✳ WARNING:

Wait until the engine is completely cool before beginning this procedure.

✳✳ WARNING:

The air conditioning system is under high pressure. DO NOT loosen any fittings or remove any components until after the system has been discharged. Air conditioning refrigerant must be properly discharged into an EPA-approved container at a dealership service department or an automotive air conditioning repair facility. Always wear eye protection when disconnecting air conditioning system fittings.

✳✳ WARNING:

These models have airbags. Always disable the airbag system before working in the vicinity of any airbag system component to avoid the possibility of accidental deployment of the airbag(s), which could cause personal injury (see Chapter 12).

✳✳ CAUTION:

If the battery is disconnected, several systems must be relearned before they will work properly (see Chapter 5, Section 3).

➡ **Note: This is a very difficult procedure for the home mechanic, involving numerous hard-to-find fasteners, clips and electrical connectors.**

1 Have the air conditioning system discharged (see **Warning** above).

2 Remove the engine covers. Disconnect and remove the battery (see Chapter 5).

3 Drain the cooling system (see Chapter 1). Refer to the coolant **Warning** in Section 1.

4 Mark, then disconnect the hoses at the heater core inlet and outlet on the engine side of the firewall (see illustration 11.5).

➡ **Note: If the hoses are stuck to the pipes, cut them off and replace them with new ones upon installation.**

5 Disconnect the heater core tubes from the heater core (see Section 11).

6 Remove the air conditioning line fastener from the evaporator core fitting at the firewall.

7 Remove the instrument panel (see Chapter 11).

8 Remove the passenger side airbag (see Chapter 12).

9 Remove the center console support brace. Remove the upper and lower air ducts from the heating/air conditioning unit.

10 From the engine compartment side, disconnect the electrical connection fasteners and heater A/C housing fastener.

11 Disconnect the electrical connectors at the right side of the instrument panel.

12 Remove the fasteners from the right side of the cross beam support, unclip the main harness from the back side of the cross beam support, then pull the beam forward.

13 With the help of an assistant, remove the cross beam support from the vehicle.

14 Carefully remove the housing assembly from the vehicle.

15 Installation is the reverse of removal.

16 Refill and bleed the cooling system (see Chapter 1).

17 Have the system evacuated, recharged and leak tested by the shop that discharged it.

18 Check for proper operation.

13 Air conditioning compressor - removal and installation

▶ **Refer to illustration 13.8 and 13.9**

✳✳ WARNING:

The air conditioning system is under high pressure. DO NOT loosen any fittings or remove any components until after the system has been discharged. Air conditioning refrigerant must be properly discharged into an EPA-approved container at a dealership service department or an automotive air conditioning repair facility. Always wear eye protection when disconnecting air conditioning system fittings.

✳✳ CAUTION:

If the battery is disconnected, several systems must be relearned before they will work properly (see Chapter 5, Section 3).

➡ **Note: The receiver-drier (see Section 14) should be replaced whenever the compressor is replaced.**

1 Have the air conditioning system discharged (see **Warning** above).

2 Remove the engine cover (see Chapter 1, Section 7). Disconnect the negative battery cable (see Chapter 5).

3 Raise the front of the vehicle and support it securely on jackstands.

4 Remove the under-vehicle splash shield (see Chapter 1, Section 6).

5 Remove the drivebelt (see Chapter 1).

6 Clean the compressor thoroughly around the refrigerant line fittings.

7 Disconnect the electrical connector from the back of the air conditioning compressor.

13.8 Air conditioning compressor mounting bolt locations - five-cylinder engine shown, others similar

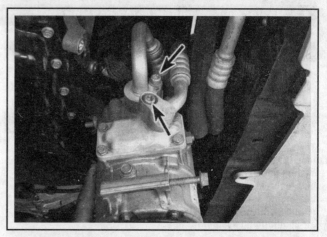

13.9 Air conditioning compressor suction and discharge line bolt locations

8 Remove the compressor mounting bolts (see illustration). Detach the compressor from the mounting bracket and lower the compressor from the engine compartment.

9 Disconnect the suction and discharge lines from the compressor (see illustration). Plug the open fittings to prevent the entry of dirt and moisture, and discard the seals between the plates and compressor

10 If a new compressor is being installed, pour the oil from the old compressor into a graduated container and add that exact amount of new refrigerant oil to the new compressor. Also follow any directions included with the new compressor.

➡ Note: Some replacement compressors come with refrigerant oil in them. Follow the directions with the compressor regarding the draining of excess oil prior to installation.

❊ **CAUTION:**

The oil used must be labeled as compatible with R-134a refrigerant systems.

11 Installation is the reverse of removal. When installing the line fitting bolt to the compressor, use new seals lubricated with clean refrigerant oil, and tighten the bolt securely.

12 Have the system evacuated, recharged and leak tested by the shop that discharged it.

14 Air conditioning reservoir with drier cartridge - removal and installation

❊ **WARNING:**

The air conditioning system is under high pressure. DO NOT loosen any fittings or remove any components until after the system has been discharged. Air conditioning refrigerant must be properly discharged into an EPA-approved container at a dealership service department or an automotive air conditioning repair facility. Always wear eye protection when disconnecting air conditioning system fittings.

❊ **CAUTION:**

If the battery is disconnected, several systems must be relearned before they will work properly (see Chapter 5, Section 3).

1 Have the air conditioning system discharged (see **Warning** above).

2 Remove the engine cover (see Chapter 1, Section 7).

3 Raise the front of the vehicle and support it securely on jackstands.

4 Remove the under-vehicle splash shield (see Chapter 1, Section 6).

5 Remove the front bumper and place the radiator support panel in the service position (see Chapter 11).

6 Remove the receiver-drier upper mounting fastener to the condenser, then remove the retaining clip.

7 Remove the receiver-drier lower mounting fasteners and lift the receiver drier up and out of the condenser.

8 Installation is the reverse of removal. Tighten the fasteners securely.

9 Have the system evacuated, recharged and leak tested by the shop that discharged it.

15 Air conditioning condenser - removal and installation

▶ **Refer to illustration 15.6**

❄ WARNING:

The air conditioning system is under high pressure. DO NOT loosen any fittings or remove any components until after the system has been discharged. Air conditioning refrigerant must be properly discharged into an EPA-approved container at a dealership service department or an automotive air conditioning repair facility. Always wear eye protection when disconnecting air conditioning system fittings.

1 Have the air conditioning system discharged (see **Warning** above).

2 Raise the vehicle and support it securely on jackstands.

3 Remove the under-vehicle splash shield (if equipped).

4 Remove the front bumper assembly (see Chapter 11).

5 Remove the clips that secure the protective screen to the condenser and remove the screen (if equipped).

6 Remove the condenser fasteners (see illustration) and separate the condenser from the radiator.

7 Installation is the reverse of removal. Always use new O-rings on air conditioning system fittings. If you are replacing the condenser with a new one, add fresh refrigerant oil to the new unit following the directions included with the new condenser (the oil must be R-134a compatible).

8 Have the system evacuated, recharged and leak tested by the shop that discharged it.

15.6 Condenser fastener locations - right side shown, left side similar

16 Air conditioning evaporator core - removal and installation

❄ WARNING:

The air conditioning system is under high pressure. DO NOT loosen any fittings or remove any components until after the system has been discharged. Air conditioning refrigerant must be properly discharged into an EPA-approved container at a dealership service department or an automotive air conditioning repair facility. Always wear eye protection when disconnecting air conditioning system fittings.

1 Have the air conditioning system discharged by a dealership service department or an automotive air conditioning facility.

2 Remove the heater and air conditioner housing (see Section 12).

3 Set the housing on a clean working surface.

4 Remove the evaporator core fasteners, separate the housing and carefully remove the evaporator core from the housing.

5 Installation is the reverse of removal.

➡ **Note: When reinstalling the evaporator core, make sure any original insulating/sealing materials are in place around the evaporator core pipes and around the core.**

6 Installation is the reverse of removal. Always use new O-rings on air conditioning system fittings. If you are replacing the evaporator core with a new one, add fresh refrigerant oil to the new unit following the directions included with the new evaporator (the oil must be R-134a compatible).

7 Have the system evacuated, recharged and leak tested by the shop that discharged it.

17 Air conditioning expansion valve - general information

▶ **Refer to illustration 17.2**

❄❄ **WARNING:**

The air conditioning system is under high pressure. DO NOT loosen any hose fittings or remove any components until the system has been discharged. Air conditioning refrigerant must be properly discharged into an EPA-approved recovery/recycling unit by a dealer service department or an automotive air conditioning repair facility. Always wear eye protection when disconnecting air conditioning system fittings.

There are several ways that air conditioning systems convert the hot high-pressure liquid refrigerant from the compressor to cold lower-pressure vapor. The conversion takes place at the air conditioning evaporator; the evaporator is chilled as the refrigerant passes through, cooling the airflow through the evaporator for delivery to the vents. The conversion is accomplished by a sudden change in pressure. Many vehicles have a removable controlled orifice in one of the air conditioning pipes at the firewall.

The models covered by this manual use an expansion valve that accomplishes the same purpose as a controlled orifice (see illustration). To remove the expansion valve, have the air conditioning system discharged by a licensed air conditioning technician. Disconnect the refrigerant lines from the expansion valve at the firewall, remove the two bolts securing the valve, then remove the valve.

17.2 Typical expansion valve location

Specifications

General

Coolant capacity	See Chapter 1
Refrigerant type	R-134a

Torque specifications

➡ **Note: One foot-pound (ft-lb) of torque is equivalent to 12 inch-pounds (in-lbs) of torque. Torque values below approximately 15 foot-pounds are expressed in inch-pounds, because most foot-pound torque wrenches are not accurate at these smaller values.**

	Ft-lbs (unless otherwise indicated)	Nm
Cooling fan-to-fan shroud fasteners	88 in-lbs	10
Cooling fan shroud-to-radiator fasteners	44 in-lbs	5
Thermostat housing fasteners		
Four-cylinder engines		
BPY models	133 in-lbs	15
CCTA, CBFA models	79 in-lbs	9
Five-cylinder engines		
Thermostat housing-to-cylinder block	18	25
Thermostat housing cover	44 in-lbs	5
Water pump (toothed) belt cover fasteners	79 in-lbs	9
Water pump (toothed) belt drive gear bolt	150 in-lbs	17
Water pump fasteners		
Four-cylinder engines		
BPY models	133 in-lbs	15
CCTA, CBFA models	79 in-lbs	9
Five-cylinder engines	88 in-lbs	10

Section

Reference to other Chapters

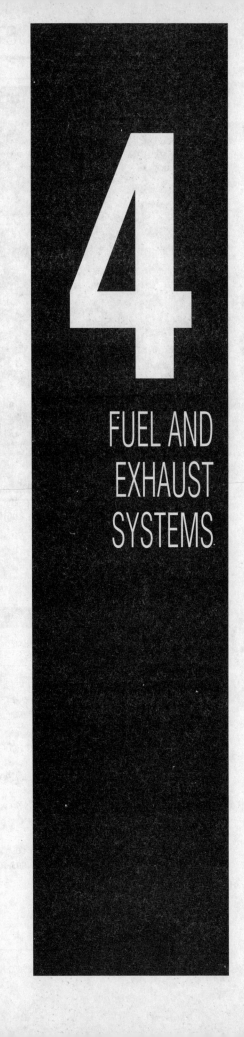

4

FUEL AND EXHAUST SYSTEMS

Typical fuel system details - five-cylinder engine shown

1	Engine compartment fuse and relay box	4	Fuel pressure relief valve	7	Fuel injectors
2	Air inlet duct	5	Intake manifold	8	Fuel rail
3	Throttle body	6	Fuel pressure test port		

1 General information

FUEL SYSTEM WARNINGS

Gasoline is extremely flammable and repairing fuel system components can be dangerous. Consider your automotive repair knowledge and experience before attempting repairs which may be better suited for a professional mechanic.

- *Don't smoke or allow open flames or bare light bulbs near the work area*
- *Don't work in a garage with a gas-type appliance (water heater, clothes dryer)*
- *Use fuel-resistant gloves. If any fuel spills on your skin, wash it off immediately with soap and water*
- *Clean up spills immediately*
- *Do not store fuel-soaked rags where they could ignite*
- *Prior to disconnecting any fuel line, you must relieve the fuel pressure (see Section 3)*
- *Wear safety glasses*
- *Have a proper fire extinguisher on hand*

FUEL SYSTEM

The fuel system consists of the fuel tank, electric fuel pump/fuel level sending unit (located in the fuel tank), fuel rail and fuel injectors. The fuel injection system is a multi-port system; multi-port fuel injection uses timed impulses to inject the fuel directly into the intake port of each cylinder. The Powertrain Control Module (PCM) controls the injectors. The PCM monitors various engine parameters and delivers the exact amount of fuel required into the intake ports.

➡ **Note: On 2.0L engine models, there are two fuel pumps: the delivery pump is located in the fuel tank and the high-pressure fuel pump is mounted to the end of the cylinder head and driven by the intake camshaft.**

Fuel is circulated from the fuel pump to the fuel rail through fuel lines running along the underside of the vehicle. Various sections of the fuel line are either rigid metal or nylon, or flexible fuel hose. The various sections of the fuel hose are connected either by quick-connect fittings or threaded metal fittings.

EXHAUST SYSTEM

The exhaust system consists of the exhaust manifold(s), catalytic converter(s), muffler(s), tailpipe and all connecting pipes, flanges and clamps. The catalytic converters are an emission control device added to the exhaust system to reduce pollutants.

2   Troubleshooting

FUEL PUMP

▶ **Refer to illustrations 2.2a and 2.2b**

1   The fuel pump is located inside the fuel tank. Sit inside the vehicle with the windows closed, turn the ignition key to ON (not START) and listen for the sound of the fuel pump as it's briefly activated. You will only hear the sound for a second or two, but that sound tells you that the pump is working. Alternatively, have an assistant listen at the fuel filler cap.

2   If the pump does not come on, check the fuel pump fuse (see illustration) and on five-cylinder models, the fuel pump relay (see illustration). All models are equipped with a fuel pump fuse, but there is no fuel pump relay on four-cylinder models; the fuel pump circuit on these models is controlled by the fuel pump control module (FPCM), which cannot be diagnosed at home.

FUEL INJECTION SYSTEM

▶ **Refer to illustration 2.9**

➡ **Note: The following procedure is based on the assumption that the fuel pump is working and the fuel pressure is adequate (see Section 4).**

3   Check all electrical connectors that are related to the system. Check the ground wire connections for tightness.

4   Verify that the battery is fully charged (see Chapter 5).

5   Inspect the air filter element (see Chapter 1).

6   Check all fuses related to the fuel system (see Chapter 12).

7   Check the air induction system between the throttle body and the intake manifold for air leaks. Also inspect the condition of all vacuum hoses connected to the intake manifold and to the throttle body.

8   Remove the air intake duct from the throttle body and look for dirt, carbon, varnish, or other residue in the throttle body, particularly around the throttle plate. If it's dirty, clean it with carb cleaner, a toothbrush and a clean shop towel.

9   With the engine running, place an automotive stethoscope against

each injector, one at a time, and listen for a clicking sound that indicates operation (see illustration).

☀ WARNING:

Stay clear of the drivebelt and any rotating or hot components.

10 If you can hear the injectors operating, but the engine is misfiring, the electrical circuits are functioning correctly, but the injectors might be dirty or clogged. Try a commercial injector cleaning product (available at auto parts stores). If cleaning the injectors doesn't help, replace the injectors.

11 If an injector is not operating (it makes no sound), disconnect the injector electrical connector and measure the resistance across the injector terminals with an ohmmeter. Compare this measurement to the other injectors. If the resistance of the non-operational injector is quite different from the other injectors, replace it.

12 If the injector is not operating, but the resistance reading is within the range of resistance of the other injectors, the PCM or the circuit between the PCM and the injector might be faulty.

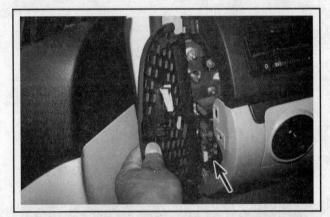

2.2a The fuel pump fuse is located in the fuse box at the left end of the instrument panel (be sure to check the guide on the end panel or in your owner's manual to locate the fuse for your particular model)

2.2b On five-cylinder models, the fuel pump relay is located at the far left end of the relay panel, which is located inside the left end of the instrument panel, to the left of the steering column. Four-cylinder models do not use a fuel pump relay. Instead, they use a control module located on the cover of the fuel level sensor

2.9 With the engine running, place an automotive stethoscope against each injector, one at a time, and listen for a clicking sound that indicates operation

3 Fuel pressure relief procedure

FOUR-CYLINDER MODELS

▶ **Refer to illustration 3.3**

1 The fuel delivery systems on 2.0L models are equipped with both a low-pressure system and a second, high-pressure system that operates at extremely high pressure. At idle, the fuel pressure in the fuel rail is about 725 psi; under certain operating conditions such as hard acceleration, the system pressure can reach 1700 psi. So before you remove or replace any component (mechanical high-pressure pump, high-pressure fuel lines, fuel rail and/or fuel injectors) in the high-pressure part of the fuel injection system, be sure to use the following procedure to relieve fuel pressure.

2 Remove the fuel pump fuse no. 27 (see illustration 2.2a) from the interior fuel panel. This opens the circuit to the Fuel Pump Control

3.3 Electrical connector on the mechanical high-pressure pump - 2.0L (BPY) model shown

Module (FPCM) so that the fuel pump inside the fuel tank will not operate.

3 Disconnect the electrical connector from the fuel pressure regulator valve on the mechanical high-pressure pump (see illustration).

4 Start the engine and allow it to idle until it stalls, then turn the ignition key to the Off position and disconnect the cable from the negative terminal of the battery (see Chapter 5). Even though the low-pressure pump inside the fuel tank is already disabled, the engine might run briefly on the residual pressure inside the high-pressure part of the system.

5 Disconnect the cable from the negative terminal of the battery (see Chapter 5).

6 At this point, the residual fuel pressure in the high side of the system might still be about 87 psi (6 bar). So when you crack open the first fitting, make sure that you are wearing safety goggles and that you completely surround the fitting with plenty of shop rags to catch any fuel that might spill out.

FIVE-CYLINDER MODELS

7 Remove the fuel filler cap to relieve any pressure built-up in the fuel tank.

8 Remove the fuel pump relay (see illustration 2.2b).

9 Attempt to start the engine; it should immediately stall. Crank the engine several more times to ensure the fuel system has been completely relieved. Disconnect the cable from the negative terminal of the battery before working on the fuel system.

10 Cover any fuel connection to be disassembled with rags to absorb the residual fuel that may leak out. Properly dispose of the rags.

11 Remove the cap from the fuel rail bleeder and surround the fitting with rags, then slowly depress the Schrader valve with a small screwdriver and allow the residual fuel pressure to bleed off.

12 The fuel system is now depressurized. Properly dispose of the rags.

4 Fuel pressure - check

▶ **Refer to illustrations 4.2a and 4.2b**

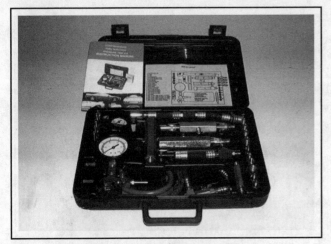

4.2a This fuel pressure testing kit contains all the necessary fittings and adapters, along with the fuel pressure gauge, to test most automotive systems

4.2b Using the proper adapters, the fuel pressure gauge can be installed between the fuel filter and the fuel line

➡ **Note: The following procedure assumes that the fuel pump is receiving voltage and runs.**

1 Raise the vehicle and support it securely on jackstands (unless you will be using Method 2 or 3 in the next Step).

2 Relieve the fuel system pressure (see Section 3), then disconnect the outlet side of the fuel filter (see *Disconnecting Fuel Line Fittings* on page 4-6). Use an adapter to connect the fuel pressure gauge between the fuel line and the fuel filter (see illustrations) (Method 1), or, if equipped, at the fuel line connection at the right-side of the engine compartment (Method 2 - see the underhood photo at the beginning of this Chapter). Alternatively, if the fuel rail is equipped with a Schrader valve, the pressure gauge can be connected to it (Method 3).

3 Start the engine and allow it to idle. Note the gauge reading as soon as the pressure stabilizes, and compare it with the pressure listed in this Chapter's Specifications.

4 If the fuel pressure is not within specifications, check the following:

  a) If the pressure is lower than specified, check for a restriction in the fuel system (kinked fuel line, plugged fuel pump inlet strainer or clogged fuel filter). If no restrictions are found, replace the fuel pressure regulator (see Section 12).

  b) If the pressure is higher than specified, replace the fuel pressure regulator (see Section 12).

5 Turn off the engine. Fuel pressure should not fall more than 8 psi over five minutes. If it does, the problem could be a leaky fuel injector, fuel line leak, or faulty fuel pump module.

6 Relieve the fuel system pressure (see Section 3), then disconnect the fuel pressure gauge.

7 Reconnect the fuel line to the fuel filter.

5 Fuel system - bleeding (five-cylinder models only)

▶ **Refer to illustration 5.1**

✳✳ **WARNING:**

Gasoline is extremely flammable. See *Fuel system warnings* in Section 1.

1 Remove the bleeder valve cap on the fuel rail (see illustration).

2 Connect an adapter from the fuel pressure test kit (see illustration 4.2a) to the Schrader valve with a drain hose inserted in an appropriate container.

3 Have an assistant, turn the ignition key to the "ON" position for 5 to 10 seconds, and fuel will flow through the adapter and drain hose into the container.

4 Once the fuel flow has little to no air bubbles clamp the drain hose off and turn the ignition key to the "OFF" position.

5 Surround the Schrader valve fitting with plenty of shop rags to catch any fuel that might spill out and remove the adapter and drain hose.

6 The fuel system is now bled. Reinstall the cap and properly dispose of the rags.

5.1 Schrader valve location (five-cylinder models only)

➡ **Note: This procedure will set a trouble code that will require a scan tool to clear the code (see Chapter 6).**

Disconnecting Fuel Line Fittings

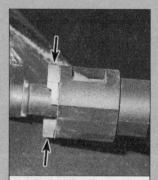

Two-tab type fitting; depress both tabs with your fingers, then pull the fuel line and the fitting apart

On this type of fitting, depress the two buttons on opposite sides of the fitting, then pull it off the fuel line

Threaded fuel line fitting; hold the stationary portion of the line or component (A) while loosening the tube nut (B) with a flare-nut wrench

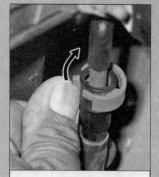

Plastic collar-type fitting; rotate the outer part of the fitting

Metal collar quick-connect fitting; pull the end of the retainer off the fuel line, and disengage the other end from the female side of the fitting . . .

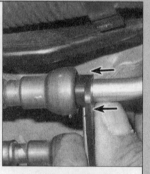

. . . insert a fuel line separator tool into the female side of the fitting, push it into the fitting until it releases the locking tabs inside the fitting, and pull the two halves of the fitting apart

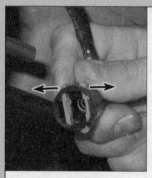

Hairpin-type clip; spread the two legs of the clip apart . . .

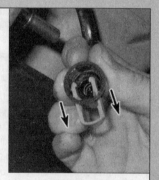

. . . pull the clip out and detach the coupling from the component (fitting detached for clarity)

Spring-lock coupling; remove the safety cover . . .

. . . install a coupling release tool and close the clamshell halves of the tool around the coupling . . .

. . . push the tool into the fitting, then pull the two lines apart

6   Fuel lines and fittings - general information and disconnection

> ✳✳ **WARNING:**
>
> Gasoline is extremely flammable. See *Fuel system warnings* in Section 1.

> ✳✳ **CAUTION:**
>
> On five-cylinder models, whenever the fuel system has been opened it must be bled (see Section 5). If the system is not bled, the catalytic converter can be damaged.

> ✳✳ **CAUTION:**
>
> Whenever the battery is disconnected, several systems must be re-learned before they will work properly (see Chapter 5, Section 3).

1   Relieve the fuel pressure before servicing fuel lines or fittings (see Section 3), then disconnect the cable from the negative battery terminal (see Chapter 5) before proceeding.

2   The fuel supply line connects the fuel pump in the fuel tank to the fuel rail on the engine. The Evaporative Emission (EVAP) system lines connect the fuel tank to the EVAP canister and connect the canister to the intake manifold.

3   Whenever you're working under the vehicle, be sure to inspect all fuel and evaporative emission lines for leaks, kinks, dents and other damage. Always replace a damaged fuel or EVAP line immediately.

4   If you find signs of dirt in the lines during disassembly, disconnect all lines and blow them out with compressed air. Inspect the fuel strainer on the fuel pump pick-up unit for damage and deterioration.

STEEL TUBING

5   It is critical that the fuel lines be replaced with lines of equivalent type and specification.

6   Some steel fuel lines have threaded fittings. When loosening these fittings, hold the stationary fitting with a wrench while turning the tube nut.

PLASTIC TUBING

7   When replacing fuel system plastic tubing, use only original equipment replacement plastic tubing.

> ✳✳ **CAUTION:**
>
> When removing or installing plastic fuel line tubing, be careful not to bend or twist it too much, which can damage it. Also, plastic fuel tubing is NOT heat resistant, so keep it away from excessive heat.

FLEXIBLE HOSES

8   When replacing fuel system flexible hoses, use only original equipment replacements.

9   Don't route fuel hoses (or metal lines) within four inches of the exhaust system or within ten inches of the catalytic converter. Make sure that no rubber hoses are installed directly against the vehicle, particularly in places where there is any vibration. If allowed to touch some vibrating part of the vehicle, a hose can easily become chafed and it might start leaking. A good rule of thumb is to maintain a minimum of 1/4-inch clearance around a hose (or metal line) to prevent contact with the vehicle underbody.

7   Exhaust system servicing - general information

▶ **Refer to illustration 7.1**

> ✳✳ **WARNING:**
>
> Allow exhaust system components to cool before inspection or repair. Also, when working under the vehicle, make sure it is securely supported on jackstands.

1   The exhaust system consists of the exhaust manifolds, catalytic converter, muffler, tailpipe and all connecting pipes, flanges and clamps. The exhaust system is isolated from the vehicle body and from chassis components by a series of rubber hangers (see illustration). Periodically inspect these hangers for cracks or other signs of deterioration, replacing them as necessary.

2   Conduct regular inspections of the exhaust system to keep it safe and quiet. Look for any damaged or bent parts, open seams, holes, loose connections, excessive corrosion or other defects which could

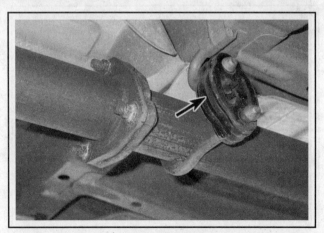

7.1 A typical exhaust system hanger. Inspect regularly and replace at the first sign of damage or deterioration

allow exhaust fumes to enter the vehicle. Do not repair deteriorated exhaust system components; replace them with new parts.

3   If the exhaust system components are extremely corroded, or rusted together, a cutting torch is the most convenient tool for removal. Consult a properly-equipped repair shop. If a cutting torch is not available, you can use a hacksaw, or if you have compressed air, there are special pneumatic cutting chisels that can also be used. Wear safety goggles to protect your eyes from metal chips and wear work gloves to protect your hands.

4   Here are some simple guidelines to follow when repairing the exhaust system:

a)   Work from the back to the front when removing exhaust system components.
b)   Apply penetrating oil to the exhaust system component fasteners to make them easier to remove.
c)   Use new gaskets, hangers and clamps.
d)   Apply anti-seize compound to the threads of all exhaust system fasteners during reassembly.
e)   Be sure to allow sufficient clearance between newly installed parts and all points on the underbody to avoid overheating the floor pan and possibly damaging the interior carpet and insulation. Pay particularly close attention to the catalytic converter and heat shield.

8   Fuel pump/fuel level sensor module - removal and installation

REMOVAL

▶ Refer to illustrations 8.3, 8.5, 8.6, 8.7 and 8.8

✳ WARNING:

Gasoline is extremely flammable, so take extra precautions when you work on any part of the fuel system. See the *Fuel system warnings* in Section 1.

✳ CAUTION:

On five-cylinder models, whenever the fuel system has been opened it must be bled (see Section 5). If the system is not bled, the catalytic converter can be damaged.

✳ CAUTION:

Whenever the battery is disconnected, several systems must be re-learned before they will work properly (see Chapter 5, Section 3).

1   Relieve the fuel system pressure (see Section 3).
2   Disconnect the cable from the negative battery terminal (see Chapter 5).
3   To access the fuel pump module inspection hole cover, remove the bench seat (see Chapter 11), then lift the carpeting back and remove the access hole cover (see illustration).
4   On four-cylinder models, the Fuel Pump Control Module (FPCM) is attached to the top of the cover, so handle the cover carefully. It's not necessary to disconnect the electrical connector from the FPCM unless you're replacing the FPCM.
5   Disconnect the fuel pump module electrical connector and lines (see illustration). Mark the lines to prevent mix-ups when reconnecting them.
6   Remove the fuel pump module lock ring. A special tool (available at most auto parts stores) is available to unscrew the lock ring, but a pair of pliers will work (see illustration). Lock one end of the pliers on the lock ring and the other end on one of the tank tabs, then slowly

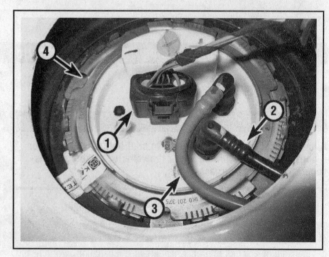

8.5 Fuel pump/fuel level sensor module connections

1   *Fuel pump/fuel level sensor electrical connector*
2   *Fuel pump supply line*
3   *Fuel return line (from filter/pressure regulator)*
4   *Module lock ring*

8.3 Fuel pump/fuel level sensor cover

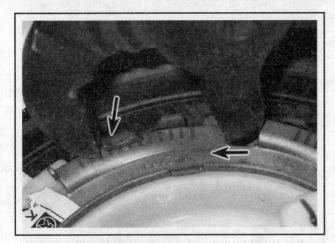

8.6 Use pliers to loosen the lock ring

8.7 Carefully remove the fuel pump/fuel level sensor module from the tank

close the pliers to move the ring counterclockwise.

7 Lift the fuel pump/fuel level sensor module out of the tank as a single assembly (see illustration). Angle the module as necessary to protect the fuel level sensor float arm.

➡ **Note: At the time this manual was written, the fuel delivery unit was not serviceable. Remove the fuel level sensor and arm from the assembly and replace the fuel pump delivery unit.**

8 Inspect the flange seal (see illustration). If the seal is damaged, replace it.

Fuel level sensor

Early version

▶ **Refer to illustration 8.9**

9 To remove the fuel level sensor, disconnect the sensor electrical connectors, then use a small screwdriver to disengage the two sensor

lock tabs that secure the sensor to the fuel pump module (see illustration). Pull the sensor straight up out of the pump module.

➡ **Note: Mark the color and location of the wires before you disconnect them.**

10 When installing the fuel level sensor module on the fuel pump module, make sure that the locking tabs snap into place.

11 No further disassembly of the fuel pump/fuel level sensor module is possible.

12 Installation is the reverse of removal.

Later version

13 Holding the fuel level sensor arm, pull the sensor in and lift the sensor up to release it from the retaining tab.

14 Disconnect the electrical wires from the sensor, noting the wire locations and colors for installation, and remove the sensor from the top of the module.

15 Install the fuel level sensor module on the fuel pump module, making sure that the locking tabs snap into place.

16 Installation is the reverse of removal.

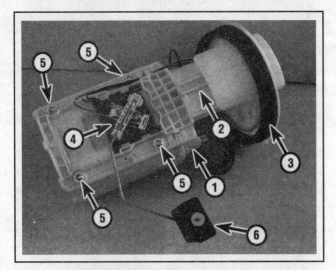

8.8 Typical fuel pump/fuel level sensor module details:

1	Fuel delivery pump	
2	Fuel pump module assembly	
3	Flange seal	
4	Fuel level sensor location	
5	Fuel pump-to-module fasteners	
6	Fuel level sensor arm and float	

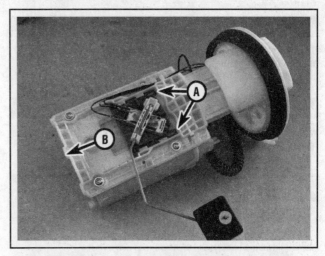

8.9 Lift up on the locking tabs (A), then slide the fuel level sensor down (B) and out - early style sensor shown

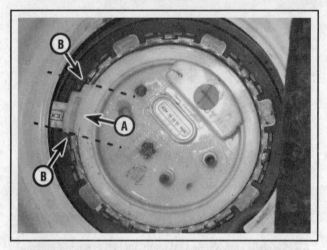

8.17 Make sure the tab (A) on the fuel delivery unit is placed in between the tabs (B) of the tank before trying to install the lock ring

8.18 Rotate the lock ring clockwise to lock the module in place

INSTALLATION

▶ **Refer to illustrations 8.17 and 8.18**

17 Install the fuel pump/fuel level sensor module in to the tank and align the tab on the module with the tank (see illustration).

➡ **Note: Use a new seal for the locking ring if the old seal is damaged.**

18 Place the locking ring over the module and lock the ring into place using a pair of pliers (see illustration).
19 Installation is the reverse of removal.
20 On five-cylinder models, bleed the fuel system (see Section 5).

9 Fuel tank - removal and installation

▶ **Refer to illustrations 9.8a, 9.8b, 9.9 and 9.12**

✳ **WARNING:**

Gasoline is extremely flammable. See *Fuel system warnings* in Section 1.

✳ **CAUTION:**

On five-cylinder models, whenever the fuel system has been opened it must be bled (see Section 5). If the system is not bled, the catalytic converter can be damaged.

✳ **CAUTION:**

Whenever the battery is disconnected, several systems must be re-learned before they will work properly (see Chapter 5, Section 3).

➡ **Note: The following procedure is much easier to perform if the fuel tank is empty.**

1 Remove the fuel tank filler cap to relieve fuel tank pressure.
2 Relieve the fuel system pressure (see Section 3).
3 Disconnect the cable from the negative battery terminal (see Chapter 5).
4 Remove the rear bench seat, disconnect the fuel pump control module (four-cylinder models), then disconnect the electrical connector and fuel supply line quick-connect fittings from the fuel pump module

(see Section 8).
5 Raise the rear of the vehicle and support it securely on jackstands.
6 Remove the right rear wheel, then remove the rear inner fender splash shield (see Chapter 11).
7 On four-cylinder BPY models, unclip the electrical wire from the filler connection, then remove the fuel filler flap mounting retainer and fuel flap assembly.
8 On four-cylinder CCTA, CBFA and all five-cylinder models, open the fuel tank filler flap and remove the mounting fastener and plastic liner (see illustrations).

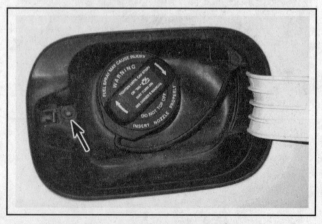

9.8a Remove the fuel filler liner mounting fastener . . .

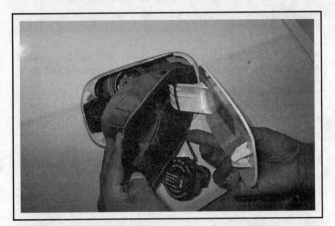

9.8b . . . then rotate the liner out

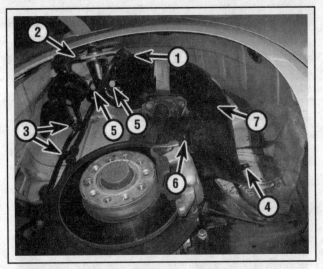

9.9 Fuel tank filler tube details

1	EVAP canister hose connection	4	Rivet
2	Vacuum line (to leak detection pump, 2010 and earlier)	5	Fuel filler tube mounting fasteners
3	Clips	6	Connector for the ABS sensor wire harness
		7	Protective shield

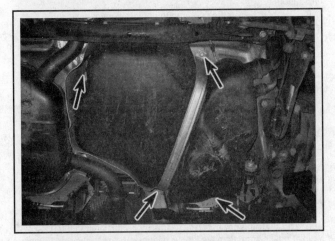

9.12 Fuel tank mounting fastener locations

9   Remove the fuel filler tube mounting fasteners and disconnect the hoses. On four-cylinder CCTA, CBFA and all five-cylinder models, unclip the ABS sensor wire from the bracket, then remove the rivet and protective shield (see illustration).

10   Disconnect the exhaust system hangers, then remove the center and rear mufflers from the vehicle (see Section 7).

11   Remove the fuel filter (see Chapter 1) and cap the fuel lines.

12   Support the fuel tank securely, then remove the fuel tank mounting fasteners, and the retaining strap mounting fastener (see illustration). Remove the strap and carefully lower the fuel tank.

13   Installation is the reverse of removal. Tighten the fuel tank mounting fasteners to the torque listed in this Chapter's Specifications. On five-cylinder models, bleed the fuel system (see Section 5).

14   Reconnect the cable to the negative battery terminal (see Chapter 5), then start the engine and check for fuel leaks.

10   Air filter housing - removal and installation

➡ **Note: This procedure applies to four-cylinder CCTA, CBFA engines only. On four-cylinder BPY and five-cylinder engines, the air filter housing is incorporated into the engine cover (see Chapter 1, Section 7 for removal and installation).**

1   Release the air guide top cover clips and remove the top cover.

2   Release the air guide lower clips and remove the guide.

3   Disconnect the electrical connector from the Mass Air Flow (MAF) sensor (see Chapter 6).

4   Loosen the clamps that secure the air intake duct to the air filter housing, then detach the intake duct from the MAF sensor.

5   Remove the air filter housing cover fasteners and cover.

➡ **Note: Do not try to completely remove the fasteners from the cover.**

6   Remove the air filter housing mounting fastener, then lift the air filter housing up and disconnect the housing from the intake air duct at the bottom of the housing.

7   While the air filter housing is out, inspect the condition of the water drain and hose.

8   Before reassembling and installing the air filter housing, thoroughly blow out all parts of the housing with compressed air.

9   Installation is the reverse of removal.

11 Throttle body/control module - removal and installation

✳✳ CAUTION:

Whenever the battery is disconnected, several systems must be re-learned before they will work properly (see Chapter 5, Section 3).

➡ Note: If a new throttle body control module is installed, the Engine Control Module (ECM) will need to be programmed using the factory scan tool.

1   Disconnect the cable from the negative battery terminal (see Chapter 5).
2   Remove the engine cover (see Chapter 1, Section 7).

11.5 Throttle body details - four-cylinder BPY model shown, other four-cylinder models similar:

1   *Electrical connector*
2   *Throttle body mounting fasteners (fourth fastener not visible)*

11.10 Throttle body air inlet hose details - five-cylinder models

1 *Throttle body*	4 *Secondary air injection*
2 *Air inlet hose*	*pump hose (if equipped)*
3 *Spring clamp*	5 *Crankcase vent hose*

➡ Note: On GTI models with four-cylinder BPY engines, remove the air inlet pipe fasteners near the headlight housing and the pipe.

FOUR-CYLINDER ENGINES

▶ Refer to illustration 11.5

3   Raise the vehicle and support it securely on jackstands.
4   Remove the charge air pipe fasteners, then disconnect the electrical connector at the pipe. Loosen the clamps at each end of the charge air pipe, and detach the pipe from the throttle body.
5   Disconnect the electrical connector from the throttle body (see illustration).
6   Remove the throttle body mounting fasteners and carefully remove the throttle body from the intake manifold.
7   Remove and inspect the throttle body gasket. If it's flattened, hardened or cracked, replace it. If it's in good condition, it can be re-used.
8   Cover the intake manifold opening with a clean shop towel to prevent anything from entering.
9   Installation is the reverse of removal. Tighten the throttle body fasteners to the torque listed in this Chapter's Specifications.

FIVE-CYLINDER ENGINES

▶ Refer to illustrations 11.10, 11.12 and 11.16

10   Disconnect the vent hose, secondary air injection pump hose and air inlet pipe clamp. Remove the air inlet pipe between the throttle body and the air filter housing (see illustration).
11   On some models, it may be necessary to remove the air guide connector-to-radiator support fasteners and the connector.
12   Disconnect the electrical connector and the vent hose, remove the throttle body mounting fasteners and carefully remove the throttle body from the intake manifold (see illustration).

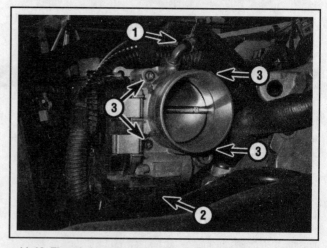

11.12 Throttle body details - five-cylinder models

1   *Vent hose*
2   *Throttle motor electrical connector*
3   *Mounting fasteners*

13 On models that use coolant to heat the throttle valve control module, once the throttle body is removed, clamp off the coolant lines to the throttle body, disconnect the clamps and remove the coolant lines.

➡ **Note: Always replace the hose clamps to the coolant lines.**

14 Remove and inspect the throttle body gasket. If it's flattened, hardened or cracked, replace it. If it's in good condition, it can be re-used.

15 Cover the intake manifold opening with a clean shop towel to prevent anything from entering.

16 Install the gasket on to the intake manifold, making sure the gasket is properly seated (see illustration).

17 Installation is the reverse of removal. Tighten the throttle body fasteners to the torque listed in this Chapter's Specifications.

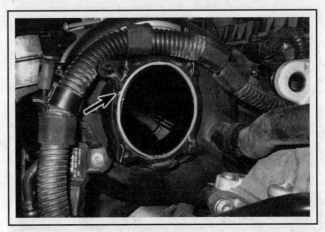

11.16 Align the tab of the throttle body seal with the notch in the intake manifold

12 Fuel pressure regulator (low pressure side) - replacement

※ **WARNING:**

Gasoline is extremely flammable, so take extra precautions when you work on any part of the fuel system. See the *Fuel system warnings* in Section 1.

※ **CAUTION:**

On five-cylinder models, whenever the fuel system has been opened it must be bled (see Section 5). If the system is not bled, the catalytic converter can be damaged.

※ **CAUTION:**

Whenever the battery is disconnected, several systems must be re-learned before they will work properly (see Chapter 5, Section 3).

1 Raise the vehicle and support it securely on jackstands.

2 Relieve the fuel system pressure (see Section 3), then disconnect the return side of the fuel filter (see *Disconnecting Fuel Line Fittings* on page 4-6).

3 Remove the fuel filter (see Chapter 1).

4 Remove the fuel pressure regulator retaining clip and remove the pressure regulator from the fuel filter.

5 Replace the pressure regulator O-ring seals.

➡ **Note: If you don't see the small O-ring seal on the pressure regulator, it might still be inside the fuel filter. Be sure to dig it out and discard it.**

Lubricate the new O-rings with a thin film of engine oil and install them on the regulator.

6 Insert the regulator into the fuel filter. Make sure that it's fully seated, then install the retaining clip.

7 On five-cylinder engines, bleed the fuel system (see Section 5).

8 Start the engine and check for leaks.

13 High-pressure fuel pump (four-cylinder models only) - removal and installation

▶ **Refer to illustrations 13.5 and 13.6**

※ **WARNING:**

Gasoline is extremely flammable, so take extra precautions when you work on any part of the fuel system. See the *Fuel system warnings* in Section 1.

※ **WARNING:**

Wait until the engine is completely cold before performing this procedure.

※ **CAUTION:**

Whenever the battery is disconnected, several systems must be re-learned before they will work properly (see Chapter 5, Section 3).

1 Relieve the fuel system pressure (see Section 3).

2 Disconnect the cable from the negative battery terminal (see Chapter 5).

3 On BPY engines, set the engine at TDC (see Chapter 2A).

4 Disconnect the electrical connector from the fuel pressure regulator valve and the low fuel pressure sensor (BPY engines only) (see illustration 3.3).

13.5 High-pressure fuel line tube nut (1) and feed line fitting (2, disconnect whichever end is easier). Hold fitting (3) with a wrench while loosing fitting (1) to prevent it from turning - typical BPY unit shown, CCTA, CBFA unit similar

5 Disconnect both fuel lines from the high-pressure pump (see illustration).

✳✳ WARNING:

Surround the fitting and wrenches with a rag before loosening the high-pressure fuel line fitting.

➡ **Note: Some models may use a banjo type bolt.**

6 Remove the high-pressure pump mounting fasteners (see illustration) and remove the pump.

14 Fuel rail and injectors - removal and installation

✳✳ WARNING:

Gasoline is extremely flammable, so take extra precautions when you work on any part of the fuel system. See the *Fuel system warnings* in Section 1.

✳✳ WARNING:

Wait until the engine is completely cool before beginning this procedure.

✳✳ CAUTION:

On five-cylinder models, whenever the fuel system has been opened it must be bled (see Section 5). If the system is not bled, the catalytic converter can be damaged.

✳✳ CAUTION:

Whenever the battery is disconnected, several systems must be re-learned before they will work properly (see Chapter 5, Section 3).

13.6 High-pressure fuel pump mounting fasteners - typical BPY unit shown; CCTA, CBFA unit similar

➡ **Note: The sleeve (cam follower) might remain in the cylinder head.**

7 Remove and discard the old pump O-ring. Always use a new O-ring when installing the pump.

8 Before installing the pump, insert the sleeve in the cylinder head, then rotate the crankshaft with a socket and breaker bar on the center bolt of the crankshaft pulley until the sleeve reaches its lowest point.

➡ **Note: Hold the sleeve down in its bore with your finger as you rotate the engine.**

9 Install the pump with a new O-ring. Install the pump mounting fasteners and tighten them, in a diagonal sequence, to the torque listed in this Chapter's Specifications.

10 Reconnect the fuel lines and tighten them securely.

11 Connect the electrical connectors to the low fuel pressure sensor and the fuel pressure regulator valve.

1 Relieve the fuel system pressure (see Section 3).

2 Disconnect the cable from the negative battery terminal (see Chapter 5).

3 Remove the engine cover (see Chapter 1, Section 7).

4 Wrap a shop rag around the fuel line connectors at the front of the engine and disconnect the fittings (see Section 6). Plug the supply line and the fuel rail.

FOUR-CYLINDER MODELS

Intake manifold with fuel rail removal

✳✳ WARNING:

The fuel system on these models operates at very high pressure (in excess of 1700 psi) and can cause serious injury. Do not attempt to work on the fuel system until you are absolutely sure that the fuel pressure has been relieved (see Section 3).

➡ **Note: A special puller tool might be required to remove the injectors from the cylinder head, and a special press tool might**

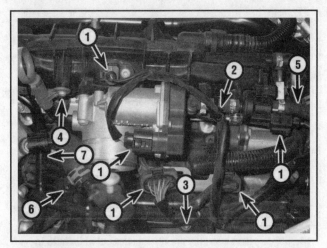

14.6 Intake manifold/fuel rail removal details - four-cylinder BPY models

1 *Electrical connectors*
2 *Harness cable tie (location and number of cable ties varies with model)*
3 *Coolant pipe mounting bracket bolt*
4 *Dipstick tube support bracket fastener*
5 *EVAP purge valve hose (disconnect from pipe on firewall)*
6 *Bracket fastener for turbocharger coolant return pipe*
7 *Turbocharger coolant return pipe*

be required to install the injectors. Special tools are also available to install and size the new Teflon O-ring on each injector, but we were able to devise a way to do this without them. Check on the availability of these tools before performing the following procedure.

➡ **Note: For intake manifold removal and installation on five-cylinder engines, refer to Chapter 2B.**

BPY engines

▶ **Refer to illustrations 14.6, 14.12, 14.14a and 14.14b**

5 Detach the intake duct from the throttle body.

6 Disconnect all electrical connectors from the intake manifold and the fuel rail (see illustration).

7 Label and disconnect all hoses from the intake manifold. On vehicles with an automatic transaxle, disconnect the vacuum hose that

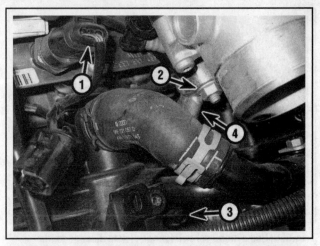

14.12 Lower intake manifold/fuel rail details - four-cylinder BPY models:

1 *Fuel pressure sensor*
2 *Support bracket nut*
3 *Support bracket bolt*
4 *Support bracket*

connects the intake manifold to the vacuum pump.

8 Remove the fasteners from both coolant pipe support brackets.

➡ **Note: On some models, it isn't necessary to disconnect the radiator hose from the coolant pipe; removing the pipe-to-manifold fasteners will allow the coolant pipe to be repositioned far enough from the manifold for removal. If you find that this is not the case on your vehicle, drain the coolant (see Chapter 1) and detach the radiator hose from the front of the coolant pipe.**

9 Remove the dipstick, remove the fastener from the dipstick tube bracket, then pull out and remove the upper part of the dipstick tube.

10 Wrap a shop rag around each of the fuel line fittings at the high-pressure pump, then disconnect both fittings (see illustration 13.5). Be prepared to catch the fuel spillage. Plug the open lines and the fuel pipes on the pump.

11 Remove the turbocharger coolant return hose from the return pipe. Remove the return pipe bracket fasteners and set the return pipe aside.

12 Disconnect the electrical connector from the fuel pressure sensor (see illustration).

13 Remove the intake manifold support bracket.

14 Remove the intake manifold fasteners (see illustrations).

14.14a Upper intake manifold fasteners - four-cylinder BPY models

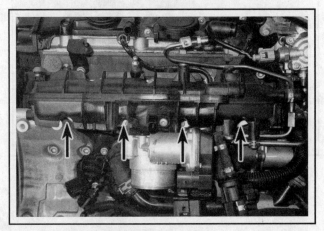

14.14b Lower intake manifold fasteners - four-cylinder BPY models

14.33a Use a small screwdriver or pick to disengage the radial compensator tabs (A) from the support ring (B), remove the support ring . . .

15 Remove the intake manifold and fuel rail as a single assembly. The injectors might come out with the fuel rail, but it's unlikely; the injectors will probably remain in the cylinder head.

16 Remove and discard the old intake manifold gasket.

17 Place the intake manifold on a clean work surface. If any injectors came out of the cylinder head when you removed the intake manifold and fuel rail, remove them from the fuel rail by simply pulling them out.

CCTA, CBFA engines

18 On models equipped with a noise generator, open the locking rings on the charge air pipe, remove the fasteners then remove the charge air pipe.

19 Remove the air filter housing (see Section 10).

20 Disconnect all electrical connectors from the intake manifold and the fuel rail.

21 Label and disconnect all hoses from the intake manifold.

14.34 Fuel injector details - four-cylinder models (later version shown, earlier version similar)

1	Combustion chamber Teflon sealing ring	3	Support ring
2	Radial compensator	4	Spacer ring
		5	Injector upper O-ring

14.33b . . . then carefully pry the injector out of its bore in the cylinder head

22 Remove the fuel supply line fasteners and lay the line out of the way.

23 Wrap a shop rag around each of the fuel line fittings at the high-pressure pump, then disconnect both fittings (see Section 13).

24 Remove the coolant line bracket fasteners and remove the manifold.

25 Raise the vehicle and support it securely on jackstands.

26 Remove the charge air pipe fasteners, then disconnect the electrical connector at the pipe. Loosen the clamps at each end of the charge air pipe, and detach the pipe from the throttle body and intercooler.

27 Remove the throttle body/control motor (see Section 11).

28 Remove the intake manifold support bracket.

➤ **Note: There are two more brackets attached to the bottom of the manifold that use push pin retainers that must be disconnected.**

29 Remove the intake manifold fasteners.

30 Remove the intake manifold and fuel rail as a single assembly.

➤ **Note: Remove the intake manifold runner electrical connector from the bottom of the manifold if it could not be disconnected earlier.**

31 Remove and discard the old intake manifold gasket.

32 Place the intake manifold on a clean work surface. If any injectors came out of the cylinder head when you removed the intake manifold and fuel rail, remove them from the fuel rail by simply pulling them out.

➤ **Note: Once the fuel rail is removed, disconnect the high pressure fuel pump line from the rail to prevent damage to the line.**

Fuel injector removal and disassembly

▶ **Refer to illustrations 14.33a, 14.33b, 14.34 and 14.35**

33 Most injectors probably did not come out of the cylinder head when you removed the fuel rail. To remove each injector from the cylinder head, disengage the tabs of the radial compensator from the support ring, remove the support ring and use a pair angled needle nose pliers to pull the injector out of the head (see illustrations). If any of the injectors are seriously stuck in the cylinder head, you might have to remove them with a special puller tool set.

34 Remove and inspect the condition of the radial compensator (see illustration). If it's damaged, replace it. Also inspect the support ring. Again, if it's damaged, replace it.

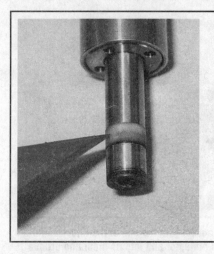

14.35 To remove the Teflon sealing ring, cut it off with a hobby knife (be careful not to scratch the injector groove)

35 Remove the old combustion chamber Teflon sealing ring and the upper O-ring from each injector (see illustration).

✷✷ CAUTION:

Be extremely careful not to damage the groove for the seal or the rib in the floor of the groove. If you damage the groove or the rib, you must replace the injector.

36 Inspect the condition of the upper spacer ring; it only needs to be replaced if it's damaged.

Intake manifold disassembly and reassembly

▶ Refer to illustrations 14.37a and 14.37b

➡ Note: No further disassembly of the intake manifold is necessary unless you're replacing some component on the manifold, or the manifold itself.

37 Remove the EVAP line fasteners and clamps from the top and underside of the intake manifold. Pull the EVAP canister purge solenoid off its mounting bracket (see illustrations) and remove the EVAP assembly.

38 Remove the fuel line clamp, unscrew the line fittings and remove the lines from the intake manifold.

39 On BPY models, carefully pry off the intake flap motor linkage, remove the intake flap motor mounting fasteners and remove the intake flap motor from the intake manifold.

40 If you're replacing the intake manifold, remove the throttle body from the intake manifold. This step is not necessary if you are simply removing or replacing the fuel rail.

41 Remove the fuel rail mounting fasteners and remove the fuel rail from the intake manifold.

42 Reassembly is the reverse of disassembly.

Injector reassembly and installation

▶ Refer to illustrations 14.47, 14.48, 14.49a, 14.49b, 14.50, 14.51a and 14.51b

43 Before installing the new Teflon seal on each injector, thoroughly clean the groove for the seal and the injector shaft. Remove all combustion residue and varnish with a clean shop rag.

Teflon seal installation using the special tools

44 The manufacturer recommends that you use the tools included in

14.37a Intake manifold disassembly details - BPY four-cylinder models

1 Fuel supply line bracket fastener
2 EVAP line bracket fastener
3 Fuel rail retaining fasteners (do not remove until you've removed everything in illustration 14.37b)

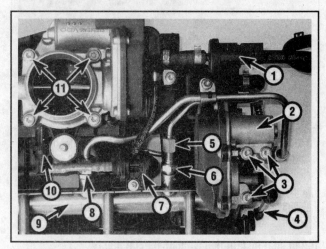

14.37b Intake manifold disassembly details - BPY four-cylinder models

1 EVAP canister purge solenoid valve
2 Intake flap motor
3 Intake flap motor mounting fasteners
4 Intake flap motor control rod
5 Low pressure fuel line fitting
6 Check valve
7 EVAP purge line
8 High pressure fuel line fitting
9 Fuel rail
10 EVAP purge line quick-connect fitting
11 Throttle body mounting fasteners

the special injector tool set to install the Teflon lower seals on the injectors: Install the special seal assembly cone on the injector, install the special sleeve on the injector and use the sleeve to push on the assembly cone, which pushes the Teflon seal into place on its groove. Do NOT use any lubricants to do so.

45 Pushing the Teflon seal into place in its groove expands it slightly. There are two sizing sleeves in the special tool set with progressively smaller inside diameters. Using a clockwise rotating motion of about 180 degrees, install the slightly larger sleeve onto the injector and over the Teflon seal until the sleeve hits its stop, then carefully

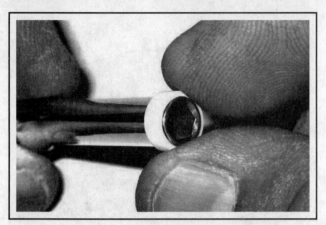

14.47 Slide the new Teflon seal onto the end of a socket that's the same diameter as the end of the fuel injector . . .

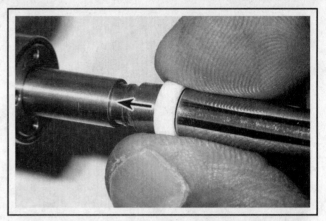

14.48 . . . align the socket with the end of the injector and slide the seal onto the injector and into its mounting groove

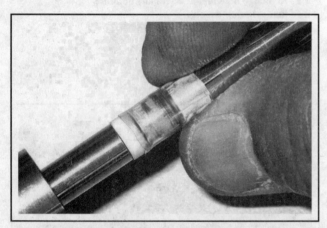

14.49a Use the socket to push a short section of plastic tubing onto the end of the injector and over the new seal . . .

turn the sleeve counterclockwise as you pull it off the injector. Use the slightly smaller sizing sleeve the same way. The seal is now sized. Repeat this step for each injector.

Teflon seal installation without special tools

46 If you don't have the special injector tool set, the Teflon seal can be installed using this method: First, find a socket that is equal or very close in diameter to the diameter of the end of the fuel injector.

47 Work the new Teflon seal onto the end of the socket (see illustration).

48 Place the socket against the end of the injector (see illustration) and slide the seal from the socket onto the injector. Do NOT use any lubricants to do so. Continue pushing the seal onto the injector until it seats into its mounting groove.

49 Because the inside diameter of the seal has to be stretched open to fit over the bore of the socket and the injector, its outside diameter is now slightly too large - it is no longer flush with the surface of the injector. It must be shrunk it back to its original size. To do so, push a piece of plastic tubing with an interference fit onto the end of the socket; a plastic straw that fits tightly on the injector will work. After pushing the plastic tubing onto the socket about an inch, snip off the rest of the tubing, then use the socket to push the tubing onto the end of the injector (see illustration) and slide it onto the injector until it completely covers the new seal (see illustration). Leave the tubing on for a few hours, then remove it. The seal should now be shrunk back its original outside diameter, or close to it.

Spacer ring and radial compensator installation

50 Install the new spacer ring at the upper end of the injector. Lubricate the new upper O-ring with clean engine oil and install it on the injector. Do NOT oil the new Teflon seal. Note that the seal is installed above the spacer (see illustration).

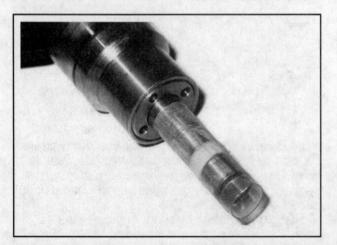

14.49b . . . then leave the plastic tubing in place for several hours to compress the new seal

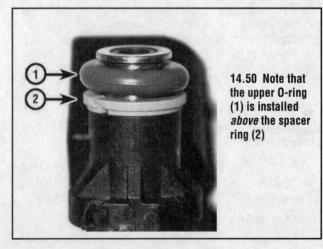

14.50 Note that the upper O-ring (1) is installed *above* the spacer ring (2)

14.51a Make sure that the locking tabs on the radial compensator are correctly aligned with the openings in the support ring . . .

14.51b . . . then push the components together so the tabs snap into place

51 Install the support ring on the top of the injector; note that the support ring can only go on the injector one way because its opening must fit around the electrical terminal. Once the support ring is in place, install the radial compensator so that the locking tabs are correctly aligned with the support ring, then push the compensator toward the upper end of the injector until the locking tabs snap into place (see illustrations).

52 Repeat this procedure until all four injectors are reassembled.

Injector installation

53 Thoroughly clean the injector bores with a small nylon brush. If any of the valves are in the way, carefully rotate the engine just enough to provide clearance to reach all of the bore.

54 Install the fuel injectors in the cylinder head (NOT in the fuel rail). You should be able to push each assembled injector into its bore in the cylinder head. The bore is tapered, so you will encounter some resistance as the Teflon seal nears the bottom of the bore. Press the injector into its bore until it stops.

Intake manifold with fuel rail installation

▶ **Refer to illustration 14.55**

55 Install a new gasket on the reassembled intake manifold (see illustration).

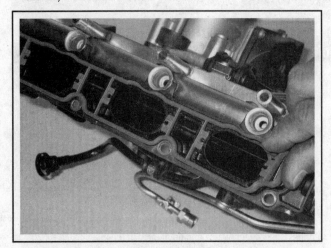

14.55 Install a new gasket on the intake manifold - BPY model shown, other models similar

56 Install the assembled intake manifold/fuel rail assembly. Make sure that the holes in the fuel rail for the fuel injectors fit onto the injectors, then push the manifold firmly until it's seated against the cylinder head. Install the intake manifold mounting fasteners and tighten them to the torque listed in this Chapter's Specifications.

➡ **Note: On CCTA and CBFA models, make sure the injectors are aligned with the notches in the cylinder head.**

57 Installation is otherwise the reverse of removal.

FIVE-CYLINDER MODELS

Removal

▶ **Refer to illustrations 14.59a, 14.59b and 14.60**

58 Disconnect the electrical connectors to the EVAP canister purge valve and fuel injectors, release the locking ring securing the valve to the transport strap then lift the hose out of the clips (see Chapter 2B, illustration 6.5).

59 Remove the fuel rail mounting fasteners (see illustration) and lift the fuel rail and injectors out from the intake manifold (see illustration).

14.59a Fuel rail mounting fastener locations - five-cylinder models

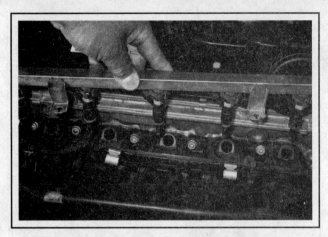

14.59b Remove the fuel rail and injectors as an assembly from the intake manifold and cylinder head - five-cylinder models

60 Remove the retaining clip from each fuel injector (see illustration), then pull the injectors out of the fuel rail.

61 Remove and discard the old injector O-rings.

➡ **Note: Even if you only removed the fuel rail assembly to replace a single injector or a leaking O-ring, it's a good idea to remove all of the injectors from the fuel rails and replace all of the O-rings at the same time.**

Installation

◆ **Refer to illustrations 14.63 and 14.64**

62 Coat the new upper and lower O-rings with clean engine oil and slide them into place on the fuel injectors.

63 Coat each upper O-ring with clean engine oil, then insert the injector into its bore in the fuel rail, then align the tab on the fuel injector with the tab on the fuel rail (see illustration) and push it into the bore until the injector is fully seated in the fuel rail.

64 Secure each injector with its retainer clip, making sure the tabs on the fuel rail and injector are seated in the clip (see illustration).

65 Coat the lower injector O-rings with clean engine oil, then install the fuel rail assemblies on the intake manifold. Tighten the fuel rail mounting fasteners securely.

66 The remainder of installation is the reverse of removal.

67 Bleed the fuel system (see Section 5) and inspect the injectors for fuel leaks.

14.60 Remove each injector retaining clip, then pull the injector out of the fuel rail - five-cylinder models

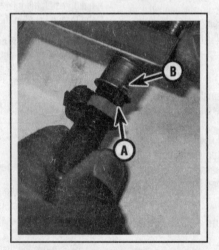

14.63 Insert the injector into the fuel rail and align the tab of the injector (A), with tab on the fuel rail (B) - five-cylinder models

14.64 The tab on the fuel rail and injector must be centered in the retaining clip, then press the clip on securely

15 Turbocharger/exhaust manifold and charge air cooler - check and replacement

CHECK

1 The turbocharger is a precision component which can be severely damaged by a lack of lubrication or from foreign material entering the air intake duct. Turbocharger failure may be indicated by poor engine performance, blue/gray exhaust smoke or unusual noises from the turbocharger. If a turbocharger failure is suspected, check the following areas:

 a) *Check the intake air duct for looseness or damage. Make sure there are no restrictions in the air intake system. Check for a dirty air filter element or damaged intercooler.*
 b) *Check the system vacuum hoses for restrictions or damage.*
 c) *Check the system wiring for damage and electrical connectors for looseness or corrosion.*
 d) *Make sure the wastegate actuator linkage is not binding.*
 e) *Check the exhaust system for damage or restrictions.*
 f) *Check the lubricating oil supply and drainback lines for damage or restrictions.*
 g) *Check the coolant supply and return lines for damage and restrictions.*
 h) *If the turbocharger requires replacement due to failure, be sure to change the engine oil and filter (see Chapter 1).*

2 Complete diagnosis of the turbocharger and control system requires special techniques and equipment. If the previous checks fail to identify the problem, take the vehicle to a dealer service department or other properly equipped repair facility for diagnosis.

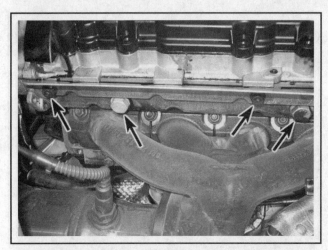

15.12 Exhaust manifold heat shield fasteners (forward-most fastener not visible in this photo) - BPY four-cylinder models

REPLACEMENT

▶ Refer to illustrations 15.12, 15.13, 15.20a, 15.20b and 15.25

✹✹ WARNING:

Wait until the engine is completely cool before beginning this procedure.

✹✹ CAUTION:

Whenever the battery is disconnected, several systems must be re-learned before they will work properly (see Chapter 5, Section 3).

3   Warm up the engine and drain the engine oil, then allow the engine to cool off and drain the cooling system (see Chapter 1).

4   Disconnect the cable from the negative terminal of the battery (see Chapter 5).

5   Loosen the right front wheel bolts, raise the front of the vehicle and support it securely on jackstands. Block the wheels at the opposite end and remove the right front wheel.

6   Remove the under-vehicle splash shield (see Chapter 1, Section 6).

7   Remove the engine cover (see Chapter 1, Section 7). Remove both side inner fender liners (see Chapter 11).

8   Remove the charge air hose from the charge air cooler. Remove the charge air pipe mounting fasteners, just below the crankshaft pulley and remove the pipe.

9   Disconnect the heater hoses at the fire-wall, then plug the hoses and heater core tubes (see Chapter 3).

10   Disconnect the coolant hose to the coolant expansion tank (see Chapter 3).

11   Disconnect the electrical connectors and harness to the ignition coils (see Chapter 5).

12   Remove the exhaust manifold heat shield fasteners and remove the heat shield (see illustration).

13   Disconnect and remove the PCV fresh air inlet hose and the EVAP hose from the engine valve cover and from the turbocharger (see illustration).

15.13 Turbocharger assembly details - BPY model shown, other models similar

1	Crankcase ventilation line	3	Coolant return line banjo bolt
2	EVAP hose (already disconnected from valve cover pipe)	4	Oil supply line banjo bolt
		5	Coolant supply line banjo bolt

14   Remove the coolant return, oil supply and coolant supply line banjo bolts from the turbocharger.

15   Disconnect the oxygen sensor electrical connectors (see Chapter 6), then remove the nuts and detach the catalytic converter from the turbocharger.

16   Remove the pendulum mount (see Chapter 2A).

17   Remove the right side driveaxle heat shield mounting fasteners and shield (see Chapter 8).

18   Remove the exhaust system mount support fasteners and mount, then lower the exhaust out of the way.

19   Disconnect and remove the air hose between the turbocharger and the charge air cooler.

20   Disconnect the electrical connectors from the wastegate bypass

15.20a Turbocharger lower details - BPY model shown, other models similar

1   Recirculating valve electrical connector
2   Wastegate bypass regulator valve electrical connector
3   Oil return line flange bolts
4   Turbocharger support brace

15.20b Turbocharger lower details - BPY model shown, other models similar

1 Oil supply line	5 Coolant supply line
2 Oil supply line banjo bolt	bracket bolt
3 Coolant supply line	6 Oil return line flange bolts
4 Coolant supply line	7 Turbocharger support brace
banjo bolt	fasteners

regulator valve and the turbocharger recirculating valve (see illustrations).

21 Remove the oil return line flange fasteners and disconnect the return line from the turbocharger. Trace the return line down to the oil pan, remove the flange fasteners and disconnect the return line from the oil pan. Remove the oil return line.

22 Remove the lower oil supply line banjo bolt from the block and remove the oil supply line.

23 Remove the lower coolant supply line banjo bolt and the coolant supply line bracket fastener, then remove the coolant supply line.

24 Remove the fastener from the lower end of the turbocharger support brace. It's not absolutely necessary to detach the upper end of the brace from the turbocharger until after you have removed the turbo from the vehicle, but if you can remove it, and the brace, it will give you a little more maneuverability when removing the exhaust manifold/turbocharger assembly. The nut for the upper brace bolt is tough to access, but even loosening it a couple of turns will allow you to move the brace as necessary when removing the exhaust manifold/turbocharger assembly.

25 Remove the exhaust manifold mounting nuts and loosen, but do not remove, the lower clamping bar nuts (see illustration).

26 Remove the exhaust manifold/turbocharger assembly.

➡ **Note: On BPY models, the engine may need to be rotated to the rear almost an inch to allow the turbocharger assembly to be removed.**

27 If you're replacing the exhaust manifold/turbocharger assembly, place the assembly on a clean work bench and remove the components that don't come with the new or remanufactured exhaust manifold/turbocharger assembly and install them on the new unit.

28 When installing the turbocharger assembly, be sure to:
   a) Coat the threads of all exhaust manifold and turbocharger fasteners and all banjo fasteners with anti-seize compound
   b) Replace all seals, gaskets and self-locking nuts
   c) Set the bottom of the exhaust manifold flange on the clamping bar, then rotate the manifold up over the upper mounting studs

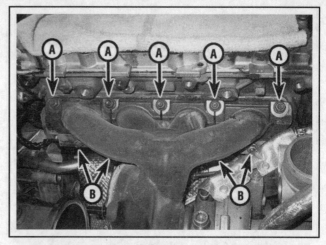

15.25 Exhaust manifold mounting nuts (A) and clamping bar nuts (B, inner nuts not visible).

➡ **Note: Loosen the clamping bar nuts a few turns, but don't remove them**

   and install the upper nuts. Tighten the fasteners evenly, a little at a time, to the torque listed in this Chapter's Specifications
   d) Use new sealing washers for all banjo fittings
   e) Tighten all turbocharger fasteners to the torque listed in this Chapter's Specifications (if no torque specification is listed, tighten the fastener securely)
   f) Add oil to the turbocharger through the oil supply line
   g) Make sure that all hoses are clean inside before installing them
   h) If you're replacing any hose clamps, the replacement clamps must be the same types as the old ones
   i) Make sure that the exhaust system is properly aligned before reconnecting it to the turbocharger
   j) Refill the engine coolant and top up the engine oil (see Chapter 1) before starting the engine
   k) After starting the engine, let it idle for about one minute to ensure an adequate oil supply to the turbocharger

29 Installation is otherwise the reverse of removal.

Charge air cooler

30 Raise the vehicle and support it securely on jackstands.

31 Remove the lower splash shield below the engine (see Chapter 1, Section 6).

32 Remove the engine cover (see Chapter 1, Section 7).

33 Remove the front bumper cover (see Chapter 11).

34 Drain the cooling system (see Chapter 1).

35 Loosen the clamps and remove the right charge air hose from the charge pipe and cooler.

36 Remove the cooling fan shroud and radiator (see Chapter 3).

37 On BPY models, remove the air guide inlet fasteners and guides from each side of the radiator support.

38 Remove the charge air cooler fasteners from the front side of the radiator support then push the cooler towards the engine and remove cooler mounts and charge air cooler

➡ **Note: On BPY models, the air conditioning condenser is mounted to the charge air cooler. Remove the air conditioning condenser mounting fasteners, secure the condenser to the radiator support then remove the charge air cooler.**

39 Installation is the reverse of removal. Replace any damaged ducts, hoses and/or hose clamps.

Specifications

Fuel system pressure

At idle	50 to 102 psi (3.5 to 7.0 bar)
Holding pressure, after 10 minutes	43 psi (3.0 bar) minimum

Torque specifications

	Ft-lbs (unless otherwise indicated)	Nm

➡ **Note:** One foot-pound (ft-lb) of torque is equivalent to 12 inch-pounds (in-lbs) of torque. Torque values below approximately 15 foot-pounds are expressed in inch-pounds, because most foot-pound torque wrenches are not accurate at these smaller values.

	Ft-lbs (unless otherwise indicated)	Nm
High-pressure fuel pump mounting fasteners	88 in-lbs	10
Intake manifold fasteners (four-cylinder models)		
BPY engine	88 in-lbs	10
CCTA, CBFA engines		
Step 1	26 in-lbs	3
Step 2	80 in-lbs	9
Exhaust manifold/turbocharger assembly (four-cylinder models)		
BPY engine		
Exhaust manifold-to-cylinder head nuts (new)	15	20
Turbocharger-to-catalytic converter fasteners/nuts	29.5	40
Oil supply line banjo fasteners (both ends)	22	30
Oil return line flange fasteners (both ends)	80 in-lbs	9
Coolant supply and return line banjo fasteners (both ends)	26	35
Support bracket fasteners	22	30
CCTA, CBFA engines		
Exhaust manifold-to-cylinder head nuts		
Step 1	44 in-lbs	5
Step 2	106 in-lbs	12
Step 3	142 in-lbs	16
Step 4	18.5	25
Turbocharger-to-catalytic converter fasteners/nuts	29.5	40
Oil supply line banjo fasteners	24	33
Oil supply line fastener	80 in-lbs	9
Oil return line flange fasteners (both ends)	80 in-lbs	9
Coolant supply and return line banjo fasteners (both ends)	28	38
Fuel tank-to-body fasteners		
BPY four-cylinder models		
M6 bolts	88 in-lbs	10
M8 bolts (new)	18.5	25
CCTA, CBFA four-cylinder and all five-cylinder models		
M6 bolts	97 in-lbs	11
M8 bolts (new)	19	26
Throttle body fasteners		
Four-cylinder models		
BPY engine	62 in-lbs	7
CCTA, CBFA engines	44 in-lbs	5
Five-cylinder models	57 in-lbs	6.5

Notes

Section

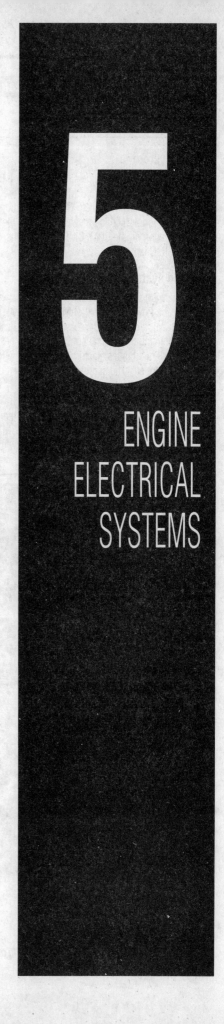

5

ENGINE
ELECTRICAL
SYSTEMS

1   General information and precautions

GENERAL INFORMATION

Ignition system

The electronic ignition system consists of the Engine speed (RPM) sensor, the Camshaft Position (CMP) sensor, the Knock Sensor (KS), the Powertrain Control Module (PCM), the ignition switch, the battery, the individual ignition coils or a coil pack, and the spark plugs. For more information on the RPM, CMP and KS sensors, as well as the PCM, refer to Chapter 6.

Charging system

The charging system includes the alternator (with an integral voltage regulator), the Powertrain Control Module (PCM), the Body Control Module (BCM), a charge indicator light on the dash, the battery, a fuse or fusible link and the wiring connecting all of these components. The charging system supplies electrical power for the ignition system, the lights, the radio, etc. The alternator is driven by a drivebelt.

Starting system

The starting system consists of the battery, the ignition switch, the starter relay, the Powertrain Control Module (PCM), the Body Control Module (BCM), the Transmission Range (TR) switch, the starter motor and solenoid assembly, and the wiring connecting all of the components.

PRECAUTIONS

Always observe the following precautions when working on the electrical system:

a) *Be extremely careful when servicing engine electrical components. They are easily damaged if checked, connected or handled improperly.*

b) *Never leave the ignition switched on for long periods of time when the engine is not running.*

c) *Never disconnect the battery cables while the engine is running.*

d) *Maintain correct polarity when connecting battery cables from another vehicle during jump starting - see the "Booster battery (jump) starting" Section at the front of this manual.*

e) *Always disconnect the cable from the negative battery terminal before working on the electrical system, but read the battery disconnection procedure first (see Section 3).*

It's also a good idea to review the safety-related information regarding the engine electrical systems located in the *Safety first!* Section at the front of this manual before beginning any operation included in this Chapter.

1.1 Engine electrical system details (five-cylinder models):

1 Battery	*4 Alternator*
2 Engine compartment fuse/relay box	*5 Ignition coils*
3 Starter motor (not visible in photo; vicinity given)	

2 Troubleshooting

IGNITION SYSTEM

1 If a malfunction occurs in the ignition system, do not immediately assume that any particular part is causing the problem. First, check the following items:

a) *Make sure that the cable clamps at the battery terminals are clean and tight.*

b) *Test the condition of the battery (see Steps 21 through 24). If it doesn't pass all the tests, replace it.*

c) *Check the ignition coil or coil pack connections.*

d) *Check any relevant fuses in the engine compartment fuse and relay box (see Chapter 12). If they're burned, determine the cause and repair the circuit.*

Check

▶ **Refer to illustration 2.3**

❋❋ WARNING:

Because of the high voltage generated by the ignition system, use extreme care when performing a procedure involving ignition components.

➡ **Note 1: The ignition system components on these vehicles are difficult to diagnose. In the event of ignition system failure that you can't diagnose, have the vehicle tested at a dealer service department or other qualified auto repair facility.**

➡ **Note 2: You'll need a spark tester for the following test. Spark testers are available at most auto supply stores.**

2 If the engine turns over but won't start, verify that there is sufficient ignition voltage to fire the spark plugs as follows.

3 On models with a coil-over-plug type ignition system, remove a coil and install the tester between the boot at the lower end of the coil and the spark plug (see illustration). On models with spark plug wires, disconnect a spark plug wire from a spark plug and install the tester between the spark plug wire boot and the spark plug.

4 Crank the engine and note whether or not the tester flashes.

❋❋ CAUTION:

Do NOT crank the engine or allow it to run for more than five seconds; running the engine for more than five seconds may set a Diagnostic Trouble Code (DTC) for a cylinder misfire.

Models with a coil-over-plug type ignition system

5 If the tester flashes during cranking, the coil is delivering sufficient voltage to the spark plug to fire it. Repeat this test for each cylinder to verify that the other coils are OK.

6 If the tester doesn't flash, remove a coil from another cylinder and swap it for the one being tested. If the tester now flashes, you know that the original coil is bad. If the tester still doesn't flash, the PCM or wiring harness is probably defective. Have the PCM checked out by a dealer service department or other qualified repair shop (testing the PCM is beyond the scope of the do-it-yourselfer because it requires expensive special tools).

7 If the tester flashes during cranking but a misfire code (related

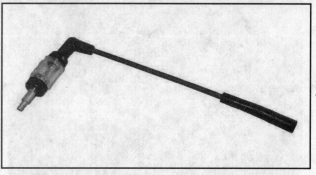

2.3 Spark tester

to the cylinder being tested) has been stored, the spark plug could be fouled or defective.

Models with spark plug wires

8 If the tester flashes during cranking, sufficient voltage is reaching the spark plug to fire it.

9 Repeat this test on the remaining cylinders.

10 Proceed on this basis until you have verified that there's a good spark from each spark plug wire. If there is, then you have verified that the coils in the coil pack are functioning correctly and that the spark plug wires are OK.

11 If there is no spark from a spark plug wire, then either the coil is bad, the plug wire is bad or a connection at one end of the plug wire is loose. Assuming that you're using new plug wires or known good wires, then the coil is probably defective. Also inspect the coil pack electrical connector. Make sure that it's clean, tight and in good condition.

12 If all the coils are firing correctly, but the engine misfires, then one or more of the plugs might be fouled. Remove and check the spark plugs or install new ones (see Chapter 1).

13 No further testing of the ignition system is possible without special tools. If the problem persists, have the ignition system tested by a dealer service department or other qualified repair shop.

CHARGING SYSTEM

14 If a malfunction occurs in the charging system, do not automatically assume the alternator is causing the problem. First check the following items:

a) *Check the drivebelt tension and condition, as described in Chapter 1. Replace it if it's worn or deteriorated.*

b) *Make sure the alternator mounting bolts are tight.*

c) *Inspect the alternator wiring harness and the connectors at the alternator and voltage regulator. They must be in good condition, tight and have no corrosion.*

d) *Check the fusible link (if equipped) or main fuse in the underhood fuse/relay box. If it is burned, determine the cause, repair the circuit and replace the link or fuse (the vehicle will not start and/or the accessories will not work if the fusible link or main fuse is blown).*

e) *Start the engine and check the alternator for abnormal noises (a shrieking or squealing sound indicates a bad bearing).*

f) *Check the battery. Make sure it's fully charged and in good condition (one bad cell in a battery can cause overcharging by the alternator).*

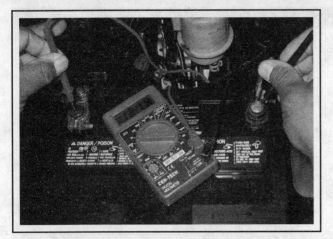

2.21 To test the open circuit voltage of the battery, touch the black probe of the voltmeter to the negative terminal and the red probe to the positive terminal of the battery; a fully charged battery should be at least 12.6 volts

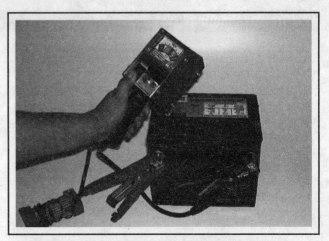

2.23 Connect a battery load tester to the battery and check the battery condition under load following the tool manufacturer's instructions

g) Disconnect the battery cables (negative first, then positive). Inspect the battery posts and the cable clamps for corrosion. Clean them thoroughly if necessary (see Chapter 1). Reconnect the cables (positive first, negative last).

Alternator - check

15 Use a voltmeter to check the battery voltage with the engine off. It should be at least 12.6 volts (see illustration 2.21).

16 Start the engine and check the battery voltage again. It should now be approximately 13.5 to 15 volts.

17 If the voltage reading is more or less than the specified charging voltage, the voltage regulator is probably defective, which will require replacement of the alternator (the voltage regulator is not replaceable separately). Remove the alternator and have it bench tested (most auto parts stores will do this for you).

18 The charging system (battery) light on the instrument cluster lights up when the ignition key is turned to ON, but it should go out when the engine starts.

19 If the charging system light stays on after the engine has been started, there is a problem with the charging system. Before replacing the alternator, check the battery condition, alternator belt tension and electrical cable connections.

20 If replacing the alternator doesn't restore voltage to the specified range, have the charging system tested by a dealer service department or other qualified repair shop.

Battery - check

▶ **Refer to illustrations 2.21 and 2.23**

21 Check the battery state of charge. Visually inspect the indicator eye on the top of the battery (if equipped with one); if the indicator eye is black in color, charge the battery as described in Chapter 1. Next perform an open circuit voltage test using a digital voltmeter.

➡ **Note: The battery's surface charge must be removed before accurate voltage measurements can be made. Turn on the high beams for ten seconds, then turn them off and let the vehicle stand for two minutes.**

With the engine and all accessories Off, touch the negative probe of the voltmeter to the negative terminal of the battery and the positive probe to the positive terminal of the battery (see illustration). The battery voltage should be 12.6 volts or slightly above. If the battery is less than the

specified voltage, charge the battery before proceeding to the next test. Do not proceed with the battery load test unless the battery charge is correct.

22 Disconnect the negative battery cable, then the positive cable from the battery.

23 Perform a battery load test. An accurate check of the battery condition can only be performed with a load tester (see illustration). This test evaluates the ability of the battery to operate the starter and other accessories during periods of high current draw. Connect the load tester to the battery terminals. Load test the battery according to the tool manufacturer's instructions. This tool increases the load demand (current draw) on the battery.

24 Maintain the load on the battery for 15 seconds and observe that the battery voltage does not drop below 9.6 volts. If the battery condition is weak or defective, the tool will indicate this condition immediately.

➡ **Note: Cold temperatures will cause the minimum voltage reading to drop slightly. Follow the chart given in the manufacturer's instructions to compensate for cold climates. Minimum load voltage for freezing temperatures (32 degrees F) should be approximately 9.1 volts.**

STARTING SYSTEM

The starter rotates, but the engine doesn't

25 Remove the starter (see Section 8). Check the overrunning clutch and bench test the starter to make sure the drive mechanism extends fully for proper engagement with the flywheel ring gear. If it doesn't, replace the starter.

26 Check the flywheel ring gear for missing teeth and other damage. With the ignition turned off, rotate the flywheel so you can check the entire ring gear.

The starter is noisy

27 If the solenoid is making a chattering noise, first check the battery (see Steps 21 through 24). If the battery is okay, check the cables and connections.

28 If you hear a grinding, crashing metallic sound when you turn the key to Start, check for loose starter mounting bolts. If they're tight, remove the starter and inspect the teeth on the starter pinion gear and flywheel ring gear. Look for missing or damaged teeth.

29 If the starter sounds fine when you first turn the key to Start, but then stops rotating the engine and emits a zinging sound, the problem is probably a defective starter drive that's not staying engaged with the ring gear. Replace the starter.

The starter rotates slowly

30 Check the battery (see Steps 21 through 24).

31 If the battery is okay, verify all connections (at the battery, the starter solenoid and motor) are clean, corrosion-free and tight. Make sure the cables aren't frayed or damaged.

32 Check that the starter mounting bolts are tight so it grounds properly. Also check the pinion gear and flywheel ring gear for evidence of a mechanical bind (galling, deformed gear teeth or other damage).

The starter does not rotate at all

33 Check the battery (see Steps 21 through 24).

34 If the battery is okay, verify all connections (at the battery, the starter solenoid and motor) are clean, corrosion-free and tight. Make sure the cables aren't frayed or damaged.

35 Check all of the fuses in the underhood fuse/relay box.

36 Check that the starter mounting bolts are tight so it grounds properly.

37 Check for voltage at the starter solenoid "S" terminal when the ignition key is turned to the start position. If voltage is present, replace the starter/solenoid assembly. If no voltage is present, the problem could be the starter relay, the Transmission Range (TR) switch (see Chapter 6) or clutch start switch (see Chapter 8), or with an electrical connector somewhere in the circuit (see the wiring diagrams at the end of Chapter 12). Also, on many modern vehicles, the Powertrain Control Module (PCM) and the Body Control Module (BCM) control the voltage signal to the starter solenoid; on such vehicles a special scan tool is required for diagnosis.

3 Battery - disconnection and reconnection

⁂ CAUTION:

Always disconnect the cable from the negative battery terminal FIRST and hook it up LAST or the battery may be shorted by the tool being used to loosen the cable clamps.

⁂ CAUTION:

If the audio system is equipped with an anti-theft system, make sure you have the correct activation code before disconnecting the battery.

Some systems on the vehicle require battery power to be available at all times, either to maintain continuous operation (alarm system, power door locks, etc.), or to maintain control unit memory (radio station presets, Powertrain Control Module and other control units). When the battery is disconnected, the power that maintains these systems is cut, and the systems must be re-learned before they will work properly. So, before you disconnect the battery, please note that on a vehicle with power door locks, it's a wise precaution to remove the key from the ignition and to keep it with you, so that it does not get locked inside if the power door locks should engage accidentally when the battery is reconnected!

Devices known as "memory-savers" can be used to avoid some of these problems. Precise details vary according to the device used. The typical memory saver is plugged into the cigarette lighter and is connected to a spare battery. Then the vehicle battery can be disconnected from the electrical system. The memory saver will provide sufficient current to maintain audio unit security codes, PCM memory, etc. and will provide power to always hot circuits such as the clock and radio memory circuits.

⁂ WARNING:

Some memory savers deliver a considerable amount of current in order to keep vehicle systems operational after the main battery is disconnected. If you're using a memory saver, make sure that the circuit concerned is actually open before servicing it.

⁂ WARNING:

If you're going to work near any of the airbag system components, the battery MUST be disconnected and a memory saver must NOT be used. If a memory saver is used, power will be supplied to the airbag, which means that it could accidentally deploy and cause serious personal injury.

To disconnect the battery for service procedures requiring power to be cut from the vehicle, loosen the cable end bolt and disconnect the cable from the negative battery terminal. Isolate the cable end to prevent it from coming into accidental contact with the battery terminal.

Battery initialization (re-learning)

Insert the key into the ignition switch and turn the key to "ON" position, then the "OFF" position.

Reset the clock and fully open all windows and sunroof to reset the auto stop functions.

Start the vehicle; the electro-mechanical steering warning light should now be on. Drive the vehicle in a straight direction for a short distance to a maximum speed of 10 to 13 mph - the steering angle sensor should now be re-initialized and the warning light turned off.

Connect a scan tool and check for any trouble codes (see Chapter 6).

4 Battery and battery tray - removal and installation

⁜ CAUTION:

If the battery is disconnected, several systems must be re-learned before they will work properly (see Section 3).

BATTERY

▶ **Refer to illustrations 4.1 and 4.3**

1 Press in the retaining tabs (see illustration) and remove the battery top cover.

2 Press in the retaining tabs at the lower edges of the battery cover and remove the side of the battery cover.

3 Disconnect the cable from the negative battery terminal first, then disconnect the cable from the positive battery terminal (see illustration).

4 Remove the battery hold-down clamp bolt and clamp.

5 Lift out the battery. Be careful - it's heavy.

➡ **Note: Battery straps and handlers are available at most auto parts stores for reasonable prices. They make it easier to remove and carry the battery.**

4.1 Location of the battery top cover retaining tab

4.9 Disconnect the wire from the fuse panel and set it to the side

6 If you are replacing the battery, make sure you get one that's identical, with the same dimensions, amperage rating, cold cranking rating, etc. Also, be sure to remove the heat shield (if equipped) from the old battery and install it on the new battery.

7 Installation is the reverse of removal. Be sure to connect the positive cable first and the negative cable last.

BATTERY TRAY

▶ **Refer to illustration 4.9 and 4.10**

8 Remove the battery (see Steps 1 through 6).

9 Remove the engine fuse panel cover (see Chapter 12), and disconnect the wire from the fuse panel (see illustration).

10 Remove the battery tray mounting fasteners (see illustration) and lift out the battery tray.

11 Installation is the reverse of removal. Be sure to connect the positive cable first and the negative cable last.

4.3 Battery removal details:

1 *Battery side cover (lift the front up to remove)*
2 *Battery negative terminal (disconnect FIRST, reconnect LAST)*
3 *Battery positive terminal*
4 *Battery hold-down clamp*

4.10 Battery tray mounting fasteners

5   Battery cables - replacement

1   When removing the cables, always disconnect the cable from the negative battery terminal first and hook it up last, or you might accidentally short out the battery with the tool you're using to loosen the cable clamps. Even if you're only replacing the cable for the positive terminal, be sure to disconnect the negative cable from the battery first.

2   Disconnect the old cables from the battery, then trace each of them to their opposite ends and disconnect them. Be sure to note the routing of each cable before disconnecting it to ensure correct installation.

3   If you are replacing any of the old cables, take them with you when buying new cables. It is vitally important that you replace the cables with identical parts.

4   Clean the threads of the solenoid or ground connection with a wire brush to remove rust and corrosion. Apply a light coat of battery terminal corrosion inhibitor or petroleum jelly to the threads to prevent future corrosion.

5   Attach the cable to the solenoid or ground connection and tighten the mounting nut/bolt securely.

6   Before connecting a new cable to the battery, make sure that it reaches the battery post without having to be stretched.

7   Connect the cable to the positive battery terminal first, then connect the ground cable to the negative battery terminal.

6   Ignition coils - removal and installation

▶ **Refer to illustrations 6.4, 6.5 and 6.6**

✳✳ CAUTION:

If the battery is disconnected, several systems must be relearned before they will work properly (see Section 3).

➡ **Note: This procedure applies to all ignition coils.**

1   Disconnect the cable from the negative battery terminal (see Section 3).

2   Remove the engine cover (see Chapter 1, Section 7).

3   On four-cylinder engines, remove the ignition coil harness fasteners.

4   On five-cylinder engines, disconnect the electrical connector from the ignition coils (see illustration). On four-cylinder engines, the ignition coil harness is rigid, so you must pull the coils up about an inch (see Step 5), disconnect all electrical connectors from the coils and pull the harness and connectors away as a unit.

5   Using special tool #T40039, slide the tool in to the top slot of the coil and pull the coil up approximately 1-1/4 inches.

➡ **Note: If the special tool is not available, use two flat blade screwdrivers or a trim panel tool to carefully pry the ignition coil up (see illustration).**

6   Grasp the ignition coil firmly and pull it straight up (see illustration).

7   Apply a little silicone dielectric compound to the inside of the spark plug boot before installing the coil. Installation is otherwise the reverse of removal.

6.4 Depress the tabs to release the connectors

6.5 Carefully pry a little on each side of the coil to raise it up

6.6 Remove each coil from the cylinder head

7   Alternator - removal and installation

⁂ WARNING:

Wait until the engine is completely cool before performing this procedure.

1   Disconnect the cable from the negative battery terminal (see Section 3).
2   Remove the engine cover.

FOUR-CYLINDER MODELS

3   Remove the air inlet hoses (see Chapter 1, Section 7).
4   Remove the turbocharger charge air pipe (see Chapter 4).

7.12 Alternator electrical connectors

7.13a Alternator upper mounting bolt location . . .

5   Remove the drivebelt (see Chapter 1).
6   Loosen the coolant pipe mounting bolts from the intake manifold, but do not completely remove the bolts.
7   Disconnect the electrical connectors from the alternator.
8   Remove the alternator mounting fasteners and remove the alternator.

FIVE-CYLINDER MODELS

▶ **Refer to illustrations 7.12, 7.13a and 7.13b**

9   Remove the air inlet from the radiator support (see Chapter 1, Section 7).
10   Place the radiator support panel in the service position (see Chapter 11).
11   Remove the drivebelts and interfering tensioners/idlers (see Chapter 1).
12   Disconnect the electrical connectors from the alternator (see illustration).
13   Remove the alternator mounting fasteners (see illustrations) and remove the alternator.

ALL MODELS

14   Installation is the reverse of removal. Be sure to tighten the alternator mounting fasteners securely.
15   Reconnect the cable to the negative terminal of the battery (see Section 3).
16   Check the charging voltage (see Section 2) to verify that the alternator is operating correctly.

7.13b . . . and lower mounting bolt location

8 Starter motor - removal and installation

▶ Refer to illustrations 8.4a, 8.4b and 8.5

⁂ CAUTION:

If the battery is disconnected, several systems must be re-learned before they will work properly (see Section 3).

1   Disconnect the cable from the negative battery terminal (see Section 3).

2   Remove the engine cover/air filter housing (see Chapter 1, Section 7).

3   Raise the vehicle and place it on jackstands. Remove the engine under-covers (see Chapter 1, Section 6).

4   Slide the protective cover off of the starter solenoid (see illustration), then disconnect the starter motor electrical connectors (see illustration) and harness retainer, if equipped.

5   Remove the plastic harness retainer fastener and retainer to access the starter motor upper mounting bolt. Remove the starter motor upper mounting bolt. On automatic transaxle models, remove the bracket nut and bracket from the lower bolt (see illustration).

6   Remove the starter lower mounting bolt and remove the starter from below.

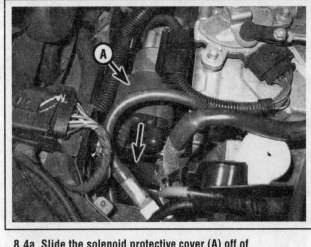

8.4a Slide the solenoid protective cover (A) off of the solenoid . . .

➡ **Note: On models equipped with a DSG transaxle, the starter motor is removed out the top of the engine compartment.**

7   Installation is the reverse of removal. Be sure to tighten the starter motor mounting fasteners securely.

8.4b . . . then disconnect the electrical connectors

8.5 Remove the bracket retaining nut (A), from the starter lower mounting bolt, then remove the harness bracket (B) from the starter

Notes

6

EMISSIONS AND ENGINE CONTROL SYSTEMS

1 General information

To prevent pollution of the atmosphere from incompletely burned and evaporating gases, and to maintain good driveability and fuel economy, a number of emission control systems are incorporated. They include the:

CATALYTIC CONVERTER

A catalytic converter is an emission control device in the exhaust system that reduces certain pollutants in the exhaust gas stream. There are two types of converters: oxidation converters and reduction converters.

Oxidation converters contain a monolithic substrate (a ceramic honeycomb) coated with the semi-precious metals platinum and palladium. An oxidation catalyst reduces unburned hydrocarbons (HC) and carbon monoxide (CO) by adding oxygen to the exhaust stream as it passes through the substrate, which, in the presence of high temperature and the catalyst materials, converts the HC and CO to water vapor (H_2O) and carbon dioxide (CO_2).

Reduction converters contain a monolithic substrate coated with platinum and rhodium. A reduction catalyst reduces oxides of nitrogen (NOx) by removing oxygen, which in the presence of high temperature and the catalyst material produces nitrogen (N) and carbon dioxide (CO_2).

Catalytic converters that combine both types of catalysts in one assembly are known as "three-way catalysts" or TWCs. A TWC can reduce all three pollutants.

EVAPORATIVE EMISSIONS CONTROL (EVAP) SYSTEM

The Evaporative Emissions Control (EVAP) system prevents fuel system vapors (which contain unburned hydrocarbons) from escaping into the atmosphere. On warm days, vapors trapped inside the fuel tank expand until the pressure reaches a certain threshold. Then the fuel vapors are routed from the fuel tank through the fuel vapor vent valve and the fuel vapor control valve to the EVAP canister, where they're stored temporarily until the next time the vehicle is operated. When the conditions are right (engine warmed up, vehicle up to speed, moderate or heavy load on the engine, etc.) the PCM opens the canister purge valve, which allows fuel vapors to be drawn from the canister into the intake manifold. Once in the intake manifold, the fuel vapors mix with incoming air before being drawn through the intake ports into the combustion chambers where they're burned up with the rest of the air/fuel mixture. The EVAP system is complex and virtually impossible to troubleshoot without the right tools and training.

EXHAUST GAS RECIRCULATION (EGR) SYSTEM

The EGR system reduces oxides of nitrogen by recirculating exhaust gases from the exhaust manifold, through the EGR valve and intake manifold, then back to the combustion chambers, where it mixes with the incoming air/fuel mixture before being consumed. These recirculated exhaust gases dilute the incoming air/fuel mixture, which cools the combustion chambers, thereby reducing NOx emissions.

The EGR system consists of the Powertrain Control Module (PCM), the EGR valve, the EGR valve position sensor and various other information sensors that the PCM uses to determine when to open the EGR valve. The degree to which the EGR valve is opened is referred to as "EGR valve lift." The PCM is programmed to produce the ideal EGR valve lift for varying operating conditions. The EGR valve position sensor, which is an integral part of the EGR valve, detects the amount of EGR valve lift and sends this information to the PCM. The PCM then compares it with the appropriate EGR valve lift for the operating conditions. The PCM increases current flow to the EGR valve to increase valve lift and reduces the current to reduce the amount of lift. If EGR flow is inappropriate to the operating conditions (idle, cold engine, etc.) the PCM simply cuts the current to the EGR valve and the valve closes.

SECONDARY AIR INJECTION (AIR) SYSTEM

Some models are equipped with a secondary air injection (AIR) system. The secondary air injection system is used to reduce tailpipe emissions on initial engine start-up. The system uses an electric motor/pump assembly, relay, vacuum valve/solenoid, air shut-off valve, check valves and tubing to inject fresh air directly into the exhaust manifolds. The fresh air (oxygen) reacts with the exhaust gas in the catalytic converter to reduce HC and CO levels. The air pump and solenoid are controlled by the PCM through the AIR relay. During initial start-up, the PCM energizes the AIR relay, the relay supplies battery voltage to the air pump and the vacuum valve/solenoid, engine vacuum is applied to the air shut-off valve which opens and allows air to flow through the tubing into the exhaust manifolds. The PCM will operate the air pump until closed loop operation is reached (approximately four minutes). During normal operation, the check valves prevent exhaust backflow into the system.

POWERTRAIN CONTROL MODULE (PCM)

The Powertrain Control Module (PCM) is the brain of the engine management system. It also controls a wide variety of other vehicle systems. In order to program the new PCM, the dealer needs the vehicle as well as the new PCM. If you're planning to replace the PCM with a new one, there is no point in trying to do so at home because you won't be able to program it yourself.

POSITIVE CRANKCASE VENTILATION (PCV) SYSTEM

The Positive Crankcase Ventilation (PCV) system reduces hydrocarbon emissions by scavenging crankcase vapors, which are rich in unburned hydrocarbons. A PCV valve or orifice regulates the flow of gases into the intake manifold in proportion to the amount of intake vacuum available.

The PCV system generally consists of the fresh air inlet hose, the PCV valve or orifice and the crankcase ventilation hose (or PCV hose). The fresh air inlet hose connects the air intake duct to a pipe on the valve cover. The crankcase ventilation hose (or PCV hose) connects the PCV valve or orifice in the valve cover to the intake manifold.

Emissions and engine control components (five-cylinder model shown)

1   Powertrain Control Module (PCM) (located under cowl)
2   Accelerator Pedal Position (APP) sensor (located behind the accelerator pedal assembly)
3   Knock sensors (located underneath the exhaust manifold, on the back side of the engine block)
4   Engine Coolant Temperature (ECT) sensor (located at the timing cover)
5   Mass Air Flow/Intake Air Temperature (MAF/IAT) sensor (removed with the engine cover assembly)
6   Transmission Range (TR) sensor
7   Heated oxygen sensor (in the exhaust manifold)
8   Downstream oxygen sensor (at back end of catalytic converter)

9   Upstream oxygen sensor (at the front of the catalytic converter)
10 Manifold Absolute Pressure (MAP) sensor (located on the intake manifold, behind the throttle body)
11 Engine speed sensor (located at the rear of the crankshaft)
12 Secondary air injection solenoid valve
13 Camshaft adjustment valve 1
14 Throttle body/control module
15 Camshaft Position (CMP) sensor
16 EVAP canister purge regulator valve
17 Engine compartment fuse and relay box
18 Crankcase pressure regulator valve for PCV system

Information Sensors

Accelerator Pedal Position (APP) sensor - as you press the accelerator pedal, the APP sensor alters its voltage signal to the PCM in proportion to the angle of the pedal, and the PCM commands a motor inside the throttle body to open or close the throttle plate accordingly

Camshaft Position (CMP) sensor - produces a signal that the PCM uses to identify the number 1 cylinder and to time the firing sequence of the fuel injectors

Crankshaft Position (CKP) sensor - produces a signal that the PCM uses to calculate engine speed and crankshaft position, which enables it to synchronize ignition timing with fuel injector timing, and to detect misfires

Engine Coolant Temperature (ECT) sensor - a thermistor (temperature-sensitive variable resistor) that sends a voltage signal to the PCM, which uses this data to determine the temperature of the engine coolant

Fuel tank pressure sensor - measures the fuel tank pressure and controls fuel tank pressure by signaling the EVAP system to purge the fuel tank vapors when the pressure becomes excessive

Intake Air Temperature (IAT) sensor - monitors the temperature of the air entering the engine and sends a signal to the PCM to determine injector pulse-width (the duration of each injector's on-time) and to adjust spark timing (to prevent spark knock)

Knock sensor - a piezoelectric crystal that oscillates in proportion to engine vibration which produces a voltage output that is monitored by the PCM. This retards the ignition timing when the oscillation exceeds a certain threshold

Manifold Absolute Pressure (MAP) sensor - monitors the pressure or vacuum inside the intake manifold. The PCM uses this data to determine engine load so that it can alter the ignition advance and fuel enrichment

Mass Air Flow (MAF) sensor - measures the amount of intake air drawn into the engine. It uses a hot-wire sensing element to measure the amount of air entering the engine

Oxygen sensors - generates a small variable voltage signal in proportion to the difference between the oxygen content in the exhaust stream and the oxygen content in the ambient air. The PCM uses this information to maintain the proper air/fuel ratio. A second oxygen sensor monitors the efficiency of the catalytic converter

Throttle Position (TP) sensor - a potentiometer that generates a voltage signal that varies in relation to the opening angle of the throttle plate inside the throttle body. Works with the PCM and other sensors to calculate injector pulse width (the duration of each injector's on-time)

Photos courtesy of Wells Manufacturing, except APP and MAF sensors.

2 On Board Diagnosis (OBD) system

GENERAL DESCRIPTION

1   All models are equipped with the second generation OBD-II system. This system consists of an on-board computer known as the Powertrain Control Module (PCM), and information sensors, which monitor various functions of the engine and send data to the PCM. This system incorporates a series of diagnostic monitors that detect and identify fuel injection and emissions control system faults and store the information in the computer memory. This system also tests sensors and output actuators, diagnoses drive cycles, freezes data and clears codes.

2   The PCM is the brain of the electronically controlled fuel and emissions system. It receives data from a number of sensors and other electronic components (switches, relays, etc.). Based on the information it receives, the PCM generates output signals to control various relays, solenoids (fuel injectors) and other actuators. The PCM is specifically calibrated to optimize the emissions, fuel economy and driveability of the vehicle.

3   It isn't a good idea to attempt diagnosis or replacement of the PCM or emission control components at home while the vehicle is under warranty. Because of a federally-mandated warranty which covers the emissions system components and because any owner-induced damage to the PCM, the sensors and/or the control devices may void this warranty, take the vehicle to a dealer service department if the PCM or a system component malfunctions.

SCAN TOOL INFORMATION

▶ **Refer to illustrations 2.4a and 2.4b**

4   Because extracting the Diagnostic Trouble Codes (DTCs) from an engine management system is now the first step in troubleshooting many computer-controlled systems and components, a code reader, at the very least, will be required (see illustration). More powerful scan tools can also perform many of the diagnostics once associated with expensive factory scan tools (see illustration). If you're planning to obtain a generic scan tool for your vehicle, make sure that it's compatible with OBD-II systems. If you don't plan to purchase a code reader or scan tool and don't have access to one, you can have the codes extracted by a dealer service department or an independent repair shop.

➡ **Note: Some auto parts stores even provide this service.**

2.4a Simple code readers are an economical way to extract trouble codes when the CHECK ENGINE light comes on

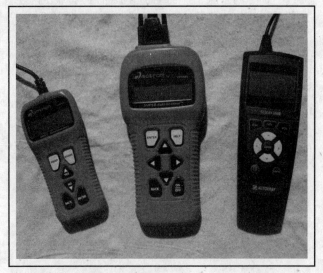

2.4b Hand-held scan tools like these can extract computer codes and also perform diagnostics

3   Obtaining and clearing Diagnostic Trouble Codes (DTCs)

All models covered by this manual are equipped with on-board diagnostics. When the PCM recognizes a malfunction in a monitored emission or engine control system, component or circuit, it turns on the Malfunction Indicator Light (MIL) on the dash. The PCM will continue to display the MIL until the problem is fixed and the Diagnostic Trouble Code (DTC) is cleared from the PCM's memory. You'll need a scan tool to access any DTCs stored in the PCM.

Before outputting any DTCs stored in the PCM, thoroughly inspect ALL electrical connectors and hoses. Make sure that all electrical connections are tight, clean and free of corrosion. And make sure that all hoses are correctly connected, fit tightly and are in good condition (no cracks or tears).

ACCESSING THE DTCS

▶ **Refer to illustration 3.1**

1   The Diagnostic Trouble Codes (DTCs) can only be accessed with a code reader or scan tool. Professional scan tools are expensive, but relatively inexpensive generic code readers or scan tools (see illustrations 2.4a and 2.4b) are available at most auto parts stores. Simply plug the connector of the scan tool into the diagnostic connector (see illustration). Then follow the instructions included with the scan tool to extract the DTCs.

2   Once you have outputted all of the stored DTCs, look them up on the accompanying DTC chart.

3   After troubleshooting the source of each DTC, make any necessary repairs or replace the defective component(s).

Clearing the DTCs

4   Clear the DTCs with the code reader or scan tool in accordance with the instructions provided by the tool's manufacturer.

DIAGNOSTIC TROUBLE CODES

5   The accompanying tables are a list of the Diagnostic Trouble Codes (DTCs) that can be accessed by a do-it-yourselfer working at home (there are many, many more DTCs available to professional mechanics with proprietary scan tools and software, but those codes cannot be accessed by a generic scan tool). If, after you have checked and repaired the connectors, wire harness and vacuum hoses (if applicable) for an emission-related system, component or circuit, the problem persists, have the vehicle checked by a dealer service department or other qualified repair shop.

3.1 The Data Link Connector (DLC) is located under the left end of the instrument panel

DIAGNOSTIC TROUBLE CODES

Code	Possible cause
P0010	Intake camshaft position actuator circuit open (bank 1)
P0011	"A" Camshaft position - timing over-advanced (bank 1)
P0012	"A" Camshaft position - timing over-retarded (bank 1)
P0013	"B" Camshaft position - actuator circuit malfunction (bank 1)
P0014	"B" Camshaft position - timing over-advanced or system performance problem (bank 1)
P0015	"B" Camshaft position - timing over-retarded (bank 1)
P0016	Crankshaft position - camshaft position correlation problem (bank 1 sensor a)
P0017	Crankshaft position - camshaft position correlation problem (bank 1 sensor b)
P0018	Crankshaft position - camshaft position correlation problem (bank 2 sensor a)
P0019	Crankshaft position - camshaft position correlation problem (bank 2 sensor b)
P0020	Intake camshaft position actuator circuit open (bank 2)
P0021	Intake camshaft position-timing over-advanced (bank 2)
P0022	Intake camshaft position-timing over-retarded (bank 2)
P0023	"B" Camshaft position - actuator circuit (bank 2)
P0024	"B" Camshaft position - timing over-advanced or system performance problem (bank 2)
P0025	"B" Camshaft position - timing over-retarded (bank 2)
P0030	HO2S heater control circuit (bank 1, sensor 1)
P0031	HO2S heater control circuit low (bank 1, sensor 1)
P0032	HO2S heater control circuit high (bank 1, sensor 1)
P0036	HO2S heater control circuit (bank 1 sensor 2)
P0037	HO2S heater control circuit low (bank 1, sensor 2)
P0038	HO2S heater control circuit high (bank 1, sensor 2)
P0040	Upstream oxygen sensors swapped from bank to bank (HO2S - bank 1, sensor 1/bank 2, sensor 1)
P0041	Downstream oxygen sensors swapped from bank to bank (HO2S - bank 1, sensor 2/bank 2, sensor 2)
P0042	HO2S heater control circuit (bank 1, sensor 3)
P0043	HO2S heater control circuit low (bank 1, sensor 3)

DIAGNOSTIC TROUBLE CODES (CONTINUED)

Code	Possible cause
P0044	HO2S heater control circuit high (bank 1 sensor 3)
P0050	HO2S heater control circuit (bank 2, sensor 1)
P0051	HO2S heater control circuit low (bank 2, sensor 1)
P0052	HO2S heater control circuit high (bank 2, sensor 1)
P0056	HO2S heater control circuit malfunction (bank 2, sensor 2)
P0057	HO2S heater control circuit low (bank 2, sensor 2)
P0058	HO2S heater control circuit high (bank 2, sensor 2)
P0068	MAP/MAF - throttle position correlation problem
P0087	Fuel rail/system pressure - too low
P0088	Fuel rail/system pressure - too high
P0089	Fuel pressure regulator 1 performance problem
P0097	Intake air temperature sensor 2 circuit low
P0098	Intake air temperature sensor 2 circuit high
P0100	Mass or volume air flow "a" circuit
P0101	Mass air flow or volume air flow circuit, range or performance problem
P0102	Mass air flow or volume air flow circuit, low input
P0103	Mass air flow or volume air flow circuit, high input
P0105	Manifold absolute pressure/barometric pressure circuit
P0106	Manifold absolute pressure or barometric pressure circuit, range or performance problem
P0107	Manifold absolute pressure/barometric pressure circuit low
P0108	Manifold absolute pressure/barometric pressure circuit high
P0111	Intake air temperature circuit, range or performance problem
P0112	Intake air temperature circuit, low input
P0113	Intake air temperature circuit, high input
P0116	Engine coolant temperature circuit range/performance problem
P0117	Engine coolant temperature circuit, low input
P0118	Engine coolant temperature circuit, high input
P0120	Throttle/pedal position sensor/switch "a" circuit

Code	Possible cause
P0121	Throttle position or pedal position sensor/switch circuit, range or performance problem
P0122	Throttle position or pedal position sensor/switch circuit, low input
P0123	Throttle position or pedal position sensor/switch circuit, high input
P0125	Insufficient coolant temperature for closed loop fuel control
P0128	Coolant Thermostat (coolant temperature below normal range)
P0130	O2 sensor circuit malfunction (bank 1, sensor 1)
P0131	O2 sensor circuit low voltage (bank 1, sensor 1)
P0132	O2 sensor circuit high voltage (bank 1, sensor 1)
P0133	O2 sensor circuit, slow response (bank 1, sensor 1)
P0134	O2 sensor circuit no activity detected (bank 1, sensor 1
P0135	O2 sensor heater circuit malfunction (bank 1, sensor 1)
P0136	O2 sensor circuit malfunction (bank 1, sensor 2)
P0137	O2 sensor circuit, low voltage (bank 1, sensor 2)
P0138	O2 sensor circuit, high voltage (bank 1, sensor 2)
P0139	O2 sensor circuit, slow response (bank 1, sensor 2)
P0140	O2 sensor circuit - no activity detected (bank 1, sensor 2)
P0141	O2 sensor heater circuit malfunction (bank 1, sensor 2)
P0142	O2 Sensor Circuit, Bank 1 Sensor 3
P0143	O2 Sensor Circuit Low Voltage, Bank 1 Sensor 3
P0144	O2 Sensor Circuit High Voltage, Bank 1 Sensor 3
P0145	O2 Sensor Circuit Slow Response, Bank 1 Sensor 3
P0146	O2 Sensor Circuit No Activity Detected, Bank 1 Sensor 3
P0147	O2 Sensor Heater Circuit, Bank 1 Sensor 3
P0150	O2 sensor circuit malfunction (bank 2, sensor 1)
P0151	O2 sensor circuit low voltage (bank 2 Sensor 1)
P0152	O2 sensor circuit high voltage (bank 2 Sensor 1)
P0153	O2 sensor circuit, slow response (bank 2, sensor 1)
P0154	O2 sensor circuit no activity detected, bank 2 sensor 1
P0155	O2 sensor heater circuit malfunction (bank 2, sensor 1)

DIAGNOSTIC TROUBLE CODES (CONTINUED)

Code	Possible cause
P0156	O2 sensor circuit malfunction (bank 2, sensor 2)
P0157	O2 sensor circuit, low voltage (bank 2, sensor 2)
P0158	O2 sensor circuit, high voltage (bank 2, sensor 2)
P0159	O2 sensor circuit, slow response (bank 2, sensor 2)
P0160	O2 sensor circuit - no activity detected (bank 2, sensor 2)
P0161	O2 sensor heater circuit malfunction (bank 2, sensor 2)
P0169	Incorrect fuel composition
P0171	System too lean (bank 1)
P0172	System too rich (bank 1)
P0174	System too lean (bank 2)
P0175	System too rich (bank 2)
P0181	Fuel temperature sensor "a" circuit range/performance problem
P0182	Fuel temperature sensor "a" circuit low
P0183	Fuel temperature sensor "a" circuit high
P0188	Fuel temperature sensor "b" circuit high
P0190	Fuel rail pressure sensor "a" circuit malfunction
P0192	Fuel rail pressure sensor "a" circuit low
P0200	Injector Circuit/Open
P0201	Injector circuit malfunction - cylinder no. 1
P0202	Injector circuit malfunction - cylinder no. 2
P0203	Injector circuit malfunction - cylinder no. 3
P0204	Injector circuit malfunction - cylinder no. 4
P0205	Injector circuit malfunction - cylinder no. 5
P0216	Injector/injection timing control circuit
P0219	Engine overspeed condition
P0221	Throttle position or pedal position sensor/switch b, range or performance problem
P0222	Throttle position or pedal position sensor/switch b circuit, low input
P0223	Throttle position or pedal position sensor/switch b circuit, high input

Code	Possible cause
P0225	Throttle/pedal position sensor/switch "c" circuit malfunction
P0226	Throttle/pedal position sensor/switch "c" circuit range/performance problem
P0227	Throttle/pedal position sensor/switch "c" circuit low
P0228	Throttle/pedal position sensor/switch "c" circuit high
P0230	System too rich at idle
P0234	Turbocharger overboost condition
P0236	Turbocharger boost sensor a circuit, range or performance problem
P0237	Turbocharger boost sensor a circuit, low
P0238	Turbocharger boost sensor a circuit, high
P0240	Turbocharger boost sensor "b" circuit range/performance problem
P0241	Turbocharger boost sensor "b" circuit low
P0242	Turbocharger boost sensor "b" circuit high
P0243	Turbocharger wastegate solenoid "a" malfunction
P0245	Turbocharger wastegate solenoid a, low
P0246	Turbocharger wastegate solenoid a, high
P0247	Turbocharger wastegate solenoid "b" malfunction
P0249	Turbocharger wastegate solenoid "b" low
P0250	Turbocharger wastegate solenoid "b" high
P0251	Injection pump fuel metering control "a" malfunction
P0252	Injection pump fuel metering control "a" range/performance problem
P0261	Cylinder no. 1 injector circuit, low
P0262	Cylinder no. 1 injector circuit, high
P0263	Cylinder no. 1 contribution/balance
P0264	Cylinder no. 2 injector circuit, low
P0265	Cylinder no. 2 injector circuit, high
P0266	Cylinder no. 2 contribution/balance
P0267	Cylinder no. 3 injector circuit, low
P0268	Cylinder no. 3 injector circuit, high
P0269	Cylinder no. 3 contribution/balance

DIAGNOSTIC TROUBLE CODES (CONTINUED)

Code	Possible cause
P0270	Cylinder no. 4 injector circuit, low
P0271	Cylinder no. 4 injector circuit, high
P0272	Cylinder no. 4 contribution/balance
P0273	Cylinder no. 5 injector circuit, low
P0274	Cylinder no. 5 injector circuit, high
P0275	Cylinder no. 5 contribution/balance
P0299	Turbocharger underboost condition
P0300	Random/multiple cylinder misfire detected
P0301	Cylinder no. 1 misfire detected
P0302	Cylinder no. 2 misfire detected
P0303	Cylinder no. 3 misfire detected
P0304	Cylinder no. 4 misfire detected
P0305	Cylinder no. 5 misfire detected
P0321	Crankshaft position (CKP) sensor/engine speed (RPM) sensor - range or performance problem
P0322	Crankshaft position (CKP) sensor/engine speed (RPM) sensor - no signal
P0324	Knock control system error
P0327	Knock sensor no. 1 circuit, low input (bank 1 or single sensor)
P0328	Knock sensor no. 1 circuit, high input (bank 1 or single sensor)
P0332	Knock sensor no. 2 circuit, low input (bank 2)
P0333	Knock sensor no. 2 circuit, high input (bank 2)
P0340	Camshaft position sensor "A" - circuit malfunction (bank 1)
P0341	Camshaft position sensor "A" - range or performance problem (bank 1)
P0342	Camshaft position sensor "A" - low input (bank 1)
P0343	Camshaft position sensor "A" - high input (bank 1)
P0345	Camshaft position sensor "A" - circuit malfunction (bank 2)
P0346	Camshaft position sensor "A" - range/performance problem (bank 2)
P0347	Camshaft position sensor "A" - low input (bank 2)
P0348	Camshaft position sensor "A" - range/performance problem (bank 2)

Code	Possible cause
P0351	Ignition coil 1 primary or secondary circuit malfunction
P0352	Ignition coil 2 primary or secondary circuit malfunction
P0353	Ignition coil 3 primary or secondary circuit malfunction
P0354	Ignition coil 4 primary or secondary circuit malfunction
P0355	Ignition coil 5 primary or secondary circuit malfunction
P0365	Camshaft position sensor "B" - circuit malfunction (bank 1)
P0366	Camshaft position sensor "B" - range/performance problem (bank 1)
P0367	Camshaft position sensor "B" - low input (bank 1)
P0368	Camshaft position sensor "B" circuit high input (bank 1)
P0390	Camshaft position sensor "B" - circuit malfunction
P0391	Camshaft position sensor "B" - range/performance problem (bank 2)
P0392	Camshaft position sensor "B" - low input (bank 2)
P0393	Camshaft position sensor "B" - high input (bank 2)
P0400	Exhaust gas recirculation flow
P0401	Exhaust gas recirculation flow insufficient detected
P0402	Exhaust gas recirculation flow excessive detected
P0403	Exhaust gas recirculation control circuit
P0404	Exhaust gas recirculation control circuit range/performance
P0411	Secondary air injection system, incorrect flow detected
P0412	Secondary air injection system switching valve A - circuit malfunction
P0413	Secondary air injection system switching valve A - open circuit
P0414	Secondary air injection system switching valve A - shorted circuit
P0416	Secondary air injection system switching valve "B" circuit open
P0417	Secondary air injection system switching valve "B" circuit shorted
P0418	Secondary air injection system, pump relay A - circuit malfunction
P0420	Catalyst system efficiency below threshold (bank 1)
P0421	Warm-up catalyst efficiency below threshold (bank 1)
P0422	Main catalyst efficiency below threshold (bank 1)
P0423	Heated catalyst efficiency below threshold (bank 1)

DIAGNOSTIC TROUBLE CODES (CONTINUED)

Code	Possible cause
P0424	Heated catalyst temperature below threshold (bank 1)
P0425	Catalyst temperature sensor circuit (bank 1, sensor 1)
P0426	Catalyst temperature sensor circuit range/performance (bank 1, sensor 1)
P0427	Catalyst temperature sensor circuit low (bank 1, sensor 1)
P0428	Catalyst temperature sensor circuit high (bank 1, sensor 1)
P0429	Catalyst heater control circuit (bank 1)
P0430	Catalyst system efficiency below threshold (bank 2)
P0431	Warm-up catalyst efficiency below threshold (bank 2)
P0432	Main catalyst efficiency below threshold (bank 2)
P0440	Evaporative emission control system malfunction
P0441	Evaporative emission control system, incorrect purge flow
P0442	Evaporative emission control system, small leak detected
P0443	Evaporative emission control system, purge control valve circuit malfunction
P0444	Evaporative emission control system, open purge control valve circuit
P0445	Evaporative emission control system, short in purge control valve circuit
P0449	Evaporative emission system vent valve/solenoid circuit
P0455	Evaporative emission (EVAP) control system leak detected (no purge flow or large leak)
P0456	Evaporative emission (EVAP) control system leak detected (very small leak)
P0458	Evaporative emission system purge control valve circuit low
P0459	Evaporative emission system purge control valve circuit high
P0480	Fan 1 control circuit
P0481	Fan 2 control circuit
P0489	Exhaust gas recirculation control circuit low
P0490	Exhaust gas recirculation control circuit high
P0491	Secondary air injection system (bank 1)
P0492	Secondary air injection system (bank 2)
P0498	Evaporative emission system vent valve control circuit low
P0499	Evaporative emission system vent valve control circuit high

Code	Possible cause
P0501	Vehicle speed sensor, range or performance problem
P0505	Idle air control system
P0506	Idle control system, rpm lower than expected
P0507	Idle control system, rpm higher than expected
P0510	Closed throttle position switch
P0544	Exhaust gas temperature sensor circuit (bank 1 sensor 1)
P0545	Exhaust gas temperature sensor circuit low (bank 1 sensor 1)
P0546	Exhaust gas temperature sensor circuit high (bank 1 sensor 1)
P0560	System voltage malfunction
P0562	System voltage low
P0563	System voltage high
P0564	Cruise control multi-function input "a" circuit
P0571	Cruise control/brake switch a, circuit malfunction
P0597	Thermostat heater control circuit/open
P0598	Thermostat heater control circuit low
P0599	Thermostat heater control circuit high
P0600	Serial communication link malfunction
P0601	Internal control module, memory check sum error
P0602	Control module programming error
P0603	Internal control module keep alive memory (KAM) error
P0604	Internal control module, random access memory (RAM) error
P0605	Internal control module, read only memory (ROM) error
P0606	PCM processor fault
P0607	Control module performance
P0608	Control module VSS output "a"
P0609	Control module VSS output "b"
P0613	TCM processor
P0614	ECM / TCM incompatible
P0627	Fuel pump "a" control circuit/open

DIAGNOSTIC TROUBLE CODES (CONTINUED)

Code	Possible cause
P0629	Fuel pump "a" control circuit high
P0638	Throttle actuator control range/performance problem (bank 1)
P0639	Throttle actuator control range/performance problem (bank 2)
P0641	Sensor reference voltage "a" circuit/open
P0642	Sensor reference voltage "a" circuit low
P0643	Sensor reference voltage "a" circuit high
P0651	Sensor reference voltage "b" circuit/open
P0652	Sensor reference voltage "b" circuit low
P0653	Sensor reference voltage "b" circuit high
P0657	Actuator supply voltage "a" circuit/open
P0658	Actuator supply voltage "a" circuit low
P0659	Actuator supply voltage "a" circuit high
P0685	ECM power relay, control - circuit open
P0686	ECM power relay control - circuit low
P0687	Engine, control relay - short to ground
P0688	Engine, control relay - short to positive
P0691	Fan 1 control circuit low
P0692	Fan 1 control circuit high
P0693	Fan 2 control circuit low
P0694	Fan 2 control circuit high
P0697	Sensor reference voltage "c" circuit/open
P0698	Sensor reference voltage "c" circuit low
P0699	Sensor reference voltage "c" circuit high
P0704	Clutch switch input circuit malfunction

4   Accelerator Pedal Position (APP) sensor - replacement

▶ **Refer to illustration 4.1**

The APP sensor is located at the top of (and is an integral component of) the accelerator pedal (see illustration). There is no reason to remove the APP sensor except to replace it. But if the APP sensor is replaced, the new unit must be programmed with a factory scan tool. If you get a Diagnostic Trouble Code indicating a problem with the APP sensor, have the sensor replaced by a dealer service department or other qualified repair shop equipped with the necessary scan tool.

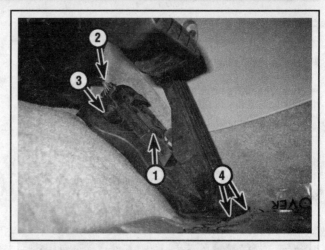

4.1 Accelerator Pedal Position (APP) sensor

1   Accelerator pedal module
2   Electrical connector
3   Mounting screw location (cap removed)
4   Opening for release tool

5   Camshaft Position (CMP) sensor - replacement

▶ **Refer to illustrations 5.3a and 5.3b**

❊❊ CAUTION:

If the battery is disconnected, several systems must be re-learned before they will work properly (see Chapter 5, Section 3).

1   Disconnect the cable from the negative battery terminal (see Chapter 5).

2   Remove the engine cover (see Chapter 1, Section 7).
3   The CMP sensor is located at the front of the cylinder head on four-cylinder timing belt (BPY) engine models (see illustration), the front side of the cylinder head cover just below the oil filler cap on four-cylinder timing chain (CCTA, CBFA) engines, or the camshaft guide frame on five-cylinder engine models (see illustration).
4   Disconnect the CMP sensor electrical connector.
5   Remove the CMP sensor mounting fastener and remove the CMP sensor.
6   Installation is the reverse of removal.

5.3a The CMP sensor is located on the front left corner of the cylinder head - four-cylinder BPY engine shown

5.3b The CMP sensor is located on the front side of the camshaft guide frame - five-cylinder engine models

---

6 Crankshaft Position (CKP)/engine speed sensor - replacement

FOUR-CYLINDER MODELS

▶ **Refer to illustration 6.3**

➡ **Note: The CKP sensor is difficult to access because it's directly behind the oil filter housing.**

1 Drain the engine oil (see Chapter 1).
2 Remove the oil filter housing.
3 Disconnect the electrical connector from the CKP sensor (see illustration).
4 Remove the CKP sensor mounting fastener and remove the CKP sensor.
5 Installation is the reverse of removal.

6.3 The CKP sensor is located on the left side of the engine block, near the flywheel (four-cylinder engine)

1   Electrical connector
2   CKP sensor (mounting bolt, which faces forward, not visible)

FIVE-CYLINDER MODELS

▶ **Refer to illustration 6.8**

6 Raise the front of the vehicle and support it securely on jackstands. Block the wheels at the opposite end and remove the right front wheel.
7 Remove the under-vehicle splash shield (see Chapter 1, Section 6).
8 Locate the engine speed sensor on the control housing, near the flywheel (see illustration).
9 Trace the engine speed sensor electrical lead to the sensor electrical connector and disconnect the connector.
10 Remove the engine speed sensor mounting fasteners and remove the sensor.
11 Installation is the reverse of removal.

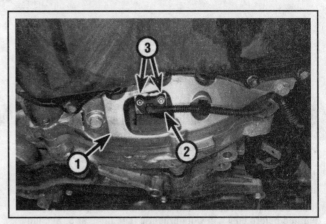

6.8 The engine speed sensor is located on the left side of the engine block, near the flywheel (five-cylinder engine)

1   Control housing
2   Engine speed sensor and electrical connector
3   Mounting fasteners

---

7 Engine Coolant Temperature (ECT) sensor - replacement

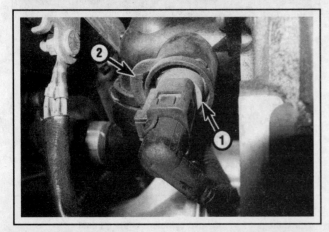

7.3 Timing belt (BPY) engine models, the ECT sensor is located at the left end of the cylinder head, on the water connection

1   ECT sensor   2   Retaining clip

❊❊ **WARNING:**

Wait until the engine has cooled completely before beginning this procedure.

1 Remove the engine cover (see Chapter 1, Section 7).
2 Partially drain the cooling system (see Chapter 1).

FOUR-CYLINDER MODELS

Timing belt (BPY) engine

▶ **Refer to illustration 7.3**

3 Disconnect the electrical connector from the ECT sensor (see illustration).
4 Pull out the retaining clip and remove the sensor. Remove and discard the sensor O-ring.

5 Before installing the ECT sensor, install a new O-ring and apply some engine coolant to the O-ring.

6 Installation is the reverse of removal.

7 Refill the cooling system (see Chapter 1).

Timing chain (CCTA, CBFA) engines

8 Raise the front of the vehicle and support it securely on jackstands.

9 Remove the under-vehicle splash shield (see Chapter 1, Section 6).

10 On models equipped with a noise generator, open the locking ring on the charge air pipe and remove the fasteners and noise generator.

11 Remove the lower section of the air charge pipe retaining fasteners, the clamps at each end and the air charge pipe.

12 Loosen the hose clamps on the lower air charge hoses-to-charge air cooler and remove the hoses.

13 Remove the throttle body (see Chapter 4).

14 Remove the intake manifold support bracket fasteners and support.

15 Disconnect the electrical connector from the ECT sensor.

16 Press the locking tabs on the sensor inwards, then pull the sensor out of the housing. Remove and discard the sensor O-ring.

17 Before installing the ECT sensor, install a new O-ring and apply some engine coolant to the O-ring.

18 Installation is the reverse of removal.

19 Refill the cooling system (see Chapter 1).

FIVE-CYLINDER MODELS

▶ **Refer to illustration 7.21**

20 Disconnect the inlet air hose from the throttle body (see Chapter 4).

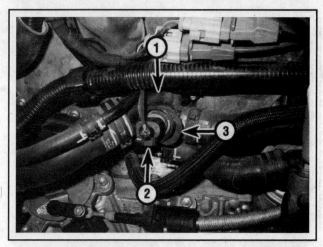

7.21 On five-cylinder models, the ECT sensor is located at the end of the timing chain cover (which is on the left end of the cylinder head)

1   *Coolant housing*
2   *ECT sensor electrical connector*
3   *Retaining clip*

21 Disconnect the electrical connector from the ECT sensor (see illustration).

22 Pull out the retaining clip and remove the sensor. Remove and discard the sensor O-ring.

23 Before installing the ECT sensor, install a new O-ring and apply some engine coolant to the O-ring.

24 Installation is the reverse of removal.

25 Refill the cooling system (see Chapter 1).

8   Knock sensor - replacement

✳✳ WARNING:

Don't attempt to remove a knock sensor when the engine is hot. If the engine has just been operated, allow sufficient time for it to cool down.

✳✳ CAUTION:

If the battery is disconnected, several systems must be re-learned before they will work properly (see Chapter 5, Section 3).

1 Remove the engine cover (see Chapter 1, Section 7).

2 Disconnect the cable from the negative battery terminal (see Chapter 5).

FOUR-CYLINDER MODELS

3 Raise the front of the vehicle and support it securely on jackstands.

4 Remove the under-vehicle splash shield (see Chapter 1, Section 6).

5 Drain the cooling system (see Chapter 1).

Timing belt (BPY) engine

▶ **Refer to illustration 8.10**

➡ **Note: There are two knock sensors - both are located under the intake manifold on the front side. Sensor 1 is located near the thermostat housing and sensor 2 is located behind the oil filter housing bracket.**

6 Remove the intake manifold (see Chapter 4).

7 Disconnect the coolant hoses and tube in front of the oil filter housing.

8 To remove knock sensor 1, remove the thermostat housing (see Chapter 3).

9 To remove knock sensor 2, remove the oil cooler mounting fasteners and the oil cooler, then disconnect the oil pressure switch electrical connector. Remove the engine oil filter housing bracket fasteners and remove the housing

8.10 On timing belt (BPY) engine models, the knock sensors are located on the left side of the block, below the intake manifold

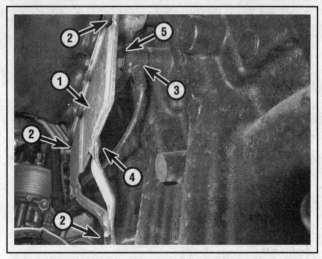

8.16 Knock sensor details - five-cylinder models

1	Knock sensor heat shield	4	Knock sensor 2
2	Heat shield mounting fasteners	5	Knock sensor 1 mounting bolt
3	Knock sensor 1		

10 Disconnect the knock sensor electrical connector (see illustration).

11 Unscrew the knock sensor(s) retaining fastener and remove the sensor(s).

Timing chain (CCTA, CBFA) engines

➡ **Note: There is one knock sensor located just above the water pump.**

12 Remove the water pump (see Chapter 3).

13 Disconnect the knock sensor(s) electrical connector.

14 Unscrew the knock sensor retaining fastener and remove the sensor.

All models

15 Installation is the reverse of removal, with the following items:

  a) Be sure to tighten the knock sensor fastener to the torque listed in this Chapter's Specifications.

✳✳ CAUTION:

Incorrectly tightening a knock sensor fastener can affect the performance of the sensor.

  b) Replace the thermostat housing gasket or water pump gasket with a new one, see Chapter 3.

  c) Replace the oil cooler and oil filter housing bracket gaskets. Tighten the fasteners evenly, a little at a time, to the torque listed in this Chapter's Specifications.

  d) Refill the cooling system, if drained (see Chapter 1).

  e) Start the engine and check for leaks.

FIVE-CYLINDER MODELS

▸ **Refer to illustration 8.16**

➡ **Note: There are two knock sensors - both are located under the exhaust manifold. Sensor 1 is located near the drivebelt end of the engine and sensor 2 is located near the transaxle end of the engine. This procedure applies to either knock sensor.**

16 Locate the knock sensors under the exhaust manifold (see illustration), then trace the electrical lead for each sensor back to the sensor electrical connector and disconnect it.

➡ **Note: The green electrical connector is for sensor 1 and the gray connector is for sensor 2.**

17 Remove the knock sensor heat shield fasteners and the heat shield.

18 Remove the knock sensor mounting fastener and remove the sensor.

19 When installing a knock sensor, be sure to tighten the sensor mounting fastener to the torque listed in this Chapter's Specifications.

✳✳ CAUTION:

Incorrectly tightening a knock sensor fastener can affect the performance of the knock sensor.

20 Installation is otherwise the reverse of removal.

9 Manifold Absolute Pressure (MAP) sensor - replacement

♦ **Refer to illustration 9.2**

➡ **Note: The MAP sensor, which is used only on 2.5L five-cylinder models, is located at the back end of the intake manifold near the throttle body. On 2009 and later models the intake air temperature sensor has been integrated with the manifold absolute pressure (MAP) sensor and is referred to as the (MAP/IAT).**

1 Remove the engine cover (see Chapter 1, Section 7).
2 Disconnect the electrical connector from the MAP sensor (see illustration).
3 Remove the MAP/IAT sensor mounting fasteners and remove the sensor.
4 Remove and discard the old MAP/IAT sensor O-ring.
5 Installation is the reverse of removal.

➡ **Note: The O-ring does not have a replacement part; it only comes with a new sensor.**

9.2 Typical MAP or (MAP/IAT) sensor location - five-cylinder models only

10 Intake Air Temperature (IAT) sensor - replacement

FOUR-CYLINDER MODELS

➡ **Note: The IAT sensor is located at the back end of the intake manifold.**

1 Remove the engine cover (see Chapter 1, Section 7).
2 Disconnect the electrical connector from the IAT sensor.
3 Remove the IAT sensor mounting fastener and remove the sensor from the intake manifold.
4 Installation is the reverse of removal.

➡ **Note: Do not discard the O-ring; the O-ring does not have a replacement part (it only comes with a new sensor).**

FIVE-CYLINDER MODELS

♦ **Refer to illustration 10.8**

➡ **Note: This procedure applies to 2008 and earlier models only. On 2009 and later five-cylinder engines, the intake air temperature sensor has been integrated with the manifold absolute pressure (MAP) sensor (see Section 9).**

5 Remove the air inlet duct (see *Air filter housing - removal and installation* in Chapter 1).
6 Loosen the hose clamp and disconnect the air intake duct from the MAF sensor body.

10.8 Rotate the sensor clockwise to remove it from the inlet air duct - 2008 and earlier five-cylinder models

7 Disconnect the electrical connector from the IAT sensor.
8 Rotate the IAT sensor clockwise and remove it from the duct (see illustration).

➡ **Note: Some models may have a clip inside of the air inlet locking the IAT sensor to the duct.**

9 Installation is the reverse of removal.

11 Mass Air Flow (MAF) sensor - replacement

FOUR-CYLINDER MODELS

Timing belt (BPY) engine models

1   Disconnect the electrical connector from the MAF sensor.
2   Remove the MAF sensor mounting fasteners and remove the sensor from the top of air filter housing.
3   Installation is the reverse of removal.

Timing chain (CCTA, CBFA) engines

4   Disconnect the electrical connector from the MAF sensor.
5   Remove the MAF sensor mounting fasteners and remove the sensor from the inlet duct.
6   Installation is the reverse of removal.

FIVE-CYLINDER MODELS

▸ Refer to illustration 11.8

➡ Note: On 2009 and later five-cylinder engines, the MAF sensor is no longer used.

7   Remove the ambient air inlet duct (see *Air filter housing - removal* and installation in Chapter 1).
8   Loosen the hose clamp and disconnect the air intake duct from the MAF sensor (see illustration).
9   Disconnect the electrical connector from the MAF sensor.

11.8 Typical MAF sensor details (2008 and earlier five-cylinder models shown):

1   *Air intake duct*
2   *Clamp*
3   *MAF sensor tube mounting fastener (other fastener not visible)*
4   *MAF sensor mounting fasteners*
5   *MAF sensor electrical connector*

10 Remove the MAF sensor mounting fasteners and remove the sensor from the housing.
11 Installation is the reverse of removal.

12 Oxygen sensors - replacement

➡ Note: Because some of the oxygen sensors are installed in the catalytic converter(s), which contracts when cool, they can be difficult to loosen when the engine is cold. Rather than risk damage to an oxygen sensor or its mounting threads, start and run the engine for a minute or two, then shut it off. Be careful not to burn yourself during the following procedure.

1   Be particularly careful when servicing an oxygen sensor:
   a) *Oxygen sensors have a permanently attached pigtail and an electrical connector that cannot be removed. Damaging or removing the pigtail or electrical connector will render the sensor useless.*
   b) *Keep grease, dirt and other contaminants away from the electrical connector and the louvered end of the sensor.*
   c) *Do not use cleaning solvents of any kind on an oxygen sensor.*
   d) *Oxygen sensors are extremely delicate. Do not drop a sensor, throw it around or handle it roughly.*
   e) *Make sure that the silicone boot on the sensor is installed in the correct position. Otherwise, the boot might melt and prevent the sensor from operating correctly.*

2   Remove the engine cover (see Chapter 1, Section 7).
3   Raise the front of the vehicle and support it securely on jackstands.
4   Remove the lower splash shield below the engine (see Chapter 1, Section 6).

UPSTREAM OXYGEN SENSORS

▸ Refer to illustrations 12.5 and 12.6

5   Locate the upstream oxygen sensor (see illustration), then trace the wiring harness to its electrical connector and disconnect the connector. Disengage the sensor harness from any harness clips.

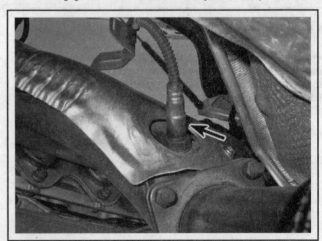

12.5 The upstream oxygen sensor is located at the upper end of the catalytic converter on four-cylinder models and at the end of the exhaust manifold on five-cylinder models

12.6 An oxygen sensor socket will allow you to work in tight quarters where a wrench would be difficult to use (and might round-off the corners of the sensor's hex)

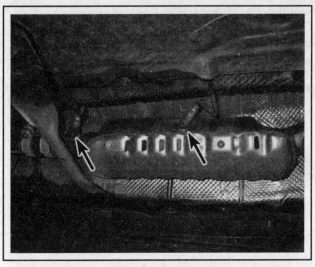

12.9 The downstream oxygen sensor(s) are located in the middle and after the catalyst (five-cylinder model shown, other models similar)

6   Unscrew the upstream oxygen sensor (see illustration).

7   If you're going to install the old sensor, apply anti-seize compound to the threads of the sensor to facilitate future removal. If you're going to install a new oxygen sensor, it's not necessary to apply anti-seize compound to the threads; the threads on new sensors already have anti-seize compound on them.

8   Installation is the reverse of removal. Be sure to tighten the oxygen sensor to the torque listed in this Chapter's Specifications.

DOWNSTREAM OXYGEN SENSORS

▶ **Refer to illustration 12.9**

9   Locate the downstream oxygen sensor(s) (see illustration), then trace the lead up to the electrical connector and disconnect the connector.

10 Unscrew the downstream oxygen sensor.

➡ **Note: Four-cylinder timing belt (BPY) engine models only have one downstream oxygen sensor, all other models have two.**

11 If you're going to install the old sensor, apply anti-seize compound to the threads of the sensor to facilitate future removal. If you're going to install a new oxygen sensor, it's not necessary to apply anti-seize compound to the threads. The threads on new sensors already have anti-seize compound on them.

12 Installation is the reverse of removal. Be sure to tighten the oxygen sensor to the torque listed in this Chapter's Specifications.

13 Transmission speed sensors - replacement

On automatic transaxles, speed sensors are integral components of the valve body/Transmission Control Module (TCM) assembly, which is located inside the transaxle. Replacing one of these sensors is beyond the scope of the home mechanic.

14 Powertrain Control Module (PCM) - removal and installation

▶ **Refer to illustration 14.4**

✳✳ CAUTION:

If the battery is disconnected, several systems must be re-learned before they will work properly (see Chapter 5, Section 3).

➡ **Note: The Powertrain Control Module (PCM), which is housed within a waterproof box in the cowl area, cannot be replaced** at home because the new unit must be reprogrammed with a proprietary scan tool. The PCM in many models is also housed inside a special metal anti-theft box and is extremely difficult to remove. This procedure is only intended for removing the PCM and electronics box for access to the clutch master cylinder.

1   Disconnect the cable from the negative battery terminal (see Chapter 5).

2   Remove the cowl cover (see Chapter 11).

3   Remove the cover from the electronics box.

4 Pry off the retaining strap from the PCM, then move the PCM aside (see illustration).

➡ **Note: Some models are equipped with an anti-theft housing or cover plate in which the PCM is mounted. The cover plate is secured with shear-head bolts. Cut slots in the shear-head bolts using a small cutting wheel or grinder and use a flat blade screwdriver to unscrew the bolts. Alternatively, drill through the bolts and use a screw extractor to remove them.**

5 Unplug the electrical connectors near the firewall.

6 Pull back the release tabs and detach the relay carrier from the electronics box, then dislodge the grommet and pull the wiring harness through the opening in the electronics box.

7 Unscrew the fasteners and remove the electronics box from the cowl area.

8 Installation is the reverse of the removal procedure.

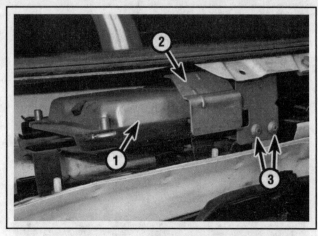

14.4 Details of the Powertrain Control Module (PCM):

1   Powertrain Control Module (PCM)
2   Anti-theft housing/cover plate
3   Shear-bolts

15 Catalytic converter - replacement

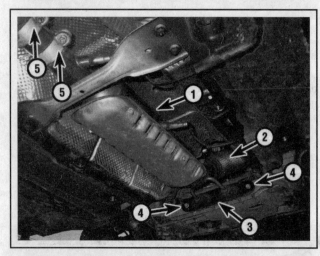

15.8 Typical catalytic converter details (five-cylinder engine shown, four-cylinder similar)

1 Catalytic converter	4 Exhaust pipe support
2 Front exhaust pipe	bracket mounting fasteners
3 Exhaust pipe support	5 Clamps
bracket	

▶ **Refer to illustration 15.8**

➡ **Note: The front exhaust pipe and catalytic converter are a single assembly.**

1 Remove the engine cover (see Chapter 1, Section 7).

2 Loosen the right-front wheel bolts, then raise the front of the vehicle and support it securely on jackstands.

3 Remove the under-vehicle splash shield (see Chapter 1, Section 6).

4 Remove the right-side inner fender liner (see Chapter 11).

5 Disconnect the electrical connectors for the downstream oxygen sensors.

6 Remove the upstream and downstream oxygen sensors from the catalytic converter (see Section 11).

7 Remove the fasteners that secure the front exhaust pipe with catalytic converter to the turbocharger.

8 Remove the front exhaust pipe support bracket bolts (see illustration) and remove the support bracket.

9 Disconnect the clamps that hold the catalytic converter to the rear exhaust.

10 Remove the catalytic converter with front exhaust pipe.

11 Remove and discard the old flange gasket and clamps.

12 Installation is the reverse of removal. Be sure to use new gaskets and self-locking nuts and tighten all fasteners securely.

16 Evaporative Emissions Control (EVAP) system - component replacement

EVAP PURGE CONTROL SOLENOID VALVE

▶ **Refer to illustrations 16.2a and 16.2b**

➡ **Note:** The purge control solenoid valve is located on the left rear part of the intake manifold (four-cylinder BPY engines), the intake manifold next to the throttle body (four-cylinder CCTA, CBFA engines), or next to fuel rail (five-cylinder engines).

1   Remove the engine cover (see Chapter 1, Section 7).
2   Disconnect the electrical connector from the purge control solenoid valve (see illustrations).
3   Disconnect the hoses from the purge control solenoid valve.
4   Remove the purge control valve from its mounting bracket.
5   Installation is the reverse of removal.

EVAP CANISTER

Four-cylinder BPY engines

➡ **Note:** The EVAP canister is located underneath the vehicle, above the rear subframe.

6   Raise the vehicle and place it securely on jackstands.
7   Remove the rear muffler, exhaust pipe and heat shield (see Chapter 4).
8   Place a floor jack securely under the subframe and loosen the mounting bolts about 3/4-inch, but do not remove the bolts (see Chapter 10) then slowly lower the subframe.
9   Disconnect the hoses from the canister. To disconnect each hose quick-connect fitting, press the release ring toward the canister (away from the hose) and simultaneously pull off the hose.
10 Remove the canister mounting fasteners and remove the canister.
11 Installation is the reverse of removal.

All other engines

▶ **Refer to illustrations 16.13 and 16.14**

➡ **Note:** The EVAP canister is located underneath the vehicle, in a recess below the spare tire well.

12 Raise the vehicle and place it securely on jackstands.
13 Remove the EVAP canister cover (see illustration).
14 Disconnect the hoses (see illustration) from the canister. To disconnect each hose quick-connect fitting, press the release ring toward the canister (away from the hose) and simultaneously pull off the hose.

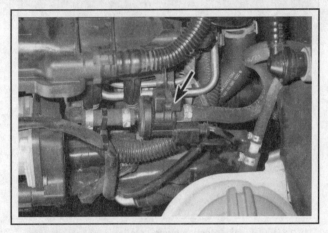

16.2a On BPY engines, the EVAP canister purge control solenoid valve is located at the left rear part of the intake manifold

16.2b On five-cylinder engines, the EVAP canister purge control solenoid valve is located next to the fuel rail

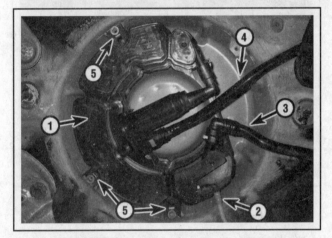

16.14 EVAP canister details

1   *EVAP canister*
2   *EVAP purge line (to purge control solenoid valve in engine compartment)*
3   *EVAP vent hose (from fuel tank)*
4   *EVAP hose (to leak detection pump)*
5   *Locking mechanism*

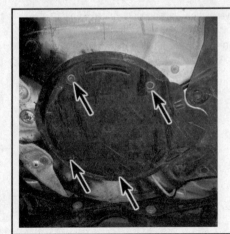

16.13 EVAP canister cover fasteners

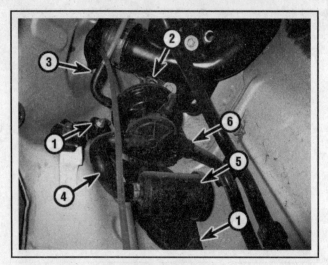

16.18 EVAP leak detection pump details

1	Mounting bracket nuts (two of three visible)	4	Air filter hose
2	Electrical connector	5	Air filter
3	Vacuum hose	6	Hose from EVAP canister

15 To remove the canister, push the release tabs towards the center using a screwdriver and remove the canister.

16 Installation is the reverse of removal.

LEAK DETECTION PUMP

▶ **Refer to illustration 16.18**

➡ **Note: The leak detection pump is located inside the left rear wheel well.**

17 Loosen the left rear wheel bolts, raise the vehicle and place it securely on jackstands. Remove the left rear wheel. Remove the left rear wheel well splash shield (see Chapter 11).

18 Remove the leak detection pump mounting bracket fasteners (see illustration), pull down the pump and mounting bracket, then disconnect the electrical connector from the leak detection pump.

19 Cut the cable ties that secure the hoses to the leak detection pump or the pump mounting bracket. Disconnect the hoses from the leak detection pump. To disconnect a hose, press the release button on the quick-connect fitting.

20 Remove the fasteners that secure the leak detection pump to its mounting bracket.

21 Installation is the reverse of removal.

17 Positive Crankcase Ventilation (PCV) system - component replacement

FOUR-CYLINDER MODELS

Timing belt (BPY) engines

1   Remove the engine cover (see Chapter 1, Section 7).
2   Remove the PCV valve housing mounting fasteners and remove

17.10 The PCV system is integrated with the valve cover (five-cylinder models)

1	PCV housing	2	Bleeder hose

the housing from the valve cover.

3   Install a new gasket to the PCV valve housing, then install the housing to the valve cover.

4   Install the mounting fasteners and tighten the fasteners securely.

Timing chain (CCTA, CBFA) engines

5   Remove the ignition coils (see Chapter 5).

6   Disconnect the hoses from the crankcase ventilation housing.

7   Remove the crankcase ventilation housing mounting fasteners and remove the housing from the top of the cylinder head cover.

8   Install a new gasket to the crankcase ventilation housing, then install the housing to the cylinder head cover.

9   Install the mounting fasteners and tighten the fasteners securely.

FIVE-CYLINDER MODELS

▶ **Refer to illustration 17.10**

10 The crankcase ventilation housing is integrated with the valve cover and can't be replaced separately (see illustration).

11 If there is a problem with the housing, the valve cover will need to be replaced (see Chapter 2B).

18 Secondary Air Injection (AIR) system (five-cylinder models) - component replacement

SECONDARY AIR INJECTION PUMP

▶ **Refer to illustrations 18.3 and 18.4**

➡ **Note: The secondary air injection pump motor is located in the lower right front corner of the engine compartment.**

1   Raise the front of the vehicle and support it securely on jackstands.

2   Remove the lower splash shield below the engine (see Chapter 1, Section 6).

3   Remove the harness retainer and disconnect the electrical connectors (see illustration).

4   Disconnect the two air tubes from the secondary AIR pump (see illustration).

5   Remove the secondary AIR pump mounting nuts.

➡ **Note: The AIR pump is mounted on three rubber mounts with studs through the middle.**

6   Slightly press the lower rubber mount downwards while removing the secondary air pump to clear the transaxle.

7   Installation is the reverse of removal.

SECONDARY AIR INJECTION SOLENOID VALVE

▶ **Refer to illustration 18.9**

8   Remove the engine cover (see Chapter 1, Section 7).

9   Disconnect the two air tubes from the secondary air injection

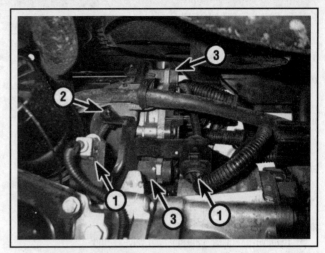

18.3 Secondary air injection pump details

1   *Electrical connectors*
2   *Harness retainer*
3   *AIR pump mounts (two of three visible)*

solenoid valve (see illustration).

10 Disconnect the electrical connector to the solenoid valve.

11 Remove the wire bracket from the base of the secondary air injection solenoid valve. Remove the mounting fasteners and remove the solenoid valve from the cylinder head.

12 Installation is the reverse of removal. Be sure to use new seals and tighten the valve mounting fasteners securely.

18.4 Secondary air injection pump tube locations:

1   *Vent tube-to-throttle body inlet tube*
2   *Pressure tube-to-secondary air injection solenoid valve*

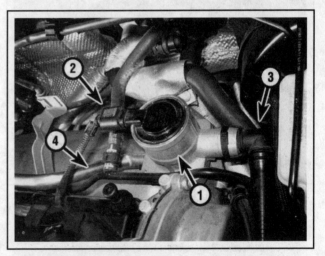

18.9 Secondary air injection solenoid valve details

1   *Secondary air injection solenoid valve*
2   *Electrical connector*
3   *Pressure tube from the air injection pump*
4   *Secondary air injection pipe to cylinder head*

19 Variable camshaft adjustment solenoid valve - replacement

FOUR-CYLINDER MODELS

Timing belt (BPY) engine

▶ **Refer to illustration 19.2**

➡ **Note: The variable camshaft adjustment solenoid is located on the back end of the cylinder head.**

1   Remove the engine cover.

2   Detach the engine harness clip from its bracket (see illustration) and push the harness aside.

3   Disconnect the electrical connector from the camshaft adjustment solenoid valve.

4   Remove the camshaft adjustment solenoid valve mounting bolt and pull the valve out of the valve cover.

5   Remove and discard the solenoid valve O-ring.

6   Installation is the reverse of removal. Use a new O-ring.

Timing chain (CCTA, CBFA) engines

➡ **Note: The variable camshaft adjustment solenoid is located on the front of the upper timing chain cover.**

7   Remove the engine cover (see Chapter 1, Section 7).

8   Disconnect the electrical connector to the camshaft adjustment

valve 1, then remove the adjustment valve retaining fasteners, the valve and seal.

➡ **Note: Always replace the adjustment valve seal and O-ring on the adjustment valve.**

9   Disconnect the electrical connector from the camshaft adjustment valve.

10 Remove the camshaft adjustment solenoid valve mounting fasteners and pull the valve out of the upper timing chain cover.

11 Remove and discard the solenoid valve O-ring.

12 Installation is the reverse of removal. Lubricate the new O-ring with engine oil.

FIVE-CYLINDER MODELS

▶ **Refer to illustration 19.14**

13 Remove the engine cover (see Chapter 1, Section 7).

14 Disconnect the electrical connector from the camshaft adjustment solenoid valve (see illustration).

15 Remove the camshaft adjustment solenoid valve mounting fastener and pull the valve out of the cylinder head.

16 Remove and discard the solenoid valve O-ring.

17 Installation is the reverse of removal. Use a new O-ring.

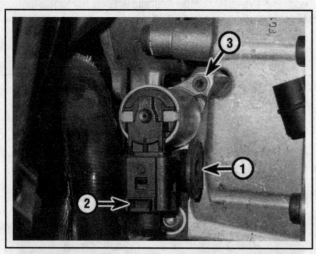

19.2 Variable camshaft adjustment solenoid valve details (timing belt [BPY] engine)

1   Harness clip bracket (clip already disengaged from bracket)
2   Camshaft adjustment solenoid valve electrical connector
3   Solenoid valve mounting bolt

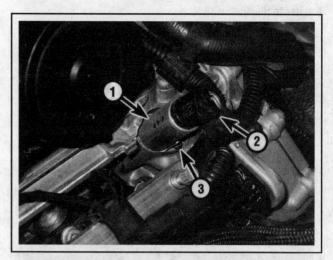

19.14 Variable camshaft adjustment solenoid valve details (five-cylinder engine)

1   Variable camshaft adjustment solenoid valve
2   Camshaft adjustment solenoid valve electrical connector
3   Solenoid valve mounting fastener

20 Variable intake manifold - component replacement

TIMING BELT (BPY) ENGINE

♦ **Refer to illustrations 20.4, 20.5 and 20.8**

※※ WARNING:

Wait until the engine is completely cool before performing this procedure.

1   Remove the engine cover (see Chapter 1, Section 7).

2   Remove the intake manifold support bracket fasteners and bracket (see Chapter 4).

3   Remove the air intake hose between the air charge cooler and the throttle body (see Chapter 4).

4   Remove the two fasteners (see illustration) that secure the electrical connector bracket to the coolant pipe.

5   Disconnect all electrical connectors from the area adjacent to the intake flap motor (see illustration).

6   Cut the cable ties that secure the wiring harnesses to the coolant pipe, move the harnesses out of the way and remove the connector bracket.

7   Remove the bolt that secures the coolant pipe bracket (see illustration 20.5) and push the coolant pipe out of the way.

8   Using a screwdriver, disengage the intake flap motor control rod from the crank arm on the intake manifold (see illustration).

9   Remove the intake flap motor mounting fasteners and remove the motor.

10 Installation is the reverse of removal.

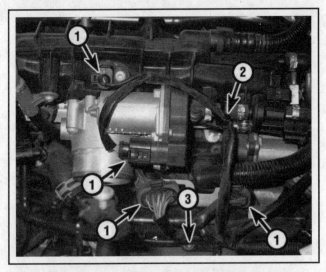

20.5 Intake flap motor details (timing belt [BPY] engine)

1   Electrical connectors
2   Harness cable tie (other cable ties not visible in this photo)
3   Coolant pipe mounting bracket bolt

TIMING CHAIN (CCTA, CBFA) ENGINES

※※ WARNING:

Wait until the engine is completely cool before performing this procedure.

➡ **Note: The intake flap in controlled by a vacuum actuator mounted to the end of the intake manifold below the high pressure fuel pump.**

11 Remove the engine cover (see Chapter 1, Section 7).
12 Disconnect the vacuum hose to the vacuum actuator.
13 Disconnect the vacuum actuator-to-crank arm linkage.
14 Remove the actuator fasteners and actuator from the manifold.
15 Installation is the reverse of removal.

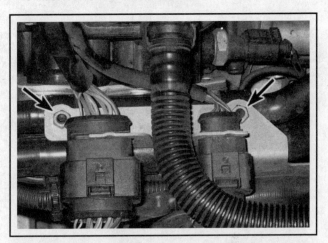

20.4 Connector bracket fasteners, intake manifold removed for clarity (timing belt [BPY] engine)

20.8 Intake flap motor removal details (intake manifold removed for clarity) (timing belt [BPY] engine):

1   Control rod connection to crank arm on intake manifold
2   Intake flap motor mounting fasteners

Torque specifications	Ft-lbs (unless otherwise indicated)	Nm

➡ **Note:** One foot-pound (ft-lb) of torque is equivalent to 12 inch-pounds (in-lbs) of torque. Torque values below approximately 15 foot-pounds are expressed in inch-pounds, because most foot-pound torque wrenches are not accurate at these smaller values.

Engine oil cooler	18.5	25
Engine oil filter bracket housing		
Step 1	133 in-lbs	15
Step 2	Tighten an additional 90-degrees	
Knock sensor mounting fastener	15	20
Oxygen sensors	41	55

Section

1 General information
2 Shift cables - adjustment
3 Manual transaxle - removal and installation
4 Manual transaxle overhaul - general information
5 Back-up light switch - removal and installation
6 Oil seals - replacement

Reference to other Chapters

Manual transaxle lubricant change - See Chapter 1
Manual transaxle lubricant level check - See Chapter 1
Transaxle mount replacement - See Chapter 7B

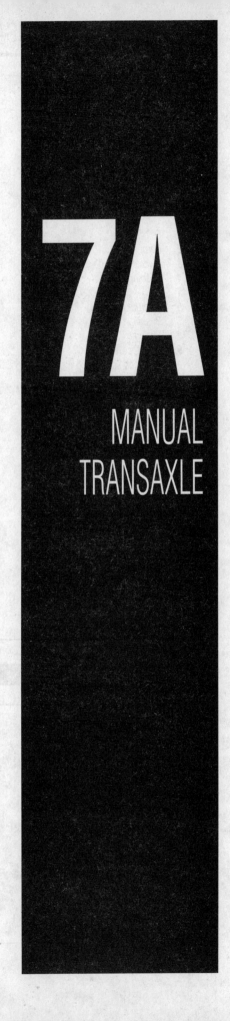

7A

MANUAL
TRANSAXLE

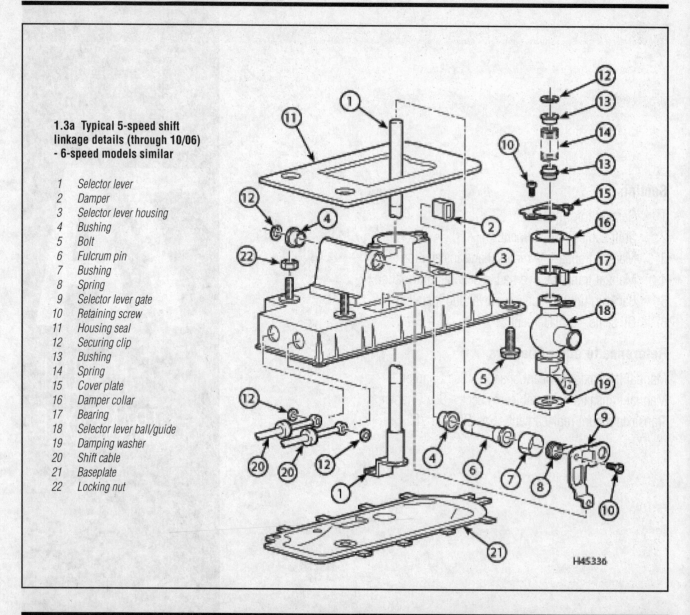

1.3a Typical 5-speed shift linkage details (through 10/06) - 6-speed models similar

1   Selector lever
2   Damper
3   Selector lever housing
4   Bushing
5   Bolt
6   Fulcrum pin
7   Bushing
8   Spring
9   Selector lever gate
10   Retaining screw
11   Housing seal
12   Securing clip
13   Bushing
14   Spring
15   Cover plate
16   Damper collar
17   Bearing
18   Selector lever ball/guide
19   Damping washer
20   Shift cable
21   Baseplate
22   Locking nut

H45336

1   General information

1.3b Transaxle end of the shift cables

▶ **Refer to illustrations 1.3a and 1.3b**

The manual transaxle is bolted directly to the left-hand end of the engine. The transaxle case is aluminum alloy.

Drive from the crankshaft is transmitted through the clutch to the transaxle input shaft, which is splined to the clutch friction disc.

All gears including reverse incorporate a synchromesh engagement. The floor-mounted shift lever is connected to the transaxle by shift cables (see illustrations).

2 Shift cables - adjustment

▶ Refer to illustrations 2.3, 2.4, 2.5 and 2.6

❋❋ CAUTION:

If the battery is disconnected, several systems must be re-learned before they will work properly (see Chapter 5, Section 3).

1   Remove the engine cover/air filter housing (see Chapter 1, Section 7).

2   Remove the battery and battery tray (see Chapter 5).

3   With the shift lever in the neutral position, push the two locking collars (one on each cable) forwards to compress the springs, then turn them clockwise to lock into position (see illustration).

4   Press down on the selector shaft on the top of the transaxle. Push the locking pin (special tool #T10027) into the transaxle while turning it clockwise until it engages and locks the selector shaft (see illustration).

5   Working inside the vehicle, unclip the shift lever boot from the center console. Still in the neutral position, move the shift lever as far to the left as possible and insert a screwdriver (or drill bit) through the hole in the base of the gear lever and into the hole in the housing (see illustration).

6   Working back in the engine compartment, turn the two locking collars on the cables counterclockwise so that the springs will release them back into position and lock the cables (see illustration).

7   With the cable adjustment set, the locking pin can now be turned counterclockwise to its original position (pointing upwards) and the selector shaft can be moved.

8   Inside the vehicle, remove the drill bit from the shift lever, then check the operation of the selector mechanism. When the shift lever is at rest in neutral, it should be centered, ready to select 3rd or 4th. The shift lever boot can now be installed to the center console.

9   The remaining installation is the reverse of removal.

2.3 Push the collar down and lock it in position - 5-speed model shown, 6-speed models similar

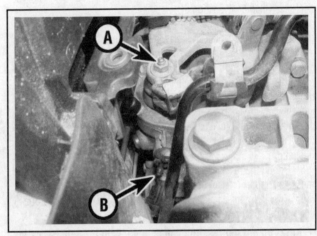

2.4 Press down on the selector shaft (A), then rotate the locking lever (B) while pushing the lever in to lock the shaft - 5-speed model shown, 6-speed models similar

2.5 Lock the gear lever in position with a drill bit - 5-speed model shown, 6-speed models similar

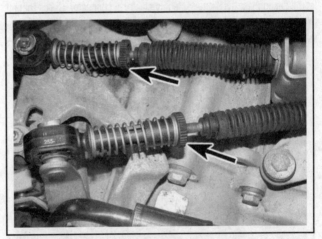

2.6 Release the two locking collars back into position - 5-speed model shown, 6-speed models similar

3 Manual transaxle - removal and installation

❋❋ CAUTION:

If the battery is disconnected, several systems must be re-learned before they will work properly (see Chapter 5, Section 3).

REMOVAL

◆ Refer to illustration 3.5, 3.7, 3.22a and 3.22b

1   Select a solid, level surface to park the vehicle upon. Give yourself enough space to move around it easily. Apply the parking brake and chock the rear wheels.

2   Remove the battery and battery tray (see Chapter 5). Also remove the engine cover (see Chapter 1, Section 7).

3   Loosen the front wheel bolts and the driveaxle/hub bolts.

4   Raise the front of the vehicle and support it securely on jackstands. Remove the splash guard from under the engine compartment (see Chapter 1, Section 6).

5   On models equipped with a metal relay lever, remove the clips from the shift lever cables and relay lever (see illustration). Remove the cables and lever from the top of the transaxle.

6   On models equipped with a plastic relay lever, push the two locking collars (one on each cable) forwards to compress the springs, then turn them clockwise to lock into position (see illustration 2.3). Using a small screwdriver, press the retaining tab down at the relay lever and slide the cables and relay off as a unit.

7   Remove the shift cable mounting bracket bolts and bracket (see illustration).

8   Unbolt the release cylinder hydraulic line bracket, the remove the transaxle support bracket bolts and bracket.

9   Unbolt the release cylinder from the transaxle, and tie it to one side without disconnecting the hydraulic line.

➡ **Note: Do not depress the clutch pedal with the release cylinder removed.**

10   Disconnect the electrical connector from the back-up light switch on the transaxle.

11   Disconnect the starter solenoid electrical connector. Check that all wiring and ground straps have been disconnected from the transaxle.

3.5 On models with metal relay levers, use a small screwdriver to disconnect the retaining clip

12   Remove the starter motor (see Chapter 5).

13   Support the engine from above with an engine support fixture (see Chapter 2C).

14   Remove the transaxle-to-engine bolts accessible from above.

15   Remove the inner fender liner (see Chapter 11). Remove the suspension level control sensor, if equipped (see Chapter 10).

16   On 6-speed models, remove the lower balljoint mounting nuts and separate the balljoint from the control arm (see Chapter 10).

17   Remove the front portion of the exhaust system (see Chapter 4). Take care not to excessively bend the flexible section of the front pipe.

18   Remove the driveaxles (see Chapter 8).

19   From under the vehicle, remove the pendulum support mounting bolt and support (see Chapter 2).

20   Support the transaxle on a jack, preferably one made for this purpose. Secure the transaxle to the jack with a safety chain. Unbolt the transaxle mount complete with rubber bushing.

21   Using the support fixture, lower the engine and transaxle until the left side mount bolts can be accessed and removed.

22   Make sure that the transaxle is adequately supported, then

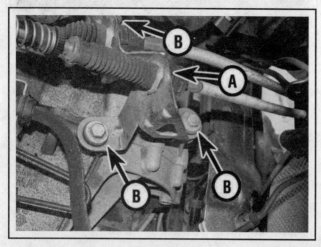

3.7 Remove the shift cable bracket (A), by removing the mounting bolts (B) and set the assembly to the side

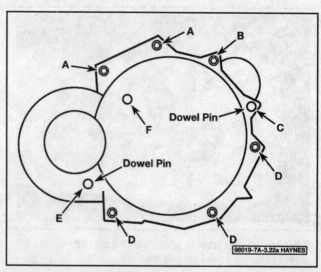

3.22a 5-speed mounting bolt identification (refer to letters for torque specifications when installing)

unscrew the remaining bolts securing the transaxle to the engine (see illustrations).

23 With the help of an assistant, withdraw the transaxle from the locating dowels on the rear of the engine, making sure that the input shaft does not hang on the clutch. Make sure that the driveshafts are supported clear of the transaxle.

❈ WARNING:

Make sure that the transaxle remains steady on the jack head. Keep the transaxle level until the input shaft is fully withdrawn from the clutch friction plate.

➡ **Note: On 6-speed models, the transaxle is pressed to the engine dowels and will have to be slowly and carefully separated.**

24 Lower the transaxle to the ground.

INSTALLATION

25 Before installing the transaxle, make sure that the location dowels are correctly positioned in the engine cylinder block rear face.

26 Installation of the transaxle is a reversal of the removal procedure, but note the following points:

a) *Check the rear rubber mounts and replace them if necessary.*

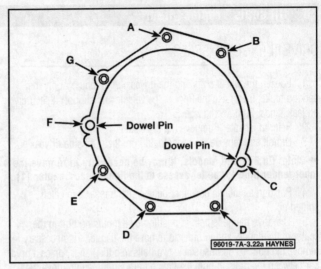

3.22b 6-speed mounting bolt identification (refer to letters for torque specifications when installing)

b) *Apply a little high-melting-point grease to the splines of the transaxle input shaft.*
c) *Tighten all fasteners (see illustration 3.22a or 3.22b) to the specified torque.*
d) *On completion, refer to Section 2 and check the shift cable adjustment.*

4 Manual transaxle overhaul - general information

1 Overhauling a manual transaxle unit is a difficult and involved job for the home mechanic. In addition to disassembling and reassembling many small parts, clearances must be precisely measured and, if necessary, changed by selecting shims and spacers. Internal transaxle components are also often difficult to obtain and in many instances, extremely expensive. Because of this, if the transaxle develops a fault or becomes noisy, the best course of action is to have the unit overhauled by a transaxle specialist or to obtain an exchange reconditioned unit.

2 Nevertheless, it is not impossible for the more experienced mechanic to overhaul the transaxle if the special tools are available and the job is carried out in a deliberate step-by-step manner, to ensure that nothing is overlooked.

3 The tools necessary for an overhaul include internal and external snap-ring pliers, bearing pullers, a slide hammer, a set of pin punches, a dial test indicator and possibly a hydraulic press. In addition, a large, sturdy workbench and a vise will be required.

4 During disassembly of the transaxle, make careful notes of how each component is fitted to make reassembly easier and accurate.

5 Before disassembling the transaxle, it will help if you have some idea of where the problem lies. Certain problems can be closely related to specific areas in the transaxle which can make component examination and replacement easier. Refer to the *Troubleshooting* Section in the front of this manual for more information.

5 Back-up light switch - removal and installation

1 Raise the vehicle and support it securely on jackstands.
2 Remove the splash shield under the engine (see Chapter 1, Section 6).
3 Remove the engine cover/air filter housing (see Chapter 1, Section 7).
4 On 2.0L engines, disconnect and remove the battery and battery tray (see Chapter 5).

5 Disconnect the back-up light switch electrical connector.
6 Unscrew the back-up light switch from the transaxle.
7 Installation is the reverse of the removal; tighten the switch securely.

6 Oil seals - replacement

DRIVE FLANGE OIL SEALS

1 Loosen the wheel bolts and the driveaxle/hub bolts. Apply the parking brake, then raise the front of the vehicle and support it securely on jackstands. Remove the wheel.

2 Refer to Chapter 8 remove the driveaxle.

3 Unbolt and remove the heat shield from the right side driveaxle.

➡ **Note: On 6-speed models, it may be necessary to remove the inner fender liner for better access to the flange (see Chapter 11).**

4 Position a suitable container beneath the transaxle to catch spilled oil.

5 The drive flange is held in position by a mounting bolt in the center of the flange, and in order to remove the flange, it is necessary to remove the bolt. To do this, screw two bolts into the flange, place a pry bar between the bolts to hold the flange from turning and remove the flange mounting bolt. Remove the flange and compression spring from the transaxle.

➡ **Note: Some 5-speed models use a two piece flange seal on the right side flange.**

6 With the flange out, note the installed depth of the oil seal in the housing, then pry it out using a large flat-bladed screwdriver.

7 Clean all traces of dirt from the area around the oil seal opening, then apply a smear of grease to the lips of the new oil seal.

8 Ensure the seal is correctly positioned, with its sealing lip facing inwards, and tap it squarely into position, using a suitable tubular drift (such as a socket) which bears only on the hard outer edge of the seal. If the surface of the flange is good, make sure the seal is installed at the same depth in its housing as originally noted.

9 Clean the oil seal and apply a smear of multi-purpose grease to its lips.

10 Insert the drive flange with compression spring through the oil seal, engaging it with the differential gear.

11 Install the flange mounting bolt and tighten the bolt to the torque listed in this Chapter's Specifications.

12 Install the driveaxle (see Chapter 8).

13 Install the wheel, then lower the vehicle to the ground. Check, and if necessary top up, the transaxle oil level.

SELECTOR SHAFT OIL SEAL

14 Apply the parking brake, then raise the front of the vehicle and support it securely on jackstands.

15 Unscrew the locking nut and slide the shift lever from the selector shaft.

16 Using a small screwdriver, carefully pry the oil seal from the housing, taking care not to damage the surface of the selector shaft or housing.

17 Wipe clean the oil seal seating and selector shaft, then smear a little multi-purpose grease on the new oil seal lips and locate the seal over the end of the shaft. Make sure the closed side of the seal faces outwards. To prevent damage to the oil seal, temporarily wrap some adhesive tape around the end of the shaft.

18 Tap the oil seal squarely into position, using a suitable tubular drift which bears only on the hard outer edge of the seal.

19 Install the gearshift coupling and tighten the locking bolt.

20 Lower the vehicle to the ground.

Specifications

General

Lubricant type and capacity   See Chapter 1

Torque specifications	Ft-lbs (unless otherwise indicated)	Nm

➡ **Note:** One foot-pound (ft-lb) of torque is equivalent to 12 inch-pounds (in-lbs) of torque. Torque values below approximately 15 foot-pounds are expressed in inch-pounds, because most foot-pound torque wrenches are not accurate at these smaller values.

	Ft-lbs	Nm
Driveaxle flange mounting bolt	24	33
Driveaxle heat shield-to-engine bolts	26	35
Transaxle-to-engine bolts (see illustrations 3.22a and 3.22b)		
5-speed models		
Bolts A (M12 x 65mm)	59	80
Bolts B (M12 x 150mm)	59	80
Bolts C (M12 x 165mm)	59	80
Bolt D (M10 x 50mm)	30	40
Bolt E (M12 x 85mm)	59	80
Bolt F (M6 x 8mm)	88 in-lbs	10
6-speed models		
Bolts A (M12 x 55mm short thread)	59	80
Bolts B (M12 x 55mm long thread)	59	80
Bolts C (M12 x 70mm)	59	80
Bolt D (M10 x 50mm)	30	40
Bolt E (M10 x 105mm)	30	40
Bolt F (M12 x 165mm)	59	80
Bolt G (M12 x 165mm)	59	80
Transaxle mount-to-body bolts*		
Step 1	44	60
Step 2	Tighten an additional 90-degrees	
Lubricant level filler/check plug and drain plug	See Chapter 1	

*Do not reuse bolts - always replace bolts with new ones.

Notes

Section

Reference to other Chapters

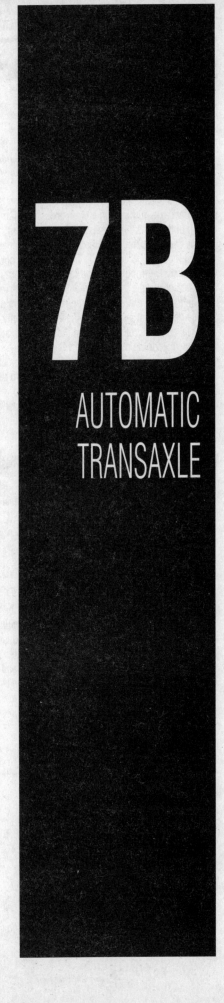

7B

AUTOMATIC TRANSAXLE

1 General information

♦ **Refer to illustration 1.3**

The automatic transaxles on the covered models are either a six-speed or a six-speed DSG (Direct Shift Transaxle).

The DSG transaxle uses two multi-disc clutch packs instead of a conventional torque converter. This allows the driver to shift manually through the gears without a clutch pedal.

The identification of the transaxle designation is the first three digits of the transaxle number. On all transaxles, the numbers are located on the top of the transaxle on a pad (see illustration).

The overall operation of the transaxle is managed by the Engine Control Module (ECM) and the Transaxle Control Module (TCM). Comprehensive troubleshooting can therefore only be carried out using dedicated electronic test equipment such as a factory scan tool.

The transaxle range sensor replacement should be left to a dealer service department or other qualified repair facility; the sensor requires a special calibration tool to adjust the sensor once it has been removed. If the special tool is not used, the vehicle will not start or shift properly.

Due to the complexity of the transaxle and its control system, major repairs and overhaul operations should be left to a dealer service department or other qualified repair facility, who will be equipped to carry out troubleshooting and repair. The information in this Chapter is

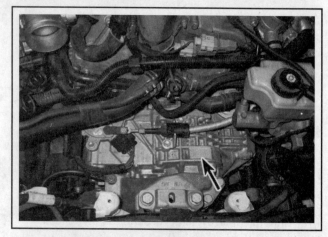

1.3 Transaxle identification number location

therefore limited to a description of the removal and installation of the transaxle as a complete unit. The removal, installation and adjustment of the shift cable and key interlock cable is also described.

2 Diagnosis - general

Automatic transaxle malfunctions may be caused by five general conditions:

a) *Poor engine performance*
b) *Improper adjustments*
c) *Hydraulic malfunctions*
d) *Mechanical malfunctions*
e) *Malfunctions in the computer or its signal network*

Diagnosis of these problems should always begin with a check of the easily repaired items: fluid level and condition (see Chapter 1) and shift cable adjustment. Next, perform a road test to determine if the problem has been corrected or if more diagnosis is necessary. If the problem persists after the preliminary tests and corrections are completed, additional diagnosis should be done by a dealer service department or transaxle repair shop. Refer to the *Troubleshooting* Section at the front of this manual for information on symptoms of transaxle problems.

PRELIMINARY CHECKS

1   Drive the vehicle to warm the transaxle to normal operating temperature.

2   Check the fluid level as described in Chapter 1.

a) *If the fluid level is unusually low, add enough fluid to bring it up to the proper level, then check for external leaks (see below).*
b) *If the fluid level is abnormally high, drain off the excess, then check the drained fluid for contamination by coolant. The presence of engine coolant in the automatic transaxle fluid indicates that a failure has occurred in the transaxle fluid cooler.*
c) *If the fluid is foaming, drain it and refill the transaxle, then check for coolant in the fluid.*

3   Look for a CHECK ENGINE light glowing on the instrument panel (see Chapter 6 for information).

➡ **Note: If the engine or its control network is malfunctioning, do not proceed with the preliminary checks until it has been repaired and runs normally.**

4   Inspect the shift cable (see Section 3). Make sure that it's properly adjusted and that it operates smoothly.

FLUID LEAK DIAGNOSIS

5   Most fluid leaks are easy to locate visually. Repair usually consists of replacing a seal or gasket. If a leak is difficult to find, the following procedure may help.

6   Identify the fluid. Make sure it's transaxle fluid and not engine oil or brake fluid.

7   Try to pinpoint the source of the leak. Drive the vehicle several miles, then park it over a large sheet of cardboard. After a minute or two, you should be able to locate the leak by determining the source of the fluid dripping onto the cardboard.

8   Make a careful visual inspection of the suspected component and the area immediately around it. Pay particular attention to gasket mating surfaces. A mirror is often helpful for finding leaks in areas that are hard to see.

9   If the leak still cannot be found, clean the suspected area thoroughly with a degreaser or solvent, then dry it.

10 Drive the vehicle for several miles at normal operating temperature and varying speeds. After driving the vehicle, visually inspect the suspected component again.

11 Once the leak has been located, the cause must be determined before it can be properly repaired. If a gasket is replaced but the sealing

flange is bent, the new gasket will not stop the leak. The bent flange must be straightened.

12 Before attempting to repair a leak, check to make sure that the following conditions are corrected or they may cause another leak.

➡ **Note: Some of the following conditions cannot be fixed without highly specialized tools and expertise. Such problems must be referred to a transaxle shop or a dealer service department.**

Gasket leaks

13 Check the pan periodically. Make sure the bolts are tight, no bolts are missing, the gasket is in good condition and the pan is flat (dents in the pan may indicate damage to the valve body inside).

14 If the pan gasket is leaking, the fluid level may be too high, the vent may be plugged, the pan bolts may be too tight, the pan sealing flange may be warped, the sealing surface of the transaxle housing may be damaged, the gasket may be damaged or the transaxle casting may be cracked or porous. If sealant instead of gasket material has been used to form a seal between the pan and the transaxle housing, it may be the wrong sealant.

Seal leaks

15 If a transaxle seal is leaking, the fluid level may be too high, the vent may be plugged, the seal bore may be damaged, the seal itself may be damaged or improperly installed, the surface of the shaft protruding through the seal may be damaged or a loose bearing may be causing excessive shaft movement.

16 Make sure the fluid drain/check plug in the transaxle fluid pan is in good condition. If leaking transaxle fluid is evident, replace the O-ring on the drain plug.

Case leaks

17 If the case itself appears to be leaking, the casting is porous and will have to be repaired or replaced.

18 Make sure the oil cooler hose fittings are tight and in good condition.

Fluid comes out vent pipe

19 If this condition occurs, the transaxle is overfilled, there is coolant in the fluid, the vent is plugged or the drain-back holes are plugged.

---

3 Shift cable - removal, installation and adjustment

REMOVAL

▶ **Refer to illustrations 3.4 and 3.5**

➡ **Note: On 03/2009 and later models, the shift cable cannot be separated from the shift lever assembly and must be replaced as a unit.**

1 Place the shift lever in the S position.

2 Remove the engine cover (see Chapter 1, Section 7).

3 Remove the battery and battery tray (see Chapter 5).

4 At the transaxle end of the cable, use a screwdriver to pry the end of the shift cable up from the transaxle lever (see illustration).

5 On 02/2009 and earlier models, squeeze the shift lever cable tabs inwards and release the cable from the bracket on the transaxle case (see illustration). Remove the cable. On 03/2009 and later models, remove the clip holding the shift lever cable to the bracket and remove the cable.

6 Apply the parking brake, then raise the front of the vehicle and support it securely on jackstands.

7 Unscrew the bolt and detach the support bracket and cable from the side of the transaxle.

8 Working under the vehicle, lower the exhaust system (see Chapter 4) and remove the heat shield fasteners and heat shield.

9 Remove the selector housing fasteners, then carefully pry off the housing from under the shifter lever. Slide the housing down the shift cable.

10 Locate the shift cable end, then pull and hold the pin retainer down.

➡ **Note: The pin retainer is plastic and can be damaged if it is pulled down too far.**

11 While holding down the pin retainer, use a screwdriver to push the pin out of the shift lever and cable eyelet.

12 Remove the shift cable from the shift lever assembly and separate the selector housing from the cable.

3.4 Carefully pry the shift cable from the selector shaft lever

3.5 On 02/2009 and earlier models, squeeze the tabs in and slide the shift cable out of the bracket

INSTALLATION

13 Installation is a reversal of removal, but lightly grease the cable end fittings, not the cable.

14 Before lowering the vehicle to the ground and before reconnecting the cable to the transaxle lever, adjust the cable as follows.

ADJUSTMENT

▶ **Refer to illustration 3.17**

15 Apply the parking brake, then raise the front of the vehicle and support it securely on jackstands.

16 Place the shift lever in the P position.

17 Loosen the selector lever adjustment bolt (see illustration).

18 Move the selector shaft lever into the P position. Tighten the selector lever bolt.

19 Verify that the transaxle is in park by rotating both front wheels by hand until the park lock actuator engages in the transaxle, and the front wheels can no longer be rotated in the same direction at the same time. If the wheels can still be rotated, move the selector shaft lever forward until the park lock engages.

20 Lightly press the shift handle button on the shifter handle and make sure the handle is still in the P position.

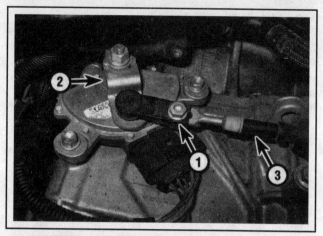

3.17 Shift cable adjustment details

1 Selector lever adjustment bolt
2 Selector shaft lever
3 Shift cable

21 Tighten the selector lever adjustment bolt to the torque listed in this Chapter's Specification.

22 Move the shift lever through the gear ranges and verify that the shifter operates correctly.

4 Shift interlock system - description and check

✳✳ **WARNING:**

These models are equipped with airbags. Always disable the airbag system before working in the vicinity of any airbag system component to avoid the possibility of accidental deployment of the airbag(s), which could cause personal injury (see Chapter 12).

✳✳ **WARNING:**

Do not use a memory saving device to preserve the ECM's memory when working on or near airbag system components.

DESCRIPTION

1 The shift lock system prevents the shift lever from being shifted out of Park or Neutral until the brake pedal is applied and the button on the lever is pushed in. It also prevents the ignition key from being turned to the Lock position until the shift lever has been placed in the Park position.

SOLENOID CHECK

▶ **Refer to illustration 4.3**

2 Remove the center console (see Chapter 11).

3 Follow the wiring harness to the shift lock solenoid electrical connector, then unplug the connector (see illustration). Using a pair of jumper wires, momentarily apply battery voltage and ground to the solenoid terminals and verify that there's an audible click.

✳✳ **CAUTION:**

Don't apply battery voltage any longer than necessary to perform this check.

4 If the shift lock solenoid doesn't click when energized, the solenoid is defective.

➡ **Note: The shift solenoid is not removable from the shift lever and must be replaced as a complete assembly.**

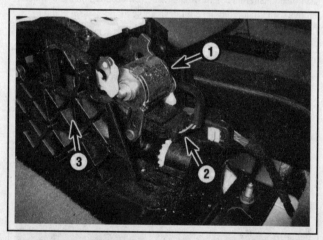

4.3 Shift lock solenoid details

1 Shift lock solenoid   3 Shift lever assembly
2 Electrical connector

5   Automatic transaxle - removal and installation

✳✳ CAUTION:

If the battery is disconnected, several systems must be re-learned before they will work properly (see Chapter 5, Section 3).

REMOVAL

▶ **Refer to illustrations 5.4, 5.11 and 5.19**

1   Select a solid, level surface to park the vehicle upon. Give yourself enough space to move around it easily. Apply the parking brake and chock the rear wheels.

2   Remove the engine cover (see Chapter 1, Section 7). Remove the battery and battery tray (see Chapter 5).

3   With the selector lever in position P, carefully disconnect the inner cable from the shift lever, then unbolt the support bracket. Position the cable to one side (see Section 3).

4   Support the engine with a three-bar engine support locating on the front fender inner channels (see illustration). The engine should be supported using both the front and rear lifting eyes. Depending on the engine, temporarily remove components as necessary to attach the support fixture.

5   Unscrew and remove the transaxle-to-engine mounting bolts accessible from the top of the engine compartment.

6   Loosen the front wheel bolts and driveaxle/hub bolts, then raise the front of the vehicle and support it securely on jackstands. Remove both front wheels.

7   Remove the under-vehicle splash shield (see Chapter 1, Section 6).

8   Remove the exhaust system (see Chapter 4).

9   Disconnect the wiring from the sensors on the transaxle (see Chapter 6).

10   Identify the electrical connectors on the transaxle, then unplug them. Loosen and detach the wiring support, and position the wiring to one side.

11   Remove the heat shield fasteners and shield from over the inner end of the driveaxle (see illustration).

12   Remove the driveaxles (see Chapter 8).

5.4   An engine support fixture can be obtained at most equipment rental yards

13   Position a suitable container beneath the transaxle to collect spilled fluid.

14   Detach the cooler lines from the transaxle, and recover the sealing rings. Plug the openings in the transaxle housing to prevent entry of dust and dirt.

15   Support the transaxle on a jack, preferably one made for this purpose. Secure the transaxle to the jack with a safety chain. Unbolt the right-hand transaxle mount complete with rubber bushing.

16   Remove the left and right-hand transaxle mounts, keeping track of the location of various-length bolts (see Section 7). At the rear of the transaxle, remove the nuts securing the rear mount to the crossmember, then remove the rear crossmember.

17   Unscrew the transaxle-to-engine mounting bolts accessible from under the car.

18   Remove the starter motor (see Chapter 5).

19   On 09G transaxles, remove the converter nut access plug (see illustration), then turn the engine to locate one of the torque converter-to-driveplate nuts in the opening. Unscrew and remove the

5.11   Driveaxle heat shield mounting fastener locations

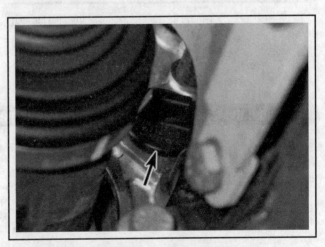

5.19   Torque converter fastener cover plug location

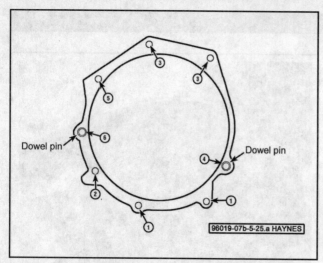

5.25a Transaxle bolt locations - 09G transaxles

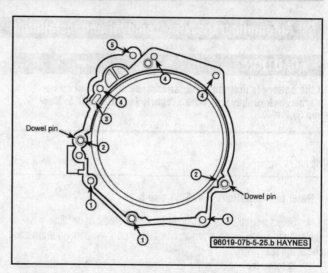

5.25b Transaxle bolt locations - DSG (02E) transaxles

nuts while preventing the engine from turning using a wide-bladed screwdriver engaged with the ring gear teeth on the driveplate. Unscrew the remaining five fasteners, turning the engine a third of a turn at a time to locate them. Mark the relationship of the torque converter to the driveplate so balance will be preserved when reinstalling the transaxle.

20 Remove the balljoint nuts and separate the balljoints from the control arms (see Chapter 10). On DSG (02E) transaxles, remove the subframe and left control arm (see Chapter 10).

21 On DSG (02E) transaxles, remove the small cover plate (above the right driveaxle flange).

22 With the help of an assistant, withdraw the transaxle from the locating dowels on the rear of the engine, making sure that the torque converter remains fully engaged with the transaxle input shaft. If necessary, use a pry bar to release the torque converter from the driveplate.

23 When the locating dowels are clear of their mounting holes, lower the transaxle to the ground using the jack. Strap a restraining bar across the front of the bellhousing to keep the torque converter in position.

❊❊ WARNING:

Make sure that the transaxle remains steady on the jack head.

24 Where necessary, remove the intermediate plate from the locating dowels.

INSTALLATION

▶ **Refer to illustrations 5.25a and 5.25b**

25 Installation of the transaxle is a reversal of the removal procedure, but note the following points:

a) As the torque converter is reinstalled, ensure that the drive pins at the center of the torque converter hub engage with the recesses in the automatic transaxle fluid pump inner wheel.

b) When installing the transaxle, make sure the marks on the torque converter and driveplate are in alignment.

c) Install the bellhousing bolts in the specific location (see illustrations), then tighten the bolts and torque converter-to-driveplate nuts to the specified torque. Always replace self-locking nuts and bolts.

d) Replace the O-ring seals on the fluid pipes and filler tube attached to the transaxle casing.

e) Tighten the transaxle mounting bolts to the correct torque.

f) Tighten the driveaxle inner CV joint bolts to the torque values listed in the Chapter 8 Specifications.

g) Check the final drive oil level and transaxle fluid level as described in Chapter 1.

h) Check the shift cable adjustment (see Section 3).

6 Automatic transaxle overhaul - general information

In the event of a fault occurring, it will be necessary to establish whether the fault is electrical, mechanical or hydraulic in nature, before repair work can be contemplated. Diagnosis requires detailed knowledge of the transaxle's operation and construction, as well as access to specialized test equipment, and so is deemed to be beyond the scope of this manual. It is therefore essential that problems with the automatic transaxle are referred to a dealer service department or other qualified repair facility for assessment. .

Note that a faulty transaxle should not be removed before the vehicle has been assessed by a knowledgeable technician equipped with the proper tools, as troubleshooting must be performed with the transaxle installed in the vehicle.

7   Transaxle mounts - check and replacement

✳✳ WARNING:

The weight of the entire engine and transaxle will be supported by the mounts not being removed during this procedure. Never place any part of your body directly under the engine or transaxle when performing this procedure.

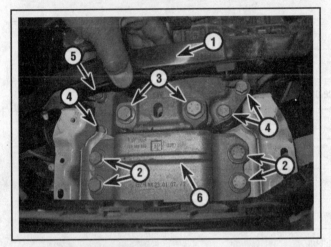

7.8 Transaxle mount details

1   *Electrical harness retainer*
2   *Transaxle mount-to-body mounting fasteners*
3   *Transaxle mount-to-transaxle bracket mounting fasteners*
4   *Transaxle bracket-to-transaxle mounting fasteners*
5   *Transaxle bracket-to-transaxle mounting studded fastener*
6   *Transaxle mount*

CHECK

1   Raise the vehicle and support it securely on jackstands.
2   Insert a large screwdriver or prybar between the transaxle and the subframe and try to pry the transaxle up slightly.
3   The transaxle should not move much at all - if the mount is cracked or torn, replace it.

REPLACEMENT

▶ **Refer to illustration 7.8**

4   Working from above in the engine compartment, remove the engine cover (see Chapter 1, Section 7).
5   Remove the battery and battery tray (see Chapter 5).
6   Remove the electrical harness retainer from the top of the mount, if equipped.
7   Support the transaxle with a floor jack. Place a block of wood on the jack head to act as a cushion.
8   Remove the bolts and nuts attaching the mount to the subframe and transaxle (see illustration).

✳✳ WARNING:

Do not disconnect more than one mount at a time, except during engine or transaxle removal.

9   Raise the transaxle slightly with the jack and remove the mount.
10 Installation is the reverse of removal. Use thread-locking compound on the mount bolts and be sure to tighten them securely.

8   Electronic control system

TROUBLE CODES

The electronic control system for the transaxle has some self-diagnostic capabilities. If certain kinds of system malfunctions occur, the PCM stores the appropriate diagnostic trouble code in its memory and the CHECK ENGINE indicator light illuminates to inform the driver.

The diagnostic trouble codes can only be extracted from the PCM using a SCAN tool that can be linked to the On Board Diagnostic (OBD II) computer via the Data Link connector (DLC). Codes are listed below for reference, but can only be extracted with the correct scan tool connected to the Data Link connector (DLC) under the left side of the instrument panel (refer to Chapter 6 for additional information).

TROUBLE CODES

Code	Code identification
P0700	Transaxle control system (mil request)
P0701	Transaxle control system range/performance problem
P0702	Transaxle control system electrical
P0704	Clutch switch input circuit malfunction
P0705	Transaxle range sensor "a" circuit (PRNDL input)
P0706	Transaxle range sensor "a" circuit range/performance problem
P0710	Transaxle fluid temperature sensor "a" circuit
P0711	Transaxle fluid temperature sensor "a" circuit range/performance problem
P0712	Transaxle fluid temperature sensor "a" circuit low
P0713	Transaxle fluid temperature sensor "a" circuit high
P0714	Transaxle fluid temperature sensor "a" circuit intermittent
P0715	Input/turbine speed sensor "a" circuit
P0716	Input/turbine speed sensor "a" circuit range/performance problem
P0717	Input/turbine speed sensor "a" circuit no signal
P0720	Generator control circuit
P0721	Output speed sensor circuit range/performance problem
P0722	Output speed sensor circuit no signal
P0725	Engine speed input circuit
P0726	Engine speed input circuit range/performance problem
P0727	Engine speed input circuit no signal
P0729	Gear 6 incorrect ratio
P0730	Incorrect gear ratio
P0731	Gear 1 incorrect ratio
P0732	Gear 2 incorrect ratio
P0733	Gear 3 incorrect ratio
P0734	Gear 4 incorrect ratio
P0735	Gear 5 incorrect ratio

Code	Code identification
P0736	Reverse incorrect ratio
P0740	Torque converter clutch circuit/open
P0741	Torque converter clutch circuit performance problem/stuck off
P0743	Torque converter clutch circuit electrical problem
P0746	Pressure control solenoid "a" performance problem/stuck off
P0747	Pressure control solenoid "a" stuck on
P0748	Pressure control solenoid "a" electrical problem
P0749	Pressure control solenoid "a" intermittent
P0751	Shift solenoid "a" performance problem/stuck off
P0752	Shift solenoid "a" stuck on
P0753	Shift solenoid "a" electrical problem
P0756	Shift solenoid "b" performance problem/stuck off
P0757	Shift solenoid "b" stuck on
P0758	Shift solenoid "b" electrical problem
P0761	Shift solenoid "c" performance problem/stuck off
P0762	Shift solenoid "c" stuck on
P0763	Shift solenoid "c" electrical
P0766	Shift solenoid "d" performance problem/stuck off
P0768	Shift solenoid "d" electrical
P0771	Shift solenoid "e" performance problem/stuck off
P0773	Shift solenoid "e" electrical
P0776	Pressure control solenoid "b" performance problem/stuck off
P0777	Pressure control solenoid "b" stuck on
P0778	Pressure control solenoid "b" electrical problem
P0779	Pressure control solenoid "b" intermittent
P0780	Shift error
P0781	1-2 shift
P0782	2-3 shift
P0783	3-4 shift

TROUBLE CODES (CONTINUED)

Code	Code identification
P0784	4-5 shift
P0785	Shift timing solenoid "a"
P0791	Intermediate shaft speed sensor "a" circuit
P0796	Pressure control solenoid "c" performance problem/stuck off
P0797	Pressure control solenoid "c" stuck on
P0798	Pressure control solenoid "c" electrical problem
P0799	Pressure control solenoid "c" intermittent
P0811	Excessive clutch "a" slippage
P0820	Gear lever x-y position sensor circuit
P0821	Gear lever x position circuit
P0822	Gear lever y position circuit
P0829	5-6 shift
P0840	Transaxle fluid pressure sensor/switch "a" circuit
P0841	Transaxle fluid pressure sensor/switch "a" circuit range/performance problem
P0842	Transaxle fluid pressure sensor/switch "a" circuit low
P0845	Transaxle fluid pressure sensor/switch "b" circuit
P0846	Transaxle fluid pressure sensor/switch "b" circuit range/performance problem
P0863	TCM communication circuit
P0864	TCM communication circuit range/performance problem
P0865	TCM communication circuit low
P0884	TCM power input signal intermittent
P0886	TCM power relay control circuit low
P0887	TCM power relay control circuit high
P0889	TCM power relay sense circuit range/performance problem
P0890	TCM power relay sense circuit low
P0891	TCM power relay sense circuit high
P0892	TCM power relay sense circuit intermittent

Code	Code identification
P0914	Gear shift position circuit
P0915	Gear shift position circuit range/performance problem
P0918	Gear shift position circuit intermittent
P0919	Gear shift position control error
P0929	Gear shift lock solenoid control circuit range/performance problem

Specifications

General

Designations

6-speed automatic	09G
6-speed automatic direct shift transaxle	02E
Automatic transaxle fluid type and capacity	See Chapter 1

Torque specifications	Ft-lbs (unless otherwise indicated)	Nm

➡ **Note: One foot-pound (ft-lb) of torque is equivalent to 12 inch-pounds (in-lbs) of torque. Torque values below approximately 15 foot-pounds are expressed in inch-pounds, because most foot-pound torque wrenches are not accurate at these smaller values.**

Automatic selector cable bracket bolt	80 in-lbs	9
Transaxle oil cooler fasteners		
6-speed (09G) transaxle	27	36
6-speed DSG (02E) transaxle		
Step 1	15	20
Step 2	Tighten an additional 90 degrees	
Driveplate-to-torque converter (new bolts)	44	60
09G transaxle-to-engine mounting fasteners (see illustration 5.25a)		
All 2010 and earlier models and all 2011 five-cylinder models		
Bolts 1 (M10 x 65mm)	30	40
Bolt 2 (M10 x 76mm)	30	40
Bolts 3 (M12 x 65mm)	59	80
Bolt 4 (M12 x 95mm)	59	80
Bolt 5 (M12 x 170mm)	59	80
Bolt 6 (M12 x 170mm)	59	80
All 2011 four-cylinder models		
Bolts 1 (M10 x 55mm)	30	40
Bolt 2 (M10 x 65mm)	30	40
Bolts 3 (M12 x 55mm)	59	80
Bolt 4 (M12 x 70mm)	59	80
Bolt 5 (M12 x 165mm)	59	80
Bolt 6 (M12 x 165mm)	59	80
02E DSG transaxle-to-engine mounting fasteners (see illustration 5.25b)		
Bolts 1 (M10 x 50mm)	30	40
Bolts 2 (M12 x 70mm)	59	80
Bolt 3 (M10 x 40mm)	30	40
Bolts 4 (M12 x 55mm)	59	80
Bolt 5 (M10 x 45mm)	30	40
Transaxle mount*		
Mount-to-transaxle bracket bolts (driver side)		
Step 1	29.5	40
Step 2	Tighten an additional 90 degrees	
Mount-to-body bracket bolts (driver side)		
Step 1	44	60
Step 2	Tighten an additional 90 degrees	

*Replace all mount bolts with new ones.

Section

8

CLUTCH AND
DRIVELINE

1 General information

The information in this Chapter deals with the components from the rear of the engine to the drive wheels, except for the transaxle, which is dealt with in Chapters 7A and 7B. Included in this Chapter is service information on the clutch and its release system, and the driveaxles.

Since nearly all the procedures covered in this Chapter involve working under the vehicle, make sure it's securely supported on sturdy jackstands or a hoist where the vehicle can be easily raised and lowered.

2 Clutch - description and check

1 All models with a manual transaxle use either a "Sachs" or "LuK" single dry plate, diaphragm spring type clutch. The clutch disc has a splined hub which allows it to slide along the splines of the transaxle input shaft. The clutch and pressure plate are held in contact by spring pressure exerted by the diaphragm in the pressure plate.

2 The clutch release system is hydraulically operated. The release system consists of the clutch pedal, the clutch master cylinder, the clutch release cylinder and the hydraulic line between the master cylinder and release cylinder. On 6-speed transaxles, the release cylinder and release bearing are one unit.

3 When pressure is applied to the clutch pedal to release the clutch, the clutch master cylinder transmits this movement to the clutch release cylinder, which moves the clutch release lever. As the lever pivots, the release bearing pushes against the fingers of the diaphragm spring of the pressure plate assembly, which in turn releases the clutch plate.

4 Terminology can be a problem regarding the clutch components because common names have in some cases changed from that used by the manufacturer. For example, the clutch release cylinder is sometimes referred to as a slave cylinder, the driven plate is also called the clutch plate or disc, the pressure plate assembly is also known as the clutch cover, and the clutch release bearing is sometimes called a throw-out bearing.

5 Other than replacing components that have obvious damage, some preliminary checks should be performed to diagnose a clutch system failure.

a) *To check clutch spin down time, run the engine at normal idle speed with the transaxle in Neutral (clutch pedal up, engaged). Disengage the clutch (pedal down), wait several seconds and shift the transaxle into Reverse. No grinding noise should be heard. A grinding noise would most likely indicate a problem in the pressure plate or the clutch disc.*

b) *To check for complete clutch release, run the engine (with the parking brake applied to prevent movement) and hold the clutch pedal approximately 1/2-inch from the floor. Shift the transaxle between 1st gear and Reverse several times. If the shift is not smooth, component failure is indicated.*

c) *Visually inspect the clutch pedal pivot at the top of the clutch pedal to make sure there is no sticking or excessive wear.*

d) *Make sure that the hydraulic lines aren't leaking at either the master cylinder or the release cylinder (see Sections 3 and 4). Bleed the system if necessary (see Section 5).*

3 Clutch master cylinder - removal and installation

✵✵ WARNING:

The models covered by this manual are equipped with Supplemental Restraint Systems (SRS), more commonly known as airbags. Always disable the airbag system before working in the vicinity of any airbag system components to avoid the possibility of accidental deployment of the airbags, which could cause personal injury (see Chapter 12).

✵✵ CAUTION:

If the battery is disconnected, several systems must be relearned before they will work properly (see Chapter 5, Section 3).

REMOVAL

1 Disconnect the cable from the negative terminal of the battery (see Chapter 5).

2 Remove the clutch pedal assembly (see Section 8).

3 Using a pin punch or small screwdriver, disconnect the clip tabs on each side of the clutch pedal that hold the clutch master cylinder push rod to the pedal.

4 Place a spacer approximately 1-1/2 inches (40 mm) long between the clutch pedal and clutch pedal stop.

➡ **Note: A standard half inch drive socket could be used.**

5 Release the lock from the clutch master cylinder to the clutch pedal assembly, then rotate the clutch master cylinder counterclockwise and pull the clutch master cylinder from the pedal bracket.

INSTALLATION

6 Remove the spacer and insert the clutch master cylinder into the pedal bracket, then insert the clip on to the end of the pushrod.

7 Place the spacer between the clutch pedal and clutch pedal stop, then push the master cylinder into the clutch pedal bracket. Rotate the cylinder clockwise to lock it in place.

8 Push the master cylinder push rod into the pedal until the clip on the end of the pushrod is heard or felt locking into the pedal.

9 Install the clutch pedal assembly (see Section 8).

10 Installation is otherwise the reverse of removal, with the following points:

a) *Tighten all fasteners to the torque values listed in this Chapter's Specifications.*

b) *Bleed the clutch hydraulic system (see Section 5).*

c) *Check the brake fluid level in the brake fluid reservoir, adding as necessary to bring it to the appropriate level (see Chapter 1).*

4   Clutch release cylinder - removal and installation

REMOVAL

➡ **Note:** On 5-speed models, the release cylinder is located on the top of the transaxle housing and access is from the engine compartment. On 6-speed models, the release cylinder and release bearing are a single unit, located in the bellhousing of the transaxle; see Section 7 for removal and installation.

1   Disconnect the cable from the negative terminal of the battery (see Chapter 5).

2   Remove the engine top cover/air filter assembly (see Chapter 1, Section 7).

3   Remove the battery and battery tray (see Chapter 5).

4   Disconnect the gear selector cables from the gear selector levers, as described in Chapter 7A. Remove the clip and remove the relay lever. Unscrew the nut and remove the selector lever from the top of the transaxle.

5   Remove the transaxle support bracket mounting fasteners and bracket.

6   Have some rags handy, as some fluid will be spilled when the line is disconnected.

7   Pull the fluid pipe retaining clip from the union on the release cylinder, then pull the pipe from the union.

8   Remove the release cylinder mounting fasteners, and remove the release cylinder from the transaxle.

INSTALLATION

9   Lubricate the end of the pushrod with copper grease. Apply lithium-base grease to the area of the boot that seats in the bore in the transaxle. Install the release cylinder, inserting it straight into its bore (otherwise the pushrod may not seat in its pocket in the release lever).

10 Connect the pressure line to the cylinder. Insert the clip and make sure the line is completely attached and won't pull off.

11 Install the release cylinder mounting bolt and tighten it to the torque listed in this Chapter's Specifications.

12 The remainder of installation is the reverse of removal, with the additional following points:

   a) *Bleed the system (see Section 5).*

   b) *Check the fluid level in the brake fluid reservoir, adding as necessary to bring it to the appropriate level (see Chapter 1).*

   c) *Wash off any spilled brake fluid with water.*

5   Clutch hydraulic system - bleeding

▶ **Refer to illustration 5.3**

1   The hydraulic system should be bled of all air whenever any part of the system has been removed or if the fluid level has been allowed to fall so low that air has been drawn into the master cylinder. The procedure is similar to bleeding a brake system.

2   Fill the brake master cylinder with new brake fluid conforming to DOT 4 specifications.

3   Remove the engine cover (see Chapter 1, Section 7). Locate the bleeder screw on the clutch release cylinder (see illustration). Remove the dust cap from the bleeder screw and push a length of snug-fitting (preferably clear) hose over the screw. Place the other end of the hose into a clear container with about two inches of brake fluid in it. The hose end must be submerged in the fluid.

4   Have an assistant depress the clutch pedal and hold it. Open the bleeder screw on the release cylinder, allowing fluid to flow through the hose. Close the bleeder screw when fluid stops flowing from the hose. Once closed, have your assistant release the pedal.

5   Continue this process until all air is evacuated from the system, indicated by a full, solid stream of fluid being ejected from the bleeder

5.3 Typical bleeder valve location - early model 5-speed transaxle shown

screw each time and no air bubbles in the hose or container. Keep a close watch on the fluid level inside the brake master cylinder reservoir; if the level drops too low, air will be sucked back into the system and the process will have to be started over again.

6   Install the dust cap on the bleeder screw. Check carefully for proper operation before placing the vehicle in normal service.

7   Lower the vehicle.

8   Recheck the brake fluid level.

6 Clutch components - removal, inspection and installation

☀☀ WARNING:

Dust produced by clutch wear and deposited on clutch components is hazardous to your health. DO NOT blow it out with compressed air and DO NOT inhale it. DO NOT use gasoline or petroleum-based solvents to remove the dust. Brake system cleaner should be used to flush the dust into a drain pan. After the clutch components are wiped clean with a rag, dispose of the contaminated rags and cleaner in a labeled, covered container.

REMOVAL

▶ **Refer to illustrations 6.4 and 6.6**

1   Access to the clutch components is normally accomplished by removing the transaxle, leaving the engine in the vehicle. If, of course, the engine is being removed for major overhaul, then the opportunity should always be taken to check the clutch for wear and replace worn components as necessary. However, the relatively low cost of the clutch components compared to the time and labor involved in gaining access to them warrants their replacement any time the engine or transaxle is removed, unless they are new or in near-perfect condition. The following procedures assume that the engine will stay in place.

2   Remove the transaxle from the vehicle (see Chapter 7A). Support the engine while the transaxle is out. Preferably, an engine hoist or support fixture should be used to support it from above. However, if a jack is used underneath the engine, make sure a piece of wood is used between the jack and oil pan to spread the load.

3   The release lever and release bearing (on 5-speed models) or release bearing and release cylinder (on 6-speed models) can remain attached to the transaxle; however, you should inspect them (see Section 7) while the transaxle is removed.

4   Carefully inspect the flywheel and pressure plate for indexing marks. If they cannot be found, scribe marks yourself so the pressure plate and the flywheel will be in the same alignment during installation

(see illustration). Of course, this won't be necessary if you're planning on replacing the pressure plate with a new one.

➡ **Note: Two types of pressure plates are used - a "Sachs" or a "LuK." The components are not interchangeable so make sure you replace them with the same type.**

5   Slowly loosen the pressure plate-to-flywheel bolts. Work in a criss-cross pattern and loosen each bolt a little at a time until all spring pressure is relieved.

6   Hold the pressure plate securely and completely remove the bolts, followed by the pressure plate and clutch disc (see illustration).

7   Inspect the pilot bearing recessed into the end of the crankshaft for wear or damage. If the needle bearings are good, clean the area and apply new grease to the needle bearings. If the bearing is damaged, insert a puller (available at most auto parts stores) and pull the bearing out from the crankshaft.

8   Using a bearing driver, drive the pilot bearing into the crankshaft with the letters on the needle bearing facing the outside. The bearing should be inserted 1/8-inch below the edge of the crankshaft. Lubricate the bearing with high-temperature grease.

INSPECTION

▶ **Refer to illustrations 6.11, 6.13a and 6.13b**

9   Ordinarily, when a problem occurs in the clutch, it can be attributed to wear of the clutch driven plate assembly (clutch disc). However, all components should be inspected at this time.

10   Inspect the flywheel for cracks, heat checking, score marks and other damage. If the imperfections are slight, a machine shop can resurface it to make it flat and smooth. Refer to Chapter 2A or 2B for the flywheel removal procedure.

11   Inspect the lining on the clutch disc. There should be at least 1/16-inch of lining above the rivet heads. Check for loose rivets, distortion, cracks, broken springs and other obvious damage (see illustration). As mentioned above, ordinarily the clutch disc is replaced as a matter of course, so if in doubt about the condition, replace it with a new one.

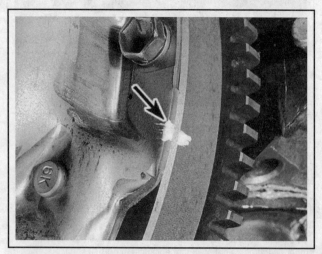

6.4 Mark the relationship of the pressure plate to the flywheel (in case you're going to re-use the same pressure plate)

6.6 When removing the pressure plate, be careful not to let the clutch disc fall out

12 The release bearing should be replaced along with the clutch disc (see Section 7).

13 Check the machined surface and the diaphragm spring fingers of the pressure plate (see illustrations). If the surface is grooved or otherwise damaged, replace the pressure plate assembly. Also check for obvious damage, distortion, cracking, etc. Light glazing can be removed with emery cloth or sandpaper. If a new pressure plate is indicated, new or factory rebuilt units are available.

INSTALLATION

▶ **Refer to illustrations 6.15 and 6.16**

14 Position the clutch disc and pressure plate with the clutch held in place with an alignment tool. Make sure the disc is installed properly. Find the word "Getriebeseite" which means "transmission side" stamped on the hub of the disc; this side must face the pressure plate.

15 Tighten the pressure plate-to-flywheel bolts only finger tight, working around the pressure plate. On models equipped with a new "LuK" clutch assembly (only), make sure both edges of the adjusting ring are located between the notches in the clutch cover cut-outs (see illustration). If the adjusting ring is in a different position with a new pressure plate, do not install the pressure plate and replace it with a new one and check again.

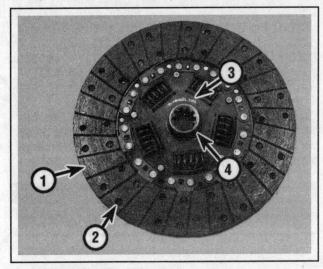

6.11 The clutch disc

1   *Lining* - this will wear down in use
2   *Rivets* - these secure the lining and will damage the flywheel or pressure plate if allowed to contact the surfaces
3   *Markings* - "Getriebeseite" or "Flywheel side" or something similar
4   *Hub* - be sure this is installed facing the proper direction (see the text)

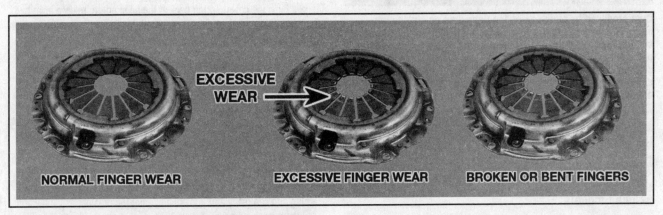

EXCESSIVE WEAR

NORMAL FINGER WEAR   EXCESSIVE FINGER WEAR   BROKEN OR BENT FINGERS

6.13a Replace the pressure plate if excessive wear is noted

6.13b Examine the pressure plate friction surface for score marks, cracks and evidence of overheating

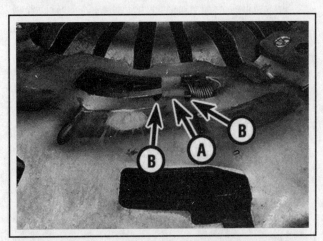

6.15 If installing a new LuK pressure plate, make sure the edges of the adjusting ring (A) are located between the notches in the clutch cover cut-outs (B) (one of three cut-outs shown)

16 Center the clutch disc by ensuring the alignment tool is through the splined hub and into the recess in the crankshaft (see illustration). Wiggle the tool up, down or side-to-side as needed to bottom the tool. Tighten the pressure plate-to-flywheel bolts a little at a time, working in a criss-cross pattern to prevent distortion of the cover. After all of the bolts are snug, tighten them to the torque listed in this Chapter's Specifications. Remove the alignment tool.

17 Using moly-base grease, lubricate the inner surface of the release bearing and the face of the bearing where it contacts the fingers of the pressure plate diaphragm spring. Also place grease on the release lever contact areas and the transaxle input shaft.

❋❋ CAUTION:

Don't use too much grease.

18 Install the clutch release bearing (see Section 7).

19 Install the transaxle and all components removed previously, tightening all fasteners to the proper torque specifications.

6.16 Center the clutch disc with a clutch alignment tool, then tighten the pressure plate bolts a little at a time, in a criss-cross pattern, to the torque listed in this Chapter's Specifications

7 Clutch release bearing and lever - removal, inspection and installation

❋❋ WARNING:

Dust produced by clutch wear and deposited on clutch components is hazardous to your health. DO NOT blow it out with compressed air and DO NOT inhale it. DO NOT use gasoline or petroleum-based solvents to remove the dust. Brake system cleaner should be used to flush it into a drain pan. After the clutch components are wiped clean with a rag, dispose of the contaminated rags and cleaner in a labeled, covered container.

REMOVAL

1 Remove the transaxle as described in Chapter 7A.

5-speed models

▶ **Refer to illustrations 7.3 and 7.4**

2 Remove the leaf spring mounting bolt at the end of the clutch release lever and remove the spring.

3 Push the detent spring back at the pivot end to release lever by pushing it through the hole (see illustration). This will release the pivot end of the lever. Withdraw the lever together with the release bearing from the guide sleeve.

4 Use a screwdriver to depress the tabs and separate the bearing from the lever (see illustration).

5 Remove the plastic pivot from the ballstud. The release lever locates on the plastic pivot.

6-speed models

6 Remove the clip securing the breather assembly to the end of the release unit on the outside of the transaxle.

7 Separate the breather assembly from the release cylinder. Have a plug and cap ready and immediately plug the breather assembly and cap the release cylinder.

8 From inside the transaxle housing, remove the release cylinder/ release bearing unit mounting fasteners and unit.

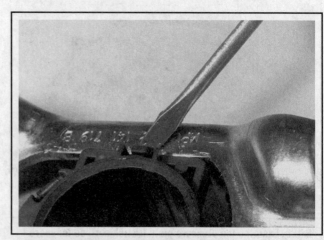

7.3 Push the detent back to release the lever - 5-speed models

7.4 Pry inward on the plastic tabs retaining the bearing to the lever, then separate the bearing from the lever - 5-speed models

7.9 To check the bearing, hold it by the outer race and rotate the inner race while applying pressure; if the bearing doesn't turn smoothly or if it's noisy, replace it - 5-speed models

INSPECTION

5-speed models

 Refer to illustration 7.9

9 Hold the bearing by the outer race and rotate the inner race while applying pressure (see illustration). If the bearing doesn't turn smoothly, or if it's noisy, replace the bearing with a new one. Wipe the bearing with a clean rag and inspect it for damage, wear and cracks. Don't immerse the bearing in solvent; it's sealed for life and to do so would ruin it. Also check the release lever for cracks and bends.

6-speed models

10 Check for any sign of leaks, then hold the release unit and rotate the release bearing while applying pressure. If there are signs of leaks or the bearing doesn't turn smoothly, or if it's noisy, replace the release cylinder/release bearing unit with a new one. Wipe the bearing with a clean rag and inspect it for damage, wear and cracks. Don't immerse the assembly in solvent; to do so would ruin it. Also check the release cylinder housing for cracks and bends.

➡ **Note: The release cylinder and bearing are one piece and cannot be separated. If either component is bad, the entire assembly must be replaced.**

INSTALLATION

5-speed models

▸ **Refer to illustration 7.12**

11 Begin installation by lubricating the ballstud and plastic pivot

7.12 Press the release lever onto the ballstud until the spring clip holds it in position - 5-speed models

with a little copper grease. Smear a little grease on the release bearing surface which contacts the diaphragm spring fingers and the release lever, and also on the guide sleeve.

12 Install the spring onto the release lever, making sure the plastic pivot is in place on the ball stud. Position the lever and bearing and press the release lever onto the ballstud until the spring holds it in position (see illustration).

13 Install the transaxle (see Chapter 7A).

6-speed models

14 Slide the release cylinder/bearing onto the input shaft, install and tighten the mounting fasteners (in small amounts) to the torque listed in this Chapter's Specifications.

❋❋ **CAUTION:**

If the mounting fasteners are not tightened in small, even amounts, the ears on the release cylinder/release bearing could break off.

15 Replace the O-ring on the end of the release cylinder.

16 Install the transaxle (see Chapter 7A).

17 Connect the breather assembly to the release cylinder and push the clip in to lock the line.

18 The remainder of installation is the reverse of removal, with the additional following points:

  a) *Bleed the system (see Section 5).*

  b) *Check the fluid level in the brake fluid reservoir, adding as necessary to bring it to the appropriate level (see Chapter 1).*

  c) *Wash off any spilled brake fluid with water.*

8   Clutch pedal assembly - removal and installation

▶ **Refer to illustration 8.4**

✳✳ **CAUTION:**

If the battery is disconnected, several systems must be re-learned before they will work properly (see Chapter 5, Section 3).

1   Disconnect the cable from the negative terminal of the battery (see Chapter 5).
2   Remove the engine cover (see Chapter 1, Section 7).
3   Place enough rags on the floor under the clutch pedal to absorb any brake fluid that may spill.
4   Working in the engine compartment, clamp the fluid supply hose leading from the brake fluid reservoir to the clutch master cylinder using a brake hose clamp, then remove the clamp and detach the hose from the clutch master cylinder (see illustration). Have a plug ready and immediately plug the line.
5   Pull out the clip and separate the pressure line from the clutch master cylinder. Plug the line to prevent excessive fluid loss and the entry of contaminants.

➡ **Note: There is a seal on the end of pressure line which can stay in the clutch master when the line is removed. Use a small pick or screwdriver to remove the seal from the master cylinder and always replace the seal with a new one.**

6   Disconnect the clutch pedal switch electrical connector from the switch and leave the switch connected to the master cylinder.

➡ **Note: If the clutch master is going to be replaced, remove the clutch pedal switch (see Section 9).**

7   Remove the driver's side under cover, if equipped, and knee bolster (see Chapter 11).
8   Remove the impact bolster support fasteners and support the instrument panel.

9   Remove the clutch pedal cover push fasteners from the pedal bracket and remove the cover (if equipped).
10   Remove the pedal bracket fasteners and remove the pedal assembly from the firewall.
11   Install the pedal assembly and tighten the fasteners to the torque listed in this Chapter's Specifications.
12   The remainder of installation is the reverse of removal, with the additional following points:

  a) *Bleed the system (see Section 5).*
  b) *Check the fluid level in the brake fluid reservoir, adding as necessary to bring it to the appropriate level (see Chapter 1).*
  c) *Wash off any spilled brake fluid with water.*

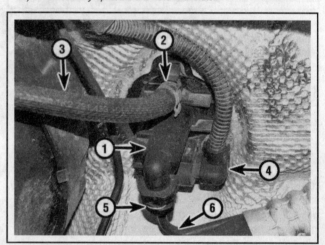

8.4 Typical clutch master cylinder details

1	Clutch master cylinder	4	Clutch position sensor
2	Supply hose clamp	5	Retaining clip
3	Supply hose	6	Pressure line (to release cylinder)

9   Clutch pedal switch - removal and installation

✳✳ **CAUTION:**

If the battery is disconnected, several systems must be re-learned before they will work properly (see Chapter 5, Section 3).

➡ **Note: The clutch pedal switch is also called the clutch position sensor in the scan tool diagnostic code references.**

REMOVAL

▶ **Refer to illustration 9.5**

1   Disconnect the cable from the negative terminal of the battery (see Chapter 5).
2   Remove the engine cover (see Chapter 1, Section 7).
3   Remove the battery and battery tray (see Chapter 5).
4   On models equipped with a pressure line that has a round dial

type component, remove the pressure line retaining clip, then disconnect and plug the line.

➡ **Note: There is a seal on the end of pressure line which can stay in the clutch master when the line is removed. Use a small pick or screwdriver to remove the seal from the master cylinder and always replace the seal with a new one.**

5 Using a small screwdriver, depress the tab on clutch pedal switch (see illustration), then pull the switch down, disconnect the switch electrical connector and remove the switch.

INSTALLATION

6 Connect the pedal switch electrical connector to the switch, then place the clutch pedal switch under the clutch master cylinder and press the switch up, making sure the switch engages with the clutch master cylinder until the switch locks in place.
7 Bleed the clutch system if the pressure line was removed (see Section 5).
8 The remainder of installation is the reverse of removal.

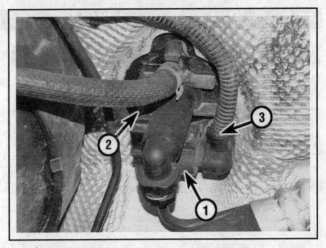

9.5 Typical clutch (pedal) position sensor details

1 Clutch position sensor   3 Electrical connector
2 Mounting tab

10 Clutch pedal and over-center spring - removal and installation

✴ CAUTION:

If the battery is disconnected, several systems must be re-learned before they will work properly (see Chapter 5, Section 3).

1 Disconnect the cable from the negative terminal of the battery (see Chapter 5).
2 Remove the driver's side under-dash cover, if equipped, and knee bolster (see Chapter 11).
3 Remove the impact bolster support fasteners and support the instrument panel.
4 Remove the clutch pedal cover push fasteners from the pedal bracket and remove the cover (if equipped).
5 Remove the clutch pedal through-bolts and nut from the pedal bracket.

6 Maneuver the clutch pedal downwards slightly, then remove the over-center spring from the slot in the pedal bracket.
7 Using a pin punch or small screwdriver, disconnect the clip tabs on each side of the clutch pedal that hold the clutch master cylinder push rod to the pedal, and remove the pedal.
8 Push the master cylinder push rod into the pedal until the clip on the end of the pushrod is heard or felt locking into the pedal.
9 Install the over-center spring into the pedal bracket.
10 Using a flat-blade screwdriver or VW special tool #T10178, push the over-spring back and install the clutch pedal to the bracket. Make sure the pivot end of the pedal sits squarely in the center of the over-center spring.
11 To align the holes for the through-bolt, push the spring in with the pedal and install the through-bolt, then tighten the nut to the torque listed in this Chapter's Specifications.

11 Driveaxles - general information and inspection

1 Power is transmitted from the transaxle to the front wheels through a pair of driveaxles. The inner end of the driveaxle is either bolted to a drive flange protruding from the differential or splined to the differential in the transaxle; the outer end of each driveaxle has a stub shaft that is splined to the hub and bearing assembly and locked in place with a large bolt.
2 The inner ends of the driveaxles are equipped with sliding constant velocity (CV) joints, which are capable of both angular and axial motion. Each inner CV joint assembly consists of a either a triple rotor-type bearing or a ball-and-cage type bearing and a housing in which the joint is free to slide in-and-out as the driveaxle moves up-and-down with the wheel.
3 The outer ends of the driveaxles are equipped with ball-and-cage type CV joints, which are capable of angular but not axial movement. Each outer CV joint consists of six ball bearings running between an inner race and an outer cage.

4 The boots should be inspected periodically for damage and leaking lubricant. Torn CV joint boots must be replaced immediately or the joints will be damaged. If either boot of a driveaxle is damaged, that driveaxle must be removed in order to replace the boot (see Section 13).
5 Should a boot be damaged, the CV joint can be disassembled and cleaned, but if any parts are damaged, the entire driveaxle assembly may have to be replaced as a unit - check with your local auto parts store regarding the availability of replacement parts and CV joints (see Section 12).
6 The most common symptom of worn or damaged CV joints, besides lubricant leaks, is a clicking noise in turns, a clunk when accelerating after coasting and vibration at highway speeds. To check for wear in the CV joints and driveaxle shafts, grasp each axle (one at a time) and rotate it in both directions while holding the CV joint housings, feeling for play indicating worn splines or sloppy CV joints. Also check the driveaxle shafts for cracks, dents and distortion.

12 Driveaxle - removal and installation

❊❊ WARNING:

The manufacturer recommends replacing the driveaxle/hub bolt with a new one whenever it is removed.

REMOVAL

1   Remove the wheel trim/hub cap (as applicable) and loosen the driveaxle/hub bolt 1/4-turn with the vehicle resting on its wheels. Also loosen the wheel bolts.

2   Raise the front of the vehicle and support it securely on jackstands. Block the rear wheels to prevent the vehicle from rolling off the stands. Remove the wheel.

3   Remove the lower splash shield below the engine (see Chapter 1, Section 6).

Driveaxle models VL90, VL100, VL107, AAR3300i

▶ **Refer to illustration 12.4**

4   Unscrew the bolts securing the inner CV joint to the transaxle drive flange or half shaft and remove the retaining plates from underneath the bolts (see illustration). Support the driveaxle by suspending it with a strap - do not allow it to hang under its weight, or the joint may be damaged.

Driveaxle model AAR2600i

▶ **Refer to illustration 12.5**

5   Place a drain pan under the CV joint to be removed, then pry the inner CV joint out of the transaxle slightly, using a large screwdriver or prybar positioned between the transaxle and the CV joint housing (see illustration). Be careful not to damage the differential seal. Support the driveaxle by suspending it with a strap - do not allow it to hang under its weight, or the joint may be damaged.

All models

▶ **Refer to illustrations 12.9a and 12.9b**

6   Pull the ABS wheel speed sensor partially out of its mounting hole in the steering knuckle (see Chapter 9). This will prevent it from becoming damaged as the driveaxle is withdrawn from the hub.

7   Remove the driveaxle/hub bolt.

8   Remove the balljoint mounting nuts and separate the steering knuckle and balljoint from the control arm (see Chapter 10).

➡ **Note: Disconnect the front level control sensor arm-to-control arm nut and separate the sensor arm from the control arm, if equipped.**

9   If the splines of the outer joint are stuck in the hub, tap the joint out of the hub using a brass drift. If this fails to free it from the hub, the joint will have to be pressed out using a puller (see illustration). Carefully swing the steering knuckle outwards and withdraw the driveaxle outer constant velocity joint from the hub (see illustration).

10   Maneuver the driveaxle out from underneath the vehicle. Remove the gasket from the end of the inner constant velocity joint, if present. Discard the gasket; a new one should be used on installation.

11   Don't allow the vehicle to rest on its wheels with one (or both) driveaxle(s) removed, as damage to the wheel bearing(s) may result. If moving the vehicle is unavoidable, temporarily insert the outer end of the driveaxle(s) in the hub(s) and tighten the driveaxle/hub bolt(s); in this case, the inner end(s) of the driveaxle(s) must be supported, for example by suspending with string from the vehicle underbody. Do not allow the driveaxle to hang down, as the joint may be damaged.

INSTALLATION

Driveaxle models VL90, VL100, VL107, AAR3300i

12   Ensure that the transaxle drive flange and inner joint mating surfaces are clean and dry.

13   Ensure that the outer joint and hub splines and threads are clean, then lubricate the splines with a light coat of multi-purpose grease.

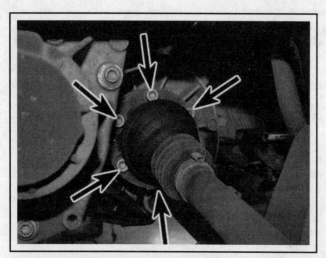

12.4 Driveaxle inner CV joint fastener locations, five of six shown - VL90, VL100, VL107, AAR3300i models

12.5 Carefully pry the inner end of the driveaxle from the transaxle at opposite points - AAR2600i models

12.9a If necessary, press the joint out of the hub using a puller

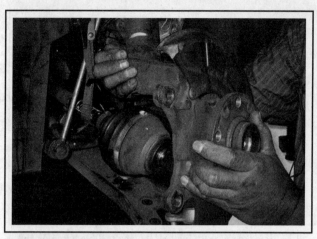

12.9b Carefully swing the knuckle assembly away from the driveaxle

14 Maneuver the driveaxle into position and engage the outer joint with the hub. Install a new bolt and tighten it to draw the joint fully into position. Don't tighten it completely yet (wait until the wheel is installed and the vehicle has been lowered to the ground).

15 Connect the steering knuckle and balljoint to the control arm, tightening the balljoint nuts to the torque listed in the Chapter 10 Specifications.

16 Align the driveaxle inner joint with the transaxle flange and install the retaining bolts and plates. Tighten the bolts to the torque listed in this Chapter's Specifications.

Driveaxle model AAR2600i

17 Pry the old spring clip from the inner end of the driveaxle and install a new one. Lubricate the seal with multi-purpose grease and raise the driveaxle into position while supporting the CV joints.

➡ **Note: Position the spring clip with the opening facing down; this will ease insertion of the driveaxle and prevent damage to the clip.**

18 Push the splined end of the inner CV joint into the differential side gear and make sure the spring clip locks in its groove.

19 Apply a light coat of multi-purpose grease to the outer CV joint

splines, pull out on the steering knuckle assembly and install the stub axle into the hub.

20 Insert the balljoint studs into the control arm and tighten the nuts to the torque listed in the Chapter 10 Specifications.

21 Install a new bolt and tighten it to draw the joint fully into position. Don't tighten it completely yet (wait until the wheel is installed and the vehicle has been lowered to the ground).

22 Grasp the inner CV joint housing (not the driveaxle) and pull out to make sure the driveaxle has seated securely in the transaxle.

All models

23 Ensure that the outer joint is drawn fully into position, then install the wheel and lower the vehicle to the ground.

24 The remainder of installation is the reverse of removal, with the following points:

a) Tighten the driveaxle/hub bolt to the torque and angle of rotation listed in this Chapter's Specifications.

b) Once the driveaxle/hub bolt is correctly tightened, tighten the wheel bolts to the torque listed in the Chapter 1 Specifications and install the wheel trim/hub cap.

c) Refill the transaxle fluid (see Chapter 1) if any was removed.

13 Driveaxle boot replacement and CV joint inspection

➡ **Note: If the CV joints exhibit signs of wear indicating need for an overhaul (usually due to torn boots), explore all options before beginning the job. Complete rebuilt driveaxles are available on an exchange basis, which eliminates much time and work. Whichever route you choose to take, check on the cost and availability of parts before disassembling the driveaxle.**

1 Remove the driveaxle from the vehicle as described in Section 12.

OUTER CV JOINT (ALL MODELS)

▶ **Refer to illustrations 13.2, 13.4, 13.5a, 13.5b, 13.5c, 13.7, 13.8, 13.9, 13.10, 13.17, 13.20a, 13.20b, 13.22a and 13.22b**

2 Secure the driveaxle in a vise equipped with soft jaws, then cut the two outer joint boot retaining clamps off (see illustration).

3 Slide the boot down the shaft to expose the constant velocity (CV) joint and wipe off as much grease as possible.

13.2 Cut the CV joint boot clamps off with a pair of diagonal cutters and discard them

13.4 Drive the outer CV joint off the shaft with a hammer and a brass punch

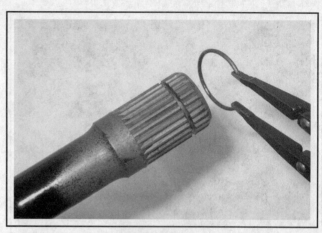

13.5a Remove the snap-ring from the end of the shaft . . .

13.5b . . . the thrust washer . . .

13.5c . . . and the dished washer

13.7 Mark the relationship of the bearing cage, inner race and housing

4   Using a hammer and a brass punch, tap the joint off the end of the driveaxle (see illustration).

✳✳ CAUTION:

Place the punch on the inner race of the CV joint only.

5   Remove the snap-ring from the driveaxle groove (see illustration), then slide the thrust washer and dished washer (if equipped), noting which way they are installed (see illustrations).
6   Slide the boot off the driveaxle and discard it.
7   Clean the outer CV joint assembly to remove as much grease as

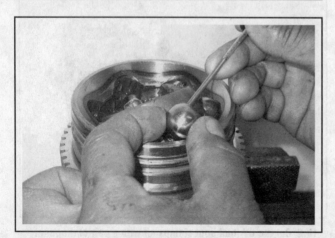

13.8 If necessary, pry the balls out with a screwdriver

13.9 Tilt the inner race and cage 90-degrees, then align the windows in the cage with the lands and rotate the inner race up and out of the outer race

13.10 Align the inner race with the cage windows and rotate the inner race out of the cage

13.17 Apply grease through the splined hole, then insert a wooden dowel into the hole and push down - the dowel will force the grease into the joint

possible. Mark the relative position of the bearing cage, inner race and housing (see illustration).

8 Mount the outer CV joint in a vise equipped with soft jaws. Push down on one side of the cage and remove the ball bearing from the opposite side. Repeat this procedure until all of the balls are removed (see illustration). If the joint is tight, tap on the inner race (not the cage) with a hammer and brass punch.

9 Remove the cage and inner race assembly from the housing by tilting it vertically and aligning two opposing cage windows in the area between the ball grooves (see illustration).

10 Turn the inner race 90-degrees to the cage and align one of the spherical lands with a cage window. Raise the land into the window and swivel the inner race out of the cage (see illustration).

11 Clean all of the parts with solvent and dry them off.

12 Inspect the housing, splines, balls and races for damage, corrosion, wear and cracks. Check the inner race for wear and scoring in the races. If any of the components are not serviceable, the entire CV joint assembly must be replaced with a new one. If the joint is in satisfactory condition, obtain a boot replacement kit; kits usually contain a new boot and retaining clamps, a constant velocity joint snap-ring and the correct type of grease. Only use CV joint grease.

13 Coat all of the CV joint components with CV joint grease before beginning reassembly.

14 Install the inner race in the cage and align the marks made in Step 7.

15 Install the inner race and cage assembly into the CV joint housing, aligning the marks on the inner race and cage assembly with the

mark on the housing.

16 Install the balls into the holes, one at a time, until they are all in place.

17 Apply CV joint grease through the hole in the inner race, then force a wooden dowel down through the hole (see illustration). This will force the grease into the joint. Continue this procedure until the joint is completely packed. Pack the joint with as much grease as you can, then place the remainder of the grease in the boot.

18 Place the axleshaft in the vise. Clean the end of the axleshaft, then slide the new clamp and boot into place.

➡ **Note: It's a good idea to wrap the axleshaft splines with electrical tape to prevent damage to the boot.**

Apply the remainder of the grease from the kit into the CV joint boot.

19 Remove the protective tape from the driveaxle splines.

20 Install a new snap-ring in the groove on the driveaxle (see illustrations), use a small screwdriver to depress the snap-ring, then tap the joint onto the driveaxle until the snap-ring engages with the groove in the inner race. Make sure the joint is securely retained by the snap-ring.

21 Ease the boot over the joint, making sure that the boot lips are correctly located on both the driveaxle and CV joint. Lift the outer sealing lip of the boot to equalize air pressure within the boot.

22 Install the large retaining clamp on the boot. Pull the small clamp

13.20a Install a new snap-ring in the driveaxle groove . . .

13.20b . . . push the snap-ring in and tap the joint into place

13.22a Pull the small clamp as tight as possible and locate the hooks on the clamp in their slots

13.22b Secure the boot clamps with a clamp crimping tool like this, available at most auto parts stores

13.24 Cut the CV joint boot clamps off with a pair of diagonal cutters, then pull the boot back on the shaft

as tight as possible and locate the hooks on the clamp in their slots (see illustration). Tighten the clamp by crimping the raised area with a special boot clamp tool (see illustration). Due to the relatively hard composition of the boots, this type of tool is required to apply adequate crimping force on the clamps. Secure the large retaining clamp using the same procedure.

23 Make sure the constant velocity joint moves freely in all directions, then install the driveaxle as described in Section 12.

INNER CV JOINT

Triple-roller type joint (AAR2600i models)

◆ Refer to illustrations 13.24, 13.25, 13.26, 13.27a, 13.27b, 13.28, 13.32, 13.35 and 13.37

24 Remove the boot clamps (see illustration).
25 Pull the boot back from the inner CV joint and slide the joint housing off. Be sure to mark the relationship of the tri-pod to the outer race (see illustration).
26 Use a center punch to mark the tri-pod and axleshaft to ensure that they are reassembled properly (see illustration).
27 Spread the ends of the stop-ring apart, slide it towards the center of the shaft, then remove the retainer clip from the end of the axleshaft (see illustrations).
28 Use a hammer and a brass punch to drive the tri-pod joint from

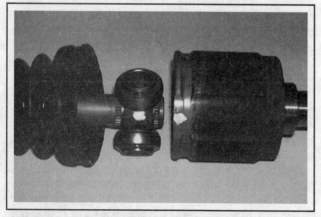

13.25 Mark the relationship of the tri-pod assembly to the outer race

13.26 Use a center punch to place marks on the tri-pod and the driveaxle to ensure that they are properly reassembled

13.27a Spread the ends of the stop-ring apart and slide it towards the center of the shaft . . .

13.27b . . . then slide the tri-pod assembly back and remove the retainer clip

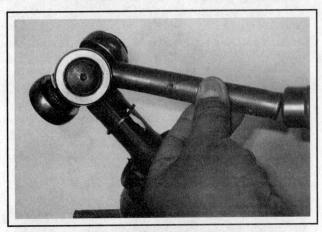

13.28 Drive the tri-pod joint from the axleshaft with a brass punch and hammer - make sure you don't damage the bearing surfaces or the splines on the shaft

the driveaxle (see illustration).

29 Remove the stop-ring from the axleshaft and discard it.

30 Clean the old grease from the outer race and the tri-pod bearing assembly. Carefully disassemble each section of the tri-pod assembly, one at a time so as not to mix up the parts. Clean the needle bearings with solvent.

31 Inspect the rollers, tri-pod, bearings and outer race for scoring, pitting or other signs of abnormal wear, which will warrant the replacement of the inner CV joint.

32 Slide the clamps and boot onto the axleshaft. It's a good idea to wrap the axleshaft splines with tape to prevent damaging the boot (see illustration).

33 Install a new stop-ring on the axleshaft, but don't seat it in its groove; position it on the shaft past the groove.

34 Place the tri-pod on the shaft (making sure the marks are aligned) and install a new bearing retainer clip. Now slide the tri-pod up against the retainer clip and seat the stop-ring in its groove.

35 Apply CV joint grease to the tri-pod assembly, the inside of the joint housing and the inside of the boot (see illustration).

36 Slide the boot into place.

37 Position the CV joint mid-way through its travel, then equalize the pressure in the boot (see illustration).

38 Tighten the boot clamps (see illustrations 9.22a and 9.22b).

39 Install the driveaxle assembly (see Section 12).

13.37 Equalize the pressure inside the boot by inserting a small, dull screwdriver between the boot and the outer race

13.32 Wrap the splined area of the axleshaft with tape to prevent damage to the boot when installing it

13.35 Pack the outer race with CV joint grease and slide it over the tri-pod assembly - make sure the match marks on the CV joint housing and tri-pod line up

Triple-roller type joint (AAR3300i models)

▶ Refer to illustrations 13.41a, 13.41b, 13.42, 13.43, 13.44, 13.45, 13.47, 13.48, 13.49, 13.50, 13.51 and 13.52

40 Remove the boot clamps and discard them (see illustration 13.24), then pull the boot back on the shaft

41 Mount the driveaxle in a vise equipped with soft jaws, then mark

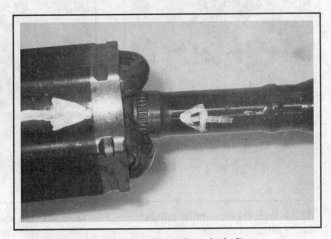

13.41a Mark the joint housing to the axleshaft

13.41b Attach a slide hammer to the triple-roller housing and pull the housing straight off the triple roller

13.42 Mark the triple-roller spider to the axleshaft

the relationship of the joint housing to the axleshaft (see illustration). Attach a slide hammer to the housing and pull the housing off the joint (see illustration).

42 Mark the relationship of the triple-roller to the axleshaft (see illustration).

➡ **Note: All parts must be installed in their original location or the axle joint may be noisy when driving.**

43 Remove the snap-ring from the end of the axleshaft (see illustration).

44 Mark the relationship of the triple-roller spider to the end of the axle shaft (see illustration), then slide the triple-roller off the shaft.

➡ **Note: If the triple-roller won't slide off or tap off easily, it will be necessary to push it off with a hydraulic press.**

45 Remove the inner snap-ring (see illustration), then clean all of the components with solvent. Inspect all components for pitting and other signs of wear (shiny, polished spots are normal and won't affect operation). If any signs of wear are found, replace the entire joint.

46 Install the new small clamp and the new boot onto the shaft. It's a good idea to wrap the splines of the shaft with electrical tape to prevent damage to the boot.

47 Install a new inner snap-ring onto the axle shaft, making sure its seated in the groove (see illustration).

13.43 Using a pair of snap-ring pliers, remove the outer snap-ring from the axleshaft end

13.44 Mark the triple-roller splines to the axleshaft splines

13.45 Using a pair of snap-ring pliers, remove the inner snap-ring from the axleshaft groove

13.47 Install the new inner snap-ring, making sure the snap-ring is seated into the groove

13.48 The triple-roller should be seated against both snap-rings

48 Install the triple-roller on the shaft, aligning the marks made in Step 44. If necessary, use a deep socket or a piece of pipe to drive the triple-roller onto the shaft until it contacts the inner snap-ring. Install a new outer snap-ring, making sure it seats completely in its groove (see illustration).

49 Apply about half of the grease into the boot side of the joint and the remaining grease into the housing (see illustration).

50 Mount the driveaxle in a vise equipped with soft jaws, using a block of wood and hammer, tap the housing onto the triple-roller (see illustration).

⁜ CAUTION:

Do not let the housing tilt while installing it, as it could be damaged.

51 Install the boot onto the housing, then position the housing mid-way through its in-and-out travel. Hold the joint in this position and equalize the pressure in the boot by inserting a small screwdriver between the boot and the housing (see illustration).

52 Place the crimp part of the large clamp in between the bolt hole flanges (see illustration), then tighten both clamps with a pair of clamp

13.51 Position the housing mid-way through its travel, then insert a screwdriver between the housing and boot to equalize the pressure

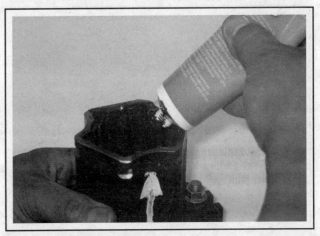

13.49 Apply half of the CV joint grease directly into the housing before installing it onto the axle shaft

13.50 Use a block of wood and hammer to reinstall the housing over the rollers

crimping pliers.

53 Make sure the CV joint moves freely, then install the driveaxle as described in Section 12.

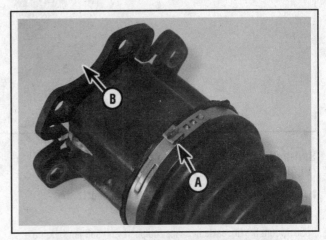

13.52 Make sure the crimped part of the clamp (A) is centered between the bolt hole flanges (B)

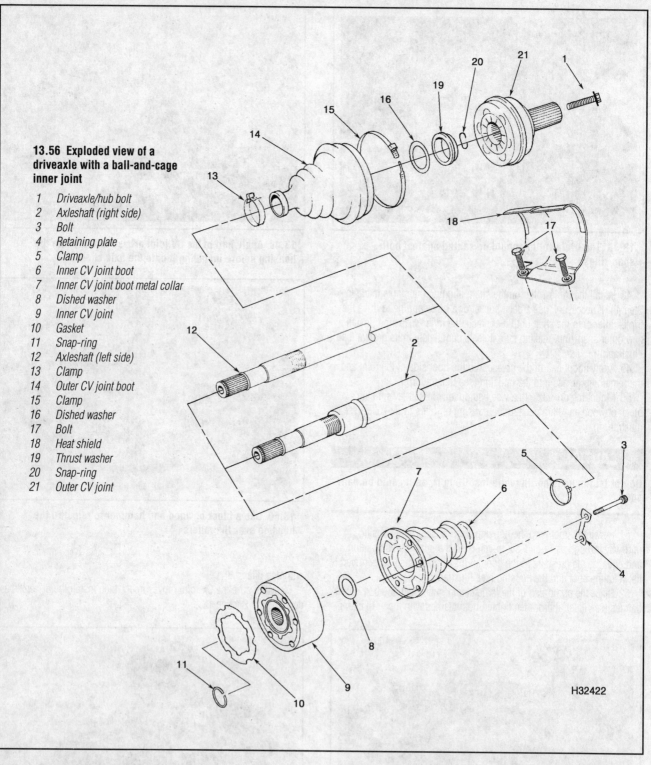

13.56 Exploded view of a driveaxle with a ball-and-cage inner joint

1   Driveaxle/hub bolt
2   Axleshaft (right side)
3   Bolt
4   Retaining plate
5   Clamp
6   Inner CV joint boot
7   Inner CV joint boot metal collar
8   Dished washer
9   Inner CV joint
10 Gasket
11 Snap-ring
12 Axleshaft (left side)
13 Clamp
14 Outer CV joint boot
15 Clamp
16 Dished washer
17 Bolt
18 Heat shield
19 Thrust washer
20 Snap-ring
21 Outer CV joint

H32422

Ball-and-cage type joint (VL90, VL100 and VL107 models)

▶ **Refer to illustrations 13.56, 13.59, 13.66 and 13.67**

54 Remove the boot clamp and discard it.

55 Mount the driveaxle in a vise equipped with soft jaws. Using a hammer and a punch, knock the boot cap off the inner CV joint.

56 Using a pair of snap-ring pliers, remove the snap-ring from its groove in the end of the driveaxle (see illustration).

57 Pull the inner joint off the end of the axleshaft. If it is stuck, use a hammer and a brass punch to drive it off the shaft; apply force to the inner race of the joint only. If it still won't come off, it'll be necessary to push it off with a hydraulic press. Remove the dished washer from the shaft, then pull off the boot.

58 Wipe the grease off the joint and mark the relationship of the inner race, cage and housing.

59 Rotate the cage and inner race 90-degrees and remove it from the housing (see illustration).

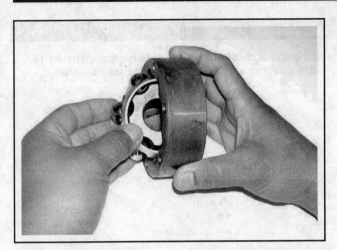

13.59 Turn the cage and inner race 90-degrees and rotate it out of the housing

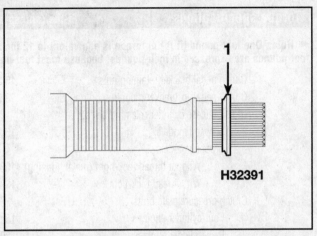

13.66 The concave side of the dished washer (1) must face the end of the axleshaft (ball-and-cage inner CV joint)

60 Remove each ball bearing from the cage, keeping track of their positions so they can be reinstalled in the same spot.

61 Turn the inner race 90-degrees in the cage, align one of the grooves with the edge of the cage and rotate the inner race out.

62 Clean all of the components and inspect for worn or damaged splines, race grooves, ball bearings and cage. Shiny spots are normal and won't affect operation. Replace the joint with a new one if any of the components show signs of wear.

63 Coat the components of the joint with CV joint grease, then assemble the inner race and cage, aligning the marks made in Step 58.

64 Press the ball bearings into their openings, then insert the inner race, cage and balls into the housing. The chamfered side of the splines must face the larger diameter side of the housing. When the components are rotated into place, the wide-spaced grooves of the inner race must be lined up with the wide-spaced grooves in the housing.

65 Install the new boot and clamp on the axleshaft. It's a good idea to wrap the splines of the axleshaft with electrical tape to prevent damage to the boot.

66 Remove the tape and install the dished washer on the axleshaft with the concave side facing the end of the shaft (see illustration).

67 If you're replacing the boot, seat the inner end of the boot in between the smaller diameter portion of the axleshaft (see illustration).

68 Place the inner joint assembly on the axleshaft and install a new snap-ring. Make sure the snap-ring seats in its groove completely.

69 Pack the CV joint with approximately 120 grams (4.2 ounces) of CV joint grease. Place 1/3 of the grease in the joint and the other 2/3 on the inner side of the joint and in the boot.

70 Seat the cap of the boot on the joint housing, aligning the bolt

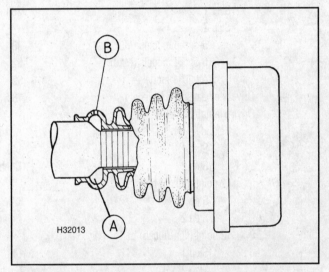

13.67 The inner end of the right inner CV joint boot must be positioned on the axleshaft like this, so the edge of the vent chamber (A) seats on the tube; the vent hole (B) must not be obstructed

holes. Make sure the boot is not twisted or deformed in any way.

71 Clean the surface of the joint housing, then stick a new gasket onto the housing.

72 Make sure the constant velocity joint moves freely in all directions, then install the driveaxle as described in Section 12.

Torque specifications

	Ft-lbs (unless otherwise indicated)	Nm

➡ **Note: One foot-pound (ft-lb) of torque is equivalent to 12 inch-pounds (in-lbs) of torque. Torque values below approximately 15 foot-pounds are expressed in inch-pounds, because most foot-pound torque wrenches are not accurate at these smaller values.**

	Ft-lbs (unless otherwise indicated)	Nm
Clutch pedal bracket retaining nuts*	18.5	25
Clutch pedal-to-bracket mounting bolt/nut*	18.5	25
Clutch release cylinder retaining bolts		
5-speed models	15	20
6-speed models		
Without thread lock-tight (metal housing)	106 in-lbs	12
With thread lock-tight	133 in-lbs	15
Clutch pressure plate bolts		
Four cylinder engines	15	20
Five-cylinder engines	120 in-lbs	13
Flywheel bolts	See Chapter 2A or 2B	
Driveaxle flange bolts		
Step 1	88 in-lbs	10
Step 2		
5-speed models (M8)	30	40
6-speed models (M10)	52	70
All 2011 models	52	70
Driveaxle heat shield fasteners	18.5	25
Driveaxle/hub bolt*		
Hex bolt		
Step 1	148	200
Step 2	Tighten an additional 180-degrees (1/2-turn)	
12 point (ribbed) bolt		
Step 1	52	70
Step 2	Tighten an additional 90-degrees (1/4-turn)	
12 point (non-ribbed) bolt		
Step 1	148	200
Step 2	Tighten an additional 180-degrees (1/2-turn)	

➡ **Note: The ribbed section of the driveaxle/hub bolt is the contact surface under the bolt head.**

Replace with new fastener(s)

Section

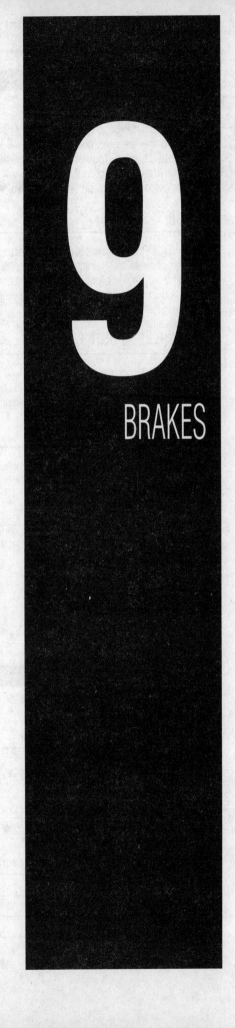

9

BRAKES

1 General information

The vehicles covered by this manual are equipped with hydraulically operated front and rear brake systems. The front brakes are disc type and the rear brakes are either disc or drum type. Both the front and rear brakes are self-adjusting. The disc brakes automatically compensate for pad wear, while the drum brakes incorporate an adjustment mechanism which is activated as the parking brake is applied.

HYDRAULIC SYSTEM

The hydraulic system consists of two separate circuits. The master cylinder has separate reservoirs for the two circuits, and in the event of a leak or failure in one hydraulic circuit, the other circuit will remain operative. A dual proportioning valve on the firewall provides brake balance between the front and rear brakes.

POWER BRAKE BOOSTER

The power brake booster, utilizing engine manifold vacuum and atmospheric pressure to provide assistance to the hydraulically operated brakes, is mounted on the firewall in the engine compartment.

PARKING BRAKE

The parking brake operates the rear brakes only, through cable actuation. It's activated by a lever mounted in the center console.

SERVICE

After completing any operation involving disassembly of any part of the brake system, always test drive the vehicle to check for proper braking performance before resuming normal driving. When testing the brakes, perform the tests on a clean, dry, flat surface. Conditions other than these can lead to inaccurate test results.

Test the brakes at various speeds with both light and heavy pedal pressure. The vehicle should stop evenly without pulling to one side or the other. Avoid locking the brakes, because this slides the tires and diminishes braking efficiency and control of the vehicle.

Tires, vehicle load and wheel alignment are factors which also affect braking performance.

PRECAUTIONS

There are some general cautions and warnings involving the brake system on this vehicle:

a) *Use only brake fluid conforming to DOT 3 specifications.*
b) *The brake pads contain fibers which are hazardous to your health if inhaled. Whenever you work on brake system components, clean all parts with brake system cleaner. Do not allow the fine dust to become airborne. Also, wear an approved filtering mask.*
c) *Safety should be paramount whenever any servicing of the brake components is performed. Do not use parts or fasteners which are not in perfect condition, and be sure that all clearances and torque specifications are adhered to. If you are at all unsure about a certain procedure, seek professional advice. Upon completion of any brake system work, test the brakes carefully in a controlled area before putting the vehicle into normal service. If a problem is suspected in the brake system, don't drive the vehicle until it's fixed.*

Troubleshooting

PROBABLE CAUSE	CORRECTIVE ACTION
No brakes - pedal travels to floor	
1 Low fluid level 2 Air in system	1 and 2 Low fluid level and air in the system are symptoms of another problem - a leak somewhere in the hydraulic system. Locate and repair the leak
3 Defective seals in master cylinder	3 Replace master cylinder
4 Fluid overheated and vaporized due to heavy braking	4 Bleed hydraulic system (temporary fix). Replace brake fluid (proper fix)
Brake pedal slowly travels to floor under braking or at a stop	
1 Defective seals in master cylinder	1 Replace master cylinder
2 Leak in a hose, line, caliper or wheel cylinder	2 Locate and repair leak
3 Air in hydraulic system	3 Bleed the system, inspect system for a leak

PROBABLE CAUSE	CORRECTIVE ACTION

Brake pedal feels spongy when depressed

1 Air in hydraulic system	1 Bleed the system, inspect system for a leak
2 Master cylinder or power booster loose	2 Tighten fasteners
3 Brake fluid overheated (beginning to boil)	3 Bleed the system (temporary fix). Replace the brake fluid (proper fix)
4 Deteriorated brake hoses (ballooning under pressure)	4 Inspect hoses, replace as necessary (it's a good idea to replace all of them if one hose shows signs of deterioration)

Brake pedal feels hard when depressed and/or excessive effort required to stop vehicle

1 Power booster faulty	1 Replace booster
2 Engine not producing sufficient vacuum, or hose to booster clogged, collapsed or cracked	2 Check vacuum to booster with a vacuum gauge. Replace hose if cracked or clogged, repair engine if vacuum is extremely low
3 Brake linings contaminated by grease or brake fluid	3 Locate and repair source of contamination, replace brake pads or shoes
4 Brake linings glazed	4 Replace brake pads or shoes, check discs and drums for glazing, service as necessary
5 Caliper piston(s) or wheel cylinder(s) binding or frozen	5 Replace calipers or wheel cylinders
6 Brakes wet	6 Apply pedal to boil-off water (this should only be a momentary problem)
7 Kinked, clogged or internally split brake hose or line	7 Inspect lines and hoses, replace as necessary

Excessive brake pedal travel (but will pump up)

1 Drum brakes out of adjustment	1 Adjust brakes
2 Air in hydraulic system	2 Bleed system, inspect system for a leak

Excessive brake pedal travel (but will not pump up)

1 Master cylinder pushrod misadjusted	1 Adjust pushrod
2 Master cylinder seals defective	2 Replace master cylinder
3 Brake linings worn out	3 Inspect brakes, replace pads and/or shoes
4 Hydraulic system leak	4 Locate and repair leak

Brake pedal doesn't return

1 Brake pedal binding	1 Inspect pivot bushing and pushrod, repair or lubricate
2 Defective master cylinder	2 Replace master cylinder

Brake pedal pulsates during brake application

1 Brake drums out-of-round	1 Have drums machined by an automotive machine shop
2 Excessive brake disc runout or disc surfaces out-of-parallel	2 Have discs machined by an automotive machine shop
3 Loose or worn wheel bearings	3 Adjust or replace wheel bearings
4 Loose lug nuts	4 Tighten lug nuts

Brakes slow to release

1 Malfunctioning power booster	1 Replace booster
2 Pedal linkage binding	2 Inspect pedal pivot bushing and pushrod, repair/lubricate
3 Malfunctioning proportioning valve	3 Replace proportioning valve
4 Sticking caliper or wheel cylinder	4 Repair or replace calipers or wheel cylinders
5 Kinked or internally split brake hose	5 Locate and replace faulty brake hose

Troubleshooting (continued)

PROBABLE CAUSE	CORRECTIVE ACTION

Brakes grab (one or more wheels)

1 Grease or brake fluid on brake lining	1 Locate and repair cause of contamination, replace lining
2 Brake lining glazed	2 Replace lining, deglaze disc or drum

Vehicle pulls to one side during braking

1 Grease or brake fluid on brake lining	1 Locate and repair cause of contamination, replace lining
2 Brake lining glazed	2 Deglaze or replace lining, deglaze disc or drum
3 Restricted brake line or hose	3 Repair line or replace hose
4 Tire pressures incorrect	4 Adjust tire pressures
5 Caliper or wheel cylinder sticking	5 Repair or replace calipers or wheel cylinders
6 Wheels out of alignment	6 Have wheels aligned
7 Weak suspension spring	7 Replace springs
8 Weak or broken shock absorber	8 Replace shock absorbers

Brakes drag (indicated by sluggish engine performance or wheels being very hot after driving)

1 Brake pedal pushrod incorrectly adjusted	1 Adjust pushrod
2 Master cylinder pushrod (between booster and master cylinder) incorrectly adjusted	2 Adjust pushrod
3 Obstructed compensating port in master cylinder	3 Replace master cylinder
4 Master cylinder piston seized in bore	4 Replace master cylinder
5 Contaminated fluid causing swollen seals throughout system	5 Flush system, replace all hydraulic components
6 Clogged brake lines or internally split brake hose(s)	6 Flush hydraulic system, replace defective hose(s)
7 Sticking caliper(s) or wheel cylinder(s)	7 Replace calipers or wheel cylinders
8 Parking brake not releasing	8 Inspect parking brake linkage and parking brake mechanism, repair as required
9 Improper shoe-to-drum clearance	9 Adjust brake shoes
10 Faulty proportioning valve	10 Replace proportioning valve

Brakes fade (due to excessive heat)

1 Brake linings excessively worn or glazed	1 Deglaze or replace brake pads and/or shoes
2 Excessive use of brakes	2 Downshift into a lower gear, maintain a constant slower speed (going down hills)
3 Vehicle overloaded	3 Reduce load
4 Brake drums or discs worn too thin	4 Measure drum diameter and disc thickness, replace drums or discs as required
5 Contaminated brake fluid	5 Flush system, replace fluid
6 Brakes drag	6 Repair cause of dragging brakes
7 Driver resting left foot on brake pedal	7 Don't ride the brakes

PROBABLE CAUSE	CORRECTIVE ACTION

Brakes noisy (high-pitched squeal)

1 Glazed lining	1 Deglaze or replace lining
2 Contaminated lining (brake fluid, grease, etc.)	2 Repair source of contamination, replace linings
3 Weak or broken brake shoe hold-down or return spring	3 Replace springs
4 Rivets securing lining to shoe or backing plate loose	4 Replace shoes or pads
5 Excessive dust buildup on brake linings	5 Wash brakes off with brake system cleaner
6 Brake drums worn too thin	6 Measure diameter of drums, replace if necessary
7 Wear indicator on disc brake pads contacting disc	7 Replace brake pads
8 Anti-squeal shims missing or installed improperly	8 Install shims correctly

➡ **Note: Other remedies for quieting squealing brakes include the application of an anti-squeal compound to the backing plates of the brake pads, and lightly chamfering the edges of the brake pads with a file. The latter method should only be performed with the brake pads thoroughly wetted with brake system cleaner, so as not to allow any brake dust to become airborne.**

Brakes noisy (scraping sound)

1 Brake pads or shoes worn out; rivets, backing plate or brake shoe metal contacting disc or drum	1 Replace linings, have discs and/or drums machined (or replace)

Brakes chatter

1 Worn brake lining	1 Inspect brakes, replace shoes or pads as necessary
2 Glazed or scored discs or drums	2 Deglaze discs or drums with sandpaper (if glazing is severe, machining will be required)
3 Drums or discs heat checked	3 Check discs and/or drums for hard spots, heat checking, etc. Have discs/drums machined or replace them
4 Disc runout or drum out-of-round excessive	4 Measure disc runout and/or drum out-of-round, have discs or drums machined or replace them
5 Loose or worn wheel bearings	5 Adjust or replace wheel bearings
6 Loose or bent brake backing plate (drum brakes)	6 Tighten or replace backing plate
7 Grooves worn in discs or drums	7 Have discs or drums machined, if within limits (if not, replace them)
8 Brake linings contaminated (brake fluid, grease, etc.)	8 Locate and repair source of contamination, replace pads or shoes
9 Excessive dust buildup on linings	9 Wash brakes with brake system cleaner
10 Surface finish on discs or drums too rough after machining (especially on vehicles with sliding calipers)	10 Have discs or drums properly machined
11 Brake pads or shoes glazed	11 Deglaze or replace brake pads or shoes

Brake pads or shoes click

1 Shoe support pads on brake backing plate grooved or excessively worn	1 Replace brake backing plate
2 Brake pads loose in caliper	2 Loose pad retainers or anti-rattle clips
3 Also see items listed under Brakes chatter	

Troubleshooting (continued)

PROBABLE CAUSE	CORRECTIVE ACTION

Brakes make groaning noise at end of stop

1 Brake pads and/or shoes worn out	1 Replace pads and/or shoes
2 Brake linings contaminated (brake fluid, grease, etc.)	2 Locate and repair cause of contamination, replace brake pads or shoes
3 Brake linings glazed	3 Deglaze or replace brake pads or shoes
4 Excessive dust buildup on linings	4 Wash brakes with brake system cleaner
5 Scored or heat-checked discs or drums	5 Inspect discs/drums, have machined if within limits (if not, replace discs or drums)
6 Broken or missing brake shoe attaching hardware	6 Inspect drum brakes, replace missing hardware

Rear brakes lock up under light brake application

1 Tire pressures too high	1 Adjust tire pressures
2 Tires excessively worn	2 Replace tires
3 Defective proportioning valve	3 Replace proportioning valve

Brake warning light on instrument panel comes on (or stays on)

1 Low fluid level in master cylinder reservoir (reservoirs with fluid level sensor)	1 Add fluid, inspect system for leak, check the thickness of the brake pads and shoes
2 Failure in one half of the hydraulic system	2 Inspect hydraulic system for a leak
3 Piston in pressure differential warning valve not centered	3 Center piston by bleeding one circuit or the other (close bleeder valve as soon as the light goes out)
4 Defective pressure differential valve or warning switch	4 Replace valve or switch
5 Air in the hydraulic system	5 Bleed the system, check for leaks
6 Brake pads worn out (vehicles with electric wear sensors - small probes that fit into the brake pads and ground out on the disc when the pads get thin)	6 Replace brake pads (and sensors)

Brakes do not self adjust

Disc brakes

1 Defective caliper piston seals	1 Replace calipers. Also, possible contaminated fluid causing soft or swollen seals (flush system and fill with new fluid if in doubt)
2 Corroded caliper piston(s)	2 Same as above

Drum brakes

1 Adjuster screw frozen	1 Remove adjuster, disassemble, clean and lubricate with high-temperature grease
2 Adjuster lever does not contact star wheel or is binding	2 Inspect drum brakes, assemble correctly or clean or replace parts as required
3 Adjusters mixed up (installed on wrong wheels after brake job)	3 Reassemble correctly
4 Adjuster cable broken or installed incorrectly (cable-type adjusters)	4 Install new cable or assemble correctly

Rapid brake lining wear

1 Driver resting left foot on brake pedal	1 Don't ride the brakes
2 Surface finish on discs or drums too rough	2 Have discs or drums properly machined
3 Also see Brakes drag	

3   Anti-lock Brake System (ABS) and Electronic Stability Program (ESP) - general information

1   The Anti-lock Brake System (ABS) and Electronic Stabilization Program (ESP) are designed to help maintain vehicle steerability, directional stability and optimum deceleration under severe braking or maneuvering conditions and on most road surfaces. The ABS system is primarily designed to prevent wheel lockup during heavy or panic braking situations. It works by monitoring the rotational speed of each wheel and controlling the brake line pressure to each wheel when engaged. Data provided by the ABS wheel speed sensors is shared with the Electronic Stabilization Program. This very sophisticated system helps with traction control, over/under-steering and acceleration control under all driving conditions. Overall, these systems aid in vehicle control and handling. Other systems added to vehicles with ESP are Electronic Differential Lock (EDL) and Acceleration Slip Regulation (ASR).

COMPONENTS

Actuator assembly

▸ **Refer to illustration 3.2**

2   The actuator assembly is mounted in the engine compartment and consists of an electric hydraulic pump and solenoid valves (see illustration).

a) *The electric pump provides hydraulic pressure to charge the reservoirs in the actuator, which supplies pressure to the braking system. The pump and reservoirs are housed in the actuator assembly.*

b) *The solenoid valves modulate brake line pressure during ABS, ESP or ASR operation.*

Wheel speed sensors

3   There is a wheel speed sensor for each wheel. Each sensor generates a signal in the form of a low-voltage electrical current or a frequency when the wheel is turning. A variable signal is generated as a result of a square-toothed ring (tone-ring, exciter-ring, reluctor, etc.) that rotates very close to the sensor. The signal is directly proportional to the wheel speed and is interpreted by an electronic module (computer).

4   The front sensors are mounted on the steering knuckles.

5   The rear sensors are mounted in the rear suspension knuckles.

ABS/ESP computer

6   The ABS/ESP control module or computer is mounted with the actuator and is the brain of these systems (see illustration 3.2). The function of the computer is to accept and process information received from the wheel speed sensors to control the hydraulic line pressure, avoiding wheel lock up or wheel spin. The computer also constantly monitors the system, even under normal driving conditions, to find faults within the system.

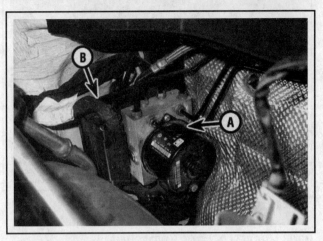

3.2 Typical ABS/ESP actuator (A) and control module (B) assembly

DIAGNOSIS AND REPAIR

7   If a dashboard warning light comes on and stays on while the vehicle is in operation, the ABS or ESP system requires attention. Although special electronic diagnostic testing tools are necessary to properly diagnose the system, you can perform a few preliminary checks before taking the vehicle to a dealer service department.

a) *Check the brake fluid level in the reservoir.*

b) *Verify that the computer electrical connectors are securely connected.*

c) *Check the electrical connectors at the hydraulic control unit.*

d) *Check the fuses.*

e) *Follow the wiring harness to each wheel and verify that all connections are secure and that the wiring is undamaged.*

8   If the above preliminary checks do not rectify the problem, the vehicle should be diagnosed by a dealer service department or other qualified repair shop. Due to the complexity of this system, all actual repair work must be done by a qualified automotive technician.

✳✳ WARNING:

Do NOT try to repair an ABS/ESP wiring harness. These systems are sensitive to even the smallest changes in resistance. Repairing the harness could alter resistance values and cause the system to malfunction. If the wiring harness is damaged in any way, it must be replaced.

✳✳ CAUTION:

Make sure the ignition is turned off before unplugging or reattaching any electrical connections.

3.12a Front wheel speed sensor location

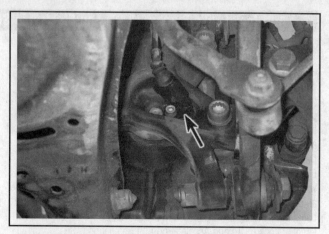

3.12b Rear wheel speed sensor location

WHEEL SPEED SENSOR - REMOVAL AND INSTALLATION

▶ **Refer to illustrations 3.12a and 3.12b**

9   Loosen the wheel lug nuts, raise the vehicle and support it securely on jackstands. Remove the wheel.

10   Make sure the ignition key is turned to the "OFF" position.

11   Trace the wiring back from the sensor, detaching all brackets and clips while noting its correct routing, then disconnect the electrical connector.

12   Remove the mounting bolt and carefully pull the sensor out from the knuckle (see illustrations).

13   Installation is the reverse of the removal procedure. Tighten the mounting fastener securely.

14   Install the wheel and bolts, tightening them securely. Lower the vehicle and tighten the bolts to the torque listed in the Chapter 1 Specifications.

4   Disc brake pads (front) - replacement

▶ **Refer to illustration 4.4**

✳✳ **WARNING:**

Disc brake pads must be replaced on both front wheels at the same time - never replace the pads on only one wheel. Also, the dust created by the brake system is harmful to your health. Never blow it out with compressed air and don't inhale any of it. An approved filtering mask should be worn when working on the brakes. Do not, under any circumstances, use petroleum-based solvents to clean brake parts. Use brake system cleaner only!

✳✳ **WARNING:**

All bolts used to mount the brake calipers are self-locking and designed to be used only once. The manufacturer states to replace caliper mounting bolts any time they are removed.

1   Remove the cap from the brake fluid reservoir. Remove about two-thirds of the fluid from the reservoir, then reinstall the cap.

✳✳ **WARNING:**

Brake fluid is poisonous - never siphon it by mouth. Use a suction gun or old poultry baster. If a baster is used, never again use it for the preparation of food.

✳✳ **CAUTION:**

Brake fluid will damage paint. If any fluid is spilled, wash it off immediately with plenty of clean, cold water.

2   Loosen the front wheel bolts, raise the front of the vehicle and support it securely on jackstands. Block the wheels at the opposite end.

3   Remove the wheels. Work on one brake assembly at a time, using the assembled brake for reference if necessary.

4   Before removing anything, thoroughly clean the caliper and disc with brake system cleaner (see illustration).

4.4 Before disassembling the brake, wash it thoroughly with brake system cleaner and allow it to dry - position a drain pan under the brake to catch the residue - DO NOT use compressed air to blow off the brake dust!

4.5 Before removing the caliper, be sure to depress the piston into its bore in the caliper with a large C-clamp to make room for the new pads

REMOVAL

▶ **Refer to illustrations 4.5, 4.6a, 4.6b, 4.7, 4.8, 4.9a and 4.9b**

5 Push the piston back into the bore to allow the caliper to be removed easily, and to make room for the new, thicker pads (see illustration).

6 Disconnect the brake pad wear indicator electrical connector (see illustration), and remove it from the bracket. Carefully unclip the pad retaining spring and remove it from the brake caliper (see illustration).

7 Remove the end caps from the guide bushing to gain access to the caliper guide pins (see illustration).

8 Unscrew the caliper guide pins, then lift the caliper away from the mounting bracket. Tie the caliper to the suspension strut using a suitable piece of wire; do not allow it to hang unsupported from the flexible brake hose (see illustration).

4.6a Disconnect the brake pad wear indicator sensor connector and remove the sensor connector from the bracket

4.6b Unclip the pad retaining spring and remove it from the caliper

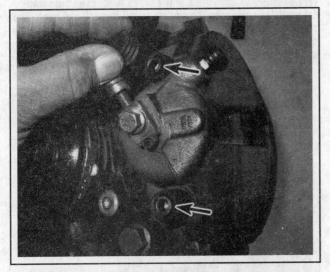

4.7 Remove the protective caps from the guide pins and remove the pins

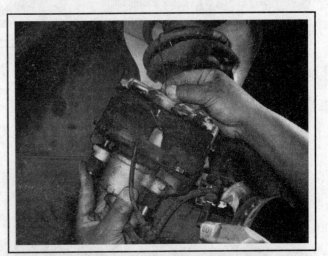

4.8 Remove the caliper from the mounting bracket and support it with a length of wire

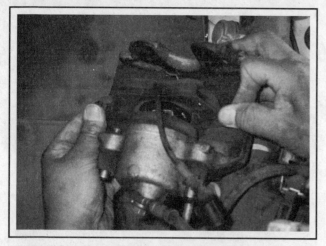

4.9a Unclip the inner pad from the caliper piston . . .

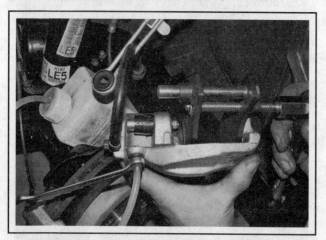

4.12 Connecting a bleeder bottle and opening the bleeder screw while pushing the piston into the caliper will prevent contaminated fluid from being pushed back into the hydraulic system (typical)

9   Unclip the inner pad from the caliper piston and remove the outer pad from the mounting bracket (see illustrations).

INSPECTION

10 Inspect the brake disc carefully as outlined in Section 7. If

4.13a Clip the inner pad into the caliper . . .

4.9b . . . and remove the outer pad from the mounting bracket

machining is necessary, follow the information in that Section to remove the disc, at which time the pads can be removed as well.

11 Prior to fitting the pads, check that the guide pins are free to slide easily in the caliper body bushings, and are a reasonably tight fit. If they're OK, lubricate them with high-temperature brake grease and reinstall them. Use brake system cleaner to clean the caliper and piston. Inspect the dust seal around the piston for damage, and the piston for evidence of fluid leaks, corrosion or damage. If any of these components require attention, the caliper should be replaced.

INSTALLATION

▶ **Refer to illustrations 4.12, 4.13a, 4.13b, 4.14 and 4.16**

12 To make room for the new pads, the caliper piston(s) must be pushed back into the cylinder. Either use a piston retraction tool or a C-clamp. Connect a brake bleeding kit to the caliper bleed screw (see illustration). Open the bleed screw as the piston is retracted; the surplus brake fluid will then be collected in the bleed kit container. Tighten the bleed screw as soon as the piston is retracted to prevent air from being drawn into the system.

➡ **Note: The ABS unit contains hydraulic components that are very sensitive to impurities in the brake fluid. Even the smallest particles can cause the system to fail through blockage. The pad retraction method described here prevents any debris in the brake fluid expelled from the caliper from being passed back to the ABS hydraulic unit.**

13 Clip the inner pad into the caliper piston and fit the outer pad to

4.13b . . . and place the outer pad into the mounting bracket

4.14 Pull out the guide pins and clean them, then apply a coat of high temperature grease to the pins and reinstall the pins in the caliper

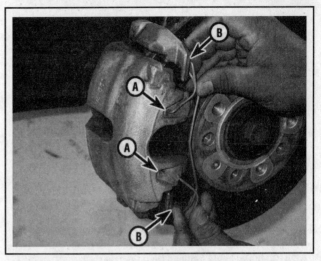

4.16 Install the return spring into the caliper body holes (A), and set the ends of the spring under the caliper mounting bracket (B)

the mounting bracket (see illustrations), ensuring its friction material is against the brake disc. Note that the outer pad has an arrow stamped onto its outer lower edge; this should point in the normal direction of rotation of the brake disc. Remove the adhesive foil backing from the outer pad, if equipped.

14 Lubricate the caliper guide pins with a light coat of high-temperature brake grease (see illustration). Maneuver the caliper into position, then install the caliper guide pins and tighten them to the torque listed in this Chapter's Specifications.

15 Install the end caps to the caliper guide pins.

16 Install the pad retaining spring, ensuring its ends are correctly located in the caliper body holes. Press the inner edge of the spring into position so that its ends are firmly in contact with the surface of the caliper bracket (see illustration).

17 Lock the brake pad wear indicator electrical connector into the bracket and reconnect the electrical connector.

18 Depress the brake pedal repeatedly, until the pads are pressed into contact with the brake disc, and a firm brake pedal feel is obtained.

19 Repeat the above procedure on the remaining front brake caliper.

20 Install the wheels and wheel bolts, then lower the vehicle to the ground and tighten the bolts to the torque listed in the Chapter 1 Specifications.

21 Once again, firmly depress the brake pedal a few times to bring the pads into contact with the disc.

22 Check and, if necessary, top-up the brake fluid level as described in Chapter 1.

23 Test the operation of the brakes carefully before placing the vehicle into normal service.

※ WARNING:

New pads will not give full braking efficiency until they have bedded in. Be prepared for this, and avoid hard braking as much as possible for the first hundred miles or so after pad replacement.

5 Disc brake pads (rear) - replacement

▶ **Refer to illustrations 5.2a, 5.2b, 5.3, 5.4, 5.5a, 5.5b, 5.5c and 5.7**

※ WARNING:

Disc brake pads must be replaced on both rear wheels at the same time - never replace the pads on only one wheel. Also, the dust created by the brake system is harmful to your health. Never blow it out with compressed air and don't inhale any of it. An approved filtering mask should be worn when working on the brakes. Do not, under any circumstances, use petroleum-based solvents to clean brake parts. Use brake system cleaner only!

※ WARNING:

All bolts used to mount the brake calipers are self-locking and designed to be used only once. The manufacturer states to replace caliper mounting bolts any time they are removed.

1 Loosen the rear wheel bolts. Block the front wheels, then raise the rear of the vehicle and support it securely on jackstands. Remove the rear wheels.

2 Disengage the cable end from the parking brake lever (see illustration), slide an open-end wrench over the cable end, then push the

5.2a Slide the cable ball end from the lever . .

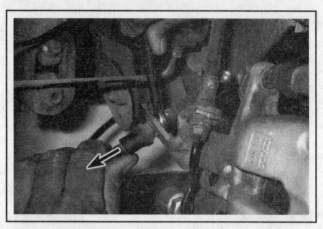

5.2b . . . then, using an open-end wrench, compress the parking brake cable retaining tabs and pull the cable out of the bracket

5.3 When removing the mounting bolts, use an open-end wrench to hold the guide pins and prevent them from rotating

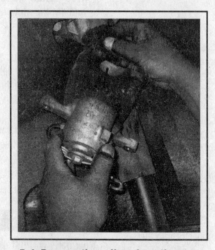

5.4 Remove the caliper from the mounting bracket and support it with a length of wire . . .

5.5a . . . then remove the outer pad . . .

wrench down over the retaining collar to compress the retaining tabs. Once the tabs are compressed, pull the parking brake cable out from the mounting bracket (see illustration).

3   Unscrew the caliper mounting bolts, while holding the guide pins with an open-end wrench to prevent them from rotating (see illustration). Discard the mounting bolts - new bolts must be used on installation.

4   Lift the caliper away from the brake pads (see illustration), and tie it to the suspension strut using a length of wire. Do not allow the caliper to hang unsupported on the flexible brake hose.

5   Remove the brake pads and anti-rattle springs from the caliper

5.5b . . . and the inner pad . . .

5.5c . . . then the anti-rattle springs from the caliper mounting bracket

mounting bracket (see illustrations).

6   Prior to installing the new pads, check that the anti-rattle springs are not damaged and fit tightly to the caliper mounting bracket, check that the guide pins are free to slide easily in the caliper bracket, and check that the rubber guide pin boots are undamaged. Pull the guide pins out and inspect them for signs of wear. If they're OK, lubricate them with high-temperature brake grease and reinstall them. Clean the caliper and piston with brake system cleaner. Inspect the dust seal around the piston for damage, and the piston for evidence of fluid leaks, corrosion or damage. If necessary, replace the caliper.

7   To make room for the new brake pads, it will be necessary to retract the piston fully into the caliper bore by rotating it in a clockwise direction using a retraction tool, or a pair of needle-nose pliers (see illustration).

❉❉ CAUTION:

Do not attempt to push the piston into the caliper with a C-clamp - it must be rotated into its bore as it is being depressed.

Connect a brake bleeding kit to the caliper bleed screw. Open the bleed screw as the piston is retracted; the surplus brake fluid will then be collected in the bleed kit container (see illustration 4.12). Tighten the bleed screw as soon as the piston is retracted to prevent air from being drawn into the system.

➡ **Note: The ABS unit contains hydraulic components that are very sensitive to impurities in the brake fluid. Even the smallest particles can cause the system to fail through blockage. The pad retraction method described here prevents any debris in the brake fluid expelled from the caliper from being passed back to the ABS hydraulic unit.**

8   Peel the protective sheet from the pad backing plates (if equipped), then install the pads in the mounting bracket, ensuring that each pad's friction material is facing the brake disc.

9   Slide the caliper back into position over the pads, making sure the pad anti-rattle springs are correctly positioned against the inner surface of the caliper body and are not jammed in the inspection aperture.

➡ **Note: New mounting bolts must be used when the caliper is installed.**

10 Press the caliper into position, then install the new mounting

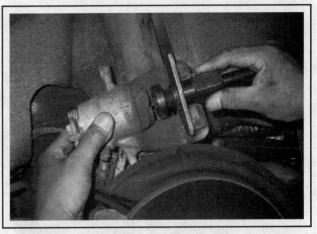

5.7 Using a retraction tool to push and rotate the piston back into the caliper

bolts, tightening them to the torque listed in this Chapter's Specifications while preventing the guide pins from turning with an open-end wrench.

11 Repeat the above procedure on the remaining rear brake caliper.

12 Connect and adjust the parking brake cables (see Section 14).

13 Depress the brake pedal repeatedly to force the pads into firm contact with the discs. Once normal pedal feel has returned, check that the discs rotate freely.

14 Install the wheels and wheel bolts, then lower the vehicle to the ground and tighten the wheel bolts to the torque listed in the Chapter 1 Specifications.

15 Check and, if necessary, top-up the brake fluid level as described in Chapter 1.

16 Test the operation of the brakes carefully before placing the vehicle into normal service.

❉❉ WARNING:

New pads will not give full braking efficiency until they have bedded in. Be prepared for this, and avoid hard braking as much as possible for the first hundred miles or so after pad replacement.

6   Disc brake caliper - removal and installation

❉❉ WARNING:

Dust created by the brake system is harmful to your health. Never blow it out with compressed air and don't inhale any of it. An approved filtering mask should be worn when working on the brakes. Do not, under any circumstances, use petroleum-based solvents to clean brake parts. Use brake system cleaner only!

❉❉ WARNING:

Bolts used to mount the rear brake calipers and mounting brackets are self-locking and designed to be used only once. The manufacturer states to replace caliper mounting bolts any time they are removed.

➡ **Note: Always replace the calipers in pairs - never replace just one of them.**

REMOVAL

◆ **Refer to illustrations 6.3a, 6.3b, 6.3c and 6.4**

1   Loosen the front or rear wheel bolts, raise the front or rear of the vehicle and support it securely on jackstands. Block the wheels at the opposite end. Remove the front or rear wheel.

2   If you are removing a rear caliper, disconnect the cable from the parking brake lever and disengage the cable retaining clips (see illustrations 5.2a and 5.2b).

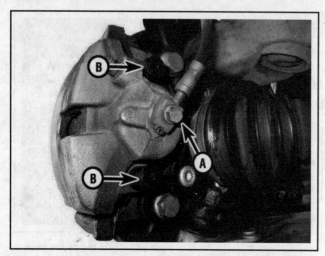

6.3a On front calipers, remove the brake line banjo bolt (A), cap the line and hole, then remove the caps and caliper guide pins (B)

3   If you're removing a front caliper, remove the banjo fitting bolt and disconnect the brake hose from the caliper (see illustration). Discard the sealing washers from each side of the hose fitting (see illustration). Plug the brake hose to prevent fluid loss and the entry of contaminants (see illustration).

4   If you're removing a rear caliper, unscrew the brake line fitting from the caliper, using a flare-nut wrench to prevent rounding-off the corners of the fitting. Remove the brake hose retaining clip (see illustration) and pull the line away from the bracket, then plug the fitting to prevent fluid loss and the entry of contaminants.

➡ **Note: If you're removing the caliper for access to other components, don't disconnect the hose. Suspend the caliper with a piece of wire to prevent damaging the brake hose.**

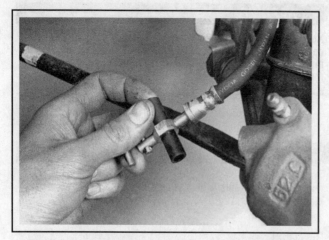

6.3c The front brake hose can be plugged using a snug-fitting piece of tubing

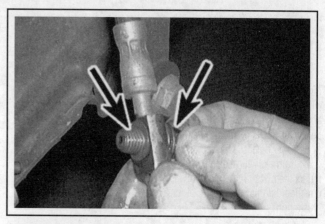

6.3b There is a sealing washer on either side of the front brake hose inlet fitting; be sure to replace these with new ones when reconnecting the hose

5   Remove the caliper guide pins or the mounting bolts and detach the caliper (see Section 4 [front] or 5 [rear]).

INSTALLATION

6   Installation is the reverse of removal. If you're installing a front caliper, use new sealing washers on each side of the brake hose inlet fitting, and tighten the fitting bolt to the torque listed in this Chapter's Specifications. Tighten the mounting fasteners to the torque listed in this Chapter's Specifications.

7   Bleed the brake system (see Section 12). Make sure there are no leaks from the hose connections. Pump the brake pedal several times before driving the vehicle, and test the brakes carefully before returning the vehicle to normal service.

6.4 On rear calipers, disconnect the brake line (A), then remove the brake line retaining clip (B) and maneuver the line out of the bracket

7   Brake disc - inspection, removal and installation

> ✷✷ **WARNING:**
>
> Bolts used to mount the rear brake calipers and mounting brackets are self-locking and designed to be used only once. The manufacturer states to replace caliper mounting bolts any time they are removed.

INSPECTION

▶ Refer to illustrations 7.4, 7.5a, 7.5b, 7.6a and 7.6b

1   Loosen the wheel bolts, raise the vehicle and support it securely on jackstands. Remove the wheel.

2   Remove the brake caliper as outlined in Section 6. It's not necessary to disconnect the brake hose for this procedure. After removing the caliper bolts, suspend the caliper out of the way with a piece of wire. Don't let the caliper hang by the hose and don't stretch or twist the hose.

3   Reinstall the wheel bolts to hold the disc securely against the hub, if necessary. It may be necessary to install washers between the disc and the wheel bolts to take up space.

4   Visually check the disc surface for score marks, cracks and other damage. Light scratches and shallow grooves are normal after use and may not always be detrimental to brake operation. Deep score marks or cracks may require disc refinishing by an automotive machine shop or disc replacement (see illustration). Be sure to check both sides of the disc. If pulsating has been noticed during application of the brakes, suspect disc runout.

➡ **Note: The most common symptoms of damaged or worn brake discs are pulsation in the brake pedal when the brakes are applied or loud grinding noises caused from severely worn brake pads. If these symptoms are extreme, it is very likely that the discs will need to be replaced.**

5   To check disc runout, place a dial indicator at a point about 1/2-inch from the outer edge of the disc (see illustration). Set the indicator to zero and turn the disc. Although the manufacturer doesn't give a runout specification, an indicator reading that exceeds 0.003 inch could cause pulsation upon brake application and will require disc refinishing by an automotive machine shop or disc replacement.

➡ **Note: If disc refinishing or replacement is not necessary, you can de-glaze the brake pad surface on the disc with emery cloth or sandpaper (use a swirling motion to ensure a non-directional finish) (see illustration).**

7.4 The brake pads on this vehicle were obviously neglected, as they wore down completely and cut deep grooves into the disc - wear this severe means the disc must be replaced

7.5a Use a dial indicator to check disc runout; if the reading exceeds the maximum allowable runout limit, the disc will have to be machined or replaced

6   It's absolutely critical that the disc not be machined to a thickness under the specified minimum thickness. The minimum (or discard)

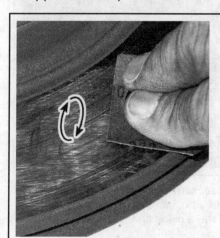

7.5b Using a swirling motion, remove the glaze from the disc surface with sandpaper or emery cloth

7.6a The minimum wear dimension is typically cast or etched into the disc. Inspect all areas (front, back, edges, etc.) of the disc closely to find this information

7.6b Use a micrometer to measure disc thickness

7.7b . . . and this is a typical rear caliper mounting bracket - as viewed from behind

7.8 A disc retaining screw holds the disc to the hub flange

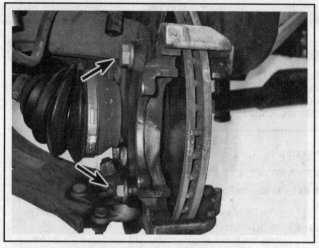

7.7a Remove the caliper mounting bracket fasteners and detach the mounting bracket - this is a typical front caliper mounting bracket . . .

thickness is cast or stamped into the disc (see illustration). The disc thickness can be checked with a micrometer (see illustration).

REMOVAL AND INSTALLATION

▶ Refer to illustrations 7.7a, 7.7b, 7.8, 7.9a and 7.9b

7   Remove the brake caliper and suspend it out of the way with a piece of wire (don't disconnect the line/hose). Remove the caliper mounting bracket (see illustrations).

8   Remove the disc retaining screw and any wheel bolts installed during inspection, and remove the disc (see illustration). If it's stuck, use a mallet to loosen it from the hub.

9   Clean the hub flange and the inside of the brake disc thoroughly; removing any rust or corrosion (see illustrations). Apply a thin film of anti-seize compound between the hub flange and inside of the disc to prevent rust and corrosion prior to the next brake service.

7.9a Clean any rust and corrosion from the areas of the hub flange that contact the disc. A wire brush or sanding tool, designed to be used with a power drill, can make the job a lot easier

10 Install the disc onto the hub and tighten the retaining screw securely.

11 Install the brake caliper mounting bracket and tighten the bolts to the torque listed in this Chapter's Specifications.

12 Install the brake pads and caliper, tightening the bolts to the torque listed in this Chapter's Specifications.

13 Install the wheel, then lower the vehicle to the ground. Tighten the wheel bolts to the torque listed in the Chapter 1 Specifications. Depress the brake pedal a few times to bring the brake pads into contact with the disc. Bleeding of the system will not be necessary unless the brake hose was disconnected from the caliper. Check the operation of the brakes carefully before placing the vehicle into normal service. Also, check the parking brake operation and adjust if necessary.

7.9b Clean any rust or corrosion from the area inside the disc that contacts the hub flange. Again, power tools are very useful for this job

8   Drum brake shoes - replacement

▶ **Refer to illustrations 8.1a, 8.1b, 8.7a, 8.7b, 8.7c, 8.8, 8.9a, 8.9b, 8.10, 8.15a, 8.15b, 8.15c, 8.16, 8.17a, 8.17b, 8.18 and 8.26**

✳✳ WARNING:

Brake shoes must be replaced on both rear wheels at the same time - never replace the shoes on only one wheel, as uneven braking may result. Also, dust created by the brake system is harmful to your health. Never blow it out with compressed air and don't inhale any of it. An approved filtering mask should be worn when working on the brakes. Do not, under any circumstances, use petroleum-based solvents to clean brake parts. Use brake system cleaner only!

1   Raise the rear of the vehicle and support it securely on jackstands, then chock the front wheels to prevent the vehicle from rolling. Release the parking brake, remove the brake drum retaining screw

(similar to the disc retaining screw shown in illustration 7.8), then slide the drum off the hub. If the drum won't come off, insert a screwdriver through one of the wheel bolt holes and pry up on the adjuster wedge; this will retract the shoes away from the drum (see illustrations).

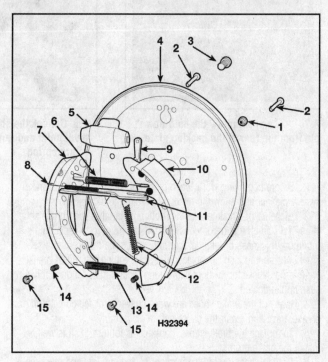

8.1b Drum brake components - exploded view

1	Plug	9	Adjuster wedge
2	Hold-down pin	10	Leading shoe
3	Wheel cylinder bolt	11	Pushrod
4	Backing plate	12	Adjuster spring
5	Wheel cylinder	13	Lower return spring
6	Upper return spring	14	Hold-down spring
7	Trailing shoe	15	Spring cup
8	Locating spring		

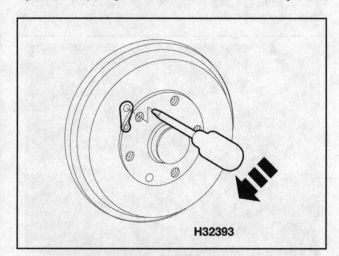

8.1a If the brake drum is tight, release the brake shoes by inserting a flat-bladed screwdriver through a hole in the drum and pry up the adjuster wedge

8.7a Remove the spring cup . . .

8.7b . . . then remove the hold-down spring . . .

8.7c . . . and withdraw the hold-down pin from the rear of the backing plate

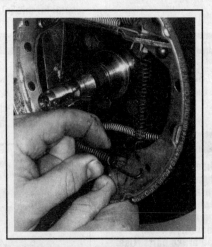

8.8 Unhook the shoes from the lower pivot point and remove the lower return spring

8.9a Free the shoes from the wheel cylinder (note the rubber band used to retain pistons) . . .

2   Before beginning work, wash off the brake assembly with brake system cleaner and allow the residue to drain into a drip pan.

3   Measure the thickness of the friction material of each brake shoe at several points; if either shoe is worn at any point to the specified minimum thickness or less, all four shoes must be replaced as a set. The shoes should also be replaced if any are fouled with oil or grease; there is no satisfactory way of degreasing friction material once it has been contaminated.

4   If any of the brake shoes are worn unevenly, or fouled with oil or grease, trace and repair the cause before reassembly.

5   To replace the brake shoes, continue as follows. If all is well, install the brake drum.

6   Note the position of the brake shoes and springs, and mark the webs of the shoes, if necessary, to aid installation.

7   Remove the hold-down cups and springs by depressing and turning them 90-degrees. This can be accomplished with a special hold-down spring tool or, if you're careful, a pair of pliers. With the cups removed, lift off the springs and withdraw the hold-down pins (see illustrations).

8   Ease the shoes out one at a time from the lower pivot point to release the tension of the return spring, then disconnect the lower return spring from both shoes (see illustration).

9   Ease the upper end of both shoes out from their wheel cylinder locations, taking care not to damage the wheel cylinder seals, and disconnect the parking brake cable from the lever on the trailing shoe. The

8.9b . . . then detach the parking brake cable and remove the shoe from the vehicle

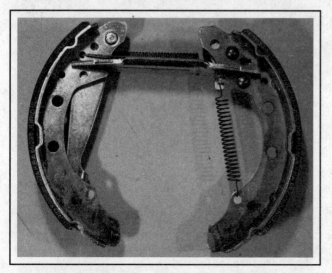

8.10 Prior to disassembly, note the correct installed location of the shoe assembly components

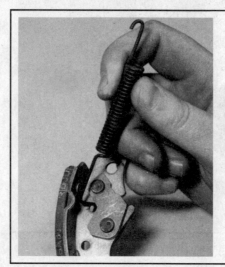

8.15a Hook the locating spring into the leading shoe . . .

brake shoe assembly can then be maneuvered out of position and away from the backing plate. Do not depress the brake pedal until the brakes are reassembled; wrap a strong rubber band around the wheel cylinder pistons to retain them (see illustrations).

10 Make a note of the correct installed positions of all components (see illustration), then unhook the upper return spring, and disengage the adjuster wedge spring.

11 Unhook the locating spring, and remove the pushrod from the trailing shoe, together with the wedge key.

12 Examine all components for signs of wear or damage and replace as necessary.

➡ **Note: All return springs should be replaced, regardless of their apparent condition.**

13 Peel back the protective caps, and check the wheel cylinder for fluid leaks or other damage; check that both cylinder pistons are free to move easily. Refer to Section 9, if necessary, for the wheel cylinder replacement procedure.

14 Apply a little high-temperature brake grease to the contact areas of the pushrod and parking brake lever.

15 Hook the locating spring into the leading shoe. Engage the

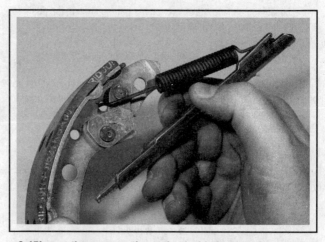

8.15b . . . then engage the pushrod with the opposite end of the spring . . .

pushrod with the opposite end of the spring, and pivot the pushrod into position on the shoe (see illustrations).

16 Install the adjuster wedge between the leading shoe and pushrod, making sure it is installed correctly (see illustration).

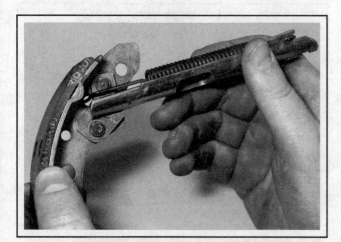

8.15c . . . and pivot the pushrod into position on the shoe

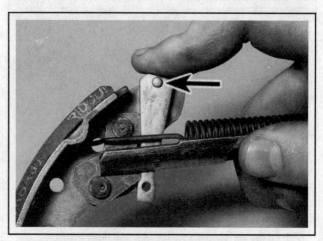

8.16 Slide the adjuster wedge into position in its slot, making sure its raised dot is facing away from the shoe

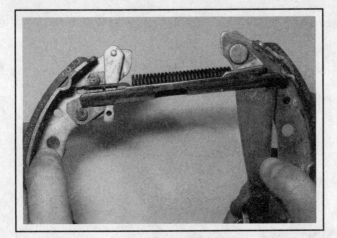

8.17a Locate the trailing shoe in the pushrod . . .

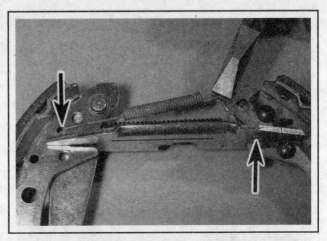

8.17b . . . and hook the upper return spring into position in the trailing shoe and pushrod

17 Locate the parking brake lever on the trailing shoe in the pushrod, and install the upper return spring using a pair of pliers (see illustrations).

18 Install the spring on the adjuster wedge and hook it onto the leading shoe (see illustration).

19 Clean the backing plate and apply a thin film of high-temperature brake grease or anti-seize compound to the shoe contact areas on the backing plate and to the wheel cylinder pistons and lower pivot point. Do not allow the lubricant to contact the friction material.

20 Remove the rubber band installed on the wheel cylinder, then install the shoe assembly.

21 Connect the parking brake cable to the parking brake lever, then locate the top of the shoes in the wheel cylinder piston slots.

22 Install the lower return spring between the shoes, then lever the bottom of the shoes onto the bottom anchor.

23 Tap the shoes to centralize them with the backing plate, then install the shoe hold-down pins and springs, securing them in position with the spring cups.

24 Install the brake drum and retaining screw.

25 Repeat the above procedure on the other rear brake.

26 Before installing the drum it should be checked for cracks, score marks, deep scratches and hard spots, which will appear as small discolored areas. If the hard spots cannot be removed with sandpaper

or emery cloth, or if any of the other conditions listed above exist, the drum must be taken to an automotive machine shop to have it resurfaced.

➡ **Note: Professionals recommend resurfacing the drums whenever a brake job is done. Resurfacing will eliminate the possibility of out-of-round or tapered drums. If the drums are worn so much that they can't be resurfaced without exceeding the maximum allowable diameter (stamped into the drum), then new ones will be required. At the very least, if you elect not to have the drums machined, remove the glazing from the surface with sandpaper or emery cloth using a swirling motion (see illustration).**

27 Once both sets of rear shoes have been replaced, install the brake drums and adjust the lining-to-drum clearance by repeatedly depressing the brake pedal until normal (non-assisted) pedal pressure returns.

28 Check and, if necessary, adjust the parking brake as described in Section 14.

29 Check the brake fluid level as described in Chapter 1.

➡ **Note: New shoes will not give full braking efficiency until they have bedded-in. Be prepared for this, and avoid hard braking as far as possible for the first hundred miles or so after shoe replacement.**

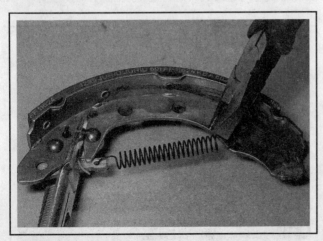

8.18 Fit the spring to the wedge key, and hook it onto the leading shoe

8.26 Remove the glaze from the drum surface with sandpaper or emery cloth

9 Wheel cylinder - removal and installation

✳✳ WARNING:

Dust created by the brake system is harmful to your health. Never blow it out with compressed air and don't inhale any of it. An approved filtering mask should be worn when working on the brakes. Do not, under any circumstances, use petroleum-based solvents to clean brake parts. Use brake system cleaner only!

REMOVAL

▶ **Refer to illustration 9.4**

1   Remove the brake drum as described in Section 8. Clean the brake assembly with brake cleaner and allow the residue to drain into a drip pan.

2   Using pliers, carefully unhook the upper brake shoe return spring and remove it from both brake shoes. Pull the upper ends of the shoes away from the wheel cylinder to disengage them from the pistons.

3   Minimize fluid loss by first removing the master cylinder reservoir cap, then tighten it down with a piece of cellophane to obtain an airtight seal.

4   Using a flare nut wrench, if available, unscrew the brake line fitting nut at the wheel cylinder (see illustration). Carefully ease the line out of the wheel cylinder and plug its end to prevent dirt entry. Wipe off any spilled fluid immediately.

5   Unscrew the wheel cylinder retaining bolt from the rear of the backing plate and remove the cylinder; take great care not to allow brake fluid to contaminate the brake shoe linings.

INSTALLATION

6   Ensure that the backing plate and wheel cylinder mating surfaces are clean, then spread the brake shoes and maneuver the wheel cylinder into position.

7   Engage the brake line and screw in the fitting nut two or three turns to ensure that the thread has started.

8   Insert the wheel cylinder retaining bolt and tighten it to the torque listed in this Chapter's Specifications. Tighten the brake line fitting nut securely.

9   Remove the cellophane from the master cylinder reservoir cap.

10 Ensure that the brake shoes are correctly located in the cylinder pistons, then carefully install the brake shoe upper return spring, using a screwdriver to stretch the spring into position.

11 Install the drum.

12 Bleed the brake hydraulic system as described in Section 12. Providing precautions were taken to minimize loss of fluid, it should only be necessary to bleed the relevant rear brake.

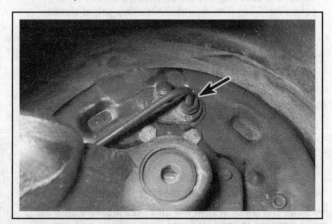

9.4 Unscrew the brake line fitting from the wheel cylinder with a flare-nut wrench to prevent rounding off the corners of the fitting

10 Master cylinder - removal and installation

REMOVAL

▶ **Refer to illustrations 10.4 and 10.8**

✳✳ CAUTION:

Brake fluid will damage paint or finished surfaces. Refer to the Precautions in Section 1.

✳✳ CAUTION:

If the battery is disconnected, several systems must be re-learned before they will work properly (see Chapter 5, Section 3).

➡ **Note:** The master cylinder is not serviceable; replace it with a new or rebuilt unit if it's defective.

1   Remove the engine cover (see Chapter 1, Section 7).

2   Disconnect the cable from the negative battery terminal (see Chapter 5).

3   Remove the battery and battery tray (see Chapter 5).

4   Unplug the electrical connectors for the brake fluid level warning switch, and on 11/2005 and later models, the brake light switch (see illustration).

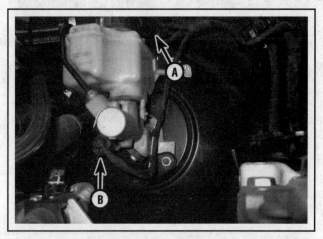

10.4 Disconnect the brake fluid level warning switch (A), and on 11/2005 and later models, the brake light switch (B)

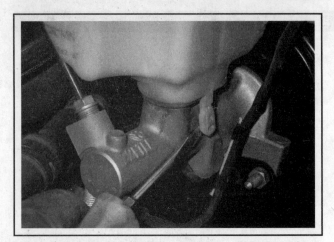

10.8 Carefully pull the locking tabs outwards on each side of the reservoir

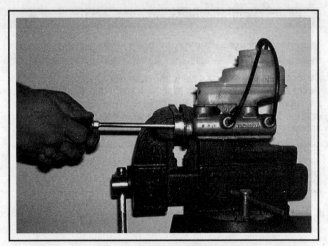

10.12 The best way to bleed air from the master cylinder before installing it on the vehicle is with a pair of bleeder tubes that direct brake fluid into the reservoir during bleeding

5   Remove the reservoir cap and siphon as much fluid as possible from the reservoir with a syringe or equivalent.

6   On manual transaxle models, disconnect and plug the clutch master cylinder hose from the back of the brake master cylinder reservoir.

7   On 11/2005 and later models, remove the brake light mounting fastener and the switch (see Section 16).

8   Carefully pull the locking tabs on the reservoir outwards (see illustration) and lift the reservoir up and out from the master cylinder.

9   Clean the area around the brake line fittings at the master cylinder and the ABS/ESP actuator assembly thoroughly with brake cleaner. Place rags beneath the fittings to catch fluid, then detach the brake lines. Cap or plug all openings to prevent contamination.

10 Remove the master cylinder mounting nuts, then detach the master cylinder and heat shield (if equipped) from the power booster.

➡ **Note: If a new master cylinder is being installed, be sure to install new seals when transferring the reservoir.**

INSTALLATION

▶ **Refer to illustration 10.12**

11 Bench bleed the new master cylinder before installing it. Mount the master cylinder in a vise, with the jaws of the vise clamping on the mounting flange.

12 Attach a pair of master cylinder bleeder tubes to the outlet ports of the master cylinder (see illustration).

13 Fill the reservoir with brake fluid of the recommended type (see Chapter 1).

14 Slowly push the pistons into the master cylinder (a large Phillips screwdriver can be used for this) - air will be expelled from the pressure chambers and into the reservoir. Because the tubes are submerged in fluid, air can't be drawn back into the master cylinder when you release the pistons.

15 Repeat the procedure until no more air bubbles are present.

16 Remove the bleed tubes, one at a time, and install plugs in the open ports to prevent fluid leakage and air from entering. Install the reservoir cap.

17 Install the master cylinder over the studs on the power brake booster and tighten the attaching nuts only finger tight at this time.

18 Thread the brake line fittings into the master cylinder. Since the master cylinder is still a bit loose, it can be moved slightly in order for the fittings to thread in easily. Do not strip the threads as the fittings are tightened.

19 Tighten the mounting nuts to the torque listed in this Chapter's Specifications, then tighten the brake line fittings securely.

20 On manual transaxle models, connect the clutch master cylinder hose from the back of the brake master cylinder reservoir.

➡ **Note: The clutch system will also need bleeding after the brake system has been bled (see Chapter 8).**

21 Fill the master cylinder reservoir with fluid, then bleed the master cylinder and the brake system as described in Section 12. To bleed the cylinder on the vehicle, have an assistant depress the brake pedal and hold the pedal to the floor. Loosen the fitting to allow air and fluid to escape. Repeat this procedure on both fittings until the fluid is clear of air bubbles.

✳ CAUTION:

Have plenty of rags on hand to catch the fluid - brake fluid will ruin painted surfaces. After the bleeding procedure is completed, rinse the area under the master cylinder with clean water.

22 Test the operation of the brake system carefully before placing the vehicle into normal service.

✳ WARNING:

Do not operate the vehicle if you are in doubt about the effectiveness of the brake system. It is possible for air to become trapped in the anti-lock brake system hydraulic control unit, so, if the pedal continues to feel spongy after repeated bleedings or the BRAKE or ANTI-LOCK light stays on, have the vehicle towed to a dealer service department or other qualified shop to be bled with the aid of a scan tool.

11 Brake hoses and lines - inspection and replacement

INSPECTION

1   Once a year, with the vehicle raised and supported securely on jackstands, the rubber hoses which connect the steel brake lines with the front and rear brake assemblies should be inspected for cracks, chafing of the outer cover, leaks, blisters and other damage. These are important and vulnerable parts of the brake system and inspection should be complete. A light and mirror will be helpful for a thorough check. If a hose exhibits any of the above conditions, replace it with a new one.

REPLACEMENT

Front brake hose

▶ **Refer to illustration 11.3**

2   Loosen the wheel bolts, raise the vehicle and support it securely on jackstands. Remove the wheel.

3   At the frame bracket (see illustration), note how the small tabs of the hose fitting sit in the bracket and keep it from rotating.

4   Support the hose fitting with an open-end wrench, and unscrew the brake line fitting from the hose. Use a flare-nut wrench to prevent rounding off the corners of the nut and be careful not to lose the spring clip on the end of the hose fitting.

5   At the caliper end of the hose, remove the inlet fitting bolt and discard the old sealing washers (see illustration 6.3a). Disconnect the brake hose from the caliper.

6   Remove the spring clip from the bracket at the lower end of the strut, then lift the hose from the bracket.

7   To install the hose, place the hose into the bracket on the strut and install the spring clip, using new sealing washers and making sure the hose isn't twisted. Tighten the inlet fitting bolt at the caliper to the torque listed in this Chapter's Specifications.

8   Place the brake hose fitting into the frame bracket while making sure the hose isn't twisted between the caliper and the frame bracket.

9   Connect the brake line fitting to the hose, starting the threads by hand. Install the spring clip then tighten the fitting securely.

10 Bleed the caliper (see Section 12).

11 Install the wheel and bolts, lower the vehicle and tighten the bolts to the torque listed in the Chapter 1 Specifications.

Rear brake hose

▶ **Refer to illustration 11.12**

12 The rear brake hose has a fitting at each end, with a mounting bracket at the body and the caliper, secured by spring clips (see illustration).

13 Support the hose fitting with an open-end wrench, and unscrew the brake line fitting from the hose, using pliers remove the spring clip that locks the hose to the bracket.

➡ **Note: Use a flare-nut wrench to prevent rounding off the corners of the nut.**

14 At the caliper end of the hose, use a flare nut wrench to separate the hose fitting from the caliper.

15 Connect the hose fitting to the caliper and tighten it with a flare-nut wrench.

16 On models with rear drum brakes, unscrew the brake line fitting from the wheel cylinder (see illustration 9.4).

17 Detach the line from the plastic clips along the rear axle and remove the line from the vehicle.

18 Installation is the reverse of removal. Tighten the line securely and bleed the caliper or wheel cylinder served by the line that was replaced (see Section 12).

19 Install the wheel and bolts, then lower the vehicle and tighten the bolts to the torque listed in the Chapter 1 Specifications.

Metal brake lines

20 When replacing brake lines, be sure to use the correct parts. Don't use copper tubing for any brake system components. Purchase

11.3 Typical front brake hose details

1   Brake hose
2   Hose fitting
3   Frame bracket/spring clip
4   Strut bracket/spring clip

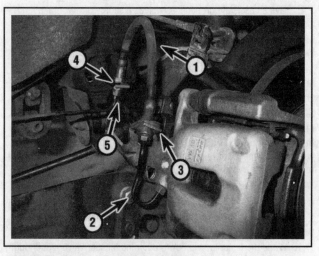

11.12 Typical rear brake hose details

1   Brake hose
2   Caliper brake line
3   Caliper bracket/spring clip
4   Brake hose bracket/spring clip
5   Brake line

genuine steel brake lines from a dealer or auto parts store.

21 Prefabricated brake line, with the tube ends already flared and fittings installed, is available at auto parts stores and dealer parts departments.

22 When installing the new line, make sure it's securely supported in the brackets and has plenty of clearance between moving or hot components.

23 After installation, check the master cylinder fluid level and add fluid as necessary. Bleed the brake system (see Section 12) and test the brakes carefully before driving the vehicle in traffic.

12 Brake hydraulic system - bleeding

▶ **Refer to illustration 12.8**

❄❄ **WARNING:**

Wear eye protection when bleeding the brake system. If the fluid comes in contact with your eyes, immediately rinse them with water and seek medical attention.

➡ **Note: Bleeding the hydraulic system is necessary to remove any air that manages to find its way into the system when it's been opened during removal and installation of a hose, line, caliper or master cylinder.**

1   You'll probably have to bleed the system at all four brakes if air has entered it due to low fluid level, or if the brake lines have been disconnected at the master cylinder.

2   If a brake line was disconnected only at a wheel, then only that caliper must be bled. If a brake line is disconnected at a fitting located between the master cylinder and any of the brakes, that part of the system served by the disconnected line must be bled.

3   Raise the vehicle about one foot and support it securely on jackstands.

4   Remove any residual vacuum from the brake power booster by pressing the brake pedal several times with the engine off.

5   Remove the master cylinder reservoir cap and fill the reservoir with brake fluid. Reinstall the cover.

➡ **Note: Continue to add fluid while bleeding the system to prevent the fluid level from dropping too low; if this happens, air will enter the master cylinder.**

6   Have an assistant on hand, as well as a supply of new brake fluid, a clear container partially filled with clean brake fluid, a length of clear tubing to fit over the bleeder valve and a wrench to open and close the bleeder valve.

7   Beginning at the left front wheel, loosen the bleeder valve slightly, then tighten it to a point where it's snug but can still be loosened quickly and easily.

➡ **Note: Use a six-point box-end wrench or socket to loosen the bleeder valve. For bleeder valves that appear to be stuck, clean the area where the valve screws into the caliper with a small wire brush, then apply penetrating oil to the threads and allow it to soak in for awhile.**

8   Place one end of the tubing over the bleeder valve and submerge the other end in brake fluid in the container (see illustration).

9   Have the assistant depress the brake pedal slowly, then hold the pedal down firmly.

10 While the pedal is held down, open the bleeder valve just enough to allow a flow of fluid to leave the valve. Watch for air bubbles to exit the submerged end of the tube. When the fluid flow slows after a couple of seconds, close the valve and have your assistant release the pedal.

11 Repeat Steps 9 and 10 until no more air is seen leaving the tube, then carefully tighten the bleeder valve and proceed to the right front wheel, the left rear wheel and the right rear wheel, in that order, and perform the same procedure. Be sure to check the fluid in the master cylinder reservoir frequently.

12 Never use old brake fluid. It contains moisture that can boil, rendering the brake system inoperative.

13 Refill the master cylinder with fluid at the end of the operation.

14 Check the operation of the brakes. The pedal should feel solid when depressed, with no sponginess. If necessary, repeat the entire process.

❄❄ **WARNING:**

Do not operate the vehicle if you are in doubt about the effectiveness of the brake system. It's possible for air to become trapped in the ABS hydraulic control unit, so, if the pedal continues to feel spongy after repeated bleedings or the BRAKE or ABS light stays on, have the vehicle towed to a dealer service department or other qualified repair shop to be bled.

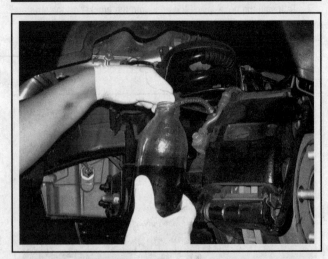

12.8 When bleeding the brakes, a hose is connected to the bleeder valve at the caliper and the other end is submerged in brake fluid. Air will be seen as bubbles in the tube and container. All air must be expelled before moving to the next wheel

13 Power brake booster - check, removal and installation

❊❊ CAUTION:

If the battery is disconnected, several systems must be re-learned before they will work properly (see Chapter 5, Section 3).

➡ Note: On some models equipped with an automatic transaxle, a vacuum pump supplies vacuum to the power brake booster in addition to manifold vacuum. The pump is mounted near the ABS/ESP hydraulic unit and has a vacuum hose routed to the brake booster. Vehicles equipped with a brake booster vacuum pump require diagnosis by a dealer service department if the system appears to be defective.

➡ Note: The power brake booster is not serviceable; replace it with a new or rebuilt unit if it's defective.

➡ Note: The master cylinder is removed along with the power brake booster as an assembly. They are separated after they are removed.

OPERATING CHECK

1 Depress the brake pedal several times with the engine off and make sure there's no change in the pedal reserve distance.

2 Depress the pedal and start the engine. If the pedal goes down slightly, operation is normal.

AIRTIGHTNESS CHECK

3 Start the engine and turn it off after one or two minutes. Depress the brake pedal slowly several times. If the pedal depresses less each time, the booster is airtight.

4 Depress the brake pedal while the engine is running, then stop the engine with the pedal depressed. If there's no change in the pedal reserve travel after holding the pedal for 30 seconds, the booster is airtight.

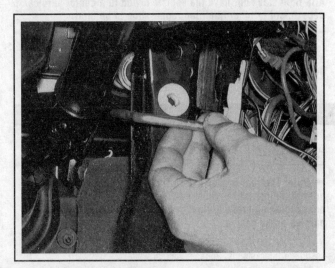

13.11b The tool is used to push on the plastic retaining lugs to release the brake pedal

REMOVAL

▶ Refer to illustrations 13.11a, 13.11b, 13.11c, 13.13 and 13.17

❊❊ CAUTION:

Brake fluid will damage paint or finished surfaces. Refer to the Precautions in Section 1.

5 With the engine off, press the brake pedal several times to remove any stored vacuum in the power brake booster.

6 Remove the engine cover (see Chapter 1, Section 7).

7 Disconnect the cable from the negative battery terminal (see Chapter 5).

8 Remove the battery and battery tray (see Chapter 5).

9 Remove the driver's side knee bolster (see Chapter 11).

10 On 11/2005 and earlier production models, remove the brake light switch (see Section 16).

11 Detach the booster pushrod from the brake pedal (see illustrations).

12 Working inside the engine compartment, remove the master cylinder (see Section 10).

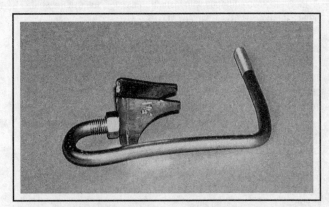

13.11a A tool, fabricated from a modified exhaust clamp, can be used to detach the booster pushrod from the brake pedal

13.11c The retaining lugs and pedal assembly viewed from the rear

13.13 Brake booster check valve

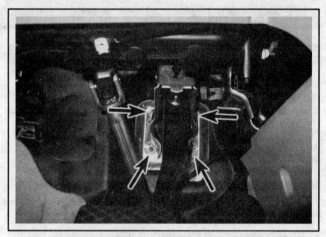

13.17 To detach the brake booster from the firewall, remove the mounting nuts

13 Remove the vacuum hose from the brake booster (see illustration).

14 Disconnect the brake booster vacuum sensor electrical connector, if equipped.

➡ **Note: If the booster is being replaced, pull the vacuum sensor from the booster and install it on the new booster.**

15 On models equipped with manual transaxles, remove the shift cables and bracket (see Chapter 7A).

16 On models equipped with automatic transaxles, clamp off and disconnect the transaxle cooler line (see Chapter 7B).

17 Working inside of the vehicle, remove the lower trim panel and the booster mounting nuts (see illustration). Carefully remove the booster out from the cowl compartment. Separate the master cylinder from the booster.

INSTALLATION

18 Assemble the master cylinder to the power brake booster. Make sure to match the pushrod to the master cylinder correctly during assembly.

19 The remainder of the installation procedures are essentially the reverse of removal.

a) *Tighten all mounting fasteners to the torque values listed in this Chapter's Specifications.*

b) *To bleed the master cylinder on the vehicle, have an assistant pump the brake pedal several times slowly, then hold the pedal to the floor. Loosen the line fittings one at a time to allow air and fluid to escape. Repeat this procedure on both fittings until the fluid is clear of air bubbles.*

✶✶ CAUTION:

Have plenty of rags on hand to catch the fluid - brake fluid will ruin painted surfaces.

c) *Bleed the brake system (see Section 12) and test the operation of the brakes before putting the vehicle into normal service.*

✶✶ WARNING:

Do not operate the vehicle if you are in doubt about the effectiveness of the brake system. It's possible for air to become trapped in the ABS hydraulic control unit, so, if the pedal continues to feel spongy after repeated bleedings or the BRAKE or ABS light stays on, have the vehicle towed to a dealer service department or other qualified repair shop to be bled.

➡ **Note: The clutch system will also need bleeding after the brake system has been bled (see Chapter 8).**

14 Parking brake - check and adjustment

CHECK

1 Pulling up the parking brake lever five clicks should engage the parking brake fully. If the number of clicks is much less, there's a chance the parking brake might not be releasing completely resulting in brake drag. If the number of clicks is much more, the parking brake may not hold the vehicle on an incline.

2 One method of checking the parking brake is to park the vehicle on a steep hill with the parking brake set and the transmission in Neutral (be sure to stay in the vehicle for this check!). If the parking brake cannot prevent the vehicle from rolling, it's in need of adjustment.

ADJUSTMENT

➡ **Note: The rear brakes are self-adjusting, and do not require normal maintenance adjustments. Adjustment is only required after replacing brake drums, brake shoes, wheel cylinders or parking brake cables.**

3 Block the front wheels, raise the rear of the vehicle and support it securely on jackstands. Remove the rear wheels.

4 Remove the center console (see Chapter 11, Section 26).

5 Apply the brake pedal several times then release the pedal, then apply the parking brake several times and release the parking brake to center the cables.

Rear drum brake models

6   With the parking brake set on the fourth notch of the ratchet mechanism, tighten the adjusting nut until it is difficult to turn both rear wheels. Once this is so, fully release the parking brake lever and check that the wheels/hub rotate freely. Check the adjustment by applying the brake fully and counting the clicks emitted from the parking brake ratchet. If necessary, re-adjust.

7   Once adjustment is correct, hold the adjusting nuts and securely tighten the locknuts.

8   Installation is the reverse of removal.

Rear disc brake models

▶ **Refer to illustration 14.9**

9   Insert a 1/16-inch (1.5 mm) feeler gauge between each rear caliper lever and the stop (see illustration).

10   Tighten the adjusting nut at the parking brake lever until there is a slight drag on the feeler gauges.

11   Remove the feeler gauges and set the parking brake fully. Release the parking brake and confirm the gap between the caliper lever and the stop is between 3/64 and 1/8-inch (1 to 3 mm).

12   Apply the parking brake and confirm the brake holds.

14.9 Measure the gap between the parking brake lever and the stop on the rear caliper

13   Release the parking brake and confirm that the brakes don't drag when the rear wheels are turned.

14   Installation is the reverse of removal.

15 Brake pedal - removal and installation

▶ **Refer to illustrations 15.5 and 15.6**

1   Remove the driver's side knee bolster for access (see Chapter 11).

2   Disconnect the brake light switch electrical connector (see Section 16), if equipped.

3   Disconnect the brake booster pushrod from the brake pedal (see Section 13).

4   Remove the pedal bracket support retaining nut, if equipped.

5   Loosen the nuts securing the pedal support bracket to the firewall/booster (see illustration), enough to allow the bracket some movement. Do not remove the nuts completely.

6   Remove the pivot shaft nut (see illustration) and slide the pivot shaft to the left, until the pedal is free. Remove the pedal and pivot bushings.

7   Installation is the reverse of removal.

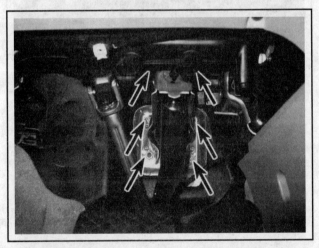

15.5 Brake pedal bracket mounting nut locations (top nuts only visible from under the instrument panel)

15.6 Location of the pedal pivot shaft nut

16 Brake light switch - removal and installation

BRAKE PEDAL MOUNTED SWITCH (11/2005 AND EARLIER PRODUCTION MODELS)

▶ **Refer to illustration 16.2**

➡ **Note: For the purpose of a secure fit, the manufacturer recommends installing the brake light switch only once.**

1   Remove the driver's side knee bolster for access (see Chapter 11).
2   Disconnect the brake light switch electrical connector (see illustration).
3   Rotate the switch about 45 degrees counterclockwise, then carefully remove it from the bracket.
4   Before installing the switch, pull the plunger on the switch out fully.
5   With the brake pedal fully released (up), install the switch in its bracket in the opposite manner that it was removed. The switch will self-adjust by design when installed correctly.

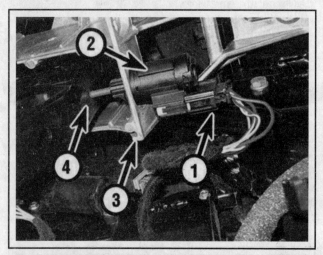

16.2 Typical brake light switch mounting details - 11/2005 and earlier production models

1 *Electrical connector*	4 *Switch plunger and brake*
2 *Brake light switch*	*pedal*
3 *Mounting bracket*	

6   Connect the electrical connector. Confirm that the brake lights are operating properly.
7   Replace the knee bolster.

MASTER CYLINDER MOUNTED SWITCH (11/2005 AND LATER PRODUCTION MODELS)

▶ **Refer to illustration 16.10**

8   Remove the engine cover (see Chapter 1, Section 7).
9   Remove the air inlet hoses (see *Air filter - removal and installation* in Chapter 4).
10 Disconnect the brake light switch electrical connector (see illustration).
11 Remove the brake light switch mounting fastener.
12 Slide the brake light switch down and out from the retaining tab.
13 Install the switch and tighten the retaining fastener securely. The switch will self-adjust by design when installed correctly.
14 Connect the electrical connector. Confirm that the brake lights are operating properly.
15 Install the air inlet hoses and engine cover.

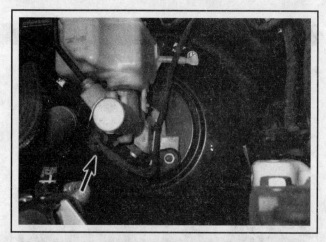

16.10 Typical brake light switch location - 11/2005 and later production models

17 Brake system vacuum pump - removal and installation

♦ **Refer to illustration 17.3**

➡ **Note: A vacuum pump is used on models equipped with an automatic transaxle.**

1 Remove the engine cover (see Chapter 1, Section 7).

2 Disconnect the cable from the negative battery terminal (see Chapter 5).

3 Disconnect the vacuum line from the pump (see illustration).

➡ **Note: The vacuum pump is located on the front side of the transaxle.**

4 Disconnect the vacuum pump electrical connector and the harness connectors, and set the harness to the side.

5 Remove the vacuum pump mounting bracket retaining bolts and remove the pump and bracket as an assembly.

6 Remove the vacuum pump-to-bracket retaining bolts and separate the pump from the bracket.

7 Installation is the reverse of removal.

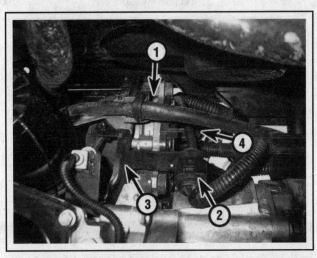

17.3 Vacuum pump details

1	Vacuum pump	3	Mounting bracket
2	Electrical connector	4	Vacuum hose connector

Specifications

General

Brake fluid type	See Chapter 1
Parking brake adjustment gap	0.060 inch (1.5 mm)

Disc brakes

Minimum brake pad thickness	See Chapter 1
Disc minimum thickness	Cast into disc
Disc runout limit	Not specified (see Section 7 of this Chapter)

Rear drum brakes

Shoe friction material minimum thickness	See Chapter 1
Maximum inside diameter	Cast into drum
Maximum out-of-round	Not specified (see Section 8, Step 26 of this Chapter)

Torque specifications

	Ft-lbs (unless otherwise indicated)	Nm

➥ **Note:** One foot-pound (ft-lb) of torque is equivalent to 12 inch-pounds (in-lbs) of torque. Torque values below approximately 15 foot-pounds are expressed in inch-pounds, because most foot-pound torque wrenches are not accurate at these smaller values.

Brake disc retaining screw	35 in-lbs	4
Caliper guide pins (mounting bolts)		
Front	22	30
Rear*	26	35
Caliper mounting bracket bolts		
Front	140	190
Rear*		
Step 1	66	90
Step 2	Tighten an additional 1/4-turn (90-degrees)	
Brake hose-to-caliper banjo bolt (front)	28	38
Brake hose-to-caliper (rear)	120 in-lbs	14
Master cylinder-to-brake booster nuts	18	25
Brake booster nuts	18	25
Vacuum pump-to-bracket bolts	72 in-lbs	8
Vacuum pump bracket-to-automatic transaxle bolts	18	25
Wheel bolts	See Chapter 1	
Wheel cylinder bolt	72 in-lbs	8

*Replace with new fasteners

Section

Reference to other Chapters

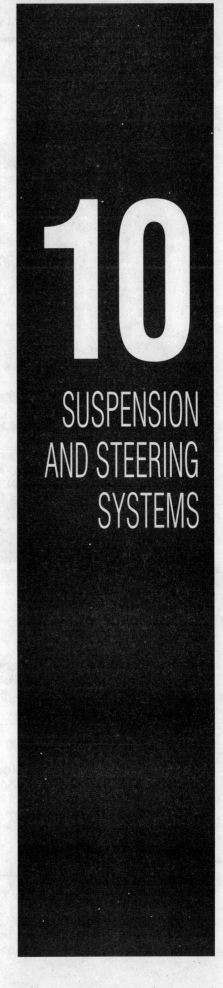

10

SUSPENSION AND STEERING SYSTEMS

1.1 Front suspension components

1	Control arm	3	Balljoint	5	Tie-rod end
2	Strut and spring assembly	4	Stabilizer bar (end)	6	Subframe

1 General information and precautions

FRONT SUSPENSION

▶ **Refer to illustration 1.1**

The front suspension is a MacPherson strut design. The upper end of each strut is attached to the vehicle's body strut support. The lower end of the strut is connected to the upper end of the steering knuckle. The steering knuckle is attached to a balljoint mounted on the outer end of the suspension control arm (see illustration).

REAR SUSPENSION

▶ **Refer to illustration 1.2**

The rear suspension on all except some 2011 Jetta models consists of a multi-link suspension which incorporates upper and lower control arms (or transverse links), trailing arms, knuckle and hub assemblies,

rear tie-rods connected to the knuckles, shock absorbers, coil springs, and a stabilizer bar (see illustration). On some 2011 Jetta models, a solid beam rear axle, shock absorbers and coil springs are used.

STEERING

The steering column is connected to the steering gear by a universal joint.

The steering gear is mounted on the front subframe and is connected by two tie-rods, with balljoints at their outer ends, to the steering arms projecting rearwards from the steering knuckles.

An electromechanical power steering system is used on all 2010 and earlier models, consisting of a power steering servo (motor) mounted to the steering gear, ECM, torque sensor and angle rotation sensor. Some 2011 Jetta models are equipped with a hydraulic power steering system that is powered by a belt driven pump, driven off of the crankshaft pulley.

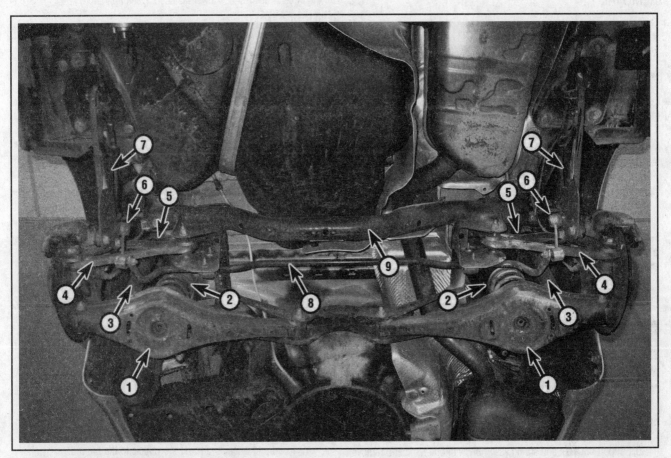

1.2 Rear suspension components

1 Lower control arm (transverse link)	4 Tie-rod	7 Trailing arm
2 Coil spring	5 Upper control arm (transverse link)	8 Stabilizer bar
3 Shock absorber	6 Stabilizer bar link	9 Subframe

PRECAUTIONS

Frequently, when working on the suspension or steering system components, you may come across fasteners which seem impossible to loosen. These fasteners on the underside of the vehicle are continually subjected to water, road grime, mud, etc., and can become rusted or frozen, making them extremely difficult to remove. In order to unscrew these stubborn fasteners without damaging them (or other components), be sure to use lots of penetrating oil and allow it to soak in for a while. Using a wire brush to clean exposed threads will also ease removal of the nut or bolt and prevent damage to the threads. Sometimes a sharp blow with a hammer and punch will break the bond between a nut and bolt threads, but care must be taken to prevent the punch from slipping off the fastener and ruining the threads. Heating the stuck fastener and surrounding area with a torch sometimes helps too, but isn't recommended because of the obvious dangers associated with fire. Long breaker bars and extension, or cheater, pipes will increase leverage, but never use an extension pipe on a ratchet - the ratcheting mechanism could be damaged. Sometimes tightening the nut or bolt first will help to break it loose. Fasteners that require drastic measures to remove should always be replaced with new ones. Many of the fasteners (nuts

and bolts) that are used to mount the suspension components are self-locking (prevailing torque) and designed to be used only once. The manufacturer requires replacement of self-locking fasteners whenever they are loosened or removed.

Since most of the procedures dealt with in this Chapter involve jacking up the vehicle and working underneath it, a good pair of jackstands will be needed. A hydraulic floor jack is the preferred type of jack to lift the vehicle, and it can also be used to support certain components during various operations.

❋❋ WARNING:

Never, under any circumstances, rely on a jack to support the vehicle while working on it. Whenever any of the suspension or steering fasteners are loosened or removed they must be inspected and, if necessary, replaced with new ones of the same part number or of original equipment quality and design. Torque specifications must be followed for proper reassembly and component retention. Never attempt to heat or straighten any suspension or steering components. Instead, replace any bent or damaged part with a new one.

2 Strut assembly - removal, inspection and installation

REMOVAL

▶ **Refer to illustrations 2.4 and 2.10**

1 Remove the wheel trim/hub cap and loosen the driveaxle bolt and wheel bolts by half a turn with the vehicle resting on its wheels.

2 Chock the rear wheels of the car, firmly apply the parking brake, then raise the front of the vehicle and support it securely on jackstands. Remove the wheel and axle bolt.

3 Disconnect the stabilizer bar link from the strut (see Section 6).

4 Remove the fastener and bracket that holds the brake hose and ABS sensor harness connector to the strut (see illustration).

5 Remove the strut-to-knuckle nut and knock the bolt out with a hammer and punch.

6 Remove the balljoint-to-control arm nuts and separate the control arm from the balljoint (see Section 8).

➡ **Note: Disconnect the front level control sensor arm-to-control arm nut and separate the sensor arm from the control arm, if equipped.**

7 Separate the strut from the steering knuckle (see Chapter 8) and support the driveaxle.

⁂ **CAUTION:**

The driveaxle must be supported once its removed from the knuckle or damage will occur to the inner CV joint.

8 Temporarily re-connect the control arm to the steering knuckle and support it with a floor jack.

9 Remove the cowl panel (see Chapter 11).

10 Support the strut and spring assembly with one hand and remove

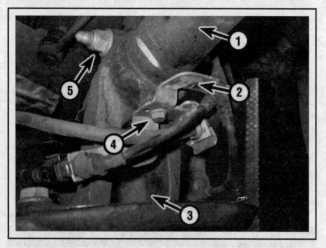

2.4 Strut mounting details

1	Strut	4	Bracket fastener
2	Bracket	5	Strut-to-knuckle pinch
3	Steering knuckle		bolt/nut

the three strut-to-shock tower fasteners (see illustration).

INSPECTION

11 Check the strut body for leaking fluid, dents, cracks and other obvious damage that would warrant repair or replacement.

12 Check the coil spring for chips or cracks in the spring coating (this can cause premature spring failure due to corrosion). Inspect the spring seat for cuts, hardness and general deterioration.

13 If any undesirable conditions exist, proceed to the strut disassembly procedure (see Section 4).

INSTALLATION

14 Guide the strut assembly up into the fenderwell and install the mounting bolts. This is most easily accomplished with the help of an assistant, as the strut is quite heavy and awkward.

➡ **Note: There are two arrows on the top of the strut bearing retainer; make sure to align one of the two arrows pointing towards the front of the car.**

15 Slide the steering knuckle into the strut flange and insert the bolt. Install the nut and tighten it to the torque listed in this Chapter's Specifications.

16 Reattach the brake hose and speed sensor wiring harness bracket to the strut.

17 Separate the control arm from the steering knuckle. Install the driveaxle into the hub splines and connect the control arm to the balljoint (see Chapter 8).

18 Tighten the three upper mounting fasteners to the torque listed in this Chapter's Specifications.

19 Install the wheel and lower the vehicle to the ground.

20 Tighten the driveaxle/hub bolt to the torque listed in the Chapter 8 Specifications, then tighten the wheel bolts to the torque listed in the Chapter 1 Specifications.

21 Installation is the reverse of the removal procedure.

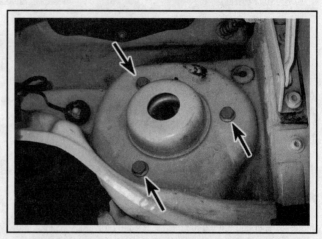

2.10 Remove the strut upper mounting fasteners

3   Strut/coil spring assembly - replacement

♦ Refer to illustrations 3.3, 3.4, 3.5a, 3.5b, 3.5c, 3.5d and 3.9

✳✳ WARNING:

Always replace the struts or coil springs in pairs - never replace just one of them, as handling peculiarities may result.

✳✳ WARNING:

Before attempting to disassemble the strut/coil spring assembly, obtain a tool to hold the coil spring in compression. Do not attempt to use makeshift methods. Uncontrolled release of the spring could cause damage and personal injury or even death. Use a high-quality spring compressor, and carefully follow the tool manufacturer's instructions provided with it. After removing the coil spring with the compressor still installed, place it in a safe, isolated area.

1   If the front suspension strut/coil springs exhibit signs of wear (leaking fluid, loss of damping capability, sagging or cracked coil springs), they should be disassembled and overhauled as necessary. The struts themselves cannot be serviced, and should be replaced if faulty; the springs and related components can be replaced individually. To maintain balanced characteristics on both sides of the vehicle, the components on both sides should be replaced at the same time.

2   With the assembly removed from the vehicle (see Section 2),

3.3 Make sure the spring compressor tool is on securely

clean away all external dirt, then mount the assembly in a vise.

3   Install the coil spring compressor tools (ensuring that they are fully engaged), and compress the spring until all tension is relieved from the upper mount (see illustration).

4   Hold the strut piston rod with an Allen key and unscrew the thrust bearing retaining nut with a box-end wrench (see illustration).

5   Withdraw the top mount, upper spring seat and spring, followed by the boot, bearing and bump stop (see illustrations).

3.4 Loosen and remove the piston rod nut

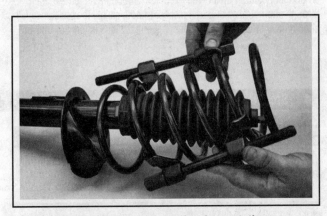

3.5a Remove the upper mount and spring seat, then carefully remove the spring . . .

3.5b . . . followed by the boot . . .

3.5c . . . the spring seat bearing . . .

3.5d . . . and the bump stop

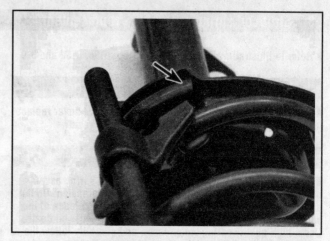

3.9 When installing the spring, make sure the ends fit into the recessed portion of the seats

6   If a new spring is to be installed, the original spring must now be carefully released from the compressor. If it is to be re-used, the spring can be left in compression.

7   With the strut assembly now completely disassembled, examine all the components for wear and damage, and check the bearing for smoothness of operation. Replace components as necessary.

8   Examine the strut for signs of fluid leakage. Check the piston rod for signs of pitting along its entire length, and check the strut body for signs of damage. Test the operation of the strut, while holding it in an upright position, by moving the piston through a full stroke, then through short strokes of 2 to 4 inches. In both cases, the resistance felt should be smooth and continuous. If the resistance is jerky or uneven,

or if there is any visible sign of wear or damage, replacement is necessary.

9   Reassembly is the reverse of disassembly, noting the following points:

  a)   *The coil springs must be installed with the paint mark at the bottom.*

  b)   *Make sure that the coil spring ends are correctly located in the upper and lower seats before releasing the compressor (see illustration).*

  c)   *Tighten the piston rod nut to the specified torque.*

4   Steering knuckle - removal and installation

※※ WARNING:

The manufacturer recommends replacing the driveaxle/hub bolt, control arm pivot bolts and nuts and all other self-locking nuts with new ones whenever they are removed (see Section 1).

➡ **Note: Remove the hub and wheel bearing assembly if the steering knuckle is going to be replaced (see Section 5).**

REMOVAL

1   Remove the wheel cover and loosen the driveaxle/hub bolt with the vehicle resting on its wheels. Loosen the wheel bolts.

2   Chock the rear wheels of the car, firmly apply the parking brake, then raise the front of the car and support it securely on jackstands. Remove the front wheel.

3   Remove the driveaxle/hub bolt.

4   Remove the ABS wheel speed sensor as described in Chapter 9.

5   Remove the brake caliper (don't disconnect the hose) and brake disc (see Chapter 9). Using a piece of wire or string, tie the caliper to the coil spring - don't let the caliper hang by the hose.

6   Detach the tie-rod end from the steering knuckle (see Section 20).

7   Detach the lower balljoint from the steering knuckle (see Section 8).

➡ **Note: Disconnect the front level control sensor arm-to-control arm nut and separate the sensor arm from the control arm, if equipped.**

8   Remove the strut-to-knuckle nut and knock the bolt out with a hammer and punch (see Section 2).

➡ **Note: It may be necessary to spread open the gap where the strut slides into the knuckle.**

9   Carefully pull the knuckle assembly outwards while pushing the driveaxle from the hub. If necessary, tap the CV joint out of the hub using a soft-faced hammer. If this fails to free it from the hub, the joint will have to be pressed out using a puller. Support the driveaxle with wire or an equivalent and never let it hang (see Chapter 8).

※※ CAUTION:

Be careful not to overextend the inner CV joint.

INSTALLATION

10   Lubricate the splines of the driveaxle with multi-purpose grease.

11   Maneuver the knuckle/hub assembly into position and engage it with the driveaxle stub shaft. Install a new driveaxle/hub bolt, but don't attempt to tighten it yet.

12 Connect the strut to the knuckle, pushing the strut into the bore as far as possible. Install the new nut and bolt, and tighten the bolt and nut to the torque listed in this Chapter's Specifications.

13 Connect the control arm to the balljoint. Install new nuts and tighten them to the torque listed in this Chapter's Specifications.

14 Engage the tie-rod end with the steering knuckle, then install the retaining nut. Tighten the nut to the torque values listed in this Chapter's Specifications.

15 Install the brake disc and caliper, tightening the caliper mounting bracket bolts (if equipped) and caliper guide pins to the torque values listed in the Chapter 9 Specifications.

16 Install the ABS wheel speed sensor as described in Chapter 9.

17 Install the wheel and lower the vehicle to the ground.

18 Tighten the driveaxle/hub bolt to the torque listed in the Chapter 8 Specifications, then tighten the wheel bolts to the torque listed in the Chapter 1 Specifications.

5 Hub and wheel bearing (front) - removal and installation

REMOVAL

▶ **Refer to illustrations 5.6 and 5.7**

※※ **WARNING:**

The manufacturer recommends replacing the driveaxle/hub bolt, control arm pivot bolts and nuts and all other self-locking nuts with new ones whenever they are removed (see Section 1).

1 Loosen the driveaxle/hub bolt (see Chapter 8).

2 Loosen the wheel bolts, raise the vehicle and support it securely on jackstands. Remove the wheel.

3 Remove the brake caliper, the caliper mounting bracket and the brake disc from the hub (see Chapter 9).

※※ **CAUTION:**

Be sure to support the brake caliper with a length of wire or rope.

4 Remove the wheel speed sensor (see Chapter 9).

5 Remove the driveaxle/hub bolt and tap the CV joint out of the hub as far as possible using a soft-faced hammer. If this fails to free it from the hub, the joint will have to be pressed out using a puller.

6 Remove the shield from the steering knuckle (see illustration).

7 Remove the hub/bearing assembly mounting bolts from the rear of the steering knuckle (see illustration).

➡ **Note: If the tool you are using cannot engage the fasteners with the driveaxle in place, remove the driveaxle (see Chapter 8).**

8 Remove the hub/bearing assembly from the steering knuckle and driveaxle. Be careful not to allow the inner CV joint of the driveaxle overextend.

INSTALLATION

9 Make sure that the mounting surfaces inside the steering knuckle and on the driveaxle splines are smooth and free of burrs and nicks prior to installing the hub/bearing assembly.

10 Lubricate the driveaxle splines with multi-purpose grease, then guide the axle into the hub/bearing assembly as the hub/bearing is mated to the steering knuckle. Install a new driveaxle/hub bolt, but don't attempt to tighten it yet.

11 Tighten the hub/bearing bolts to the torque listed in this Chapter's Specifications.

12 Install the brake disc, the caliper mounting bracket and the caliper; tighten the fasteners to the torque values listed in the Chapter 9 Specifications.

13 Install the wheel, remove the jackstands and lower the vehicle.

14 Tighten the driveaxle/hub bolt to the torque listed in the Chapter 8 Specifications.

15 Tighten the wheel bolts to the torque listed in the Chapter 1 Specifications.

5.6 Remove the disc shield mounting bolts

5.7 Front hub and bearing mounting bolts

6 Stabilizer bar and bushings (front) - removal and installation

▶ Refer to illustrations 6.3 and 6.6

✳✳ WARNING:

The manufacturer recommends replacing the stabilizer bar link nuts and stabilizer bar clamp bolts with new ones whenever they are removed (see Section 1).

1   Raise the front of the vehicle and support it securely on jackstands.

2   Remove the lower splash shield below the engine (see Chapter 1, Section 6).

3   Remove the fasteners and detach the stabilizer bar links from the stabilizer bar (see illustration).

4   Remove the pendulum mount (see Chapter 2A or 2B) and disconnect the steering column U-joint coupler from the steering gear (see illustration 22.6b).

5   Remove the exhaust pipe support bracket fasteners from the subframe.

6   Remove the stabilizer bar bushing clamp fasteners (see illustration).

➡ **Note: Disconnect the front level control sensor arm-to-control arm nut and separate the sensor arm from the control arm, if equipped.**

7   Place a floor jack under the subframe, remove the rear subframe fasteners and loosen the front subframe fasteners. Lower the subframe no more than three inches.

8   Detach the stabilizer bar bushing clamps and remove the stabilizer bar from the subframe.

9   Inspect the clamp bushings and the link bushings. If they're cracked, hardened or deteriorated in any way, replace them.

10 Installation is the reverse of the removal procedure. Tighten the fasteners to the torque values listed in this Chapter's Specifications.

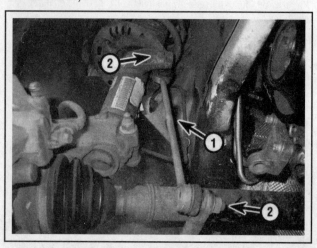

6.3 Front stabilizer link details

1	Stabilizer bar link	3	Stabilizer bar link-to-bar nut
2	Stabilizer bar link-to-strut nut		

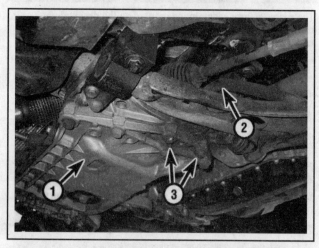

6.6 Front stabilizer bar details (right side shown)

1	Subframe	3	Stabilizer bar fasteners
2	Stabilizer bar		

7 Control arm (front) - removal, bushing replacement and installation

✳✳ WARNING:

The manufacturer recommends replacing the control arm pivot bolts and nuts, the balljoint nuts and the strut through-bolt/nut with new ones whenever they are removed (see Section 1).

REMOVAL

▶ Refer to illustration 7.3

1   Remove the wheel trim/hub cap (as applicable) and loosen the driveaxle/hub bolt 1/4-turn with the vehicle resting on its wheels. Loosen the wheel bolts.

2   Raise the front of the vehicle and support it securely on jackstands. Block the rear wheels to prevent the vehicle from rolling off the stands. Remove the wheel and driveaxle/hub bolt.

➡ **Note: There are two types of hub bolts used; always replace the driveaxle/hub bolt with the same type (see Chapter 8).**

3   Remove the balljoint-to-control arm nuts (see illustration).

4   Pull the control arm down and separate the control arm from the balljoint.

➡ **Note: Disconnect the front level control sensor arm-to-control arm nut and separate the sensor arm from the control arm, if equipped.**

2009 and earlier models

▶ Refer to illustration 7.9

5   Remove the fasteners and detach the stabilizer bar links from the stabilizer bar (see illustration 6.3).

6   Remove the pendulum mount (see Chapter 2A or 2B) and disconnect the steering column U-joint coupler from the steering gear (see

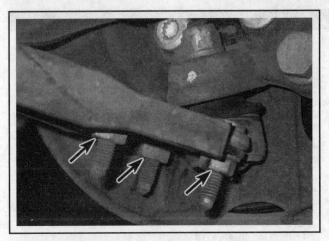

7.3 Balljoint-to-control arm nuts

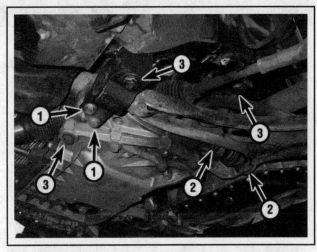

7.9 2009 and earlier control arm details - left side shown

1	Control arm bracket bolts	3	Subframe-to-body bolts
2	Control arm through-bolt/nut		

illustration 22.6b).

7   Remove the exhaust pipe support bracket fasteners from the subframe.

8   Disconnect the tie-rod ends from the steering knuckle (see Section 20).

9   Remove the control arm bracket mounting bolts at the rear end of the control arm (see illustration).

10   Remove the through-bolt and nut at the front end of the control arm. To allow the through-bolt to be withdrawn, the subframe must be lowered. To do this, support the subframe with a floor jack, then loosen and withdraw the subframe securing bolts (see illustration 17.9). Note that the bolts are threaded through the inner of the two sets of subframe bolt holes.

11   Lower the subframe slightly, withdraw the control arm inner pivot bolt, then remove the arm from the vehicle.

2010 and later models

Right side control arm

➡ **Note: This procedure applies to both left and right control arms on vehicles equipped with a manual transaxle.**

12   Remove the control arm through-bolt/nut (horizontal) from the front of the arm.

13   Remove the control arm mounting bolt (vertical) from the rear of the arm.

14   Maneuver the arm towards the rear of the vehicle, then pull the front of the control arm out and remove it from the vehicle.

Left side control arm

➡ **Note: This procedure applies to the left control arm on vehicles equipped with an automatic or DSG transaxle. On models with a manual transaxle, see Steps 12 through 14.**

15   Remove the pendulum mount (see Chapter 2A or 2B) and disconnect the steering column U-joint coupler from the steering gear (see illustration 22.6b).

16   Remove the exhaust pipe support bracket fasteners from the subframe. Also detach the power steering pressure line from the transaxle.

17   Disconnect the tie-rod ends from the steering knuckle (see Section 17).

18   Remove the control arm through-bolt/nut (horizontal) at the front

of the control arm and the bolt (vertical) from the rear of the control arm.

19   To allow the through-bolt to be withdrawn, the rear of the subframe must be lowered. To do this, support the subframe with a floor jack, unscrew and remove the two outer most subframe-to-body bolts, loosen the front subframe bolts and lower the rear of the subframe, but no more than 3-15/16 inches (10 cm).

20   Remove the control arm from the subframe.

BUSHING REPLACEMENT

21   Thoroughly clean the arm, removing all traces of dirt, thread locking compound and undercoating if necessary, then check carefully for cracks, distortion or any other signs of wear or damage, paying particular attention to the inner pivot bushing and balljoint. Note that the inner bushing has a hydraulic action; fluid leakage indicates that the bushing has been damaged and must be replaced. The balljoint is an integral part of the lower arm and cannot be replaced separately.

22   Replacement of the inner pivot bushing will require the use of a hydraulic press and several spacers and is therefore best entrusted to an automotive machine shop. If such equipment is available, press out the old bushing and install the new one using a spacer which bears only on the bushing outer edge. Ensure the bushing is correctly positioned so that the cavities are aligned with the center axis of the arm.

INSTALLATION

23   Installation is the reverse of removal, noting the following points:

 a) Use new control arm and subframe fasteners.
 b) Ensure that the control arm inboard securing bolt passes through the inner of the two sets of subframe bolt holes.
 c) Raise the outer end of the control arm with a floor jack to simulate normal ride height before tightening the inner pivot bolt/nut.
 d) Tighten all suspension fasteners to the torque values listed in this Chapter's Specifications.
 e) Lower the vehicle and tighten the wheel bolts to the torque listed in the Chapter 1 Specifications.
 f) Have the front end alignment checked and, if necessary, adjusted.

8 Balljoints - check and replacement

CHECK

1   Inspect the control arm balljoints for looseness anytime either of them is separated from the steering knuckle. See if you can turn the ballstud in its socket with your fingers. If the balljoint is loose, or if the ballstud can be turned, replace the balljoint. You can also check the balljoints with the suspension assembled as follows.

2   Raise the front of the vehicle and support it securely on jackstands placed under the frame rails.

3   Place a floor jack under the front lower control arm and raise it slightly. Attempt to move the steering knuckle up and down; a large prybar underneath the tire, or a prybar placed between the end of the control arm and the steering knuckle will be helpful. If any play is felt, replace the control arm and balljoint as an assembly (the balljoint is not replaceable separately).

4   Also try to move the steering knuckle in-and-out. If any play is felt, replace the control arm/balljoint assembly.

5   Check the balljoint boot for cracks and tears. If any are present, replace the upper control arm/balljoint assembly.

REPLACEMENT

▶ **Refer to illustrations 8.8 and 8.11**

✳✳ WARNING:

The manufacturer recommends replacing all self-locking nuts whenever they are removed.

8.8 Loosen the balljoint nut a couple of turns but do not completely remove it at this time

6   Remove the wheel trim/hub cap (as applicable) and loosen the driveaxle/hub bolt 1/4-turn with the vehicle resting on its wheels. Also loosen the wheel bolts.

7   Raise the front of the vehicle and support it securely on jackstands. Block the rear wheels to prevent the vehicle from rolling off the stands. Remove the wheel and driveaxle/hub bolt.

➡ **Note: There are two types of hub bolts used; always replace the driveaxle/hub bolt with the same type (see Chapter 8).**

8   Loosen the balljoint-to-steering knuckle nut (see illustration), but don't remove it yet.

9   Remove the balljoint-to-control arm nuts (see Section 7).

10 Separate the control arm from the balljoint (see Section 7).

11 Push the driveaxle out of the hub far enough to install a small balljoint separator, then pop the balljoint stud from the steering knuckle (see illustration).

12 Unscrew the nut and remove the balljoint from the steering knuckle.

13 Install the new balljoint into the steering knuckle and install the nut, but don't tighten it completely yet.

14 Connect the balljoint to the lower arm and tighten the fasteners to the torque listed in this Chapter's Specifications. Also tighten the balljoint-to-steering knuckle nut to the torque listed in this Chapter's Specifications.

15 Install the wheel and bolts, lower the vehicle and tighten the wheel bolts to the torque listed in the Chapter 1 Specifications.

16 Install a new driveaxle/hub bolt and tighten it to the torque listed in the Chapter 8 Specifications.

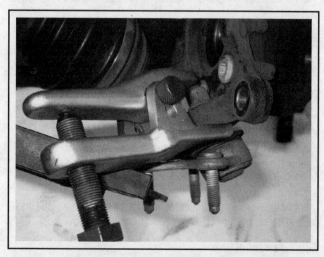

8.11 Separate the balljoint from the steering knuckle (the nut has been loosened but not completely removed - this will prevent the components from separating violently)

9 Shock absorber (rear) - removal and installation

▶ **Refer to illustration 9.3**

❊❊ **WARNING:**

The manufacturer recommends replacing the shock absorber lower mounting bolt and nut with new ones whenever they are removed.

❊❊ **WARNING:**

Always replace the shock absorbers in pairs - never replace just one of them, as handling peculiarities may result.

1   Loosen the rear wheel bolts. Chock the front wheels to keep the vehicle from rolling, then raise the rear of the vehicle and support it securely on jackstands. Remove the rear wheel.

2   On models with multi-link rear suspension, support the lower control arm with a floor jack positioned near the outer end of the arm. On 2011 Jetta models equipped with a torsion beam rear axle, place the floor jack below the coil spring pocket.

❊❊ **WARNING:**

The jack must remain in position throughout the entire procedure.

3   Remove the shock absorber lower mounting fastener (see illustration).

4   Remove the shock absorber upper mounting fasteners and remove the shock absorber.

5   Guide the shock absorber into position and install the upper mounting bolts and a new lower mounting bolt (and nut, on 2011 Jetta models with a torsion beam axle). Don't tighten the lower mounting fastener(s) yet.

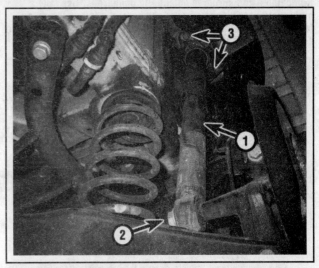

9.3 Rear shock absorber details - multi-link suspension shown, torsion axle suspension similar

1   Rear shock absorber   3   Upper mounting fasteners
2   Lower mounting fastener

6   Tighten the upper mounting bolts to the torque listed in this Chapter's Specifications.

7   Raise the rear axle to simulate normal ride height, then tighten the lower mounting bolt/nut to the torque listed in this Chapter's Specifications.

➡ **Note: The long collar of the shock absorber must face to the rear and sit into the center of the knuckle housing arm seat.**

8   Repeat the procedure to replace the other rear shock absorber.

9   Install the wheels and lower the vehicle. Tighten the wheel bolts to the torque listed in the Chapter 1 Specifications.

10 Coil spring (rear) - removal and installation

▶ **Refer to illustration 10.2**

❊❊ **WARNING:**

Always replace the coil springs in pairs - never replace just one of them.

1   Loosen the wheel bolts. Chock the front wheels to prevent the vehicle from rolling, then raise the rear of the vehicle and support it securely on jackstands placed under the rocker panel flanges. Remove the wheels.

2   Following the tool manufacturer's instructions, install a spring compressor (which can be obtained at most auto parts stores or equipment yards on a daily rental basis) on the spring and compress it enough to relieve the tension on the other suspension components (see illustration). This can be verified by wiggling the spring.

10.2 Compress the rear coil spring with the special tool

※※ WARNING:

Removing a coil spring is potentially dangerous. Use only a high-quality spring compressor and carefully follow the manufacturer's instructions furnished with the tool. After removing the coil spring, set it aside in a safe, isolated area.

3   Remove the spring and the upper and lower spring seats. Check the spring for cracks and chips, replacing the springs as a set if any defects are found. Also check the upper and lower seats for damage and deterioration, replacing them as necessary.

➡ **Note: If the lower spring seat is removed, it has a location pin that must be inserted back into the lower control arm or axle beam to center the seat.**

4   Installation is the reverse of the removal procedure, but make sure the lower spring seat is positioned with the pin on the seat inserted into the hole in the control arm or axle beam, and the coil springs positioned with the end of the spring up against the spring seat stop.

5   Lower the vehicle and tighten the wheel bolts to the torque listed in the Chapter 1 Specifications.

11 Hub and wheel bearing (rear) - removal and installation

▶ **Refer to illustrations 11.4 and 11.5**

1   Loosen the rear wheel bolts, raise the rear of the vehicle and support it securely on jackstands. Remove the wheel.

2   On rear drum brake models, remove the brake drum (see Chapter 9).

3   On rear disc brake models, remove the brake caliper (don't detach the hose), mounting bracket and disc (see Chapter 9). Hang the caliper with a piece of wire - don't let it hang by the brake hose.

4   Remove the dust cap from the hub (see illustration).

➡ **Note: Always replace the dust cap with a new one whenever it's removed.**

5   Unscrew the hub bearing bolt (see illustration) and remove the hub and bearing assembly.

6   Installation is the reverse of removal, noting the following points:

a) *Make sure the mating surfaces on the knuckle or stub axle and the hub and bearing assembly are clean before installation.*

b) *Tighten the mounting bolt to the torque listed in this Chapter's Specifications.*

c) *Install the brake caliper (see Chapter 9), tightening the mounting bolts to the torque listed in the Chapter 9 Specifications.*

d) *Install the brake drum and adjust the parking brake (see Chapter 9).*

e) *Install the wheel and wheel bolts. Lower the vehicle and tighten the bolts to the torque listed in the Chapter 1 Specifications.*

11.4 Remove the dust cap from the rear hub

11.5 Rear hub and bearing mounting bolt

12 Knuckle (rear, multi-link suspension) - removal and installation

※※ WARNING:

The manufacturer recommends replacing all fasteners whenever they are removed.

1   Loosen the wheel bolts, raise the rear of the vehicle and support it securely on jackstands, then remove the wheel.

2   Remove the rear brake caliper, caliper mounting bracket and brake disc (see Chapter 9). Support the caliper with a length of wire - don't let it hang by the hose.

3   Remove the ABS rear wheel speed sensor (see Chapter 9).

4   Remove the rear coil spring (see Section 10).

5   Detach the shock absorber from the knuckle (see Section 9).

6   Detach the lower control arm from the knuckle (see Section 15).

7   Detach the tie-rod from the knuckle (see Section 15).

8   Detach the upper control arm from the knuckle (see Section 15).

9   Detach the trailing arm from the knuckle (see Section 15), then remove the knuckle.

➥ **Note: Make reference marks on the adjusting fasteners before removing the arm.**

10 Installation is the reverse of removal, noting the following points:

a) *Use a new upper control arm-to-rear knuckle bolt, washer and nut, lower control arm-to-rear knuckle nut, trailing arm-to-rear knuckle nuts and bolts, and tie-rod bar-to-rear knuckle nut.*

b) *Don't tighten any of the suspension fasteners until the rear suspension has been raised to simulate normal ride height (this will prevent bushing distortion). Tighten all suspension fasteners to the torque values listed in this Chapter's Specifications.*

c) *Install the brake disc, caliper mounting bracket and caliper (see Chapter 9). Tighten the brake fasteners to the torque values listed in the Chapter 9 Specifications.*

d) *Install the wheel and tighten the bolts securely, then lower the vehicle and tighten the bolts to the torque listed in the Chapter 1 Specifications.*

13 Stub axle (rear, torsion beam suspension) - removal and installation

⁂ **WARNING:**

The manufacturer recommends replacing all nuts and bolts whenever they are removed.

1 Loosen the rear wheel bolts, raise the rear of the vehicle and support it securely on jackstands. Remove the wheel.

2 Loosen the tension from the parking brake, then remove the drum retaining screw and drum (see Chapter 9).

3 Remove the brake shoes and wheel cylinder (see Chapter 9).

4 Remove the dust cap from the hub (see illustration 11.4).

➥ **Note: Always replace the dust cap with a new one whenever it's removed.**

5 Remove the hub bearing assembly from the stub axle (see Section 11).

6 Remove the backing plate-to-axle beam bolts and remove the backing plate and stub axle together. Separate the stub axle from the backing plate.

7 Installation is the reverse of removal, noting the following points:

a) *Make sure the mating surfaces on the knuckle or stub axle and the hub and bearing assembly are clean before installation.*

b) *Tighten the mounting bolt to the torque listed in this Chapter's Specifications.*

c) *Install the wheel cylinder, brake shoes and brake drum, then bleed the brake system (see Chapter 9).*

d) *Adjust the parking brake (see Chapter 9).*

e) *Install the wheel and wheel bolts. Lower the vehicle and tighten the bolts to the torque listed in the Chapter 1 Specifications.*

14 Stabilizer bar and bushings (rear, multi-link suspension) - removal and installation

◗ **Refer to illustrations 14.2 and 14.3**

⁂ **WARNING:**

The manufacturer recommends replacing all self-locking nuts whenever they are removed.

1 Loosen the rear wheel bolts, raise the rear of the vehicle and support it securely on jackstands. Block the front wheels to keep the vehicle from rolling off the stands. Remove the rear wheels and lower control arm stone trim protector (if equipped).

2 Remove the mounting fasteners from the stabilizer bar links, then separate the links from the bar (see illustration).

3 Remove the stabilizer bar clamp mounting fasteners (see illustration) and remove the stabilizer bar.

4 Inspect the stabilizer bar bushings and link bushings for cracks, tears and other signs of deterioration. Replace as necessary. Also check the ballstuds at the ends of the links for looseness, replacing the links if necessary.

5 Installation is the reverse of removal. Tighten all fasteners to the torque values listed in this Chapter's Specifications.

6 Tighten the wheel bolts to the torque listed in the Chapter 1 Specifications.

14.2 Remove the stabilizer link fastener and separate the link from the bar - right side shown, left side identical

14.3 Rear stabilizer bar clamp bolts - right side shown, left side identical

15 Rear suspension arms - removal and installation

✳✳ WARNING:

The manufacturer recommends replacing all fasteners that are removed or loosened.

1   Loosen the rear wheel bolts, raise the rear of the vehicle and support it securely on jackstands. Block the front wheels to keep the vehicle from rolling off the stands. Remove the rear wheel.

UPPER CONTROL ARM (TRANSVERSE LINK)

▶ **Refer to illustration 15.5**

2   Remove the coil spring (see Section 10).
3   Using a floor jack, support the subframe on the same side from which the upper arm will be removed.
4   Unhook the speed sensor wire from the upper arm.
5   Mark the relationship of the adjuster cam on the upper control arm-to-subframe and fastener (see illustration).
6   Remove the upper control arm-to-subframe fasteners.
7   Remove the upper arm-to-knuckle fastener, then remove the arm.

➡ **Note: Mark the location of the washer on the arm-to-knuckle fastener; it must reinstalled in the same location, with a gap between the washer and the backing plate.**

8   Inspect the bushings for damage and wear. The bushings can be replaced, but a press and special adapters are required. If the bushings need to be replaced, take the arm to an automotive machine shop.
9   Installation is the reverse of removal, noting the following points:

a) *Use new fasteners (see the* **Warning** *at the beginning of this Section).*
b) *Don't tighten any of the suspension fasteners until the rear suspension has been raised to simulate normal ride height (this will prevent bushing distortion). Tighten all suspension fasteners to*

the torque values listed in this Chapter's Specifications.
c) *Align the cam adjuster with its mark made during removal, then tighten the control arm fasteners to the torque listed in this Chapter's Specifications.*
d) *Install the wheel and wheel bolts, then lower the vehicle and tighten the wheel bolts to the torque listed in the Chapter 1 Specifications.*
e) *Have the rear wheel alignment checked and, if necessary, adjusted.*

LOWER CONTROL ARM (TRANSVERSE LINK)

▶ **Refer to illustration 15.14**

10 On vehicles equipped with automatic leveling headlamps, disconnect the vehicle level sensor linkage from the lower control arm.

➡ **Note: On some models it will be necessary to disconnect and lower the rear part of the exhaust system (see Chapter 4).**

11 Remove the rear coil spring (see Section 10).
12 Mark the relationship of the cam adjuster to the lower control arm at the subframe.
13 Remove the lower control arm-to-knuckle mounting fastener and separate the arm from the knuckle.
14 Remove the lower control arm-to-subframe mounting fastener, the front mounting nut, the eccentric washer and the eccentric bolt (adjuster cam) (see illustration).
15 Detach the arm from the subframe and remove it from the vehicle.
16 Inspect the bushings for damage and wear. The bushings can be replaced, but special tools are required. If the bushings need to be replaced, take the arm to an automotive machine shop.
17 Installation is the reverse of removal, noting the following points:

a) *Use new fasteners (see the* **Warning** *at the beginning of this Section).*

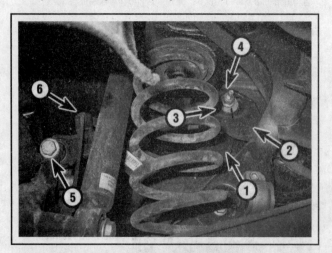

15.5 Upper control arm (transverse link) details

1   Rear upper control arm (transverse link)
2   Rear subframe
3   Adjuster cam
4   Upper control arm-to-subframe fastener
5   Upper control arm-to-knuckle fastener
6   Speed sensor wire clip

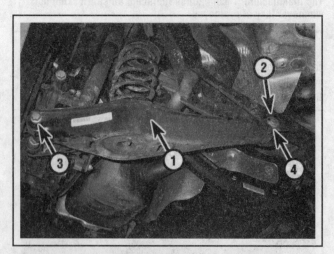

15.14 Lower control arm (transverse link) details

1   Lower control arm (transverse link)
2   Adjuster cam (one on each side)
3   Control arm-to-knuckle fastener
4   Control arm-to-subframe fastener

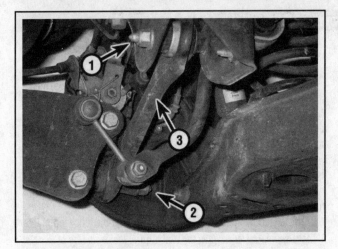

15.20 Rear tie-rod details

1   Tie-rod-to-subframe   2   Tie-rod-to-knuckle fastener
    fastener   3   Tie-rod

b) *Don't tighten any of the suspension fasteners until the rear suspension has been raised to simulate normal ride height (this will prevent bushing distortion). Tighten all suspension fasteners to the torque values listed in this Chapter's Specifications.*

c) *Align the adjuster cam with its mark made during removal, then tighten the control arm fasteners to the torque listed in this Chapter's Specifications.*

d) *Install the wheel and wheel bolts, then lower the vehicle and tighten the wheel bolts to the torque listed in the Chapter 1 Specifications.*

e) *Have the rear wheel alignment checked and, if necessary, adjusted.*

TIE-ROD

▶ **Refer to illustration 15.20**

18 Remove the coil spring (see Section 10).

19 Disconnect the stabilizer links and stabilizer bar brackets (see Section 14).

20 Remove the tie-rod-to-subframe mounting fasteners (see illustration).

21 Remove the tie-rod-to-knuckle mounting fasteners, then remove the tie-rod.

22 Inspect the bushings for damage and wear. The bushings are not replaceable separately; if they are damaged, the tie-rod must be replaced

23 Installation is the reverse of removal, noting the following points:

a) *Use new fasteners (see the* **Warning** *at the beginning of this Section).*

b) *Don't tighten the tie-rod mounting fasteners until the suspension has been raised to simulate normal ride height.*

c) *Tighten the wheel bolts to the torque listed in the Chapter 1 Specifications.*

d) *Have the rear wheel alignment checked and, if necessary, adjusted.*

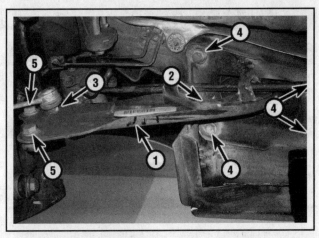

15.27 Trailing arm details

1   Trailing arm
2   Parking brake cable bracket (with push-pin fastener)
3   Stabilizer link-to-trailing arm (nut on opposite side)
4   Trailing arm bracket fasteners (two of four fasteners shown)
5   Trailing arm-to-knuckle fasteners

TRAILING ARM

▶ **Refer to illustration 15.27**

24 Remove the rear coil spring (see Section 10).

25 Remove the parking brake cable bracket fastener and separate the bracket from the trailing arm.

➡ **Note: Some models are equipped with a parking brake cable bracket mounted to the trailing arm with a rivet. To remove the rivet, push the center of the rivet in and remove the bracket from the arm.**

26 Disconnect the stabilizer link from the trailing arm (see Section 14).

27 Remove the trailing arm-to-knuckle mounting fasteners, then remove the trailing arm bracket-to-body fasteners (see illustration).

28 Detach the arm from the knuckle, then from the body and remove it from the vehicle.

29 Once the trailing arm is out of the vehicle, remove the trailing arm-to-bracket through-bolt/nut and separate the arm from the bracket.

30 Inspect the bushings for damage and wear. The bushings can be replaced, but special tools are required. If the bushings need to be replaced, take the arm to an automotive machine shop.

31 Installation is the reverse of removal, noting the following points:

a) *Use new fasteners (see the* **Warning** *at the beginning of this Section).*

b) *Don't tighten any of the suspension fasteners until the rear suspension has been raised to simulate normal ride height (this will prevent bushing distortion). Tighten all suspension fasteners to the torque values listed in this Chapter's Specifications.*

c) *Install the wheel and wheel bolts, then lower the vehicle and tighten the wheel bolts to the torque listed in the Chapter 1 Specifications.*

d) *Have the rear wheel alignment checked and, if necessary, adjusted.*

16 Rear axle beam (some 2011 Jetta models) - removal and installation

✳✳ WARNING:

The manufacturer recommends replacing all fasteners that are removed or loosened.

✳✳ CAUTION:

If the vehicle is raised using a hoist or lift, the rear of the vehicle must be tied to the lifting points to prevent it from lifting off of the rear lifting points and falling off once the rear axle beam is removed.

1   Loosen the rear wheel bolts, raise the rear of the vehicle and support it securely on jackstands. Block the front wheels to keep the vehicle from rolling off the stands. Remove the rear wheels.

2   Release the parking brake and loosen the parking brake adjustment nut until the cables can be disconnected from the brake cable equalizer (see Chapter 9).

3   Disconnect the rear wheel speed sensors (see Chapter 9).

4   Remove the coil springs (see Section 10).

5   Using a floor jack, raise the axle beam until the crossbrace is in a horizontal position. Remove the crossbrace-to-rear axle fasteners and separate the crossbrace from the rear axle.

6   Disconnect the brake lines from each side of the rear axle, then remove the clips attaching the lines to the rear axle (see Chapter 9).

7   Remove the rear axle bracket fasteners from the right side, then remove just the through-bolt/nut from the left side.

➡ **Note: The rear axle mounting bracket fasteners are different lengths - be sure to mark them as you remove them for installation.**

8   Remove the rear shock absorber-to-rear axle fasteners and lower the rear axle from the vehicle.

9   Installation is the reverse of removal, noting the following points:

a) Use new fasteners (see the **Warning** at the beginning of this Section).

b) Don't tighten the rear axle mounting fasteners until the suspension has been raised to simulate normal ride height.

c) Bleed the brake system (see Chapter 9).

d) Tighten the wheel bolts to the torque listed in the Chapter 1 Specifications.

e) Have the rear wheel alignment checked and, if necessary, adjusted.

17 Subframe - removal and installation

✳✳ WARNING:

The manufacturer recommends replacing the subframe mounting bolts (if they are corroded), all self-locking nuts for the tie-rod end-to-steering knuckle and steering gear, and the steering shaft U-joint pinch bolt with new ones whenever they are removed.

FRONT

▶ **Refer to illustration 17.9**

1   Raise the front of the vehicle and support it securely on jackstands.

2   Remove the lower splash shield below the engine (see Chapter 1, Section 6).

3   Remove the heat shield fasteners and heat shield from the subframe.

4   Remove the exhaust system bracket fasteners from the subframe.

5   Remove the pendulum mount (see Chapter 2A or 2B).

6   Disconnect the lower control arms from the balljoints (see Section 7).

7   Disconnect the tie-rod ends from the steering knuckles (see Section 20).

8   Disconnect the stabilizer bar links and remove the stabilizer bar clamp fasteners (see Section 6).

9   Remove the steering gear-to-subframe fasteners (see illustration).

➡ **Note: The steering gear can be left in-vehicle or removed with the subframe. This procedure explains how to remove the subframe while leaving the steering gear in the vehicle. To remove the steering gear with the subframe, see Section 22.**

10 Support the subframe with a floor jack, then loosen and withdraw the subframe securing bolts and lower the subframe from the vehicle.

➡ **Note: On 2011 models, note the location of the shims between the subframe and the body, if equipped.**

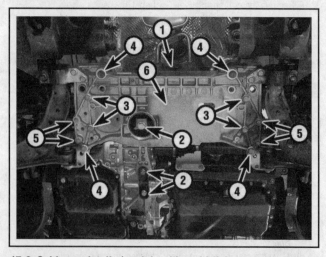

17.9 Subframe details (models with multi-link rear suspension)

1	Exhaust bracket	4	Subframe-to-body bolts
2	Pendulum mount bolts	5	Subframe-to-stabilizer bar
3	Subframe-to-steering gear bolts		clamp bolts
		6	Front subframe

11 Installation is the reverse of removal, noting the following points:

a) *Use new fasteners (see the* **Warning** *at the beginning of this Section).*

b) *Don't tighten the control arms, tie-rod fasteners until the suspension has been raised to simulate normal ride height.*

c) *Tighten the wheel bolts to the torque listed in the Chapter 1 Specifications.*

d) *Have the front wheel alignment checked and, if necessary, adjusted.*

REAR

Multi-link suspension

▶ **Refer to illustration 17.21 and 17.22**

✳✳ CAUTION:

If the vehicle is raised using a hoist or lift, the rear of the vehicle must be tied to the lifting points to prevent it from lifting off of the rear lifting points and falling off once the rear subframe is removed.

12 Loosen the rear wheel bolts, raise the rear of the vehicle and support it securely on jackstands. Block the front wheels to keep the vehicle from rolling off the stands. Remove the rear wheels.

13 Remove the exhaust system (see Chapter 4).

14 On vehicles equipped with automatic leveling headlamps, disconnect the vehicle level sensor linkage from the lower control arm.

15 Remove the ABS wheel speed sensors (see Chapter 9).

16 Remove the coil springs (see Section 10).

17 Remove the shock absorber-to knuckle fastener (see Section 9).

18 Remove the rear calipers and parking brake cable housing fasteners (see Chapter 9). Support the caliper with a length of wire - don't let it hang by the hose.

19 Remove the ABS sensor wire harness from the bracket on the upper control arm.

20 Remove the brake hose retaining clips from both sides of the vehicle (see Chapter 9).

21 Support the subframe and suspension assembly with a floor jack and slowly remove the trailing arm-to-body bracket fasteners (see illustration).

22 Remove the subframe fasteners and slowly lower the subframe assembly out of the vehicle (see illustration).

23 Installation is the reverse of removal, noting the following points:

a) *Use new fasteners (see the* **Warning** *at the beginning of this Section).*

b) *Don't tighten the control arms or tie-rod fasteners until the suspension has been raised to simulate normal ride height.*

c) *Tighten the wheel bolts to the torque listed in the Chapter 1 Specifications.*

d) *Have the rear wheel alignment checked and, if necessary, adjusted.*

Axle beam suspension

24 Remove the rear axle beam (see Section 16).

25 Remove the subframe fastener and lower the subframe.

26 Installation is the reverse of removal, noting the following points:

a) *Use new fasteners (see the* **Warning** *at the beginning of this Section).*

b) *Tighten the wheel bolts to the torque listed in the Chapter 1 Specifications.*

c) *Have the rear wheel alignment checked and, if necessary, adjusted.*

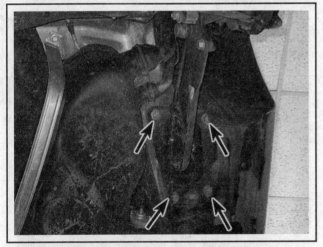

17.21 Trailing arm bracket-to-body fastener locations - multi-link rear suspension

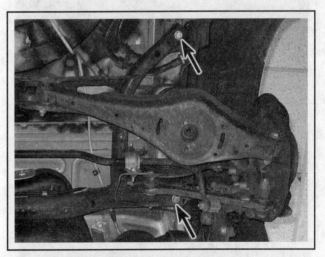

17.22 Rear subframe fastener locations (right side shown, left side similar) - multi-link rear suspension

18 Steering wheel - removal and installation

⚹⚹ WARNING:

These models are equipped with airbags. Always disable the airbag system before working in the vicinity of any airbag system component to avoid the possibility of accidental deployment of the airbag(s), which could cause personal injury (see Chapter 12).

⚹⚹ WARNING:

Do not use a memory saving device to preserve the ECM's memory when working on or near airbag system components.

⚹⚹ CAUTION:

If the battery is disconnected, several systems must be re-learned before they will work properly (see Chapter 5, Section 3).

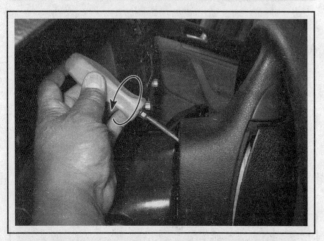

18.3a Rotate the steering wheel 90-degrees from center (counterclockwise), insert a flat-blade screwdriver into the right side opening on the steering wheel and twist it toward the left to release the retainer

18.3b Rotate the steering wheel 180-degrees to the right, insert the screwdriver into the left side opening and twist it towards the right to unlock the left side retainer, then carefully lift the airbag module off of the steering wheel

➡ **Note:** On 2011 models, the steering electronic control module and steering angle sensor are incorporated into the clockspring and are replaced as a single unit.

REMOVAL

▶ Refer to illustrations 18.3a. 18.3b, 18.4, 18.7, 18.8, 18.10, 18.11a, 18.11b, 18.12, 18.13 and 18.15

1   Park the vehicle with the wheels pointing straight ahead. Disconnect the cable from the negative battery terminal (see Chapter 5).

2   Refer to Chapter 12 and disable the airbag system.

3   To detach the airbag module from the steering wheel, rotate the steering wheel 90-degrees from center (counterclockwise) and insert a flat-blade screwdriver into the right rear side opening on the steering wheel. Turn the screwdriver towards the driver's door to unlock the right side lock (see illustration). Rotate the steering wheel 180-degrees (clockwise) and insert the screwdriver into the left rear side opening on the steering wheel. Turn the screwdriver towards the passenger door to unlock the left side lock and carefully lift the airbag module off of the steering wheel (see illustration).

4   Remove the connector lock and disconnect the airbag module and horn electrical connectors (see illustration).

5   Set the module aside in a safe, isolated area, with the airbag side of the module facing UP.

⚹⚹ WARNING:

When carrying the airbag module, keep the driver's (trim) side of it away from your body and, when you set it down, make sure the driver's side is facing up.

6   Disconnect any other electrical connectors needed for removal and turn the steering wheel to the center position.

18.4 Typical airbag module electrical connection details

1   Airbag module
2   Airbag module electrical connector lock

3   Airbag module electrical connector

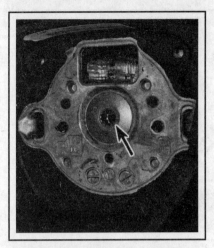

18.7 Remove the steering wheel mounting fastener; a 12 mm, 12-point spline-drive bit is required

18.8 After removing the bolt, check for alignment marks on the steering wheel and steering shaft - if there aren't any, make your own

18.10 Remove the steering electronic control module-to-clockspring fastener

7   Remove the steering wheel bolt using a 12 mm, 12-point spline-drive bit (see illustration).

8   Mark the position of the steering wheel to the steering shaft if marks don't already exist or don't line up (see illustration).

9   Lift the steering wheel from the shaft, noting how any electrical wire harnesses are routed. If the steering wheel is tight, tap it up near the center using the palm of your hand, or twist it from side-to-side while pulling upwards.

✳ CAUTION:

Don't hammer on the shaft to remove the wheel.

✳ WARNING:

Don't allow the steering shaft to turn after the steering wheel is removed or damage to the airbag clockspring could occur. Also, do not allow the hub of the clockspring to turn.

Steering electronic control module (2010 and earlier models)

➡ **Note: The steering column switches must be removed in order, starting with the steering electronic control module, then the clockspring and steering angle sensor. The new steering electronic control module must be calibrated with a factory scan tool. For this reason, if a new module is needed, it is best to have a VW dealer perform this job.**

10   Remove the steering electronic control module-to-clockspring fastener (see illustration).

11   Insert a drill bit or punch into the hole (see illustration), and release the center retaining clip from the steering column (see illustration).

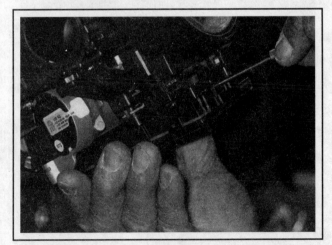

18.11a Insert a drill bit or punch through the hole in the front of the control module to release the mounting clip

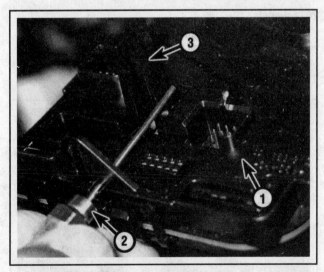

18.11b Steering electronic control module removal details

1   Steering electronic control module
2   Drill bit or punch
3   Retaining clip release tab

18.12 Disconnect the electrical connectors to the control module

12 Remove the steering electronic control module from the column and disconnect the electrical connectors (see illustration).

Clockspring

2010 and earlier models

13 If it is necessary to remove the clockspring, remove the steering column covers (see Chapter 11), remove the steering electronic control module (see Steps 10 through 12), then disengage the clockspring retaining clips and detach it from the steering column (see illustration).

✳✳ CAUTION:

Do not allow the clockspring to rotate.

Installation is the reverse of removal.

2011 models

14 If it is necessary to remove the steering electronic control module/clockspring, remove the steering column covers (see Chapter 11), disconnect the electrical connectors and the three retaining screws, then detach it from the steering column.

18.15 Carefully disengage the steering angle sensor from the steering column base switch assembly

18.13 Disconnect the clockspring retaining clips and remove the clockspring

✳✳ CAUTION:

Do not allow the clockspring to rotate.

Installation is the reverse of removal.

Steering angle sensor (2010 and earlier models)

➡ **Note: The new steering angle sensor must be calibrated with a factory scan tool. For this reason, if a new sensor is needed, it is best to have a VW dealer perform this job.**

15 If it is necessary to remove the steering angle sensor, remove the clockspring (see Step 13). Depress the tabs and slide the steering gear sensor from the switch (see illustration). Installation is the reverse of removal.

INSTALLATION

▶ **Refer to illustration 18.16**

16 2010 and earlier models: Before installing the steering wheel, make sure steering angle sensor (if removed) is locked in place, the air-

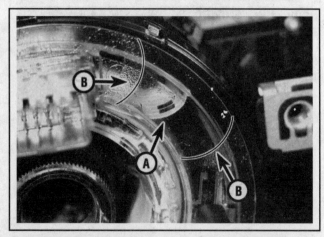

18.16 The black-marked band (A), must be located in the viewing window (B) before installing the steering wheel.
➡ **Note: On some models, the window is in the 10 o'clock position and the mark on the band is yellow**

bag clockspring is centered (see illustration) and all of the clip fasteners are locked into place.

17 2010 and earlier models: Connect the electrical connectors to the steering electronic control module, place the module on to the steering column and press the module in place. Make sure the module retaining clips lock in place, then the steering angle sensor and clockspring are firmly plugged in to the control module. Install the module to clockspring fastener.

18 Install the wheel onto the steering shaft, aligning the index marks and routing any wiring harnesses.

19 Install a new steering wheel bolt and tighten it to the torque listed in this Chapter's Specifications.

✳✳ WARNING:

Do not reuse the steering wheel bolt.

20 Connect the electrical connectors for the horn and the airbag module.

21 Position the airbag module onto the steering wheel and lock the module in place.

22 Refer to Chapter 12 for the procedure to enable the airbag system.

19 Steering column - removal and installation

✳✳ WARNING:

These models are equipped with airbags. Always disable the airbag system before working in the vicinity of any airbag system component to avoid the possibility of accidental deployment of the airbag(s), which could cause personal injury (see Chapter 12).

✳✳ WARNING:

Do not use a memory saving device to preserve the ECM's memory when working on or near airbag system components.

✳✳ CAUTION:

If the battery is disconnected, several systems must be re-learned before they will work properly, (see Chapter 5, Section 3).

REMOVAL

▶ **Refer to illustration 19.12**

1 Park the vehicle with the wheels pointing straight ahead. For models with an automatic transaxle, place the shift lever in PARK. Disconnect the cable from the negative battery terminal (see Chapter 5). Disable the airbag system (see Chapter 12).

2 Remove the steering column cover (see Chapter 11).

3 Remove the steering wheel (see Section 18). Prevent the steering shaft from turning.

✳✳ CAUTION:

If this is not done, the airbag clockspring could be damaged.

4 Remove the lower instrument panel trim (under the steering column) (see Chapter 11).

5 Remove the airbag system clockspring (see Section 18).

6 Remove the multi-function switch (see Chapter 12).

7 Disconnect the wiring harness clips, harness connectors and ground wire from the steering column.

8 Press the tabs on both sides of the cable guide cover towards the inside and remove the cover from the guide on the steering column.

9 On manual transaxle models, remove the clutch pedal crash brace fastener and brace from the column, if equipped.

10 Secure the lower section of the steering column to the upper section by passing a length of wire through the hole in the lower section of the column and through the spring on the upper section.

11 Remove the footwell trim panel and mark the relationship of the steering shaft lower universal joint to the steering gear input shaft, then remove the pinch bolt securing the universal joint (see Section 22).

12 Remove the steering column mounting bolts (see illustration), then separate the universal joint from the steering gear input shaft and guide the column out from the instrument panel.

INSTALLATION

13 Guide the column into position, connecting the U-joint with the steering gear input shaft. Install the pinch bolt, but don't tighten it yet.

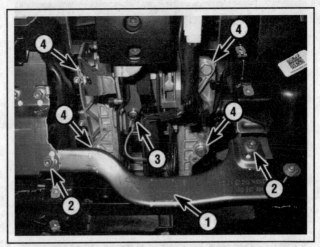

19.12 Steering column mounting details - 2010 and earlier model shown, other models similar

1	Instrument panel brace	3	Ground wire
2	Brace fasteners	4	Steering column fasteners

14 Install the steering column mounting bolts, but don't tighten them yet.

15 Remove the wire installed in Step 10. If a new steering column was installed, remove the protective materials used for transport from the column.

16 The remainder of installation is the reverse of the removal procedure, noting the following points:

   a) When installing the steering wheel, be sure the airbag clockspring is centered (see Section 18), and tighten the steering wheel bolt to the torque listed in this Chapter's Specifications.

   b) With the steering column in position, tighten the column mounting bolts to the torque listed in this Chapter's Specifications.

   c) Reconnect the shift interlock cable (see Chapter 12).

   d) Tighten the U-joint pinch bolt to the torque listed in this Chapter's Specifications after the steering column mounting fasteners have been tightened.

20 Tie-rod ends (front) - removal and installation

REMOVAL

▶ **Refer to illustrations 20.2a, 20.2b and 20.4**

1 Loosen the front wheel lug nuts. Apply the parking brake, raise the front of the vehicle and support it securely on jackstands. Remove the front wheel.

2 Hold the tie-rod with a pair of locking pliers or wrench and loosen the jam nut enough to mark the position of the tie-rod end in relation to the threads (see illustrations).

3 Loosen (but don't remove) the nut on the tie-rod end stud.

4 Disconnect the tie-rod end from the steering knuckle arm with a puller (see illustration). Remove the nut and detach the tie-rod end.

5 Unscrew the tie-rod end from the tie-rod.

INSTALLATION

6 Thread the tie-rod end on to the marked position and insert the stud into the steering knuckle arm. Tighten the jam nut securely.

7 Install the nut on the stud and tighten it to the torque listed in this Chapter's Specifications.

8 Install the wheel and lug nuts. Lower the vehicle and tighten the lug nuts to the torque listed in the Chapter 1 Specifications.

9 Have the alignment checked and, if necessary, adjusted.

20.2a Loosen the jam nut . . .

20.2b . . . then mark the position of the tie-rod end in relation to the threads

20.4 Disconnect the tie-rod end from the steering knuckle arm with a puller

21 Steering gear boots - replacement

♦ **Refer to illustration 21.3**

1   Loosen the lug nuts, raise the vehicle and support it securely on jackstands. Remove the wheel.

2   Remove the tie-rod end and jam nut (see Section 20).

3   Remove the outer steering gear boot clamp with a pair of pliers (see illustration). Cut off the inner boot clamp with a pair of diagonal cutters. Slide off the boot.

4   Before installing the new boot, wrap the threads and serrations on the end of the steering rod with a layer of tape so the small end of the new boot isn't damaged.

5   Slide the new boot into position on the steering gear until it seats in the groove in the steering rod and install new clamps.

6   Remove the tape and install the tie-rod end (see Section 20).

7   Install the wheel and lug nuts. Lower the vehicle and tighten the lug nuts to the torque listed in the Chapter 1 Specifications.

21.3 The outer ends of the steering gear boots are secured by spring-type clamps (A); they're easily released with a pair of pliers. The inner ends of the steering gear boots are retained by boot clamps which must be cut off and discarded (B)

22 Steering gear - removal and installation

♦ **Refer to illustrations 22.6a and 22.6b**

❋❋ **WARNING:**

These models are equipped with airbags. Always disable the airbag system before working in the vicinity of any airbag system component to avoid the possibility of accidental deployment of the airbag, which could cause personal injury (see Chapter 12). Also, don't allow the steering wheel to turn after the steering gear has been removed. To prevent this, pass the seat belt through the steering wheel and plug it into its latch.

❋❋ **WARNING:**

Do not use a memory saving device to preserve the ECM's memory when working on or near airbag system components.

❋❋ **CAUTION:**

If the battery is disconnected several systems must be re-learned before they will work properly, see Chapter 5, Section 3.

➡ **Note: The steering gear cannot be repaired, if the steering gear is worn or damaged it must be replaced.**

1   Park the vehicle with the front wheels pointing straight ahead.

Apply the parking brake and chock the rear wheels, then loosen the front wheel bolts. Raise the front of the vehicle and support it securely on jackstands. Remove both front wheels.

2   Remove the battery from the engine compartment (see Chapter 5).

3   Turn the steering wheel to the center position, then remove the ignition key to engage the steering lock.

❋❋ **CAUTION:**

Ensure that the steering column remains in the straight-ahead position throughout the remainder of this procedure, or the airbag contact unit may become misaligned, leading to the failure of the airbag system.

4   Remove the driver's side under-dash panel (see Chapter 11).

5   Secure the lower section of the steering column to the upper section as described in Section 19.

❋❋ **CAUTION:**

Do not allow the upper and lower sections of the steering column to become separated while the steering column is detached from the steering gear, as this can cause the internal components to become detached and misaligned.

22.6a Remove the footwell cover fasteners, then remove cover . . .

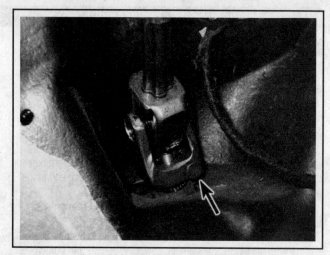

22.6b . . . and remove the pinch bolt at the base of the steering column

6   Remove footwell cover fasteners and cover (see illustration), then the pinch bolt securing the universal joint to the input shaft of the steering gear (see illustration).

7   Pull the steering column universal joint off the steering gear input shaft and move it to one side. Pull the input shaft cover from the firewall and into the vehicle, if equipped.

2011 JETTA MODELS EQUIPPED WITH HYDRAULIC POWER STEERING

8   Siphon the fluid from the power steering fluid reservoir. If a suitable implement is not readily available to siphon the fluid from the system, it can be drained into a container when the hydraulic lines are detached from the steering gear.

9   Apply hose clamps to the fluid lines leading to and from the steering gear. Take care to avoid causing damage to the hoses by pinching.

ALL MODELS

10   Remove the lower splash shield below the engine (see Chapter 1, Section 6).

11   Remove the heat shield fasteners and heat shield from the subframe, if equipped.

12   Remove the exhaust system bracket fasteners from the subframe.

13   Remove the pendulum mount (see Chapter 2B, Section 15).

14   Disconnect the lower control arms from the balljoints (see Section 8).

15   Disconnect the tie-rods from the steering knuckles (see Section 20).

16   Disconnect the stabilizer bar links and remove the stabilizer bar clamps fasteners (see Section 6).

17   Remove the steering gear-to-subframe fasteners (see illustration 17.9).

Models equipped with electromechanical steering gear

18   Support the subframe with a floor jack and remove the rear subframe bolts (see illustration 17.9). Lower the rear of the subframe slightly.

➡ **Note: Make sure no electrical wiring is being stretched while lowering the subframe.**

19   Remove the steering gear heat shield fasteners and heat shield.

20   Disconnect the cable guide clips from the subframe.

21   Disconnect the electrical connectors to the steering gear.

22   Carefully lower the rear of the subframe using the floor jack, enough to lift the steering gear off the subframe and out of the vehicle.

※※ **CAUTION:**

To avoid damaging the steering gear control module, do not set the steering gear down on top of the control module.

23   Install the steering gear on to the subframe and connect the electrical connectors.

24   Align the steering gear mounting holes with the holes in the subframe, then install the mounting bolts and tighten the bolts to the torque listed is this Chapter's Specifications.

25   The remainder of the installation procedure is a reversal of removal, noting the following points:

 a) Refer to Section 17 to reconnect the subframe.
 b) Refer to Section 20 to reconnect the tie-rod ends.
 c) Tighten the wheel bolts to the torque listed in the Chapter 1 Specifications.
 d) Finally, have the wheel alignment checked and, if necessary, adjusted.

Models equipped with hydraulic steering gear

26 Unscrew the fittings and disconnect the fluid supply and return lines from the steering gear. Clean the connections before they are detached. Drain any fluid remaining in the system into a container for disposal. Tie the lines back away from the work area, and seal off their ends to prevent further leakage and keep dirt from entering the system.

27 Support the subframe with a floor jack and remove the rear subframe bolts (see illustration 17.9). Lower the rear of the subframe enough to lift the steering gear off the subframe and out of the vehicle.

➡ **Note: Make sure no electrical wiring is being stretched while lowering the subframe.**

28 Maneuver the steering gear on to the subframe and align the steering gear mounting holes with the holes in the subframe.

29 Install the steering gear-to-subframe mounting bolts and tighten the bolts to the torque listed is this Chapter's Specifications.

30 The remainder of the installation procedure is a reversal of removal, noting the following points:
  a) *Connect the pressure and return line fittings to the steering gear. Tighten the pressure line to the torque listed in this Chapter's Specifications.*
  b) *Refer to Section 20 to reconnect the tie-rod ends.*
  c) *Top up the fluid level as described in Chapter 1 and bleed the system as described in Section 24.*
  d) *Tighten the wheel bolts to the torque listed in the Chapter 1 Specifications.*
  e) *Finally, have the wheel alignment checked and, if necessary, adjusted.*

23 Power steering pump - removal and installation

1 Raise the front of the vehicle and support it securely on jackstands.

2 Remove the lower splash shield below the engine (see Chapter 1, Section 6).

3 Loosen the power steering pump pulley bolts, then remove the drivebelt (see Chapter 1).

4 Using brake hose clamps, clamp both the supply and return hoses near the power steering fluid reservoir. This will minimize fluid loss during subsequent operations.

5 Wipe clean the area around the power steering pressure and return line fittings.

6 Unscrew and disconnect the pressure line from the pump; be prepared for fluid spillage, and position a container beneath the pipe while unscrewing the line. Plug the end of the line and the steering pump orifice, to minimize fluid leakage and to keep dirt out of the hydraulic system.

7 Loosen the clamp and disconnect the fluid supply hose from the rear of the power steering pump. Plug the end of the hose and cover the pump fluid port to prevent contamination.

8 Remove the pump pulley bolt and pulley, then remove the pump mounting fasteners and detach the pump from its bracket.

9 If the power steering pump is faulty, it must be replaced. The pump is a sealed unit and cannot be overhauled.

10 If a new pump is to be installed, it must be primed with fluid first, to ensure adequate lubrication during its initial stages of operation. Failure to do this could cause noisy operation and may lead to early pump failure. To prime the pump, pour the specified grade of hydraulic fluid into the fluid supply port on the pump, and simultaneously rotate the pump pulley. When the fluid exits from the pressure port, it is primed and ready for use.

11 Maneuver the pump into position, then install its mounting bolts and tighten them to the torque listed in this Chapter's Specifications.

12 Install the pulley to the pump, then install the pulley mounting bolts and tighten them securely at this time.

13 Connect the pressure line to the pump and carefully screw the line in to the pump. Ensure the line is correctly routed, then tighten the line to the torque listed in this Chapter's Specifications.

14 Reconnect the supply hose to the pump and secure it in position with the retaining clip. Remove the hose clamps used to minimize fluid loss.

15 Install the power steering pump drivebelt (see Chapter 1) and tighten the pulley pump fasteners to the torque listed in this Chapter's Specifications.

16 Install the under-vehicle splash shield. Reconnect the negative battery cable.

17 Top up the hydraulic system (see Chapter 1), then bleed the system as described in Section 24.

24 Power steering system - bleeding

1 Following any operation in which the power steering fluid lines have been disconnected, the power steering system must be bled to remove all air and obtain proper steering performance.

2 With the front wheels in the straight ahead position, check the power steering fluid level and, if low, add fluid until it is up to the MIN mark on the dipstick.

3 Raise the front of the vehicle and support it securely on jackstands.

4 Turn the steering wheel back-and-forth repeatedly, lightly hitting the stops.

⁎⁎ CAUTION:

Don't hold the steering wheel in the full-right or full-left position, as this could damage the pump.

5   Start the engine and allow it to run at fast idle. Recheck the fluid level and add more if necessary until it is up to the MIN mark.

6   Bleed the system by turning the wheels from side to side, just barely contacting the stops. This will work the air out of the system. Keep the reservoir full of fluid as this is done.

7   When the air is worked out of the system and the fluid level stabilizes, return the wheels to the straight ahead position and leave the vehicle running for several more minutes before shutting it off. Lower the vehicle.

8   Road test the vehicle to be sure the steering system is functioning normally and noise-free.

9   Recheck the fluid level to be sure it is up to the HOT mark on the dipstick while the engine is at normal operating temperature. Add fluid if necessary (see Chapter 1).

25 Wheels and tires - general information

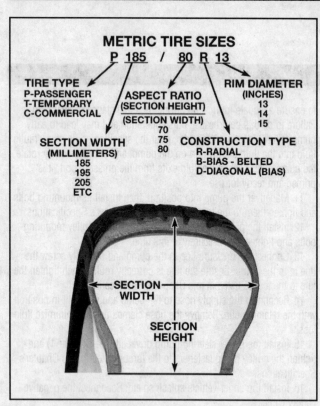

25.1 Metric tire size code

▶ **Refer to illustration 25.1**

1   All vehicles covered by this manual are equipped with metric-sized steel belted radial tires (see illustration). Use of other size or type of tires may affect the ride and handling of the vehicle. Don't mix different types of tires, such as radials and bias belted, on the same vehicle as handling may be seriously affected. It's recommended that tires be replaced in pairs on the same axle, but if only one tire is being replaced, be sure it's the same size, structure and tread design as the other.

2   Because tire pressure has a substantial effect on handling and wear, the pressure on all tires should be checked at least once a month or before any extended trips (see Chapter 1).

3   Wheels must be replaced if they are bent, dented, leak air, have elongated bolt holes, are heavily rusted, out of vertical symmetry or if the wheel bolts won't stay tight. Wheel repairs that use welding or peening are not recommended.

4   Tire and wheel balance is important in the overall handling, braking and performance of the vehicle. Unbalanced wheels can adversely affect handling and ride characteristics as well as tire life. Whenever a tire is installed on a wheel, the tire and wheel should be balanced by a shop with the proper equipment.

26 Wheel alignment - general information

▶ **Refer to illustration 26.2**

A wheel alignment refers to the adjustments made to the wheels so they are in proper angular relationship to the suspension and the ground. Wheels that are out of proper alignment not only affect vehicle control, but also increase tire wear.

The angles normally measured are camber, caster and toe-in (see illustration). Camber and caster are not always adjustable but are usually checked to see if any suspension components are worn or damaged. The toe-in angle is commonly adjusted on all vehicles in the front and on the rear of vehicles with independent rear suspension.

Getting the proper wheel alignment is a very exacting process, one in which complicated and expensive machines are necessary to perform the job properly. Because of this, you should have a technician with the proper equipment perform these tasks. We will, however, use this space to give you a basic idea of what is involved with a wheel alignment so you can better understand the process and deal intelligently with the shop that does the work.

Toe-in is the turning in of the wheels. The purpose of a toe specification is to ensure parallel rolling of the wheels. In a vehicle with zero toe-in, the distance between the front edges of the wheels will be the same as the distance between the rear edges of the wheels. The actual amount of toe-in is normally only a fraction of an inch. On the front end, toe-in is controlled by the tie-rod end position on the tie-rod. Incorrect toe-in will cause the tires to wear improperly by making them scrub against the road surface.

Camber is the tilting of the wheels from vertical when viewed from one end of the vehicle. When the wheels tilt out at the top, the camber is said to be positive (+). When the wheels tilt in at the top the camber is negative (-). The amount of tilt is measured in degrees from vertical and this measurement is called the camber angle. This angle affects the amount of tire tread that contacts the road and compensates for changes in the suspension geometry when the vehicle is cornering or traveling over an undulating surface.

Caster is the tilting of the front steering axis from the vertical. A tilt toward the rear is positive caster and a tilt toward the front is negative caster.

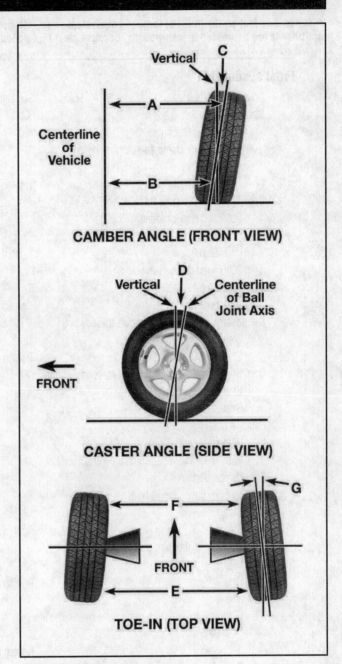

CAMBER ANGLE (FRONT VIEW)

CASTER ANGLE (SIDE VIEW)

TOE-IN (TOP VIEW)

26.2 Wheel alignment details

A minus B = C (degrees camber)
D = degrees caster
E minus F = toe-in (measured in inches)
G = toe-in (expressed in degrees)

Torque specifications	Ft-lbs (unless otherwise indicated)	Nm

→ **Note:** One foot-pound (ft-lb) of torque is equivalent to 12 inch-pounds (in-lbs) of torque. Torque values below approximately 15 foot-pounds are expressed in inch-pounds, because most foot-pound torque wrenches are not accurate at these smaller values.

Front suspension

Driveaxle/hub bolt	See Chapter 8	
Stabilizer bar		
Connecting link nuts	48	65
Stabilizer bar clamp-to-subframe bolts		
Step 1	15	20
Step 2	Tighten an additional 90-degrees (1/4-turn)	
Control arm-to-subframe through-bolt		
2009 and earlier models		
Step 1	52	70
Step 2	Tighten an additional 180-degrees (1/2-turn)	
2010 and later models		
Step 1	52	70
Step 2	Tighten an additional 90-degrees (1/4-turn)	
Control arm rear mounting bracket-to-body bolt		
Step 1	52	70
Step 2	Tighten an additional 90-degrees (1/4-turn)	
Control arm rear mounting bracket-to-console bolts		
Step 1	37	50
Step 2	Tighten an additional 90-degrees (1/4-turn)	
Balljoint nuts		
With steel control arm	44	60
With sheet steel or aluminum control arm	74	100
Strut damper shaft nut	44	60
Strut-to-body strut support bolts		
Step 1	15	20
Step 2	Tighten an additional 90-degrees (1/4-turn)	
Strut-to-lower control arm bolt/nut		
Step 1	52	70
Step 2	Tighten an additional 90-degrees (1/4-turn)	
Subframe		
Subframe-to-body mounting bolts (through console)		
Step 1	52	70
Step 2	Tighten an additional 90-degrees (1/4-turn)	
Console-to-subframe bolts		
Step 1	15	20
Step 2	Tighten an additional 90-degrees (1/4-turn)	
Console-to-body bolt		
Step 1	52	70
Step 2	Tighten an additional 90-degrees (1/4-turn)	
Pendulum-to-subframe bolt		
Step 1	74	100
Step 2	Tighten an additional 90-degrees (1/4-turn)	
Pendulum support-to-transaxle bolts		
Step 1	30	40
Step 2	Tighten an additional 90-degrees (1/4-turn)	

Torque specifications	Ft-lbs (unless otherwise indicated)	Nm

➡ **Note: One foot-pound (ft-lb) of torque is equivalent to 12 inch-pounds (in-lbs) of torque. Torque values below approximately 15 foot-pounds are expressed in inch-pounds, because most foot-pound torque wrenches are not accurate at these smaller values.**

Front suspension (continued)

Wheel bearing assembly mounting bolts
Step 1	52	70
Step 2	Tighten an additional 90-degrees (1/4-turn)	

Rear suspension

Control arms (transverse link)
Lower control arm-to-subframe bolt/nut	70	95

Lower control arm-to-knuckle bolt/nut
Step 1	66	90
Step 2	Tighten an additional 90-degrees (1/4-turn)	

Upper control arm-to-knuckle bolt/nut
Step 1	96	130
Step 2	Tighten an additional 90-degrees (1/4-turn)	

Upper control arm-to-subframe
eccentric bolt/nut	70	95

Rear tie-rod-to-knuckle bolt/nut
Step 1	96	130
Step 2	Tighten an additional 90-degrees (1/4-turn)	

Rear tie-rod-to-subframe bolt/nut
Step 1	66	90
Step 2	Tighten an additional 90-degrees (1/4-turn)	

Rear trailing arm bracket-to-body bolt/nut
Step 1	37	50
Step 2	Tighten an additional 90-degrees (1/4-turn)	

Rear trailing arm-to-knuckle bolt/nut
Step 1	66	90
Step 2	Tighten an additional 45-degrees (1/8-turn)	

Rear axle beam (some 2011 Jetta models)

Mounting bracket-to-rear axle beam through-bolts/nuts
Step 1	52	70
Step 2	Tighten an additional 90-degrees (1/4-turn)	

Mounting bracket-to-body fasteners
Step 1	37	50
Step 2	Tighten an additional 90-degrees (1/4-turn)	

Crossbrace (axle beam suspension) fasteners
Step 1	52	70
Step 2	Tighten an additional 90-degrees (1/4-turn)	

Shock absorber-to-rear axle bolt
Step 1	30	40
Step 2	Tighten an additional 90-degrees (1/4-turn)	

Rear wheel bearing hub bolt
Step 1	59	80
Step 2	Tighten an additional 90-degrees (1/4-turn)	

Torque specifications	Ft-lbs (unless otherwise indicated)	Nm

➡ **Note:** One foot-pound (ft-lb) of torque is equivalent to 12 inch-pounds (in-lbs) of torque. Torque values below approximately 15 foot-pounds are expressed in inch-pounds, because most foot-pound torque wrenches are not accurate at these smaller values.

Rear suspension (continued)

	Ft-lbs	Nm
Shock absorber upper mounting bolts		
Step 1	37	50
Step 2	Tighten an additional 45-degrees (1/8-turn)	
Shock absorber-to-lower control arm bolt/nut		
2009 and earlier models	133	180
2010 and later models		
Step 1	30	40
Step 2	Tighten an additional 90-degrees (1/4-turn)	
Stabilizer bar (multi-link suspension)		
Connecting link-to-stabilizer bolt	33	45
Connecting link-to-trailing arm/knuckle nut	33	45
Clamp bolts		
Step 1	18.5	25
Step 2		
2009 and earlier models	Tighten an additional 45-degrees (1/8-turn)	
2010 and later models	Tighten an additional 90-degrees (1/4-turn)	
Stub axle bolts (2010 and later models)		
Step 1	22	30
Step 2	Tighten an additional 90-degrees (1/4-turn)	
Subframe bolts		
Front		
Step 1	52	70
Step 2	Tighten an additional 90-degrees (1/4-turn)	
Rear		
2010 and earlier models		
Step 1	66	90
Step 2	Tighten an additional 90-degrees (1/4-turn)	
2011 models		
Step 1	66	90
Step 2	Tighten an additional 90-degrees (1/4-turn)	
Step 3	Loosen one full turn (360-degrees)	
Step 4	66	90
Step 2	Tighten an additional 90-degrees (1/4-turn)	

Torque specifications	Ft-lbs (unless otherwise indicated)	Nm

➡ **Note:** One foot-pound (ft-lb) of torque is equivalent to 12 inch-pounds (in-lbs) of torque. Torque values below approximately 15 foot-pounds are expressed in inch-pounds, because most foot-pound torque wrenches are not accurate at these smaller values.

Steering

Steering column		
Mounting bolts	15	20
Universal joint pinch bolt/nut		
Step 1	15	20
Step 2	Tighten an additional 90-degrees (1/4-turn)	
Steering gear*		
Mounting bolts		
Step 1	37	50
Step 2	Tighten an additional 90-degrees (1/4-turn)	
Servo motor with control module-to-steering gear bolts	26	35
Tie-rod end-to-knuckle nut*		
Step 1	15	20
Step 2	Tighten an additional 90-degrees (1/4-turn)	
Tie-rod end (lock nut)	41	55
Steering wheel bolt*		
Step 1	22	30
Step 2	Tighten an additional 90-degrees (1/4-turn)	
Power steering pump (2011 models)		
Pulley mounting bolts	16.5	22
Mounting bolts	17	23
Pressure line fitting	23.5	32

* Note: The manufacturer states to replace the fasteners whenever they are removed.

Wheels

Wheel bolts	See Chapter 1	

Notes

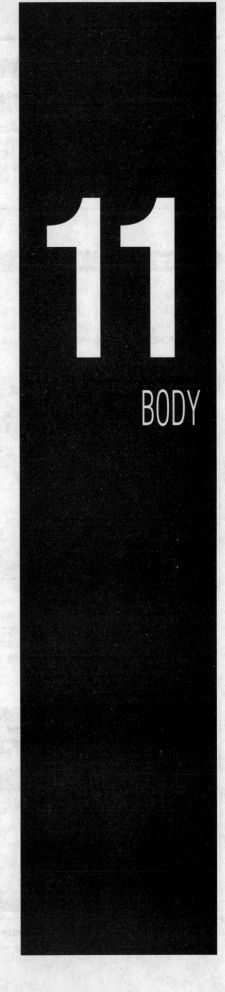

11

BODY

Section

1 General information

✽✽ WARNING:

The models covered by this manual are equipped with Supplemental Restraint Systems (SRS), more commonly known as airbags. Always disable the airbag system before working in the vicinity of any airbag system components to avoid the possibility of accidental deployment of the airbags, which could cause personal injury (see Chapter 12).

Certain body components are particularly vulnerable to accident damage and can be unbolted and repaired or replaced. Among these parts are the hood, doors, tailgate, liftgate, bumpers and front fenders.

Only general body maintenance practices and body panel repair procedures within the scope of the do-it-yourselfer are included in this Chapter.

2 Repair minor paint scratches

No matter how hard you try to keep your vehicle looking like new, it will inevitably be scratched, chipped or dented at some point. If the metal is actually dented, seek the advice of a professional. But you can fix minor scratches and chips yourself. Buy a touch-up paint kit from a dealer service department or an auto parts store. To ensure that you get the right color, you'll need to have the specific make, model and year of your vehicle and, ideally, the paint code, which is located on a special metal plate under the hood or in the door jamb.

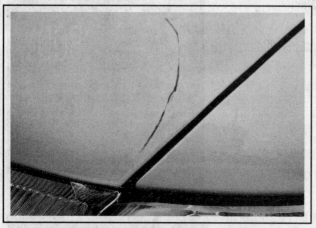

Make sure the damaged area is perfectly clean and rust free. If the touch-up kit has a wire brush, use it to clean the scratch or chip. Or use fine steel wool wrapped around the end of a pencil. Clean the scratched or chipped surface only, not the good paint surrounding it. Rinse the area with water and allow it to dry thoroughly

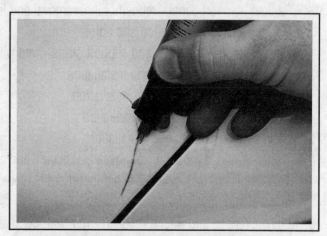

Thoroughly mix the paint, then apply a small amount with the touch-up kit brush or a very fine artist's brush. Brush in one direction as you fill the scratch area. Do not build up the paint higher than the surrounding paint

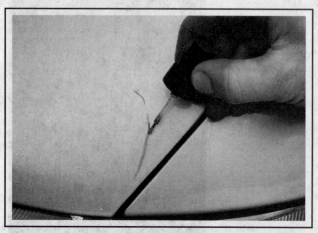

If the vehicle has a two-coat finish, apply the clear coat after the color coat has dried

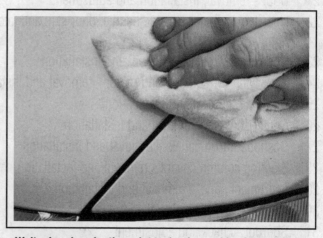

Wait a few days for the paint to dry thoroughly, then rub out the repainted area with a polishing compound to blend the new paint with the surrounding area. When you're happy with your work, wash and polish the area

PLASTIC BODY PANELS

The following repair procedures are for minor scratches and gouges. Repair of more serious damage should be left to a dealer service department or qualified auto body shop. Below is a list of the equipment and materials necessary to perform the following repair procedures on plastic body panels.

> *Wax, grease and silicone removing solvent*
> *Cloth-backed body tape*
> *Sanding discs*
> *Drill motor with three-inch disc holder*
> *Hand sanding block*
> *Rubber squeegees*
> *Sandpaper*
> *Non-porous mixing palette*
> *Wood paddle or putty knife*
> *Curved-tooth body file*
> *Flexible parts repair material*

Flexible panels (bumper trim)

1   Remove the damaged panel, if necessary or desirable. In most cases, repairs can be carried out with the panel installed.

2   Clean the area(s) to be repaired with a wax, grease and silicone removing solvent applied with a water-dampened cloth.

3   If the damage is structural, that is, if it extends through the panel, clean the backside of the panel area to be repaired as well. Wipe dry.

4   Sand the rear surface about 1-1/2 inches beyond the break.

5   Cut two pieces of fiberglass cloth large enough to overlap the break by about 1-1/2 inches. Cut only to the required length.

6   Mix the adhesive from the repair kit according to the instructions included with the kit, and apply a layer of the mixture approximately 1/8-inch thick on the backside of the panel. Overlap the break by at least 1-1/2 inches.

7   Apply one piece of fiberglass cloth to the adhesive and cover the cloth with additional adhesive. Apply a second piece of fiberglass cloth to the adhesive and immediately cover the cloth with additional adhesive in sufficient quantity to fill the weave.

8   Allow the repair to cure for 20 to 30 minutes at 60-degrees to 80-degrees F.

9   If necessary, trim the excess repair material at the edge.

10 Remove all of the paint film over and around the area(s) to be repaired. The repair material should not overlap the painted surface.

11 With a drill motor and a sanding disc (or a rotary file), cut a "V" along the break line approximately 1/2-inch wide. Remove all dust and loose particles from the repair area.

12 Mix and apply the repair material. Apply a light coat first over the damaged area; then continue applying material until it reaches a level slightly higher than the surrounding finish.

13 Cure the mixture for 20 to 30 minutes at 60-degrees to 80-degrees F.

14 Roughly establish the contour of the area being repaired with a body file. If low areas or pits remain, mix and apply additional adhesive.

15 Block sand the damaged area with sandpaper to establish the actual contour of the surrounding surface.

16 If desired, the repaired area can be temporarily protected with several light coats of primer. Because of the special paints and techniques required for flexible body panels, it is recommended that the vehicle be taken to a paint shop for completion of the body repair.

STEEL BODY PANELS

⯈ **See photo sequence**

Repair of dents

17 When repairing dents, the first job is to pull the dent out until the affected area is as close as possible to its original shape. There is no point in trying to restore the original shape completely as the metal in the damaged area will have stretched on impact and cannot be restored to its original contours. It is better to bring the level of the dent up to a point that is about 1/8-inch below the level of the surrounding metal. In cases where the dent is very shallow, it is not worth trying to pull it out at all.

18 If the backside of the dent is accessible, it can be hammered out gently from behind using a soft-face hammer. While doing this, hold a block of wood firmly against the opposite side of the metal to absorb the hammer blows and prevent the metal from being stretched.

19 If the dent is in a section of the body which has double layers, or some other factor makes it inaccessible from behind, a different technique is required. Drill several small holes through the metal inside the damaged area, particularly in the deeper sections. Screw long, self-tapping screws into the holes just enough for them to get a good grip in the metal. Now pulling on the protruding heads of the screws with locking pliers can pull out the dent.

20 The next stage of repair is the removal of paint from the damaged area and from an inch or so of the surrounding metal. This is easily done with a wire brush or sanding disk in a drill motor, although it can be done just as effectively by hand with sandpaper. To complete the preparation for filling, score the surface of the bare metal with a screwdriver or the tang of a file or drill small holes in the affected area. This will provide a good grip for the filler material. To complete the repair, see the Section on filling and painting.

Repair of rust holes or gashes

21 Remove all paint from the affected area and from an inch or so of the surrounding metal using a sanding disk or wire brush mounted in a drill motor. If these are not available, a few sheets of sandpaper will do the job just as effectively.

22 With the paint removed, you will be able to determine the severity of the corrosion and decide whether to replace the whole panel, if possible, or repair the affected area. New body panels are not as expensive as most people think and it is often quicker to install a new panel than to repair large areas of rust.

23 Remove all trim pieces from the affected area except those which will act as a guide to the original shape of the damaged body, such as headlight shells, etc. Using metal snips or a hacksaw blade, remove all loose metal and any other metal that is badly affected by rust. Hammer the edges of the hole in to create a slight depression for the filler material.

24 Wire-brush the affected area to remove the powdery rust from the surface of the metal. If the back of the rusted area is accessible, treat it with rust inhibiting paint.

25 Before filling is done, block the hole in some way. This can be done with sheet metal riveted or screwed into place, or by stuffing the hole with wire mesh.

26 Once the hole is blocked off, the affected area can be filled and painted. See the following subsection on filling and painting.

These photos illustrate a method of repairing simple dents. They are intended to supplement Body repair - minor damage in this Chapter and should not be used as the sole instructions for body repair on these vehicles.

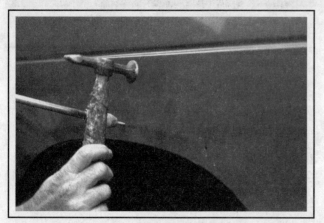

1 If you can't access the backside of the body panel to hammer out the dent, pull it out with a slide-hammer-type dent puller. Tap with a hammer near the edge of the dent to help 'pop' the metal back to its original shape, about 1/8-inch below the surface of the surrounding metal

2 Using coarse-grit sandpaper, remove the paint down to the bare metal. Clean the repair area with wax/silicone remover.

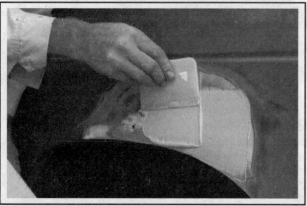

3 Following label instructions, mix up a batch of plastic filler and hardener, then quickly press it into the metal with a plastic applicator. Work the filler until it matches the original contour and is slightly above the surrounding metal

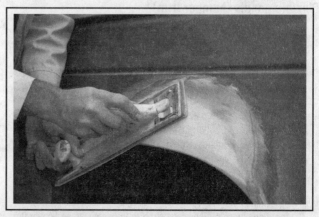

4 Let the filler harden until you can just dent it with your fingernail. File, then sand the filler down until it's smooth and even. Work down to finer grits of sandpaper - always using a board or block - ending up with 360 or 400 grit

5 When the area is smooth to the touch, clean the area and mask around it. Apply several layers of primer to the area. A professional-type spray gun is being used here, but aerosol spray primer works fine

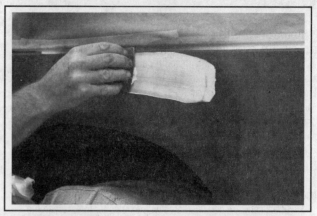

6 Fill imperfections or scratches with glazing compound. Sand with 360 or 400-grit and re-spray. Finish sand the primer with 600 grit, clean thoroughly, then apply the finish coat. Don't attempt to rub out or wax the repair area until the paint has dried completely (at least two weeks)

Filling and painting

27 Many types of body fillers are available, but generally speaking, body repair kits which contain filler paste and a tube of resin hardener are best for this type of repair work. A wide, flexible plastic or nylon applicator will be necessary for imparting a smooth and contoured finish to the surface of the filler material. Mix up a small amount of filler on a clean piece of wood or cardboard (use the hardener sparingly). Follow the manufacturer's instructions on the package, otherwise the filler will set incorrectly.

28 Using the applicator, apply the filler paste to the prepared area. Draw the applicator across the surface of the filler to achieve the desired contour and to level the filler surface. As soon as a contour that approximates the original one is achieved, stop working the paste. If you continue, the paste will begin to stick to the applicator. Continue to add thin layers of paste at 20-minute intervals until the level of the filler is just above the surrounding metal.

29 Once the filler has hardened, the excess can be removed with a body file. From then on, progressively finer grades of sandpaper should be used, starting with a 180-grit paper and finishing with 600-grit wet-or-dry paper. Always wrap the sandpaper around a flat rubber or wooden block, otherwise the surface of the filler will not be completely flat. During the sanding of the filler surface, the wet-or-dry paper should be periodically rinsed in water. This will ensure that a very smooth finish is produced in the final stage.

30 At this point, the repair area should be surrounded by a ring of bare metal, which in turn should be encircled by the finely feathered edge of good paint. Rinse the repair area with clean water until all of the dust produced by the sanding operation is gone.

31 Spray the entire area with a light coat of primer. This will reveal any imperfections in the surface of the filler. Repair the imperfections with fresh filler paste or glaze filler and once more smooth the surface with sandpaper. Repeat this spray-and-repair procedure until you are satisfied that the surface of the filler and the feathered edge of the paint are perfect. Rinse the area with clean water and allow it to dry completely.

32 The repair area is now ready for painting. Spray painting must be carried out in a warm, dry, windless and dust free atmosphere. These conditions can be created if you have access to a large indoor work area, but if you are forced to work in the open, you will have to pick the day very carefully. If you are working indoors, dousing the floor in the work area with water will help settle the dust that would otherwise be in the air. If the repair area is confined to one body panel, mask off the surrounding panels. This will help minimize the effects of a slight mismatch in paint color. Trim pieces such as chrome strips, door handles, etc., will also need to be masked off or removed. Use masking tape and several thickness of newspaper for the masking operations.

33 Before spraying, shake the paint can thoroughly, then spray a test area until the spray painting technique is mastered. Cover the repair area with a thick coat of primer. The thickness should be built up using several thin layers of primer rather than one thick one. Using 600-grit wet-or-dry sandpaper, rub down the surface of the primer until it is very smooth. While doing this, the work area should be thoroughly rinsed with water and the wet-or-dry sandpaper periodically rinsed as well. Allow the primer to dry before spraying additional coats.

34 Spray on the top coat, again building up the thickness by using several thin layers of paint. Begin spraying in the center of the repair area and then, using a circular motion, work out until the whole repair area and about two inches of the surrounding original paint is covered. Remove all masking material 10 to 15 minutes after spraying on the final coat of paint. Allow the new paint at least two weeks to harden, then use a very fine rubbing compound to blend the edges of the new paint into the existing paint. Finally, apply a coat of wax.

4 Body repair - major damage

1 Major damage must be repaired by an auto body shop specifically equipped to perform body and frame repairs. These shops have the specialized equipment required to do the job properly.

2 If the damage is extensive, the frame must be checked for proper alignment or the vehicle's handling characteristics may be adversely affected and other components may wear at an accelerated rate.

3 Due to the fact that all of the major body components (hood, fenders, etc.) are separate and replaceable units, any seriously damaged components should be replaced rather than repaired. Sometimes the components can be found in a wrecking yard that specializes in used vehicle components, often at considerable savings over the cost of new parts.

5 Upholstery, carpets and vinyl trim - maintenance

UPHOLSTERY AND CARPETS

1 Every three months remove the floormats and clean the interior of the vehicle (more frequently if necessary). Use a stiff whiskbroom to brush the carpeting and loosen dirt and dust, then vacuum the upholstery and carpets thoroughly, especially along seams and crevices.

2 Dirt and stains can be removed from carpeting with basic household or automotive carpet shampoos available in spray cans. Follow the directions and vacuum again, then use a stiff brush to bring back the "nap" of the carpet.

3 Most interiors have cloth or vinyl upholstery, either of which can be cleaned and maintained with a number of material-specific cleaners or shampoos available in auto supply stores. Follow the directions on the product for usage, and always spot-test any upholstery cleaner on an inconspicuous area (bottom edge of a backseat cushion) to ensure that it doesn't cause a color shift in the material.

4   After cleaning, vinyl upholstery should be treated with a protectant.

➡ **Note: Make sure the protectant container indicates the product can be used on seats - some products may make a seat too slippery.**

✳ CAUTION:

Do not use protectant on vinyl-covered steering wheels.

5   Leather upholstery requires special care. It should be cleaned regularly with saddlesoap or leather cleaner. Never use alcohol, gasoline, nail polish remover or thinner to clean leather upholstery.

6   After cleaning, regularly treat leather upholstery with a leather conditioner, rubbed in with a soft cotton cloth. Never use car wax on leather upholstery.

7   In areas where the interior of the vehicle is subject to bright sunlight, cover leather seating areas of the seats with a sheet if the vehicle is to be left out for any length of time.

VINYL TRIM

8   Don't clean vinyl trim with detergents, caustic soap or petroleum-based cleaners. Plain soap and water works just fine, with a soft brush to clean dirt that may be ingrained. Wash the vinyl as frequently as the rest of the vehicle.

9   After cleaning, application of a high-quality rubber and vinyl protectant will help prevent oxidation and cracks. The protectant can also be applied to weather-stripping, vacuum lines and rubber hoses, which often fail as a result of chemical degradation, and to the tires.

6   Fastener and trim removal

▸ **Refer to illustration 6.4**

1   There is a variety of plastic fasteners used to hold trim panels, splash shields and other parts in place in addition to typical screws, nuts and bolts. Once you are familiar with them, they can usually be removed without too much difficulty.

2   The proper tools and approach can prevent added time and expense to a project by minimizing the number of broken fasteners and/or parts.

3   The following illustration shows various types of fasteners that are typically used on most vehicles and how to remove and install them

Fasteners

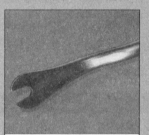

This tool is designed to remove special fasteners. A small pry tool used for removing nails will also work well in place of this tool

A Phillips head screwdriver can be used to release the center portion, but light pressure must be used because the plastic is easily damaged. Once the center is up, the fastener can easily be pried from its hole

Here is a view with the center portion fully released. Install the fastener as shown, then press the center in to set it

This fastener is used for exterior panels and shields. The center portion must be pried up to release the fastener. Install the fastener with the center up, then press the center in to set it

This type of fastener is used commonly for interior panels. Use a small blunt tool to press the small pin at the center in to release it . . .

. . . the pin will stay with the fastener in the released position

Reset the fastener for installation by moving the pin out. Install the fastener, then press the pin flush with the fastener to set it

This fastener is used for exterior and interior panels. It has no moving parts. Simply pry the fastener from its hole like the claw of a hammer removes a nail. Without a tool that can get under the top of the fastener, it can be very difficult to remove

(see illustration). Replacement fasteners are commonly found at most auto parts stores, if necessary.

4   Trim panels are typically made of plastic and their flexibility can help during removal. The key to their removal is to use a tool to pry the panel near its retainers to release it without damaging surrounding areas or breaking-off any retainers. The retainers will usually snap out of their designated slot or hole after force is applied to them. Stiff plastic tools designed for prying on trim panels are available at most auto parts stores (see illustration). Tools that are tapered and wrapped in protective tape, such as a screwdriver or small pry tool, are also very effective when used with care.

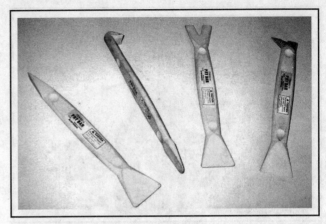

6.4 These small plastic pry tools are ideal for prying off trim panels

7   Hinges and locks - maintenance

Once every 3000 miles, or every three months, the hinges and latch assemblies on the doors, hood and trunk should be given a few drops of light oil or lock lubricant. The door latch strikers should also be lubricated with a thin coat of grease to reduce wear and ensure free movement. Lubricate the door and trunk locks with spray-on graphite lubricant.

8   Windshield and fixed glass - replacement

Replacement of the windshield and fixed glass requires the use of special fast-setting adhesive/caulk materials and some specialized tools and techniques. These operations should be left to a dealer service department or a shop specializing in glass work.

9   Radiator support panel - repositioning, removal and installation

1   The radiator support panel is the section of bodywork that is mounted across the front of the vehicle. The radiator support panel and its associated components can be removed as an assembly; the radiator support panel can also be moved forward several inches to the service position without having to disconnect all the components mounted on it. Once the radiator support panel is placed in the service position, access to components at the front of the engine are greatly improved.

PLACING THE RADIATOR SUPPORT PANEL IN THE SERVICE POSITION

▸ **Refer to illustration 9.6, 9.9, 9.11, 9.12 and 9.13**

➡ **Note: To carry out this procedure, it will be necessary to use two 8 to 10 inch long bolts.**

2   Raise the front of the vehicle and support it securely on jackstands.

3   Remove the lower splash shield below the engine (see Chapter 1, Section 6).

➡ **Note: On models equipped with an auxiliary heater, remove the three fasteners from the splash shield.**

4   Remove the engine cover (see Chapter 1, Section 7).

5   Remove the front bumper (see Section 12).

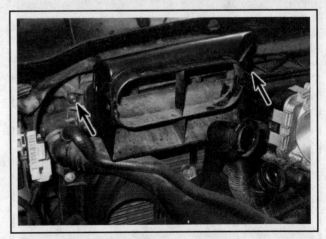

9.6 Air intake duct fasteners

6   Remove the intake air duct (see illustration).

7   Open the hood cable release coupler, disconnect the cable and unclip the coupler from the radiator support (see Section 11).

8   On turbo models, disconnect the air duct from the air charge cooler, then remove the air duct hoses to the air charge cooler. Unclip the A/C hose from the bracket.

9.9 Disconnect the electrical connector to the A/C high pressure switch

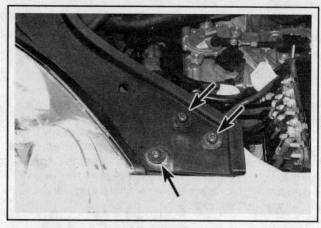

9.11 Radiator support panel upper fasteners and radiator support panel-to-fender fasteners

9 Disconnect the harness connector for the A/C high pressure switch (see illustration).

10 Remove the horns (see Chapter 12).

11 Remove the upper fasteners for the radiator support panel to the fenders (see illustration).

➡ **Note: On 2011 models, remove the headlight housing-to-radiator support and fender mounting fasteners.**

12 Remove one of the bumper support bracket fasteners from each side of the bumper support, then thread the service tool or bolt where the fasteners were and remove the remainder of the bumper support bracket fasteners (see illustration).

13 Carefully draw the radiator support panel away from the front of the engine compartment as far as possible without disconnecting the coolant hoses (see illustration).

14 Secure the service position by aligning the rear bolt holes at the top with the front bolt holes and inserting the bolts to retain the radiator support in position.

15 The radiator support panel can be refitted by following the repositioning procedure in reverse. Ensure that all the fasteners are tightened securely. On completion, check the positioning of the headlights and adjust if necessary (see Chapter 12).

REMOVAL AND INSTALLATION

❉ **WARNING:**

Wait until the engine is completely cool before beginning this procedure.

❉ **WARNING:**

The air conditioning system is under high pressure. DO NOT loosen any fittings or remove any components until after the system has been discharged. Air conditioning refrigerant should be properly discharged into an EPA-approved container at a dealership service department or an automotive air conditioning facility. Always wear eye protection when disconnecting air conditioning system fittings.

16 Remove the A/C condenser from the radiator (refer to Chapter 3 for mounting details), but do not disconnect the refrigerant lines. Tie the condenser to the lower corners of the fenders using a suitable piece of wire; do not allow it to hang unsupported from the flexible hoses.

9.12 Thread the service tool or bolt where the fasteners were, then remove the remainder of the bumper support bracket fasteners

9.13 With the bolts in place, pull the radiator support forward

If the condenser cannot be properly secured prior to removal, have the air conditioning system discharged by a dealership service department or an automotive air conditioning facility.

17 Refer to Steps 1 through 15 and place the radiator support panel in the service position.

18 Drain the coolant as described in Chapter 1.

19 Disconnect the coolant hoses from the radiator as described in Chapter 3. On models with air conditioning, also unbolt the refrigerant lines from the condenser and disconnect the electrical connectors from the A/C high pressure switch (see Chapter 3).

20 Disconnect the hood release cable from the hood latch mechanism (see Section 11).

21 Disconnect the electrical connectors for the headlights, the side marker lights and, if equipped, the headlight aiming control motors. Also disconnect the electrical connectors located at the left hand corner of the engine compartment.

22 Disconnect the power steering lines to the oil cooler and remove the cooler.

23 On models equipped with an automatic transaxle, disconnect the transaxle cooler lines and cap the ends of the lines.

24 With the help of an assistant to support the panel, remove the nuts from the ends of the service tools, then withdraw the radiator support panel from the front of the vehicle.

25 Installation is the reverse of removal. Check the operation of the front lights, and the hood lock and safety catch. Refill and bleed the cooling system as described in Chapter 1, and have the headlights checked for correct alignment.

10 Hood - removal, installation and adjustment

➡ **Note: The hood is awkward to remove and install - at least two people should perform this procedure.**

REMOVAL AND INSTALLATION

▸ **Refer to illustration 10.4**

1 Use blankets or pads to cover the cowl area of the body and the fenders.

2 Remove the wiper washer cover; disconnect the windshield washer hose and electrical connector.

3 Remove the harness cover from the hood hinge by sliding the locking tab to the left, then pull the cover off and disconnect the electrical harness.

4 Make alignment marks around the hinge plates using a permanent marker to insure the same installation (see illustration).

5 On 2010 and earlier models, have an assistant support the hood and detach the upper end of the hood support strut (see Section 11).

6 Remove the hinge-to-hood nuts and lift off the hood.

7 Installation is the reverse of removal.

ADJUSTMENT

▸ **Refer to illustration 10.10**

8 Fore-and-aft and side-to-side adjustment of the hood is done by moving the hood in relation to the hinge plates after loosening the nuts.

9 Loosen the nuts and move the hood into correct alignment. Move it only a little at a time. Tighten the hinge nuts and carefully lower the hood to check the alignment.

10 Adjust the hood bumpers on the hood by turning them in or out to make the hood flush with the fenders when closed (see illustration).

11 The safety latch assembly can also be adjusted up-and-down and side-to-side after loosening the nuts.

12 Adjust the buffer stops on each side of the radiator support by screwing the stop in or out.

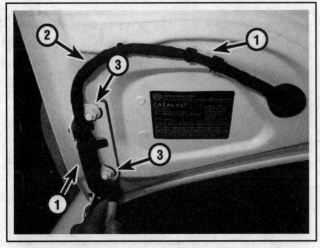

10.4 Hood hinge details

1	Harness clips	3	Mounting fasteners
2	Harness and washer hose		

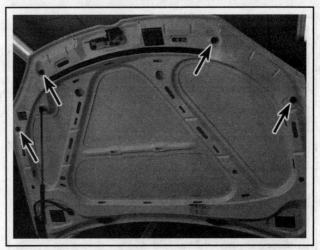

10.10 Adjust the hood height by screwing the hood bumpers in or out

11 Hood latch, release cable and support struts - removal and installation

LATCH

▶ **Refer to illustrations 11.2, 11.3 and 11.4**

1　Open the hood and remove the grille (see Section 13).
2　Open the release coupling and disconnect the hood latch cable (see illustration).
3　Remove the latch fasteners, lift the latch assembly out of the radiator support and disconnect the electrical connector from the latch assembly (see illustration).
4　Disconnect the retaining clip and detach the cable from the latch assembly (see illustration).
5　Installation is the reverse of removal.

11.2 Hood cable release coupling details

1　Release coupling cover
2　Release lever-to-coupling cable
3　Hood latch-to-release coupling cable

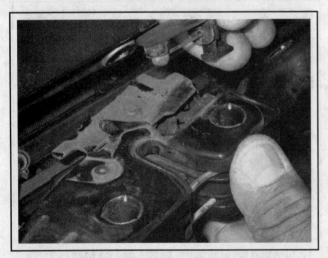

11.4 Pry the cable retaining clip end back and detach the cable from the latch

CABLE

▶ **Refer to illustrations 11.7 and 11.9**

➡ **Note: The hood release cable is divided in two sections, from the hood release lever (inside the vehicle)-to-release coupling and the release coupling-to-hood latch.**

6　To detach the release coupling-to-hood latch cable section, follow Steps 1 through 4.
7　From inside the vehicle, insert a small screwdriver into the gap between operating lever and clip, then pry the clip back and remove the lever (see illustration).
8　Pry up the front section of the sill trim and driver's side kick panel (see Section 27).
9　Pull the cable housing from the release lever and disconnect the cable end from the release arm (see illustration). Remove the cable.

11.3 Latch assembly mounting fastener locations

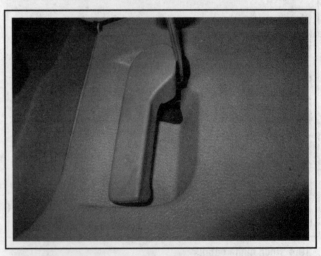

11.7 Insert a screwdriver into the gap and pry back the retaining clip

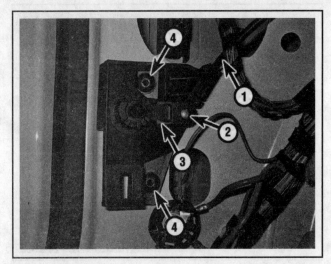

11.9 Hood release handle details

1 Hood release cable housing
2 Hood release cable end
3 Release lever arm
4 Release lever mounting fasteners

10 Attach a wire or string to the end of the old cable in the engine compartment.

11 Working inside the passenger compartment, pull the cable through the cowl and into the passenger compartment.

12 Connect the string or wire to the new cable and pull it through the cowl into the engine compartment.

13 The remainder of installation is the reverse of removal. Be sure to fasten all of the cable retaining clips in their original locations.

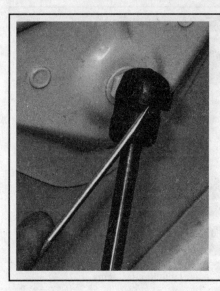

11.15 Pry the clip off to release the hood support strut

SUPPORT STRUT

◆ **Refer to illustration 11.15**

➡ **Note: This procedure only applies to 2010 and earlier models; 2011 models use a removable hood support rod.**

14 Open the hood and support it securely.

15 Use a small screwdriver to carefully lift the retaining springs (see illustration) at both ends of the support strut. Then pry or pull the strut from the ballstud to detach it from the vehicle.

16 Installation is the reverse of removal.

12 Bumper covers - removal and installation

1 Front and rear bumpers are composed of a fascia, or bumper (exterior) cover, and a metal structural beam.

FRONT BUMPER COVER

◆ **Refer to illustrations 12.3, 12.4, 12.5, 12.6, and 12.10**

2 Raise the front of the vehicle and support it securely on jackstands.

3 Remove the lower splash shield below the engine (see Chapter 1, Section 6) and the lower bumper cover fasteners (see illustration).

12.3 Bumper cover lower mounting fasteners

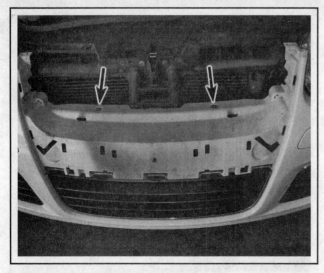

12.4 Bumper cover upper mounting fasteners

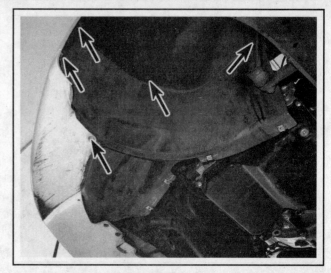

12.5 Remove the mounting fasteners securing the lower section of the inner fender splash shield

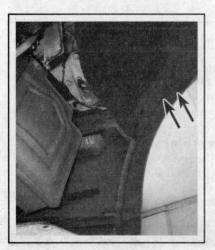

12.6 Remove the fasteners securing the bumper cover to the front fenderwells

12.10 Remove the bumper cover, sliding it squarely from each side

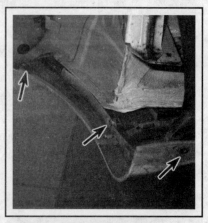

12.13 Rear bumper cover-to-wheelwell fasteners

4   Open the hood, remove the radiator grille (see Section 13) and remove the upper mounting fasteners (see illustration).

➡ Note: On Rabbit models, there are four upper mounting fasteners: two vertical and two horizontal. On 2011 Jetta models, there are six upper fasteners.

5   Remove the mounting fasteners and remove the lower section of the inner fender splash shield (see illustration).

6   Working at each front wheelwell, remove the fasteners from the bumper cover (see illustration) and unclip the rear edge of the bumper cover.

7   On Rabbit models, use a screwdriver to release the two retaining tabs located behind the lower grilles on both sides of the bumper.

8   If equipped, remove the foglights from the bumper (see Chapter 12, if necessary). On certain models, the ambient temperature sensor is mounted on the rear surface of the bumper; disconnect the electrical connector.

9   If equipped with a front spoiler, remove the spoiler mounting fasteners from below and remove the spoiler from the bumper cover.

10 Carefully withdraw the bumper assembly by sliding it squarely away from the front of the vehicle (see illustration). If equipped with headlight wipers, pull the bumper out to the point where the washer hose can be detached from its bumper-to-cross panel connection before fully withdrawing the bumper.

➡ Note: The height of the bumper can be altered by adjusting the position of the threaded sleeves inside the bumper mounting tubes.

11 If the bumper cover needs to be removed from the metal bumper, simply remove the fasteners and release catches and separate the two components.

12 Installation is the reverse of removal. Loosely install all fasteners before fully tightening them.

REAR BUMPER COVER

▶ Refer to illustration 12.13, 12.14, 12.15 and 12.16

13 Working at the rear wheelwells, remove the fasteners for the liner to the lower rear corner, fold the wheelwell liner back and remove the fasteners securing the bumper cover to the wheelwell (see illustration).

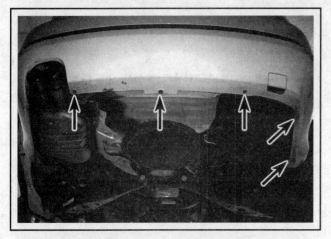

12.14 Rear bumper cover lower mounting fasteners

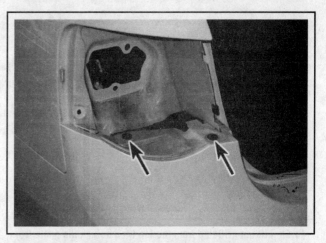

12.15 Rear bumper cover upper mounting fasteners

14 Remove the rear bumper cover lower fasteners from under the bumper (see illustration).

15 Remove the taillight housing (see Chapter 12) and remove the bumper cover upper fasteners (see illustration).

16 Carefully withdraw the bumper cover assembly by sliding it squarely away from the rear of the vehicle. Disengage the locking tabs from the edges one at a time by grasping the lower edge of the bumper just to the rear of the wheelwell and pivoting it upwards and away from the rear quarter panel to release it (see illustration).

17 The bumper support brackets can be removed from the bumper by removing the fasteners.

18 Installation is the reverse of removal. Loosely install all fasteners before fully tightening them.

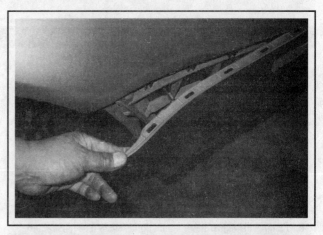

12.16 Unclip the trailing edge of the bumper cover from its retaining bracket, then pull the rear bumper away from the vehicle

13 Radiator grille - removal and installation

▶ **Refer to illustrations 13.1, 13.2a and 13.2b**

1 Open the hood and remove the upper grill fasteners (see illus-

tration), then use a small screwdriver to disengage the clips from the grille.

2 Remove the lower grille fasteners (if equipped) and remove the

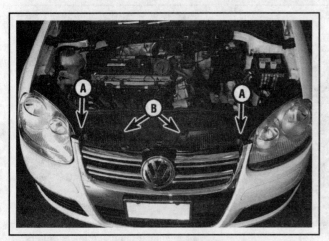

13.1 Remove the upper grille mounting fasteners (A), then remove the clips (B) - Jetta shown, other models similar

13.2a Remove the grille lower mounting fasteners (Jetta and GTI models only)

13.2b Lift the grille up from the top then detach the grille from the bumper cover (Jetta models shown, GTI models similar)

grille (see illustrations).

➡ **Note: On Rabbit and 2011 Jetta models, tilt the grille out from the top slightly, then pull the bottom of the grille outwards to disengage the clips from the bumper cover.**

3   Installation is the reverse of removal.

14 Front fender - removal and installation

▶ **Refer to illustrations 14.4, 14.6, 14.7 and 14.8**

1   Loosen the wheel bolts, then raise the front of the vehicle and support it securely on jackstands. Remove the wheel

2   Remove the lower splash shield below the engine (see Chapter 1, Section 6).

3   Remove the front bumper cover (see Section 12).

4   Remove the inner fender splash shield fasteners and remove the inner fender splash shield (see illustration).

5   Open the door and remove the two fender-to-door pillar fasteners in the door jamb.

6   Remove the fender lower mounting fasteners (see illustration).

7   Remove the fasteners for the fender to the front support brace and the lower inner fenderwell brace (see illustration).

8   Remove the fasteners securing the top of the fender (see illustration). Detach the hood release cable from the fender (right side).

9   Detach the fender. It's a good idea to have an assistant support the fender while it's being moved away from the vehicle to prevent damage to the surrounding body panels.

10   Installation is the reverse of the removal procedure. Tighten all fasteners securely.

14.4 Remove the inner fender splash shield mounting fasteners

11   Tighten the wheel bolts to the torque listed in the Chapter 1 Specifications.

14.6 Remove the lower fender fasteners

14.7 Remove the fender support brace and front fender fasteners

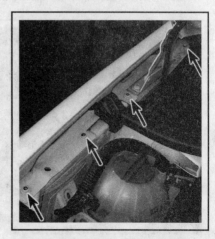

14.8 Fender top mounting fasteners

15 Cowl cover - removal and installation

▶ **Refer to illustrations 15.2, 15.3 and 15.4**

1   Open the hood, then refer to Chapter 12 and remove the windshield wiper arms.

2   Pry the side cowl seals up from both ends of the cowl (see illustration).

3   Remove the cowl weather strip; start on one side and pull the strip forward until it reaches the opposite side. Remove the louvered cowl cover (see illustration).

➡ **Note: On 2011 models, the louvered cowl cover is made of two overlapping pieces, attached only by clips along the perimeter of the cowl panels.**

4   Remove the cowl cover retaining fasteners (see illustration).

5   Lift the plastic cowl cover upwards and out.

6   Installation is the reverse of removal.

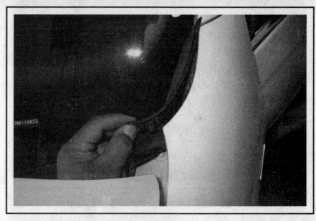

15.2 Side cowl seal retaining clip

15.3 Remove the louvered cowl cover - 2010 and earlier model shown

15.4 Remove the cowl mounting fasteners and cowl panel - 2010 and earlier model shown

16 Trunk lid (sedan models) - removal, installation and adjustment

▶ **Refer to illustrations 16.2, 16.3, 16.4 and 16.6**

➡ **Note: The trunk lid is heavy and somewhat awkward to remove and install - at least two people should perform this procedure.**

1   Open the trunk lid and cover the edges of the trunk compartment with pads or cloths to protect the painted surfaces when the lid is removed.

2   Slide the cover off of the truck latch, then separate the trunk emergency release handle halves and remove the cable from the handle (see illustration). Pull the release handle from the socket and remove the mounting screw and cover.

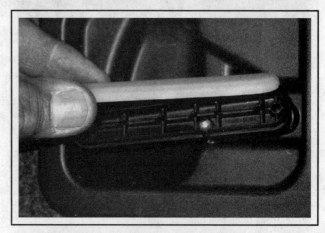

16.2 Separate the trunk release handle halves, remove the cable end and pop the handle out of the socket

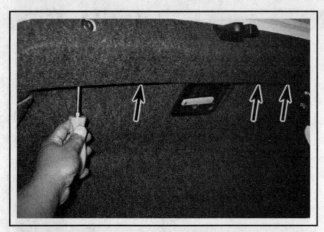

16.3 Remove the trunk lid panel mounting fasteners

16.4 Use a trim tool to pry around the edges of the panel

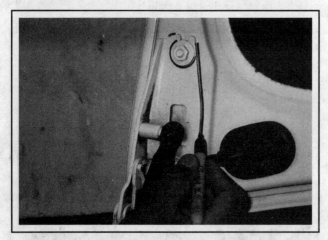

16.6 Use a marking pen to outline the hinge plate and mounting nuts

3   Remove the trim panel mounting fasteners from the trunk lid (see illustration).

4   Use a trim tool to pry off the trunk trim panel (see illustration).

5   Disconnect the electrical harness connectors and pull the harness out from the trunk lid.

6   Mark the relationship between the trunk lid and the hinges by drawing around the outside of each hinge with a marker (see illustration).

7   Remove the trunk lid support struts (see Section 17).

8   With the help of an assistant to support the trunk lid, remove the hinge-to-trunk lid retaining nuts, and lift the lid clear.

9   Installation is the reverse of removal. Check the trunk lid for correct alignment. If necessary, loosen the hinge nuts to adjust, then retighten them; there should be an even gap of approximately 1/8 inch (3 mm) between the outside edge of the trunk lid and the surrounding bodywork. Adjust the trunk lid height (if necessary) by removing rubber caps on the buffer stops on each side of the trunk lid and screwing the stop in or out as necessary.

17   Trunk lid latch, lock cylinder and support struts (sedan models) - removal and installation

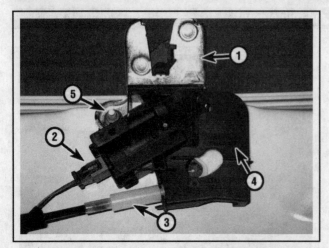

17.2 Trunk latch mounting details

1	Truck latch	4	Plastic cover
2	Electrical connector	5	Retaining nut (second nut is
3	Actuating cable		under plastic cover)

LATCH

▶ **Refer to illustration 17.2**

1   Refer to Section 16 and remove the inner trim panel from the trunk lid.

2   Disconnect the lock actuating cable from the latch (see illustration).

3   Mark the installed position of the latch with a marker. Remove the plastic cover, then the retaining nuts and withdraw the lock unit from the trunk lid. As it is withdrawn, unplug the electrical connector from the lock.

4   Installation is the reverse of removal.

➥ **Note: When reinstalling the trunk lid latch, align the bolt heads with the marks made during removal.**

LOCK CYLINDER

5   Detach the operating cable from the joint by unclipping the plastic fastener and rotating the joint while pulling the cable from the lever.

6   Disconnect the wiring from the lock cylinder unit as it becomes accessible.

7   Remove the lock cylinder mounting fasteners and remove the lock.

8   Installation is the reverse of removal.

SUPPORT STRUTS

9   The trunk lid supports are removed in the same manner as the hood support struts. Refer to Section 11 for this procedure.

18 Liftgate (coupe and wagon models) - removal, installation and adjustment

▶ **Refer to illustration 18.8**

➡ **Note: The liftgate is heavy and somewhat awkward to remove and install - at least two people should perform this procedure.**

1   Open the liftgate, then remove the trim panel/grab handle fasteners at the center of the lower edge of the liftgate.

2   Remove the fasteners at the left and right hand sides, then carefully pry the lower section of the trim panel from the liftgate using just enough force to release the spring clips. Similarly, unclip the upper section of the trim panel from the liftgate rear window opening.

3   Disconnect the wiring from the liftgate components (lock switch, wiper motor, and rear light units) at the connectors. Note the routing and attachment locations of the wires.

4   Mark the relationship between the liftgate and its hinges using a marker.

5   With an assistant to help support the liftgate, use a small screwdriver to carefully lift the retaining springs (see illustration 11.15) at both ends of the support strut.

6   Pry or pull the strut from the ballstud to detach it from the vehicle.

7   Carefully pry the hinge covers off and remove the covers.

8   Remove the liftgate-to-hinge fasteners (see illustration), and lift the liftgate clear of the vehicle.

9   Installation is the reverse of removal. Check that the liftgate is correctly aligned before fully tightening the liftgate hinge bolts.

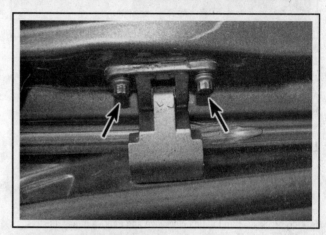

18.8 Liftgate hinge fasteners

10   The latch assembly can also be adjusted up-and-down after loosening the nuts.

11   The closed position of the liftgate can be adjusted by altering the positions of the rubber liftgate stops towards the top of the liftgate opening.

12   Unclip the plastic cover from the liftgate stop and adjust the center adjusting screw in or out as necessary.

19 Liftgate latch, lock cylinder and support struts (coupe and wagon models) - removal and installation

COUPE MODELS

▶ **Refer to illustrations 19.1a, 19.1b, 19.2, 19.6, 19.7a and 19.7b**

1   Open up the liftgate and remove the trim panel as described in Section 18.

➡ **Note: If the lock is inoperative, the tailgate can be opened manually by opening the emergency access cover from inside the vehicle (see illustrations).**

19.1a Remove the emergency cover . . .

19.1b . . . and operate the lever to open the liftgate

Liftgate lock

2   Disconnect the wiring from the lock (see illustration).

3   Remove the retaining fasteners and remove the lock from the tailgate.

4   Installation is the reverse of removal.

Liftgate handle/release unit

5   Remove the rear wiper motor as described in Chapter 12.

6   Disconnect the wiring from the handle/release unit (see illustration).

7   Remove the retaining fasteners holding the unit to the liftgate and locking brackets. Turn the unit clockwise and remove it (see illustrations).

19.6 Disconnect the wiring

19.7a Remove the retaining fasteners . . .

19.2 Disconnect the wiring from the liftgate lock

8   Installation is a reversal of removal; however, before installing the trim panel, check the operation of the lock components.

WAGON MODELS

9   Open up the liftgate and remove the trim panel as described in Section 18.

Liftgate lock

10 Disconnect the electrical connector on the rear side of the lock.

11 Remove the retaining fasteners and remove the lock from the liftgate.

12 Installation is the reverse of removal.

Liftgate handle/release button

13 Disconnect the electrical connector from the back side of the handle button.

14 Remove the two retaining fasteners and the threaded pin, then pull off the cover.

15 Remove the handle/release button from the liftgate.

16 Installation is a reversal of removal; however, before installing the trim panel, check the operation of the lock components.

SUPPORT STRUTS (ALL MODELS)

17 The liftgate support struts are removed in the same manner as the hood support struts. Refer to Section 11 for this procedure.

19.7b . . . and remove the liftgate handle/release unit

20 Door trim panels - removal and installation

DRIVER'S DOOR

▶ **Refer to illustrations 20.2a, 20.2b, 20.3, 20.4, 20.5, 20.6a, 20.6b and 20.7**

1 On 2011 models, open the door and carefully pry the upper trim from the door panel.

2 Lift the armrest from the trim panel by carefully inserting a screwdriver or similar tool under its inner, rear lip, and prying upwards. Disconnect the wiring from the switches (see illustrations).

3 Remove the two trim panel screws located in the armrest recess (see illustration).

4 Remove the fasteners from the lower edge of the trim panel (see illustration).

➡ **Note: Some early models may have an upper fastener at the front corner of the door panel.**

5 To release the door trim panel retaining clips, carefully pry between the panel and door with a trim tool (see illustration). Work around the outside of the panel, and when all the retaining clips are released, lift the door trim panel upwards and off the window slot.

6 Disconnect the harness retaining clips and electrical connectors (see illustrations).

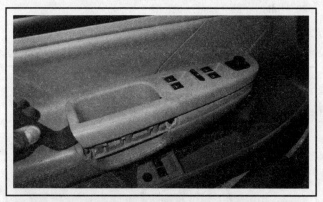

20.2a Carefully pry up the driver's side armrest . . .

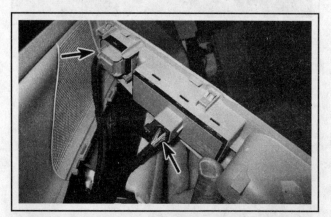

20.2b . . . then disconnect the electrical connectors from the switches

20.3 Remove the door panel fasteners under the arm rest

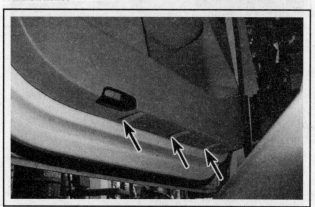

20.4 Lower trim panel fasteners

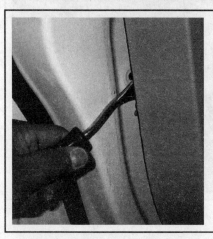

20.5 Use a trim tool to pry the door trim panel back to disengage the fasteners

20.6a Disconnect the electrical connectors . . .

20.6b . . . and harness clips

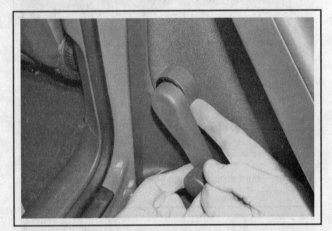

20.16a Press the spacer/clip from the backside of the handle . . .

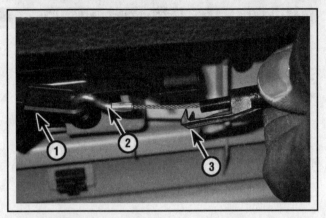

20.7 Interior door handle details

1 Interior handle
2 Operating cable
3 Operating cable molded
    mounting clip

20.16b . . . and slide the handle from the splines

7 Disconnect the cable from the door panel then unhook the cable from the inner door handle (see illustration). Lift the trim panel away from the door, noting the positions of the molded clips mounted along the sides.

8 Installation is the reverse of removal. Ensure that the wiring and connections are secure and correctly routed, clear of the window regulator and latch/lock components.

FRONT PASSENGER'S DOOR

9 Using a screwdriver, carefully unclip the upper trim cover from the door grab handle and remove it.

10 Remove the trim retaining fasteners located inside the door handle.

11 Remove the fasteners from the upper front corner and lower edge of the trim panel.

12 To release the door trim panel retaining clips, carefully pry between the panel and door with a trim tool. Work around the outside of the panel, and when all the retaining clips are released, lift the door trim panel upwards and off the window slot.

13 Disconnect the wiring from the speaker and door control unit.

14 Disconnect the cable from the door panel then unhook the cable from the inner door handle (see illustration 20.7). Lift the trim panel away from the door, noting the positions of the molded clips mounted along the sides.

15 Installation is the reverse of removal. Ensure that the wiring and

connections are secure and correctly routed, clear of the window regulator and latch/lock components.

REAR DOORS

▶ **Refer to illustrations 20.16a, 20.16b, 20.17a, 20.17b, 20.18, 20.19, 20.20 and 20.22**

16 On models with manually-operated windows, note the closed position of the handle, then press the spacer/clip located under the han-

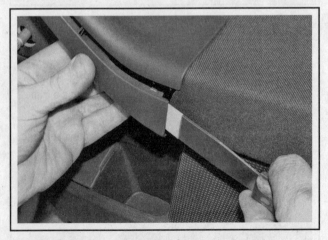

20.17a Carefully pry the upper trim cover out . . .

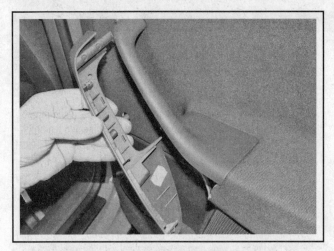

20.17b . . . and remove it from the grab handle

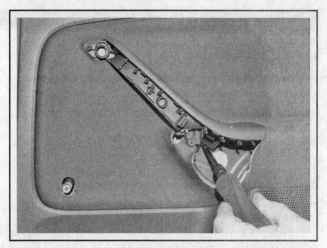

20.18 Location of the upper retaining screws

20.19 Location on the lower retaining screw

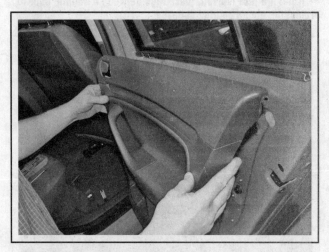

20.20 Remove the door trim panel

dle towards the front of the car, and slide the handle from the splines (see illustrations).

17 Using a screwdriver, carefully unclip the upper trim cover from the door grab handle and remove it (see illustrations).

18 Remove the trim retaining fasteners located inside the grab handle (see illustration).

19 Remove the fasteners from the lower edge of the trim panel (see illustration).

20 To release the door trim panel retaining clips, carefully pry between the panel and door with a trim tool. Work around the outside of the panel, and when all the retaining clips are released, lift the door trim panel upwards and off the window slot (see illustration).

21 Where applicable, disconnect the wiring from the trim panel.

22 Unhook the cable from the inner door handle, and remove the trim panel from the vehicle (see illustration).

23 Installation is the reverse of removal.

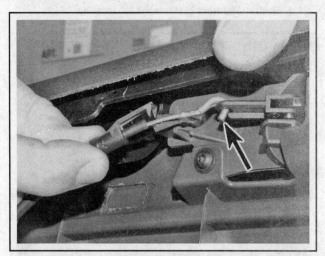

20.22 Unhook the cable from the inner door handle

21 Door - removal, installation and adjustment

▶ Refer to illustrations 21.1, 21.5, 21.6 and 21.8

➡ Note: The hinge bolts must always be replaced if loosened.

1 Open the door and disconnect the rubber boot by pressing the tab (see illustration) on the top of the boot and pulling it away from the door.

2 Disconnect the wiring harness connector by pulling the locking lever down and disconnect the wiring connector.

3 Each hinge has a guide bolt screwed into it, although, the bolt is not threaded into the pillar, but acts purely as a guide. **Do not** remove these bolts.

➡ Note: On 2011 models, remove the door strap fasteners and remove the strap.

4 Place a jack under the door or have an assistant on hand to support it when the lower hinge bolts are removed.

➡ Note: If a jack is used, place rags between it and the door to protect the door's painted surfaces.

5 Scribe a line around the lower hinge with a marking pen, then remove the lower hinge bolts (see illustration).

6 Remove the upper bolt from the upper hinge (see illustration) and carefully remove the door.

7 Installation is the reverse of removal, making sure to align the hinge with the marks made during removal before tightening the bolts.

8 Following installation of the door, check the alignment and adjust it if necessary as follows:

a) *Up-and-down and in-and-out adjustments are made by loosening the hinge-to-door bolts/nuts and moving the door as necessary.*

b) *Forward-and-backward adjustments are made by loosening the hinge-to-body bolts and moving the door as necessary.*

c) *The door lock striker can also be adjusted both up-and-down and sideways to provide positive engagement with the lock mechanism. This is done by loosening the fasteners and moving the striker as necessary (see illustration).*

21.1 Electrical harness boot release tab location

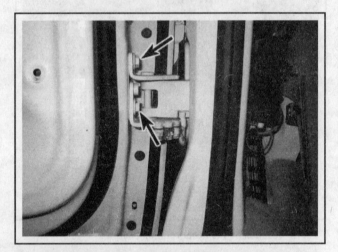

21.5 Remove the lower hinge fasteners

21.6 Remove the upper hinge fastener and lift off the door

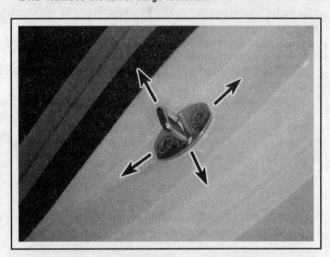

21.8 The striker can be loosened and moved slightly to achieve secure latch engagement

22 Door lock cylinder, outside handle, door skin and latch - removal and installation

LOCK CYLINDER

▶ Refer to illustrations 22.1, 22.2 and 22.3

➡ Note: The lock cylinder is only on the driver's side door. The passenger's side door uses an end cap. The removal procedure is the same for both.

1 Open the driver's door and remove the trim panel from the end of the door (see illustration).
2 Remove the lock cylinder cover cap and turn the Torx bolt counterclockwise until it stops. This moves the locking arm to the rear and releases the lock cylinder (see illustration).

➡ Note: On 2011 models, use a small screwdriver to pry the cap from the end of the lock cylinder.

3 Remove the lock cylinder from the outside door handle (see illustration).
4 Installation is the reverse of removal.

OUTSIDE HANDLE

▶ Refer to illustrations 22.6 and 22.7

5 Remove the lock cylinder as described in steps 1 through 3.

22.1 Remove the trim panel from the end of the door

6 Using a small screwdriver, pry the release cable out form the handle (see illustration).
7 Rotate the end of the handle outwards and towards the front of the door to remove it (see illustration).

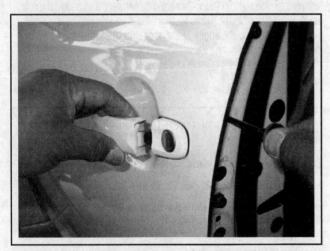

22.2 Unscrew the Torx bolt counterclockwise until it stops - do not try to remove the bolt

22.3 Remove the lock cylinder (or end cap on passenger's side door) from the door

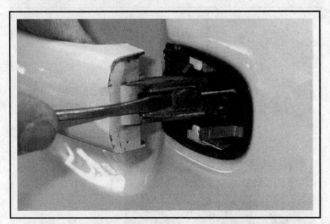

22.6 Disconnect the release cable from the handle

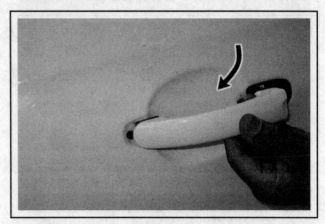

22.7 Rotate the end of the door handle outwards, then remove

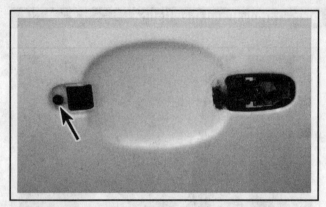

22.12 Remove the door handle bearing bracket-to-door skin fastener

8   Installation is the reverse of removal.

DOOR SKIN

▶ **Refer to illustrations 22.12, 22.13a, 22.13a and 22.14**

➡ **Note: 2011 models do not have a detachable door skin - the door is a one piece shell.**

9   Remove the door trim panel and water shield if equipped (see Section 20).
10 Remove the lock cylinder and outside handle as described in

22.13b . . . bottom and rear edge of the door

22.14 Carefully lift the door skin from the door frame

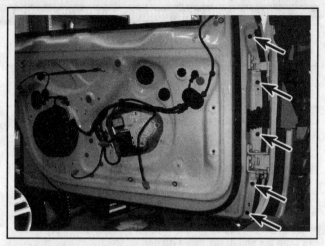

22.13a Remove the door skin mounting fasteners from the front edge . . .

Steps 1 through 7.
11 Pry the trim panels from each end of the door.
12 Remove the outside handle frame mounting fastener (see illustration).
13 Working around the door edges, remove the door skin mounting fasteners (see illustrations). Make sure to note the each location of the fasteners as you remove them; they are different sizes and styles. If the fasteners are installed in the wrong location, the door skin can be damaged.
14 Apply tape to the edges of the door skin to protect the paint, then remove the door skin (see illustration).
15 Installation is the reverse of removal.

LATCH

16 Remove the door trim panel and water shield, if equipped (see Section 20).

2010 and earlier models

▶ **Refer to illustrations 22.18, 22.19 and 22.20**

➡ **Note: To access the latch, the outer door skin must be removed (see Steps 9 through 14).**

17 Remove the lock cylinder, outside handle and door skin as described in Steps 1 through 14.
18 Disconnect the door handle bearing bracket rubber retainer (see

22.18 Disconnect the handle bearing bracket rubber retainer

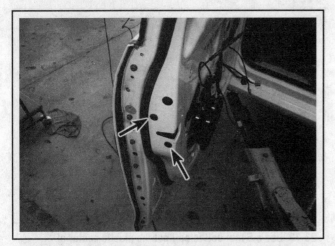

22.19 Remove the latch mounting fasteners

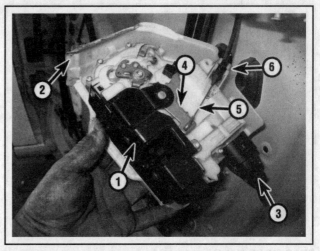

22.20 Door latch details

1	Lock unit	4	Actuator lever
2	Latch cover	5	Operating cable
3	Power door lock electrical connector	6	Operating cable housing

illustration) and slide the bearing bracket out.

19 Remove the two fasteners, and withdraw the lock unit with its cover from the door (see illustration).

20 Disconnect the operating cable housing from the lock unit and the electrical connector (see illustration).

21 Unhook the interior handle operation cable from the lock unit by pulling the cable end straight out of the actuator lever (see illustration 22.20).

22 Installation is the reverse of the removal.

2011 models

23 Pry the cover up from the bottom and remove the access panel from the door.

24 Disconnect the electrical harness connector at the door.

25 Remove the lock cylinder or end cap as described in Steps 1 through 3.

26 Remove the two fasteners, and with-draw the lock unit with its cover from the door.

27 Disconnect the operating cable from the door handle and unclip the cable from the lock assembly. Make a note of the cable location.

28 Disconnect the operating cable housing from the lock unit.

29 To unhook the interior handle operation cable from the lock unit, rotate the cable end 90 degrees and unclip the cable.

30 Installation is the reverse of the removal.

23 Door window glass - removal and installation

FRONT DOOR WINDOW GLASS

▶ **Refer to illustration 23.2**

➥ **Note: On 2010 and earlier models, there are two different ways to remove the door window glass; the first is described in this Section and the second is described in Section 24. The window glass fasteners are accessible from both sides. If removing the fasteners from the inside, use a reverse Torx and turn the fasteners clockwise to loosen.**

1 Remove the door trim panel (see Section 20).

2 Remove the window glass fastener access caps (see illustration), then lower the window until the fasteners are visible.

3 Loosen the window glass fasteners but do not remove them.

4 Raise the glass up from the clamps, then tilt the front of the glass downwards and remove the glass from the door.

5 Install the glass into the door and hand tighten the fasteners.

6 Raise the window up into the frame and make sure the glass is aligned. Lower the window until the fasteners are visible in the access holes and tighten the window glass fasteners securely.

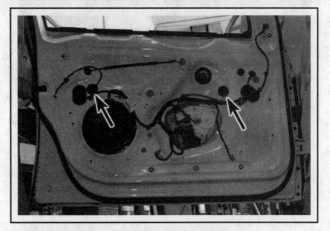

23.2 Window glass fastener access cap locations

7 Check that the window glass moves properly in the window frame. The remainder of installation is the reverse of the removal procedure.

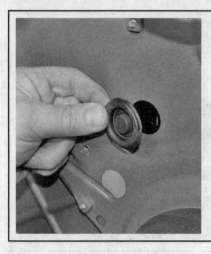

23.9 Remove the access cap

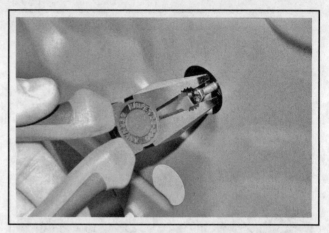

23.10 Use a 5 mm bolt to pull out the plastic center of the roll-pin

REAR DOOR WINDOW GLASS

▶ **Refer to illustrations 23.9, 23.10 and 23.12**

8 Remove the door trim panel (see Section 20).

9 Remove the window glass fastener access cap (see illustration), then lower the window until the plastic roll-pin is visible in access hole.

10 Screw in a 5 mm x 70 mm long bolt into plastic center of the roll-pin and pull out the bolt (with pin) (see illustration).

11 Screw in an 8 mm x 80 mm long bolt into the outer part of the roll-pin and pull the roll-pin out of the clamping bracket. When screwing the bolt into the outer part of the roll-pin, do not use excessive force or the roll-pin may fall inside the door.

23.12 Remove the window channel rubber molding from the window frame

➡ **Note: On Jetta models, remove the window regulator motor (see Section 24), and lower window glass.**

12 Remove the window channel rubber molding from the window frame (see illustration).

13 Remove the window channel fasteners and channel from the door.

14 Remove the rear window from the regulator carrier.

15 The remainder of the installation is the reverse of the removal procedure.

REAR DOOR FIXED WINDOW GLASS

16 Remove the door outer skin as follows:

a) Pry out the clips and remove the cover from the rear edge of the door - start at the bottom and work upwards.

b) Pry out the clips and remove the cover from the front edge of the door.

c) Remove the bolt securing the mounting plate. The bolt is located through the handle opening.

d) To make sure the panel is installed in the same position, mark the bolts and outer skin panel in relation to each other.

e) Remove all the perimeter bolts, however, note the location of each bolt as they are of different lengths.

f) Remove the skin from the door.

17 Remove the door window glass (see Steps 8 through 14).

18 Pull out the rubber guide channel, then the fasteners and remove the center rib from the channel.

19 Using a screwdriver, separate the guide channel and fixed window from the door frame, and remove.

20 Installation is a reversal of removal.

24 Door window regulator and motor - removal and installation

WINDOW REGULATOR

2010 and earlier models
Removal

▶ **Refer to illustrations 24.3, 24.4a, 24.4b and 24.5**

1 Remove the door trim panel (see Section 20).
2 Remove the door skin (see Section 22).
3 Remove the side impact protection bar fasteners (see illustration).
4 Loosen the door windows glass clamp fasteners and remove the window glass from the door (see illustrations).
5 Remove the window regulator fasteners, then remove the regulator and power window motor as an assembly (see illustration).

➡ **Note: Disconnect the power window motor electrical connection from the motor.**

Installation

6 Install the regulator brackets and mounting plate and tighten the fasteners securely.
7 Install the window glass and tighten the clamp fasteners securely.
8 Install the side impact protection bar and tighten the bolts to the torque listed in this Chapter's Specifications.
9 Install the door outer skin (see Section 22).
10 Install the door trim panel.

2011 models
Removal

11 Remove the door trim panel (see Section 20).
12 Remove the door window glass (see Section 23).

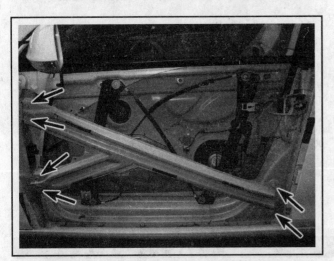

24.3 Side impact protection support fastener locations

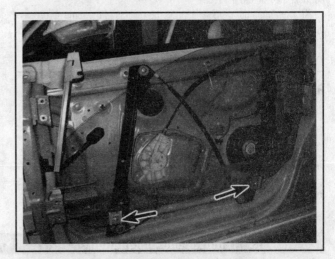

24.4a Loosen the window glass clamp fasteners . . .

24.4b . . . and remove the glass from the vehicle

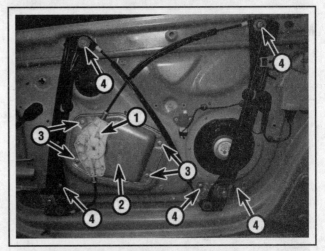

24.5 Front door window regulator details - 2010 and earlier models

1   Window regulator drive (power window motor)
2   Mounting plate (power window motor)
3   Mounting plate fasteners
4   Window regulator mounting fasteners

13 Remove the power window motor fasteners, unplug the electrical connectors and remove the motor.

14 Release the hooks on the cable reel and push the reel into the door.

15 Working through the access holes at the bottom of the door, remove the two regulator frame mounting nuts and push the bottom of the regulator frame into the door.

16 Loosen the top two regulator frame mounting nuts, and slide the nuts towards the two openings in the door, then push them into the door.

17 Remove the window regulator and window glass as an assembly from the door opening.

Installation

18 Install the window regulator and reel through the door opening, and align the top mounting nuts with the openings. Push the regulator lower studs through the lower opening, install the nuts and tighten the regulator mounting nuts securely.

19 Insert the guides on the cable reel through the door panel and connect the hook to the reel.

20 The remainder of installation is the reverse of the removal procedure.

WINDOW MOTOR (WITH CONTROL MODULE)

Removal

▶ **Refer to illustration 24.23**

21 Remove the door trim panel (see Section 20).

22 With the window fully closed, use adhesive tape to hold the glass in position.

23 Use a screwdriver to carefully disconnect the electrical connectors from the motor (see illustration).

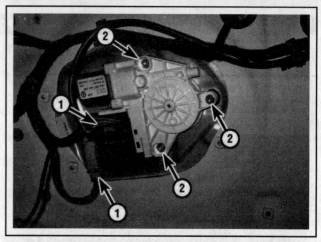

24.23 Window motor mounting details

| 1 | Electrical connectors | 2 | Mounting fasteners |

24 Remove the mounting fasteners and remove the motor (with control module) from the mounting plate.

Installation

25 Place the motor (with control module) on the mounting plate and install the mounting fasteners hand-tight.

26 Reconnect the electrical connectors, then remove the tape and move the window down and up a short distance to allow the splines between the motor and cable drum to engage.

27 Tighten the motor mounting fasteners securely.

28 Raise and lower the window twice to its upper and lower stops to normalize the window and activate the safety pinch/roll-back function.

29 Install the door trim panel.

25 Mirrors - removal and installation

INTERIOR MIRROR

Without rain sensor

▶ **Refer to illustrations 25.1 and 25.2**

1 Rotate the mirror 90-degrees counterclockwise until the retaining spring disengages and remove the mirror from the retaining plate (see illustration). If the vehicle is equipped with an automatic mirror, unclip the cover and detach the wiring harness and mirror connector, then rotate the mirror 90-degrees and remove the mirror.

2 To install the mirror, align it 90-degrees from the installed position (vertical with the front and rear of the vehicle). Engage the mirror with the retaining plate, then rotate it clockwise until the mirror locks in

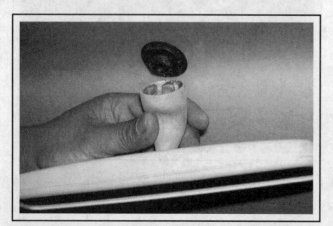

25.1 Pull the inside mirror off its retaining bracket at an angle

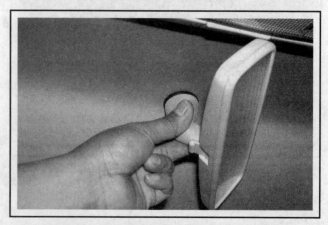

25.2 Align the mirror vertically in the vehicle and rotate it 90-degrees until it locks into place

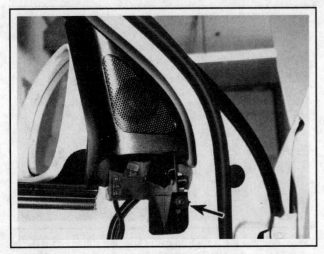

25.9 Remove the sail trim panel fastener and pry the panel off of the door

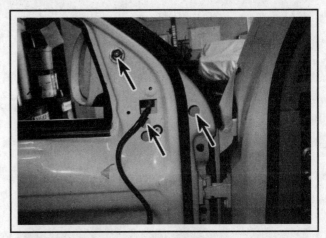

25.10 Exterior mirror mounting fasteners - 2010 and earlier model shown, later model similar

EXTERIOR MIRROR

▶ **Refer to illustrations 25.9 and 25.10**

8 Remove the door panel (see Section 20).
9 Remove the sail trim panel fastener and carefully pry the trim cover from the door (see illustration).
10 Remove the mirror mounting fasteners and detach the mirror from the door (see illustration). Work the mirror harness through the hole in the door.
11 Disconnect the electrical connector for the mirror and carefully withdraw the connector.
12 Installation is the reverse of removal.

place (see illustration).
3 If the vehicle is equipped with an automatic mirror, connect the wiring harness, mirror connector and the mirror trim cover.

With rain sensor

4 Pry off the trim caps from each side of the mirror.
5 If the vehicle is equipped with an automatic mirror, disconnect the wiring harness mirror connector.
6 Loosen the clips from each side of the mirror base, the slide the mirror off of the base.
7 Installation is the reverse of removal.

26 Center console - removal and installation

▶ **Refer to illustrations 26.3a, 26.3b, 26.5, 26.6, 26.7, 26.8a, 26.8b, 26.9, 26.10a, 26.10b, 26.11, 26.12a and 26.12b**

※ WARNING:

The models covered by this manual are equipped with Supplemental Restraint Systems (SRS), more commonly known as airbags. Always disable the airbag system before working in the vicinity of any airbag system components to avoid the possibility of accidental deployment of the airbags, which could cause personal injury (see Chapter 12).

※ CAUTION:

If the battery is disconnected, several systems must be re-learned before they will work properly (see Chapter 5, Section 3).

➡ Note: On 2011 models, the center console is one piece; remove all the mounting fasteners in the similar locations and order as earlier models, then remove the center console as a single unit.

1 Place the shift lever in the neutral position and pull up the parking brake handle.

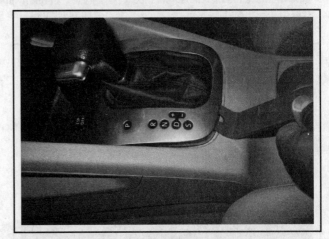

26.3a Carefully pry the shift cover and boot up . . .

2 On manual transaxle models, remove the gear shift lever boot (see Chapter 7A).
3 On automatic transaxle models, pry up the shift cover from the rear, then press the locking sleeve tabs in from the sides and remove the cover and boot (see illustrations).

26.3b . . . then press the locking sleeve tabs in and remove the cover and boot assembly

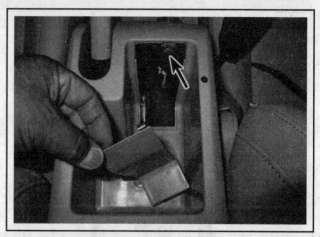

26.5 Remove the inner trim panel from the storage panel, then remove the fastener - 2010 and earlier Jetta models shown, other models similar

26.6 Remove the fasteners from the rear of the console

26.7 Carefully pry the rear trim panel off the end of the storage console

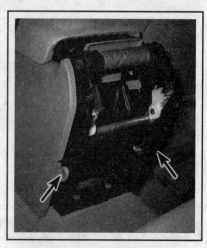

26.8a Remove the storage console fasteners . . .

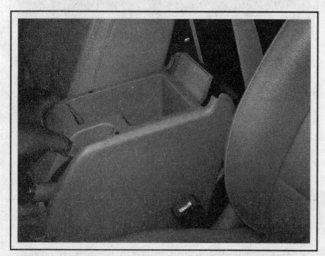

26.8b . . . then lift the storage console up and around the parking brake lever

4   On vehicles equipped with a CD changer, remove the changer from the console and the switch panel (see Chapter 12).

5   On Rabbit and GTI models, remove the rubber mat. On Jetta and Golf models, remove the small trim panel from the center of the console, then remove the fastener (see illustration).

➡ **Note: If equipped with cool storage, the panel with nozzle is unclipped and the nozzle stays with the trim panel.**

6   Remove the fasteners from the rear of the console (see illustration).

➡ **Note: On models equipped with rear cup holders, open the holder and remove the fasteners.**

7   Using a trim tool, remove the rear section from the console (see illustration).

8   Remove the rear fasteners for the console storage and remove the center console storage panel (see illustrations).

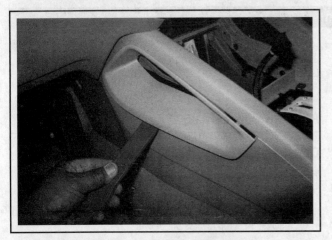

26.9 Pry the console inserts out from each side

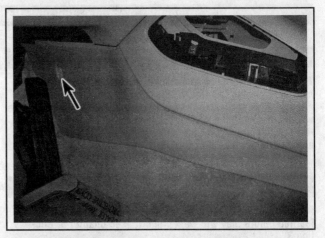

26.10a Remove the fastener cover and fastener . . .

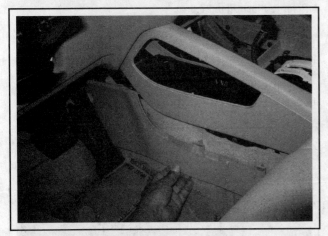

26.10b . . . then slide the panel down and out

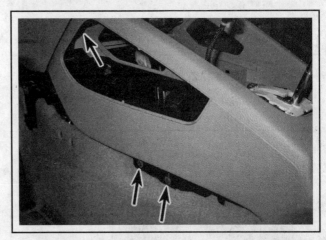

26.11 Center console front and side fasteners

9 Using a trim tool, remove the console side insert panels (see illustration).

10 Remove the console lower side trim panel fastener cover and fastener, then pull the side trim panel down and out (see illustrations).

11 Remove the center front and lower fasteners (see illustration).

12 Remove the cup holder mat and fastener from the rear of the

console, then remove the console (see illustrations). Disconnect any electrical connectors as the console is withdrawn.

13 Installation is the reverse of removal. Ensure that the clips at the front lower edges of the console engage with the instrument panel support framework.

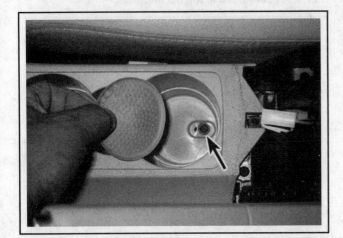

26.12a Remove the cup holder mat and fastener . . .

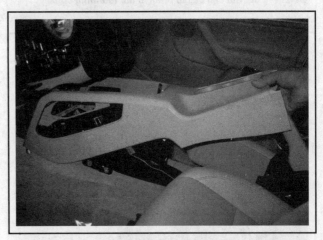

26.12b . . . then remove the center console

27 Dashboard trim panels - removal and installation

☀ WARNING:

The models covered by this manual are equipped with Supple-mental Restraint Systems (SRS), more commonly known as airbags. Always disable the airbag system before working in the vicinity of any airbag system components to avoid the possibil-ity of accidental deployment of the airbags, which could cause personal injury (see Chapter 12).

☀ CAUTION:

If the battery is disconnected, several systems must be re-learned before they will work properly (see Chapter 5, Sec-tion 3).

DASHBOARD END CAPS

► **Refer to illustration 27.2**

1   The end caps are held in place by clips.

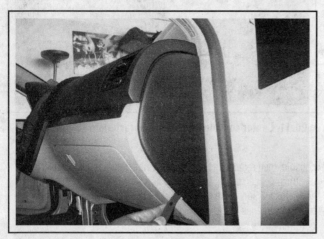

27.2 Pry out the end cap to release the retaining clips

27.8 Use a small screwdriver to pry out the emblem and remove the upper A-pillar fastener

2   Pry out the cover with a trim tool to release the mounting clips (see illustration).
3   Installation is the reverse of removal.

A-PILLAR TRIM PANELS

Center A-pillar

► **Refer to illustration 27.5**

4   Remove the dashboard end caps (see illustration 27.2).
5   Pry the center A-pillar out from the instrument panel (see illustration).
6   Installation is the reverse of removal.

Upper A-pillar

► **Refer to illustration 27.8**

7   Remove the center A-pillar trim (see Steps 4 and 5).
8   On 2010 and earlier models, carefully pry the airbag emblem out and remove the fastener (see illustration). On 2011 models, remove the fastener at the bottom of the trim panel.
9   Pull the A-pillar trim panel away from the windshield towards the inside of the vehicle.

27.5 Pry out the center A-pillar trim panel

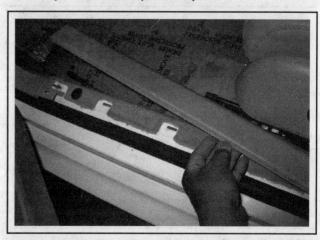

27.12 Pry up the front section of the sill trim from the door entry

27.14a Remove the kick panel fastener (driver's side only) . . .

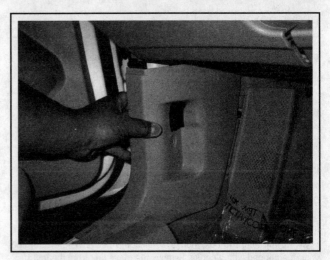

27.14b . . . then pry out on the kick panel to release the retaining clips

➡ **Note: The A-pillar trim starts from the windshield and stops at the top of the door.**

10 Installation is the reverse of removal.

KICK PANELS

▶ **Refer to illustrations 27.12, 27.14a and 27.14b**

11 Remove the dashboard end caps (see illustration 27.2) and center A-pillar trim panel (see illustration 27.5).

12 Pry up the front section of the sill trim panel from the floorboard (see illustration).

13 Pull the kick panel away from the A-pillar and unclip the lower section of the trim panel.

14 On the driver's side, remove the hood release handle (see Section 11), then remove the fastener and pry out the kick panel (see illustrations).

15 Installation is the reverse of removal.

DRIVER'S KNEE BOLSTER (DRIVER'S SIDE STORAGE COMPARTMENT)

▶ **Refer to illustrations 27.19a and 27.19b**

16 Remove the left dashboard end cap to access two side fasteners (see illustration 27.2).

17 Pry up the trim piece from the end of the steering column upper trim panel and the instrument cluster.

18 Remove the headlight switch (see Chapter 12).

19 Remove the driver's knee bolster upper and lower fasteners (see illustrations), pull the panel away, disconnect any electrical connectors and remove the panel.

➡ **Note: On models equipped with a storage drawer, remove the drawer to access the lower mounting fasteners.**

20 Installation is the reverse of removal.

27.19a Remove the knee bolster lower fasteners . . .

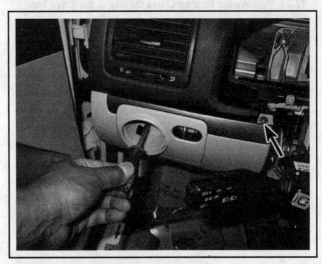

27.19b . . . then the upper fasteners

GLOVE BOX

▶ **Refer to illustrations 27.23, 27.24 and 27.25**

21 Remove the right dashboard end cap (see illustration 27.2).

22 Remove the center A-pillar trim (see illustration 27.5) and kick panel (see Steps 12 through 14).

23 Carefully pry out and remove the center cover panel (see illustration).

24 Remove the glove box lower fasteners from the outside of the instrument panel (see illustration).

25 Open the glove box and remove the fasteners at the top of the glove box (see illustration).

26 Slide the glove box out and separate the glove box from the instrument panel.

27 Lower the glove box, then disconnect the electrical connector and vent, if equipped with a cooler. Remove the glove box from the instrument panel.

28 Installation is the reverse of removal.

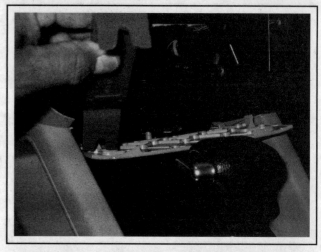

27.23 Carefully pry the center trim cover out from the bottom of the instrument panel

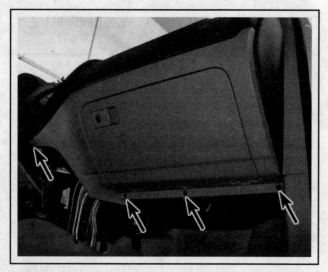

27.24 Remove the fasteners from outside of the glove box

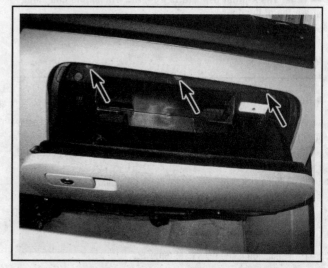

27.25 Open the glove box and remove the top fasteners

28 Steering column covers - removal and installation

▶ **Refer to illustration 28.2 and 28.3**

1 Pry up the trim piece from the end of the column and instrument cluster (see Chapter 12).

2 Pull down on the steering column tilt lever, lower the column and remove the lower trim and fastener (see illustration).

3 Pry up the upper cover and remove it (see illustration). With the upper cover removed, rotate the steering wheel and remove the lower cover fasteners at the front of the cover.

4 Remove the lower cover.

5 Installation is the reverse of removal.

28.2 Remove the lower cover mounting fastener

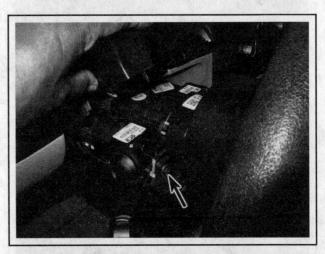

28.3 Carefully pull up on the upper trim and disconnect the clips, then remove the lower cover mounting fasteners (one of two shown)

29 Instrument panel - removal and installation

▶ **Refer to illustrations 29.9, 29.10a, 29.10b, 29.10c, 29.11a, 29.11b, 29.12, 29.13a, 29.13b, 29.13c, 29.13d and 29.13e**

✳✳ WARNING:

The models covered by this manual are equipped with Supplemental Restraint Systems (SRS), more commonly known as airbags. Always disable the airbag system before working in the vicinity of any airbag system components to avoid the possibility of accidental deployment of the airbags, which could cause personal injury (see Chapter 12).

✳✳ CAUTION:

This is a difficult procedure for the home mechanic, involving tedious disassembly and the disconnection/reconnection of numerous electrical connectors. If you do attempt this procedure, make sure you take good notes and mark all matching connectors (and their mounting points) to aid reassembly.

✳✳ CAUTION:

If the battery is disconnected, several systems must be re-learned before they will work properly (see Chapter 5, Section 3).

1 Disconnect the negative battery cable (see Chapter 5).

2 Remove the center console (see Section 26).

3 Remove the steering wheel (see Chapter 10).

4 Remove the steering column covers (see Section 28).

5 Remove all of the dashboard trim panels (see Section 27).

➡ **Note: On 2011 models, the instrument cluster trim, left vent and center vent are all one piece (see Chapter 12, Section 11 for removal).**

6 Remove the audio components, the multi-function switch and the instrument cluster (see Chapter 12).

7 Disconnect the electrical connector for the passenger's side airbag (see Chapter 12).

➡ **Note: The passenger's side airbag remains in the vehicle as the panel is removed.**

8 Remove the headlight switch (see Chapter 12).

9 Carefully pry out the optical photo sensor cover at the top of the instrument panel (see illustration), disconnect the sensor from the electrical connector and remove the sensor.

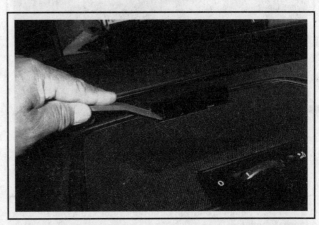

29.9 Pry out the optical sensor trim using a small screwdriver

29.10a Remove the air outlet vent fastener . . .

29.10b . . . pry off the air outlet vent cover . . .

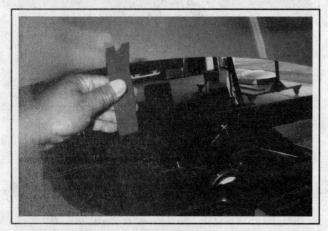

29.10c . . . and remove the air adjuster housing

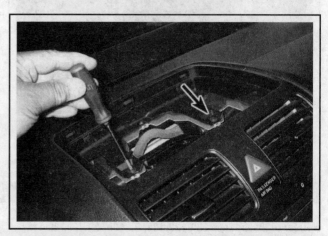

29.11a Remove the center vent mounting fasteners . . .

10 On 2010 and earlier models, remove the air outlet vent cover fastener and carefully pry out the cover, then remove the air adjuster housing (see illustrations). If equipped with a storage tray, lift the storage tray mat out and remove the storage tray mounting fasteners.

➥ **Note: On later models, the air outlet vent cover and adjuster housing are removed as a single unit.**

11 On 2010 and earlier models, remove the center vent fasteners, then use a trim tool to remove the center vent from the instrument panel (see illustrations).

12 Remove the instrument panel end caps (see Section 27), then remove the left and right vents (see illustration).

13 Remove the remaining fasteners securing the instrument panel

29.11b . . . and carefully pry out the center vents - 2010 and earlier models

29.12 Pry out and remove the vents from each end of the instrument panel - left side shown

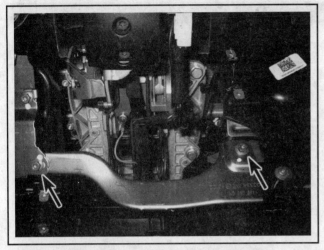

29.13a Remove the knee bolster support bracket-to-instrument panel fasteners

29.13b Remove the airbag-to-instrument panel fasteners

29.13c Remove the left side instrument panel fasteners

29.13d Remove the right side instrument panel fastener

(see illustrations), and disconnect any electrical connectors still attached to the panel. Have an assistant help you pull the panel back and out of the vehicle.

14 Installation is the reverse of removal.

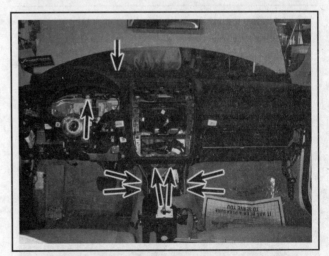

29.13e Remove the center instrument panel fasteners

30 Seats - removal and installation

✳✳ WARNING:

The models covered by this manual are equipped with Supplemental Restraint Systems (SRS), more commonly known as airbags. Always disable the airbag system before working in the vicinity of any airbag system components to avoid the possibility of accidental deployment of the airbags, which could cause personal injury (see Chapter 12).

✳✳ WARNING:

The front and rear seats on some models are equipped with side-impact airbags at the upper outside of the seat back. Refer to Chapter 12 to disable the airbag system before working on the seats.

✳✳ CAUTION:

If the battery is disconnected, several systems must be relearned before they will work properly (see Chapter 5, Section 3).

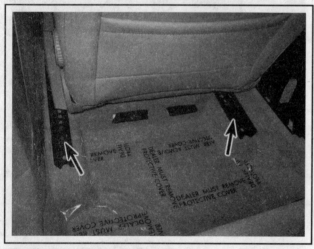

30.3 Remove the plastic buttons in the seat track covers, then remove the rear mounting fasteners

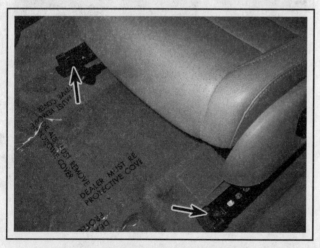

30.4 Remove the front seat mounting fasteners

FRONT

▶ **Refer to illustrations 30.3 and 30.4**

1   Disconnect the negative battery cable (see Chapter 5).
2   Remove the drawer from the seat, if equipped.
3   Slide the seat forward and remove the seat track covers, remove the rear seat track fasteners and unplug any electrical connectors attached to the seat (see illustration).
4   Slide the seat all the way to the back, remove the seat track covers, unplug any electrical connectors and remove the front seat track fasteners (see illustration). Remove the seat from the vehicle.
5   Installation is the reverse of removal.

REAR

Seat cushion

▶ **Refer to illustration 30.7**

6   At the rear of the seat cushion, unclip the four guides from the child seat mountings.
7   Lift the front edge of the cushion from the location sockets, then push the cushion to the rear and pull upwards (see illustration).

➥ **Note: On wagon models, lift the front edge of the cushion up from each side and press the seat cushion hooks out of the mounts.**

8   Remove the rear seat cushion from the vehicle. Installation is the reverse of removal.

Seat back

▶ **Refer to illustrations 30.10, 30.11a and 30.11b**

9   Remove the seat cushion as described in Steps 6 through 8.

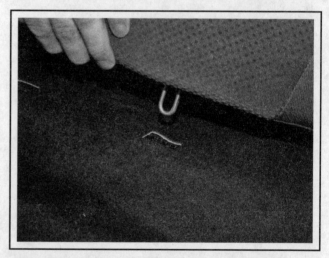

30.7 Pull up on the corners of the rear seat cushion to disengage the cushion from the mount

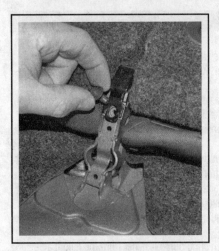

30.10 Pry up the trim cover and remove the seat back fastener

30.11a Lift the seat back off the center mount . . .

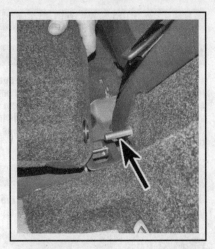

30.11b . . . then slide it off the outer mounting pin

10 Fold the backrest forwards, then pull back the carpet. Remove the cover from the center mount and remove the clamp fastener (see illustration).

11 Remove the right backrest by lifting it from the center mount and sliding it off the outer mounting pin (see illustrations).

12 Remove the left backrest by lifting it from the center mounting

and sliding it off the outer mounting pin.

13 Remove the side cushion fasteners and pull the cushion out of the mounts.

14 Installation is the reverse of removal. Tighten the seat back fasteners securely.

31 Sunroof - check and adjustment

CHECK

1 If the sunroof motor fails to operate, first check the relevant fuse. If the fault cannot be traced and rectified, the sunroof can be opened and closed manually using an Allen key to turn the motor spindle (an Allen key is supplied with the vehicle, and should be in the vehicle tool kit in the trunk). To gain access to the motor, remove the overhead console (see Chapter 12). Insert the Allen key fully into the motor opening (against spring pressure). Rotate the key to move the sunroof to the required position.

ADJUSTMENT

▶ **Refer to illustration 31.5**

2 The position of the glass panel can be adjusted in the following manner.

3 Open the interior sunshade all the way back and operate the sunroof until it is tilted open.

4 There are glass fasteners on each side of the sunroof opening, inside the vehicle. Unclip the bellows from each side.

5 Loosen the front fasteners and lower the sunroof (see illustration). Set the front edge of the glass approximately 0.039-inch (1 mm) below the surface of the roof when closed. Tighten the front fasteners.

6 Loosen the rear glass adjustment fasteners and adjust the glass approximately 0.039-inch (1 mm) above the roof at the rear. Tighten the rear fasteners.

7 When the adjustment is correct, tilt the sunroof open and reinstall the plastic covers over the glass rails.

8 Due to the complexity of the sunroof mechanism, considerable expertise is needed to repair or replace the sunroof components successfully. Removal of the sunroof first requires the headliner to be removed, which is a complex and tedious operation, and not a task to be undertaken lightly. Therefore, any repairs with the sunroof should be referred to a VW dealer or other qualified repair shop.

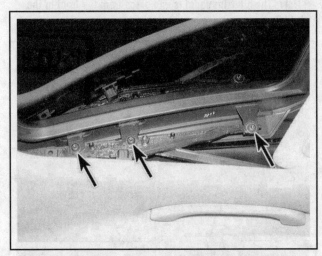

31.5 The sunroof glass has three fasteners on each side (arrows) used to adjust the fit of the glass to the roof

32 Seat belts - removal and installation

❄ WARNING:

The models covered by this manual are equipped with Supplemental Restraint Systems (SRS), more commonly known as airbags. Always disable the airbag system before working in the vicinity of any airbag system components to avoid the possibility of accidental deployment of the airbags, which could cause personal injury (see Chapter 12).

❄ WARNING:

Do not use electrical test equipment on the belt tensioner system; it could cause the pyrotechnic belt tensioner to discharge.

❄ WARNING:

An auxiliary voltage input device (memory saver) must not be used when working near airbag system components.

❄ WARNING:

Never strike the pillars or floorpan with a hammer or use an impact-driver tool in these areas unless the system is disabled.

❄ CAUTION:

If the battery is disconnected, several systems must be re-learned before they will work properly (see Chapter 5, Section 3).

FRONT SEAT BELTS

▶ Refer to illustrations 32.7, 32.8 and 32.10

1 Raise the seat to the highest point.
2 Disconnect the negative battery cable (see Chapter 5).
3 Open the front and rear doors and remove the sill trim panel.

➡ Note: The sill trim panel is one piece from the front to the rear door.

4 Using a small screwdriver, remove the airbag emblem from the B-pillar upper trim panel. Remove the fastener and pry the panel from the pillar.
5 Remove the two fasteners from the base of the B-pillar lower trim panel and remove the panel.
6 Remove the belt anchor fastener and remove the anchor from the body.
7 Use a small screwdriver to open the wire retainer and disconnect the electrical connector from the belt module (see illustration).
8 Remove the belt retractor fastener from the base of the B-pillar and remove the belt tensioner (see illustration).
9 Remove the belt guide fasteners from the B-pillar and remove the guide.
10 Remove the belt pivoting guide fastener from the height adjuster and remove the belt (see illustration).
11 Installation is the reverse of removal. Make sure the belt is not twisted before installing the lower seat mount side.

Belt latch replacement

12 Remove the front seat (see Section 30).

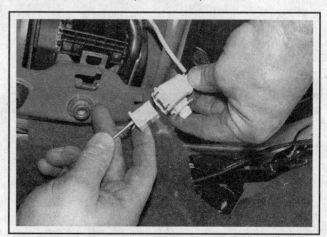

32.7 Disconnect the electrical connector to the seat belt retractor

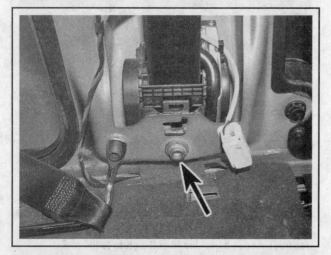

32.8 Remove the belt retractor mounting fastener

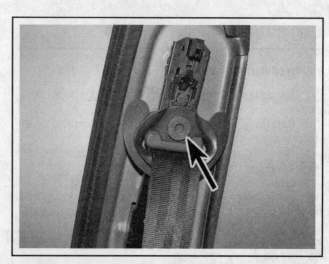

32.10 Remove the belt pivot guide from the height adjuster

13 Remove the latch fastener and latch from the base of the seat.
14 Installation is the reverse of removal.

REAR SEAT BELTS

15 Disconnect the negative battery cable (see Chapter 5).
16 Remove the seat (see Section 30) and remove the lower anchor point fastener and belt end.
17 Remove the C-pillar trim and rear parcel shelf trim on sedans (see Section 33).
18 From inside the rear luggage compartment, remove the trim and loosen the belt retractor fastener. Slide the tensioner assembly back, up and out.
19 Use a small screwdriver to open the yellow retainer and disconnect the electrical connector from the belt module.
20 Installation is the reverse of removal. Make sure the belt is not twisted before installing the lower seat mount side.

Belt latch replacement

21 Remove the seat cushion and seat back (see Section 30).
22 Remove the latch fastener and latch from the floorpan.
23 Installation is the reverse of removal. Make sure the belt is not twisted before installing the lower mount side.

33 Rear parcel shelf - removal and installation

✳ WARNING:

The models covered by this manual are equipped with Supplemental Restraint Systems (SRS), more commonly known as airbags. Always disable the airbag system before working in the vicinity of any airbag system components to avoid the possibility of accidental deployment of the airbags, which could cause personal injury (see Chapter 12).

✳ WARNING:

The front and rear seats on some models are equipped with side-impact airbags at the upper outside of the seat back. Refer to Chapter 12 to disable the airbag system before working on the seats.

✳ CAUTION:

If the battery is disconnected, several systems must be re-learned before they will work properly (see Chapter 5, Section 3).

1   Disconnect the negative battery cable (see Chapter 5).
2   Remove the rear seat and side trim panels (see Section 30).
3   Using a small screwdriver, pry the airbag emblem out from the C-pillar trim panel. Remove the fastener and pry the panel upwards then out from the pillar.
4   Use a small screwdriver to open the yellow/blue wire retainer and disconnect the electrical connector from the belt module.
5   Remove the belt retractor fastener from the base and remove the belt retractor.
6   Remove the child seat anchors, if equipped.
7   Pull up on the front section of the shelf and disconnect the front three retaining clips. Pull the shelf forward to disengage the rear clips and remove the shelf.
8   Installation is the reverse of removal.

Torque specifications

Side impact protection bar bolts	15 ft-lbs	20 Nm

Section

12

CHASSIS ELECTRICAL SYSTEM

1   General information

The electrical system is a 12-volt, negative ground type. Power for the lights and all electrical accessories is supplied by a lead/acid-type battery that is charged by the alternator.

This Chapter covers repair and service procedures for the various electrical components not associated with the engine. Information on the battery, alternator, ignition system and starter motor can be found in Chapter 5.

It should be noted that when portions of the electrical system are serviced, the negative cable should be disconnected from the battery to prevent electrical shorts and/or fires.

2   Electrical troubleshooting - general information

▶ **Refer to illustrations 2.5a, 2.5b, 2.6 and 2.9**

A typical electrical circuit consists of an electrical component, any switches, relays, motors, fuses, fusible links or circuit breakers related to that component and the wiring and connectors that link the component to both the battery and the chassis. To help you pinpoint an electrical circuit problem, wiring diagrams are included at the end of this Chapter.

Before tackling any troublesome electrical circuit, first study the appropriate wiring diagrams to get a complete understanding of what makes up that individual circuit. Trouble spots, for instance, can often be narrowed down by noting if other components related to the circuit are operating properly. If several components or circuits fail at one time, chances are the problem is in a fuse or ground connection, because several circuits are often routed through the same fuse and ground connections.

Electrical problems usually stem from simple causes, such as loose or corroded connections, a blown fuse, a melted fusible link or a failed relay. Visually inspect the condition of all fuses, wires and connections in a problem circuit before troubleshooting the circuit.

If test equipment and instruments are going to be utilized, use the diagrams to plan ahead of time where you will make the necessary connections in order to accurately pinpoint the trouble spot.

The basic tools needed for electrical troubleshooting include a circuit tester or voltmeter (a 12-volt bulb with a set of test leads can also be used), a continuity tester, which includes a bulb, battery and set of test leads, and a jumper wire, preferably with a circuit breaker incorporated, which can be used to bypass electrical components (see illustrations). Before attempting to locate a problem with test instruments, use the wiring diagram(s) to decide where to make the connections.

VOLTAGE CHECKS

Voltage checks should be performed if a circuit is not functioning properly. Connect one lead of a circuit tester to either the negative battery terminal or a known good ground. Connect the other lead to a connector in the circuit being tested, preferably nearest to the battery or fuse (see illustration). If the bulb of the tester lights, voltage is present, which means that the part of the circuit between the connector and the battery is problem free. Continue checking the rest of the circuit in the same fashion. When you reach a point at which no voltage is present, the problem lies between that point and the last test point with voltage. Most of the time the problem can be traced to a loose connection.

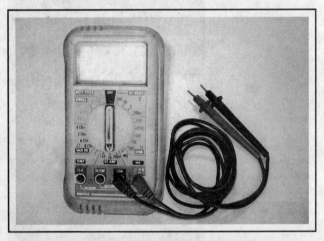

2.5a The most useful tool for electrical troubleshooting is a digital multimeter that can check volts, amps, and test continuity

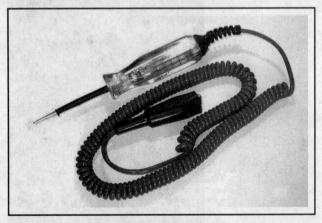

2.5b A test light is a very handy tool for checking voltage

2.6 In use, a basic test light's lead is clipped to a known good ground, then the pointed probe can test connectors, wires or electrical sockets - if the bulb lights, the part being tested has battery voltage

➡ **Note: Keep in mind that some circuits receive voltage only when the ignition key is in the Accessory or Run position.**

FINDING A SHORT

One method of finding shorts in a circuit is to remove the fuse and connect a test light or voltmeter in place of the fuse terminals. There should be no voltage present in the circuit. Move the wiring harness from side-to-side while watching the test light. If the bulb goes on, there is a short to ground somewhere in that area, probably where the insulation has rubbed through. The same test can be performed on each component in the circuit, even a switch.

GROUND CHECK

Perform a ground test to check whether a component is properly grounded. Disconnect the battery and connect one lead of a continuity tester or multimeter (set to the ohms scale), to a known good ground. Connect the other lead to the wire or ground connection being tested. If the resistance is low (less than 5 ohms), the ground is good. If the bulb on a self-powered test light does not go on, the ground is not good.

CONTINUITY CHECK

A continuity check is done to determine if there are any breaks in a circuit - if it is passing electricity properly. With the circuit off (no power in the circuit), a self-powered continuity tester or multimeter can be used to check the circuit. Connect the test leads to both ends of the circuit (or to the power end and a good ground), and if the test light comes on the circuit is passing current properly (see illustration). If the resistance is low (less than 5 ohms), there is continuity; if the reading is 10,000 ohms or higher, there is a break somewhere in the circuit. The same procedure can be used to test a switch, by connecting the continuity tester to the switch terminals. With the switch turned On, the test light should come on (or low resistance should be indicated on a meter).

2.9 With a multimeter set to the ohms scale, resistance can be checked across two terminals - when checking for continuity, a low reading indicates continuity, a high reading indicates lack of continuity

FINDING AN OPEN CIRCUIT

When diagnosing for possible open circuits, it is often difficult to locate them by sight because the connectors hide oxidation or terminal misalignment. Merely wiggling a connector on a sensor or in the wiring harness may correct the open circuit condition. Remember this when an open circuit is indicated when troubleshooting a circuit. Intermittent problems may also be caused by oxidized or loose connections.

Electrical troubleshooting is simple if you keep in mind that all electrical circuits are basically electricity running from the battery, through the wires, switches, relays, fuses and fusible links to each electrical component (light bulb, motor, etc.) and to ground, from which it is passed back to the battery. Any electrical problem is an interruption in the flow of electricity to and from the battery.

3   Fuses - general information

FUSES

▶ **Refer to illustrations 3.1a, 3.1b and 3.3**

The electrical circuits of the vehicle are protected by a combination of fuses, circuit breakers and fusible links. The main fuse/relay panel is in the engine compartment (see illustration), while the interior fuse/relay panel is located inside the passenger compartment (see illustration). Each of the fuses is designed to protect a specific circuit, and the various circuits are identified on the fuse panel itself.

Several sizes of fuses are employed in the fuse blocks. There are small, medium and large sizes of the same design, all with the same blade terminal design. The medium and large fuses can be removed with your fingers, but the small fuses require the use of pliers or the small plastic fuse-puller tool found in most fuse boxes.

If an electrical component fails, always check the fuse first. The best way to check the fuses is with a test light. Check for power at the

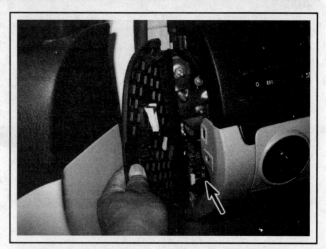

3.1a The interior fuse box is located at the left end of the instrument panel, under a cover

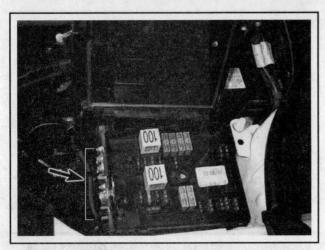

3.1b The engine compartment fuse box is located in the left-rear corner of the engine compartment

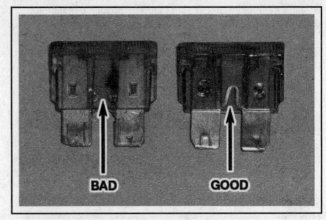

3.3 When a fuse blows, the element between the terminals melts

exposed terminal tips of each fuse. If power is present at one side of the fuse but not the other, the fuse is blown. A blown fuse can also be identified by visually inspecting it (see illustration).

Be sure to replace blown fuses with the correct type. Fuses (of the same physical size) of different ratings may be physically interchangeable, but only fuses of the proper rating should be used. Replacing a fuse with one of a higher or lower value than specified is not recommended. Each electrical circuit needs a specific amount of protection. The amperage value of each fuse is molded into the top of the fuse body.

If the replacement fuse immediately fails, don't replace it again until the cause of the problem is isolated and corrected. In most cases, this

will be a short circuit in the wiring caused by a broken or deteriorated wire.

HIGH AMPERAGE FUSES

Some circuits are protected by high amperage fuses, known as "SA" fuses, which are fastened to the studs on the front of the underhood fuse/relay box (see illustration 3.1b). These are used in circuits which are not ordinarily fused, or which carry high current, such as the circuit between the alternator and the battery. If you have to replace an SA fuse, make sure that you replace it with one of the same specification. If the replacement fuse blows in the same circuit, make sure that you troubleshoot the circuit in which the fuse melted BEFORE installing another one.

4   Circuit breakers - general information

Circuit breakers protect certain circuits, such as the power windows or heated seats. Depending on the vehicle's accessories, there may be one or two circuit breakers, located in the fuse/relay box in the engine compartment.

Because the circuit breakers reset automatically, an electrical overload in a circuit breaker-protected system will cause the circuit to fail momentarily, then come back on. If the circuit does not come back on, check it immediately.

For a basic check, pull the circuit breaker up out of its socket on the fuse panel, but just far enough to probe with a voltmeter. The breaker should still contact the sockets. With the voltmeter negative lead on a good chassis ground, touch each end prong of the circuit breaker with the positive meter probe. There should be battery voltage at each end. If there is battery voltage only at one end, the circuit breaker must be replaced.

Some circuit breakers must be reset manually.

5   Relays - general information

Several electrical accessories in the vehicle, such as the fuel injection system, horns, starter, and fog lamps use relays to transmit the electrical signal to the component. Relays use a low-current circuit (the control circuit) to open and close a high-current circuit (the power cir-

cuit). If the relay is defective, that component will not operate properly. Most relays are mounted in the engine compartment and interior fuse/relay boxes (see illustrations 3.1a and 3.1b).

6 Electrical connectors - general information

Most electrical connections on these vehicles are made with mul-tiwire plastic connectors. The mating halves of many connectors are secured with locking clips molded into the plastic connector shells. The mating halves of some large connectors, such as some of those under the instrument panel, are held together by a bolt through the center of the connector.

To separate a connector with locking clips, use a small screwdriver to pry the clips apart carefully, then separate the connector halves. Pull only on the shell, never pull on the wiring harness as you may damage the individual wires and terminals inside the connectors. Look at the connector closely before trying to separate the halves. Often the locking clips are engaged in a way that is not immediately clear. Additionally, many connectors have more than one set of clips.

Each pair of connector terminals has a male half and a female half.

When you look at the end view of a connector in a diagram, be sure to understand whether the view shows the harness side or the component side of the connector. Connector halves are mirror images of each other, and a terminal shown on the right side end-view of one half will be on the left side end-view of the other half.

It is often necessary to take circuit voltage measurements with a connector connected. Whenever possible, carefully insert a small straight pin (not your meter probe) into the rear of the connector shell to contact the terminal inside, then clip your meter lead to the pin. This kind of connection is called "backprobing." When inserting a test probe into a terminal, be careful not to distort the terminal opening. Doing so can lead to a poor connection and corrosion at that terminal later. Using the small straight pin instead of a meter probe results in less chance of deforming the terminal connector.

Electrical connectors

Most electrical connectors have a single release tab that you depress to release the connector

Some electrical connectors have a retaining tab which must be pried up to free the connector

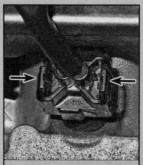

Some connectors have two release tabs that you must squeeze to release the connector

Some connectors use wire retainers that you squeeze to release the connector

Critical connectors often employ a sliding lock (1) that you must pull out before you can depress the release tab (2)

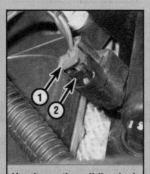

Here's another sliding-lock style connector, with the lock (1) and the release tab (2) on the side of the connector

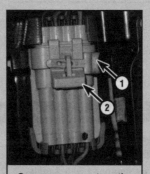

On some connectors the lock (1) must be pulled out to the side and removed before you can lift the release tab (2)

Some critical connectors, like the multi-pin connectors at the Powertrain Control Module employ pivoting locks that must be flipped open

7 Key fob - battery replacement and transmitter programming

BATTERY REPLACEMENT

▶ **Refer to illustrations 7.3a, 7.3b and 7.4**

1 Replace the battery when the key fob transmitter doesn't operate the locks at a distance of 10 feet. Normal range should be about 30 feet.

2 Before replacing the key fob battery, open the driver's door with the key.

3 Use a small screwdriver to carefully separate transmitter from the key half, then split the case halves (see illustrations).

4 Replace the transmitter battery with a new battery (see illustration).

5 Snap the case halves together, then insert the transmitter into the key half and perform the synchronization procedure.

TRANSMITTER PROGRAMMING (SYNCHRONIZATION)

6 Open the door with the key.

7 Press the unlock button of the key fob.

8 Insert the key into the ignition lock and turn the ignition to the "ON" position.

9 Turn the ignition off and remove the key.

10 Press the unlock button on the key fob.

7.3a Use a small screwdriver to separate the fob half from the key half . . .

➡ **Note: The synchronization procedure should be completed within 30 seconds.**

11 The locking system should respond - if not, remove and install the key fob battery and begin again.

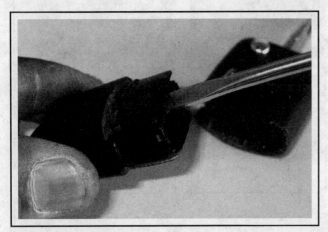

7.3b . . . then split the fob halves

7.4 Remove the battery; note which way the battery is facing before you remove it

8 Ignition switch and key lock cylinder - replacement

⁂ WARNING:

The models covered by this manual are equipped with Supplemental Restraint Systems (SRS), more commonly known as airbags. Always disable the airbag system before working in the vicinity of any airbag system components to avoid the possibility of accidental deployment of the airbags, which could cause personal injury (see Section 25).

⁂ CAUTION:

If the battery is disconnected, several systems must be re-learned before they will work properly (see Chapter 5, Section 3).

1 The steering lock housing is located under the steering column electronic control module on the steering column (switch on the left,

8.5 Disconnect the electrical connector for the electronic immobilizer induction coil

8.6 Access hole location

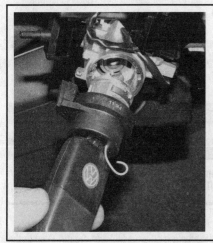

8.7 Insert a paper clip into the access hole and pull out the assembly

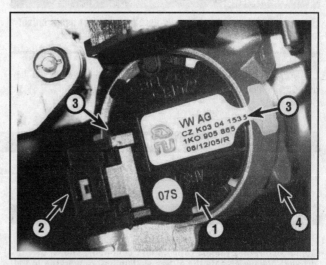

8.11 Ignition switch details - without keyless entry (KESSY) system

1	Ignition switch	3	Ignition switch locking tabs
2	Electrical connector	4	Lock housing

➡ **Note: The electronic immobilizer induction coil is integrated into the lock cylinder and can't be replaced separately.**

8   When installing the key lock cylinder, align it in its original position (still in the "ON" position with the key in), then push the cylinder in until it snaps in place. Remove the paper clip, turn the key to the Lock position and remove the key.

9   Installation is the reverse of removal.

IGNITION SWITCH

Without keyless entry (KESSY) system

▶ **Refer to illustration 8.11**

10 Loosen the steering column mounting bolts and lower the steering column (see Chapter 10).

11 Disconnect the electrical connector to the ignition switch (see illustration).

12 Unlock the switch by depressing the tabs in the lock housing using a small screwdriver.

13 Pull the ignition switch out from the lock housing.

key lock cylinder on the right). It is comprised of a cast-metal housing, the ignition lock cylinder, the ignition switch and the electronic immobilizer induction coil.

2   Disconnect the cable from the negative terminal of the battery (see Chapter 5).

3   Remove the steering column covers (see Chapter 11), steering wheel and clockspring (see Chapter 10), and steering column switch assembly (see Section 9).

KEY LOCK CYLINDER

▶ **Refer to illustrations 8.5, 8.6 and 8.7**

4   On models with automatic transaxles, the shift linkage must be in Park before removing/installing the lock cylinder. Insert the key into the lock and turn it to the "ON" position.

5   Disconnect the electrical connector from the electronic immobilizer induction coil (see illlustration).

6   To remove the key lock cylinder, keep the key in the lock and rotated to the "ON" position and align the access hole with the mark on the trim (see illustration).

7   Insert the straightened end of a large paper clip into the hole in the cylinder (see illustration) and pull the key, lock cylinder and induction coil from the lock cylinder housing as an assembly.

With keyless entry (KESSY) system

14 Instead of an ignition switch in the steering column, vehicles equipped with the keyless entry system (KESSY) have a start system button in the center console.

15 Remove the center console (see Chapter 11).

16 Disconnect the electrical connector from the switch.

17 Open the tabs on the switch and remove it from the console.

18 Installation is the reverse of removal.

LOCK HOUSING

▶ **Refer to illustration 8.21**

19 Loosen the steering column mounting bolts and lower the steering column (see Chapter 10).

❊❊ CAUTION:

The mounting brackets are easily damaged; do not use a chisel to remove the shear bolt heads.

20 Disconnect the electrical connector to the ignition switch and the electronic immobilizer induction coil.

8.21 Lock housing shear bolt locations

21 To remove the housing, locate the shear bolt heads (see illustration) then drill the bolt heads out from the top of steering column bracket.

22 Installation is the reverse of removal. Tighten the new shear bolts until their heads break off.

9   Steering column switches - replacement

▶ **Refer to illustrations 9.5a and 9.5b**

❊❊ WARNING:

The models covered by this manual are equipped with Supplemental Restraint Systems (SRS), more commonly known as airbags. Always disable the airbag system before working in the vicinity of any airbag system components to avoid the possibility of accidental deployment of the airbags, which could cause personal injury (see Section 25).

❊❊ CAUTION:

If the battery is disconnected, several systems must be re-learned before they will work properly (see Chapter 5, Section 3).

1   The steering column switch base carrier is located on the top of the steering column. All the steering column switches are mounted to the base carrier, including the steering column electronic control module, the turn signal, headlight dimmer, windshield wiper/washer, clockspring, steering angle sensor and, if equipped, cruise control functions.

9.5a Insert a feeler gauge as shown to release the fastener on the inside of the switch . . .

9.5b . . . then release the clip on the outside of the switch and remove the switch

➡ **Note:** On 06/2010 and later models, the turn signal, headlight dimmer, windshield wiper/washer and, if equipped, cruise control function switches cannot be disassembled and must be replaced as a complete unit.

2 Disconnect the cable from the negative terminal of the battery (see Chapter 5). Remove the airbag module and steering wheel (see Chapter 10).

3 Remove the steering column covers (see Chapter 11).

4 Remove the clockspring (see Chapter 10, Section 18).

5 Release the individual switch fasteners (see illustrations) and disconnect the switch(es) from the base carrier.

6 Installation is the reverse of removal.

10 Instrument panel switches - replacement

❊❊ WARNING:

The models covered by this manual are equipped with Supplemental Restraint Systems (SRS), more commonly known as airbags. Always disable the airbag system before working in the vicinity of any airbag system components to avoid the possibility of accidental deployment of the airbags, which could cause personal injury (see Section 25).

HEADLIGHT SWITCH

▶ **Refer to illustration 10.1**

1 Turn the headlight switch knob counterclockwise until it stops at the zero position. Push in on the switch and twist it to the right (clockwise), then withdraw it from the instrument panel (see illustration).

2 Pull the switch out far enough to disconnect the electrical connector and remove the switch.

3 Installation is the reverse of removal.

DASH LIGHT DIMMER SWITCH

▶ **Refer to illustration 10.6**

4 Remove the headlight switch as described in Steps 1 and 2.

5 Remove the driver's side dashboard trim panel (see Chapter 11) and disconnect the electrical connector.

6 Squeeze the switch retaining tabs together and remove the dimmer switch (see illustration).

7 Installation is the reverse of removal.

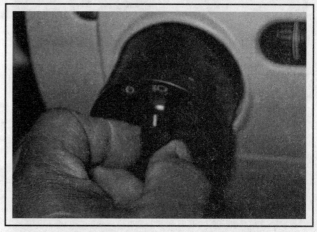

10.1 Push in on the switch and turn it clockwise, then withdraw it from the instrument panel

HAZARD FLASHER SWITCH

▶ **Refer to illustrations 10.9 and 10.10**

8 Remove the instrument panel center vent assembly (see Chapter 11).

9 Disconnect the electrical connectors to the front passenger airbag indicator lamp and the hazard flasher switch (see illustration).

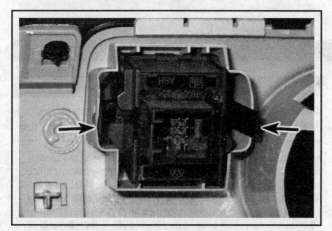

10.6 Squeeze the mounting tabs in and remove the dimmer switch from the panel

10.9 Disconnect the electrical connectors to the front passenger airbag indicator lamp (A), and the hazard flasher switch (B)

10.10 Pull the tabs open and remove the hazard switch

10.15 Remove the switch panel fasteners

10 Carefully open the tabs (see illustration) and remove the switch.
11 Installation is the reverse of removal.

CENTER CONSOLE SWITCHES

▶ **Refer to illustrations 10.15 and 10.16**

12 Depending on the options of the vehicle, there may be one or more switches on the center console, including seat heaters and rear window defogger.

13 All of the aforementioned switches are located in the switch panel at the top of the center console.

14 Remove the shift cover (see Chapter 11).

15 Remove the switch panel fasteners (see illustration), and lift up the panel.

16 All of the switches are removed the same way. Disconnect the electrical connector and push the switch out from the back side of the panel (see illustration).

17 Installation is the reverse of removal.

10.16 Press the switch out of the panel from the backside

11 Instrument cluster - removal and installation

▶ **Refer to illustration 11.3**

✳ WARNING:

The models covered by this manual are equipped with Supplemental Restraint Systems (SRS), more commonly known as airbags. Always disable the airbag system before working in the vicinity of any airbag system components to avoid the possibility of accidental deployment of the airbags, which could cause personal injury (see Section 25).

✳ CAUTION:

If the battery is disconnected, several systems must be re-learned before they will work properly (see Chapter 5, Section 3).

➡ **Note:** The instrument cluster is not serviceable and must be replaced as a complete unit. The instrument cluster control module data must be saved using a factory scan tool prior to removal. The new cluster must be programmed with a factory scan tool. For this reason it is best to have a VW dealer (or other qualified repair shop) perform this job if replacement of the unit is required.

1   Disconnect the negative cable from the battery (see Chapter 5).

2   Remove the steering column upper trim cover (see Chapter 11) and on 2011 models only, remove the radio (see Section 12). Remove the center vent fasteners from the radio opening in the instrument panel, then pry the left hand vent, instrument cluster trim and center vent out from the instrument panel (all one piece).

3   Remove the screws securing the cluster to the instrument panel (see illustration).

4   Pull the instrument cluster out from the instrument panel and remove the cluster.

❋❋ CAUTION:

The instrument cluster is plugged in to the dash; pull the cluster straight out to prevent damaging the electrical connector pins.

5   Installation is the reverse of removal.

11.3 Instrument cluster fasteners

12 Radio and speakers - removal and installation

❋❋ WARNING:

The models covered by this manual are equipped with Supplemental Restraint Systems (SRS), more commonly known as airbags. Always disable the airbag system before working in the vicinity of any airbag system components to avoid the possibility of accidental deployment of the airbags, which could cause personal injury (see Section 25).

❋❋ CAUTION:

If the battery is disconnected, several systems must be re-learned before they will work properly (see Chapter 5, Section 3).

➡ **Note: The audio system is part of the diagnostic network of the vehicle. Any problems with the radio, antenna or speakers may set a trouble code that can be retrieved with a scan tool.**

RADIO

◆ Refer to illustrations 12.4a, 12.4b, 12.5a and 12.5b

❋❋ CAUTION:

On models equipped with the "Premium 8" radio, the transport mode must be activated before removing and deactivated after installation.

1   Turn the ignition switch to the Off position and remove the key. Also turn the radio to Off.

2   On models with a "Premium 8" radio, turn the unit ON, then press and hold the CD player forward, reverse and skip buttons at the same time. After 5 seconds, "CDC transportation safeguard activated" will appear in the radio display.

3   On 2010 and earlier models, remove the instrument panel center trim and vent panel (see Chapter 11).

➡ **Note: On 2011 Jetta models, use a plastic trim tool to pry off the radio and A/C control trim panel.**

4   Remove the radio and A/C control trim panel fasteners and pry the trim panel off of the instrument panel (see illustrations).

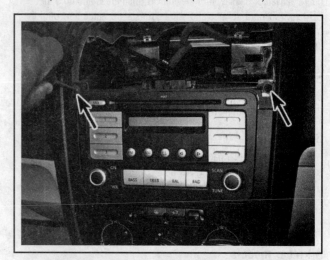

12.4a Remove the radio and A/C control trim panel fasteners . . .

12.4b . . . then carefully pry the radio and A/C control trim panel out from the instrument panel

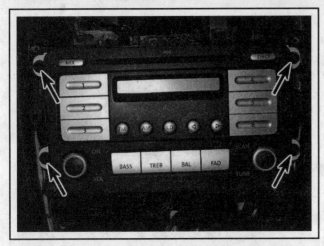

12.5a Remove the radio mounting fasteners . . .

12.5b . . . and rotate the electrical connector lock to disconnect the connector from the rear of the radio

5   Remove the radio fasteners, pull the radio out from the instrument panel, release the electrical connector lock, and disconnect the connector from the back of the radio (see illustrations).

6   Installation is the reverse of removal. Deactivate the Anti-theft system. On "Premium 8" radio, cancel the "CDC transportation safeguard activated" display; turn the unit ON, then press and hold the CD player forward, reverse and skip buttons at the same time until the "deactivation" button appears on the touch screen. Press the "deactivation" button on the screen and transportation safeguard is deactivated.

SATELLITE RADIO

7   Turn the ignition switch to the Off position and remove the key.

Sedan models

8   Remove the rear package tray (see Chapter 11) and loosen the satellite radio tuner mounting screws.

9   Open the trunk and slide the tuner back until the screws come through the openings in the sheet metal.

10   Disconnect the electrical connectors and remove the unit.

11   Installation is the reverse of the removal procedure.

All other models

12   Remove the passenger's side front seat (see Chapter 11).

13   Remove the mounting fasteners, then disconnect the electrical connectors and remove the unit.

14   Installation is the reverse of the removal procedure.

CD CHANGER

▶ **Refer to illustration 12.18**

15   Turn the ignition switch to the Off position and remove the key.

16   Open the armrest and remove any CDs in the changer.

17   Push the two tools into the slots on either side of the CD changer (see illustration).

18   Pull the changer out of the console, disconnect the connectors, and remove the CD changer from the vehicle.

19   Installation is the reverse of the removal procedure.

SPEAKERS

Door bass speakers

▶ **Refer to illustration 12.21**

20   Remove the door panel (see Chapter 11).

21   Disconnect the electrical connector at the speaker, then drill the rivets out and remove the speaker (see illustration).

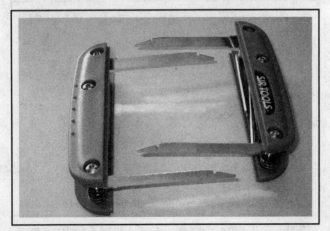

12.18 Typical CD changer removal tools

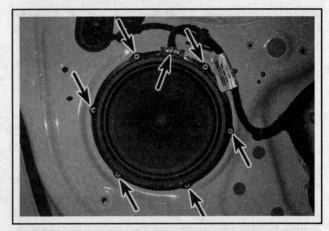

12.21 Disconnect the electrical connector and drill out the rivets

22 Installation is the reverse of the removal procedure.

➡ **Note: Do not use sheet metal screws to replace the rivets.**

Door midrange and treble speakers

➡ **Note: On rear door treble speakers, the plastic tab clips must be cut off and melted back in place using a soldering gun.**

23 Remove the door panel and sail panel (see Chapter 11).
24 Disconnect the electrical connector at the speaker, remove the

mounting fasteners and remove the speaker from the sail panel.
25 Installation is the reverse of the removal procedure.

Subwoofer (sedans)

26 Open the trunk and remove the subwoofer-to-parcel shelf fasteners.
27 Lower the subwoofer and disconnect the electrical connector
28 Remove the subwoofer from inside the trunk. Installation is the reverse of the removal procedure.

13 Antenna - removal and installation

➡ **Note: There are two types of antennas used on these models: a grid type and roof-mounted type. The grid type is an integral component of the rear window (or windows, depending on model). To replace these antennas you must replace the rear window or side window(s).**

1 Remove the rear headliner trim and D-pillar trim from both sides.

2 Remove the rear reading light or luggage compartment light (wagons) housing (see Section 19).
3 Disconnect the antenna cable(s).
4 Carefully pull down the headliner at the rear.
5 Remove the mounting nut and antenna from the roof.
6 Installation is reverse of removal.

14 Rear window defogger - check and repair

1 The rear window defogger consists of a number of horizontal heating elements baked onto the inside surface of the glass. Power is supplied through a large fuse from the fuse/relay box in the dash area. Refer to the wiring diagrams at the end of Chapter 12. The heater is controlled by the instrument panel switch.

2 Small breaks in the element can be repaired without removing the rear window.

CHECK

▶ **Refer to illustrations 14.5, 14.6 and 14.8**

3 Turn the ignition switch and defogger switch to the ON position.
4 Using a voltmeter, place the positive probe against the defogger grid positive terminal and the negative probe against the ground termi-

nal. If battery voltage is not indicated, check the fuse, defogger switch, defogger relay and related wiring. If voltage is indicated, but all or part of the defogger doesn't heat, proceed with the following tests.

5 When measuring voltage during the next two tests, wrap a piece of aluminum foil around the tip of the voltmeter positive probe and press the foil against the heating element with your finger (see illustration). Place the negative probe on the defogger grid ground terminal.

6 Check the voltage at the center of each heating element (see illustration). If the voltage is 5 to 6 volts, the element is okay (there is no break). If the voltage is 0 volts, the element is broken between the center of the element and the positive end. If the voltage is 10 to 12 volts, the element is broken between the center of the element and the ground side. Check each heating element.

7 If none of the elements are broken, connect the negative probe to a good chassis ground. The voltage reading should stay the same - if it doesn't, the ground connection is bad.

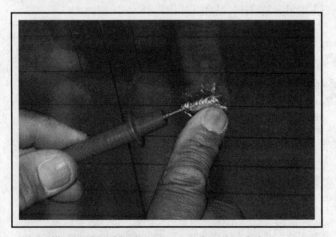

14.5 When measuring the voltage at the rear window defogger grid, wrap a piece of aluminum foil around the positive probe of the voltmeter and press the foil against the wire with your finger

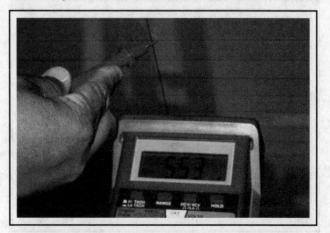

14.6 To determine if a heating element has broken, check the voltage at the center of each element - if the voltage is 6-volts, the element is unbroken

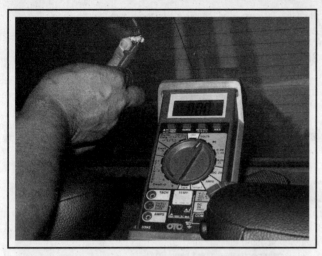

14.8 To find the break, place the voltmeter negative lead against the defogger ground terminal, place the voltmeter positive lead with the foil strip against the heat wire at the positive terminal end and slide it toward the negative terminal end - the point at which the voltmeter deflects from several volts to zero volts is the point at which the wire is broken

8   To find the break, place the voltmeter negative probe against the defogger ground terminal. Place the voltmeter positive probe with the foil strip against the heating element at the positive side and slide it toward the negative side. The point at which the voltmeter deflects from several volts to zero is the point where the heating element is broken (see illustration).

REPAIR

▶ **Refer to illustration 14.14**

9   Repair the break in the element using a repair kit specifically for

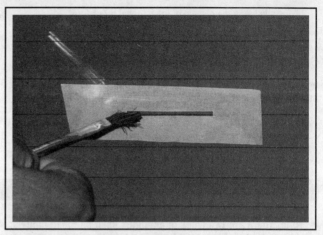

14.14 To use a defogger repair kit, apply masking to the inside of the window at the damaged area, then brush on the special conductive coating

this purpose, such as DuPont paste No. 4817 (or equivalent). The kit includes conductive plastic epoxy.
10 Before repairing a break, turn off the system and allow it to cool for a few minutes.
11 Lightly buff the element area with fine steel wool, then clean it thoroughly with rubbing alcohol.
12 Use masking tape to mask off the area being repaired.
13 Thoroughly mix the epoxy, following the kit instructions.
14 Apply the epoxy material to the slit in the masking tape, overlapping the undamaged area by about 3/4-inch on either end (see illustration).
15 Allow the repair to cure for 24 hours before removing the tape and using the system.

15 Headlight housing - replacement

15.1 Disconnect the electrical connector from the headlight housing - 2007 model shown, other models similar

MODELS WITH HALOGEN BULBS

▶ **Refer to illustrations 15.1 and 15.4**

1   Disconnect the electrical harness connector from the headlight housing (see illustration).

➡ **Note: On 2010 models, the headlight housing electrical connector can only be disconnected after the housing has been moved forward.**

2   Remove the bumper cover (see Chapter 11).
3   Apply masking tape onto the body areas surrounding the headlight housing to prevent damage.
4   Remove the upper fastener and lower fasteners (see illustration).
5   Pull the headlight housing all the way out.
6   Installation is the reverse of the removal procedure. Refer to Section 17 for adjusting procedures after the headlight housing is installed.

15.4 Headlight housing fastener details - 2007 model shown, other models similar

MODELS WITH XENON (HID) BULBS

✳✳ WARNING:

Some models use High Intensity Discharge (HID) bulbs instead of halogen bulbs. These can be identified by the high-voltage warning sticker on the headlight housing. According to the manufacturer, the high voltages produced by this system can be fatal in the event of a shock. Also, the voltage can remain in the circuit even after the headlight switch has been turned to OFF and the ignition key has been removed. Therefore, for your safety, we don't recommend that you try to remove one these headlight housings. Instead, have this service performed by a dealer service department or other qualified repair shop.

✳✳ WARNING:

Never attempt to check for voltage at the bulb socket of an HID headlight.

16 Headlight bulbs - replacement

HALOGEN BULBS

✳✳ WARNING:

Halogen bulbs are gas-filled and under pressure and may shatter if the surface is scratched or the bulb is dropped. Wear eye protection and handle the bulbs carefully, grasping only the base whenever possible. Don't touch the surface of the bulb with your fingers because the oil from your skin could cause it to overheat and fail prematurely. If you do touch the bulb surface, clean it with rubbing alcohol.

Low beam

❖ **Refer to illustrations 16.1 and 16.2**

1   Rotate the bulb cover counterclockwise and remove the cover (see illustration).

2   Rotate the bulb holder counterclockwise and remove the bulb holder and bulb from the contacts (see illustration).

3   Remove the old bulb from the holder.

4   Handling the new bulb only with gloves or a clean rag, insert the new bulb in the holder.

5   Installation is the reverse of the removal procedure.

16.1 Rotate the low beam cover counterclockwise and pull the cover off - 2007 model shown, other models similar

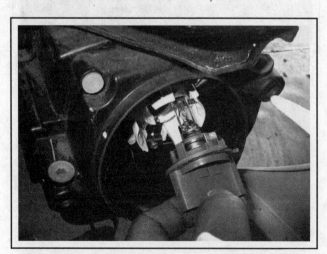

16.2 Rotate the low-beam bulb holder counterclockwise and remove the bulb holder and bulb - 2007 model shown, other models similar

16.6 Remove the rubber cover from the back of the housing - 2007 model shown, other models similar

16.8 Snap the high-beam lock spring over and open the cover - 2007 model shown, other models similar

High beam

▶ Refer to illustrations 16.6, 16.8 and 16.9

6 Pull the rubber cap off of the headlight housing (see illustration).
7 Disconnect the electrical connector.
8 Push the retaining spring clips in towards the center and to the

left to release the bulb (see illustration).
9 Pull the bulb straight out of the socket (see illustration). Make sure to avoid touching the new bulb with your fingers (see **Warning** at the beginning of this Section).
10 Installation is the reverse of removal.

XENON (HID) BULBS

⚹ **WARNING:**

Some models use High Intensity Discharge (HID) bulbs instead of halogen bulbs. These can be identified by the high-voltage warning sticker on the headlight housing. According to the manufacturer, the high voltages produced by this system can be fatal in the event of a shock. Also, the voltage can remain in the circuit even after the headlight switch has been turned to OFF and the ignition key has been removed. Therefore, for your safety, we don't recommend that you try to remove one these headlight housings. Instead, have this service performed by a dealer service department or other qualified repair shop.

⚹ **WARNING:**

Never attempt to check for voltage at the bulb socket of an HID headlight.

16.9 Carefully remove the high-beam bulb without contacting the glass surface of the bulb

17 Headlights - adjustment

▶ **Refer to illustrations 17.1 and 17.2**

❊❊ WARNING:

The headlights must be aimed correctly. If adjusted incorrectly, they could temporarily blind the driver of an oncoming vehicle and cause an accident or seriously reduce your ability to see the road. The headlights should be checked for proper aim every 12 months and any time a new headlight is installed or front-end bodywork is performed. The following procedure is only an interim step to provide temporary adjustment until the headlights can be adjusted by a properly equipped shop.

➡ **Note: Some models are equipped with a headlight leveling system. This adjustment procedure will not apply to those models. Have the headlights adjusted by a dealer service department or other qualified repair shop.**

1   These models are equipped with headlight housings with three adjustment screws, one controlling left-and-right movement and one for up-and-down movement for both high and low beam and a third for just low beam up-and-down movement (see illustration).

➡ **Note: The third adjustment screw is used to raise or lower the low beam separately once the high beam has been adjusted.**

2   There are several methods of adjusting the headlights. The simplest method requires an open area with a blank wall and a level floor (see illustration).

3   Position masking tape vertically on the wall in reference to the vehicle centerline and the centerlines of both headlights.

4   Position a horizontal tape line in reference to the centerline of all the headlights.

➡ **Note: It may be easier to position the tape on the wall with the vehicle parked only a few inches away.**

5   Adjustment should be made with the vehicle parked 25 feet from the wall, sitting level, the gas tank half-full and no unusually heavy load in the vehicle.

6   Starting with the high beam adjustment, position the high intensity zone so it is two inches below the horizontal line and two inches to the side of the vertical headlight line, away from oncoming traffic. Twist the adjustment screws until the desired level has been achieved.

7   Adjust the low beam, position the high intensity zone so it is two inches below the horizontal line and two inches to the side of the vertical headlight line, away from oncoming traffic. Twist the adjustment screws until the desired level has been achieved.

8   With the high beams on, the high intensity zone should be vertically centered with the exact center just below the horizontal line.

9   Have the headlights adjusted by a dealer service department at the earliest opportunity.

17.1 Headlight adjustment screws - 2007 model shown, other models similar

1   High/low beam vertical (up-and-down) adjuster
2   High/low beam horizontal (side-to-side) adjuster
3   Low beam vertical (up-and-down) adjuster

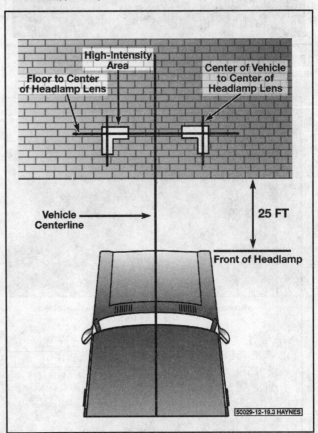

17.2 Headlight adjustment details

18 Taillight housing - removal and installation

▶ **Refer to illustrations 18.2 and 18.3**

1   Fold back the trim panel that covers the taillight housing and the wheel housing.

✳✳ CAUTION:

Do not leave the trunk side panel bent or out of shape too long, or it will permanently deform it.

2   Disconnect the electrical connectors from the taillight housing (see illustration).

3   Remove the taillight housing nuts, press up the release tabs (see illustration) and remove the taillight housing.

4   Installation is the reverse of removal.

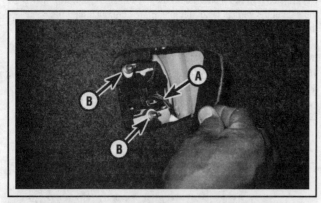

18.2 Disconnect the electrical connector (A), then remove the mounting nuts (B) - Sedan model shown, other models similar

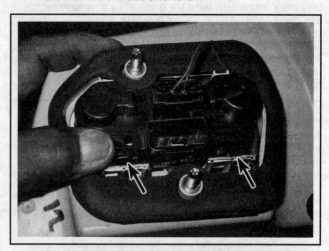

18.3 Press up the locking tabs to disengage the housing and pull the taillight housing out - Sedan model shown, other models similar

Bulb removal

To remove many modern exterior bulbs from their holders, simply pull them out

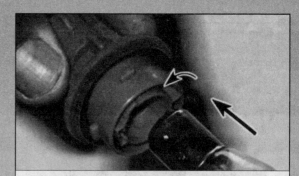

On bulbs with a cylindrical base ("bayonet" bulbs), the socket is spring-loaded; a pair of small posts on the side of the base hold the bulb in place against spring pressure. To remove this type of bulb, push it into the holder, rotate it 1/4-turn counterclockwise, then pull it out

If a bayonet bulb has dual filaments, the posts are staggered, so the bulb can only be installed one way

To remove most overhead interior light bulbs, simply unclip them

19 Bulb - replacement

☀☀☀ WARNING:

Bulbs can remain hot for up to twenty minutes after they're turned off. Be sure bulbs are off and cool before you touch them.

FRONT TURN SIGNAL LIGHT

▶ **Refer to illustration 19.2**

1   Remove any interfering engine compartment covers/air intake ducts for access to the headlight housing.
2   Rotate the bulb holder counterclockwise and remove the bulb holder and bulb from the contacts (see illustration).
3   Push the bulb into the holder, rotate the bulb counterclockwise and remove the bulb from the holder.
4   Installation is the reverse of the removal procedure.

FRONT PARKING LIGHT

▶ **Refer to illustration 19.7**

5   Remove any interfering engine compartment covers/air intake ducts for access to the headlight housing.
6   Open the plastic cover for the high-beam bulb on the back of the headlight housing (see illustration 16.6).
7   Pull the parking light bulb holder out of the headlight housing (see illustration), then pull the bulb from the holder.

➡ **Note: On 2011 models, the bulb holder must be rotated counterclockwise, then removed.**

8   Installation is the reverse of removal.

SIDE-MARKER LIGHTS

Rabbit and GTI models

9   Push the front of the marker light in slightly, then push the back

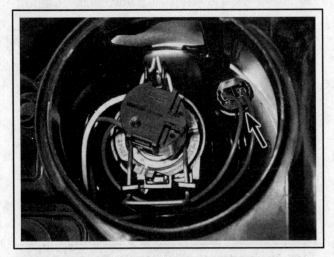

19.7 Front parking light bulb location - 2010 and earlier models shown, later model similar

19.2 Rotate the bulb holder counterclockwise and pull the holder from the housing

of the marker light housing forward and lift it out of the fender.
10 Twist the bulb holder counterclockwise to remove it.
11 Installation is the reverse of the removal procedure. Make sure the hook (forward) end of the light housing goes in first, then snap the housing in place until the tab is engaged.

Jetta models

▶ **Refer to illustration 19.13**

12 Remove the under-vehicle splash shield (see Chapter 1, Section 6).
13 Press the retaining tab forward and remove the marker light from the front bumper cover (see illustration).
14 Twist the bulb holder counterclockwise to remove it.

➡ **Note: The marker bulb can be removed from the marker light from under the vehicle without removing the marker light.**

15 Installation is the reverse of the removal procedure. Make sure the tab end of the light housing goes in first, then snap the housing in place until the tab is engaged.

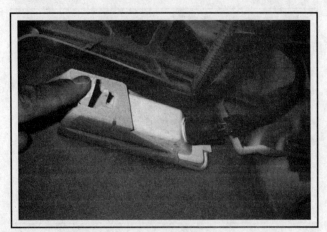

19.13 Disengage the side marker light by pressing the retaining tab forward

19.20 Spread the release clips apart (Jetta models)

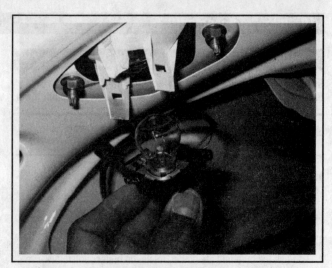

19.22 Remove the housing and remove the bulb

TAIL/STOP/TURN/BACK-UP LIGHTS

16 Remove the rear taillight housing (see Section 18).

17 Squeeze the release tabs to unlock the bulb assembly and remove the bulb holder from the housing. Twist the bulbs counterclockwise to remove them.

18 Installation is the reverse of removal.

TAIL/REAR FOG LIGHT

▶ Refer to illustrations 19.20 and 19.22

19 The tail/rear fog lights are located on the trunk lid or hatch. Open the lid or hatch and the trim access panel.

20 On Jetta models, spread the release clips apart to unlock the bulb assembly (see illustration).

21 On Rabbit and GTI models, rotate the bulb holder counterclockwise to release the holder.

22 Pull out the bulb housing and disconnect the electrical connectors (see illustration). Twist the bulb counterclockwise to remove it.

23 Installation is the reverse of removal.

HIGH-MOUNT BRAKE LIGHT

➡ **Note: The high-mount brake light must be replaced as a unit; the individual LED lights are not serviceable.**

Sedans

▶ Refer to illustrations 19.24 and 19.25

24 Remove the trim for the roof end strip (see illustration) directly against the rear window.

25 Disconnect the electrical connector and press the light assembly towards the rear window (see illustration) to release it from the mounting clips.

26 Installation is the reverse of removal.

Rabbit, GTI and Wagon models

27 From the outside of the vehicle, carefully pry the top of the brake light downwards to disengage the mounting tabs.

28 Pull the housing out and disconnect the electrical connector.

29 Installation is the reverse of the removal procedure.

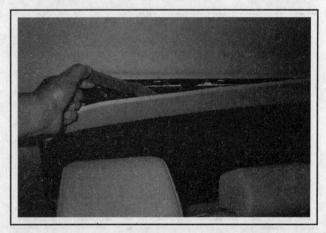

19.24 On sedan models, carefully pry out the roof end trim panel

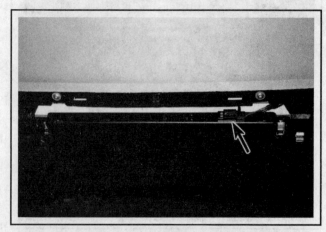

19.25 Disconnect the electrical connector, then push the high-mount brake light housing towards the window and out

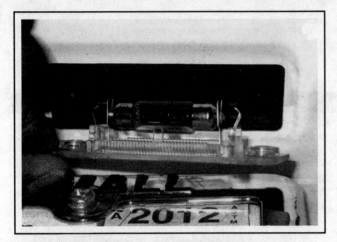

19.30 Remove the license plate light housing

19.34a Carefully pry off the lens cover using a small flat-blade screwdriver . . .

LICENSE PLATE LIGHT BULB

◗ **Refer to illustration 19.30**

30 Use a small screwdriver to remove the license plate light housing mounting screws, then tilt and pull out the light housing (see illustration).

31 Remove the bulb from the bulb holder.

32 Installation is the reverse of removal.

INTERIOR LIGHTS

Instrument cluster lights

33 The instrument cluster is illuminated by LEDs that are part of the printed circuit board. There are no user-replaceable bulbs behind the instrument cluster. Consult with a dealer service department or other qualified repair shop; some facilities might be equipped to repair the cluster, or might offer an exchange program. If the instrument cluster is replaced, it will have to be programmed with a proprietary scan tool.

Front dome lights

◗ **Refer to illustrations 19.34a and 19.34b**

34 Remove the dome light lens (see illustration), then remove the bulb(s) by pulling straight out (see illustration).

35 Installation is the reverse of removal.

Front reading/map lights

◗ **Refer to illustration 19.36**

36 Remove the front light lens cover (see illustration). Remove the bulb(s) (see illustration 19.34b).

➡ **Note: Not all models have a reading/map light lens that can be removed. If the lens can't be removed, pry the trim panel off at the rear of the housing, then remove the fasteners and swing the overhead console down. Remove the bulb holders and replace the bulbs.**

37 Installation is the reverse of removal.

Vanity lights

38 Pry the light out of the headliner carefully with a small screwdriver.

39 Unhook the bulb cover, then remove the bulb by pulling it straight out (see Illustration 19.34b).

40 Installation is the reverse of removal.

Glovebox light

41 Open the glovebox door and pry the light housing out of the glovebox carefully with a small screwdriver.

42 Remove the bulb by pulling it straight out of the bulb holder.

43 Installation is the reverse of removal.

19.34b . . . then remove the bulbs

19.36 Carefully pry the lens cover off the front reading light using a small flat-blade screwdriver

Luggage compartment lights

44 Pry the light assembly from the trunk lid, liftgate or trunk floor opening depending on the model and disconnect the electrical connector.

45 Remove the bulb by pulling it straight out of the light assembly.

46 Installation is the reverse of removal.

20 Horns - replacement

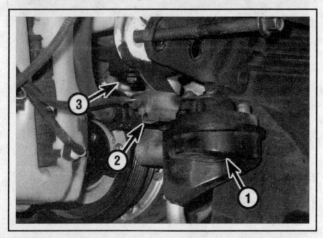

20.2 Typical horn details - right side shown, left side identical

1 *Low-tone horn*   3 *Mounting fastener*
2 *Electrical connector*

◆ **Refer to illustration 20.2**

➡ **Note: There are two horns, located behind the front bumper cover and bolted to each end of the front bumper reinforcement bar. The low- tone horn is on the passenger's side, and the high-tone horn is on the driver's side.**

1 Remove the bumper cover (see Chapter 11).

2 Disconnect the electrical connector, remove the fastener and detach the horn (see illustration).

3 Installation is the reverse of removal.

21 Wiper motor - replacement

FRONT WIPER MOTOR

◆ **Refer to illustrations 21.4 and 21.6**

1 Turn the ignition switch to the Off position and remove the key.

2 Mark the positions of the wiper arm(s) on the windshield, remove the nuts, then remove the wiper arm using a rocking motion.

3 Remove the windshield cowl cover and weatherstrip (see Chapter 11).

4 Disconnect the wiper motor electrical connector and remove the windshield wiper motor/linkage assembly fasteners (see illustration).

5 Lift the windshield wiper motor assembly from the cowl area.

6 Remove the wiper motor-to-linkage nut, then the motor-to-bracket fasteners and separate the motor from the linkage bracket (see illustration).

7 Installation is the reverse of removal.

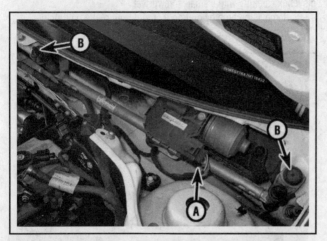

21.4 Disconnect the electrical connector (A), then remove the mounting fasteners (B) and windshield wiper motor and linkage

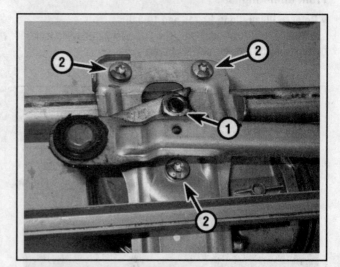

21.6 Windshield wiper motor details

1 *Wiper motor-to-linkage nut*
2 *Linkage bracket-to-wiper motor fasteners*

REAR WIPER MOTOR

▶ **Refer to illustration 21.14**

8   Turn the ignition switch to the Off position and remove the key.

9   Mark the position of the wiper arm on the window, then carefully pry the base cap apart and lift off.

10   Detach the rear spray jet and loosen, but do not remove, the wiper arm nut.

11   Carefully rock the wiper arm back and forth until it is loose and remove nut and wiper arm.

12   Remove the inner trim panel from the hatch area (see Chapter 11).

13   Disconnect the wiper motor harness connector and remove the wiper motor mounting fasteners.

14   Lift the wiper motor assembly from the hatch/liftgate area (see illustration).

15   Installation is the reverse of removal.

21.14 Remove the rear wiper motor from the hatch/liftgate

22 Cruise control system - description and check

These vehicles have an electrically controlled throttle body. The accelerator pedal communicates with the throttle body through the Powertrain Control Module (PCM) (see Chapters 4 and 6 for more information about the electronic throttle control system). The PCM also controls the cruise control system, which is now an integral function of the electronic throttle control system. If the system malfunctions, begin diagnosis by checking to see if any trouble codes have been set (see Chapter 6). If that doesn't lead to the problem, take it to a dealer service department or other qualified repair shop for further diagnosis.

23 Power window system - general information

➡ **Note: These vehicles are equipped with various control modules that govern the door locks, the power windows, the ignition lock and security system, the interior and exterior lights, the headlights, the horn, the windshield wipers/washers, the heating/air conditioning system, the audio system and the power mirrors. In the event of a malfunction with one of these systems, have the vehicle diagnosed by a dealership service department or other qualified automotive repair facility if no obvious problems are found.**

The power window system operates electric motors, mounted on the doors, which lower and raise the windows. The system consists of the control switches, the motors, regulators, glass mechanisms and associated wiring.

The power windows can be lowered and raised from the master control switch by the driver or by the switch located at the passenger window. Each window has a separate motor that is reversible. The position of the control switch determines the polarity and therefore the direction of operation.

The circuit is protected by fuses and a circuit breaker. Check the fuses in the fuse panel at the left end of the instrument panel. Each motor is equipped with an internal circuit breaker; this prevents one stuck window from disabling the whole system. Refer to the wiring diagrams at the end of Chapter 12. Problems within this system can only be diagnosed with a professional-grade scan tool. If you have eliminated the obvious causes of a problem, have the vehicle checked at a dealership service department or other properly equipped repair shop.

24 Power door lock system - general information

➡ **Note: These vehicles are equipped with various control modules that govern the door locks, the power windows, the ignition lock and security system, the interior and exterior lights, the headlights, the horn, the windshield wipers/washers, the heating/air conditioning system, the audio system and the power mirrors. In the event of a malfunction with one of these systems, have the vehicle diagnosed by a dealership service department or other qualified automotive repair facility if no obvious problems are found.**

The central locking system uses an actuator (motor) integrated into each door lock. The actuators are not serviceable separately and if one is bad the entire lock assembly must be replaced. The power door lock systems operate bi-directional motors. The first motor locks the exterior door and the second motor locks the interior door latch assembly, called the safe function. This no longer allows the doors to open from the interior door handles when the doors are locked.

➡ **Note: In the event of an accident in which the airbags have been deployed, the locking system control module will open all locked doors.**

The central locking system control module is located behind the glove box. Each door also has a control module located towards the front of each door. Problems within these modules can only be diagnosed with a factory scan tool. If you have eliminated the obvious causes of a problem, have the vehicle checked at a dealership service department or other properly equipped repair shop.

25 Airbag system - general information and system component removal and installation

These models are equipped with a Supplemental Restraint System (SRS), more commonly known as airbags, designed to protect the driver and the passenger from serious injury in the event of a head-on or side collision. All models have a diagnostic control unit, located on the floor under the center console.

✳✳ WARNING:

If your vehicle is ever involved in a flood, or the interior carpeting is soaked for any reason, disconnect the battery and do not start the vehicle until the airbag system can be checked by your dealer. If the SRS system is subjected to flooding, the airbags could go off upon starting the vehicle, even without an accident taking place.

AIRBAG MODULES

Driver's airbag

The airbag inflator module contains a housing incorporating the cushion (airbag) and inflator unit, mounted in the center of the steering wheel. The inflator assembly is mounted on the back of the housing over a hole through which gas is expelled, inflating the bag almost instantaneously when an electrical signal is sent from the system. A spiral cable (or clockspring) assembly on the steering column under the steering wheel carries this signal to the module. This clockspring can transmit an electrical signal regardless of steering wheel position.

Passenger's airbag

The airbag is mounted inside the right side of the instrument panel, in the area above the glove box. It's similar in design to the driver's airbag, except that it's larger than the steering wheel unit. The trim cover (on the side of the instrument panel that faces toward the passenger) is textured and colored to match the instrument panel and has a molded seam that splits open when the bag inflates.

Side impact airbags

Some models are equipped with side-impact airbags located in the outer part of the front seat backs. Additionally some models have side impact airbags integrated into the outside rear seat bolsters.

Side curtain airbags

In addition to the side-impact airbags, extra side-impact protection is also provided by side-curtain airbags on some models. These are long airbags that, in the event of a side impact, come out of the headliner at each side of the car and come down between the side windows and the seats. They are designed to protect the heads of both front seat and rear seat passengers.

SENSING AND DIAGNOSTIC MODULE

The sensing and diagnostic module supplies the current to the airbag system in the event of a collision, even if battery power is cut off. It checks this system every time the vehicle is started, causing the "AIR BAG" light to go on then off, if the system is operating properly. If there is a fault in the system, the light will go on and stay on, flash, or the dash will make a beeping sound. If this happens, the vehicle should be taken to your dealer immediately for service. This module is mounted under the center console. There is also a roll-over sensor located directly behind it on later models.

SEAT BELT PRE-TENSIONERS

All models are equipped with pyrotechnic (explosive) units in the front seat belt retracting mechanisms. During an impact that would trigger the airbag system, the airbag control unit also triggers the seat belt retractors. When the pyrotechnic charges go off, they accelerate the retractors to instantly take up any slack in the seat belt system to more fully prepare the driver and front seat passenger for impact.

The airbag system should be disabled any time work is done to or around the seats.

✳✳ WARNING:

Never strike the pillars or floorpan with a hammer or use an impact-driver tool in these areas unless the system is disabled.

DISARMING THE SYSTEM AND OTHER PRECAUTIONS

✳✳ WARNING:

Failure to follow these precautions could result in accidental deployment of the airbag and personal injury.

✳✳ WARNING:

Any time you are working in the vicinity of airbag wiring or components, DISARM THE SRS SYSTEM.

✳✳ WARNING:

An auxiliary voltage input device (memory saver) must NOT be used when working near airbag system components.

Whenever working in the vicinity of the steering wheel, steering column or any of the other SRS system components, the system must be disarmed.

To disarm the airbag system:

a) *Turn the steering wheel to the straight-ahead position and turn the ignition switch to the Lock position, then remove the key.*
b) *Disconnect the negative battery cable (see Chapter 5).*
c) *Wait at least two minutes for the back-up power supply to be depleted.*
d) *Before touching any airbag system component, ground yourself to a metal part of the vehicle to discharge any static electricity built up in your body.*

To re-arm the airbag system:

a) *Turn the ignition switch to the On position.*

b) *Make sure there is nobody inside the vehicle and that there are no objects near any of the airbag modules, then reconnect the cable to the negative terminal of the battery.*

c) *Turn the ignition switch to the Off position, wait ten seconds, then turn it to the On position. The AIR BAG light on the instrument panel should come on continuously for about six seconds, then turn off.*

➡ **Note: The light might take up to 30 seconds to come on after the key is turned to the On position (during this time the Restraints Control Module is performing a self-check of the system). If the light fails to come on, or if it flashes, or if a chime sounds in patterns of five sets of five beeps, have the vehicle diagnosed by a dealer service department or other qualified repair shop.**

Whenever handling an airbag module:

Always keep the airbag opening (the trim side) pointed away from your body. Never place the airbag module on a bench or other surface with the airbag opening facing the surface. Always place the airbag module in a safe location with the airbag opening facing up.

Never measure the resistance of any SRS component. An ohmmeter has a built-in battery supply that could accidentally deploy the airbag.

Never use electrical welding equipment on a vehicle equipped with an airbag without first disconnecting the electrical connector for each airbag.

Never dispose of a live airbag module. Return it to a dealer service department or other qualified repair shop for safe deployment and disposal.

COMPONENT REMOVAL AND INSTALLATION

Driver's side airbag module and spiral cable

Refer to Chapter 10, *Steering wheel - removal and installation,* for the driver's side airbag module and clockspring removal and installation procedures.

Passenger's airbag module and other airbag modules

Even if you ever have to remove the instrument panel, it's not necessary to remove the passenger airbag module to do so; it can simply remain installed in the instrument panel. We don't recommend removing any of the other airbag modules either. These jobs are best left to a professional.

26 Wiring diagrams - general information

Since it isn't possible to include all wiring diagrams for every year and model covered by this manual, the following diagrams are those that are typical and most commonly needed.

Prior to troubleshooting any circuits, check the fuses and circuit breakers (if equipped) to make sure they're in good condition. Make sure the battery is properly charged and check the cable connections (see Chapter 1).

When checking a circuit, make sure that all connectors are clean, with no broken or loose terminals. When disconnecting a connector, do not pull on the wires. Pull only on the connector housings themselves.

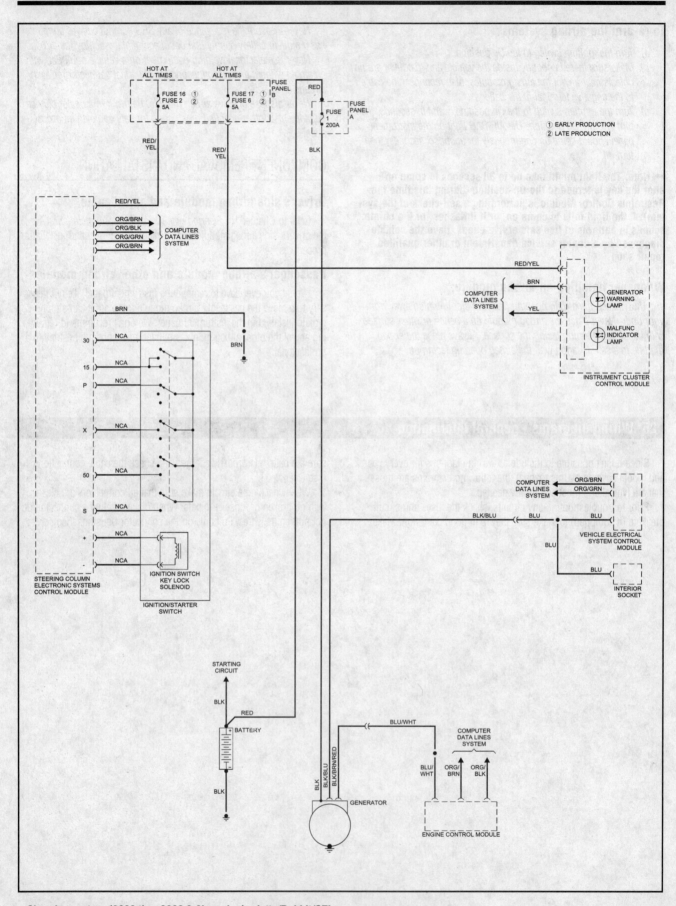

Charging system (2006 thru 2008 2.0L engine) - Jetta/Rabbit/GTI

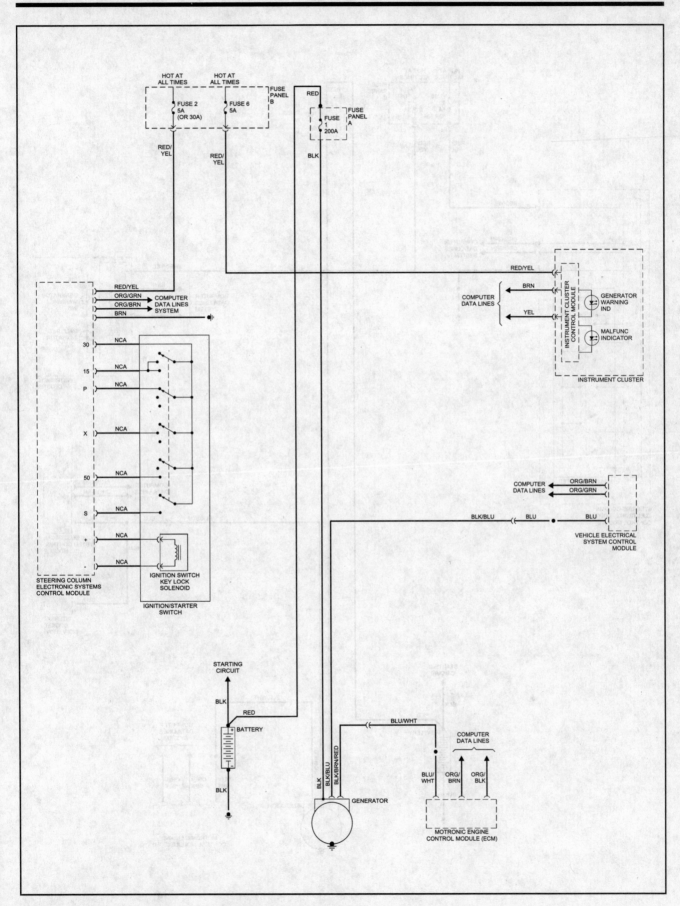

Charging system (2009 and later 2.0L engine) - Jetta/GTI

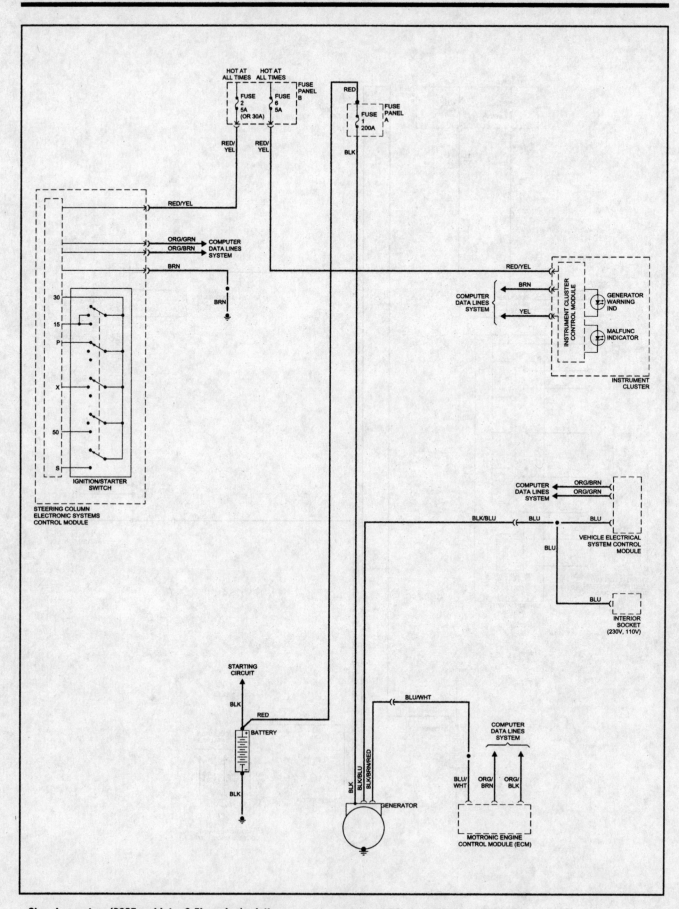

Charging system (2005 and later 2.5L engine) - Jetta

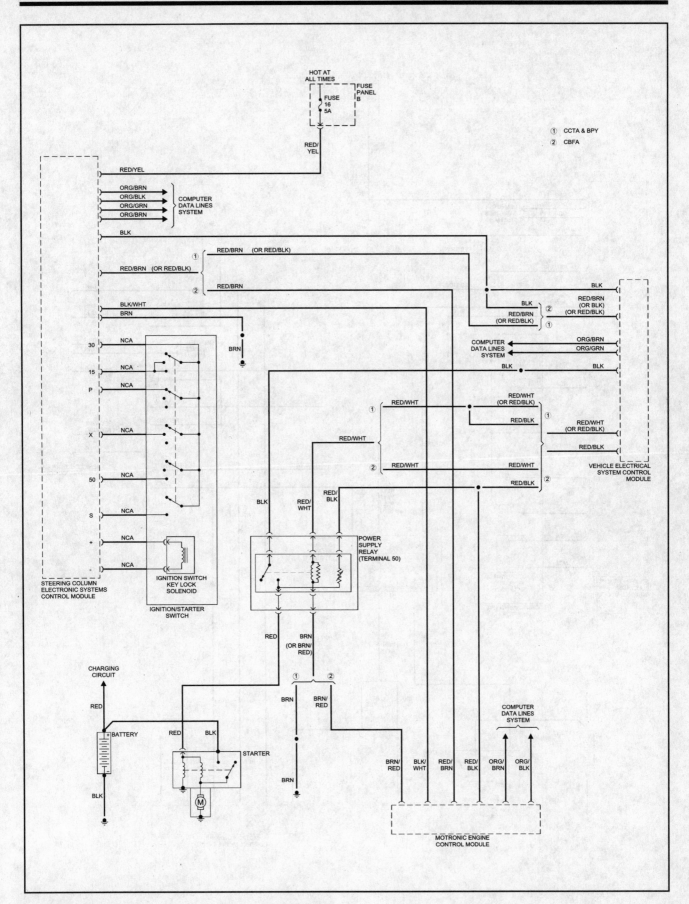

Starting system (2006 thru 2008 2.0L engine) - Jetta/Rabbit/GTI

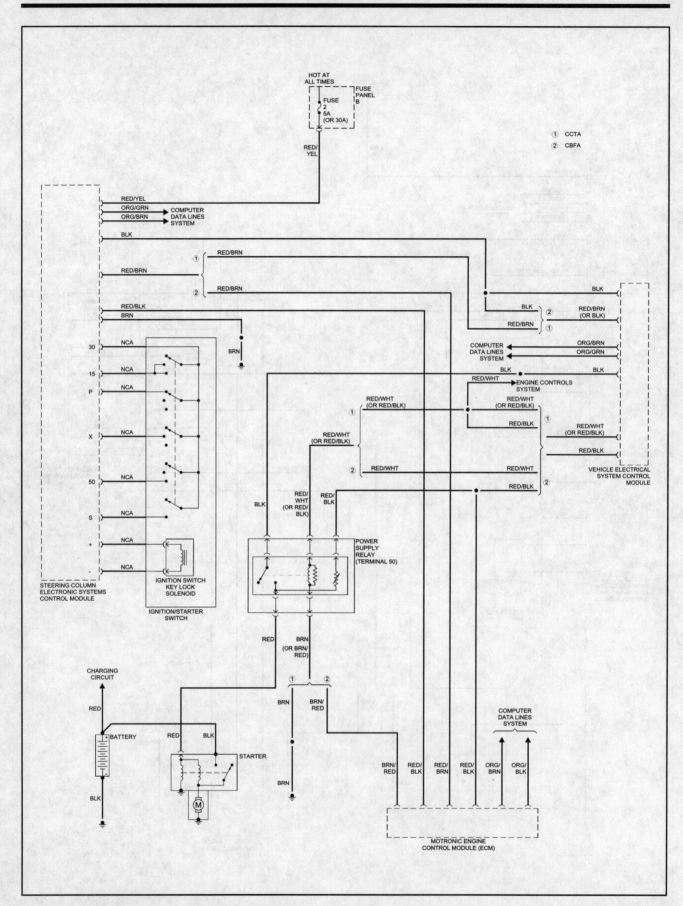

Starting system (2009 and later 2.0L engine) - Jetta/GTI

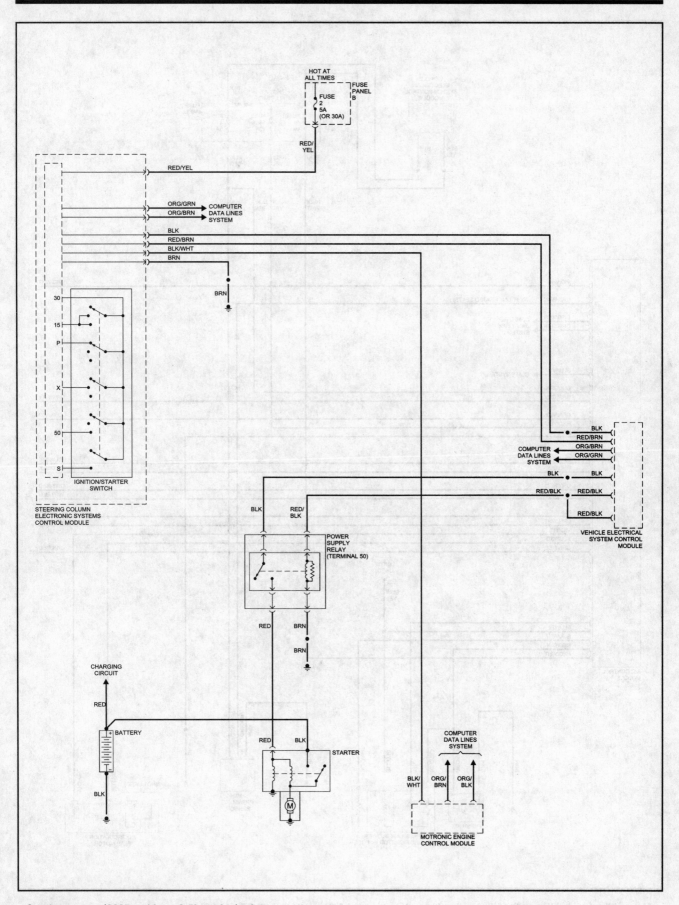

Starting system (2005 and later 2.5L engine) - Jetta

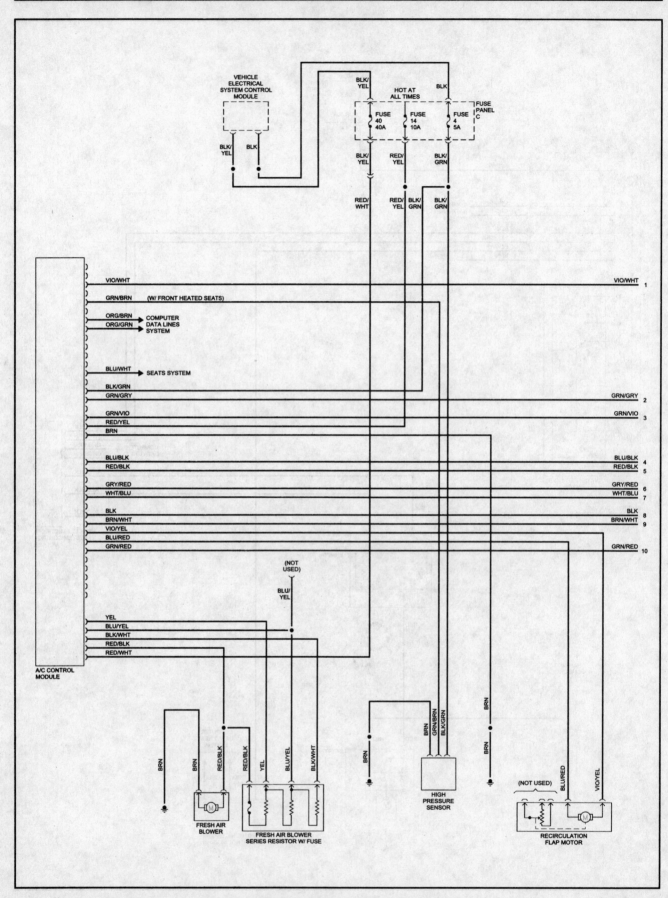

Air conditioning, heating and engine cooling fan system (manual A/C) - Jetta/Rabbit/GTI (1 of 2)

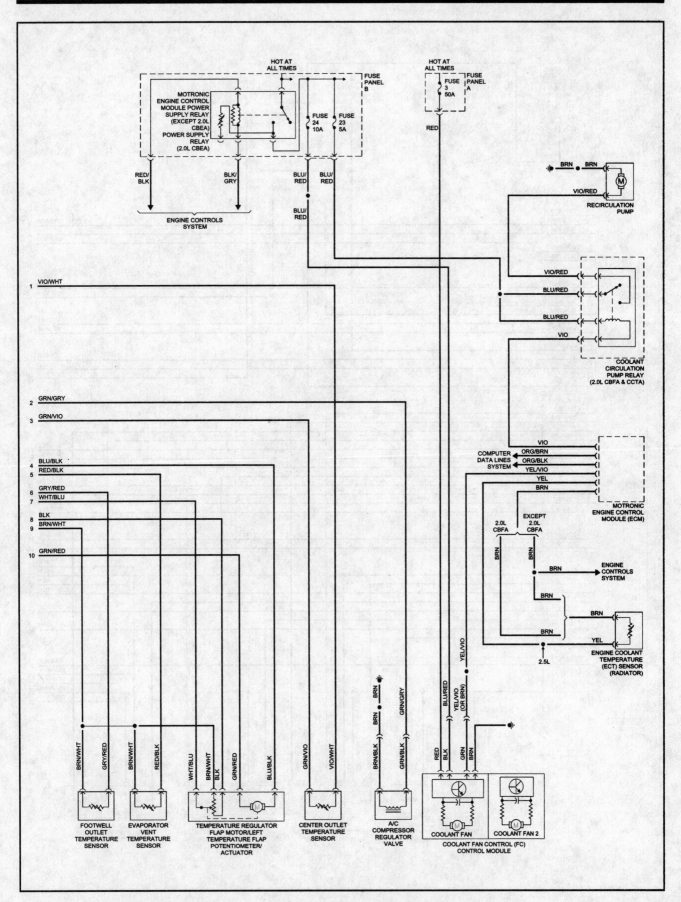

Air conditioning, heating and engine cooling fan system (manual A/C) - Jetta/Rabbit/GTI (2 of 2)

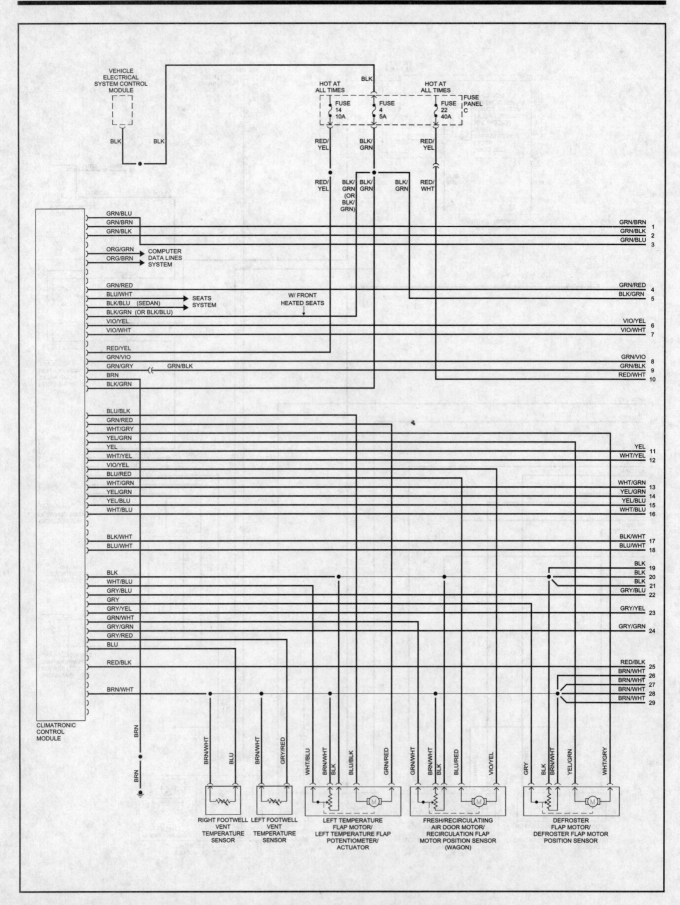

Air conditioning, heating and engine cooling fan system (Automatic A/C) - Jetta/Rabbit/GTI (1 of 3)

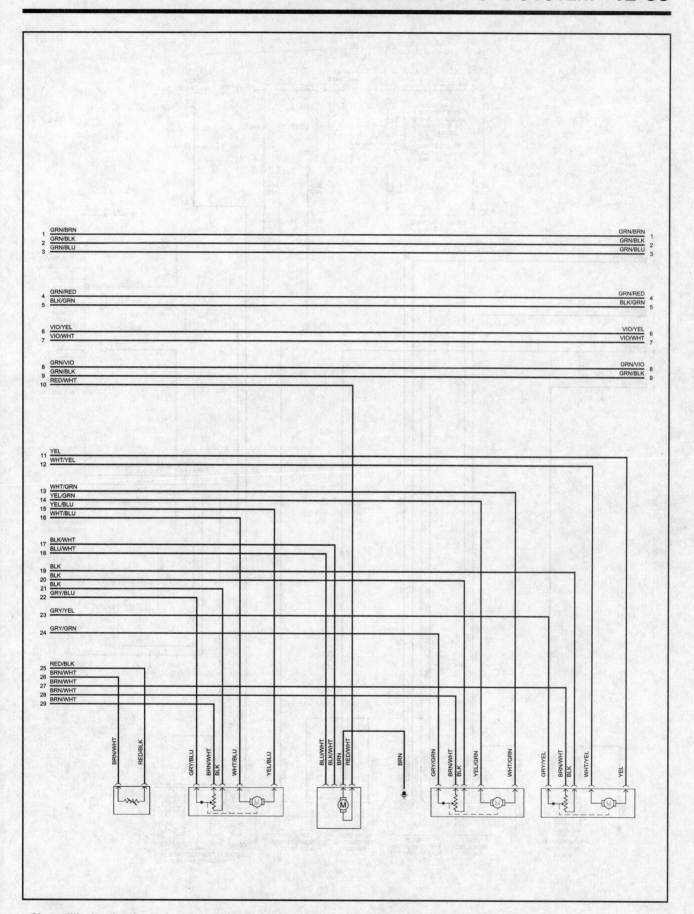

Air conditioning, heating and engine cooling fan system (Automatic A/C) - Jetta/Rabbit/GTI (2 of 3)

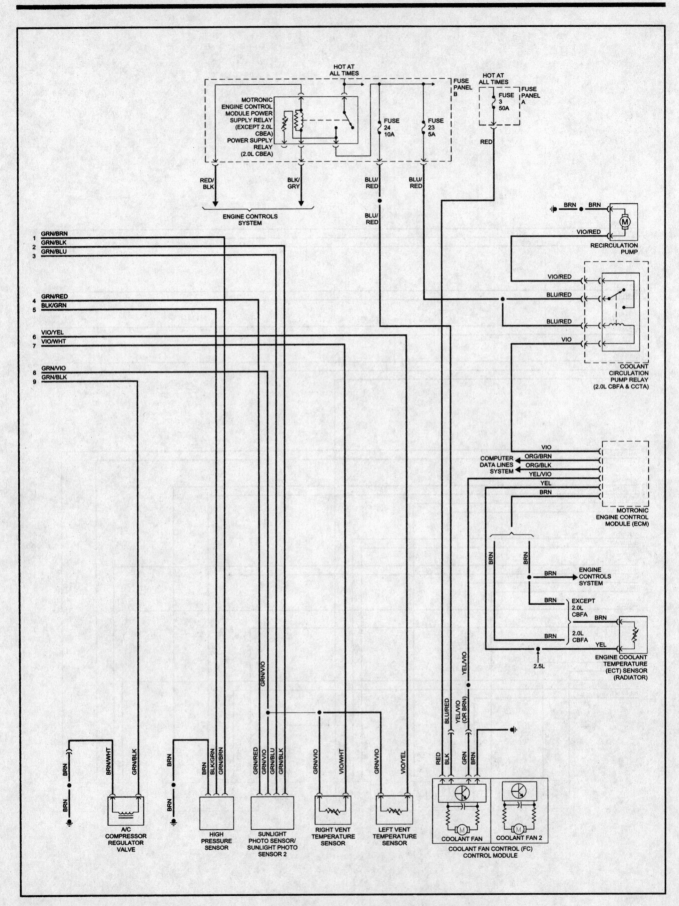

Air conditioning, heating and engine cooling fan system (Automatic A/C) - Jetta/Rabbit/GTI (3 of 3)

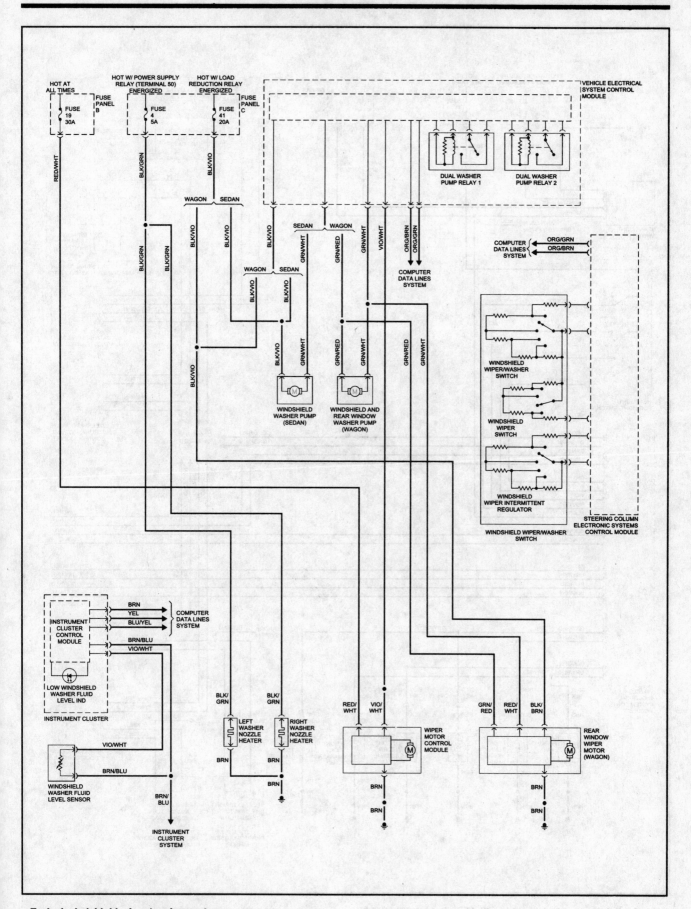

Typical windshield wiper/washer system

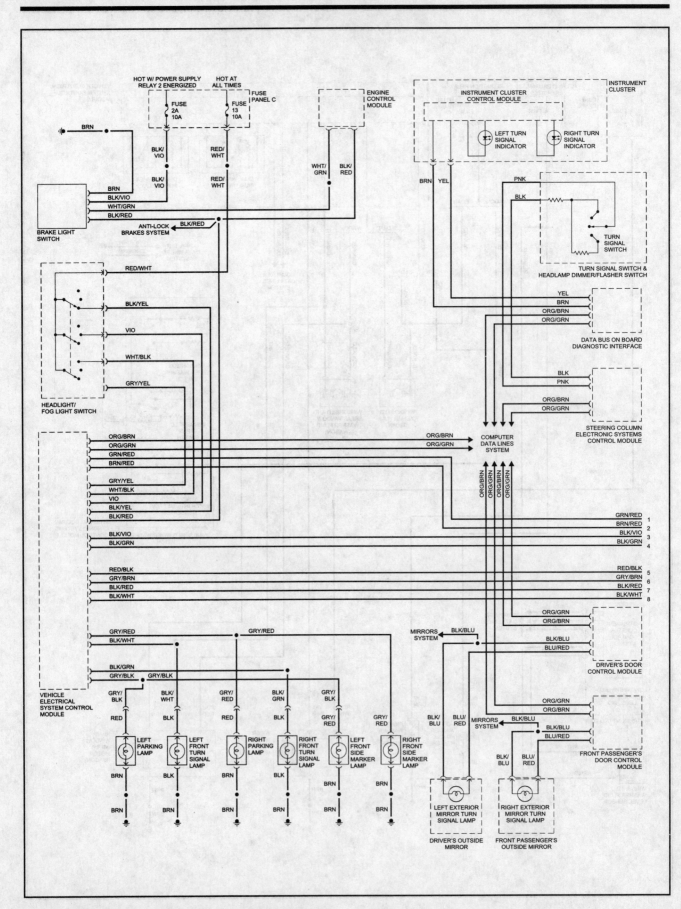

Exterior lighting system (except headlights) - Rabbit/GTI (1 of 2)

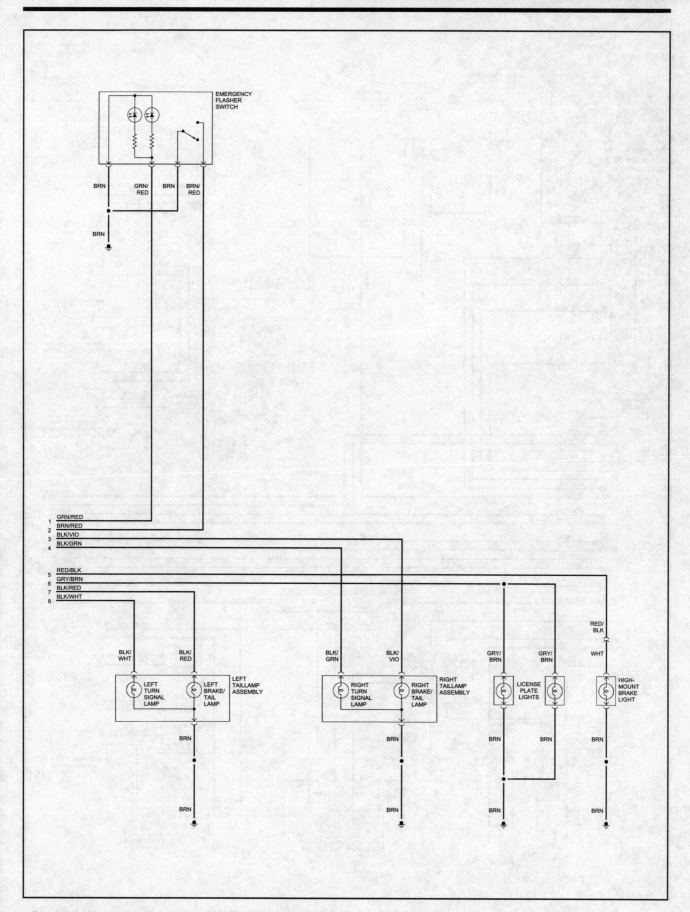

Exterior lighting system (except headlights) - Rabbit/GTI (2 of 2)

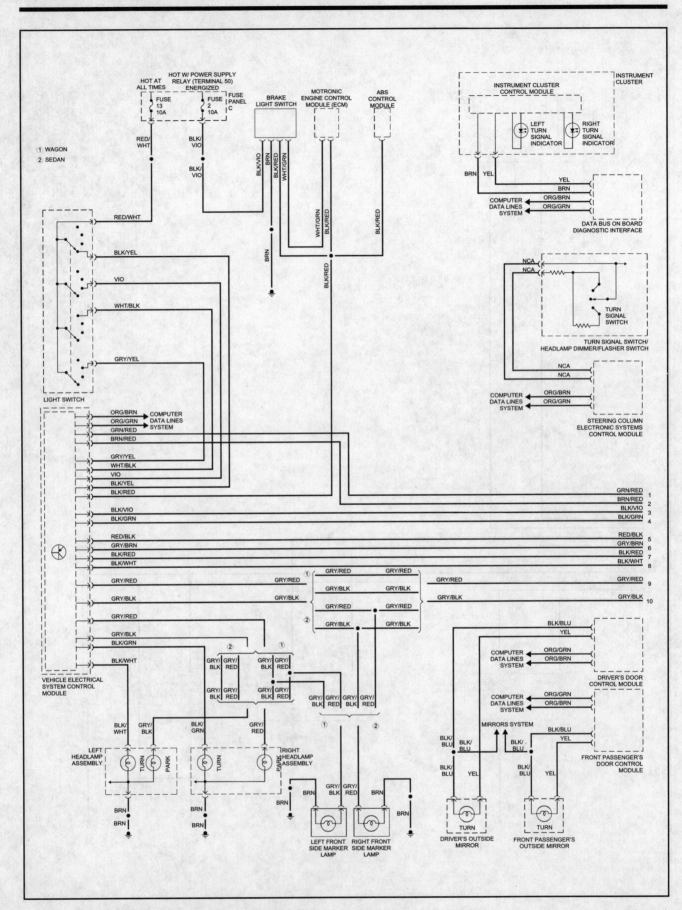

Exterior lighting system (except headlights) - Jetta (1 of 2)

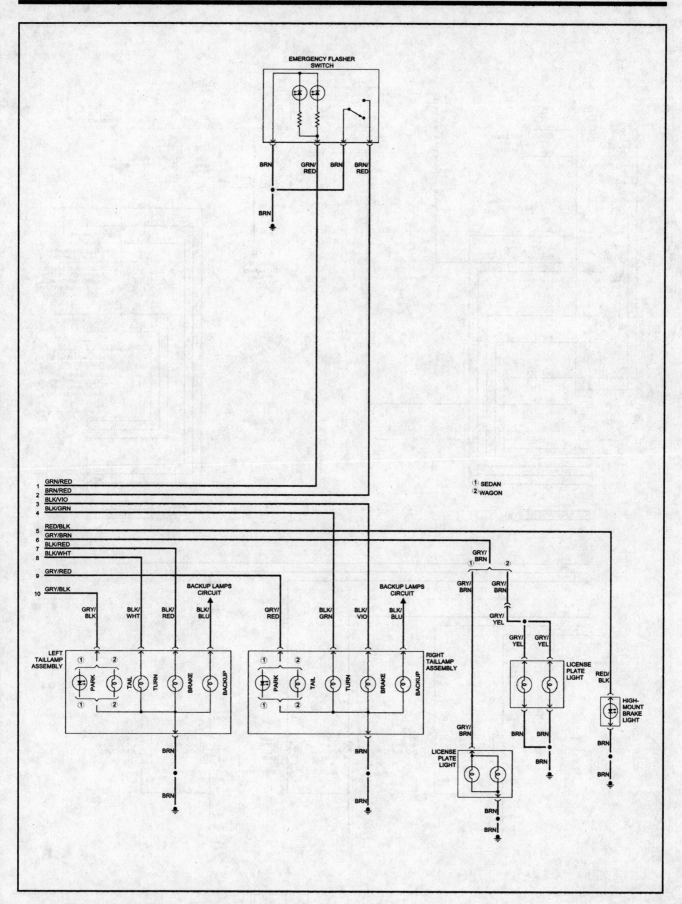

Exterior lighting system (except headlights) - Jetta (2 of 2)

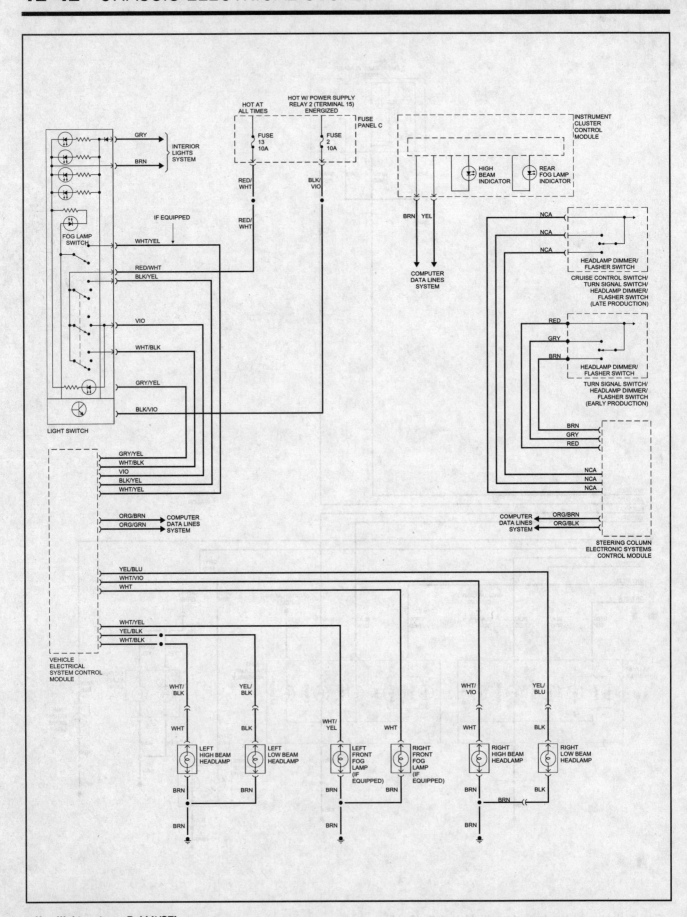

Headlight system - Rabbit/GTI

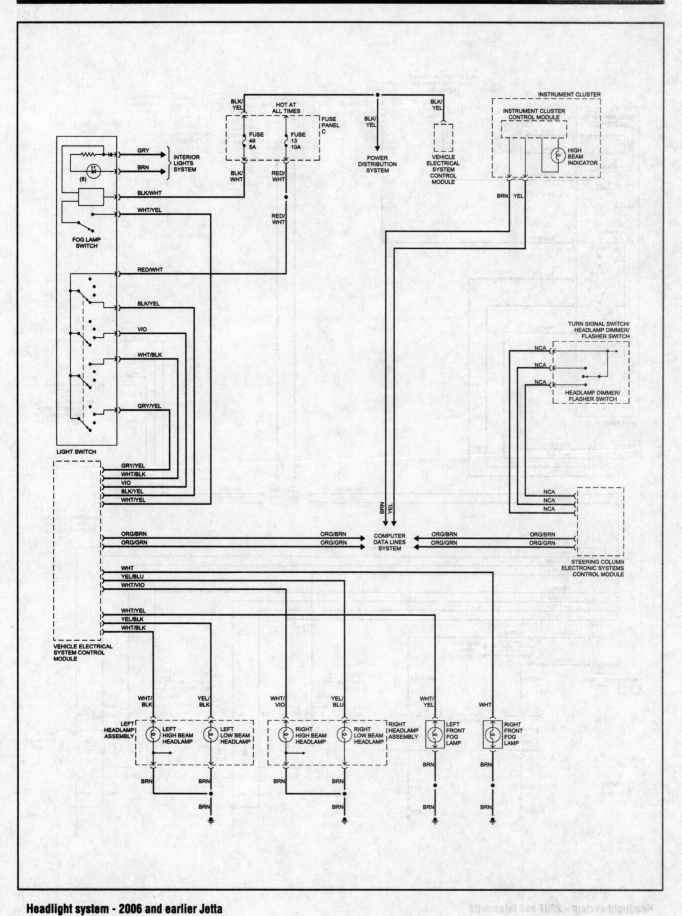

Headlight system - 2006 and earlier Jetta

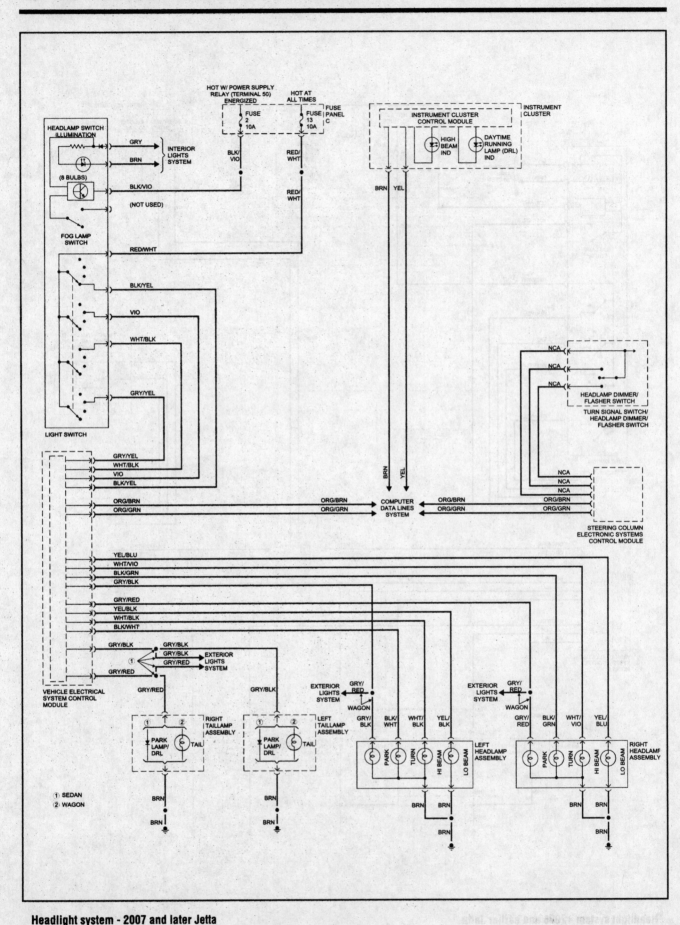

Headlight system - 2007 and later Jetta

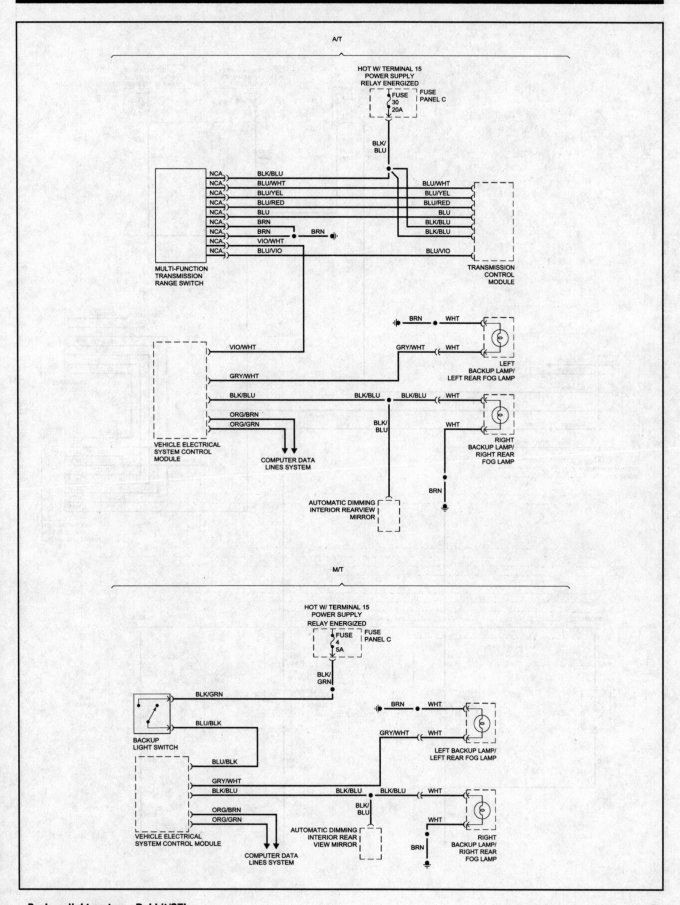

Back-up light system - Rabbit/GTI

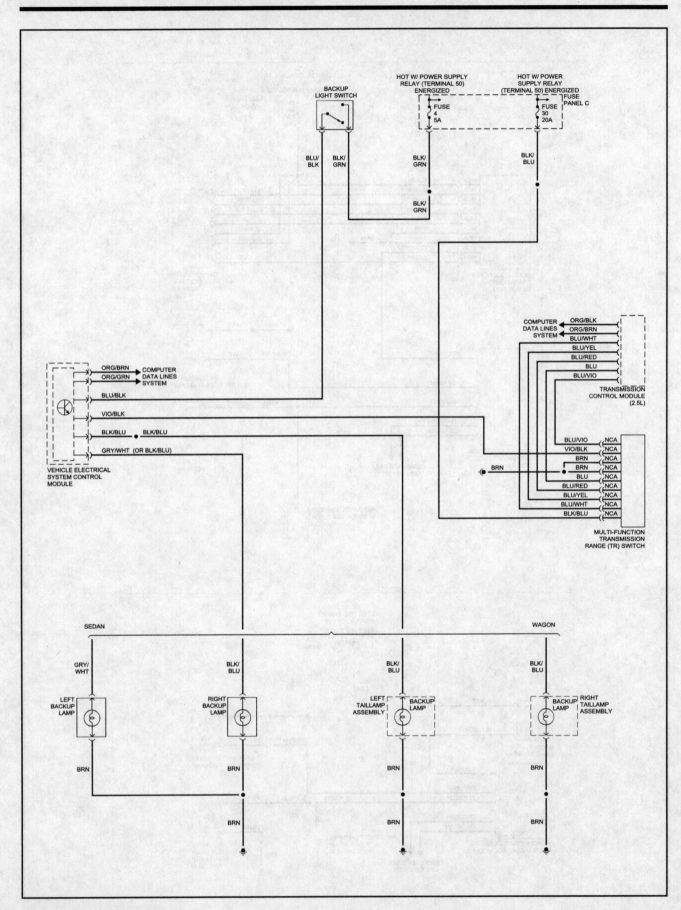

Back-up light system - Jetta

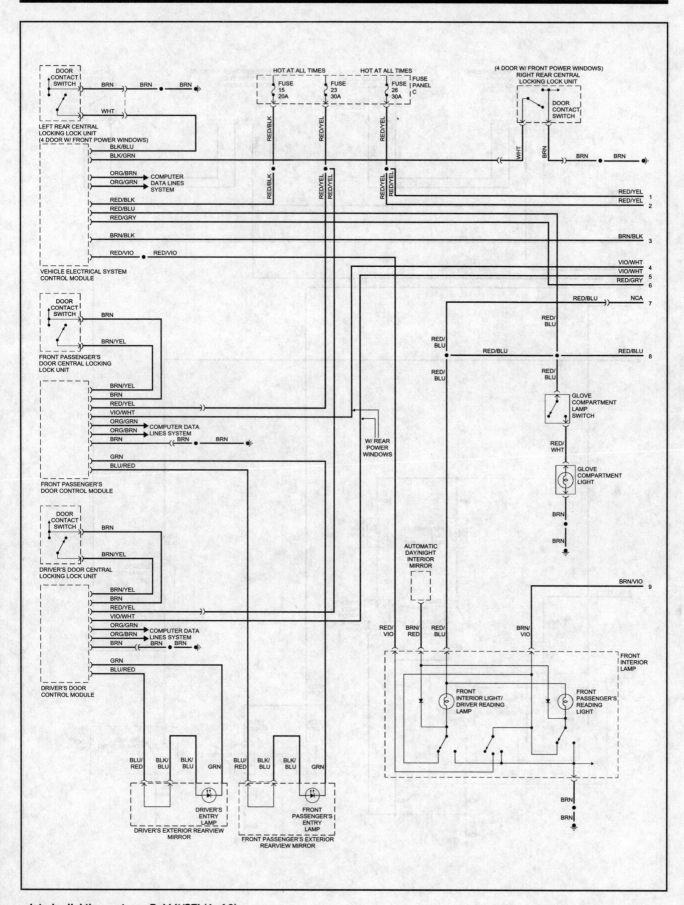

Interior lighting system - Rabbit/GTI (1 of 2)

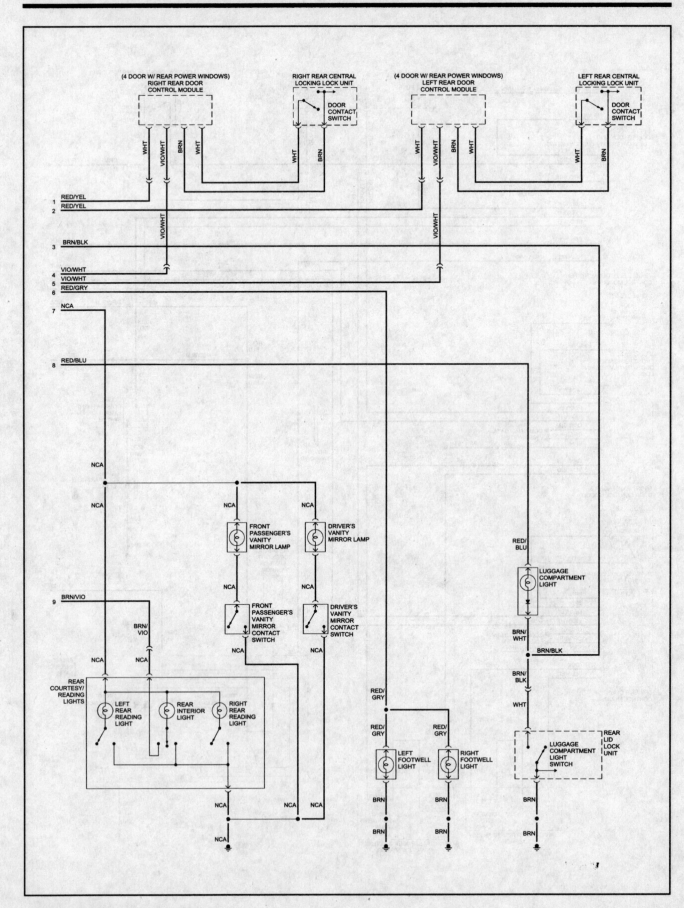

Interior lighting system - Rabbit/GTI (2 of 2)

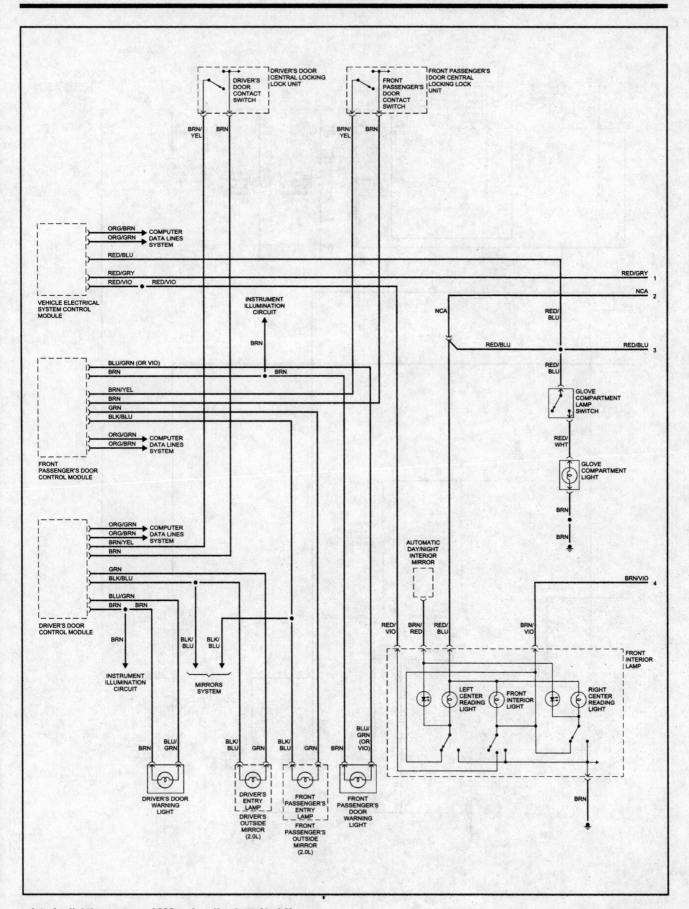

Interior lighting system - 2006 and earlier Jetta (1 of 2)

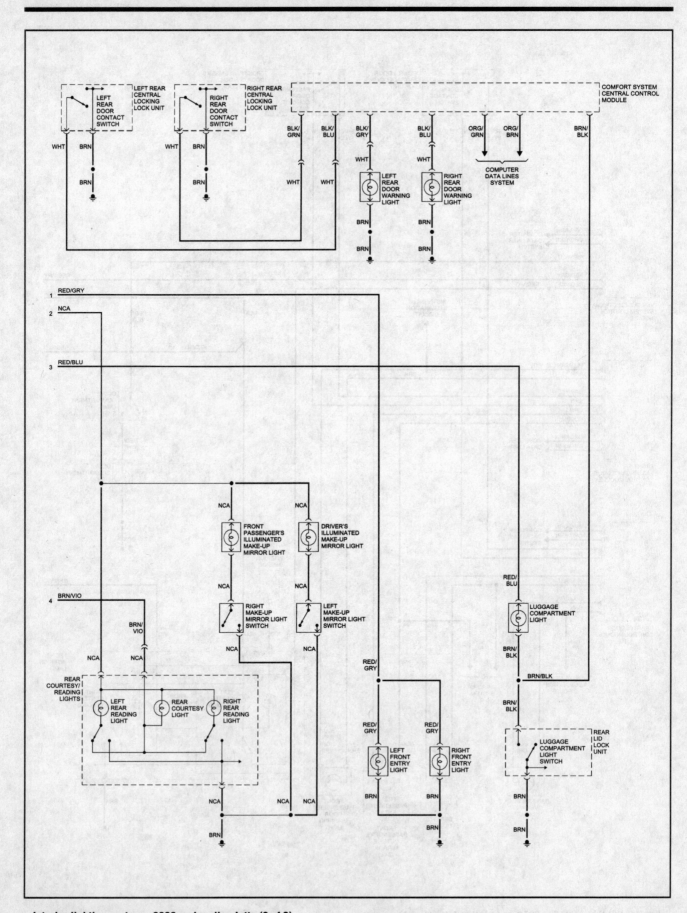

Interior lighting system - 2006 and earlier Jetta (2 of 2)

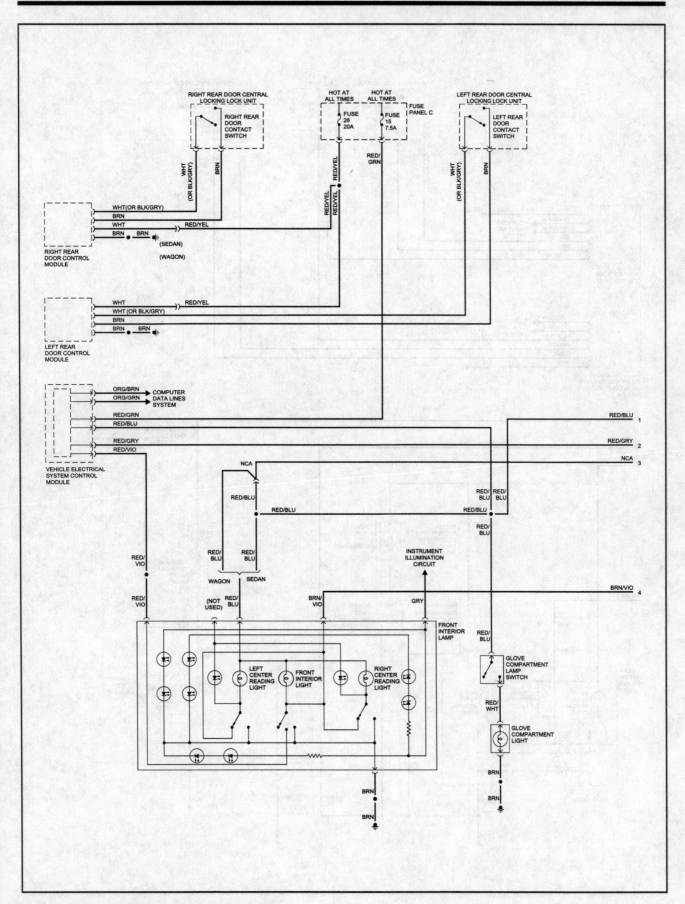

Interior lighting system - 2007 and later Jetta (1 of 2)

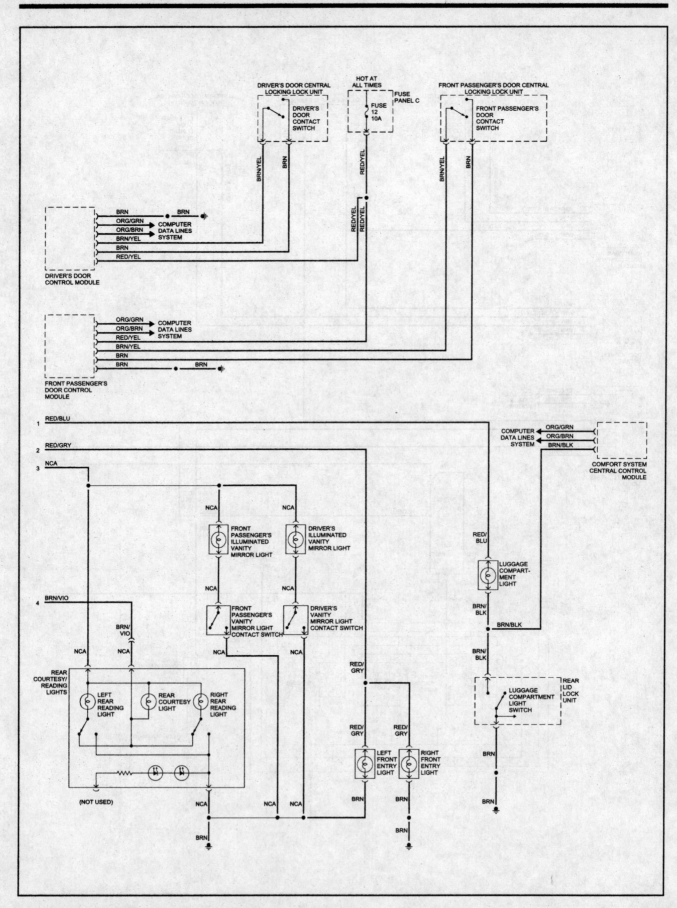

Interior lighting system - 2007 and later Jetta (2 of 2)

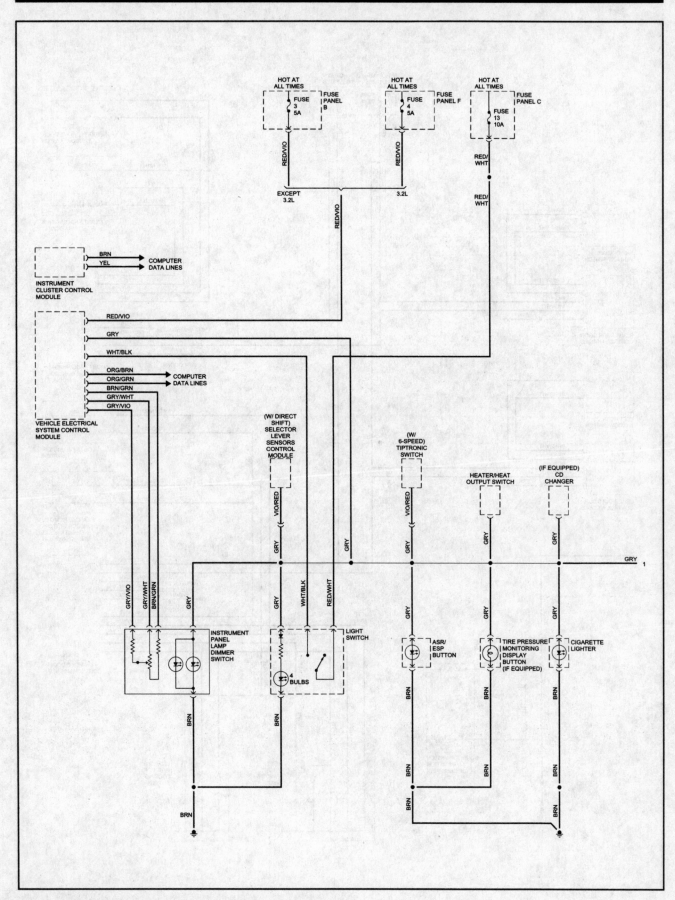

Instrument panel and switch illumination - Rabbit/GTI (1 of 2)

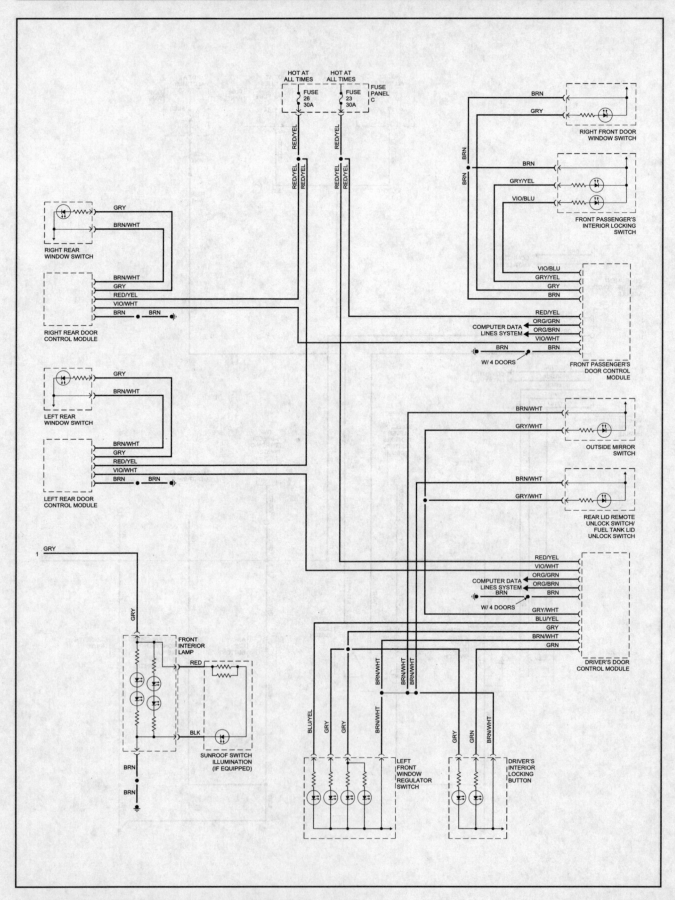

Instrument panel and switch illumination - Rabbit/GTI (2 of 2)

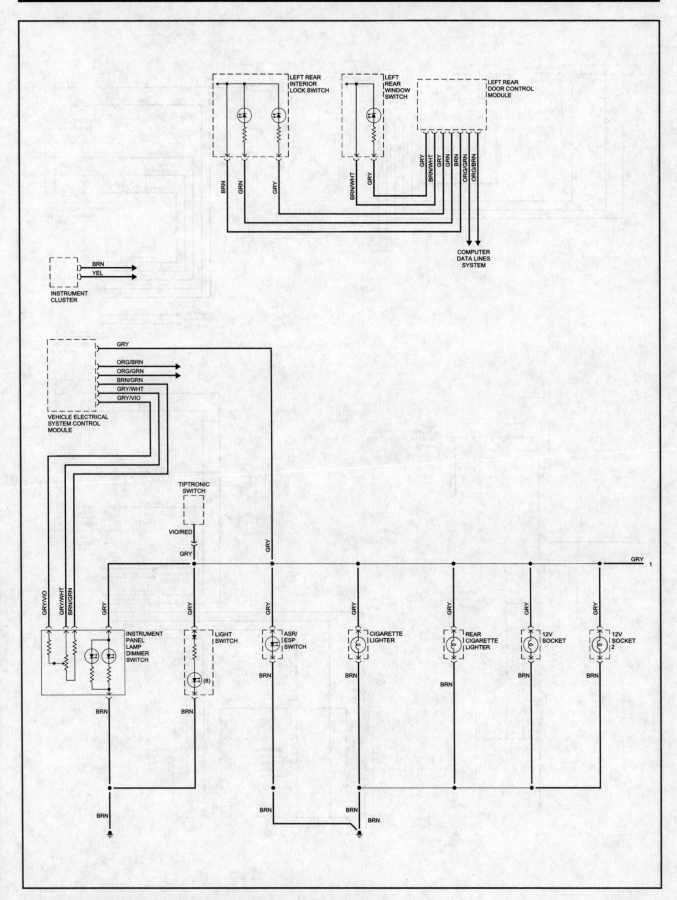

Instrument panel and switch illumination - 2006 and earlier Jetta (1 of 2)

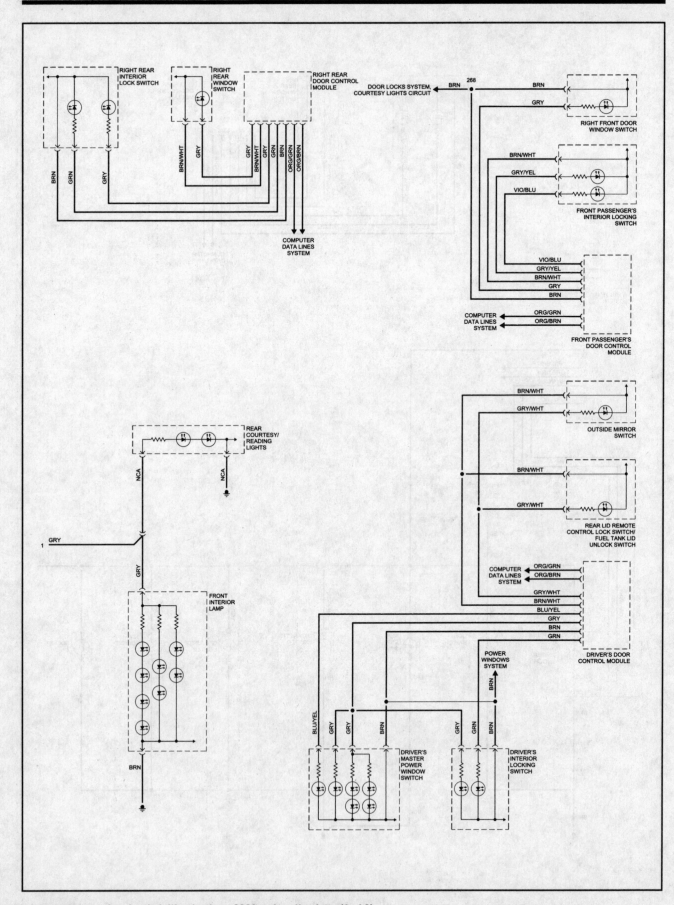

Instrument panel and switch illumination - 2006 and earlier Jetta (2 of 2)

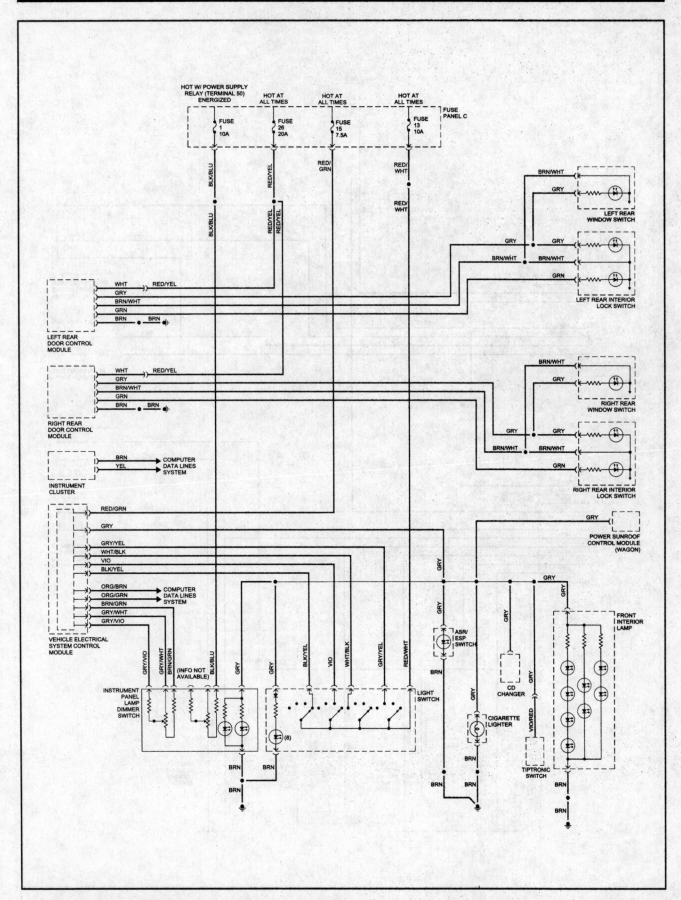

Instrument panel and switch illumination - 2007 and later Jetta (1 of 2)

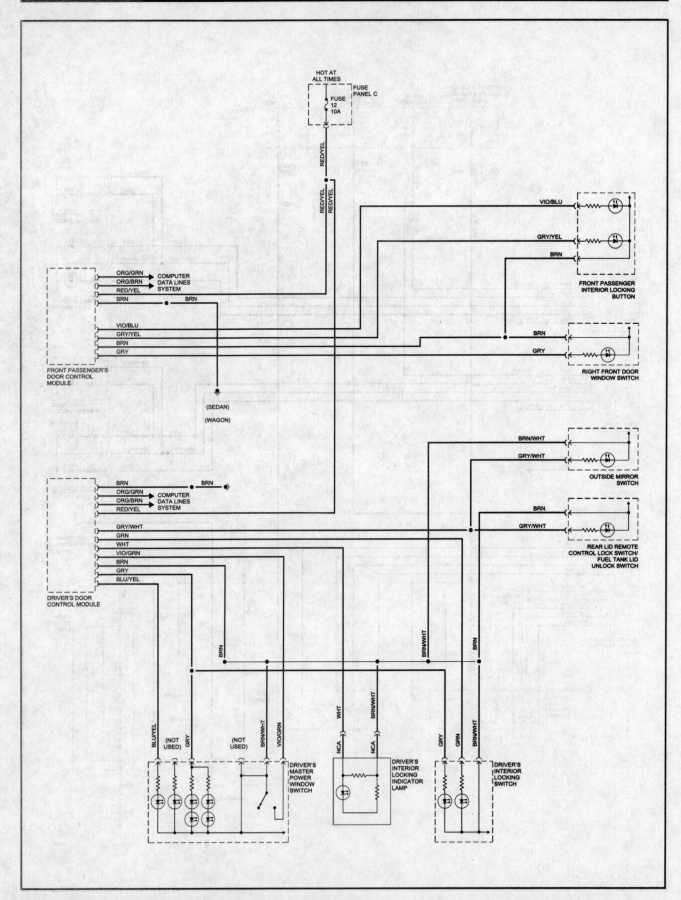

Instrument panel and switch illumination - 2007 and later Jetta (2 of 2)

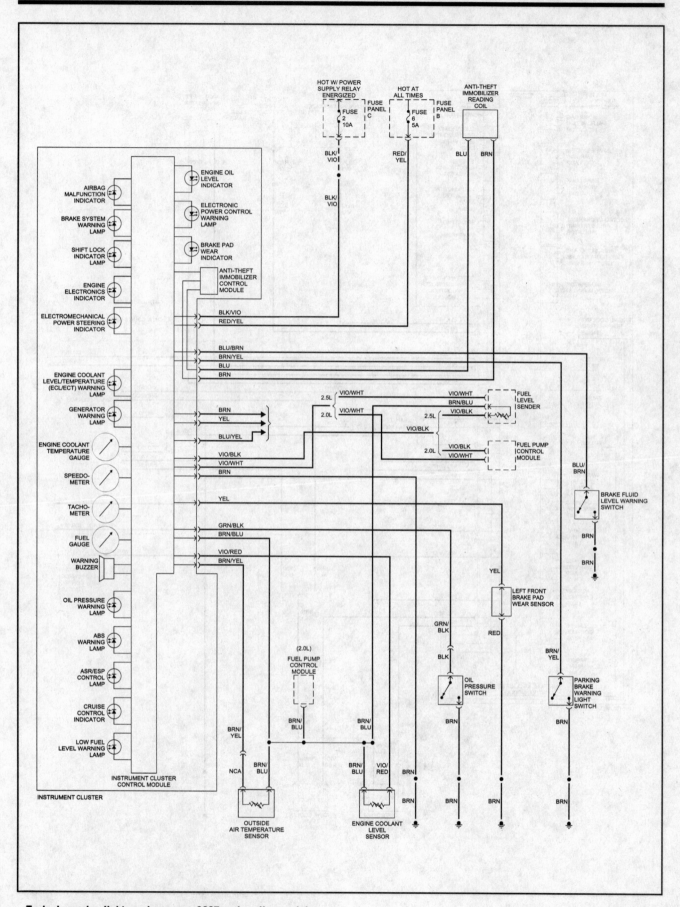

Typical warning lights and gauges - 2007 and earlier models

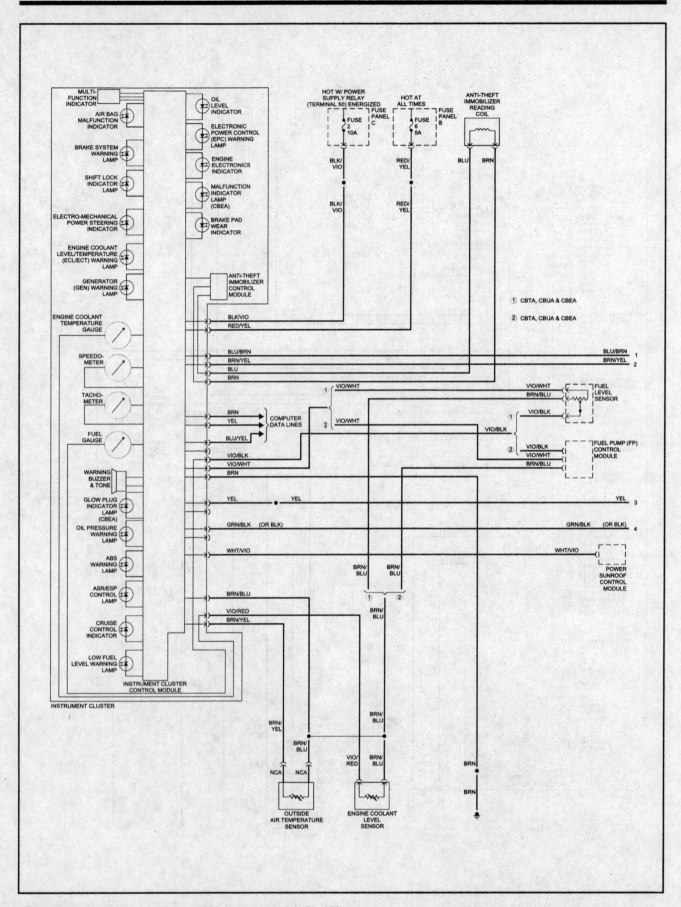

Typical warning lights and gauges - 2008 and later models (1 of 2)

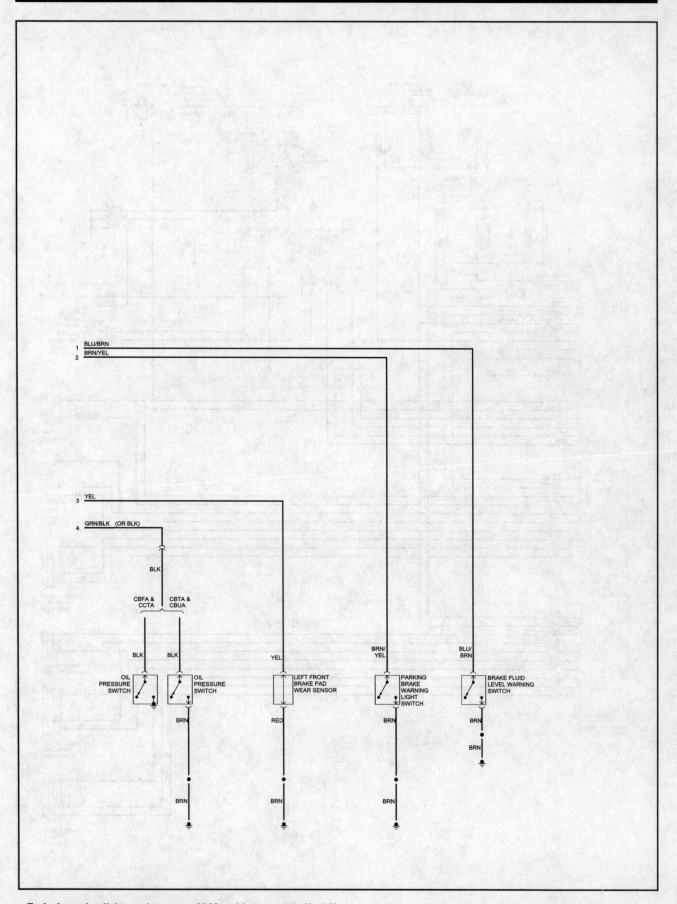

Typical warning lights and gauges - 2008 and later models (2 of 2)

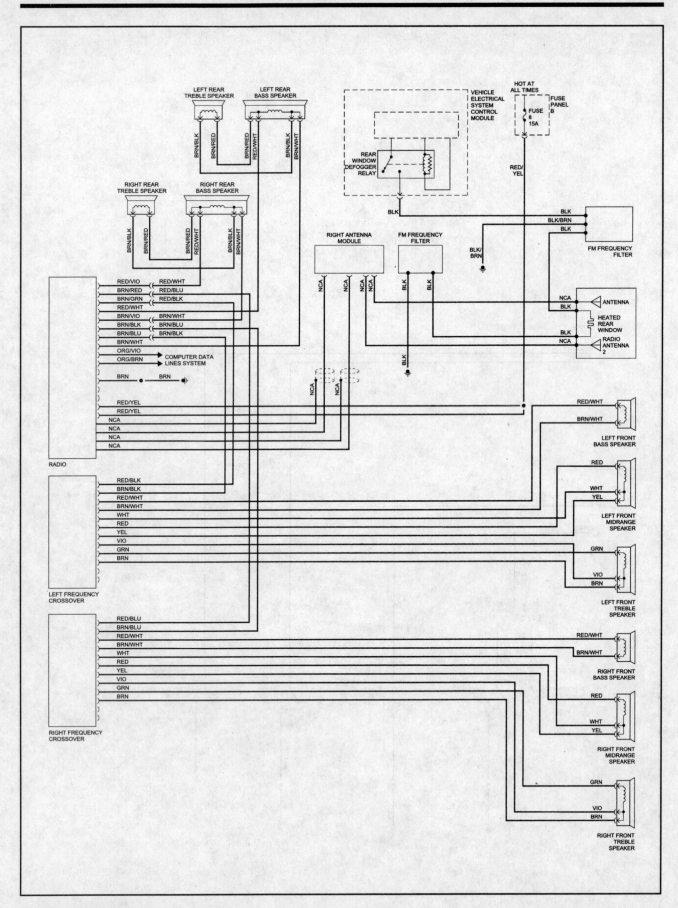

Typical audio system (base) - all models

GLOSSARY

AIR/FUEL RATIO: The ratio of air-to-gasoline by weight in the fuel mixture drawn into the engine.

AIR INJECTION: One method of reducing harmful exhaust emissions by injecting air into each of the exhaust ports of an engine. The fresh air entering the hot exhaust manifold causes any remaining fuel to be burned before it can exit the tailpipe.

ALTERNATOR: A device used for converting mechanical energy into electrical energy.

AMMETER: An instrument, calibrated in amperes, used to measure the flow of an electrical current in a circuit. Ammeters are always connected in series with the circuit being tested.

AMPERE: The rate of flow of electrical current present when one volt of electrical pressure is applied against one ohm of electrical resistance.

ANALOG COMPUTER: Any microprocessor that uses similar (analogous) electrical signals to make its calculations.

ARMATURE: A laminated, soft iron core wrapped by a wire that converts electrical energy to mechanical energy as in a motor or relay. When rotated in a magnetic field, it changes mechanical energy into electrical energy as in a generator.

ATMOSPHERIC PRESSURE: The pressure on the Earth's surface caused by the weight of the air in the atmosphere. At sea level, this pressure is 14.7 psi at 32°F (101 kPa at 0°C).

ATOMIZATION: The breaking down of a liquid into a fine mist that can be suspended in air.

AXIAL PLAY: Movement parallel to a shaft or bearing bore.

BACKFIRE: The sudden combustion of gases in the intake or exhaust system that results in a loud explosion.

BACKLASH: The clearance or play between two parts, such as meshed gears.

BACKPRESSURE: Restrictions in the exhaust system that slow the exit of exhaust gases from the combustion chamber.

BAKELITE: A heat resistant, plastic insulator material commonly used in printed circuit boards and transistorized components.

BALL BEARING: A bearing made up of hardened inner and outer races between which hardened steel balls roll.

BALLAST RESISTOR: A resistor in the primary ignition circuit that lowers voltage after the engine is started to reduce wear on ignition components.

BEARING: A friction reducing, supportive device usually located between a stationary part and a moving part.

BIMETAL TEMPERATURE SENSOR: Any sensor or switch made of two dissimilar types of metal that bend when heated or cooled due to the different expansion rates of the alloys. These types of sensors usually function as an on/off switch.

BLOWBY: Combustion gases, composed of water vapor and unburned fuel, that leak past the piston rings into the crankcase during normal engine operation. These gases are removed by the PCV system to prevent the buildup of harmful acids in the crankcase.

BRAKE PAD: A brake shoe and lining assembly used with disc brakes.

BRAKE SHOE: The backing for the brake lining. The term is, however, usually applied to the assembly of the brake backing and lining.

BUSHING: A liner, usually removable, for a bearing; an anti-friction liner used in place of a bearing.

CALIPER: A hydraulically activated device in a disc brake system, which is mounted straddling the brake rotor (disc). The caliper contains at least one piston and two brake pads. Hydraulic pressure on the piston(s) forces the pads against the rotor.

CAMSHAFT: A shaft in the engine on which are the lobes (cams) which operate the valves. The camshaft is driven by the crankshaft, via a belt, chain or gears, at one half the crankshaft speed.

CAPACITOR: A device which stores an electrical charge.

CARBON MONOXIDE (CO): A colorless, odorless gas given off as a normal byproduct of combustion. It is poisonous and extremely dangerous in confined areas, building up slowly to toxic levels without warning if adequate ventilation is not available.

CARBURETOR: A device, usually mounted on the intake manifold of an engine, which mixes the air and fuel in the proper proportion to allow even combustion.

CATALYTIC CONVERTER: A device installed in the exhaust system, like a muffler, that converts harmful byproducts of combustion into carbon dioxide and water vapor by means of a heat-producing chemical reaction.

CENTRIFUGAL ADVANCE: A mechanical method of advancing the spark timing by using flyweights in the distributor that react to centrifugal force generated by the distributor shaft rotation.

CHECK VALVE: Any one-way valve installed to permit the flow of air, fuel or vacuum in one direction only.

CHOKE: A device, usually a moveable valve, placed in the intake path of a carburetor to restrict the flow of air.

CIRCUIT: Any unbroken path through which an electrical current can flow. Also used to describe fuel flow in some instances.

CIRCUIT BREAKER: A switch which protects an electrical circuit from overload by opening the circuit when the current flow exceeds a predetermined level. Some circuit breakers must be reset manually, while most reset automatically.

COIL (IGNITION): A transformer in the ignition circuit which steps up the voltage provided to the spark plugs.

COMBINATION MANIFOLD: An assembly which includes both the intake and exhaust manifolds in one casting.

COMBINATION VALVE: A device used in some fuel systems that routes fuel vapors to a charcoal storage canister instead of venting them into the atmosphere. The valve relieves fuel tank pressure and allows fresh air into the tank as the fuel level drops to prevent a vapor lock situation.

COMPRESSION RATIO: The comparison of the total volume of the cylinder and combustion chamber with the piston at BDC and the piston at TDC.

CONDENSER: 1. An electrical device which acts to store an electrical charge, preventing voltage surges. 2. A radiator-like device in the air conditioning system in which refrigerant gas condenses into a liquid, giving off heat.

CONDUCTOR: Any material through which an electrical current can be transmitted easily.

CONTINUITY: Continuous or complete circuit. Can be checked with an ohmmeter.

COUNTERSHAFT: An intermediate shaft which is rotated by a mainshaft and transmits, in turn, that rotation to a working part.

CRANKCASE: The lower part of an engine in which the crankshaft and related parts operate.

CRANKSHAFT: The main driving shaft of an engine which receives reciprocating motion from the pistons and converts it to rotary motion.

CYLINDER: In an engine, the round hole in the engine block in which the piston(s) ride.

CYLINDER BLOCK: The main structural member of an engine in which is found the cylinders, crankshaft and other principal parts.

CYLINDER HEAD: The detachable portion of the engine, usually fastened to the top of the cylinder block and containing all or most of the combustion chambers. On overhead valve engines, it contains the valves and their operating parts. On overhead cam engines, it contains the camshaft as well.

DEAD CENTER: The extreme top or bottom of the piston stroke.

DETONATION: An unwanted explosion of the air/fuel mixture in the combustion chamber caused by excess heat and compression, advanced timing, or an overly lean mixture. Also referred to as "ping".

DIAPHRAGM: A thin, flexible wall separating two cavities, such as in a vacuum advance unit.

DIESELING: A condition in which hot spots in the combustion chamber cause the engine to run on after the key is turned off.

DIFFERENTIAL: A geared assembly which allows the transmission of motion between drive axles, giving one axle the ability to turn faster than the other.

DIODE: An electrical device that will allow current to flow in one direction only.

DISC BRAKE: A hydraulic braking assembly consisting of a brake disc, or rotor, mounted on an axle, and a caliper assembly containing, usually two brake pads which are activated by hydraulic pressure. The pads are forced against the sides of the disc, creating friction which slows the vehicle.

DISTRIBUTOR: A mechanically driven device on an engine which is responsible for electrically firing the spark plug at a predetermined point of the piston stroke.

DOWEL PIN: A pin, inserted in mating holes in two different parts allowing those parts to maintain a fixed relationship.

DRUM BRAKE: A braking system which consists of two brake shoes and one or two wheel cylinders, mounted on a fixed backing plate, and a brake drum, mounted on an axle, which revolves around the assembly.

DWELL: The rate, measured in degrees of shaft rotation, at which an electrical circuit cycles on and off.

ELECTRONIC CONTROL UNIT (ECU): Ignition module, module, amplifier or igniter. See Module for definition.

ELECTRONIC IGNITION: A system in which the timing and firing of the spark plugs is controlled by an electronic control unit, usually called a module. These systems have no points or condenser.

END-PLAY: The measured amount of axial movement in a shaft.

ENGINE: A device that converts heat into mechanical energy.

EXHAUST MANIFOLD: A set of cast passages or pipes which conduct exhaust gases from the engine.

FEELER GAUGE: A blade, usually metal, or precisely predetermined thickness, used to measure the clearance between two parts.

FIRING ORDER: The order in which combustion occurs in the cylinders of an engine. Also the order in which spark is distributed to the plugs by the distributor.

FLOODING: The presence of too much fuel in the intake manifold and combustion chamber which prevents the air/fuel mixture from firing, thereby causing a no-start situation.

FLYWHEEL: A disc shaped part bolted to the rear end of the crankshaft. Around the outer perimeter is affixed the ring gear. The starter drive engages the ring gear, turning the flywheel, which rotates the crankshaft, imparting the initial starting motion to the engine.

FOOT POUND (ft. lbs. or sometimes, ft.lb.): The amount of energy or work needed to raise an item weighing one pound, a distance of one foot.

FUSE: A protective device in a circuit which prevents circuit overload by breaking the circuit when a specific amperage is present. The device is constructed around a strip or wire of a lower amperage rating than the circuit it is designed to protect. When an amperage higher than that stamped on the fuse is present in the circuit, the strip or wire melts, opening the circuit.

GEAR RATIO: The ratio between the number of teeth on meshing gears.

GENERATOR: A device which converts mechanical energy into electrical energy.

HEAT RANGE: The measure of a spark plug's ability to dissipate heat from its firing end. The higher the heat range, the hotter the plug fires.

HUB: The center part of a wheel or gear.

HYDROCARBON (HC): Any chemical compound made up of hydrogen and carbon. A major pollutant formed by the engine as a byproduct of combustion.

HYDROMETER: An instrument used to measure the specific gravity of a solution.

INCH POUND (inch lbs.; sometimes in.lb. or in. lbs.): One twelfth of a foot pound.

INDUCTION: A means of transferring electrical energy in the form of a magnetic field. Principle used in the ignition coil to increase voltage.

INJECTOR: A device which receives metered fuel under relatively low pressure and is activated to inject the fuel into the engine under relatively high pressure at a predetermined time.

INPUT SHAFT: The shaft to which torque is applied, usually carrying the driving gear or gears.

INTAKE MANIFOLD: A casting of passages or pipes used to conduct air or a fuel/air mixture to the cylinders.

JOURNAL: The bearing surface within which a shaft operates.

KEY: A small block usually fitted in a notch between a shaft and a hub to prevent slippage of the two parts.

MANIFOLD: A casting of passages or set of pipes which connect the cylinders to an inlet or outlet source.

MANIFOLD VACUUM: Low pressure in an engine intake manifold formed just below the throttle plates. Manifold vacuum is highest at idle and drops under acceleration.

MASTER CYLINDER: The primary fluid pressurizing device in a hydraulic system. In automotive use, it is found in brake and hydraulic clutch systems and is pedal activated, either directly or, in a power brake system, through the power booster.

MODULE: Electronic control unit, amplifier or igniter of solid state or integrated design which controls the current flow in the ignition primary circuit based on input from the pick-up coil. When the module opens the primary circuit, high secondary voltage is induced in the coil.

NEEDLE BEARING: A bearing which consists of a number (usually a large number) of long, thin rollers.

OHM: (Ω) The unit used to measure the resistance of conductor-to-electrical flow. One ohm is the amount of resistance that limits current flow to one ampere in a circuit with one volt of pressure.

OHMMETER: An instrument used for measuring the resistance, in ohms, in an electrical circuit.

OUTPUT SHAFT: The shaft which transmits torque from a device, such as a transmission.

OVERDRIVE: A gear assembly which produces more shaft revolutions than that transmitted to it.

OVERHEAD CAMSHAFT (OHC): An engine configuration in which the camshaft is mounted on top of the cylinder head and operates the valve either directly or by means of rocker arms.

OVERHEAD VALVE (OHV): An engine configuration in which all of the valves are located in the cylinder head and the camshaft is located in the cylinder block. The camshaft operates the valves via lifters and pushrods.

OXIDES OF NITROGEN (NOx): Chemical compounds of nitrogen produced as a byproduct of combustion. They combine with hydrocarbons to produce smog.

OXYGEN SENSOR: Use with the feedback system to sense the presence of oxygen in the exhaust gas and signal the computer which can reference the voltage signal to an air/fuel ratio.

PINION: The smaller of two meshing gears.

PISTON RING: An open-ended ring with fits into a groove on the outer diameter of the piston. Its chief function is to form a seal between the piston and cylinder wall. Most automotive pistons have three rings: two for compression sealing; one for oil sealing.

PRELOAD: A predetermined load placed on a bearing during assembly or by adjustment.

PRIMARY CIRCUIT: the low voltage side of the ignition system which consists of the ignition switch, ballast resistor or resistance wire, bypass, coil, electronic control unit and pick-up coil as well as the connecting wires and harnesses.

PRESS FIT: The mating of two parts under pressure, due to the inner diameter of one being smaller than the outer diameter of the other, or vice versa; an interference fit.

RACE: The surface on the inner or outer ring of a bearing on which the balls, needles or rollers move.

REGULATOR: A device which maintains the amperage and/or voltage levels of a circuit at predetermined values.

GL-4 GLOSSARY

RELAY: A switch which automatically opens and/or closes a circuit.

RESISTANCE: The opposition to the flow of current through a circuit or electrical device, and is measured in ohms. Resistance is equal to the voltage divided by the amperage.

RESISTOR: A device, usually made of wire, which offers a preset amount of resistance in an electrical circuit.

RING GEAR: The name given to a ring-shaped gear attached to a differential case, or affixed to a flywheel or as part of a planetary gear set.

ROLLER BEARING: A bearing made up of hardened inner and outer races between which hardened steel rollers move.

ROTOR: 1. The disc-shaped part of a disc brake assembly, upon which the brake pads bear; also called, brake disc. 2. The device mounted atop the distributor shaft, which passes current to the distributor cap tower contacts.

SECONDARY CIRCUIT: The high voltage side of the ignition system, usually above 20,000 volts. The secondary includes the ignition coil, coil wire, distributor cap and rotor, spark plug wires and spark plugs.

SENDING UNIT: A mechanical, electrical, hydraulic or electromagnetic device which transmits information to a gauge.

SENSOR: Any device designed to measure engine operating conditions or ambient pressures and temperatures. Usually electronic in nature and designed to send a voltage signal to an on-board computer, some sensors may operate as a simple on/off switch or they may provide a variable voltage signal (like a potentiometer) as conditions or measured parameters change.

SHIM: Spacers of precise, predetermined thickness used between parts to establish a proper working relationship.

SLAVE CYLINDER: In automotive use, a device in the hydraulic clutch system which is activated by hydraulic force, disengaging the clutch.

SOLENOID: A coil used to produce a magnetic field, the effect of which is to produce work.

SPARK PLUG: A device screwed into the combustion chamber of a spark ignition engine. The basic construction is a conductive core inside of a ceramic insulator, mounted in an outer conductive base. An electrical charge from the spark plug wire travels along the conductive core and jumps a preset air gap to a grounding point or points at the end of the conductive base. The resultant spark ignites the fuel/air mixture in the combustion chamber.

SPLINES: Ridges machined or cast onto the outer diameter of a shaft or inner diameter of a bore to enable parts to mate without rotation.

TACHOMETER: A device used to measure the rotary speed of an engine, shaft, gear, etc., usually in rotations per minute.

THERMOSTAT: A valve, located in the cooling system of an engine, which is closed when cold and opens gradually in response to engine heating, controlling the temperature of the coolant and rate of coolant flow.

TOP DEAD CENTER (TDC): The point at which the piston reaches the top of its travel on the compression stroke.

TORQUE: The twisting force applied to an object.

TORQUE CONVERTER: A turbine used to transmit power from a driving member to a driven member via hydraulic action, providing changes in drive ratio and torque. In automotive use, it links the driveplate at the rear of the engine to the automatic transmission.

TRANSDUCER: A device used to change a force into an electrical signal.

TRANSISTOR: A semi-conductor component which can be actuated by a small voltage to perform an electrical switching function.

TUNE-UP: A regular maintenance function, usually associated with the replacement and adjustment of parts and components in the electrical and fuel systems of a vehicle for the purpose of attaining optimum performance.

TURBOCHARGER: An exhaust driven pump which compresses intake air and forces it into the combustion chambers at higher than atmospheric pressures. The increased air pressure allows more fuel to be burned and results in increased horsepower being produced.

VACUUM ADVANCE: A device which advances the ignition timing in response to increased engine vacuum.

VACUUM GAUGE: An instrument used to measure the presence of vacuum in a chamber.

VALVE: A device which control the pressure, direction of flow or rate of flow of a liquid or gas.

VALVE CLEARANCE: The measured gap between the end of the valve stem and the rocker arm, cam lobe or follower that activates the valve.

VISCOSITY: The rating of a liquid's internal resistance to flow.

VOLTMETER: An instrument used for measuring electrical force in units called volts. Voltmeters are always connected parallel with the circuit being tested.

WHEEL CYLINDER: Found in the automotive drum brake assembly, it is a device, actuated by hydraulic pressure, which, through internal pistons, pushes the brake shoes outward against the drums.

A

MASTER INDEX

B

BACK-UP LIGHT SWITCH, REMOVAL AND INSTALLATION, 7A-5
BALANCE SHAFTS, FOUR-CYLINDER ENGINES, REMOVAL AND INSTALLATION, 2A-29
BALLJOINTS, CHECK AND REPLACEMENT, 10-10
BATTERY
and battery tray, removal and installation, 5-6
cables, check and replacement, 5-7
check, maintenance and charging, 1-14
disconnection and reconnection, 5-5
BLOWER MOTOR, REMOVAL AND INSTALLATION, 3-14
BODY REPAIR
major damage, 11-5
minor damage, 11-3
BOOSTER BATTERY (JUMP) STARTING, 0-19
BRAKE
Anti-lock Brake System (ABS) and Electronic Stability Program (ESP), general information, 9-7
caliper, removal and installation, 9-13
disc, inspection, removal and installation, 9-15
fluid
    change, 1-25
    level check, 1-8
    type, 1-33
general information and precautions, 9-2
hoses and lines, inspection and replacement, 9-23
hydraulic system, bleeding, 9-24
light switch, removal and installation, 9-28
master cylinder, removal and installation, 9-21
pads, replacement
    front, 9-8
    rear, 9-11
parking brake,
    check and adjustment, 9-26
    pedal, removal and installation, 9-27
power brake booster, check, removal and installation, 9-25
shoes, replacement, 9-17
system check, 1-20
system vacuum pump, removal and installation, 9-29
troubleshooting, 9-2
wheel cylinder, removal and installation, 9-21
BULB REPLACEMENT, 12-19
BUMPER COVERS, REMOVAL AND INSTALLATION, 11-11
BUYING PARTS, 0-9

C

CABIN AIR FILTER REPLACEMENT, 1-19
CABLE REPLACEMENT
battery, 5-7
hood release, 11-10

CALIPER, DISC BRAKE, REMOVAL AND INSTALLATION, 9-13
CAMSHAFT POSITION (CMP) SENSOR, REPLACEMENT, 6-17
CAMSHAFT TIMING CHAIN AND TENSIONER, FIVE-CYLINDER ENGINES, REMOVAL AND INSTALLATION, 2B-7
CAMSHAFTS, ROLLER ROCKER ARMS AND LASH ADJUSTERS, REMOVAL, INSPECTION AND INSTALLATION
five-cylinder engines, 2B-10
four-cylinder engines, 2A-11
CAPACITIES, FLUIDS AND LUBRICANTS, 1-33
CARPETS, MAINTENANCE, 11-5
CATALYTIC CONVERTER, REPLACEMENT, 6-24
CENTER CONSOLE, REMOVAL AND INSTALLATION, 11-29
CHARGING SYSTEM
alternator, removal and installation, 5-8
check, 5-3
CHASSIS ELECTRICAL SYSTEM, 12-1
CHEMICALS AND LUBRICANTS, 0-20
CIRCUIT BREAKERS, GENERAL INFORMATION, 12-4
CLUTCH
components, removal, inspection and installation, 8-4
description and check, 8-2
fluid
    level check, 1-8
    type, 1-33
hydraulic system, bleeding, 8-3
master cylinder, removal and installation, 8-2
pedal
    and over-center spring, removal and installation, 8-9
    assembly, removal and installation, 8-8
    switch, removal and installation, 8-8
release bearing and lever, removal, inspection and installation, 8-6
release cylinder, removal and installation, 8-3
COIL SPRING (REAR), REMOVAL AND INSTALLATION, 10-11
COILS, IGNITION, REPLACEMENT, 5-7
COMPRESSOR, AIR CONDITIONING, REMOVAL AND INSTALLATION, 3-17
CONDENSER, AIR CONDITIONING, REMOVAL AND INSTALLATION, 3-19
CONTROL ARM
removal and installation
    front, 10-8
    rear, lower, 10-14
    rear, upper, 10-14
bushing replacement (front), 10-8
CONTROL HOUSING COVER (FIVE-CYLINDER ENGINE), REMOVAL AND INSTALLATION, 2C-19
CONVERSION FACTORS, 0-21
COOLANT
Engine Coolant Temperature (ECT) sensor, replacement, 6-18
level check, 1-7
temperature gauge sending unit, check and replacement, 3-14
type, 1-33